THE OXFORD HANDBOOK OF

DANCE AND THE POPULAR SCREEN

THE OXFORD HANDBOOK OF

DANCE AND THE POPULAR SCREEN

Edited by

MELISSA BLANCO BORELLI

OXFORD
UNIVERSITY PRESS

OXFORD
UNIVERSITY PRESS

Oxford University Press is a department of the University of Oxford.
It furthers the University's objective of excellence in research, scholarship,
and education by publishing worldwide.

Oxford   New York
Auckland   Cape Town   Dar es Salaam   Hong Kong   Karachi
Kuala Lumpur   Madrid   Melbourne   Mexico City   Nairobi
New Delhi   Shanghai   Taipei   Toronto

With offices in
Argentina   Austria   Brazil   Chile   Czech Republic   France   Greece
Guatemala   Hungary   Italy   Japan   Poland   Portugal   Singapore
South Korea   Switzerland   Thailand Turkey Ukraine Vietnam

Oxford is a registered trademark of Oxford University Press
in the UK and certain other countries.

Published in the United States of America by
Oxford University Press
198 Madison Avenue, New York, NY 10016

Library of Congress Cataloging-in-Publication Data
The Oxford handbook of dance and the popular screen / edited by Melissa Blanco Borelli. pages
cm
Includes bibliographical references and index.
ISBN 978–0–19–989782–7 (hardcover : alk. paper)   ISBN 978-0-19-066154-0 (PB)
1. Dance in motion pictures, television, etc.
I. Blanco Borelli, Melissa editor of compilation.
GV1779.O95 2013
791.436578—dc23
2013018975

1 3 5 7 9 8 6 4 2
Printed in the United States of America
on acid-free paper

CONTENTS

PART II THE COMMERCIAL BIG SCREEN

PART III MUSIC VIDEO AND TELEVISUAL BODIES

PART IV SCREENING NATIONHOOD

PART V CYBER SCREENS

PART VI CONCLUSION

List of Contributors

Takiyah Nur Amin is Assistant Professor of World Dance at the University of North Carolina at Charlotte.

Inna Arzumanova received her PhD from University of Southern California's Annenberg School for Communication and Journalism and is now a Lecturer at the University of Southern California.

Stephanie L. Batiste is an Associate Professor in the Departments of Black Studies and English at the University of California at Santa Barbara.

Harmony Bench is Assistant Professor of Dance at The Ohio State University.

Kathaleen Boche is a PhD candidate in the Department of History at Florida State University.

Melissa Blanco Borelli is a Senior Lecturer in Dance at Royal Holloway, University of London.

Derek A. Burrill is Associate Professor of Media and Cultural Studies at the University of California, Riverside.

Rosemary Candelario is Assistant Professor of Dance at Texas Woman's University.

Thomas F. DeFrantz is Professor of Dance and African American Studies at Duke University.

Sherril Dodds is Professor of Dance and Chair of the Dance Department at Temple University.

Colleen Dunagan is an Associate Professor of Dance at California State University, Long Beach.

Roxane Fenton is on the dance faculty at Santa Ana College and at California State University, Long Beach.

Mary Fogarty is Assistant Professor in Dance at York University (Toronto, Canada).

Victor Fowler is a noted Cuban teacher and essayist. He is a frequent collaborator in the most relevant Cuban cultural publications and his critical works as well as his poems have been distributed in Venezuela, Colombia, Nicaragua, England, France, Italy, Belgium, and the United States.

Cindy García is an Assistant Professor in the Department of Theatre Arts and Dance at the University of Minnesota, Twin Cities.

Alexandra Harlig is a PhD candidate in The Ohio State University Department of Dance.

Chih-Chieh Liu is a post-doctoral fellow in music at the University of Hong Kong.

Raquel L. Monroe is an Assistant Professor in Dance at Columbia College Chicago.

Amita Nijhawan is Lecturer in Dance Studies at the University of Surrey.

Ariel Osterweis is Assistant Professor of Dance and Performance Studies at Wayne State University in Detroit, Michigan.

Clare Parfitt-Brown is a Senior Lecturer in Dance at the University of Chichester.

Karyn T.D. Recollet is a member of the Department of Indigenous Studies at Sudbury University (Sudbury, Ontario).

Laura Robinson is Lecturer in Dance Studies at the University of Surrey.

Mary Simonson is Assistant Professor of Film and Media Studies and of Women's Studies at Colgate University.

Philippa Thomas is a PhD candidate at Goldsmiths College and lectures at London Contemporary Dance School.

Susie Trenka is a PhD fellow and research assistant in Film Studies at the University of Zurich, Switzerland.

Alexis A. Weisbrod is an Associate Faculty member at Mt. San Jacinto College.

About the Companion Website

www.oup.com/us/ohdps

Oxford has created a website to accompany *The Oxford Handbook of Dance and the Popular Screen*. Examples that cannot be made available in a book, namely the examples accompanying chapter 7, are provided here. The reader is encouraged to consult this resource in conjunction with reading the chapter. Examples available online are signaled with Oxford's symbol ⊙.

THE OXFORD HANDBOOK OF

DANCE AND THE POPULAR SCREEN

INTRODUCTION: DANCE ON SCREEN

MELISSA BLANCO BORELLI

THIS anthology seeks to establish a body of contemporary readings about dance in a popular screen context. It offers ways to engage with the multi-layered meanings of the dancing body in film, television, music videos, Internet sites such as YouTube, commercials, and video games by specifically utilizing methodologies from critical dance studies, performance studies, and film/media analysis. It does not pretend to be a comprehensive historical narrative of dance on the popular screen, but rather, it posits the significance of dance as an object of study. It demonstrates how dance on the popular screen might be read, analyzed, and considered through the different mediated bodies and choreographies. This collection aims to position the field of critical dance studies alongside film and media analysis in order to enrich, enliven, and further theorize the role that dance and screen bodies play in popular culture. The anthology positions the popular as a viable and valuable field of inquiry, instantiating popular dance studies scholar Sherril Dodds's claim that "popular dance constitutes a site of social and economic power that has the capacity to destabilize and transgress cultural norms" (2011, 3). Ultimately, it is this destabilization that allows the dance practices addressed in this volume to complicate our encounter with them through the popular screen.

Among the questions the anthology considers include: How do dance and choreography function within the filmic apparatus? What types of bodies are associated with specific dances and how does this affect how dance(s) is/are perceived in the everyday? How do the dancing bodies on screen negotiate power, access, and agency? How are multiple choreographies of identity (e.g., race, class, gender, sexuality, and nation) set in motion through the narrative, dancing bodies, and/or dance style? What types of corporeal labors (dance training, choreographic skill, rehearsal, the constructed notion of "natural talent") are represented or ignored? What role(s) do(es) a specific film have in the genealogy of Hollywood dance films? How do the narrative and filmic conventions of Hollywood inform how dance operates in cultural meaning-making? What kinds of communities has social media and its reliance on the popular screen helped to develop? How does the experience of gaming through dance complicate notions of embodiment, sociality, and choreography?

The main motivation for compiling this anthology was not only an interest in dance on popular screens, but also the growing interest among students at both undergraduate and graduate levels to do research on dance and its mediated representations. Because dance on the popular screen can be so heavily entangled in the zeitgeist, finding scholarly material on a recent music video, dance film, or YouTube trend poses a challenge. Furthermore, not all dance scholars engage with the popular, which leads to a dearth of material on popular screen dance. This poses a challenge to those interested in engaging immediately and discursively with popular screen dance. Often, I have found myself spontaneously theorizing a mediated dance spectacle during a lecture. I also spend research time surfing the Internet, voraciously reading blogs or watching the popular videos on VeVo or YouTube in order to get an immediate analysis on a controversial, topical, or popular screen choreography. Popular culture spills out into our everyday interactions and it is perhaps the most important site from which one might engage in dynamic discussions (with undergraduates particularly) about politics, class, sexuality, or consumer capitalism.

In my lectures, I often incorporate references to music videos, films, or celebrity culture in order to make the theoretical topic more relevant and accessible to my undergraduate students. For example, one of my favorite ways of elucidating Marcel Mauss's *Techniques of the Body* is through George Michael's *Flawless (Go to the City)* video.[1] Put simply, Mauss argues that there is no such thing as a natural body. All of us learn efficient ways of moving through cultural/social indoctrination, imitation, and repetition. To elucidate his point and demonstrate his anthropological training, he explains various types of everyday techniques: walking, sitting, and brushing one's teeth.[2] His analysis of bodily techniques informs dance studies with its focus on the moving body and the different dance techniques that shape dancing bodies. Taking Mauss's premise about efficient body techniques and applying it to the myriad of corporeal activities occurring in Michael's video offers a visible example of how bodies enact everyday choreographies.

Flawless (Go to the City) takes place in a hotel room. It begins with a white man performing his morning bathroom ritual at the toilet. Fortunately, we witness this masculine technique of the body from behind. Slowly, more and more people enter and exit the room, providing a stunning array of the different bodies that have inhabited the room before. One, then two, then three, five, ten, thirteen, twenty, twenty-plus other bodies join him. They remain oblivious to one another as the video cleverly attempts to show that they have all, at some point, *been* in that same hotel room before, albeit at different times. As the song progresses, these hotel room guests wash, walk, bathe, do sit-ups, dance on the bed, get dressed, brush their teeth; in other words, they perform different techniques of their everyday activities as well as corporeal gestures pertaining to their character (e.g., the yogi sits in lotus position on the far left of the screen, the detective looks in the corners and crevices of the room, the drag queen begins to apply her makeup for an upcoming performance, the Latina with the bamboo earrings talks on the phone). George Michael portrays the omniscient observer who walks around, sits on the bed and unobtrusively watches the encircling activities around him (Fig. 0.1).

As the camera gradually pans out to a wide shot of the entire room, the room has quickly filled with more than twenty people (Fig. 0.2).

FIGURE 0.1 Screen Capture, George Michael, *Flawless (Go to the City)* music video (2004). George Michael (center, dressed in black) sits on the hotel bed as the other guests' bodies engage in different activities around him.

FIGURE 0.2 Screen Capture, George Michael, *Flawless (Go to the City)* music video (2004). Wider shot of the activity going on around George Michael.

Suddenly, they all face forward and begin to dance in unison: step, side, step, touch, repeat to the other side, repeat backward, add a turn, then freestyle (Fig. 0.3). This sudden choreographic eruption presents an opportunity to watch these different bodies perform the same movement phrase differently. Not one person does it like the other. I cannot think of a better way to begin a conversation about the body and the effects that

FIGURE 0.3 Screen Capture, George Michael, *Flawless (Go to the City)* music video (2004). The ensemble choreography in which all the bodies execute the same 16-count phrase.

social inscription, dance training, identity, and representation have on it than that unexpected 16-count phrase.

Once the unison routine finishes, they break away from the group formation and continue with their personal tasks: looking in the mirror, buttoning a shirt, dancing around. One by one, they begin to exit the room until its first occupant, the white man in boxer shorts, sits back down to watch television and eat his dinner provided by room service. Does his ability to finally remain alone and enjoy the comfort of the room comment upon the type of access and privilege white male capitalist bodies have? Perhaps. Yet, what I primarily want to highlight in this example is the theoretical potential that popular dance on screen offers.

Sherril Dodds's book *Dance on Screen: Genres and Media from Hollywood to Experimental Art* (Palgrave, 2001) took on board the topic of dance on screen as a viable object of study. It set a crucial scholarly foundation for the significance of dance in screen contexts by establishing the analysis of dance on screen as critically and methodologically important. Dodds's monograph examines dance on screen from commercially popular films like *Flashdance* to avant-garde filmmakers working with concepts of dance and choreography for the screen. Many of the contributors in this volume cite her important work. Judy Mitoma, Elizabeth Zimmer, and Dale Ann Steiber's edited volume *Envisioning Dance on Film and Video* (Routledge, 2002) looks at a wide array of dance in both popular and experimental films. It also considers the ethnographic dance film/documentary and choreographers who have worked with film and the moving image.[3] This anthology continues the trajectory set up by these works but focuses exclusively on the popular screen.

Critical dance studies emerges as the primary methodology through which to read the multiplicity of choreographies on the screen. Whether it is the now iconic backward bend of Neo in *The Matrix*, or Baby's leap into Johnny Castle's arms in *Dirty Dancing*, dance studies provides tools to facilitate literacy in how bodies signify and this handbook addresses the lack of accessible scholarship on popular dance in film, television, music videos, the Internet, advertisements, and video games. I envision this anthology as a useful resource for students and teachers who can read through its pages, view the attached links, and see how analysis about dance on the popular screen might be done. After the following chapter summaries, which provide a cursory overview of the content in the anthology, I will provide some suggestions for students on how to engage with watching, analyzing, and writing critically about dance on popular screens.

SCREENED HISTORIES

The anthology consists of five sections, with each focusing on a specific type of screen where popular dance takes place. The first section, *Screened Histories*, features films that tell a story of a particular dance history (the can-can in *Moulin Rouge!*, hip-hop in *Breakin'* and *Wild Style*); films that belong within dance film histories (*Dance Girl Dance, Stormy Weather*); or films that feature a dance (*Swan Lake* featured in *Black Swan*) that is part of a specific dance history. Clare Parfitt-Brown's "An Australian in Paris: Techno-Choreographic Bohemianism in *Moulin Rouge!*" examines the cancan in Baz Luhrmann's *Moulin Rouge!* and introduces the concept of "prosthetic memory," which facilitates a new way to read the dancing in the film (Chapter 1). Parfitt-Brown "is particularly interested in how the on-screen bodies, layered with historical and cultural references and set in motion by choreography and the camera, affect the bodies on the other side of the screen." Her analysis advocates an embodied spectatorship, not a passive ocular-centric one. This is of special interest to students of dance on the popular screen who can read this chapter and begin to consider what it means to be kinesthetically involved while watching dancing bodies on screen. How does this change our role as spectator and what new opportunities for embodied interactions with film does Parfitt-Brown set up through her analysis of *Moulin Rouge!*?

Mary Simonson's chapter about Dorothy Arzner's film *Dance, Girl, Dance* (1941) gets its title from a comment well-known columnist Hedda Hopper made about the film, namely that it was a different kind of ballet (Chapter 2). Simonson argues that "the evolving identities and careers of the film's female characters are as much a critique of national artistic identity as a critique of contemporary gender roles: in *Dance, Girl, Dance*, it is on and through the female body that American art—and our ways of experiencing and understanding it—is negotiated and defined." This film also engages with the hierarchies constructed between popular dance and ballet and how the female characters practicing these respective dances (Lucille Ball as the show girl, Maureen O'Hara as the ballerina) become archetypes of paradoxical femininities. Films about dance often establish these types of binaries between dance forms, and this chapter teases out the cultural signifiers of white femininities that continue to have currency.

Alexandra Harlig's chapter "emphasizes three different moments in social dance history where the popular screen had a similar impact, spreading locally or socially narrow forms across the country from their communities of origin to wider communities of practice" (Chapter 3). By focusing on the newsreels of Vernon and Irene Castle, as well as the Charleston and the Twist on American Bandstand in the 1950s, Harlig's chapter makes a case for the significant impact that film and television screens have on audience spectatorship and participation in dance. Harlig provides a historical overview of these three moments and ultimately argues that "through these cycles of dissemination, development, and re-mediation, geographically and socio-economically disparate groups became connected through embodied practice and the ritual of watching." Harlig's chapter helps to situate how watching dances on screen creates audience, fans, and community; it also makes clear the ways in which we experience dance on screen today, particularly the communities that emerge from learning similar choreographies via the screen (Gangnam Style, Beyoncé's *Single Ladies*, and the Harlem Shake, to name a few).

Ariel Osterweis's chapter operates in a two-fold manner (Chapter 4). First, it references the significance of *Swan Lake* within canonical ballet history. Second, it uses the virtuosity expected to perform the 32 *fouettés* of Odette's solo to begin a discussion on how dance, virtuosity, and ambition function in Darren Aronofsky's *Black Swan*. Although the film is about a ballerina who longs to perform the challenging dual role of Odile/Odette in *Swan Lake, Black Swan* is not necessarily about dance. Instead, dance plays a secondary role to lead character Nina's psychological demise. It is dance though, particularly the virtuosic expectations of ballet technique and the perfectionist tendencies it creates, that drives Nina to madness. Osterweis demonstrates how a theoretically informed reading of technique, virtuosity, and ballet offers new insights into this popular and highly discussed film.

Singin' in the Rain (1952), another popular film featuring the iconic dance number of Gene Kelly frolicking in the rain, comprises Fogarty's chapter (Chapter 5). Fogarty sets out to "follow the sociological impulse to question how 'creativity' is assigned to particular artists, directors and dancers, and how certain societal factors contribute to the making of performances and importantly, to comparisons between performances." She examines the iconic dance number alongside its reiteration in a Volkswagen advertisement where Kelly's face becomes superimposed on a poppin', lockin', break-dancing body. Issues surrounding the value of popular dance, authenticity, and creative genius meander through Fogarty's discussion of Kelly's rain-soaked choreography and its refashioning for the purposes of brand marketing.

Stormy Weather (1943) features another famous dance on screen scene. Lena Horne looks wistfully through a window and the camera follows her gaze to reveal Katherine Dunham standing out in the rain. From there, a dissolve brings the viewer to an imaginary moment featuring one of the many memorable dance numbers in the film. Trenka examines the variety of dance numbers in *Stormy Weather* through issues of appreciation, appropriation, and assimilation (Chapter 6). She argues that *"Stormy Weather's* fragmentary entertainment history self-reflexively and paradoxically—and to some degree involuntarily—reveals Hollywood's strategies in the exploitation of black talent. Though carelessly anachronistic at times, the film's panoply of styles and stars self-referentially chronicles the history of black dance in white Hollywood in all its contradictory ambivalence." Her careful reading of a popular film that celebrates black cultural achievement despite the corrosive racial environment of 1940s America demonstrates how popular screen entertainments often act as palliatives to social ills, with dance functioning as the opportunity to temporarily forget (and idealistically correct) all wrongs. Trenka, along with the other contributors in this volume, reveals how the social component of dance, that is, the where, who, and why of people dancing, merits careful consideration.

Thomas DeFrantz's chapter traces a genealogy of hip-hop in films: *Fame* (1980), *Flashdance* (1983), *Wild Style* (1983), *Beat Street* (1984), *Breakin'* (1984), *Breakin' 2* (1984), and *Style Wars* (1985) (Chapter 7). He suggests that Hollywood subsumed these "breaksploitation" films as hip-hop became more mainstream by the 1990s, thereby paving the way for the dance and competition films of the 90s and 00s (e.g., *Save the Last Dance, Step Up, Stomp the Yard*). A hip-hop body emerges on screen and DeFrantz asserts that "the hip[-]hop body produced in Hollywood films is one that stands as representative of racial and cultural exchange, indicates the possibility of progressive group politics, and restricts structures of hierarchical, old-guard authority." By elucidating this history, DeFrantz positions black social dance forms, its innovators, performers, and practitioners as crucial components in the history of the Hollywood dance film.

THE COMMERCIAL BIG SCREEN

This section showcases chapters that analyze different aspects of commercial dance films through identity politics, commercialism, technology, and the politics of moving bodies. In these narratives cultural signifiers about race, gender, class, and sexuality (among others) appear, reappear, and circulate. In many of these films, the filmic apparatus perpetuates ideological binaries: high/low art, ballet/social dance, white/black (othered) bodies, and boy/girl (heteronormative) relationships. These films also construct dance and its practice as a form of self-discovery and individual expression. The scholars in this section highlight how these binaries, ideologies, and constructions shape the narratives, characters, and dance in their respective chapters. In so doing, they demonstrate the types of analyses a student might engage in when watching or researching the types of danced representations present in such films.

The classic Hollywood dance film, *Dirty Dancing* (1987) begins this foray into the commercial screen. Roxane Fenton and Colleen Dunagan's chapter explains how dance helps to shape Baby's transition from "baby" to woman (Chapter 8). By looking at how race, class, gender, and sexuality literally partner throughout the film, Fenton and Dunagan argue that the "film presents Baby's character learning and adopting normative notions of femininity as she learns to dance. Further, by changing her body, Baby moves from a state of idealistic naivety to one of mature, sexualized womanhood." Fenton and Dunagan particularly examine how the camerawork and editing facilitate Baby's transition, thereby demonstrating how the camera can certainly function as a choreographer in dance on screen. They also point out that despite the film taking place in 1963, during the American Civil Rights Movement, these historically significant social upheavals make no appearance in the film. Baby's emerging womanhood, although occurring among the differently raced and classed bodies that dance in the sheds behind the resort, becomes the central narrative. Those brown and black bodies dancing alongside her and by extension enabling her to become more comfortable with her sexuality serve a narrative function. Through the activity of dancing, of moving one's body, the visible differences between Baby's body and theirs disappear. Dance in *Dirty Dancing* not only functions as a liberating practice for Baby, but as one that allows for the racial and class tensions that were taking place in 1963 to disappear. Once again, dance both highlights but ultimately erases difference, with Fenton and Dunagan unpacking these differences for their readers.

The erasure of difference reverberates throughout Cindy García's chapter on the sequel (or more precisely prequel to) *Dirty Dancing: Havana Nights* (2004).[4] (Chapter 9). García problematizes the representation of American and *Cubana* femininities in the film, arguing that Katey's white American body and its practice of Cuban social dance leads to the displacement of *Cubana* femininity in the film. Katey's relationship with Javier, the Cuban boy, and her dedication to learn Cuban dance so that she can be his dance partner in a competition at a local nightclub leads her to practice with a *Cubana*. García's chapter focuses on a brief exchange between Katey and the *Cubana* hotel employee who teaches Katey how to be more "feminine." Rather than focus on the heteronormative romance plot in this film, García's intention "to offer an alternate reading based on the homosocial interactions that occur in the periphery" points to how the multiple layers of signification in this exchange foreground the power relationships inherent in corporeal interactions between differently raced and classed bodies.

Inna Arzumanova's chapter on *Save the Last Dance* (another favorite essay topic for undergraduate dance studies students) explores how the interracial, heteronormative romance narrative told through dance hints to a post-racial logic (Chapter 10). This chapter questions how dance narratives enable post-racial fantasies to emerge where the racial stereotypes associated with the bodies dancing become elided, while gender and sexuality move to the forefront. Arzumanova argues that, "[i]n narrating the nation as a utopia of racial harmony and easy social and racial mobility, [*Save the Last Dance*] deflects from the current realities plaguing interracial coupling, obscuring subtle but mainstream racist discourse and the sustained effort to mark, identify and contain difference at all costs." Again, dance functions as the activity through which these tensions manifest. Arzumanova continues to suggest what other contributors in this section do; that the filmic apparatus positions dance as an innocuous, almost utopian activity that allows for transcendence from social realities. The social, that which inscribes our bodies with raced, classed, and gendered modes of being and moving, can be escaped by moving those very same raced, classed, and gendered bodies. This type of circular (and perhaps even faulty) logic shapes how Hollywood dance films continue to erase the value of difference while at the same time highlighting it as a distinguishing characteristic among the variety of dancing bodies on the screen.

Like García, Raquel Monroe's chapter on *Step Up 2: The Streets* pays close attention to the peripheral character of the unnamed double-dutch-playing girl as a way to problematize the construction of white femininity as portrayed by the character of Andie (Chapter 11). Monroe shares her frustration as she recounts memories of when she was a teenager longing to see black female characters dancing as leads in films. For her, *Step Up 2* showcases white female exceptionalism in black social dance forms at the expense of black bodies. One notable moment in the film is when Andie reverberates her butt during a dance class. As Monroe articulates, "the filmic apparatus choreographs Andie's dancing as an integral part of her embodied cultural experience, yet shrouds the labor of the young black bodies with which she aligns herself. Taken from the playground and placed in other contexts, black girls' jiggling flesh transgresses, while Andie elevates her white flesh as an accomplished, aesthetically pleasing spectacle." Monroe's analysis complicates a seemingly benign dance gesture (coded as self-expression in the film's narrative) and shifts it into a space where discourses of race, power, and appropriation reside.

Discourses about race, space, and affect permeate Stephanie Batiste's chapter on the dance documentary *Rize* (2005). Chapter 12 titled "Affect-ive Moves," explores the dance practices of clowning and krumping as featured in David LaChappelle's film. Batiste states that "the creative acts of krump and clown dancing express young L.A. dancers' sense of self and community through kinetic affect, that is, through a complex expressive matrix of joy, disappointment, ownership, ecstasy, and danger that they embed in the dance." She continues further in the chapter to examine "krump's engagement with violence to reveal dancers' complicated relationship to this aspect of urban life." Furthermore, Batiste focuses on the affective ties to community and urban space that krumping and clowning provide. She writes, "for krumpers, dance and the body serve as sites for processing, absorbing, deflecting, claiming urban space, not over-simply resisting victimization to it. The dance practice carves out social space." Although the film, like others analyzed in this volume, is not without its problematic representational strategies, Batiste's cogent analysis of *Rize* demonstrates how to unpack multiple layers of meaning within a film that, on the surface, merely attempts to showcase an exciting urban dance form. Interesting to note is that one of the dancers featured in *Rize*, L'il C, is now a judge on the popular television dance competition show *So You Think You Can Dance* (which has a chapter dedicated exclusively to it in this volume).

Continuing with the theme of racialized bodies and their representation, Blanco Borelli's chapter centers around the mulatta body in the films *Sparkle* (1976), *Flashdance* (1983), and *Honey* (2003) (Chapter 13). Blanco Borelli's analysis of this mulatta film "trilogy" seeks to unravel how the Hollywood filmic apparatus engages with signifiers of raced sexuality and hierarchies of dance styles to enforce and reify mythic narratives about dance, dancing raced bodies, and dance-making. By establishing a genealogy of the mulatta body in a US context through dance and/or performance films, these juxtapositions illustrate how the mulatta subject develops from tragic figure (through the character of Sister in *Sparkle*) to an independent and self-reliant one (in *Honey*).

The last chapter in this section does not focus on a dance film specifically, yet theories of the body inform it. Burrill examines the bodies in motion in *The Matrix* (1999) and in so doing sets up "how bodies on screen are not only imagined and choreographed, but also how they are rehearsed, captured, digitized, reproduced, bought, sold, presented and commodified" (Chapter 14). Explaining Neo's now famous corporeal gesture, Burrill states that "when Neo bends over backwards, it is a signal that the greater culture is feeling equally strained. But, at the same time, the attendant excitement is equally palpable. It is as if we are re-learning our bodies in our collision with the digital and the virtual. Considering that Neo dodges all the bullets save one, the scene is also a potent reminder that our bodies will always be subject to growing pains, mistakes and obsolescence, no matter how virtuosic our digital or real performance is or how seductive the mode of representation may be." In this statement, Burrill links the gesture of the backbend to our contemporary moment, where the many discomforts of global capitalism, technological advancement, and terror warnings keep our bodies alert. This chapter thus sets up a framework through which one might view specific movements, gestures, or everyday choreographies as symptomatic of our neoliberal condition. In other words, moving bodies, regardless of whether they are moving in time to music and dancing or moving in self-defense, materialize their social realities (even if, according to *The Matrix*, reality is an illusion).

Music Video and Televisual Bodies

The third section focuses on the impact that music videos have had on popular dance and its dissemination. Here, the anthology engages with the role that dancing plays in music video and television competition shows. Like earlier sections, these contributors focus on factors such as gender, representation, appropriation, capitalism, and the impact social media has by enabling multiple understandings of these televisual bodies and the dancing that they do. Takiyah Nur Amin's chapter on Beyoncé's video *Girls Run the World* makes a case for how the seemingly innocuous glamorized performance of Beyoncé actually articulates a complex historical-political matrix that surrounds black women's bodies (Chapter 15). Nur Amin pays particular attention to circulating images of Michelle Obama, nineteenth-century circulations, and constructions of black femininity in order to tease out the multi-layered problems operating subliminally within Beyoncé's video performance. She asserts, "The video, with its apparent pronouncement and celebration of women's empowerment circulates in a public sphere that is contextualized by long-standing historical discourses that render its message ironic and inert, especially when considered in relationship to the real business of 'runnin' the world.'"

Chih-Chieh Liu's chapter on the music video performances of Chinese-American superstar Coco Lee, particularly in her video *Hip Hop Tonight* (2006), calls into question the claims of authenticity, naturalism and sexiness that circulate around Coco's performance (Chapter 16). As a transnational celebrity, Coco's body signifies in multiple ways. Liu argues "that Coco's dancing body is a symbolic battlefield: it is context- and media-specifically constructed according to Mandarin pop's logic of spectacle. This process is marked by a constant negotiation, resulting in a paradoxical formation which is full of contradictions." These contradictions become the crux of her analysis. Liu, like Nur Amin, demonstrates how to critically engage and expand on a short, polysemic text.

Notions of authenticity also revolve around Philippa Thomas's chapter on Beyoncé's 2009 hit song/video *Single Ladies (Put a Ring on It)* (Chapter 17). By looking at the original video and issues of choreographic authenticity, queer fan iterations on YouTube, and flash mob performances, Thomas "seeks to explore how cultural texts disseminated online are made and remade, challenged and championed; the mutability inherent to all texts becoming literally visible in this specific environment." What Thomas makes clear in this chapter is what she calls "the tangled politics inherent in cultural consumption," specifically by examining the complex web of "audience, authorship, authenticity, racism, gender and power."

Dancing televisual bodies continue to enthrall audiences, particularly in recent dance competition reality shows. Laura Robinson's chapter on UK television dance competitions focuses on the performances of race, masculinity, and virtuosity by UK hip-hop dance crews *Diversity*, *Flawless*, and *Animaniax* (Chapter 18). As she explains, her chapter "aims to equip the reader with the critical methods for exploring meaning within male group urban dance performances on the UK popular screen." Robinson demonstrates these methods by focusing on how the television show, operating within a market-driven consumer capitalist framework, represents the predominantly black British male dancing bodies. Discourses about spectacularization, black masculinity, and commodification of dance emerge.

Robinson's chapter partners exceptionally well with Alexis Weisbrod's chapter on *So You Think You Can Dance* (SYTYCD) (Chapter 19). Weisbrod claims that this "show alters and recontextualizes dancing bodies in order to make its images accessible for a wide audience. The result is not a legitimization of a pre-existing form of dance but, instead, a popularization of a new practice, a carefully constructed bricolage of dance that spectacularizes white and non-white bodies alike through a particular rhetoric." For Weisbrod, the judges' comments contain potent discourse. She "considers how the show's lexicon, specifically the words and rhetoric used by the judges, creates bodies and racially marks dance movement and genres as a tool for audience use as they read dance in the mediated space of *SYTYCD*." Weisbrod takes her reader through the organizational logic of the show, "and provides examples from the various seasons to showcase how *SYTYCD* continually constructs and legitimizes bodies and their technical dance training." For those students who are fans of the show, this chapter opens up a critical perspective without necessarily undermining the value and enjoyment of the show. More importantly, it also demonstrates how dance partners with language in order to construct many of the ideas crucial to this anthology: race, gender, nation, class, and heteronormativity.

Screening Nationhood

The inextricable link between dance and national identity shapes the different chapters in this section, which range from dances in Hollywood musicals of the 1950s, to post-Revolutionary Cuban films, to an American performance documentary, and to a Bollywood-inspired film. Kathaleen Boche's chapter on Western musicals and their choreographed numbers from the end of World War II through the 1950s analyzes some of the most popular western musicals from this period, including *Seven Brides for Seven Brothers* (1954), *Annie Get Your Gun* (1950), and *Oklahoma!* (1955). Boche focuses "on how improvisational ingenuity serves as a vehicle to express elements of American post-war whiteness through the dancing bodies of the frontiersmen and women in these films. The idea that necessity breeds creativity is not a new one, and it is also not a uniquely American one, yet this chapter seeks to demonstrate how these qualities manifested in the choreographies created and used in the musicals." What Boche's chapter makes clear is how film, dance, and choreography function as products of the socio-historical moment in which they develop. Furthermore, the ideologies of traditional gender roles, rugged individualism, and (white) American exceptionalism not only appear in these musicals as products, but served as potential guidelines for social choreographies by audiences who were restructuring their understandings of themselves and the world after the social, political, and historical upheavals created by World War II. In other words, not only are these musicals representative of their historical moment, but they also contributed to the appropriation and enactment of the aforementioned (so-called) American ideals.

Victor Fowler's chapter on several dance sequences in post-Revolutionary Cuban films also articulates a politics of national identity (Chapter 21). For Fowler, dance operates as a quintessential Cuban structure of feeling.[5] As the Cuban film industry began to develop under state-controlled support, the representation of Cuba as a pluralistic dancing society began to circulate in films post-1959. Like Boche, Fowler looks at several moments on celluloid that elucidate components of a national identity. Again, each film (*Cuba Baila* (1960), *Un Día en el Solar* (1965), *Los del Baile* (1965), *Memorias del Subdesarrollo* (1965), *Son o No Son* (1980), and *Solo Habana* (2000)) provides a window into a specific historical moment in post-Revolutionary Cuban history. The presence of the dancing Cuban body (whether male, female, white, mulatto, or black) functions as a discursive site that, according to Fowler, demonstrates something about the Cuban people: "their capacity to resist, and their stubborn hope."

Rosemary Candelario's chapter on *David Chapelle's Block Party* does not pretend to be about dance (Chapter 22). Like Burrill, Candelario analyzes the bodies in the film to make a case for how moving, gesturing, and speaking bodies generate critical discourse. In Candelario's case, the bodies of *Block Party* address a politics of the American nation, one that is multi-racial and, in this performative instance, utopian. Candelario writes that in "addressing the commodification of their bodies and their culture, the attendees of the block party enact alterity, and in the process offer up a vision of a (utopian) national body as young, black, predominantly male, and significantly both urban and rural." Both the film and the block party "enact not a carnivalesque rehearsal of revolution, but a utopic vision of community." Candelario's analysis adroitly maneuvers through a variety of interdisciplinary theorists to demonstrate how theories of the body can inform film analysis. Regardless of whether bodies dance, theories about the body facilitate ways in which to read the signifying processes that bodies set into motion.

Amita Nijhawan's chapter on *Bride and Prejudice* (2004) looks to four dance sequences in the film to make a case for how dance mobilizes the social class and value that the different bodies in the film possess (Chapter 23). Nijhawan writes, "the dance sequences in *Bride and Prejudice* are not just glamorous interludes, but they are an essential tactic that delineates class structure within India, as well as between India and its economic others. Just like manners figure in Austen's novel to distinguish between the worth of various characters, in the film, dance sequences, bodily movement, and deportment demarcate lines of breeding, morality, and economic worth. It is the dancing bodies that tell us the difference between who is worthy and who is less so. In other words, the dances construct the class and moral hierarchy of the film." Again, the methodology of critical dance studies enables a rigorous analysis of dance on the popular screen. What this chapter makes clear is how cross-cultural exchange and, in Darcy's case, transformation, occurs through the physical practice of dance. Additionally, that shift into a new physicality has greater significance when read within the context of the relationship India has with itself and other nations.

CYBER SCREENS

The popularity of YouTube and video games provides new screens through which to consider the role of dance, particularly its practice and dissemination. In this section, some contributors examine choreographies made specifically for Internet viewing and circulation, while others analyze the significance of gaming and the impact that dance video games, specifically *Dance Central*, have on concepts of embodiment, choreography, and dance pedagogy.

Harmony Bench's chapter on Michael Jackson's *Thriller* video presents her interest in the deceased pop icon's body of work, specifically how it addresses notions community (Chapter 24). She looks to the numerous renditions of Thriller's choreography—the Cebu Filipino prisoners, the flash mobs set up after Jackson's death, the version in the film *13 Going on 30*—to articulate a politics of social belonging. Bench's interest lies in "the way dancers asserted a collective ownership over the choreography, which they deployed in both private and public settings." She goes on to argue that, "as a shared cultural artifact, 'Thriller' became a privileged site for articulating a collective sense of belonging that pushed against pervasive discourses of threat after September 11, 2001 and of insecurity amidst a euphemistically labeled 'global economic downturn'. Further, through the rupturing effects of flash mobs, 'Thriller' also offered a way to resignify public spaces that had given themselves over to the fear and suspicion of a population caught up in the 'War on Terror.' " Bench makes explicit the connections that this globally popular choreography has with current geopolitical economic upheavals. Bench suggests that the participation in the choreography "offered American audiences a counter-discourse to the War on Terror and a failing economy, one that incorporated the monstrous in order to exorcise fear and promoted a mode of collective and affective belonging through performance." Social media facilitates the creation of online communities; communities that exist whether members are fans of a particular YouTube video, gamers, or possess shared modes of identity.

Karyn Recollet's investigation of contemporary Indigenous thought and cultural expression through hip-hop traces the relationship Canadian Indigenous communities have to hip-hop (Chapter 25). For them, hip-hop offers a performative and expressive space through which to dialogue and discuss their own conceptualizations and understandings of Native identity. Recollet explores "the significance of dancing 'between the break beats' where *between* spaces are portals to creativity and the life force that connects us all. [She] look[s] at the hip-hop crew as an important site for the reconfiguration of rich and complex Native identities and the expression of how *embodiment* functions to transcend colonialism." Recollet specifically examines the YouTube videos made by the indigenous media collective A Tribe Called Red (ATCR). By combining Hollywood images/scenes that feature Native bodies with electronic beats and pow wow rhythms (something they call "electric pow wow"), ATCR reconfigures indigeneity. Recollet states that "they are using these images as the dominant-cultural raw materials to create alternative identities through mash ups and the critical use of color, form and subject matter in film." Recollet's analysis points to how social media and the accessibility to a computer screen provides a necessary forum for communities (particularly historically marginalized ones) to contest, create, and circulate their perceptions about the complexity inherent in national (tribal) identity.

Burrill and Blanco Borelli's chapter focuses on another type of community: the gaming community, particularly ones that play *Dance Central* (Chapter 26). The structure of this co-authored chapter attempts to "mirror the relationship between the player's body and the player's brain, both working together during the game, yet often in conflict when in comes to that difficult (or simple) move." Furthermore, the two authorial voices relate to the two competing bodies in the new version of *Dance Central*, where players can battle over whose interpretation of the choreography receives the most points. To be fair, this chapter does not purport to performatively render a competition between Burrill and Blanco Borelli, but to draw on their individual research strengths in order to begin a discussion about how "*Dance Central* (as well as other games played with the body, on the Wii or the Xbox Kinect system, for example) enable[s] new ways of learning and embodiment through social choreographies, while at the same time de- and re-materializing the demonstrative visceral body of the choreographer." What does it mean for popular dance to literally dance alongside and through the digital? This chapter provides some thoughts and preliminary theorizations for further discussion. It is the hope that students who have an interest in dance gaming may pursue this line of questioning further and establish exciting theorizations of their own.

Sherril Dodds's essay concludes this anthology with some insightful thoughts on the importance and relevance of new methods of inquiry into dance on the popular screen (Chapter 27). An advocate of popular dance as a rich site for analysis, Dodds states that popular screen dance "presents enticing moments of virtuosity, transformation, humour, fantasy and desire, concepts which should not be readily devalued." She makes a claim for the role that moving bodies play and the value that they circulate. Because of the significance of her book *Dance on Screen* to the field, her chapter contribution thus "revisits what might be central to the way in which we study popular screen dance, what ought we to value and what still requires some investment in our intellectual efforts." Dodds's reflection piece serves as a fitting conclusion to an anthology that owes an intellectual debt to her important monograph.

FINAL NOTES ON WATCHING AND WRITING DANCE (ON THE POPULAR SCREEN)

Because popular dance on the screen continually shifts, develops, and changes (and dance fads come and go), it is crucial to have a theoretical framework set up from which to begin to analyze the plethora of choreographies, bodies, and filmic nuances that occur. As such, the chapters in this anthology provide tools through which a student of popular dance on screen can begin to engage with the practice. Each chapter can be examined to identify the rhetorical strategies the specific author utilizes to materialize the moving screen bodies on the page. Another useful tactic would be to identify how the specific author(s) utilize their respective theorists to support, undergird, and/ or expand their analysis. In this way, students can begin to explore how dance theorizes identity politics, space, or nation and what theories emerge as productive ways into a particular set of moving images, choreography, or bodies. Furthermore, each chapter provides an avenue into the methodological diversity available for dance and performance analysis.

What do we do, then, after we watch dance on screen? Passive spectatorship belies the urgency of our critical engagement with these performances. As students of popular dance on screen, one of the most important ways to contribute to ongoing discussions, debates, and scholarship about popular dance is to think about the politics of its written representation and to conceive new ways of making the dance *dance* on the page. An introductory question such as, "What is the body doing?" allows the spectator to direct her focus to the body, its appearance, and movements. Another question then follows: How is the body doing "it"? Here, one would engage with active verbs to ascertain the movement(s) and then add adverbial qualifiers to indicate the quality of the movement. If, for example, the dancer juts her hip, how is she doing it? Is it a forceful jutting? Or is it subtle? How about a seductive jut? Or a lazy jut? Or possibly even a static jut? Each of these four descriptions describes a different quality of movement. It is important to think about the specifics about the body movement and find the most suitable words that can best describe the complexity of the dancing body. Other elements to consider include the location of the camera. Where is it placed as this particular hip lazily juts out? Is it capturing her body in a full frontal body shot? Is the camera close-up, angled alongside her lazily jutting hip? The choreography of the camera, the camera as a body unto itself, where it looks and where it gazes from, contributes to the reading of the dancing as it progresses. A close-up of the seductive jutting hip, for example, might be sexualizing this particular body. If so, what other possible signifiers of sexuality might one identify? What histories of sexualized bodies is the filmic apparatus calling upon? By filmic apparatus, I mean the term that developed within cinema studies that argues that film is ideological due to the ideological nature of its methods of representation, such as the camera or the editing.[6] Other questions to consider include: What themes become evident as the dancing body continues to move around the screen? What cultural signifiers/representations and/or stereotypes are being circulated? What bodies tend to get associated with certain dance styles? What are the underlying historical, social, cultural, and/or political implications behind these representations? These are the kinds of questions the contributors to this anthology surely engage with as they carefully watch, write, and analyze.

Audiences engage with spectatorship in ideological ways, since we read and make meaning about what we watch from our cultural positioning and understanding of our social environment. Thus, as audiences who spend time watching a variety of popular screens on a daily basis (admittedly, some more than others), we must develop the analytical tools to understand the role that patriarchal capitalist ideologies can play in the way images get constructed, circulated, (re)invented, problematized, and commodified. When these images contain dancing and signifying bodies literally setting the multiplicity of ideological representations into motion, it becomes clear why popular dance on screen offers such a rich site for critical engagement and enquiry.

NOTES

1. George Michael, *Flawless (Go to the City)* http://youtu.be/QgGDcn46aW8 [accessed March 2, 2012].
2. Marcel Mauss, "Techniques of the Body" in *Incorporations*, ed. Jonathan Crary and Sanford Kwinter (New York: Zone Books, 1992).
3. Carol Vernallis's *Experiencing Music Video: Aesthetics and Cultural Context* (New York: University of Columbia Press, 2004) provides a good foundation for how to engage with the music video genre through media and film analysis. Dianne Railton and Paul Watson's *Music Video and the Politics of Representation* (Edinburgh: University of Edinburgh Press, 2011) focuses on specific music videos to examine different modes of representational analysis, such as gender and race.

4. *Dirty Dancing* (1987) takes place in 1963. *Dirty Dancing: Havana Nights* (2004) takes place in 1958 prior to the Cuban Revolution. Patrick Swayze makes a cameo in *Havana Nights*, thereby showing the audience how he may have gained and developed his Latin dance skills before moving from Cuba to upstate New York.

5. Cultural theorist Raymond Williams coined the term "structure of feeling" to express how individuals create a common set of perceptions and values within their historical moment to understand and define their lived reality and cultural experience. Raymond Williams, *Marxism and Literature* (New York: Oxford Paperbacks, 1977).

6. Phillip Rosen, ed., *Narrative, Apparatus, Ideology: A Film Theory Reader* (New York: Columbia University Press, 1986).

BIBLIOGRAPHY

Dodds, Sherril. *Dance on Screen: Genres and Media from Hollywood to Experimental Art.* Basingstoke: Palgrave MacMillan, 2001.

Dodds, Sherril. *Dancing on the Canon: Embodiments of Value in Popular Dance.* Basingstoke: Palgrave MacMillan, 2011.

Mitoma, Judy, Elizabeth Zimmer, and Dale Ann Steiber, eds. *Envisioning Dance on Film and Video.* London & New York: Routledge, 2002.

PART I

SCREENED HISTORIES

CHAPTER 1

·······································

AN AUSTRALIAN IN PARIS: TECHNO-CHOREOGRAPHIC BOHEMIANISM IN *MOULIN ROUGE!*

·······································

CLARE PARFITT-BROWN

THE film *Moulin Rouge!* (2001) might be thought of as a historical and cultural vortex, drawing in, fragmenting, and recombining art and popular culture of the last two centuries to produce a bohemian-inspired, turn-of-the-millennium film musical. The production and consumption of this cinematic eclecticism have been considered by scholars primarily in musical and filmic terms.[1] This chapter, however, takes bodies as its starting point—those on screen and those watching the film. It is particularly interested in how the on-screen bodies, layered with historical and cultural references and set in motion by choreography and the camera, affect the bodies on the other side of the screen. This is an important consideration for an analysis of *Moulin Rouge!*, as critical reviews of the film suggest that it elicits a particularly visceral response in its spectators. José Arroyo, reviewer for *Sight and Sound*, described being "walloped by talent and frazzled by cleverness";[2] Peter Travers, writing for *Rolling Stone*, "felt mauled";[3] and *The Observer*'s Philip French was "targeted by a squadron of kamikaze bombers loaded with sugary marshmallow."[4] This chapter explores these physical experiences of spectatorship, focusing on the film's dance sequences. It argues that in these sequences, choreography and digital technology (including computer-generated imagery and editing) combine to allow spectators to physically experience on-screen bodies that are historically and culturally complex, distant, and "other." In so doing, *Moulin Rouge!* aligns itself with a bohemian tradition of cross-cultural and transhistorical self-performance, while reconfiguring that tradition for a twenty-first-century context.

"Not What It Was, but What It Felt Like to Be There"

The dominant mode of contemporary filmmaking is a cinematic naturalism that invites spectators to view realistic action as if through a keyhole or window. Baz Luhrmann, the director of *Moulin Rouge!*, has sought in his trilogy of "Red Curtain" films to break these naturalistic conventions by using non-realistic devices of dance and song to keep the audience aware that they are watching a film.[5] In so doing, Luhrmann encourages viewers to adopt a more active form of spectatorship.[6] In particular, he aims to induce a physical and emotional response in the spectator, like those described by the critics above.

> "You're constantly awaking the audience so they participate," Luhrmann says. "Just when you think, 'This is so cheesy, I'm going to throw up,' I'm going to kick you in the stomach. In that state, there's an agreement that they know they are going to be emotionally manipulated, and they surrender to it."[7]

Luhrmann acknowledges that this form of "audience participatory cinema"[8] is no longer common in Western feature-length filmmaking. Indeed, film historian Tom Gunning argues that although a participatory aesthetic characterized the early "cinema of attractions" from 1895 to about 1907, the rise of narrative cinema forced it "underground" into genres such as the musical, where it was contained within song-and-dance numbers separated by narrative sequences.[9] *Moulin Rouge!*, therefore, is intended as an experiment in transposing a cinematic language across time and space to a historical and cultural context in which it is no longer the norm.[10] Luhrmann cites Hollywood and Bollywood musicals as sources for his construction of a participatory film musical, while refusing to be defined by these totalizing modes of production, positioning *Moulin Rouge!* as an Australian film.[11]

Through the historically and culturally dislocated cinematic form of the film musical, spectators of *Moulin Rouge!* are invited to physically engage in an even more distant constructed past, a reimagined version of the Moulin Rouge of the 1890s. Luhrmann approaches this by seeking in his depiction of the cabaret not visual authenticity but sensory authenticity, that is, an evocation of how it would have *felt*. This involves translating the feeling of watching the cancan in the 1890s, for example, into comparable experiences in contemporary popular culture, through which the audience can physically connect with the past. Luhrmann explains, "we did come out of a historical reality, we just manipulated them [*sic*] to make some sort of code for us to understand—not what it was, but what it felt like to be there. That's quite a distinction. What the can-can was—a violent, sexy dance. What it would look like was a lot of leaping around in funny costumes. What it felt like was Fatboy Slim, people doing break-dancing, very funky. It's this kind of decoding, just helping the audience figure where they are in a given moment."[12] Elements of late twentieth-century hip-hop culture and the British

FIGURE 1.1 Screen capture of *Moulin Rouge!*, director Baz Luhrmann, (2001), "Zidler's Rap".

dance music scene of the 1990s are incorporated into the cancan number through the soundtrack (Fatboy Slim wrote *Because We Can* [2001] for the film), MTV-style editing, and the section entitled "Zidler's Rap," in which the Moulin Rouge manager, Harold Zidler, addresses the camera directly, flanked by female cancan dancers, in the style of a hip-hop music video (Fig. 1.1).[13] Luhrmann attempts to convey the exhilarating edginess of watching the cancan in the 1890s through these contemporary popular cultural references.

The film's choreographer, John O'Connell, similarly tried to convey a sensory experience, a taste or a feeling, rather than a particular historical image in the dance scenes. After extensive research, including reading books on the cancan, watching film musicals and Bollywood films, and learning Argentine tango and Indian classical dance, O'Connell brought these together "subliminally" in the rehearsal room, aiming "for the flavor of it rather than trying to recreate or recycle something."[14] By evoking familiar dance, music, and film cultures of the late twentieth century, *Moulin Rouge!* seeks to offer spectators a sensory encounter with a distant past beyond their living memories.

Media scholar Alison Landsberg uses the term "prosthetic memory" to describe memories transmitted by technologies of mass culture, such as cinema and experiential museums, which allow spectators to physically experience a past through which they did not live.[15] She argues that through films or museum exhibits about the Holocaust, for example, spectators can embody the memories of others, altering their subjectivity, and enabling empathy across boundaries of race, class, and gender. Landsberg and Luhrmann share a conviction that technological mediation does not foreclose, but rather allows the physical and emotional engagement of the audience with the film, by acting as a vehicle for the construction and transfer of memories. The notion of prosthetic memory provides a framework for thinking about how *Moulin Rouge!* creates a physical connection between spectators and the fin-de-siècle Parisian past.

A Bohemian Sensory Otherness

In pitching the play within the film, "Spectacular, Spectacular!," to the wealthy Duke, Zidler describes it as "the world's first completely modern, entirely electric, totally bohemian, all-singing, all-dancing stage spectacular." If Gilles Deleuze is right to assert that the play within the film often takes as its object the film itself,[16] then Zidler's hyperbolic assertion suggests that technology, bohemia, singing, and dancing are also fundamental elements of *Moulin Rouge!*. Zidler's statement implies that technology and bohemia are linked to song and dance in contributing to the spectacular qualities of the play/film, and therefore its relationship to the spectator. The next two sections will focus on the ways in which bohemia, dancing, and technology participate in the construction of prosthetic memory in *Moulin Rouge!*.

Luhrmann's previous theatrical direction of the opera *La Bohème* (1990) influenced the formative development of the *Moulin Rouge!* project:

> About ten years ago when we were researching *La Bohème*, the Puccini opera, and we went to the Moulin Rouge in Paris.... I was reminded... of a time and place—when Picasso was passing through there—when the popular culture of the 20th century was sediment that moved downstream from that place and time. It stuck with me. Finally, when we were looking for a place to set our Orphean world, it became not the idealistic bohemianism of 1830, but the commercialized bohemia of 1890/1900. This is a great reflection on us at this time, a time of incredible technological change, a time when the world is moving forwards and backwards. Armed with those three things, we had a starting point.[17]

Here, Luhrmann draws connections between the 1830s bohemian setting of *La Bohème*, the fin-de-siècle bohemianism at the heart of *Moulin Rouge!*, and the contemporary turn-of-the-millennium context. In particular, he notes the recurring theme of simultaneous nostalgia and innovation in these three historical moments. Perhaps, in choosing a fin-de-siècle bohemian setting for *Moulin Rouge!*, he recognized parallels between bohemian art and his own practice of scavenging from cultural history as a means of contemporary artistic reinvention. Indeed, bohemianism can be detected in Luhrmann's filmmaking not only as the cultural backdrop of several of his productions, but also as an artistic and cinematic philosophy.

English scholar Mike Sell identifies two particular characteristics of bohemia, "theatricalized authenticity" and "exoticism."[18] Following Sell, it might be observed that these elements have often combined in the bohemian attempt to fashion an "authentic" existence through performances of historical and cultural otherness. For example, Henri de Toulouse-Lautrec frequently performed gender and cultural cross-dressing in photographic portraits (a tendency referenced in *Moulin Rouge!* through the kimono he wears to echo the "Elephant Love Melody," evoking his costume in Maurice Guibert's photograph of 1892). Sell points out that *Moulin Rouge!* reproduces this practice of cross-cultural performance, citing references to blackness and the Roma gypsies that surround Satine. All of the main characters have orientalized equivalents in the play "Spectacular, Spectacular!" (for example, the Duke is orientalized as the maharajah, played by Zidler), and Christian is doubly exoticized since his role as the penniless sitar player is played by the Unconscious Argentinean, notably in the tango scene. Taking into account the nationalities of the film's actors adds another layer of cultural complexity. For example, the Australian actress Nicole Kidman plays the French courtesan Satine, who plays an Indian courtesan in "Spectacular, Spectacular!" Sell points out that "the theatre of bohemian exoticism can be simultaneously a memory theatre, too,"[19] making the past as ripe for bohemian appropriation as other cultures. For example, Catherine Martin, production designer of *Moulin Rouge!*, costumed Satine to evoke the feminine icons of film history. According to Martin, "The first moment we see Satine she is a combination of Marilyn Monroe (*How to Marry a Millionaire* [1953]), Marlene Dietrich (*Blue Angel* [1930]), with a sprinkle of *Cabaret* [1972] and a nod to Rita Hayworth in *Gilda* [1946]."[20] These cross-cultural and transhistorical performances in *Moulin Rouge!* might be considered a form of what Sell calls "bohemian memory,"[21] the rediscovery and glorification of forgotten cultural artifacts, especially those disdained by bourgeois arbiters of taste and defenders of sexual, racial, gender, or class boundaries.

The purpose of bohemian appropriations of the past and other cultures in *Moulin Rouge!* is partly narrative; Luhrmann claims that in the tango scene, for example, "the synchronicity [...] is really alive between a piece of existing culture [the 1978 song *Roxanne* by The Police] and our needs as storytellers."[22] Luhrmann reveals another purpose of his cross-cultural scavenging while reflecting on his collaboration with hip-hop artist Missy Elliot on the *Moulin Rouge!* soundtrack: "The great thing about the hip-hop folk is that they are fearless and culturally blind. [...] Their ability to steal from culture without judgement, without a decision about what is right or wrong or good or bad, *it's just does it affect you emotionally or not*, that blindness to pretension gets me going."[23] Perhaps Luhrmann admires Elliot's ability to create an emotional connection with the listener by "sampling" across cultural boundaries because this reflects his own aspirations. Luhrmann layers *Moulin Rouge!* with historical and cultural references with which the audience may already be familiar (Bollywood, rap culture, the golden era of Hollywood) in order to facilitate their emotional and physical connection to a time and place with which they may be less familiar (the *Moulin Rouge!* version of fin-de-siècle Paris). The result is "a heightened or created world that is at once familiar yet exotic, distant."[24] In *Moulin Rouge!*, audience participatory cinema and historical/cultural sampling combine to offer spectators a mode of sensory, emotional engagement with a constructed past.

Luhrmann recognizes that physical encounters across cultural and historical boundaries have been the foundation of popular, bohemian-influenced entertainment since at least the International Exhibitions of the nineteenth century.[25] Like the fin-de-siècle Moulin Rouge, *Moulin Rouge!* offers spectators a form of cultural and historical tourism.[26] Film scholar Anne Friedberg contends that cinema, from its emergence to the present day, has invited spectators to adopt a mobile, virtual gaze, allowing them to be virtually transported into worlds and bodies beyond their direct experience.[27] *Moulin Rouge!* makes visible, in both form and content, its inheritance of this notion of entertainment as a virtual, but sensory, encounter with culturally and historically distant bodies. It traces a complex ancestral web, from bohemia through the World's Fairs, the Moulin Rouge and early cinema, "underground"[28] into the Hollywood film musical, and across continents into Bollywood cinema, to a point of convergence in *Moulin Rouge!* itself. The film does not learn from and discard these ancestors, but accumulates them, leading to the sense expressed by a number of commentators that it is a museum film,[29] "a journey through the cultural history of film itself."[30] It is, however, as Brian McFarlane specifies, "not the kind of museum in which, say, the coins of the last 200 years are arranged neatly in glass cases (and very interesting, no doubt, for numismatists), but the kind to which you might take your children, feeling sure they and probably you will have a good time."[31] It is, in other words, an experiential museum of the kind described by Landsberg, in which visitors are invited to participate with their whole bodies, and in the process, perhaps, take on prosthetic memories. In *Moulin Rouge!*, bohemian memory becomes prosthetic memory; the cross-cultural/historical role-playing of the individual artist becomes a mass cultural technology for physically experiencing other worlds.

Techno-Choreographic Bohemianism

Deleuze writes that in some musicals, "dance is no longer the movement of dream which outlines a world, but now acquires depth, grows stronger as it becomes the sole means of entering into another world, that is, into another's world, into another's dream or past."[32] Film studies scholar Annette Kuhn has observed dance playing this role in the recollections of film spectators of the 1930s.[33] Several of her interviewees spoke of the moments in Fred Astaire and Ginger Rogers musicals when the dance number took the actors and spectators seamlessly from the "realistic" space of the narrative into the fantasy space of the musical number. Some interviewees remembered these moments as making them want to, and believe they could, dance. Kuhn summarizes their accounts: "The sensation imbues your body, and carries you out of your local picture house onto the familiar streets of your neighbourhood, and you are moved to dance along the pavement all the way home."[34] In these spectators' recollections, paradoxically, the non-naturalistic cinematic device of opening the dance into a fantasy space gave them the greatest sense of physical engagement with the film, making them want to dance themselves. As Walter Benjamin wrote of cinema in 1936 at the height of Astaire and Roger's fame, "The equipment-free aspect of reality here has become the height of artifice,"[35] that is, technological intervention is necessary to produce an unmediated experience of film. In these musical moments, dance and technology combine to break down the barrier between the spectator and the world of the film, inviting their physical engagement with the dancing bodies on screen.

Moulin Rouge! at first appears to treat dance in an opposite way to the Astaire and Rogers films. While Astaire was renowned for maintaining the integrity of the dancing body by using long takes and full-body shots, the editing of many of the dance numbers in *Moulin Rouge!* (by Jill Bilcock, Luhrmann's collaborator on all the "Red Curtain" films) deliberately breaks up the shape and rhythm of the original choreography and fragments the dancing bodies. This is most evident in the cancan number, which attempts to convey the exhilaration of Christian's first visit to the Moulin Rouge with a flurry of legs, faces and petticoats. Indeed, O'Connell was disappointed that the speed of the editing made it difficult to see his choreography.[36] Following in the tradition of Busby Berkeley and Gene Kelly, the choreography in *Moulin Rouge!* is no longer solely accomplished by a choreographer working with live bodies, but now also involves an editor working with the raw material of the rushes. For Luhrmann, this editing phase of the choreographic process can enhance the spectators' physical engagement with the characters and their emotional journey, rather than detracting from it. Therefore, in many of the musical numbers Luhrmann uses the opposite cinematic technique to Astaire—fragmentation of the body and rapid editing—to achieve the same effect, an unmediated, physical experience of the dancing bodies on screen. In fact, Astaire was not adverse to the technological manipulation of his dancing image to achieve this effect, and some of these techniques are echoed by Luhrmann, as shown in the example below. Therefore, despite Luhrmann's rejection of the full-body shot and the long take, his cinematic treatment of dance has more in common with Astaire's than it might at first appear.

The "Your Song" number in *Moulin Rouge!* makes evident the parallels between Astaire's and Luhrmann's technological manipulation of the dancing image to achieve the physical and emotional engagement of the audience. Christian woos Satine in her boudoir by singing Elton John's "Your Song" (1970). As they begin to dance, they spin together in a ballroom dancing hold, bringing to mind the ballroom-influenced style of Astaire and Rogers. This spin initiates a shift from the realistic space of the boudoir to a fantasy space in the sky above Paris (Fig. 1.2). Aurally, this shift is signaled by the replacement of Christian's voice with the operatic voice of Luciano Pavarotti, which appears to emanate from the man-in-the-moon (based on Georges Méliès's *Le Voyage dans la Lune* [1902]). Visually, the couple leaps from the window of the boudoir into the clouds, settling on a Parisian rooftop. Astaire had also evoked the feeling of being in love by using trick photography to dance in the air, dancing up to and on the Washington Square Arch in *The Belle of New York* (1952) and on the walls and ceiling in *Royal Wedding* (1951). In "Your Song," the aural shift into an operatic register combines with the couple's liberation from gravity to produce a sense of suspended reality, beyond the demands and complications of the underworld they have left behind. In this new world, anything is possible. Christian acquires an umbrella, skips with it in circles across the clouds, and hangs from the Eiffel Tower as if it were a lamppost, referring to another famous cinematic moment of love-inspired liberatory dancing: Gene Kelly's title number from *Singin' in the Rain* (1952). The final sequence of movement evokes Astaire and Rogers once again as Satine spins toward Christian, flaring her Rogers-esque dress, before Christian lifts her, still spinning, into his arms. As the song ends, the sky fades into the familiar surroundings

FIGURE 1.2 Screen capture of *Moulin Rouge!*, director Baz Luhrmann, (2001), "Your Song".

of the boudoir, where the couple are performing the same movement, suggesting that their emotions, rather than their physical bodies, had been dancing in the sky. The choreography of the scene invites the spectator to participate in the characters' emotional arc, rather than merely following their literal movements. And yet, echoing the Astaire and Rogers numbers in unrealistic fantasy spaces, Luhrmann chooses to convey this *genuine* emotion via a sequence which draws attention to its *artificiality* through obviously computer-generated imagery, unsubtle intertextual references, and juxtapositions of scale (Christian is half the size of the Eiffel Tower).

Luhrmann's comment on the use of a familiar pop song in this scene could equally apply to the dancing: "Now I have seen this scene with audiences all around the world.... And so there's this kind of laughter, realisation, unsettled, 'oh I can't believe it' moment. But [...] for all of the over-sentiment, actually you can hear the audience being drawn in and, as ridiculously romantic as it is, truly engage in the emotional feeling that's being generated between the two."[37] Unlike the 1930s audiences of Astaire and Rogers films, early twenty-first-century Euro-American audiences have been conditioned by the rejection of film musical artifice in the post-war era. Late twentieth-century teen musicals attempted to soften the jarring effect of the shift from narrative to musical number by using a non-diegetic soundtrack to avoid a non-naturalistic "bursting into song" moment.[38] Luhrmann, however, not only returns to characters singing, but intensifies the synthetic quality of this sequence, while retaining its function as a vehicle of uncynical, sincere emotion. This seeming contradiction exemplifies Luhrmann's cinematic philosophy of "The Big Lie that reveals the Big Truth."[39] In an act of Sell's bohemian "theatricalized authenticity," Luhrmann uses an unashamedly artificial technological device to convey apparently universal aspects of human experience.[40]

Jay David Bolter and Richard Grusin have argued that this paradox is a condition of contemporary media culture.[41] They see in media technologies the convergence of two apparently opposite tendencies with long historical genealogies: hypermediacy, the desire to increase the layers and channels of mediation (Luhrmann's "Big Lie"); and immediacy, the desire to create a sense of presence by erasing the traces of mediation (Luhrmann's "Big Truth"). These trajectories coalesce in new digital media that are defined by "remediation," "the representation of one medium in another."[42] In *Moulin Rouge!*, a film which makes extensive use of digital technologies in its construction of artifice, remediation is highly evident. In "Your Song," for example, *digital* technologies are used to reconstruct a cinematic illusion (dancing in the sky) associated with the era of *celluloid* film. Two media are merged in a cinematic choreography designed to *reduce* the audience's sense of mediation, to invite them to join the dance.

In *Moulin Rouge!*, mediation paradoxically produces an immediacy between dancing bodies on screen and the bodies of spectators, allowing the latter to experiment with "other" physical identities. This might be considered a form of virtual bohemianism, a historical and cultural role-play facilitated by cinematic spectatorship. Dance functions here to unite on-screen and off-screen bodies, counterbalancing hypermediacy with the sensation of presence. This aesthetic might be called "Techno Boho," following Australian journalist Sacha Molitorisz's coining of the term to describe one of the style tribes of Sydney,[43] the city in which *Moulin Rouge!* was filmed and where Luhrmann bases his production company, Bazmark. Molitorisz describes the Techno Bohos as "a thriving subculture of new Bohemians, who make music, films, visual art and mixed media installations."[44] According to Molitorisz, female Techno Bohos often wear burlesque or vintage clothes, embodying the past in a way reminiscent of *Moulin Rouge!*. However, in *Moulin Rouge!* it is specifically the combination of dance and technological remediation that allows spectators to become virtual bohemians. The expanded term "techno-choreographic bohemianism" might, therefore, be more appropriate for this aesthetic in *Moulin Rouge!*.

THE END OF HISTORY?

The erasure of historical, cultural, and bodily boundaries through techno-choreographic bohemianism in *Moulin Rouge!* has proved unsettling to a number of critics. Media scholar Jim Collins has summarized critical responses to films that exhibit such "hyperconscious eclecticism": "hyperconscious eclecticism is a sign of (choose one): a) the end of "Narrative"; b) the end of "the Real," "History," etc.' c) the end of art and entertainment for anyone other than overstimulated promiscuous teenagers; d) a sign of all-purpose moral and intellectual decay."[45] All of these criticisms have been leveled at *Moulin Rouge!*. This section analyzes these critiques in relation to the effects of techno-choreographic bohemianism on narrative, history, memory, and the body in the film.

In *Moulin Rouge!*, the bohemian performance of authenticity becomes digitally remastered as postmodern hyperreality,[46] a term defined by Umberto Eco as a cultural condition of the proliferation of the "absolute fake," in which "absolute reality is offered as a real presence."[47] This term resonates with Luhrmann's notion of "real artificiality," which refers to the amount of labor necessary to construct the artifice of the real.[48] Eco notes that America's hyperreal museums commit the "original sin of 'the lev-elling of pasts,' the fusion of copy and original."[49] A number of theorists have noted this tendency in twentieth-century culture,[50] and particularly in twentieth-century film. Deleuze describes the coexistence of "sheets of past" in film as a type of time-image, a cinematic form in which time is no longer produced as narrative by the characters' actions, but made directly visible, allowing multiple temporalities to be experienced at once.[51] The spectator is opened up to "a whole temporal 'panorama', an unstable set of floating memories, images of a past in general which move past at dizzying speed, as if time were achieving a profound freedom."[52] Deleuze argues that this can produce in film a "crystal-image" in which the actual and the virtual, present and past, constantly trans-form into one another.[53]

This sense of time is palpable in *Moulin Rouge!*, particularly in Satine's opening number. As she is lowered into the Moulin Rouge dance hall on a trapeze, Toulouse describes her as "the sparkling diamond." She sits on the rotating trapeze, her costume and jewelry twinkling like a crystal turning in the light (Fig. 1.3), and her spoken lyrics, tying together love, death, and jewels, predict her own demise. On the word "die," the camera cuts momentarily to an image of her lifeless body, forming what Deleuze would call an "internal circuit,"[54] a moment of simultaneity, between this moment, Christian's opening announcement of her death, and her actual death in the finale. She is costumed to evoke past female cinematic icons (as listed earlier) whose images jostle with the con-temporary star image of Kidman to form deeper circuits that dive in and out of the spec-tator's visual memory. Satine's pale skin, deliberately enhanced by blue light, becomes a ghostly surface on which images of past female bodies play. In deed, Luhrmann consid-ers that Kidman's "white reflective skin" identifies her physically with 1950s Hollywood actresses such as Marilyn Monroe, whose skin allowed them to "shine in the frame" despite limited lighting.[55] Sell argues that her "luminously pale" skin also alludes to Edouard Manet's painting *Olympia* (1863).[56] Like the nude prostitute in *Olympia*, Satine

FIGURE 1.3 Screen capture of *Moulin Rouge!*, director Baz Luhrmann, (2001), "Sparkling Diamonds".

is contrasted physically with her black companion, the Moulin Rouge dancer Chocolat, while sharing in his highly saleable exoticism. In Satine's first moments on screen, her body has already become a "crystal-image" with many temporal facets, reflecting both her own future within the film's narrative, and the history of white, female bodies in Euro-American visual culture.

These historical references proliferate in the song-and-dance number that follows Satine's entrance. She sings "Diamonds Are a Girl's Best Friend," echoing Monroe's rendition in *Gentlemen Prefer Blondes* (1953), and O'Connell's choreography at times echoes Jack Cole's, such as the framing of Kidman/Monroe by a sea of suited men. Lyrical reference is also made to Madonna's *Material Girl* (1985) music video, which itself imitates Monroe's performance. This complex web of quotation not only layers the sequence with multiple temporalities and media forms—celluloid film, music video, and digital film—it also evokes Madonna's famed manipulation of historical, ethnic, and sexual identities in performance. Viewers are reminded of this through the performance by the Moulin Rouge dancers of face-framing arm movements reminiscent of Madonna's *Vogue* (1990) video, while they sing the lyrics of *Material Girl*. The choreography for *Vogue* was influenced by the gay African-American and Latino club practice of voguing, with its poses derived from photographs of Hollywood stars such as Monroe and Dietrich. Madonna disregarded copyright issues in these appropriations,[57] instead treating the movements and images as recombinable signifiers through which to construct her public profile. Through Madonna, Monroe is positioned as one of a number of historical female archetypes that can be embodied by performers for both artistic and commercial purposes. Indeed, Satine later discusses with Zidler which model of femininity she should adopt to encourage the Duke to invest: "wilting flower, bright and bubbly or smoldering temptress?" However, like bohemian role-play, Satine's performances of femininity are combined with a desire for authenticity, summed up in her ambition, first stated in this scene, to become an oxymoronic "real actress." Here, Sell's bohemian "theatricalized authenticity" and Eco's postmodern "absolute fake" coincide, highlighting the bohemian lineage of Luhrmann's postmodern approach to the film musical.

Satine's opening number exemplifies how *Moulin Rouge!* creates a prosthetic memory of fin-de-siècle Paris by recombining familiar fragments of visual and musical culture into a new sensory universe. Even before *Moulin Rouge!* was released, Luhrmann proclaimed, "We've reinvented the musical.... We've given it a postmodern form. We've taken all the culture of the last 100 years, torn it up, and pieced it back together to make our own world."[58] This can be considered a form of postmodern pastiche, a mode of cultural production that, film scholar Richard Dyer argues,[59] allows film spectators to inhabit and feel the emotional pull of images of the past, while being aware of their historical and cultural construction—precisely the purpose of Luhrmann's bohemian strategy of "real artificiality." During Satine's "Sparkling Diamonds" number, spectators may be drawn into the immediacy of the performance, much of which is filmed from the point of view of the male patrons with whom Satine dances, while recognizing the collage of historical quotations that comprise it. This positioning of the spectator both inside (physically and emotionally involved with) and outside (retaining critical distance from) the cinematic image is facilitated by the film's slippery refusal to remain ideologically bound by any single cultural form, whether Hollywood, Bollywood, or MTV.

The effects of this method on the representation of history in *Moulin Rouge!* have been scathingly critiqued by English scholar Lael Ewy:

> At best *Moulin Rouge* is a lot of fun. At worst it represents the erasure of history. *Moulin Rouge* is set in the Paris of 1900—at least ostensibly it is. The actual Paris of 1900 is the Paris of Satie, the Paris of Ravel, of Debussy. The actual Paris of 1900 is the Paris of Matisse, and at least for part of the year, the Paris of Picasso.... What we get in *Moulin Rouge*, though, is a Paris of 1900 filtered through the myopia of late 20th Century pop culture, especially pop music. We get an anachronistic melange of Madonna and Elton John, of Nirvana and Olivia Newton John. In other words, it isn't the Paris of 1900. It isn't even close.[60]

Ewy echoes the lament of many detractors of postmodernism that contemporary culture signals the "end of history."[61] The linear flow of history as a meaningful narrative is disrupted by the postmodern appropriation of images irrespective of chronology. However, Jacques Derrida "wonder[s] if the end of history is but the end of a *certain* concept of history."[62] Ewy's historical model derives from the humanist tradition of the Enlightenment, in which the past objectively exists, and therefore historical accounts either reveal its essence truthfully, or obscure it. In this framework, history is linear—it should not be repeated or manipulated after the event. This type of history has been challenged in the twentieth century, notably by Benjamin's reconceptualization of the historian's subject matter as "the constellation which his own era has formed with a definite earlier one."[63] This conception of history as a set of moving prisms through which images of the past are refracted in ever changing ways has been adopted and developed by postmodern historiography. It also reflects the way history is used in *Moulin Rouge!*.

Robert Burgoyne has argued that contemporary commercial films have the capacity to question the linearity and reality of history by using digital technology to create prosthetic memories.[64] Burgoyne notes that while Landsberg is optimistic about the political potential of prosthetic memory and its effects on conceptions of history, some critics find this tendency in contemporary film troubling. He cites the example of film historian Thomas Elsaesser, who fears that "the burning in of memories via the media—burned in to the point that they create *symptoms in the spectator*—speak not to empathy and new social alliances but rather to cultural obsession, fantasy, and trauma."[65] This suggests that the challenge of cinematic prosthetic memory to the integrity of history is also read as a challenge to the integrity of the body. If memories can be manipulated, then what of the bodies that rely on them for their sense of continuity and reality? This resonates with the testimonies of *Moulin Rouge!* critics at the beginning of this chapter who experienced the film as a physical assault. Indeed, some critics posit a direct connection between the film's disruption of linear time, its bodily impact, and its manipulation of memory. Journalist Peter Keogh writes,

> If we assume he knows what he's doing, then Baz Luhrmann's goal seems to be the *end of cinema as we know it*: i.e., a coherent art form that provides pleasure and meaning.

How else explain Moulin Rouge, a film that takes beautiful actors, sets, costumes, and production numbers, fuses (or diffuses) a century and a half of pop culture from Verdi to MTV, photographs it all like a freak show, and chops it into confetti? This is the *Memento* of movie musicals, stroboscopically edited into three-second segments *without apparent logic, cohesion, or continuity* and designed to cater to—or induce— *short-term memory disorder.*[66]

For Keogh, the disregard for linear history in *Moulin Rouge!* pathologically infects spectator's memories. Even some critics who recommend the film pathologize its effects on spectators' memories. For example, Stephanie Zacharek writes, "Luhrmann is a tricky director. I'm not sure how he does it, but his movies have a way of reshaping themselves in your memory after the fact—it's as if they have viruses built into them that spring to life a day or so later, mysterious microorganisms that go to work in your brain to smooth out a movie's flaws and heighten its most sensual or exhilarating moments."[67] Zacharek characterizes the prosthetic memories implanted by the film as technological or biological viruses, infiltrating the body in which, presumably, "authentic" memories, histories, and identities normally reside.

English literature and cultural studies scholar Grace Kehler has noted the frequency of metaphors of disease in reviews of *Moulin Rouge!* and links this to the imagery of prostitution in the film.[68] Satine reproduces the stereotype of the consumptive nineteenth-century prostitute; like Marguerite in Alexandre Dumas' novel *La dame aux Camellias* (1848) and Violetta in Giuseppe Verdi's opera *La Traviata* (1853), Satine must die in order to restore the health of society. Kehler cites Lynda Nead's argument that the prostitute's threat lies in her status as an unobtainable commodity that can be perpetually resold. The consumptive prostitute, therefore, embodies the temptations of consumer culture, as well as its threat never to deliver what it purports to sell. Conscious of its own role as a commodity, Kehler argues, *Moulin Rouge!* constructs itself as a nineteenth-century prostitute—exotically alluring, but dangerously diseased.

I propose that the connection between *Moulin Rouge!* and the stereotypical nineteenth-century prostitute is not just the sale of an impossible commodity, but also the sale of a physical encounter with other bodies, cultures, and histories, in an artificially constructed environment (the brothel or the cinematic image). This is the basis of the fin-de-siècle commercialized bohemianism that *Moulin Rouge!* takes as it subject matter, but it also becomes a structuring principle of the cultural economy of the film itself. It is experienced by the spectator as a violent attack on the "authentic" integrity of the body and its memories, and therefore rejected, like Satine, as pathological.

In this identification of the body of the film with the body of Satine, *Moulin Rouge!* rather undermines its own philosophy. While the film ostensibly encourages an openness to other bodies, it renders its embodiment of this encounter in the character of Satine, and thus itself, diseased. When Satine dies, so does the possibility of a bohemian embodiment of other times and places, leaving its audience only with Christian's disembodied, typewritten words. Thus, *Moulin Rouge!* reinforces the nineteenth-century humanist morality that pathologized the figure of the prostitute, and which informs critics' rejections of the film's seductive, technologically constructed physicality.[69]

By constructing its own techno-cinematic bohemianism as a contagious disease, *Moulin Rouge!* implies that the derivation of pleasure from viewing the film is tantamount to the psychiatric disorder of masochism. This is evident in critic Steven Aoun's response to the film: "In your face doesn't even begin to describe the experience. The film is more like a rabid dog that suddenly leaps at your throat. So, why did I enjoy being knocked to the ground and thrashed about? Well, apart from confessing my own tendency toward masochism, *Moulin Rouge!* also cries out to be loved. The film is nothing less (or more) than an attempt to revitalize the musical in a cynical and jaded age. Only a sadist could delight in resisting its infectious entreaty."[70] Landsberg's notion of prosthetic memory, however, rehabilitates the potential bodily violence of film viewing.[71] She states that although "prosthetic memories, like an artificial limb, often mark a trauma," they nevertheless create "the conditions for ethical thinking precisely by encouraging people to feel connected to, while recognizing the alterity of, the 'other.'"[72] Therefore, spectators who enter physically and emotionally into the artificial, historically and culturally eclectic world of *Moulin Rouge!* might open themselves not only to historical, mnemonic, and bodily violence, but also to cross-cultural and transhistorical encounters, engagements, and identifications. This has always been the trade-off implicit in bohemianism, one that Luhrmann reinterprets for the postmodern age.

Perhaps the most audacious historical leap made in *Moulin Rouge!* is between the bohemian tradition of "theatricalized authenticity" and postmodern forms of cinematic prosthetic memory. The film implies a parallel between the bohemian experience of otherness offered by the Moulin Rouge to its customers and the experience of physically participating in a technologically constructed past that is offered to spectators by the film itself. The film musical form provides Luhrmann with a bridge between these two contexts. In its song-and-dance numbers, the film musical retained and developed early cinema's non-linear, spectacular, audience-engaging characteristics, which had much in common with live entertainment of the 1890s.[73] This capacity to physically engage spectators also makes the film musical a powerful vehicle for conveying prosthetic memories, although it does not feature in Landsberg's argument. In the song-and-dance numbers in *Moulin Rouge!*, Luhrmann's "real artificiality" reaches its apogee, and the continuity between bohemian memory and prosthetic memory is most evident. These moments, beyond the limitations of narrative time and place, are also the height of the film's historical and cultural juxtapositions. In these scenes, the film's direct appeal to the bodies of spectators to enter physically and emotionally into Luhrmann's constructed world is most urgent. The film offers spectators two ways of interpreting these physical onslaughts: as pathological attacks on the body, or as opportunities for experiencing, empathizing with, dancing in other worlds, a possibility that underpinned the bohemian tradition, and is reinvigorated for the twenty-first century by *Moulin Rouge!*.

NOTES

1. For example, Robert A. Morace, "Delirious Postmodernism: Baz Luhrmann's Moulin Rouge." (Paper presented at Film Musicals: From the Classical Era to Postmodern Cinema, University College Cork, September 19–20, 2003); Patricia Pisters, "'Touched by a Cardboard Sword': Aesthetic Creation and Non-Personal Subjectivity in *Dancer in the Dark* and *Moulin Rouge*," in *Discern(E)Ments: Deleuzian Aesthetics/Esthéthiques Deleuziennes*, ed. Joost de Bloois, Sjef Houppermans, and Frans-Willem Korsten (Amsterdam and New York: Rodopi, 2004), 151–169; Katherine R. Larson, "Silly Love Songs: The Impact of Puccini's *La Boheme* on the Intertextual Strategies of *Moulin Rouge!*" *The Journal of Popular Culture* 42, no. 6 (2009): 1040–1052; Mina Yang, "Moulin Rouge! And the Undoing of Opera," *Cambridge Opera Journal* 20, no. 3 (2010): 269–282.

2. Jose Arroyo, review of *Moulin Rouge*, directed by Baz Luhrmann, *Sight and Sound* 11, no. 9, September 2001, 50–52.

3. Peter Travers, review of *Moulin Rouge!*, directed by Baz Luhrmann, *Rolling Stone*, June 1, 2001, http://www.rollingstone.com/movies/reviews/moulin-rouge-20010509.

4. Philip French, review of *Moulin Rouge*, directed by Baz Luhrmann, *The Guardian*, September 9, 2001, http://www.guardian.co.uk/film/2001/sep/09/philipfrench1?INTCMP=SRCH.

5. Luhrmann cited in "Behind the Story," accessed April 17, 2002, http://www.clubmoulinrouge.com/html/member/background_orph.htm (site discontinued).

6. Luhrmann cited in "Red Hot Music: An Interview with Baz Luhrmann," accessed April 3, 2003, http://www.amazon.co.uk/exec/obidos/tg/feature/-/249299/ref=br_bx_2_1/026-25374 (no longer online); Luhrmann cited in Jason Frank, "Interview: Baz Luhrmann, Director," accessed April 3, 2003, http://www.gamesfirst.com/articles/jfrank/baz_interview/baz_interview.htm.

7. John Horn, "The Land of Baz," *Newsweek*, May 27, 2001: 58.

8. Luhrmann cited in "Red Hot Music."

9. Tom Gunning, "The Cinema of Attractions: Early Film, the Spectator and the Avant-Garde," in *Early Cinema: Space, Subjectivity and Narrative*, ed. Thomas Elsaesser (London: British Film Institute, 1990), 57.

10. Luhrmann cited in Rebecca Murray, "Baz Luhrmann Talks Awards and "Moulin Rouge," accessed April 3, 2003, http://romanticmovies.about.com/library/weekly/aa030902a.htm.

11. Luhrmann cited in "Red Hot Music"; Luhrmann cited in Geoff Andrew, "Baz Luhrmann (I)," last modified 2001, accessed May 19, 2010, http://www.guardian.co.uk/film/2001/sep/07/1; see also Diane Sandars, "Highly Hybridic, Mostly Palimpsestic: Innovative Uses of Music Video in the Recent Australian Musicals, *Moulin Rouge* and *One Night the Moon*" (Paper presented at What Lies Beneath, The University of Melbourne, November 6, 2003); and Tara Brabazon, *From Revolution to Revelation: Generation X, Popular Culture and Cultural Studies* (Aldershot and Burlington: Ashgate, 2005).

12. "Interview with Baz Luhrmann," last modified May 30, 2001, accessed April 3, 2003, http://www.themoviechicks.com/may2001/mcrrtbaz.html (no longer online).

13. See Brabazon, *From Revolution to Revelation*, on the use of popular memories of musical sub-cultures in this number.

14. John O'Connell (choreographer, *Moulin Rouge!*), interview with the author, May 30, 2005.

15. Alison Landsberg, *Prosthetic Memory: The Transformation of American Remembrance in the Age of Mass Culture* (New York: Columbia University Press, 2004).

16. Gilles Deleuze, *Cinema 2: The Time-Image* (London: Continuum, 2005), 73.

17. Luhrmann cited in Andrew, "Baz Luhrmann (I)."

18. Mike Sell, "Bohemianism, the Cultural Turn of the Avantgarde, and Forgetting the Roma," *TDR: The Drama Review* 51, no. 2 (T194) (2007): 45, 47.

19. Ibid., 49.

20. Martin cited in Baz Luhrmann and Catherine Martin, *Moulin Rouge!* (New York: Newmarket Press, 2001), 78.

21. Sell, "Bohemianism," 41.

22. Baz Luhrmann, "Commentary," Disc 1, *Moulin Rouge!*, Two Disc Set, directed by Baz Luhrmann (Los Angeles, CA: Twentieth Century Fox, 2002), DVD.

23. Luhrmann cited in Andrew, "Baz Luhrmann (I)," emphasis added.

24. Luhrmann cited in "Behind the Story."

25. "Interview with Baz Luhrmann."

26. Brabazon, *From Revolution to Revelation*, 172.

27. Anne Friedberg, *Window Shopping: Cinema and the Postmodern* (Berkeley, Los Angeles, and Oxford: University of California Press, 1993).

28. Gunning, "The Cinema of Attractions," 57.

29. Brabazon, *From Revolution to Revelation*, 273; Brian McFarlane, "The Movie as Museum," *Meanjin* 60, no. 4 (2001): 212–217.

30. Michael F. Nyiri, "The Buzz Starts Here: The Best Film of 2001," last modified 2001, accessed February 23, 2010, http://www.allthingsmike.com/ElectricMovies/dvds/MoulinRouge/essay.html.

31. McFarlane, "The Movie as Museum," 212.

32. Gilles Deleuze, *Cinema II: The Time-Image* (Minneapolis: University of Minnesota Press, 1989), 60.

33. Annette Kuhn, *An Everyday Magic: Cinema and Cultural Memory* (London and New York: I. B. Tauris, 2002).

34. Ibid., 192.

35. Walter Benjamin, "The Work of Art in the Age of Mechanical Reproduction," translated by Harry Zohn, in *Illuminations*, ed. Hannah Arendt (London: Fontana, 1973), 233.

36. O'Connell cited in Michael Montgomery, "John O'Connell and Moulin Rouge," *Dance Europe* 45, October (2001): 28–30.

37. Luhrmann, "Commentary."

38. Jane Feuer, *The Hollywood Musical*, 2nd ed. (London: Macmillan, 1993), 128.

39. Luhrmann cited in "Interview: Baz Luhrmann Reveals His Love for Movies, Music, and Putting It All Together," last modified 2002, accessed April 3, 2003, http://video.barnesand-noble.com/search/Interview.asp?ctr=622158.

40. Media and culture scholar Patricia Pisters has also addressed this question "of being deeply touched by something that is obviously an illusion," in relation to *Moulin Rouge!* and Lars von Trier's film *Dancer in the Dark* (2000). Pisters, " 'Touched by a Cardboard Sword,' " 152. She draws on Gilles Deleuze's argument that film (or any aesthetic creation) is not a representation of something else, but a real experience in itself. For example, Deleuze, *Cinema II*.

41. Jay David Bolter and Richard Grusin, *Remediation: Understanding New Media* (Cambridge, MA: MIT Press, 2000).

42. Ibid., 45.

43. Sacha Molitorisz, "Tribes of Sydney," *The Sydney Morning Herald*, January 7, 2010, http://www.smh.com.au/lifestyle/life/tribes-of-the-sydney-20100107-lv15.html.

44. Ibid.

45. Jim Collins, "Genericity in the Nineties: Eclectic Irony and the New Sincerity," in *Film Theory Goes to the Movies*, ed. Jim Collins, Hilary Radner, and Ava Preacher Collins (New York and London: Routledge, 1993), 250.

46. Rachael Turk, "Children of the Digital Revolution," *Metro*, September 1, 2001: 6.

47. Umberto Eco, *Travels in Hyperreality* (San Diego and New York: Harcourt Brace & Company, 1990), 8, 7.

48. Luhrmann cited in Andrew, "Baz Luhrmann (I)."

49. Eco, *Travels in Hyperreality*, 9.

50. For example, Jean Baudrillard, "Simulacra and Simulations," in *Jean Baudrillard: Selected Writings*, ed. Mark Poster (Cambridge and Oxford: Polity Press and Basil Blackwell, 1988), 166–184.

51. Gilles Deleuze, *Cinema 2: The Time-Image* (London: Continuum, 2005), 95.

52. Ibid., 53.

53. Ibid., 67.

54. Ibid., 67.

55. McAlpine cited in Luhrmann, "Commentary."

56. Sell, "Bohemianism," 48.

57. "No Rave Reviews for Madonna's Horst Play," *The Dallas Morning News*, May 16, 1990, http://nl.newsbank.com/nl-search/we/Archives?p_product=DM&p_theme=dm&p_action=search&p_maxdocs=200&p_topdoc=1&p_text_direct-0=0ED3D101E429494A&p_field_direct-0=document_id&p_perpage=10&p_sort=YMD_date:D&s_trackval=GooglePM.

58. Luhrmann cited in "Moulin Rouge," *Entertainment Weekly*, August 18, 2000, 83.

59. Richard Dyer, "The Notion of Pastiche," in *The Aesthetics of Popular Art*, ed. Jostein Gripsrud (Bergen and Kristiansand: Senter for Kulturstudier and HøyskoleForlaget, Norwegian Academic Press, 2001), 77–89.

60. Lael Ewy, "Moulin Rouge, the Erasure of History, and the Disneyfication of the Avant Garde," *EastWesterly Review* 7 (Fall 2001), http://www.postmodernvillage.com/eastwest/issue7/7a-0003.html.

61. Fredric Jameson, *The Cultural Turn: Selected Writings on the Postmodern, 1983–1998* (London and New York: Verso, 1998), 73.

62. Jacques Derrida, *Specters of Marx: The State of Debt, the Work of Mourning and the New International*, translated by Peggy Kamuf (New York and London: Routledge, 1994), 15, original emphasis.

63. Walter Benjamin, "Theses on the Philosophy of History," in *Illuminations*, ed. Hannah Arendt (London: Fontana, 1973), 245–255.

64. Robert Burgoyne, "Memory, History and Digital Imagery in Contemporary Film," in *Memory and Popular Film*, ed. Paul Grainge (Manchester: Manchester University Press, 2003), 220–236, emphasis added.

65. Burgoyne, "Memory, History and Digital Imagery," 226, emphasis added.

66. Peter Keogh, review of *Moulin Rouge*, directed by Baz Luhrmann, "No Cancan Do: Baz Luhrmann Cuts Moulin Rouge into MTV Ribbons," *The Boston Phoenix*, May 31–June 7, 2001, http://www.bostonphoenix.com/boston/movies/documents/01655667.htm, emphasis added.

67. Stephanie Zacharek, review of *Moulin Rouge*, directed by Baz Luhrmann, May 18, 2001, http://www.salon.com/2001/05/18/moulin_rouge/.

68. Grace Kehler, "Still for Sale: Love Songs and Prostitutes from La Traviata to Moulin Rouge," *Mosaic* (Winnipeg) 38, no. 2 (2005): 145–162.
69. Cathryn Conner Bennett draws similar conclusions in her analysis of *Moulin Rouge!*, but for different reasons. Cathryn Conner Bennett, "The Gender Politics of Death: Three Formulations of *La Bohème* in Contemporary Cinema," *Journal of Popular Film and Television* 32, no. 3 (2004): 116.
70. Steven Aoun, review of *Moulin Rouge*, directed by Baz Luhrmann, "Home Box Office with Steven Aoun," *Metro*, January 1, 2003, 265.
71. See also Steven Shaviro's work on masochistic film viewing. Steven Shaviro, *The Cinematic Body* (Minneapolis and London: University of Minnesota Press, 1993).
72. Landsberg, *Prosthetic Memory*, 20, 9.
73. See Gunning, "The Cinema of Attractions."

BIBLIOGRAPHY

Adorno, Theodor. *The Culture Industry.* London and New York: Routledge, 1991.

Andrew, Geoff. "Baz Luhrmann (I)." Last modified 2001. Accessed May 19, 2010. http://www.guardian.co.uk/film/2001/sep/07/1.

Aoun, Steven. Review of *Moulin Rouge*, directed by Baz Luhrmann. "Home Box Office with Steven Aoun." *Metro*, January 1, 2003: 265.

Arroyo, Jose. "Moulin Rouge." *Sight and Sound* 11, no. 9 (Sept 2001): 50–52.

Baudrillard, Jean. "Simulacra and Simulations." In *Jean Baudrillard: Selected Writings,* edited by Mark Poster, 166–184. Cambridge and Oxford: Polity Press and Basil Blackwell, 1988.

"Behind the Story." Accessed April 17, 2002. http://www.clubmoulinrouge.com/html/member/background_orph.htm (site discontinued).

Benjamin, Walter. "Theses on the Philosophy of History." In *Illuminations*, edited by Hannah Arendt, 245–255. London: Fontana, 1973.

——. "The Work of Art in the Age of Mechanical Reproduction." Translated by Harry Zohn. In *Illuminations*, edited by Hannah Arendt, 211–244. London: Fontana, 1973.

Bolter, Jay David, and Richard Grusin. *Remediation: Understanding New Media.* Cambridge, MA: MIT Press, 2000.

Brabazon, Tara. *From Revolution to Revelation: Generation X, Popular Culture and Cultural Studies.* Aldershot and Burlington, VT: Ashgate, 2005.

Burgoyne, Robert. "Memory, History and Digital Imagery in Contemporary Film." In *Memory and Popular Film*, edited by Paul Grainge, 220–236. Manchester: Manchester University Press, 2003.

Collins, Jim. "Genericity in the Nineties: Eclectic Irony and the New Sincerity." In *Film Theory Goes to the Movies*, edited by Jim Collins, Hilary Radner, and Ava Preacher Collins, 242–263. New York and London: Routledge, 1993.

Conner Bennett, Cathryn. "The Gender Politics of Death: Three Formulations of *La Bohème* in Contemporary Cinema." *Journal of Popular Film and Television* 32, no. 3 (2004): 110–120.

Deleuze, Gilles. *Cinema 2: The Time-Image.* London: Continuum, 2005.

——. *Cinema II: The Time-Image.* Minneapolis: University of Minnesota Press, 1989.

Derrida, Jacques. *Specters of Marx: The State of Debt, the Work of Mourning and the New International.* Translated by Peggy Kamuf. New York and London: Routledge, 1994.

Dyer, Richard. "The Notion of Pastiche." In *The Aesthetics of Popular Art*, edited by Jostein Gripsrud, 77–89. Bergen and Kristiansand: Senter for Kulturstudier and HøyskoleForlaget, Norwegian Academic Press, 2001.

Eco, Umberto. *Travels in Hyperreality*. San Diego and New York: Harcourt Brace & Company, 1990.

Ewy, Lael. "Moulin Rouge, the Erasure of History, and the Disneyfication of the Avant Garde." *EastWesterly Review* 7 (Fall 2001). http://www.postmodernvillage.com/eastwest/issue7/7a-0003.html.

Feuer, Jane. *The Hollywood Musical*. 2nd ed. London: Macmillan, 1993.

Frank, Jason. "Interview: Baz Luhrmann, Director." Accessed April 3, 2003. http://www.games-first.com/articles/jfrank/baz_interview/baz_interview.htm.

French, Philip. Review of *Moulin Rouge*, directed by Baz Luhrmann. "Moulin Rouge." *The Guardian*, September 9, 2001. http://www.guardian.co.uk/film/2001/sep/09/philipfrench1?INTCMP=SRCH.

Friedberg, Anne. *Window Shopping: Cinema and the Postmodern*. Berkeley, Los Angeles, and Oxford: University of California Press, 1993.

Gunning, Tom. "The Cinema of Attractions: Early Film, the Spectator and the Avant-Garde." In *Early Cinema: Space, Subjectivity and Narrative*, edited by Thomas Elsaesser, 56–62. London: British Film Institute, 1990.

Horn, John. "The Land of Baz." *Newsweek*, May 27, 2001: 58.

"Interview with Baz Luhrmann." Last modified May 30, 2001. Accessed April 3, 2003. http://www.themoviechicks.com/may2001/mcrrtbaz.html (no longer online).

"Interview: Baz Luhrmann Reveals His Love for Movies, Music, and Putting It All Together." Last modified 2002. Accessed April 3, 2003. http://video.barnesandnoble.com/search/Interview.asp?ctr=622158.

Jameson, Fredric. *The Cultural Turn: Selected Writings on the Postmodern, 1983–1998*. London and New York: Verso, 1998.

Kehler, G. "Still for Sale: Love Songs and Prostitutes from La Traviata to Moulin Rouge." *Mosaic* (Winnipeg) 38, no. 2 (2005): 145–162.

Keogh, Peter. Review of *Moulin Rouge*, directed by Baz Luhrmann. "No Cancan Do: Baz Luhrmann Cuts Moulin Rouge into MTV Ribbons." *The Boston Phoenix*, May 31–June 7, 2001. http://www.bostonphoenix.com/boston/movies/documents/01655667.htm.

Kuhn, Annette. *An Everyday Magic: Cinema and Cultural Memory*. London and New York: I. B. Tauris, 2002.

Landsberg, Alison. *Prosthetic Memory: The Transformation of American Remembrance in the Age of Mass Culture*. New York: Columbia University Press, 2004.

Larson, Katherine R. "Silly Love Songs: The Impact of Puccini's *La Boheme* on the Intertextual Strategies of *Moulin Rouge!*" *The Journal of Popular Culture* 42, no. 6 (2009): 1040–1052.

Luhrmann, Baz. "Commentary." Disc 1. *Moulin Rouge!*, Two Disc Set DVD. Directed by Baz Luhrmann. Los Angeles, CA: Twentieth Century Fox, 2002.

Luhrmann, Baz, and Catherine Martin. *Moulin Rouge!* New York: Newmarket Press, 2001.

McFarlane, Brian. "The Movie as Museum." *Meanjin* 60, no. 4 (2001): 212–217.

Molitorisz, Sacha. "Tribes of Sydney." *The Sydney Morning Herald*, January 7, 2010. http://www.smh.com.au/lifestyle/life/tribes-of-the-sydney-20100107-lv15.html.

Montgomery, Michael. "John O'Connell and Moulin Rouge." *Dance Europe* 45, October (2001): 28–30.

Morace, Robert A. "Delirious Postmodernism: Baz Luhrmann's Moulin Rouge." Paper presented at Film Musicals: From the Classical Era to Postmodern Cinema, University College Cork, September 19–20, 2003.

"Moulin Rouge." *Entertainment Weekly*, August 18, 2000: 83.

Murray, Rebecca. "Baz Luhrmann Talks Awards and 'Moulin Rouge.'" Accessed April 3, 2003. http://romanticmovies.about.com/library/weekly/aa030902a.htm.

"No Rave Reviews for Madonna's Horst Play." *The Dallas Morning News*, May 16, 1990. http://nl.newsbank.com/nl-search/we/Archives?p_product=DM&p_theme=dm&p_action=search&p_maxdocs=200&p_topdoc=1&p_text_direct-0=0ED3D101E429494A&p_field_direct-0=document_id&p_perpage=10&p_sort=YMD_date:D&s_trackval=GooglePM.

Nyiri, Michael F. "The Buzz Starts Here: The Best Film of 2001." Last updated 2001. Accessed February 23, 2010. http://www.allthingsmike.com/ElectricMovies/dvds/MoulinRouge/essay.html.

Pisters, Patricia. "'Touched by a Cardboard Sword': Aesthetic Creation and Non-Personal Subjectivity in *Dancer in the Dark* and *Moulin Rouge*." In *Discern(E)Ments: Deleuzian Aesthetics/ Esthéthiques Deleuziennes*, edited by Joost de Bloois, Sjef Houppermans, and Frans-Willem Korsten, 151–169. Amsterdam and New York: Rodopi, 2004.

"Red Hot Music: An Interview with Baz Luhrmann." Accessed April 3, 2003. http://www.amazon.co.uk/exec/obidos/tg/feature/-/249299/ref=br_bx_2_1/026-25374 (no longer online).

Sandars, Diane. "Highly Hybridic, Mostly Palimpsestic: Innovative Uses of Music Video in the Recent Australian Musicals, *Moulin Rouge* and *One Night the Moon*." Paper presented at What Lies Beneath, The University of Melbourne, November 6, 2003.

Sell, Mike. "Bohemianism, the Cultural Turn of the Avantgarde, and Forgetting the Roma." *TDR: The Drama Review* 51, no. 2 (T194) (2007): 41–59.

Shaviro, Steven. *The Cinematic Body*. Minneapolis and London: University of Minnesota Press, 1993.

Travers, Peter. Review of *Moulin Rouge!*, directed by Baz Luhrmann. *Rolling Stone*, June 1, 2001. http://www.rollingstone.com/movies/reviews/moulin-rouge-20010509.

Turk, Rachael. "Children of the Digital Revolution." *Metro*, September 1, 2001: 6.

Wilson, Elizabeth. "The Bohemianisation of Mass Culture." *International Journal of Cultural Studies* 2, no. 1 (1999): 11–32.

Yang, Mina. "Moulin Rouge! and the Undoing of Opera." *Cambridge Opera Journal* 20, no. 3 (2010): 269–282.

Zacharek, Stephanie. Review of *Moulin Rouge*, directed by Baz Luhrmann. May 18, 2001. http://www.salon.com/2001/05/18/moulin_rouge/.

CHAPTER 2

A DIFFERENT KIND OF BALLET: REREADING DOROTHY ARZNER'S *DANCE, GIRL, DANCE*

MARY SIMONSON

DIRECTOR Dorothy Arzner's film *Dance, Girl, Dance* was hardly a blockbuster when it premiered in 1940. Though some critics raved that it was a "knockout," others were more negative: *New York Times* writer Bosley Crowther called the film a "cliché-ridden, garbled repetition" of an old story. "It's a long involved tale," Crowther deadpanned, "told by a man who stutters."[1] In the last few decades, however, *Dance, Girl, Dance* has captured the attention of feminist film critics. The film has been embraced as a true "woman's film," as it was not only created for female audiences, but also was directed by one of the few female—indeed, lesbian—directors working in Hollywood during the classical era. *Dance, Girl, Dance* has been celebrated for its pointed critique of contemporary gender roles, courtship and marriage rituals, and cinematic treatment of women: as film scholar Claire Johnston writes, here "it is the universe of the male which invites scrutiny, which is rendered strange."[2]

The body of feminist film theory and criticism that Arzner's career and films have generated is crucial to both film scholarship and cultural studies. Yet the sustained focus on gender politics in *Dance, Girl, Dance* is also reductive. Perhaps because of its de facto "women's film" label, the film has rarely captured the attention of scholars exploring dance films or film musicals; gender- and sexuality-based claims seem to preempt consideration of the film's deployment of dance. The film's dance scenes, when mentioned, tend to be understood in one of two ways: first, as a means to attract and then critique the male gaze and other modes of cinematic looking, and second, as a field across which women's relationships can be negotiated. As film scholar Judith Mayne notes, "Dance is [...] a connection through which the desires and conflicts of [the film's] female communities are experienced."[3]

For contemporary critics and audiences, however, the dance sequences in *Dance, Girl, Dance* were not merely a means of deconstructing cinematic codes. Rather, they were the film's high point, remarkable in their own right. As *Los Angeles Times* columnist Hedda Hopper promised her readers, the film offered a new and "different kind of ballet" that audiences were sure to love.[4] Created a few years after George Balanchine arrived in the United States to help found the School of American Ballet and a New York-based ballet company, two years after Martha Graham staged "American Document," and only months after the American Ballet Theatre was established, *Dance, Girl, Dance* articulates a vision of American dance and artistic identity. In addition to juxtaposing high art and popular culture, as so many scholars have claimed, this backstage dance musical narrates the transformation of European-derived Romantic ballet technique into a "modern" American aesthetic focused on realism, ethnic and racial diversity, and urban life. It is only when protagonist Judy (Maureen O'Hara) rejects the ethereal, romantic ballets she choreographed under her Russian teacher's tutelage and adopts this new aesthetic that she—and by extension, American art and entertainment—mature beyond both European models and the burlesque hall. The evolving identities and careers of the film's female characters are as much a critique of national artistic identity as a critique of contemporary gender roles: in *Dance, Girl, Dance*, it is on and through the female body that American art—and our ways of experiencing and understanding it—are negotiated and defined.

THE GAZE AND ITS BLIND SPOTS

When producer Eric Pommer set out to produce *Dance, Girl, Dance* based on a popular story by German author Vicki Baum, Roy Del Ruth was slated to direct. Yet after production difficulties and personal issues arose, Del Ruth was replaced by Arzner; she overhauled the screenplay by Tess Slesinger and Frank Davis to create a film that traces the lives and careers of Judy, an aspiring ballerina who can only find jobs dancing in burlesque shows, and Bubbles (Lucille Ball), a rising popular star and gold digger with more sex appeal than artistic vision. The two women begin in the dance troupe of Madame Basilova (Maria Ouspenskaya), an elderly woman who was once a prima ballerina in the Russian Imperial Ballet, but is now consigned to serving as a "flesh peddler" for low-class American theaters.[5] After Madame's death—she is killed in an thoroughly unrealistic hit-and-run accident—the two women find themselves working together at the Bailey Brothers burlesque hall: Bubbles is Tiger Lily White, the risqué star of the show, and Judy is her "stooge," priming the audience for Tiger Lily White's encore with a tame, pretty ballet excerpt. As both women struggle to win stardom on stage, they simultaneously compete for the heart of rich playboy Jimmie Harris (Louis Hayward). In the end, Judy's dream is fulfilled not through marriage or domestic bliss with Jimmie, but by an invitation to join the American Ballet, a "real" ballet company headed by Steve Adams (Ralph Bellamy).

As might be expected, the body of feminist scholarship on *Dance, Girl, Dance* readily acknowledges Judy's choice of her career over Jimmie. Scholars have also regularly noted the film's privileging of women's relationships with one another over heterosexual relationships. Despite Judy and Bubbles's disagreements and rivalry—the two eventually come to blows in an onstage (but unstaged) brawl—they care for one another throughout the film. When Judy is out of work and can't cover her rent, for example, Bubbles immediately pays the landlord; even when most infuriated at Bubbles, Judy gently applies her makeup backstage. Heterosexual courtship and marriage, on the other hand, are ridiculed. Over the course of the film, characters marry blithely and separate even more blithely; at least two marriages are quickly annulled, and another marriage occurs between two virtual strangers, including a groom who is too drunk to comprehend what is happening.

Yet it is the gaze and its deployment that has captured the most critical attention. As scholars including Claire Johnston and Lucy Fisher have argued, Arzner's true achievement in *Dance, Girl, Dance* is her interrogation of the "male gaze" and voyeurism so dominant in classical cinema. Arzner repeatedly uses formal means, particularly shot/reverse shot sequences, to draw our attention to the ways in which male characters look and female characters are displayed. In one scene, for instance, Bubbles and Judy's troupe dances for a club manager. As Bubbles performs a slinky hula number, shots of her coy expression and sinuous movements alternate with larger and larger close-ups of the manager's face. His eyes scan up and down as he salivates and chews on his cigar; Bubbles winks back at him, their eyelines perfectly matched. Similarly, Bubbles and Judy's performances at the burlesque hall are presented in series of alternating shots of each woman dancing onstage and the largely male audience ogling, whistling, and catcalling. The result, as Fisher writes, is a "documentation of voyeurism at work: the man's engagement, as well as the woman's complicity—the surveyor and the surveyed."[6]

In addition to making the gaze visible, *Dance, Girl, Dance* also suggests alternatives to these visual regimes. Throughout the film, male and female characters alike model ways of looking that resist both voyeurism and fetishism. Judy, for example, peers through a cracked door at the American Ballet Company: she is utterly fascinated by their performance, but as a dancer herself, she aligns herself with them rather than viewing them as "Other." Company director Steve Adams and his male choreographer, too, watch rehearsals with sharply critical eyes, but fully acknowledge the personhood and abilities of each of the dancers. Even when Madame Basilova watches Judy rehearsing in the attic, peering upward from the stairwell, it is with respect: after a few moments, Basilova returns to her office to schedule a "real" audition for Judy. The film's most striking reversal of the gaze comes during one of Judy's burlesque performances, when she abruptly halts her dance, strides to the center of the stage, and scolds her audience for objectifying her and the other performers. This scene, accomplished through a series of shot/reverse shots of the audience members squirming uncomfortably as Judy glares at them, has been read in a variety of ways. For some scholars and critics, Judy's speech robs the one-way voyeuristic look of its pleasure, indicting both the burlesque audience and, possibly, the film's own audience: we, after all, have been enjoying the "show" just as much as those sitting in the theater. For others, the scene both destroys the gaze and transgresses cinematic traditions "of the male discourse."[7] Some have highlighted the fact that it is a woman—Steve Adams's secretary, Miss Olmstead—who jumps to her feet in applause after Judy's outburst; others have argued that the cheers that eventually swell from male and female audience members alike turn the gaze back on Judy. Still others question whether the onstage wrestling match that ensues between Bubbles and Judy when Bubbles tries to retake the stage emphasizes Judy's strength, or objectifies both women, reinstating cinematic norms. Finally, film scholar Judith Mayne suggests that Judy's speech doesn't actually reverse the male gaze at all, but deploys a look that is fundamentally different, and unaccounted for within film theory: the empowered look of a female performer.[8]

With the exception of scholars Gerald Peary and Karyn Kay, who suggest that the speech is not about men, but a "rebuke against those who misuse art as a decadent mode of expression," no attention has been given to the dance numbers that attract the gaze in the first place. Even those scholars intrigued by the cinematic possibilities of women performing tend to read the film's extensive music and dance scenes as little more than a means of enacting and negotiating gender roles. Claire Johnston, for example, describes dance as representing the entwinement of economics and sexuality for women; for Lucy Fisher, dance is a forum through which the treatment of women by the entertainment industry and perhaps society as a whole, can be critiqued.[9] Others, including Mayne, read dance as a means of defining each women's character and priorities: as in so many 1930s and '40s dance musicals in which ballet is deployed as a marker of high culture and class, here Judy's ballet helps to mark her as artistic, thoughtful, and focused on her personal dreams, while Bubbles's burlesque routines carry associations with gold digging, seduction, and men. Even Peary and Kay, who devote a great deal of attention to the different types of dance performed in the film, offering close analyses of each number, suggest that Judy's struggle to "make it" as a dancer is actually less about dance than about her journey to adulthood. For them, *Dance, Girl, Dance* is not a dance film, but a coming-of-age tale, a "modern day Cinderella story."[10]

Certainly, understanding dance as an act through which gender and sexuality are constructed is an extremely useful strategy: as dance scholar Susan Foster has argued, "choreography, the tradition of codes and conventions through which meaning is constructed in dance, offers a social and historical analytic framework for the study of gender."[11] Such analyses, however, tend to stress Bubbles and Judy's commonalities as women: though their different dance styles are acknowledged, their vastly divergent dreams and conceptions of dance—which grow even wider as Judy's career evolves—are rarely mentioned. Further, these readings ignore the possibility that dance is not merely a sign in this film, but a semiotic object itself. The film's numerous dance scenes (all created by film and stage choreographer Ernst Matray with assistance from his wife, actress Maria Solveg) are hardly standard film musical fare. In addition to the more traditional song-and-dance numbers performed by Bubbles and Basilova's troupe to catchy strophic tunes like "Jitterbug Bite" and "Mother, What Do I Do Now," *Dance, Girl, Dance* features two extended ballet pieces. As Judy, Maureen O'Hara and body double Vivien Fay perform a balletic solo to an orchestrated version of the "Morning Star" theme; later, we watch the American Ballet rehearse the elaborate, jazz- and modern dance-infused *Urban Ballet* (featuring Fay as herself). Nor are these numbers staged just once, as in most film musicals. They are rehearsed and performed again and again, facilitating an unusual level of familiarity with both the performance style and the specific choreography of each.

The film's innovative choreography, carefully prepared performances, and central placement of dance becomes a bit more understandable—and reading dance as a semiotic object in its own right seems even more appropriate—when one considers that Dorothy Arzner's lifelong partner and frequent collaborator, Marion Morgan, was a well-known American dancer. Originally a physical education teacher at Manual Arts High School in Los Angeles, Morgan directed summer dance programs at the University of California at Berkeley from 1910 on and headed a dance school that offered lessons in "Greek, Interpretive, Egyptian, Oriental, Character, and Dramatic dance."[12] From 1916 until the mid-1920s, Morgan toured the nation's vaudeville theaters with the Marion Morgan Dancers, performing antiquity-themed dances; the troupe also performed in silent films including *Don Juan, Up in Mabel's Room, A Night of Love,* and *The Masked Women* (all 1926).[13] Arzner and Morgan collaborated on a number of films, as well: Morgan created the waxworks tableau in Arzner's *Get Your Man* (1927), and choreographed scenes for *Manhattan Cocktail* (1928). The women's relationship, collaborations, and mutual interests suggest that Arzner was likely well versed and invested in both filmed dance and the contemporary American dance scene.[14]

SOUNDING BALLET

From the opening moments of *Dance, Girl, Dance,* dance takes center stage. Further, though the film's establishing shot features both Judy and Bubbles onstage dancing, the film's dialogue, choreography, and score quickly make clear that Judy is the true dancer—and our heroine. The film opens in an Akron, Ohio nightclub, where Judy's troupe is performing a showy tap number, "Roll Out the Barrel," complete with top hats, sequined dresses, and mildly out-of-tune vocals. As the club is raided and the performance halted, Judy meets playboy Jimmie Harris. Immediately taken with her, he waltzes her around the empty dance floor as patrons stream out, whistling the tune that will later come to be known as "Morning Star." Yet when Bubbles whisks Jimmie out of the club, leaving Judy standing alone in the middle of the dance floor, Judy is not particularly troubled. Later that evening, as Judy and fellow troupe member Sally prepare for bed and Sally expresses her displeasure at Bubbles's behavior, Judy shrugs it off. Placing her ankle on a chair back, leg extended in front of her, she begins a series of stretches as Sally climbs into bed and turns out the light. Bubbles may be preoccupied with men, but the "only thing I really care about," Judy confides, "is dancing." Seconds later, when Bubbles bursts into the room, she too acknowledges these divergent goals. As the camera cuts between Bubbles, flopped on the bed, and Judy, performing a series of *pliés* in the center of the room, Bubbles recounts her date with Jimmy. Eyeing Judy's movements curiously, Bubbles finally shakes her head slightly. "I'll say one thing for you, Pavlova," she tells Judy. "You've certainly got ambition."

In addition to marking Judy as a "true" dancer, fully dedicated to her art, this scene also works to link Judy to music, and particularly, the "Morning Star" theme. The score for *Dance, Girl, Dance,* created by Edward Ward with songs by Chester Forrest and Bob Wright, is primarily presented as diegetic accompaniment for the film's dance scenes. Yet Judy's offstage activities, and especially her dialogues about dance, are regularly accompanied by versions of the "Morning Star" melody in the underscore. An orchestrated version of the song, for instance, sounds continuously through the cut from the Akron nightclub to the women's lodging house, then accompanies Judy's reflections on her love of dance. As she begins her exercises, her *pliés* and front *cambrés* almost seem to fall in time with the melody. Yet when Bubbles bursts through the door and flips on the lights, yanking our attention away from Judy, the melody halts abruptly. As the camera tracks Bubbles around the room, her image is accompanied not by music but by the sound of her movements and voice. Judy resumes her exercises in silence, her "accompaniment" seemingly short-circuited by Bubbles's mere presence.

Throughout the film, Judy's alignment with music—and Bubbles's separation from it—is also highlighted visually. The film's editing, for instance, stresses the repartee between Judy and the conductor and musicians at the burlesque house. Shots of an intimidated Judy dancing before the heckling audience are paired not with reverse shots of that audience, but instead with shots of the conductor urging Judy on. Similarly, after Judy's withering speech to the burlesque hall patrons (Fig. 2.1), the camera lingers on members of the orchestra as they nod and applaud wildly (Fig. 2.2). During Bubbles's performances, however, the pit orchestra and conductor remain invisible; the camera tracks only Bubbles's address to the audience and their enthusiastic responses. Even during the troupe's hula audition, Judy is captured standing behind an open record player;

FIGURE 2.1 Judy (Maureen O'Hara) breaks the fourth wall to admonish her audience at the burlesque show. Screenshot from *Dance, Girl, Dance* (dir. Dorothy Arzner, 1940).

FIGURE 2.2 Orchestra members cheer for Judy after her speech. Screenshot from *Dance, Girl, Dance* (dir. Dorothy Arzner, 1940).

Bubbles, on the other hand, is portrayed through a series of shot-reverse shots with an ogling, salivating casting agent. Despite the fact that it is Bubbles who actually produces music—she always sings during her burlesque performances—the film's score and visual representations figure the two women as incompatible, fundamentally unable to relate to one another musically. The women occupy utterly different spheres of sound, just as they occupy different spheres of dance.

DANCING A MIGRATION

Despite the musical gulf between Judy and Bubbles, Judy does share her theme with other characters. Judy's changing personal and professional alliances and her development as a dancer are narrated primarily through the development and transfer of the "Morning Star" theme. In the first half of *Dance, Girl, Dance*, the score and camerawork alike suggest a close link between Judy; her teacher and mentor, Madame Basilova; and the late nineteenth-century ballet tradition that Basilova represents. The first inkling of this relationship comes about fifteen minutes into the film, as Judy returns to New York City from the disheartening burlesque hall gig in Akron, Ohio—and her first meeting with wealthy playboy Jimmie Harris. The scene opens with a series of overhead shots that slowly descend into Times Square, accompanied by a medley of strident, syncopated, and occasionally dissonant melodies played by brass and woodwinds. The camera settles at street level before an open door, then zooms closer, mimicking an approaching visitor, before settling on a close-up of the sign that hangs to the right of the door: "Madame Lydia Basilova, formerly Ballerina of the Imperial Russian Ballet." The cut to the sign is accompanied by an abrupt shift in the underscore. A soft, lyrical string variation of the "Morning Star" theme, which is already linked to Judy from the nightclub in Ohio, begins. As the camera lingers on the sign, this melody morphs into a descending minor scale played by a solo violin, suturing Judy to Madame's past as a famed Russian dancer.

This close bond between Judy and Madame is made even clearer in the next scene. Inside the studio, as Madame hangs up the phone and laments the lack of dance gigs available for her troupe, a voice sounds from the doorway: "I'm back." The camera remains trained on a close-up of Madame, her hair pulled back severely into a bun, as she raises her eyes. A reverse shot reveals Judy, standing in the doorway with her coat and suitcase. Though Madame feigns anger at Judy's late arrival, their affection for one another shines through. In a series of shots that oscillate between Madame's wrinkled face and Judy's smooth, youthful complexion, Madame sharply distinguishes between the "art" of ballet and the world of burlesque. "True artists" like herself are ill suited to the American entertainment industry: "What a life!" Madame rages, "A flesh-peddler I have become! A jellyfish salesman." Judy, too, doesn't belong on burlesque stages: she simply doesn't have the "oomph" that matters in burlesque. Pacing around the small office, which is lined with photographs of herself dancing, Madame Basilova pauses to acknowledge that Judy does have potential and might be taught, might one day become the sort of artist Madame herself once was.

As the film proceeds, Judy's unsuitability for burlesque is affirmed again and again. Not only does her inspired "Morning Star" ballet number make her the laughing-stock and stooge in the Bailey Brothers burlesque show, but her hula solo is roundly rejected by a Hoboken manager in favor of Bubbles's version, as well. (This rejection is to be expected; after all, as Madame reminds Judy, "A hula isn't dancing. It's nothing but 'oomph.' And you haven't got it.") Yet Judy's close alignment with Madame Basilova and nineteenth-century Russian ballet slowly fades as well. After the discouraging hula audition, Madame Basilova is staring out the window of her office when she hears strains of a piano melody upstairs. She looks at the ceiling, instantly aware that it must be Judy rehearsing, and after a moment's hesitation, steps into the hallway. The piano accompaniment takes up a richly ornamented version of Judy's "Morning Star" theme, and we watch through the wavy glass panes in the office walls as Madame's blurry figure slowly ascends the adjacent staircase. The film cuts to a shot from the top of the stairs; Madame climbs just far enough to peer over the railing into the attic, then crouches back down a bit to ensure that she's hidden from Judy's view as the piano articulates a series of descending thirds (Fig. 2.3). A reprise of the "Morning Star" theme is played, and the camera pans from Madame to what she is watching: Judy, in a light-colored leotard and ballet skirt, gracefully dances on point (Fig. 2.4). As Judy's piano accompaniment again embarks on a series of descending thirds, the camera cuts back to Madame watching in the shadows, and then, as a bouncy, upbeat theme begins, we turn back to Judy's dance. The film continues to cut between the two women; eventually, Madame turns from

FIGURE 2.3 From the shadows, Madame Basilova watches Judy rehearsing her ballet. Screenshot from *Dance, Girl, Dance* (dir. Dorothy Arzner, 1940).

FIGURE 2.4 Unaware of Madame's watchful gaze, Judy choreographs her ballet. Screenshot from *Dance, Girl, Dance* (dir. Dorothy Arzner, 1940).

Judy's rehearsal and descends the stairs to her office. A slower, less ornamented version the "Morning Star" theme sounds, and the camera zooms in for a medium close-up of Judy's graceful arm gestures as she *bourrées* across the attic floor, before cutting to a shot of Madame flipping through her address book at her desk. Just as the camera zoomed in to reveal Madame's name and pedigree inscribed on the sign outside the studio as Judy's "Morning Star" theme played earlier in the film, here, strains of Judy's music drift down from the attic as Madame locates the entry she's looking for. This time, it is not Madame's own name and pedigree that we read as the camera draws us closer, but another name: Steve Adams, of the American Ballet. Glancing once more upstairs toward Judy and her melody, Madame picks up the phone and begins to dial.

That Steve Adams will replace Madame Basilova in Judy's life—and that his vision of the American ballet will overtake the old-fashioned romanticism of Basilova's pedigree—is hinted at again when Adams and Judy meet for the first time outside the American Ballet's offices a few weeks after Madame Basilova's death. Though neither is aware of the other's identity, Adams is immediately fascinated by Judy; Judy, ever-focused on her dance career, ignores his interest and abruptly departs. As she steps out of the frame, strings play the "Morning Star" theme in the underscore, then transition to the light, quick melody that follows the theme in Judy's dance. This time, the tune does not accompany Madame's gaze at Judy. Instead, the camera lingers on Steve Adams's face before revealing what he is looking at: Judy's feet as she runs down the sidewalk in the rain, gracefully weaving through pedestrians with quick dance-like steps.

The linkage between Steve Adams and Judy's future is further suggested when Judy glimpses Adams's company, The American Ballet, in rehearsal. Waiting for her appointment with Adams in the company's reception area, Judy peeks through a slightly ajar door and catches sight of a female dancer performing a balletic solo partnered by a series of men in identical hooded unitards with capes (Figs. 2.5 and 2.6). Just as Madame watched Judy from the shadows earlier in the film, imagining her future with a "real"

FIGURE 2.5 Judy peers through a cracked door at the American Ballet in rehearsal. Screenshot from *Dance, Girl, Dance* (dir. Dorothy Arzner, 1940).

FIGURE 2.6 Judy catches a glimpse of the prima ballerina (Vivian Fay) of the American Ballet. Screenshot from *Dance, Girl, Dance* (dir. Dorothy Arzner, 1940).

company, now Judy takes this position, peering through the door at the company itself. These two moments of watching—indeed, of voyeurism—are connected not only visually by the cuts between close-ups of a shadowy female face and shots of dancing women, but also musically: the same series of descending thirds featured in the underscore when Madame watched Judy are reprised here in an orchestrated version each time the camera settles on a close-up of Judy's face.[15]

As the sequence continues, visual and musical clues continue to suggest an alliance between Judy and Adams's company. The film abruptly cuts from Judy at the studio door to Steve Adams in his office, dictating to his secretary. As he describes his vision for a "new" ballet that acknowledges the realities of urban American life like "telephones, factories, cafeterias," rather than romantic "interpretations of bluebirds," a series of variations on Judy's "Morning Star" melody emerges in the underscore. The camera cuts back to Judy's watching eyes and then the rehearsal, but the music continues seamlessly, suggesting that the "Morning Star" theme has penetrated not only Adams's world, but the ballet's score as well.

Back in the studio, though, the ballet abruptly shifts: the female soloist crumples to the floor as a siren sounds, winds enter with a quick ostinato, and dancers cross the stage performing stylized pantomimes of street-cleaners, newsboys, shoe-shiners, and pedestrians. A syncopated clarinet melody reminiscent of the dissonant underscore that first introduced us to New York City accompanies the riotous action, then we hear a carnivalesque tune as an organ grinder appears, and finally, a syncopated ragtime melody as a couple in blackface cakewalk across the stage. Moments later, the female soloist reappears center stage as a distorted, brassy, and percussive rendition of the "Morning Star" theme begins. This transformed theme—a hybrid of the original melody and the harsh, dissonant motives from earlier in the number—matches the soloist's own transformation: her shimmering costume and lyricism are traded for a sharply geometric dress and quick, angular movements.

In this extended number, the American Ballet portrays not only an alternative to Judy's romantic ballet—and, for that matter, to the popular dance of the burlesque theater—but also the transformation of a ballerina's style from romanticism to modern, twentieth-century dance. As Judy watches through the cracked door, it is almost as if she is looking into a mirror of her own future: venturing away from Madame Basilova and traditional Russian ballet and toward Steve Adams's modern American aesthetic, the prima ballerina with textbook classical technique reawakens in a new, strikingly modern choreographic and musical world. Abstraction is replaced by the concrete; musical and choreographic dissonance is introduced; and heterogeneity trumps uniformity. Escapist rhapsodies—whether they be on bluebirds or morning stars—are rejected in favor of realism, plurality, and the urban. The sounds of the street—quite literally, the underscore that accompanied the camera's descent into Times Square at the beginning of the film—find their way into the dance studio, and into the "Morning Star" theme, foretelling Judy's future as a dancer. And indeed, by the end of the film, Judy has secured herself a position in the American Ballet; Adams tells his choreographer, "She was born with more than any dancer we've got. She knows less. It's our job to teach her what we know." As Judy falls into Steve Adams's arms in the closing scene, half laughing and half crying in relief, we hear the "Morning Star" theme in yet another iteration, once again tonal and string-heavy, but now modulating unpredictably toward its final, triumphant cadence.

THE AMERICAN BALLET, ON-SCREEN AND OFF

The vision of American dance that Steve Adams articulates and Judy embraces is not entirely Arzner's invention. Rather, Judy's shifting conception of dance neatly parallel and comment upon contemporary developments in American ballet. As in *Dance, Girl, Dance,* the world of American dance in the early decades of the twentieth century was populated by American dancers performing in popular venues, visiting Russian artists and teachers, uneducated but intrigued audiences, and a burgeoning population of modern dancers. By the mid-1930s, dreams of American ballet companies were being bandied about; as Lincoln Kirstein wrote in 1938, not only were American audiences interested and open-minded about ballet, they were especially supportive of American-born dancers and "starting to have an almost proprietary interest" in ballet as an art form.[16] Together with choreographer George Balanchine, Kirstein worked to develop a number of American ballet institutions: first a ballet school, then in 1935 the

American Ballet, and then smaller touring units, including the Ballet Caravan. With each, Kirstein sought to generate a unique American style, one that—like Steve Adams's invented vision—refused the legacy of Russian dance in favor of something "frank, open, fresh, and friendly," a style that captured "the rhythm of New York, symbolized by athleticism, speed, extrovert energy, the reckless dynamism in its syncopation and asymmetry, and as well a kind of impersonal mastery, an abstraction of life symbolized by the grid-land and numerical nomination of its streets and avenues."[17] With pieces like *Alma Mater* (1934, choreography by Balanchine to music by Kay Swift) and *Serenade* (1935, choreography by Balanchine to Tchaikovsky's Serenade for Strings in C, Op. 48), Kirstein hoped to offer audiences choreography that emphasized equality over hierarchy, "a democratic corps de ballet," an organic "body of dancers."[18] Other pieces, particularly those created for the Ballet Caravan, like Eugene Loring's *Yankee Clipper* (1937, music composed by Paul Bowles) and *Billy the Kid* (1937, music composed by Aaron Copland) employed not only this American aesthetic, but also American settings and characters, plots with which American audiences "could feel at home."[19]

A few years later, and just months before the release of *Dance, Girl, Dance,* another national company, The American Ballet Theatre, was formed by architect turned impresario Richard Pleasant, with support from ballerina Lucia Chase. Pleasant, too, was interested in generating a uniquely American dance aesthetic, one characterized by collaboration, diverse styles, and democratic management. Built out of Mikhail Mordkin's Russian Ballet Company, the new company was divided into wings, each with different choreographers: the Classic division (Anton Dolin and Bronislava Nijinska); the Russian division (Adolph Bolm and Michel Fokine, among others); the American wing (Eugene Loring and Agnes DeMille, then later Jerome Robbins and Michael Kidd); a Negro division; a Spanish division (Jose Fernandez); and a British wing (Anthony Tudor, Andre Howard). Dancers, too, were diverse: experienced dancers from Mordkin's troupe and other European stars mixed with fledgling American unknowns. The company's first season, which opened on January 11, 1940, at the Center Theater in New York City and ran about three weeks, featured eighteen different ballets, including DeMille's *Black Ritual,* Nijinska's *La Fille Mal Gardée,* Tudor's *The Judgment of Paris,* and *Swan Lake.* This diversity of members, choreographers, and works reflected the organization's democratic ideals: the company would perform ballets from a variety of national traditions and styles, generating a sort of onstage melting pot. Further, no one choreographer, style, or even soloist was to dominate: principal roles would alternate, very different ballets would share the same program, and the works of various choreographers would be showcased in turn. Kirstein and his followers strove to mix time-honored traditions and fresh new ideas seamlessly to create a new, uniquely American aesthetic and practice.

Placed within this historical and cultural context, Judy's journey in *Dance, Girl, Dance* is not only about her personal growth from a girl into a woman, as Karyn Kay and Gerald Peary suggest. It is also the tale of her development as a modern, mid-twentieth-century American dancer. Judy's eventual rebirth as a member of the American ballet, like Vivien Fay's "death" and transfiguration in the *Urban Ballet,* simultaneously narrate the ongoing development of an American ballet aesthetic, and serve as a prescription for

American artists and dancers. Tracing Judy's struggles, evolution, and finally her estab-lishment as a successful dancer, *Dance, Girl, Dance* gestures toward the establishment of an American ballet independent of foreign influences and able, like Judy, to speak for itself and raise American audiences to their feet in applause.

Yet this reading, too, points back to the film's gender politics in the end. In its poi-gnant critique of mid-century American dance and artistic identities, Arzner's film acknowledges dance and professional arts careers as powerful spaces in which women can take control of not only their own destinies as artists, but also the ever-elusive gaze. Throughout the film, we watch women peer through various "keyholes": Madame Basilova watches Judy dance from the shadows, Judy watches the American Ballet rehearse through a crack in the door. These moments are unusual and particularly com-pelling not only because women are doing the gazing; they're also unique in that the object of the gaze is infinitely more fascinating and meaningful to the looker on-screen than it is to most of the film's viewers. Though we can look "with" these on-screen women, we can't quite see that which they see. As artists, Judy and Madame Basilova—and indeed, Arzner herself, seated behind her movie camera—are simultaneously able to revel in their ability to gaze, and to catch glimpses of that which is otherwise invis-ible. Feminist critics have long commented on the similarity between Dorothy Arzner and Madame Basilova: both are butch female artists in neckties. Yet perhaps Arzner and her collaborators are actually more closely aligned with Judy and her new mentor Steve Adams: artistic innovators with an eye toward the future, interested in breaking bound-aries and redefining American aesthetics, and above all, engaged in the creation of social commentary through art.

NOTES

1. Bosley Crowther, "The Screen in Review," *The New York Times*, October 11, 1940, 25.
2. Claire Johnston, "Dorothy Arzner: Critical Strategies," in *Feminism and Film Theory*, ed. Constance Penley (New York: Routledge, 1988): 36–45.
3. Judith Mayne, *Directed by Dorothy Arzner* (Bloomington: Indiana University Press, 1994), 43–44.
4. Hedda Hopper, "Hedda Hopper's Hollywood," *Los Angeles Times*, August 29, 1940, A11.
5. The troupe director was originally written as a male part, Basiloff, and Maurice Moscovich was cast in the part by producer Erich Pommer and then-director Roy del Ruth. Moscovich died suddenly in late June of 1940, after three days of taping; Dorothy Arzner replaced him with Maria Ouspenskaya as Madame Basilova.
6. Lucy Fischer, "Shall We Dance? Women and the Musical," in *Shot/Countershot: Film Tradition and Women's Cinema* (Princeton, NJ: Princeton University Press, 1989), 151.
7. Johnston, "Dorothy Arzner," 6.
8. Mayne, *Directed by Dorothy Arzner*, 140.
9. Johnston, "Dorothy Arzner," 5; Alison Butler echoes this view, noting "Arzner uses dance dialectically to represent the women's economic and sexual dilemmas: Bubbles dances to attract men, performing stereotypical female sexuality; Judy dances for artis-tic self-expression, attracting a man incidentally (insofar as such a thing could ever be

incidental in a Hollywood film), but both are ultimately in pursuit of money and social mobility." Butler, *Women's Cinema: The Contested Screen* (London: Wallflower, 2002), 36; Lucy Fischer, "Shall We Dance?" 148–154.

10. Karyn Kay and Gerald Peary, "Dorothy Arzner's *Dance, Girl, Dance,*" *Velvet Light Trap* 10 (Fall 1973): 26.

11. Susan Leigh Foster, "Choreographies of Gender," *Signs: Journal of Women in Culture and Society* 24, no. 1 (1998): 5.

12. Flyer for the Marion Morgan School of Dance, Jerome Robbins Dance Division, New York Public Library for the Performing Arts.

13. Advertisements for the Marion Morgan Screen Dancers, "Producing Spectacles, Dances, and Originalities in Film Productions," *Standard Casting Directory,* September 1926, November 1926, April 1927. Jerome Robbins Dance Division, New York Public Library for the Performing Arts.

14. Interestingly, the film's ties to dance run even deeper: like Arzner, Vicki Baum, the author of the story upon which the script was based, was a musician and dance connoisseur: a professional harpist-turned-writer, Baum was particularly taken with the choreography and movement style of German modern dancer Mary Wigman, who deeply influenced early twentieth-century American dance aesthetics. See Vicki Baum, *It Was All Quite Different: The Memoirs of Vicki Baum* (Funk and Wagnalls, 1964), 242–43.

15. This descending motive is also associated with the act of watching in the scene that precedes Judy's arrival at the American Ballet Studio. As Steve Adams, his secretary, and a choreographer look on, the dancers rehearse their piece, the camera cutting between shots of the dancers and shots of the onlookers. The motive emerges as the camera comes to settle on Adams's thoughtful face.

16. Lincoln Kirstein, "Our Ballet and Our Audiences," in *Ballet: Bias and Belief* (New York: Dance Horizons, 1983), 53–57; reprinted from *The American Dancer* 11, no. 9 (July 1938): 22–23.

17. Lincoln Kirstein, "The Policy of a Ballet Company," in *Ballet: Bias and Belief* (New York: Dance Horizons, 1983), 124; reprinted from *Playbill* (New York State Theater issue, Nov. 11–30, 1975), 3–4, 6, 9–10.

18. Lincoln Kirstein, "The Policy of a Ballet Company," in *Ballet; Bias and Belief* (New York: Dance Horizons, 1983), 125; reprinted from *Playbill* (New York State Theater issue, Nov. 11–30, 1975), 3–4, 6, 9–10.

19. Lincoln Kirstein, "Blast at Ballet: a Corrective for the American Audience" (1937). In *Ballet; Bias and Belief* (New York: Dance Horizons, 1983), 199.

BIBLIOGRAPHY

Baum, Vicki. *It Was All Quite Different: The Memoirs of Vicki Baum.* New York: Funk and Wagnalls, 1964.

Butler, Alison. *Women's Cinema: The Contested Screen.* London: Wallflower, 2002.

Crowther, Bosley. "The Screen in Review." *New York Times,* October 11, 1940.

Fischer, Lucy. *Shot/Countershot: Film Tradition and Women's Cinema.* Princeton: Princeton University Press, 1989.

Foster, Susan Leigh. "Choreographies of Gender." *Signs: Journal of Women in Culture and Society* 24, no. 1 (1998): 1–33.

Hopper, Hedda. "Hedda Hopper's Hollywood." *Los Angeles Times*, August 29, 1940.

Johnston, Claire. "Dorothy Arzner: Critical Strategies." In *Feminism and Film Theory*, edited by Constance Penley. New York: Routledge, 1988.

Kay, Karyn, and Gerald Peary, "Dorothy Arzner's *Dance, Girl, Dance*," *Velvet Light Trap* 10 (Fall 1973): 26.

Kirstein, Lincoln. "Blast at Ballet: a Corrective for the American Audience." In *Ballet: Bias and Belief.* New York: Dance Horizons, 1983, 157–284.

Kirstein, Lincoln. "Our Ballet and Our Audiences." In *Ballet: Bias and Belief.* New York: Dance Horizons, 1983, 53–57. Reprinted from *The American Dancer* 11, no. 9 (July 1938): 22–23.

Kirstein, Lincoln. "The Policy of a Ballet Company." In *Ballet: Bias and Belief.* New York: Dance Horizons, 1983, 121–126. Reprinted from *Playbill*. New York State Theater issue, Nov. 11–30, 1975, 3–4, 6, 9–10.

Mayne, Judith. *Directed by Dorothy Arzner*. Bloomington: Indiana University Press, 1994.

Flyer for the Marion Morgan School of Dance, Jerome Robbins Dance Division, New York Public Library for the Performing Arts.

Advertisements for the Marion Morgan Screen Dancers, "Producing Spectacles, Dances, and Originalities in Film Productions," Standard Casting Directory, September 1926, November 1926, April 1927. Jerome Robbins Dance Division, New York Public Library for the Performing Arts.

CHAPTER 3

COMMUNITIES OF PRACTICE: ACTIVE AND AFFECTIVE VIEWING OF EARLY SOCIAL DANCE ON THE POPULAR SCREEN

ALEXANDRA HARLIG

IN this age of the Internet, social media, and video-sharing sites, much has been said about the media's role in turning dances that would have remained marginal or local fads into country- and world-wide phenomena.[1] However, this disseminating function of audio-visual media is not unique to the Internet or the present day. This chapter considers three moments in early twentieth-century American social dance history where the popular screen had a similar impact, spreading local forms across the country from their communities of origin to wider communities of practice. In particular, this chapter focuses on Vernon and Irene Castle's filmed representations of ragtime partner dances pre–World War I, the film and newsreel representations of the Charleston throughout the 1920s, and television dance party shows broadcasting the Twist and other new dances in the 1950s and 60s.

In addition to its documentary function through time, audio-visual media has proven itself an ideal vehicle for disseminating popular dance movement widely over space. In the instances discussed here, the media facilitated the embodiment and consumption of movement and meaning of music, steps, and bodies across racial and social lines. Through these cycles of dissemination, development, and mediation, geographically and socio-economically disparate groups became connected through embodied practice and the ritual of watching—both themselves and others—thereby forming a consumer-based youth culture centered on music and dance.

But the imitation of dances from mediated sources was not a passive process; the screen images and the dancing practices of their audiences were in fact engaged in a two-way dialogue that popular dance scholar Sherril Dodds calls a "sophisticated circuit of reinvention."[2] As in popular dance today, dances in the early twentieth century circulated between social and presentational settings; choreography adapted from social dances appeared in Vaudeville, on Broadway, and in film, inspiring dancing at clubs and ballrooms, and the popularity of these dance forms socially in turn spurred more theatrical representations. Feature films, newsreels, and television not only made viewers aware of the existence of popular dance forms but also, as Dodds observes about music video, served "as a pedagogical tool that circulates and distributes dance styles that audiences are keen to adopt and develop."[3] In addition to the dance styles, the popularity of these forms was often emphasized on the screen, whether through depictions of the number of people joining in on the given trend or newsreel voice-over proclamations that the dance is "sweeping the country!"[4] Through consumption of these media, dancers were connected not only to the images on screen but also to the others who were watching, and later, to those who took up the dances themselves.

In order to discuss the connections between the wide range of people who experienced the dances considered here, this chapter builds on Benedict Anderson's articulation of the *imagined community*. The imagined community—the nation, in Anderson's writing—is formed through the coherence of individuals who may never meet but who are convinced of their affiliation. He illustrates this conception through the "almost precisely simultaneous consumption" of the daily newspaper, a ritual through which "the newspaper reader, observing exact replicas of his own paper being consumed by his [...] neighbours, is continually reassured that the imagined world is visibly rooted in everyday life."[5] Merely attending a showing of a film or watching a television program did not instantly unite the audience members discussed in this chapter into a community. Instead the discourse surrounding the watching, and the dancing it inspired, helped to form real communities of practice, albeit sometimes spread across the nation.

Throughout this chapter *community of origin* denotes the community in which initial innovations in dance movements took place, and *communities of practice* refers to larger networks of practitioners that formed at a secondary or tertiary phase, whether through personal contact with a dance style or, in many cases, through the images of it on the popular screen. This transmission took place through two kinds of engagement with mediated dancing—through *affective viewing* engaged through a feeling of recognition, desire, or belonging while watching, and *active viewing*, which promotes actions, such as learning or adapting the dances. The first makes visible the "imagined" community of Anderson, while the second is involved in the disseminating process, making new communities of practice possible.

The media discussed in this chapter inspired audience members to dance themselves, due in large part to the accessible characters or practitioners who were shown doing social dances in the social settings audience members also attended, and who were sharing the same experiences and emotions as the audience. This enabled an affective viewing, a connection to the media that in turn prompted active viewing and the mimicry and adoption of the dance forms. In turn, this process led to the iconic images—both still and in motion—of audience members engaged in dance at the same time as performers, whether in ballrooms with the Castles, doing the Charleston in nightclubs and speakeasies, or in front of televisions tuned to *American Bandstand*, actively constituting the nation through communities of practice.

The Films and Influence of Vernon and Irene Castle

Irene and Vernon Castle, a husband and wife ballroom dancing team, dominated the social dance scene in the pre–World War I period, acting as cultural brokers between classes and races in the United States, and popularizing dancing as an acceptable leisure time activity for the white middle- and upper-classes. Early adopters of a multi-media marketing strategy, the Castles reached their audience through appearances in Broadway shows; exhibition performances and demonstrations at clubs, including the two they owned; print media; and two silent films.

The Castles did not specialize in a single partner dance style, instead continuously introducing new dances to a society anxious for novelty but adamant about expertise. The early ballroom dances taught and adapted by the Castles and their contemporaries included simplified, jazzed-up versions of European partner dances like the waltz and the polka, and adaptations of Latin and ragtime dances, like the Maxixe, Tango, and Foxtrot. These were danced in close holds with high centers of gravity and emphasized quick, light steps and turns. Especially popular were various "one-step" and "two-step" dances, like the Castle Walk, whose steps were simple and allowed interesting upper-body movement, and more variation in direction than styles with complicated footwork.

While the print media, including interviews, photos, and the Castles' extremely successful dance manual *Modern Dancing* did a great deal in promoting the Castles, seeing them in motion on film was much more effective in the work of convincing people of the value and desirability of dance, and inspiring them to learn. [6] Eve Golden, Castle biographer, asserts that seeing the Castles dance on film showed their talent and emotiveness in a way that still photos used for publicity simply could not.[7]

Before the Castles could fuel what early social dance historian Julie Malnig calls the "social dance revolution" of the first decade and a half of the twentieth century, they faced the challenge of popularizing dance and making it respectable.[8] Their influence is widely attributed to their "aura of acceptability." As Irene told it, "[…] we were clean-cut; we were married and when we danced there was nothing suggestive about it."[9] Malnig details the dual role that exhibition ballroom teams and especially the female partners had—at once bringing the independence and expression of dance to a larger social sphere and at the same time acting to diffuse the perceived sensuality and to moderate the dances so that the practice would be acceptable.[10] As African-American dance scholar Nadine George-Graves states, "the Castles and others whitened ragtime dance at the same time they offered their version as an escape from European constraints, deca-dence, and corruption."[11] This position as cultural intermediary, spreading a form from its communities of origin to new audiences, was realized in person through their teach-ing tours, but the impact was multiplied through their films.

Just before the release of their book *Modern Dancing* in 1914, the Castles starred in the short film *Mr. and Mrs. Castle before the Camera*. Shot at their club Castle House with a small audience of friends, it shows the couple demonstrating their most well-known steps. The film was very successful, and many similar films by professional dancing couples followed.[12] On the heels of this success, Vernon wrote their feature film *Whirl of Life* with silent-film screenwriter Catherine Carr. Loosely biographical, the film debuted in 1915, and featured the couple dancing in various venues, includ-ing at the fictional grand opening of their actual club Castles by the Sea.[13] The film was made at the height of their popularity; one title card declared that the Castles' danc-ing "swept the entire country," followed by a montage of dancing couples who varied by age, race, and class.[14] *Whirl* greatly broadened the reach of the Castles' influence. Dance critic Arlene Croce calls *Whirl of Life* the most successful dance film of the silent period, identifying the Castles as the most important impetus for the pre–World War I partner dance craze.[15]

What made both *Dancing Lessons* and *Whirl* so effective in shaping dance practice was that they, and other similar films released between 1913 and 1916, offered a medi-ated version of the familiar experiences the audiences were having in ballrooms. Even if audience members had not seen the Castles in person, they would have had similar experiences as those portrayed in the films: first watching a professional couple in an exhibition dance, then a brief lesson, and then open dancing for the rest of the night. If watching exhibition couples in the dancing clubs enabled non-professional patrons to copy and learn from them,[16] the films featuring these same dancers performed a similar function while reaching a much wider audience. Although *Whirl* was the Castles' only feature film, Croce asserts that it captured what made the Castles successful, "their abil-ity to embody and at the same time exalt the spirit of an era."[17] Their audiences, swept up in the same spirit by still and moving images of the Castles and dancers like themselves, took to the floor.

THE CHARLESTON AND FLAPPER FILMS

Like early ballroom dancing before it and the dances of the Twist era several decades later, the Charleston, according to performance studies scholar Amy Koritz, "gener-ated a discourse that intertwined apprehension about gender, class, race, and aesthetic value with both invocations of expertise and consumerist imperatives."[18] In the 1920s, the bodies and embodied practices of young adults were at the center of a debate about a new consumerism, one in which identity formation happened partially through prod-uct selection, including engagement with the jazz dances and consumption of their representations on film and newsreels. Advertisers, producers, and publishers harnessed the cultural capital of fashion, music, and live and screen performances for their own benefit, defining the styles of the day.

The Charleston is certainly the most iconic of the many dances popular in the 1920s,[19] and had a greater staying power than most, maintaining popularity for the majority of the decade where other dances were only prominent for a year or two.[20] The Charleston takes many forms, all characterized by swinging lower legs and twisting knees; at its simplest it is comprised of a tap to the front with one foot, which closes back to standing, and a tap to the back with the second foot, which also returns so the feet are side-by-side. Improvisation set individual dancers apart from the crowd, and occurred in the bending of the knees, the freeness of the torso, and the range of motion of the legs, which might kick and swing in a wide trajectory, or be placed directly in front of the dancer.

While the Southern roots of the Charleston coalesced on Harlem dance floors and appeared in many stage productions,[21] the dance became a countrywide phenomenon through its media coverage. Most important as a pedagogical tool were the Charleston's visual representations, including newsreels, and the many flapper films of the 1920s, themselves products of the Jazz Age's desire for cultural and bodily freedom and expression. In an era where individualism was emphasized, the expression of this through corporeal innovation and mastery was especially prized. The range of onscreen interpretations and the high level of variation on the dance floor made the Charleston an ideal candidate to be learned through the screen, making it ripe for transmission across racial, class, and geographic boundaries through film.

The flapper film genre, bookended by 1921's *The Girl with the Jazz Heart* and 1929's *Glorifying the American Girl*, captured the spirit of the decade through aesthetics and the social implications of the characters' actions. From its earliest instance the Charleston in film was both symbol and instigator of social change, and in many films the dance "marks a value-laden crossroad in the narrative trajectories of the central characters."[22] Flapper films were generally silent and comic, but cultural studies scholar Lori Landay suggests that "the influence that flapper films, stars, and styles had on individuals and groups of spectators and consumers attests to the ways in which the films were taken seriously."[23]

The flapper films were "taken seriously," that is to say widely imitated and discussed, because these films portrayed the characters' interaction with society and other individuals through dance in much the same way as the audience members experienced it, causing an affective viewing experience, or what Landay calls an "active subjective identification."[24] Flappers and their male counterparts on the screen and in the audience faced similar decisions and pressures about respectability, image, and how to be an individual in an increasingly mechanized world. Moreover, dancing characters were shown to be enjoying the dance and their bodies, an experience salient for the films' audience members; the movie scenes of characters dancing vigorously for their friends replicated faithfully the newfound performativity of individuals on the dance floor. The theatrical space of the popular screen took up the image of the Charleston-ing partygoer, and broadcast it across the country.

In addition to feature films, the Charleston was featured in newsreels and other shorts. These shorts show footage of Charleston-ing men and women of various age and class at Charleston contests, nightclubs, house parties, on the street, on a Navy vessel, and even on top of a propeller airplane. These clips indicated that the Charleston was being performed and experienced by people with a wide range of abilities and expertise. Watching the newsreels re-inscribed the importance and popularity of the Charleston, making evident the "imagined" community for the viewing audience, many of whom were already part of the community of practice, while offering a persuasive argument for those not yet engaged. The flapper films and Charleston newsreels afforded viewers the opportunity to identify affectively with the characters on screen through observing the embodied and kinesthetic pleasure of characters much like themselves. Remembering these experiences as their own, the audience's active viewing prompted productive exploration of the dance and lifestyles portrayed.

TWISTIN' ON TELEVISION

In the post–World War II era, television changed the media landscape. While television already operated on a local scale, the linking of the coasts by coaxial cable in 1951 was a turning point in broadcast history. John Jackson, in his book *American Bandstand*, argues that the ability to broadcast nationwide enabled television to become the "unstoppable financial and cultural force it is today," setting the scene for the influence of the show, and laying the groundwork for a youth culture cemented by the consumption and embodiment of dancing images.[25] *American Bandstand* started as the local daily Philadelphia show *Bandstand* in 1953 and went country-wide on ABC in 1957.[26] Like other teen dance party shows of the time,[27] *American Bandstand* was modeled after a record hop, featuring new records and live music introduced by a host (Dick Clark for *Bandstand*), to which a studio full of ordinary teenagers danced the afternoon away. There were other elements of the show, such as games and record-rating, but the majority of the time was spent dancing—in the studio for the show's "regulars" and in front of the TV for the home viewing audience.

American Bandstand was the first network dance show, and like the work of Vernon and Irene Castle, it both brought specific dances to the audience and promoted popular dance in general as a recreational activity for America's youth.[28] Like the other forms discussed here, a broad community of practice was achieved in part through the obscuring of the communities of origin in on-air discourse and visual representation; while most of the dances done on *American Bandstand* originated in the African-American and Latino communities, the dancers were white teenagers, first from high schools in the area around the Philadelphia studio, and later from across the country when the show moved to Los Angeles.

In their famous book *Jazz Dance,* social dance historians Marshall and Jean Stearns characterize the teens who appeared on *Bandstand* as approachable, in much the same way as the charming, married Castles were, and so too the relatable characters of the flapper films. The appeal of *Bandstand* seems to be in part the affiliation the audience felt with those on screen, whom the Stearnses describe as "awkward dancers with whom any teen-ager could identify. The girls danced like girls, and unlike professional TV dancers, the boys really danced like boys."[29] While the Charleston-dancing characters of the flapper films helped blur the distinction between social and theatrical dancing, the live broadcasted *Bandstand* further diminished the distinction between spectator and performer by featuring non-professional high schoolers doing social dance in a social—albeit filmed—setting.

With the teenagers in the studio dancing to musical guests and those viewing at home mimicking the movements of both, *American Bandstand* was a show-within-a-show in which multiple audiences participated and performed. For their live appearances on these shows, choreographers like Cholly Atkins were hired to create choreography for singing groups to perform, often including pared-down versions of popular dances,[30] many of which were already being done socially in their communities of origin. Philadelphian Louis Porter recalls, "We learned to do a lot of the dances from the singers themselves … like Chubby Checker had the twist, and if he come on stage, he did the twist, and everybody learned to do [it]."[31]

The Twist, made famous by Chubby Checker with his 1960 remake of the song of the same name,[32] was described by the singer on *American Bandstand* as putting a cigarette out with your foot while drying your back off with a towel. Like the Charleston, the Twist allowed a great deal of improvisation. It was always done with bent knees, and for variation dancers could shift their weight from one side to the other, sitting into one hip and freeing the other leg to rotate in and out in the hip socket while the upper body moved in opposition. Unlike some of the other dances popular in the previous years, one Philadelphia dance instructor mused in the early 1960s, the Twist "allows a lot more individualism […]. I think that's one of the reasons it's so popular. People are getting fed up with being automatons—whether it's on the factory production line or a dance floor."[33] While popular dance would become increasingly unstructured throughout the 1960s, in the early years of the decade the Twist was danced by Americans of all ages, classes, and races.[34]

One of the impacts of the dance party shows was spreading local, specific dances to broader audiences. Because *Bandstand* was originally a local Philadelphia show, the dances were almost all local Philadelphia dances,[35] and more specifically, almost entirely derived from the dances popular in the African-American communities, from which the mostly Italian-American participants on *Bandstand* learned many of their moves. This learning had two primary sources: direct learning through contact in the integrated Philadelphia schools, and learning from the local African-American dance party show, *The Mitch Thomas Show*. Through the dissemination by broadcast media, the dances of Philadelphia became the nation's dances, although adjusted for and by predominately white dancers and audiences.

Shows like *American Bandstand*, geared to the teenager as consumer, helped constitute both a market and a community through audience consumption of musical and embodied forms. As with Anderson's newspaper reader, tuning into *American Bandstand* at the same time every day was an affirmation of participation and membership, a "thread that stitched together different teenagers in different parts of the country into a coherent and recognizable youth culture."[36] While the studio audience danced as they watched live musical performances, teens in dens and public buildings across the country watched the television actively, dancing together to the music.

CONCLUSION

The early Ballroom dances, as well as the Charleston and the Twist, enjoyed periods of development prior to their popularity in the media, which in turn resulted in their fame and diffusion across social and racial divides. Starting in the first half of the twentieth century, the role of the media in popular dance has been to notice local or emerging trends and disseminate them to larger audiences, encouraging individuals to join a burgeoning community of practice. But dancing bodies are not dependent on media representations; new dances continued to arise in areas of the country traditionally known for dance innovation and invention, and even those teenagers who learned directly from the television and movie screen adapted moves to their own abilities and personalities. These dances—as they were when they reached mass audiences, and as symbols of nationhood, the imagined community—were created by processes of commodification, diffusion, and broadcast, but were always based in the innovations and actions of specific communities of origin and practice.

Dancing is first and foremost a corporeal physical practice, and even with the invention of new technological ways to share, dance forms continue to be passed along in person. According to dance scholar Carol Martin, "social dance's physical transmission from body to body means that it can be about both forgetting and remembering, making it an ideal vehicle for the transformation of meaning over time."[37] The popular screen makes that transformation more rapid, initiating the formation of separate but connected communities of practice, communities indexed to the images of the nationwide imagined community, and often divorced from the social and economic realities of the communities of origin.

While the enthusiasm for Ballroom dancing, the Charleston, and the Twist gave way to new styles, the influence of the dancers and movement of each time period persists in popular culture and on the dance floor in large part because of the wide dissemination of the dance forms through media and the continued access to this audio-visual record. From the kinesthetic bonds between fellow dancers across space to the affective bonds that connect dancers across media, communities of practice continue to be reinforced and reimagined through the projection and consumption of their own images on the popular screen.

NOTES

1. At the time of writing, the music video for Korean pop singer Psy's "Gangnam Style" became the first ever video to reach one billion views on YouTube.com, and did so in just five months.

2. Sherril Dodds, "From Busby Berkeley to Madonna; Music Video and Popular Dance," in *Ballroom, Boogie, Shimmy Sham, Shake*, ed. Julie Malnig (Urbana: University of Illinois Press, 2009), 259.

3. Dodds, *Busby Berkeley to Madonna*, 258–259.

4. Voice-over on a newsreel of the 1925 Roseland Ballroom Charleston Contest, Carol Téten, "1920–1929 From the Blackbottom to the Lindy Hop" on DVD *America Dances! 1897–1948: A Collectors' Edition of Social Dance in Film* (Kentfield, CA: Dancetime Publications, 2003).

5. Benedict Anderson, *Imagined Communities: Reflections on the Origin and Spread of Nationalism* (London: Verso, 1991), 35.

6. For analysis of the Castles and their contemporaries in print media, see Julie Malnig, "Athena Meets Venus: Visions of Women in Social Dance in the Teens and early 1920s," *Dance Research Journal* 31.2 (1999): 34–62; Malnig "Two-Stepping to Glory: Social Dance and the Rhetoric of Social Mobility," in *Moving History/Dancing Cultures*, ed. Ann Dils and Ann Cooper Albright (Middletown, CT: Wesleyan University Press, 2001) 271–287.

7. Eve Golden, *Vernon and Irene Castle's Ragtime Revolution* (Lexington: University Press of Kentucky, 2007), 105.

8. For the negative attitudes of society toward dancing, particularly for women, see Malnig "Two-Stepping to Glory: Social Dance and the Rhetoric of Social Mobility," in *Moving History/Dancing Cultures*, ed. Ann Dils and Ann Cooper Albright, 271–287 (Middletown, CT: Wesleyan University Press, 2001);" "Apaches, Tangos, and Other Indecencies: Women, Dance and New York Nightlife," in *Ballroom, Boogie, Shimmy Sham, Shake*, ed. Julie Malnig (Urbana: University of Illinois Press, 2009); Mark Knowles, *The Wicked Waltz and Other Scandalous Dances: Outrage at Couple Dancing in the 19th and Early 20th Centuries* (Jefferson, NC: McFarland, 2009), 3–14; Lewis A. Erenberg, "Everybody's Doin' It: The Pre-World War I Dance Craze, the Castles, and the Modern American Girl," *Feminist Studies* 3.2 (1975): 155–170.

9. Quoted in Golden, *Vernon and Irene Castle*, 49.

10. Julie Malnig, "Apaches," 81–82.

11. Nadine George-Graves, "'Just Like Being at the Zoo': Primitivity and Ragtime Dance," in *Ballroom, Boogie, Shimmy Sham, Shake*, ed. Julie Malnig, (Urbana: University of Illinois Press, 2009), 64. On the obscuring of the African-American origin of popular dances, see Malnig "Apache" esp. 81; George-Graves; Koritz 65–68; Tim Wall, "Rocking Around the Clock: Teenage Dance Fads from 1955 to 1965," in *Ballroom, Boogie, Shimmy Sham, Shake*, ed. Julie Malnig (Urbana: University of Illinois Press, 2009), 182–198; John Jackson, *American Bandstand: Dick Clark and the Making of a Rock 'n; Roll Empire* (Oxford: Oxford University Press, 1999), 208–212.

12. Including at least six short instructional films and *The Quest of Life* (1916), a feature film starring the Waltons, competitors of the Castles—notice the parallel title.

13. Eve Golden, *Vernon and Irene Castle*, 135.

14. In *The Story of Irene and Vernon Castle*, the 1939 biopic starring Fred Astaire and Ginger Rogers, they literally dance across a map of the country, leaving dancing groups in their wake.

15. Arlene Croce, "Dance in Film," in *Afterimages* (New York: Knopf, 1978), 430.

16. Malnig "Apaches," 82; "Two-Stepping," 282.

17. Croce, "Dance in Film," 430.

18. Amy Koritz, *Culture Makers: Urban Performance and Literature in the 1920s* (Urbana, University of Illinois Press, 2009), 65.

19. For attempts at tracing the Charleston's historical roots, see Barbara Cohen-Stratyner, "'A Thousand Raggy, Draggy Dances': Social Dance in Broadway Musical Comedy in the 1920s," in *Ballroom, Boogie, Shimmy Sham, Shake*, ed. Julie Malnig (Urbana: University of Illinois Press, 2009), 220–223; Koritz, *Culture Makers*, 67–8; Marshall Stearns and Jean Stearns *Jazz Dance: The Story of American Vernacular Dance* (New York: Da Capo, 1994), 111–114.

20. The Charleston was not only pervasive in its era, it survived the 1920s in the form of the Lindy Hop, the Cholly Rock step seen in B-boying (breakdancing), and the New Jack Swing move the Kid 'n Play, made famous by the Hip-Hop duo of the same name.

21. For discussion of the Charleston in Broadway Musicals, see Cohen-Stratyner, 220–223.

22. Koritz, *Culture Makers*, 77.

23. Lori Landay, "The Flapper Film: Comedy, Dance, and Jazz Age Kinaesthetics," in *A Feminist Reader in Early Cinema*, ed. Jennifer M. Bean and Diane Negra (Durham, NC: Duke University Press, 2002), 225.

24. Ibid., 234. Landay emphasizes the particular identification of female spectators with flapper actresses. Interestingly, the Charleston was danced by an almost equal number of men.

25. Jackson, *American Bandstand*, ix.

26. For a thorough history of (*American*) *Bandstand* and its hosts, influence, and scandals, see Jackson, *American Bandstand*; for an excellent analysis of the show's racial politics, see Matthew F. Delmont, *Nicest Kids in Town: American Bandstand, Rock 'n' Roll, and the Struggle for Civil Rights in 1950s Philadelphia* (Berkeley: University of California Press, 2012).

27. For an extensive list of similar shows, see Delmont, *Nicest Kids*, 160.

28. Jackson, *American Bandstand*, 207.

29. Stearns, *Jazz Dance*, 4.

30. Cholly Atkins, half of the "class-act" tap duo Coles and Atkins, had a successful second career doing "vocal choreography" for Motown's largest acts.

31. Quoted in John W. Roberts, *From Hucklebuck to Hip-Hop: Social Dance in the African-American Community in Philadelphia* (Darby, PA: Diane, 1995), 21.

32. For the complex history of the Twist and its music, see Jim Dawson, *The Twist: The Story of the Song and Dance that Changed the World* (Boston: Faber and Faber, 1995).

33. Quoted in Dawson, *The Twist*, 58.

34. In 1961 the Twist craze led to the production of at least five feature films, *Twist Around the Clock, Don't Knock the Twist*, and *It's Trad Dad!* with Checker, as well as *Hey Let's Twist* and *Twist All Night*. By all accounts, these films did not feature brilliant plots or acting.

35. Of course other regions also contributed—among other examples the Bop, which inspired the *Bandstand* music hit "At the Hop," was originally from California (Jackson, *American Bandstand*, 90; Dawson, 38), and early versions of the Twist as such were sighted on *The Buddy Deane Show* in Baltimore (Dawson, 16).

36. Delmont, *Nicest Kids*, 158.

37. Carol Martin, "Reality Dance: American Dance Marathons," in *Ballroom, Boogie, Shimmy Sham, Shake*, ed. Julie Malnig (Urbana: University of Illinois Press, 2009), 93–108.

Bibliography

Cohen-Stratyner, Barbara. "'A Thousand Raggy, Draggy Dances': Social Dance in Broadway: Musical Comedy in the 1920s." In *Ballroom, Boogie, Shimmy Sham, Shake*, edited by Julie Malnig, 217–233. Urbana: University of Illinois Press, 2009.

Dawson, Jim. *The Twist: The Story of the Song and Dance That Changed the World*. Boston: Faber and Faber, 1995.

Delmont, Matthew F. *Nicest Kids in Town: American Bandstand, Rock 'n' Roll, and the Struggle for Civil Rights in 1950s Philadelphia*. Berkeley: University of California Press, 2012.

Dodds, Sherril. "From Busby Berkeley to Madonna: Music Video and Popular Dance." In *Ballroom, Boogie, Shimmy Sham, Shake*, edited by Julie Malnig, 247–260. Urbana: University of Illinois Press, 2009.

Erenberg, Lewis A. "Everybody's Doin' It: The Pre-World War I Dance Craze, the Castles, and the Modern American Girl." *Feminist Studies* 3.2 (1975): 155–170.

George-Graves, Nadine. "'Just Like Being at the Zoo': Primitivity and Ragtime Dance." In *Ballroom, Boogie, Shimmy Sham, Shake*, edited by Julie Malnig, 55–71. Urbana: University of Illinois Press, 2009.

Golden, Eve. *Vernon and Irene Castle's Ragtime Revolution*. Lexington: University Press of Kentucky, 2007.

Jackson, John. *American Bandstand: Dick Clark and the Making of a Rock 'n Roll Empire*. Oxford: Oxford University Press, 1999.

Knowles, Mark. *The Wicked Waltz and Other Scandalous Dances: Outrage at Couple Dancing in the 19th and Early 20th Centuries*. Jefferson, NC: McFarland, 2009.

Koritz, Amy. *Culture Makers: Urban Performance and Literature in the 1920s*. Urbana: University of Illinois Press, 2009.

Landay, Lori. "The Flapper Film: Comedy, Dance, and Jazz Age Kinaesthetics." In *A Feminist Reader in Early Cinema*, edited by Jennifer M. Bean and Diane Negra, 221–246. Durham, NC: Duke University Press, 2002.

Malnig, Julie. "Apaches, Tangos, and Other Indecencies: Women, Dance and New York Nightlife." In *Ballroom, Boogie, Shimmy Sham, Shake*, edited by Julie Malnig, 72–90. Urbana: University of Illinois Press, 2009.

Malnig, Julie. "Athena Meets Venus: Visions of Women in Social Dance in the Teens and early 1920s." *Dance Research Journal* 31.2 (1999): 34–62.

Malnig, Julie. "Two-Stepping to Glory: Social Dance and the Rhetoric of Social Mobility." In *Moving History/Dancing Cultures*, edited by Ann Dils and Ann Cooper Albright, 271–287. Middletown, CT: Wesleyan University Press, 2001.

Martin, Carol. "Reality Dance: American Dance Marathons." In *Ballroom, Boogie, Shimmy Sham, Shake*, edited by Julie Malnig, 93–108. Urbana: University of Illinois Press, 2009.

Roberts, John W. *From Hucklebuck to Hip-Hop: Social Dance in the African-American Community in Philadelphia*. Darby, PA: Diane, 1995.

Stearns, Marshall, and Jean Stearns. *Jazz Dance: The Story of American Vernacular Dance*. New York: Da Capo, 1994.

Wall, Tim. "Rocking Around the Clock: Teenage Dance Fads from 1955 to 1965." In *Ballroom, Boogie, Shimmy Sham, Shake*, edited by Julie Malnig, 182–198. Urbana: University of Illinois Press, 2009.

CHAPTER 4

DISCIPLINING *BLACK SWAN*, ANIMALIZING AMBITION

ARIEL OSTERWEIS

Illuminated by a hazy spotlight on an otherwise darkened proscenium stage, a lone ballerina appears in a long diaphanous white tutu. Her right arm traces a downward *port de bras* as Tchaikovsky's unmistakable score to *Swan Lake* haunts the scene. A male dancer approaches the ballerina, thrusting her around in a jaggedly circular pattern, black feathers sprouting from his every surface. A portrait of serenity suddenly transforms into a whirling site of terror and manipulation. Preceded by faint sounds of judgmental laughter (other dancers in the wings? the soloist's alter-ego?), the feathered perpetrator rotates around the ballerina's periphery, in an oppositional centrifugal-centripetal relationship with the camera, an agent of alternating surveillance and penetration. He then releases the ballerina into a state of rapture. She brushes her hand along her cheek, revealing a face at once pained and ecstatic (Fig. 4.1). Back turned, arms rippling like avian wings, the ballerina *bourrées* away from us into the distant, waning spotlight.

"I had the craziest dream last night," utters a frail-voiced Nina Sayers, cracking her neck and toes in a bedroom painted an infantilizing pink (Fig. 4.2). While stretching in front of a mirror in the Manhattan apartment she shares with her mother, Nina continues, "I was dancing the white swan. It was different choreography. It was more like the Bolshoi's. It was the prologue, when Rothbart casts a spell." Nina's mother fails to respond and we hear breakfast being prepared—a dream fallen on deaf ears. As the first scene of *Black Swan* (2010) cuts abruptly from the stage to Nina's room, we detect director Darren Aronofsky's interest in drawing out his protagonist's confusion between dreams and reality. We are introduced to the duality of Odette/Odile, the white and black swans of the classical story ballet, *Swan Lake*. Aronofsky focuses on this duality not to portray a strict opposition, but to propose that one persona must subsume the other, that a performer's ambition is marked by the parasitical encounter of daily rigor and the "dream"[1] of stardom. As such, Aronofsky purposefully conflates the dream state with the dream that drives ambition. Nina dreams of landing the role of Odette/Odile. Day in and day out, rigorous repetition and rehearsal feeds off the dream, one that reflects back at the dancer her anxieties in all their mutated forms, disfigured, bleeding, animalistic.

FIGURE 4.1 Screen Capture of *Black Swan*, Director Darren Aronofsky (2010), during opening scene onstage.

FIGURE 4.2 Screen Capture of *Black Swan*, Director Darren Aronofsky (2010), in Nina's bedroom.

TECHNIQUE AND EMOTION

A.O. Scott begins his December 30, 2010 article for the *New York Times* with the following: "The subject of *Black Swan*—a leading candidate for the most misunderstood film of 2010—is the relationship, in art, between technique and emotion."[2] Scott notes,

> Ballet, the specific art form in question, is shown to require endless practice and grueling physical discipline. Bodies, in particular the bodies of young women, are stretched and twisted into unnatural postures, and the cost of the fleeting, breathtaking grace they attain is reckoned in close-ups of battered, bloody feet and tendons pulled almost to the snapping point. The toe shoes that are among the principal tools of this torment also seem to be surrogates and scapegoats; they are scraped,

mutilated and disfigured by the dancers in a symbolic re-enactment of the violence they perform upon themselves in their ruthless pursuit of perfection.[3]

Like the fairy tale ballet, the film avoids realism and lingers in hyperbole, even the grotesque. Of significance is the way the film relies upon technical precision to invoke the dismantling effects of technique itself, demonstrating how the pursuit of virtuosity narrates a story of the attainment, surpassing, and failure of technique. The camera supports this pursuit of virtuosity through an array of film techniques that are equal to the virtuosic displays of the dancers—close-ups, tracking point-of-view shots, accelerated sequences, purposefully unsteady shots, and special effects. By virtue of this technical equivocation between the apparatus and the dancer's body, *Black Swan* attempts to meet the challenge of adapting a story ballet whose historical trajectory has been defined by the evolution of technique itself.

By paying particular attention to the role of the dancing body in *Black Swan*, this chapter interrogates the status of virtuosity and performance in a film that insists on the horror of transformation. Aronofsky exploits the body as a canvas for the psychological pressure of ambition, portraying the pursuit of perfection as a continual struggle between technique and ecstasy, control and release. Nina's quest for perfection is defined by a transformation from the innocence of aspiration (breathy, fleeting, idealistic) to the cunning of ambition (pointed, uncompromising, cruel). Initially equating perfection with the fulfillment of technique, Nina goes on to harness technique in pursuit of the imperfect perfection of ecstasy. Nina's preoccupation becomes less rational and more carnal; withdrawing from reason and explanation, perfection enters the realm of excess. It is in that ecstatic excess—an excess that threatens the integrity of the choreography—that we can locate the crux of virtuosity, personified by Odette/Odile. Embodied by Nina (Natalie Portman) and Lily (Mila Kunis), self and *other* perform a necessarily entangled pas de deux, one in which the seemingly perfect image of the other simultaneously haunts and motivates the dancer, a figure for whom psychological control diminishes as artistic control accrues (Fig. 4.3).

For all of Aronofsky's purported disloyalty to the reality of the ballet profession in *Black Swan*, the film remains true to *Swan Lake*'s significance in dance history as the full-length work that announced the modern mark of female virtuosity in ballet from the late nineteenth century onward: the *fouetté* turn. Aronofsky unleashes the *fouetté* turn to perform a blurring between selves, Odette and Odile. This blurring marks both psychic confusion and an occupational precipice, recurring throughout the film in a particular relationship to the camera's orbit. The camera implicates us in its own hurried, erratic mode of surveillance and desire for contact with its subject matter. Marius Petipa and Lev Ivanov's revival of *Swan Lake* for the Mariinsky Theatre in 1895 (after Tchaikovsky's 1875–1876 score) featured Italian ballerina Pierina Legnani as Odette/Odile, the princess who undergoes transformation into a swan. It was in Petipa's production that the climactic trope of thirty-two *fouetté* turns that punctuates many a *grand pas de deux* became a signifier of female achievement in twentieth century ballet.[4] Aronofsky's Odette/Odile is Nina, played by Portman, who won an academy award for

FIGURE 4.3 Screen Capture of *Black Swan*, Director Darren Aronofsky (2010), dressing room mirrors.

her performance. Ambition permeates *Black Swan* on multiple levels: the film itself has been hailed an "ambitious achievement," Portman's acting and ballet training for *Black Swan* epitomizes Hollywood ambition, Nina's character is haunted by ambition's alienating effects, and Odette/Odile embodies nineteenth-century ballet's technical ambition. All these permutations of ambition operate corporeally, both literally and metaphorically: the "body" of the film within Aronofsky's "body" of work, bodily training, and the continual threat of "other" bodies penetrating or sprouting from one's own.

Significantly, in the history of Western concert performance, virtuosity emerges through the trope of the soloist, further exploited via capitalist ideology's reliance on commodity exchange and the cult of individualism. In other words, audiences flock to witness their favorite performer (ballerina) stand out from the group (*corps de ballet*), and it is impossible to extricate that performer's exceptional qualities from the economic fact of ticket sales. As a term that became popular through the advent of print journalism, virtuosity is a quality unknown to performance schemas that lie outside of systems of judgment and criticism. Virtuosity relies on the masculinist ambition (as opposed to feminized aspiration) driving the capitalist workplace, and in *Black Swan* ambition finds itself painfully grafted onto the female dancer. Aronofsky exhibits this sense of grafting on the surface of the skin, reaching its apex with the sprouting of wings in the ballet's final scene. Just as Nina is haunted by her own ambition, she finds herself in a hierarchical realm defined by tiers of scrutiny: Nina is subordinate to the judgment of her mother and the artistic director, Thomas Leroy (played by Vincent Cassell), and Thomas is subordinate to the whims and funding prerogatives of the ballet company's board of directors (Fig. 4.4).

Black Swan portrays artistic ambition through Nina's—and Odette/Odile's—erratic transformation from human to animal. *Black Swan* alludes to the *Swan Lake*'s libretto, its themes of duality, love, deception, paranoia, and transformation. Aronofsky draws out the tension between technique's mechanical, disciplining function and the unrefined,

FIGURE 4.4 Screen Capture of *Black Swan*, Director Darren Aronofsky (2010), Thomas and Nina seduction in studio.

animalistic characteristics of ecstasy. In doing so, he recognizes the idea that technique is often thought to provide formal tools with which an artist can express carnal emotion. Nina's artistic director, Thomas, commands, "Seduce us; attack it" and reiterates "Lose yourself" throughout the film. An early scene features Nina tentatively attempting to seduce her director Thomas after a less than successful audition for the role of Odette/Odile. Having released her hair from her profession's prescribed taut ballet bun, Nina enters Thomas' black and white office wearing fresh lipstick. She utters, "I practiced the coda last night and I finished." Thomas' response reemphasizes the importance of passion (over labor) in the role of Odile: "Honestly, I don't care about your technique. You should know that by now." After he tells Nina he has chosen another dancer (Veronica) for the role of Odette/Odile, Nina tries to exit only to have the door slammed in her face. "That's it?" challenges Thomas, "You're not going to try to change my mind? You must have thought it was possible. Otherwise what are you doing here all dolled up?" Nina responds, "I came to ask for the part." "The truth is," Thomas continues,

> When I look at you, all I see is the white swan. Yes you're beautiful, fearful, fragile. Ideal casting. But the black swan, it's a hard fucking job to dance both.... I see you obsessed getting each and every move perfectly right but I never see you lose yourself. Ever. All the discipline for what?

Nina says, "I just want to be perfect," and Thomas reminds her in the hyperbolically authoritarian tone Aronofsky cites from lowbrow film genres, "Perfection is not just about control. It's also about letting go." Then Thomas grabs Nina and kisses her only

FIGURE 4.5 Screen Capture of *Black Swan*, Director Darren Aronofsky (2010), Nina's bloody hangnail.

to be received with a bite. Thomas is shocked, responding, "That fuckin' hurt!" Nina's newfound impulse to cause pain marks a crucial shift in her artistry, from a technically proficient dancer to one with the potential to incite feeling.

Outwardly directed pain, however, is merely a precursor to the amplification of Nina's enactments of self-inflicted pain, the endpoint of ballet's logic of refinement. As subordinate to the ballet master's rule, the ballerina's discipline is taken to the extreme, portrayed in *Black Swan* as corporeal masochism: human body parts are mangled and removed, and what remains are wounds from which the animalistic emerges. Nina compulsively scratches the skin on her back, yanks off her toenails, and rips her hangnails until her fingers bleed (Fig. 4.5). In ballet training, technique is learned within an ideology of perfecting an imperfect body. Dancers are corrected, meaning they are expected to incrementally implement corrections from their instructor with each reiteration of a movement combination. Nina's obsession with technique is one in which the trope of the correction intensifies from correcting movements to correcting flesh. Just as the dancer must begin class each day by executing *pliés* before moving onto more complex material, sometimes Nina's wounds magically disappear, as if to invite compulsive returns, repeated acts of mutilation in the name of refinement. The muscular impulse of extended, rippling, wing-like arms in the swan's *port de bras* emerges from the shoulder blades, but Nina returns to the site with obsessive-compulsive scratching, eventually drawing blood, inscribing a masochistic stigmata (Fig. 4.6). Less of a scarring and more of an open wound, this inscription becomes the fissure from which the black swan's feathers sprout.

The most significant aspects of Nina's bodily mutilations are that they are self-inflicted and born of repetition. The ballet profession requires unending repetition of exercises, classes, and rehearsals over many years, and Nina's back scratching is a mutated substitution for and supplement to that practice. Nina's masochism stimulates transformation (from human to swan), and, as opposed to injury's hindering effects, parallels

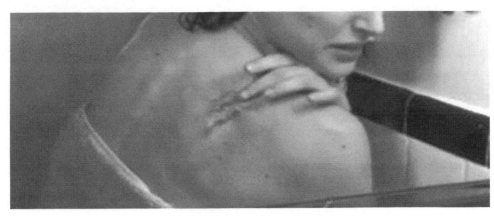

FIGURE 4.6 Screen Capture of *Black Swan*, Director Darren Aronofsky (2010), Nina's back scratch.

technique's function of improving ability. Nina's body is both disciplined and disciplining, each *fouetté* turn a repetition that demands control as it takes the body further and further out of control. That Nina grows larger-than-life black feathered wings during the culminating *fouetté* turn sequence of *Swan Lake* in the final scene of *Black Swan* is significant, marking the point at which the pinnacle of her technical achievement coincides with raw animalistic attributes associated with the ecstatic.

In *Black Swan,* ballet's corporeal practice evacuates as it supplements, and Odette/Odile defeats herself in the name of art. Throughout the film, Nina and her own "other" evoke the struggle of the artist to achieve balance between the human capability to master mechanical technique and the untamed animalistic emotion necessary to sustain ambition and evoke passion onstage. Aronofsky has stated, "I'm always very interested in performance ... and this story is about that, which gives it ... a clear connection to *The Wrestler* (2008)."[5] While *Black Swan* traces the pursuit of virtuosity in the early life of an aspiring artist, in *The Wrestler*, Aronofsky's main protagonist tries to hold onto and resuscitate the virtuosity he once possessed, from the vantage point of the latter end of a physically demanding career, one that also (but differently) straddles the artist-athlete divide. What Aronofsky understands is performance's demand for reiteration, rehearsal, and repetition, that a career in performance requires what scholars such as Richard Schechner and Judith Butler have long identified as the theoretical term *performance's* reenactments, its continuous *doing*. In other words, one is not born a virtuoso, which Aronofksy illustrates at the level of both practice and theory. Virtuosity requires repetition and achievement that lies in excess of the fulfillment of the composition.

In terms of virtuosity, *Black Swan* creates a parallel between the cinematic apparatus (the full schematic technicity of cinema, including camerawork) and the dancer's bodily technique, an alternating concealment and exposure of the mechanical. As Thomas tells Nina, if the criteria of judgment were based on nothing more than technique, she would be without peer. But he ultimately asks her to allow emotion to dictate her technique.

This can be seen as synecdochic of the problem the film poses at an analytical level and one of the potential sources of misunderstanding, for in just the same way that Nina must break free from the constraints of technique and draw upon the power of emotion, so too does Aronofsky's film insist that the spectator rely upon emotion as a point of access to the film's technique. What emerges is a palpable tension between cinematic/mediated mechanics and those executed by the human body. Both through its subject matter and its filmic apparatus, *Black Swan* fragments, mutilates, and transforms the human body in pursuit of perfection, mirroring the dialectic of ambition's temporality as that which is characterized by future-oriented desires and goals that are continually interrupted by setbacks. Tugging at the forward motion of ambition's sights, its imagining of success, is the threat and occurrence of failure. Failure takes time—time away from momentum and time to reassemble the shattered fragments ejected from linear temporality.

BODY GENRES

In *Black Swan*, intersecting temporalities manifest themselves corporeally, through bodily transformation and mutation. Aronofksy has referred to *Black Swan* as a werewolf movie, and the film points to other genres and modes, such as the psychological thriller, horror, melodrama, camp, and the backstage musical. As such, Aronofsky deploys lowbrow aesthetics to explore the pursuit of a highbrow art form. *Black Swan* is most readily associated with *The Red Shoes* (1948) in terms of its supposed glimpse into the world of ballet and the trope of female ambition's ill effects. Nevertheless, whereas a love interest is seen as detrimental to a ballerina's career in *The Red Shoes*, the ballet master in *Black Swan* encourages Nina to pursue erotic adventure in order to attain sexual maturity. While *Black Swan* does not display sex acts as explicitly as hardcore pornography, Aronofsky's film certainly amounts to an amalgamation of elements of film scholar Linda Williams's multiple genres and modes of filmic excess, namely, pornography, melodrama, and horror. Due to the withholding of visible penetration and overtly displayed genitals, Nina and Lily's bedroom scene classifies as soft-core (Fig. 4.7). The scene's importance lies in the fact that it is a fantasy, a dream ultimately alluding to Nina's own dual Odette/Odile-like persona. According to film critic Terrence Rafferty, "There are remarkably few horror movies about the terror and violence of making art, but *Black Swan* is in that tiny company."[6] Referring to these three as "body genres" (and Williams has since claimed melodrama to be a mode as opposed to a genre, per se),[7] Williams presents their "pertinent features of bodily excess":

> There is the spectacle of a body caught in the grip of intense sensation or emotion.... the focus on what could probably best be called a form of ecstasy.... In each of these genres the bodies of women figured on the screen have functioned traditionally as the primary *embodiments* of pleasure, fear, and pain.... So the bodies of women have tended to function, ever since the eighteenth century origins of these

FIGURE 4.7 Screen Capture of *Black Swan*, Director Darren Aronofsky (2010), Lily and Nina lesbian fantasy.

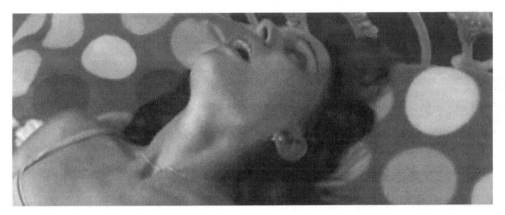

FIGURE 4.8 Screen Capture of *Black Swan*, Director Darren Aronofsky (2010), Nina's orgasm.

genres in the Marquis de Sade, Gothic fiction, and the novels of Richardson, as both the *moved* and the *moving*.[8]

The subject matter of *Black Swan* is most indisputably the *moving* body, however hyperbolized it might be. And, according to Williams, body genres depend not only the moving female body, but also on various temporal structures in alternation, such as "too late," "too early," and "right on time." *Black Swan* exercises the limits of a temporality of ambition, trying to accomplish as much movement as possible within a career known for its brevity and obsession with youth (Fig. 4.8).

Nina's primary focus is to acquire mastery over her body, regardless of what it may be doing at any given moment in the narrative. As a werewolf—or were*swan*—film that unabashedly conjures multiple body genres, *Black Swan* animalizes ambition through the coming-of-age transformation of a young woman as opposed to a teenaged boy. By re-gendering the werewolf trope, Aronofsky reverses the "horror" of the process of becoming-animal: whereas the male werewolf is perceived as a threat to those around him, injuring or destroying those in his midst, the female wereswan of *Black Swan* that is Odette-becoming-Odile is seen as a threat to herself. Others must get out of the werewolf's way, but the wereswan must get out of her own way, must "lose herself." Of course, the nocturnal mischief of the werewolf/swan presents us with another duality, a temporal binary internal to—and complicating—the temporality of ambition. As Scott observes, the film elaborates on Odette/Odile's competing Apollonian and Dionysian poles. Aronofsky's ballerina, both human and animal, strains the limits of the body-mind binary while reversing conventional notions of good and evil. Human by day and swan by night, Odette/Odile ultimately reveals the instability of epistemological binary constructions in the first place.

Reversibility

As far as binary constructions go, no trope is more symbolic of ballet's haunting duality than that of the mirror. Subway windows double as mirrors as Nina applies lipstick on her way to morning ballet class. When Nina is auditioning for the role of Odette/Odile, the studio mirror is as much a site of reflection as it is one of distortion (Fig. 4.9). After a series of *piqué* turns and *bourrées*, the camera rotates around Nina, then focuses on Thomas's face as Nina appears dancing in the mirror. Aronofsky seems to suggest that the dressing room mirror is a site of aspiration's memory, hosting images of generations

FIGURE 4.9 Screen Capture of *Black Swan*, Director Darren Aronofsky (2010), Nina in studio mirror.

of ballerinas making up their faces before performances, succumbing to ambition's corrupting effects. Breaking glass is audible in the hallway as Nina approaches aging dancer
Beth's departing tirade. Upon Beth's retirement, Nina raids the dancer's dressing room
for theatrical ephemera (used lipstick, nail file), tokens containing the promise of the
transference of stardom from one generation to another. The mirror in *Black Swan* functions both conceptually and visually: the dual character Odette/Odile is both always
mirroring herself and is mirrored by Nina's offstage persona/s, and actual mirrors figure
heavily in the film's visual landscape. Nina's reflection sometimes manifests itself as her
own image and at other times as her doppelgänger, Lily. Furthermore, Nina and Lily
"mirror" the duality of Odette/Odile's character, a classic example of the figure of the
doppelgänger, the evil other. In German, doppelgänger is comprised of the two words
meaning "double" and "walker." Thus, Lily is Nina's haunting double walker (Fig. 4.10).

Through the mirror, we are privy to reflections, breaking glass, distortion, and
images of self-scrutiny. The mirror has long served as the literal and figurative tool of
"reflection" inherent to ballet training. As a tool, the mirror is indicative of the training
process, in which the rational and emotional still interact, for it is not until the ballerina sets foot onstage that she can rely on so-called "muscle memory" and let go of the
deliberate phrasing of the studio for the relative emotional abandon of performance.
While the reliability of the glass mirror is forfeited onstage, we are privy to multiple
scenes of the glass-like substance, rosin, being crushed underfoot, and rosin provides
increased traction for the ballerina in otherwise slippery satin *pointe* shoes. In *Black
Swan*, episodes of breaking glass and crushed rosin coincide with developments in
character, as Nina's persona is continually fractured and reformed in her quest of the
role of Odette/Odile.

Aronofsky's trope of the mirror resonates with film scholar Vivian Sobchack's phenomenological concept of the reversibility of experience in the cinema and the availability of the *cinesthetic subject*. In arguing that the film and its viewer enter into a

FIGURE 4.10 Screen Capture of *Black Swan*, Director Darren Aronofsky (2010), Nina and
her double in subway station.

co-constitutive relationship with each other, Sobchack departs from the mirror's simply reflective characteristic to suggest that

> All the bodies in the film experience—those on-screen and off-screen (and possibly that of the screen itself)—are potentially subversive bodies. They have the capacity to function both figuratively and literally . . . . each exists in a figure-ground reversibility with the others.[9]

After Merleau-Ponty, Sobchack proposes a phenomenology of cinematic experience, imparting the idea that we sense film haptically, with all our senses at our disposal. To consider such a full-bodied cinematic experience is to undermine the regime of visuality. Aronofsky (inadvertently or otherwise) engages the very conflict between the mirror's mere reflection and reversibility's active exchange by forcing form to grapple with content. In fittingly Odette/Odile fashion, Aronofsky's directorial style is one in which intentionally complex cinematic technique exaggerates its subject matter, including images of actual mirrors. Thus, if mirrors ordinarily reflect the dancer's image, Aronofsky's distorted, fragmented portrayal of mirrors through cinematic techniques forces in the "viewer" a reversible experience in which she comes into phenomenological exchange with the film itself.

Importantly, "live" ballet performance does not necessarily possess the tools to make available such reversible experience, as the ballet audience member sits at a fixed distance from the stage, often unable to discern facial detail and other such "close-ups" of the dancing bodies. Paradoxically, the traditional proscenium stage may not offer the reversibility Sobchack identifies in film, and therefore it is important to point out that (for this and many other reasons) a production of *Swan Lake* could certainly not claim to possess the same levels of horror, melodrama, or heightened sexuality as *Black Swan*. One simple distinction between "viewing" experiences of classical ballet and contemporary film is that, for the most part, the dancers comprise the moving bodies in a ballet setting, whereas the camera often acts as the significant moving "body" in film, dictating much of the directionality of the "viewer's" gaze and sensibility. Additionally, the experience of film is further heightened sensorially when one takes into consideration the added elements of very deliberate sonic, musical, and editorial choices, ones that are unallowable or impossible in a classical ballet context.

Returning to the framework of Williams's body genres, we find that the "excesses" created by horror, melodrama, and pornography are nearly impossible without the technical facility of the camera and its related components. Despite—and precisely because of—its recorded nature, film is able to generate synesthetically heightened sensations of experience. It is not necessarily the *content* of Black Swan (elements such as plot, subject matter, or acting) that creates such heightened sensation for the viewer; rather, heightened sensation is created through *form* and formal qualities born of the film's apparatus, its machinery. More specifically, it is through technical elements of special effects, close-ups, distorted sound (animalistic wings amplified), and excerpts of Tchaikovsky's music that create such intensification of synesthesia. Heightened synesthesia is not necessarily inherent to film (and therefore always more possible in film than live dance), but film has the capacity to mechanically/technically intensify elements that will inevitably generate amplified sensation for the viewer. Sobchack's *cinesthetic subject* is a combination of "cinema," "synaesthesia," and "coaenesthesia," the latter two pointing to the idea that the arousal of one sense can instigate perception in another. Cinesthesia resonates with, yet departs from, dance studies' preferred term, *kinesthesia*, the idea of one's sensual awareness of one's own muscular movement. Whereas cinesthesia is involuntary, kinesthesia is self-aware. Nina scrutinizes herself in the mirror in spaces both domestic and professional, as she practices at home in a folding mirror, and rehearses in the studio in front of mirrored walls. Her own transformation from self-conscious human to involuntary swan is paralleled by her transformation from kinesthetic to cinesthetic subject. As such, Aronofsky takes us on a tour of the possibilities of our own subjective sensory-perceptive experiences of ballet and film.

Black Swan amplifies the fact that film's technical and technological components ultimately *mirror* the dancer's relationship to technique. Thus, Aronofsky draws a parallel—through the device of mirrors themselves throughout *Black Swan*—between filmic technique and balletic technique. The editor and camera thus parallel the dancer. Herein lies the theme of *virtuosity* as that which takes place in film through the cinematic apparatus and in dance through the dancer's live corporeal execution of difficult movements, especially in repetition, as in the execution of thirty-two *fouetté* turns. The fact that a body double was hired to dance many of Portman's passages is a particularly fitting (if paradoxical) example of the way film can rely on a double to assist an actor in depicting a role invested in the theme of the double itself.

Elaborating on the ecstatic nature of body genres, Williams alludes to "contemporary meanings" of ecstasy that "suggest components of direct or indirect sexual excitement and rapture."[10] She goes on to locate visual and aural attributes of such rapture as evoking a lack of control through bodily spasms and unarticulated sounds. In a fitting parallel, the drug Ecstasy figures in the film, as Lily drops an Ecstasy pill into Nina's cocktail during the rare night of debauchery that ends with Nina's fantasy lesbian romp with black-winged Lily. In *Black Swan* we become privy to Nina's flirtation with rapture through sensual (though not especially revealing) scenes of masturbation and sex, as well as the centrifugal sound of ominous bird wings preparing for flight layered over Tchaikovsky's score (Fig. 4.11). Albeit perversely, rapture is also approached through acts of abjection—vomiting, stabbing, toenail-breaking, and hangnail-ripping. These self-inflicted bodily mutilations incrementally lead Nina to what Thomas identifies as the aesthetically ideal loss of control. Nina's culminating sequence of *piqué* turns leading into *fouetté* turns whips her around and around into a near-frenzy that approaches a state of rapture, save the mechanism of technique that allows her to arrive at such feats in the first place. We finally perceive Nina's rapture in her slow-motion downward fall to a mattress on the ground in the final moment of the ballet. That this fatal climax takes place backstage underscores Aronofsky's paramount interest in the psyche of the performer, that which lies behind the façade of artistry. In this instance she is not in control of her movements through bodily technique, and she lands on her back, blood oozing outward from her center (Fig. 4.12). After Thomas runs to her and asks, "What

FIGURE 4.11 Screen Capture of *Black Swan*, Director Darren Aronofsky (2010), Nina grows black wings in final solo.

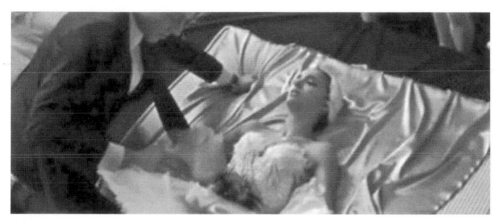

FIGURE 4.12 Screen Capture of *Black Swan*, Director Darren Aronofsky (2010), final scene; Nina utters, "I was perfect."

did you do?" she utters, "I felt it. Perfect. I was perfect." We are left to cinesthetically perceive Nina's inevitable death, her arrival at rapture, an arrival that might not be detected through unmediated channels of the live and mechanical.

In *Black Swan*, youthful aspiration becomes competitive ambition (ultimately between the self and its own other). Nina's ambition proves both necessary and detrimental; her final performance results in a display of perfection as both success and death. Nina's trajectory to becoming a swan is a metamorphosis in which each additional feather externalizes her psychological struggle as well as the disintegration of rational human composure. As a symbol of flight, her wings represent the simultaneous embodiment of perfection, on the one hand, and ambition's unfortunate repercussions, on the other: Nina's wings never lift her into the air, and soon vanish like ballet's ever-fleeting feats.

NOTES

1. I intentionally intersperse the colloquial sense of "dream," as in a wish or fantasy.
2. A.O. Scott, "Natalie Portman Embraces Monster and Victim," Dec 30, 2010.
3. Ibid.
4. Legnani is known to be the first ballerina to execute thirty-two *fouetté* turns in a row.
5. Aronofsky in Rafferty.
6. Rafferty.
7. Williams, Playing the Race Card.
8. Williams, "Film Bodies," 4.
9. Sobchack, 9.
10. Williams, "Film Bodies," 4.

BIBLIOGRAPHY

Rafferty, Terrence. "A Dark Transformation of Strains of 'Swan Lake.'" *New York Times*. Oct 30, 2010. http://www.nytimes.com/2010/10/31/movies/31raff.html?pagewanted=all.

Scott, A.O. "Natalie Portman Embraces Monster and Victim." *New York Times*. Dec 30, 2010.

Sobchack, Vivian. "What My Fingers Knew: The Cinesthetic Subject, or Vision in the Flesh." *Senses of Cinema*. Issue 5 (Special Effects/Special Affects: Technologies of the Screen – A Symposium), April 2000.

Williams, Linda. "Film Bodies: Gender, Genre, and Excess." *Film Quarterly*, Vol. 44, No. 4 (Summer, 1991): 2–13.

——. *Playing the Race Card: Melodramas of Black and White from Uncle Tom to O.J. Simpson*. Princeton, NJ: Princeton University Press, 2001.

CHAPTER 5

···

GENE KELLY: THE
ORIGINAL, UPDATED

···

MARY FOGARTY

I will not pause to argue the claim that the creative life of Kelly and Donen
has been befouled. Let me just say that our collective memory, our culture,
our pleasure have all been monkeyed with. Yes, the film survives, and can
still be seen, but its beauty and its integrity are being flagrantly interfered
with. The nature of a movie is being insidiously mocked and exploited.
And while this is not the first instance of this kind of electronic reordering
of an existing scene, it maybe a threshold to ever more indecent re-makes.

(David Thomson, *The Independent*, February 6, 2005)

It was an honor and a privilege being one of the dancers in this commercial. Gene Kelly was a great dancer, singer and actor which is a lot more
than I have to offer. It's extremely flattering having a commercial that
essentially implies that my moves are an updated version of Gene's dance
skills.

(David "Elsewhere" Bernal, kottke.org, February 11, 2005)

AT a historical moment when the concept of creativity itself is being challenged (Frith
2012), the work of Gene Kelly, one of Hollywood's most significant contributors to dance
on screen, is worth revisiting (Fig. 5.1). The site of this discussion will be the contro-
versy in 2005 surrounding a Volkswagen commercial[1] that "updated" the original solo
dance sequence from *Singin' in the Rain* (Donen and Kelly 1952) performed by Gene
Kelly in the character of Don Lockwood. The commercial features the dance moves
of David "Elsewhere" Bernal and Donnie "Crumbs" Counts, which are digitally doc-
tored to fit within the framework of Kelly's original setting, and with the superimposi-
tion of Gene Kelly's face on both dancers. I begin with a critical comparison of these
two dance sequences. Later in the chapter, Maaike Bleeker's concept of the "cover" in
choreographic practices (2012) is introduced. The "cover" is Bleeker's modification of
Mark Franko's (1989) distinction between reconstruction and reinvention. This concept

FIGURE 5.1 Gene Kelly as Don Lockwood in *Singin' in the Rain* (Donen and Kelly 1952).

is used here to compare how popular dance performances, such as those described in the commercial, are "remixes" of the qualities and values of past performers and differ from the "cover" in choreographic works. Remixes benefit from an understanding of how hip-hop dance practitioners evaluate and assess dance performances through their own measures of "creativity" and "originality."

A revisiting of Gene Kelly's films reveals a complex trajectory of discourses that informs "listening" as a serious practice in popular dance practices and receptions. Thus, this chapter concludes with examples from Kelly's films to demonstrate how contemporary listening practices are rooted in notions about acoustic space, sound, and the senses that have a history tracing back long before hip-hop culture emerged. A reflection on these residual values contributes to a broader understanding of the historical situation of popular dance performances.

The influential scene from *Singin' in the Rain* is one of the most well-known dance sequences in the history of Hollywood musicals. However, as Peter Wollen (1992) has pointed out, the acclaim for *Singin' in the Rain* accrued gradually over decades, before it was regarded as an important film. In the scene in question, toward the end of the film, Kelly dances alone in a rain-soaked street, set to the music of the film's signature melody. Comparisons between Gene Kelly's solo performance and the "remix" of the commercial reveal that measures and evaluations of creativity are, indeed, social facts (DeNora 1997, Frith 2012). These social facts are debated not only in the realm of high art but also in those popular dance styles that have been deemed in various discourses to be "lowbrow." For example, Gene Kelly's work has historically been downplayed by dance writers and historians because of his status as a popular dance performer and only began to be seriously reassessed in the 1990s (see Sheaves 1990).

Wollen designates Gene Kelly's performance in the original scene as a "summation" of his work, "echoing and developing numbers he had done in earlier films, crystallizing the principles and ideas about dance and film which he had been forming, consciously and unconsciously, since early childhood…" (p. 29). Thus, Wollen argues that although the film is a complex collaboration between choreographers, directors, assistants, musical arrangers, composers, script writers, and the like, this does not refute the overarching contribution of Gene Kelly.

Wollen's assertions reveal the investment that the auteur theory in film studies had, not only in in the concept of "creativity," but also in the notion of the "work" itself. Lydia Goehr (1992) identifies that the concept of a "work of art" takes shape around 1800 and carries forward across various disciplines, including visual arts and music, with the rise of the concert hall. In this setting, to listen properly to music one must sit attentively and in silence to properly appreciate the "work." The "work" is not located in any particular performance but rather hovers above its tangible live traces and notations, as what Goehr calls the "work-concept." The conceptions of dance parallel these developments as audiences moved into theaters to quietly contemplate dance choreography. Audiences' investments in one particular artist's career over time, and the subsequent development of theories to explain the works of great artists, resulted in this particular view of creativity centered on the "work-concept." Auteur theory, developed to explain the works of great film directors (see *Cahiers du Cinema* writers of the early 1960s for this), was the construction of film critics who saw parallels across the film "works" of particular directors that resembled their own creative "signature."

This signature is the mark of creativity: the impulse of a particular person who is "original" and, as was often referred to in times passed, possessed of "genius." In the first quotation at the start of this chapter, film critic David Thomson's acknowledgment of the "creative life" of two directors who collaborated, on what became an equal footing, speaks to his reading both of their creativity and of how that creativity was collaborative and shared. His reading fuels his suggestion that the "creative life" of Kelly and Donen, as represented through their collaborative Hollywood film musicals such as *Singin' in the Rain*, has been contaminated by the remaking of a classic dance sequence for a televised commercial.

The sociological impulse to question how creativity is assigned to particular artists, directors, and dancers is useful here. I begin by suggesting that within popular dance practices and receptions, distinctions of quality are already being made by audiences and critics and need to be recognized in the burgeoning field of popular dance studies.

As I have noted elsewhere, elitism can be found in the attitudes of participants within various dance styles categorized as popular or street dance. This is not surprising considering how much of popular dance performance, like the professional dance world itself, is centered on competition. Even for audiences, dancers are compared, and aesthetic pleasures are often experienced in the act of comparison. Gene Kelly's position as the everyday American in his various roles and film characters is defined not only through his performances but also through the ongoing comparisons that were drawn between himself and his contemporary, Fred Astaire, who was seen to represent the "aristocracy" in relation to Kelly's assertively plebian "athleticism." These distinctions were traced by press and fans alike in their physiques as well as in their movement

FIGURE 5.2 *Singin' in the Rain* (Donen and Kelly 1952).

vocabularies, and were often a focus of comment by those who observed them. For example, Cyd Charisse's husband remarked that he always knew with whom she had gone to work with that day from the state of her body: if she was bruised, it had been the rough-and-tumble Gene Kelly, as opposed to Fred Astaire (Trachtenberg 1983).

A closer look at the famous scene from *Singin' in the Rain* and its TV commercial remake will help to focus the discussion. When the scene begins, Don Lockwood (Gene Kelly) is leaving the home of his girlfriend at the point in the narrative arc when all is well in his world and most of his problems have been (temporarily) resolved. The sound of rain gives physicality to the setting, its damp discomfort offset by the upbeat, quietly nonchalant and non-diegetic orchestral music. He waves his driver away as he steps away from the door and starts singing, "doo de doo doo." When he starts to sing in the rain, about singing in the rain, he chooses to close his umbrella and embrace the moment of nighttime isolation provided by the late hour and the rain that has emptied the streets (Fig. 5.2). Some of the aspects of the scene I have just highlighted are ripe for comparison with the shortened commercial remake and point to the influence that Kelly had on future generations of dancers.

Kelly's arms are relaxed as he walks gracefully down the street. His face is perpetually grinning; his steps are loose and pedestrian with sudden moments of sharp, dynamic extensions. His use of the umbrella as a substitute dance partner transforms, as the umbrella becomes a musical instrument, an extension of his arm movements and a twirling addition as he travels across the space of the street (Figs. 5.3 and 5.4). His shoulder shrugs are comical and his movements are playful and exuberant. In most of the shots his full body is visible and the shot transitions rely on match-on-action editing, resulting in seamless transitions between Kelly's movements. Although at moments the

FIGURE 5.3 *Singin' in the Rain* (Donen and Kelly 1952).

FIGURE 5.4 *Singin' in the Rain* (Donen and Kelly 1952).

camera movements contribute to the feel of the performance for the most part the camera centers Kelly in the shot.

The updated commercial version of the scene begins similarly with the dancer playing Don Lockwood/Gene Kelly walking down the street singing "doo de doo doo," the umbrella shielding him from the rain. His arms are not as relaxed and free as in the original version, showing performed tension around the shoulder. He looks up and decides to close his umbrella and his arms extend out, but again with a more restricted and controlled inverted movement across his shoulders and chest than Kelly's movements had been during this opening sequence. As the Kelly replacement closes his umbrella, the musical pitch of the non-diegetic orchestra modifies and electronic beats kick in, matching the "hits" that the dancer makes, in keeping with the remix created by Mint Royale. The "hits" involve the isolation and quick contraction and release of various muscles. The sound of the rain, unlike in the original, disappears. Similarly, the movements of the dancer are no longer amplified with sounds of tapping feet.

The dancer begins to "wave" and "hit" with his arms as he travels sideways, handing his umbrella over to a passer-by. This is one of the other major modifications of the scene as the umbrella is given up before the dance sequence begins, rather than at the end, as in the original film version (Fig. 5.5). Now without the umbrella, the dancer represents his signature moves, along with some classic b-boy power moves and freezes added by the next dancer that plays Don Lockwood. The movements are sharper in speed than the original dance; the extensions are more angular (Fig. 5.6). When one dancer grabs a pole to set up an upside-down freeze it is the moment where the angles actually most resemble Kelly's original shapes, albeit from an upside-down point of departure (Fig. 5.7). Unlike in the film version, the new Lockwood character touches the ground with his hands for a series of acrobatic movements, including a somersault, flip, and a "1990" (this is a move in breaking when a dancer spins upside down on one arm with both legs extended above him/her) (Fig. 5.8). In doing so, the vocabulary of movement is expanded and indeed, updated.

The use of dancers with very different movement vocabularies adds to the dimension of this performance, with David "Elsewhere" Bernal providing some of the more

FIGURE 5.5 Volkswagen commercial.

FIGURE 5.6 Volkswagen commercial.

FIGURE 5.7 Volkswagen commercial.

comical and playful movements in a popping and abstract waving style and, at the other extreme, Donnie "Crumbs" Counts providing the gymnastic and b-boy moves.[2] This wide array of movements transforms and expands Gene Kelly's vocabulary in different directions, albeit in a shortened span of time. There are only eight shots to this version, adding up to about a minute in total, including the final title screen advertising the product as "The original, updated."

Film critic David Thomson's judgment that the addition of "hip hop" music (electronic, more or less) and related dance styles had "monkeyed" with "our" pleasure and

FIGURE 5.8 B-boy performing a "1990" in Volkswagen commercial.

cultural memory was not the only response to this remake, which also received praise for its technological innovations. In some ways, the rhetorical inclusion of the word "our" to describe cultural memory in Thomson's critique is precisely the type of value judgment that Sherril Dodds (2011) takes to task in *Dancing on the Canon: Embodiments of Value in Popular Dance*. Dodds questions the authority attributed to critics and scholars who make value judgments and assessments about the inherent worth of cultural producers and works. Dodds focuses her own research instead on how popular dance styles "negotiate and re-imagine the values they encounter through their dancing bodies" (p. 4).

Simon Frith (1996) looks at authority in popular culture from a different perspective, questioning why populist academics attempting to level the playing field between high and low art forms have often attempted to leave their own value judgments about popular culture outside of their academic discourses, as if they were somehow embarrassing. He suggests that not only are aesthetic judgments of value interesting and useful, but they are *already* a part of everyday conversations about popular culture. Dodds's contempt for this line of reasoning and her suggestion that academics making aesthetic judgments have a different kind of authority is understandable given the problematic commentary by dance academics and critics in the past. For example, Thomson's suggestion that the introduction of "hip hop" to a Gene Kelly remix involves a "monkeyed" rendition of a dance scene is worthy of critique as he claims to speak from an informed position about "our cultural memory."

Another model of engaging with the act of comparisons is rooted in the works of contemporary artists. Dance scholar Maaike Bleeker (2012) has recently suggested the concept of "covers" to describe choreographic performances that are "a response" to a previous work. For Mark Franko (1989) reconstruction differs from reinvention because reconstruction focuses on reproducing a past work whereas reinvention seeks to "rethink" primary source materials in a new work. Bleeker creates a further distinction with her notion of a "cover." She suggests that a cover differs from reinvention because the new work is further mediated by repertoire and recordings, rather than primary sources. The process and intention behind choreographic works engaged with the past is the central focus of this typology. For Bleeker, a cover:

> ...highlights that what is re-enacted here is works—artistic creations by other artists, as distinct from re-enactments of historical events or situations...A cover is a remake of or a response to an earlier artistic creation from the position of another artist at a later moment in time. This response is not a reinvention of the originally intended aims and effects but rather a rethinking or, as Nicole Beutler puts it, a rearticulation of artistic thought as it unfolds in the original work. (p. 20)

For the purposes of addressing popular dance performances, I suggest a further distinction. The "remix," although not a perfect metaphor, suggests that a move or series of movements is modified or reimagined without necessarily aspiring to or aligning the meaning with the intentions or process of the initial creation. A remix is a remake that is not necessarily assessed as an artistic "work" either by creators or audiences. This point will become clear with the introduction of some cultural commentary directed at the original *Singin' in the Rain* film.

Thomson's derogatory comments about the reworking of Kelly's rain sequence take on a new focus in the light of Clover's (1995) questions about the invisible and unacknowledged contributions of African American dancers to the history of tap and jazz[3] as represented in films such as *Singin' in the Rain*. Clover's analysis holds the film auteur(s) accountable as she considers this a problematic "work" that does not provide explicit reference to the contributions of African American dancers. From Clover's perspective, biographical components and context are not given any weight because her critical evaluation is about the text itself where the African American presence in dance is invisible. Clover (1995) does describe how Gene Kelly had acknowledged his debt to black performers, although her evidence is more or less a recounting by Fred Kelly, Gene's brother and dance partner in his early career. However, Clover's analysis of these autobiographical accounts and of the Hollywood musical takes its place firmly within textual criticism:

> *What Singin' in the Rain* doesn't-but-does know is that the real art of the film musical is dance, that a crucial talent source for that art is African-American performance, and that, relative to its contribution, this talent source is undercredited and underpaid. (Clover, 1995, p. 742)

For her, this problematic aspect of the film will always undermine its celebrated position as one of the most important musicals. Gene Kelly acknowledged the influence of both African American dance forms and Irish dance for his style in interviews rather than the film itself.

Gene Kelly himself appreciated the hip-hop dance styles that had emerged since his time.[4] However, the inclusion of Kelly's remarks about dance could be construed as a rhetorical device on the part of a scholar making an argument. One could just as easily foreground his interest in ballet (Chumo 1996) as a signifier of his value system and question whether or not this has any significance at all.

Embodied citations are just as valuable as verbal ones and this code of conduct is complicated by issues of race, ethnicity, gender and any visual markers of difference. If the African American dance influences on Gene Kelly were never named in his films and thus left inaudible, the influence of Gene Kelly on future developments of popular dance styles *has* been made audible in recent years. For example, international DJ and "coach" of the Soul Mavericks (UK) breaking crew, Kevin "DJ Renegade" Gopie (Fig. 5.9) points out:

> My earliest dance influences come from watching old movies like *7 Brides for 7 Brothers* and *Singin' in the Rain*. I used to enjoy watching Russ Tamblyn and Gene Kelly. Powerful dancers. It instilled in me the idea of looking strong and solid when you dance. Good form balanced with good technique. I never had any mentors as a dancer. I basically had to train myself even though I trained with others, who also trained themselves.[5]

Other internationally influential b-boys[6] from Toronto, Canada, often cited musicals as major influences on the development of their dance styles from Arnold "Gizmo" Vidad

FIGURE 5.9 Kevin "DJ Renegade" Gopie. Photo: William K, March 3, 2012.

of Bag of Trix to Karl "Dyzee" Alba of Supernaturalz crew.[7] And, unlike Clover's evaluation of the "work," this acknowledgment resembles the codes of street dance culture, where citations are both embodied and made morally and ethically audible through verbal acts of recognition to teachers, mentors, and mediated inspirations.

Issues of ownership and authorship are addressed in popular dance practice but in different ways. Popular dance practices are indebted to discourses about "creativity," and participants in street dance styles have their own debates about morality, ownership, and copyright. For example, participants are warned by others not to "bite" (steal other dancers' moves), although they are encouraged to be inspired and "flip it" (make the move their own through modifications).[8] The codes of street dance culture that are imposed by participants on each other are rooted in historical concepts about the relationship between legitimation and expression. Both "creativity" and "originality" are judged in the context of what has come before and how a dancer has both transformed movements and also expressed their own individuality. Interestingly, the practice of modifying movements is supplemented by a tactic whereby dancers can sanction other dancers to perform their moves in battles. These practices are reminiscent of oral traditions in folk practices (Schloss 2009) and involve the international circulation of knowledge by dancers (Fogarty 2012).

Dancers are evaluated by what is perceived to be their unique style or flavor, and originality is understood as an individual expression and modification of movements. Dancers are judged by measures of "creativity" that are negotiated and exerted by practitioners in their dancing and teaching. This involves a "remix" of past dance influences through an *embodied* or verbal citation. Gene Kelly's influence on DJ Renegade, mentioned earlier, was a mediated influence, just as exposure to hip-hop culture for dancers often involved radio, video, television, and films. Like other dancers outside of New York City, Renegade found influences where he could as he taught himself. Besides Gene Kelly, other figures such as James Brown, Bruce Lee, Fred Astaire, and the Nicolas Brothers have been referenced by key b-boys and b-girls as influential to the development of their style and character.

One of the most significant evaluations of popular dance is the connection between the dancers' movements and the music. Theresa Buckland (1983) has argued that popular dance practices have been distinguished from art dance through their tight relationship to popular music recordings. I suggest that a fundamental evaluative pleasure comes out of this privileged relationship and is, indeed, what is appealing about marrying music to dance. It is impossible to know what someone else is paying attention to as they listen to a song. This is precisely why good popular dance performances are so engaging. Good performances seem to demonstrate what a dancer is paying attention to *within* a song. Attentive listening is made both visible and audible to audiences through the competence of dancers to highlight music. This interest in attentive listening has historical roots that are evident through expanding considerations of music to a discussion of sound itself.

Sound is central to evaluations of popular dance performances. Popular artists are often considered creative when they foreground the relationship of sound to the moving body. The *Singin' in the Rain* film sequence at the heart of this discussion attempts to authenticate the dancing by focusing attention throughout the sequence on the sounds of tapping feet (Wollen 1992). This attention to the significance of sound is foregrounded in other films involving Gene Kelly. For example, Kelly and Donen's film musical, *On the Town* (1949) features the sights and sounds of New York City as three sailors rove around town looking for girls and adventure. In one of the sailors' first encounters, they ask a man in the subway for directions and every time the man answers them his voice is made inaudible by the sound of a train going past. The comedy of this focuses the viewer's attention on the sounds and the sheer volume of the city, and this focus on sound continues to drive the plot.

The field of sound studies offers insights into the historical contexts for popular dance practices that I will only draw on briefly in this essay. Writers such as Thompson (2002) and Sterne (2003) suggest that listening practices, and their relationship to technological innovations in recording and the senses, have historical roots in the eighteenth and nineteenth centuries. Listening becomes a specialized technique in medical practice (stethoscope), musical appreciation (gramophones), and communication (telephones). In the above example from *On the Town*, a whole narrative scenario turns out to revolve around the attention to sound through listening to the sounds of the modern city.

Gene Kelly's famous dance scenes from various films—from his alter ego dance sequence in *Cover Girl* (1944) to his classic solo dance scene in *Singin' in the Rain*—have emphasized the sound of tapping shoes. Wollen (1992) suggests that this attention to sound authenticates Gene Kelly's adherence to the conventions and values of tap dancing practices. Here I want to reverse the sound image and suggest instead that Kelly's performances, when discussed in the context of popular dance on screen, foreground the changing listening practices that emerged in modernity and with the birth of the modern city. This new attention to sound was a part of the technological transformations taking place in American cities and involved the development of new types of acoustic spaces (Thompson 2002).

In the commercial remake of "Singin' in the Rain," the enhanced reverb in the music adds an eerie quality to the outdoor city space that draws attention to the film set as indoor space, as constructed. When the street dancers remix Gene Kelly's style, the everyday pedestrian moves of Kelly are "remixed" as stiff and robotic, and then morph into a parkour-style engagement with the city, as the dancer freezes on the lamppost and somersaults down the street with authority. The electronic soundtrack and reverb are part of this mutation of the city-set.

A variety of dance styles share space and even the same body in the commercial remix. In the original film, *Singin' in the Rain*, the variety of dance styles are juxtaposed, as we follow Don Lockwood (Gene Kelly) and his good friend Cosmo Brown (Donald O'Connar) from their humble beginnings with tap dancing, to performances in touring vaudeville acts, until Don successfully makes his way to stardom on the silent screen. Broadway dance and vaudeville are evident, as is ballet. *Singin' in the Rain* also alludes to the history of modern dance. The ballet sequence when Gene Kelly partners with Cyd Charisse features a long scarf and bare feet, hinting at the influence of Isadora Duncan,

Martha Graham, and Loïe Fuller (modern dance pioneers). Although both ballet and modern dance are presented, "entertainment" dancing is the dominant feature of this film and sets the tone for popular dance performances on screen as an expression of individual emotions in the narrative plot (Wollen 1992).

In *Singin' in the Rain*, the high and low divisions of art are often parodied, especially when Don Lockwood's love interest Kathy Selden (Debbie Reynolds) conveys a snobbish tone when referring to the movies as "dumb show." Humor is often used as a device to mock an elitist divide. In the dance performance of Cosmo Brown's "Make 'Em Laugh" scene, a few lines from the song Cosmo sings sum up an argument for the central value of humor in popular dance performance:

> Now you could study Shakespeare and be quite elite. And you can charm the critics and have nothin' to eat. Just slip on a banana peel, the world's at your feet. Make 'em laugh. Make 'em laugh. Make 'em laugh.

Comedy is one feature that was often aligned with dance as "entertainment."

Singin' in the Rain provides a commentary on the distinctions drawn in American society between highbrow and lowbrow tastes. The elite read Shakespeare or go to the theater (it is implied), whereas the "masses" (i.e., the lower or lower middle class) just want to be entertained with comedy and vaudeville acts. However, movies are represented as somewhere between these two extremes whilst clearly situated as a celebrity culture.

There are a range of dance styles used to express the emotions and persona of each character. Gene Kelly's contributions as actor, director, dancer, and choreographer suggest a versatility that is uncommon and that contributed to the eclectic dance styles presented. As David "Elsewhere" Bernal points out in the quote that opened this chapter, Gene Kelly's talents far exceeded those of many dancers in their multidisciplinary scope. That reputation and Kelly's performances are clearly valued by dancers such as Bernal. However, arguing for the value of Gene Kelly's output is no simple task, and as scholars are quick to point out, the absence of any credit for the African American dancers who contributed to popular dance practices is highly problematic (Clover 1995; Gottschild 2000; Knaap 2006). While the debates persist about the hierarchies within popular dance practices themselves, new generations of dancers infuse older performances through their participation in various "remixes."

Regardless of how contemporary debates are played out—whether in cultural criticism, in the academic classroom, or through everyday conversations—what is clear is that judgments about what makes a good or bad performance are constantly enacted. As I have suggested with the "remix" perspective, popular dance practices and their receptions are not necessarily organized around the concept of a "work of art," and yet assessments about "creativity" and "originality" remain at play. Dancers are often compared to each other and the notion of the "work" is replaced by situations and events such as "battles," competition formats where dancers respond directly to their opponents with attempts at original and individual movement vocabularies. Or, in the case of the commercial remix, the status of the cultural artifact is not considered to be a "work of art," even by those that enjoyed the dancers' performances within the commercial. The point I am making here, finally, is that the category of the "work of art" may be downplayed; yet the attentive listening practices that accompanied the historical emergence of the "work-concept" continue in the reception and evaluation of popular dance performances today.

NOTES

1. http://dekku.nofatclips.com/2008/03/volkswagen-golf-singin-in-rain.html   [Accessed January 5, 2012].
2. David "Elsewhere" Bernal was in one of the most popular early viral videos when he performed at a Korean American talent show. In the underground b-boy world he is most known for performing and directing the *Detours* video. Donnie "Crumbs" Counts is part of the well-known b-boy crew Style Elements and has also trained Justin Timberlake and appeared in *You Got Served* (2004).
3. See Robert Crease (1995) for a discussion about the problems with the term "jazz" as used to describe a diverse range of music and dance.
4. See his statements in the introduction to the documentary *That's Dancing!* (Haley 1985).
5. Personal correspondence April 2, 2010.
6. B-boys are males who dance to the break of a record.
7. Personal correspondences July/August 2007.
8. See Fogarty (2011).

BIBLIOGRAPHY

Bleeker, Maaike A. 2012. "(Un)Covering Artistic Thought Unfolding." In *Dance Research Journal*. Vol. 44, No. 2, pp. 13–25.

Buckland, Theresa. 1983. "Definitions of Folk Dance: Some Explorations." In *Folk Music Journal*. Vol. 4, No. 4, pp. 315–352.

Chumo, Peter. 1996. "Dance, Flexibility, and the Renewal of Genre in *Singin' in the Rain*." In *Cinema Journal*. Vol. 36, No. 1, pp. 29–54.

Clover, Carol. 1995. "Dancin' in the Rain." In *Critical Inquiry*. Vol. 21, No. 4, pp. 722–747.

Crease, Robert. 1995. "Divine Frivolity: Hollywood Representations of the Lindy Hop, 1937–1942." In *Representing Jazz*, edited by K. Gabbard. Durham, NC: Duke University Press, pp. 207–228

DeNora, Tia. 1997. *Beethoven and the Construction of Genius: Musical Politics in Vienna, 1792–1803*. Berkeley, CA: University of California Press.

Dodds, Sherril. 2011. *Dancing on the Canon: Embodiments of Value in Popular Dance*. London: Palgrave MacMillan.

Fogarty, Mary. 2012. "Breaking Expectations: Imagined Affinities in Mediated Youth Cultures." In *Continuum: Journal of Media and Cultural Studies*. Vol. 26, No. 4, pp. 449–462.

——. 2011. *Dance to the Drummer's Beat*. Edinburgh: University of Edinburgh. PhD Dissertation.

——. 2010. "A Manifesto for the Study of Popular Dance." In *Conversations across the Field of Dance Studies*, edited by D. Robinson. Society of Dance History Scholars, pp. 4–5.

Franko, Mark. 1989. "Repeatability, Reconstruction and Radical Interpretation." In *History and Theory*. May, pp. 198–208.

Frith, Simon. 2012. "Creativity as a Social Fact." In *Musical Imaginations: Multidisciplinary Perspectives on Creativity, Performance and Perception*, edited by D. Hargreaves, D. Miell, and R. MacDonald. Oxford: Oxford University Press, pp. 62–72.

——. 1991. "The Good, the Bad, and the Indifferent: Defending Popular Culture from the Populists," *Diacritics*. Vol. 21, No. 4, pp. 101–115.

——. 1996. *Performing Rites: on the Value of Popular Music*. Oxford: Oxford University Press.

Goehr, Lydia. 1992. *The Imaginary Museum of Musical Works: An Essay in the Philosophy of Music*. Oxford: Oxford University Press.

Gottschild, Brenda Dixon. 2000. *Waltzing in the Dark: African American Vaudeville and Race Politics in the Swing Era*. New York: St. Martin's Press.

Knapp, Raymond. 2006. *The American Musical and the Performance of Personal Identity*. Princeton: Princeton University Press.

Schloss, Joseph G. 2009. *Foundation: B-boys, B-girls, and Hip-Hop Culture in New York*. New York: Oxford University Press.

Sheaves, Louise. 1990. *Gene Kelly: A Reassessment of a Popular Dance Artist*. London: Laban Centre for Movement and Dance. MA dissertation.

Sterne, Jonathan. 2003. *The Audible Past: Cultural Origins of Sound Reproduction*. Durham, NC: Duke University Press.

Thompson, Emily. 2004. *The Soundscape of Modernity: Architectural Acoustics and the Culture of Listening in America, 1900–1933*. Cambridge: The MIT Press.

Wollen, Peter. 1992. *Singin' in the Rain*. London: Palgrave MacMillan.

FILMOGRAPHY

Cover Girl. 1944. Film. Directed by Charles Vidor. USA: Columbia Pictures. 107 min.

Detours: An Experimental Dance Collaboration - Extended Trails. 2001. Film. Directed by David "Elsewhere" Bernal. USA. 2 hours and 57 min.

Flashdance. 1983. Film. Directed by Adrian Lyne. USA: Paramount Pictures. 95 min.

Gene Kelly: Anatomy of a Dancer. 1983. TV documentary. Directed by Robert Trachtenberg. USA: American Masters. 87 min.

On the Town. 1949. Film. Directed by Stanley Donen and Gene Kelly. USA: MGM. 98 min.

Singin' in the Rain. 1952. Film. Directed by Stanley Donen and Gene Kelly. USA: MGM.103 min.

That's Dancing! 1985. Film. Directed by Jack Haley Jr. Narrated by Gene Kelly. USA: MGM. 105 min.

You Got Served. 2004. Directed by Chris Stokes. USA: Columbia Pictures. 95 min.

YOUTUBE CLIPS

http://dekku.nofatclips.com/2008/03/volkswagen-golf-singin-in-rain.html Featuring David "Elsewhere" Bernal and Donnie "Crumbs" Counts. Accessed January 5, 2012.

http://www.youtube.com/watch?v=WAyTK6jF508 "David Elsewhere—Kollaboration 2001" Featuring David "Elsewhere" Bernal. Accessed September 12, 2012.

CHAPTER 6

···

APPRECIATION, APPROPRIATION, ASSIMILATION: *STORMY WEATHER* AND THE HOLLYWOOD HISTORY OF BLACK DANCE

···

SUSIE TRENKA

Stormy Weather occupies a special place among the black-cast musicals produced by Hollywood studios in the classical period. While the other films in the series belong to the subgenre of the folk musical, *Stormy Weather* is a backstage musical that lacks the moral dichotomies structuring the narratives of, for instance, *Hallelujah!* (1929) or *Cabin in the Sky* (1943).[1] On the one hand, the focus on contemporary urban show business gives *Stormy Weather* a more progressive note compared to the other black musicals, which tend to associate the modern and urban with sinful pleasures, while advocating old-fashioned rural life and religion. On the other hand, *Stormy Weather* in many ways represents the peak of what black film historian Donald Bogle has called the "Negro Entertainment Syndrome," that is, the standard Hollywood practice of reducing African American performers to the function of "only entertainers."[2] Yet, despite being produced in "white Hollywood" by a white director, *Stormy Weather* is not a one-way exploitation of black talent by the white industry. Rather, the numbers and narrative of *Stormy Weather* reflect and negotiate several complex and contradictory processes: white appropriation and exploitation of "authentic" black talent, black assimilation to supposedly "classy" white styles, but also black adaptation and appropriation of hitherto white domains of performance. *Stormy Weather* is the first Hollywood feature to explicitly celebrate black achievement, and it does so in the form of a backstage-biopic/revue musical whose underlying theme of travel, as has been noted, stresses dynamic motion and progress, suggesting an "allegory of African American movement (geographic and aesthetic)."[3]

A succession of song and dance numbers only loosely connected by a threadbare plot, *Stormy Weather* features more black musical numbers, especially dance numbers, than any other Hollywood musical. In this chapter, I look at some of the dance scenes and their narrative contexts, but also at some of the movie's gaps, exploring issues of appreciation, appropriation, and assimilation in relation to both film and dance history. Starting from the premise of the film's appreciation of African American popular culture, I argue that *Stormy Weather*'s fragmentary entertainment history self-reflexively and paradoxically—and to some degree involuntarily—reveals Hollywood's strategies in the exploitation of black talent. Though carelessly anachronistic at times, the film's panoply of styles and stars self-referentially chronicles the history of black dance in white Hollywood in all its contradictory ambivalence.

APPRECIATION: HOLLYWOOD'S RELUCTANT RECOGNITION OF CULTURAL HISTORY

Stormy Weather opens with a framing device that serves to link the film's present of 1943 to the past in which most of the story takes place. The first shot after the opening credits shows aging tap dancer Bill Williamson (Bill "Bojangles" Robinson) dancing with a group of kids on his front porch. Next, a little girl goes to fetch a magazine from the mailbox. Before the first word of dialogue is spoken, we see the cover of the magazine entitled *Theatre World* in close-up: it is a special edition devoted to "celebrating the magnificent contribution of the colored race to the entertainment of the world during the past twenty-five years." As it soon turns out, the entire magazine is dedicated to Bill, who thus comes to personify and represent black entertainment. On a diegetic level, the magazine prompts Bill to recount the story of his career and of his liaison with beautiful singer Selina Rogers (Lena Horne). But it doesn't require much of an interpretive leap to read the caption as a self-reflexive mission statement that might just as well have appeared as part of the title credits. It serves to justify the existence of the whole film, which—at a mere 78 minutes runtime containing a good 15 musical numbers—doesn't have much to offer *besides* black entertainment. Or does it?

As Arthur Knight concludes in his outstanding study of black performance in musical film, there has never been such a thing as "just" singing and dancing, particularly for African Americans.[4] Nowhere is this as obvious as in *Stormy Weather*. Tellingly, the magazine caption insinuates that "the world" is *not* "colored," and that to contribute to this world is not quite the same as to partake in it, as equals. The film never makes explicit the contact between its black protagonists and the white worlds of Hollywood and Paris, which are mentioned as the highpoints in Bill's and Selina's careers, respectively. Yet, there seems to be no escape from a larger world, both diegetically and extra-diegetically, that is not black.[5] As noted by several critics, the narrative, spanning the years from the end of World War I up to the film's present during World War II and framed by two benefit shows for black soldiers, highlights a different kind of "contribution" and needs to be seen in the context of patriotic propaganda and government efforts to promote African American enlistment.[6] While this context is no doubt important, it is nevertheless the historical dimension of entertainment that matters most in *Stormy Weather*—both in terms of the history the film purports to tell and of its own place in (black) film history.

The narrative's time frame includes the Jazz Age and the Swing Era, when first the Charleston and the Black Bottom and later the Lindy Hop/Jitterbug dance crazes swept the nation. It is also the time of the Harlem Renaissance, when African American intellectual and artistic activity reached new heights. Harlem became the capital of entertainment with its theaters, nightclubs, and ballrooms attracting large numbers of white customers fascinated by the perceived exoticism and sensuality of black music and dance. While the influence of African American vernacular music and dance on American popular culture goes back much further, the years referenced in *Stormy Weather* are especially significant due to technological innovations in the mass media. With large amounts of black music and dance made available to a mass audience for the first time through radio, records, and films, it is no exaggeration that American popular music and dance from the early 1920s to the mid-40s is not just influenced, but dominated by African American styles. In commercial terms however, white spin-offs by far outperform their black sources of inspiration in what has frequently been called the "whitening" of black culture (as, for instance, in Glenn Miller's version of big band swing).

Cinematic products of the period testify to these circumstances sometimes more, sometimes less directly through a number of phenomena:[7] the white Charleston-dancing heroines of 1920s flapper films; black "specialty acts" in otherwise white sound features of all genres; the Vitaphone shorts of the 1930s and the Soundies of the 40s; the invisible (and often uncredited) presence of black musicians on numerous soundtracks; the more or less obvious black influences on the performance styles of white tap dancers, swing musicians, and singers; and, of course, the continuation of minstrelsy's complex and contradictory blackface tradition in musicals from *The Jazz Singer* (1927) onward.[8]

In light of this history, the explicit acknowledgment of African American achievement in *Stormy Weather* is, of course, long overdue. And to choose tap dancer Bill Robinson to represent black entertainment is appropriate, particularly in a Hollywood context where the movie musical has made tap the most prominent of the African American derived art forms appropriated and popularized by whites. At the same time, Robinson is among the first black performers to attain a certain—if limited—star status in Hollywood. There is then a patronizing flavor to *Stormy Weather*'s belated appreciation of black cultural history, as the film's self-consciously declared purpose inadvertently betrays the unfairness of the enterprise, pointing to African Americans' remarkable contributions to something that is owned and controlled by whites, who collect most of the profits.

PRODUCING ASSIMILATION,
APPROPRIATING PRODUCTION

The appropriation of black music and dance idioms by white performers, who would make them more accessible for mainstream audiences and thus more profitable, has become something of a commonplace in cultural criticism of recent decades. The case of *Stormy Weather* is somewhat more complicated, since the artists are black, yet at least some of their performances feature rather "whitened" styles. This is especially apparent in some of the big production numbers. Raymond Knapp discusses the film's treatment of minstrelsy and argues that

> the most tainted of the minstrelsy-based numbers are without exception connected with the film's villains, whose villainy is signaled through their willingness to pander to prevailing (white) tastes. Thus, the cakewalk, "Diga Diga Doo," and "African Dance" are part of the milieu of the shifty and manipulative showman Chick Bailey... The consistency of this association of villainy and minstrelsy tropes (with an admixture of "jungle" themes in Chick Bailey's show) should encourage us to understand the film as "integrated" in the sense that its songs and other numbers are to some extent situational and not merely a succession of hits, and to take its governing sensibility as more subtle than is usually surmised."[9]

While Knapp makes a good point here concerning the film's overall structure, it should also be noted that the "jungle" styles exhibited in *Stormy Weather* carry their own set of historical associations. Going back to colonialist discourses of the eighteenth and nineteenth centuries, these exotic stereotypes are less directly connected with minstrelsy than with the modernist primitivism in European and American art and performance of the early twentieth century.[10] They appeared in Hollywood musicals of the 1930s and 40s as well as in many of the Panoram Soundies of the 40s. Just as importantly, they were a staple of the stage shows at Harlem's famous Cotton Club in the 1920s and 30s—a venue that provided black entertainment specifically for a white clientele.[11]

In *Stormy Weather*, the jungle numbers occur at an early point in Bill's career. When he asks impresario Chick Bailey to give him a solo dance part in his show, Chick replies "What? Let you do your cheap hoofin' in a classy show like this?" The story, however, seems to favor the "cheap" over the "classy" by first making fun of the demeaning role Bill is assigned—sitting on a tree in a ridiculous costume during "Diga Diga Doo"—and then having him upstage Chick with his spontaneous dance on the giant tom-toms (Fig. 6.1). The allegedly authentic African American form of rhythm tap is thus put above the somewhat absurd kitsch of the jungle productions. Yet, the status of the latter remains ambivalent. In "Diga Doo," after being told to put on his wig, Bill isn't seen anymore. The moment of mockery with regard to the racist stereotypes is short and the rest of the number is presented without a trace of irony, featuring chorus girls in a silly combination of striped tiger-kitten costumes and white feathers and a dance routine that

FIGURE 6.1 Bill Robinson dancing on giant tom-toms in a stereotypical "jungle" number.

looks like the precursor to a latter-day aerobics workout. By including two full-length, lavishly staged jungle numbers with solo appearances by the protagonists, the film thus suggests that this type of black entertainment is as valid as any of the other numbers— which it is, at least in terms of its popularity with white audiences.

In the generic context of a backstage musical and biopic, one would perhaps expect the hero to overcome the constraints of prevailing tastes and prove the world wrong by successfully introducing innovations. Interestingly though, Bill opposes Chick's control over the show by going back to the roots—the vernacular roots—of modern show business, resuming the allegedly improvised tap he has showcased earlier, when he joined a jam session on the riverboat taking him to Memphis.

Yet Bill's defiance of jungle stereotypes with his old-school tap performance does not help his career for the moment. Instead, it is a classy number of a different kind that seals the success of Bill and Selina's career later on. After Bill's own Harlem production has first been threatened by bankruptcy and then miraculously saved by a winning horse, the sequence is brought to a close with an elaborate production number to McHugh and Fields's "I Can't Give You Anything But Love." Bill and Selina, in tailcoat and glittering evening gown, sing the song, for the most part strutting along quite stiffly rather than dancing much. They are backed by a large chorus in equally glamorous costumes, gently swaying and elegantly tap dancing in upright posture on an enormous stage of the kind that existed only in Hollywood, accompanied by an invisible orchestra complete with strings. In other words, "I Can't Give You" is as white a Hollywood musical number as can be, and it is clearly the "classiest" of the film's performances in that it shows an opulent upper-class setting (in an implausible contrast to both the song's lyrics and the show's previous financial problems). At this point, the story seems to suggest that the true road to success for black entertainers leads neither through the colonialist exoticism of the jungle numbers nor the return to the folk roots of black dance, but rather via assimilation to the "refined" white styles of Broadway and Hollywood.

Yet this assimilation is also an appropriation. While the narrative context of Chick Bailey's production at least implicitly critiques the Cotton Club's concessions to white tastes, there are no such negative connotations to Bill's show. In addition to the glamorous production number, the show includes such varied performance idioms as blues singing, jazz dancing, and a comic blackface routine.[12] Produced in Harlem,[13] with no implications of white money or a white audience, its success is also the success of independent black enterprise. And Robinson, sporting white tie and tails in "I Can't Give You," almost inevitably calls to mind Fred Astaire, Hollywood's foremost (white) tap dance star.[14] The Harlem sequence thus suggests that black business can very well include the business of appropriating the glamour of Hollywood's white musicals. In its production numbers, *Stormy Weather* thus almost despite itself testifies to the exchange between black and white music and dance styles.

SOCIAL DANCE AND THE MARGINALIZATION OF SUBVERSION

Despite this obvious and inevitable hybridity, it is appropriate to call *Stormy Weather* a "dictionary of black dance."[15] And another way of looking at its "entries" is to consider them in terms of an opposition between professional performance and improvised social dancing, respectively. Only one number, the jam session on the riverboat, takes place outside the world of professional showbiz. Yet it still involves a group of "travelling minstrel boys," whose music makes Bill dance, which in turn establishes his career potential when a band member suggests that he get a job dancing at "one of them Beale Street cafés" in Memphis. A far cry from the fancy prancing in "I Can't Give You," the scene roots Bill's art in the improvised vernacular, and locates it in a rural Southern setting, only to later have it refashioned in terms of white urban glamour and, by consequence, commercial success. Only two more (consecutive) numbers are performed in a backstage setting rather than onstage. They occur at the point when the cast of Bill's Harlem show is trying to convince his friend Gabe, who is posing as a rich man, to invest in their bankrupt show. After Mae E. Johnson finishes singing "Salt Lake City," an unidentified male dancer jumps out onto the floor and performs a solo, with the invisible orchestra smoothly transitioning to the next song, "Nobody's Sweetheart." As with the Tramp Band on the riverboat, neither of these two solo performers is mentioned in the film's credits. By putting uncredited performances on the margins of the fictional showbiz world and—by extension—of the Hollywood star system, the allocation of diegetic performance spaces mirrors the industry's practices of exclusion and marginalization.

Less than a minute long, the dance solo by the unidentified dancer in particular is perhaps easily forgotten. Yet it deserves consideration as a particularly noteworthy instance

FIGURE 6.2 Classic Swing Charleston kicks in one of the film's few backstage numbers.

of authentic or classic jazz dance. The short tap number includes a variation on the basic step of the Swing Charleston, big twisting moves of the hips and legs, high leg-kicks, and wildly swinging arms (Fig. 6.2). Engaging the whole body and using a lot of space, the dance is somewhere halfway between Robinson's upright, legs-only variety of tap and the Nicholas Brothers' acrobatic "flash act" in the film's final sequence. With respect to setting and costume—the dancer wears simple but elegant suit pants and a white shirt—the number is equally far removed from the riverboat jam's associations with minstrelsy as from the Hollywood glamour of "I Can't Give You." Instead, we get a short glimpse of truly classic jazz dance, that is to say, the ensemble of African American vernacular dances rooted in Southern plantation culture, but further developed in the black urban centers in the 1920s to 40s, most notably Harlem, where they were danced in improvised as well as choreographed form, both socially and professionally, to a variety of jazz-inflected music styles.[16]

Even though improvised jazz dancing, and this includes tap,[17] was absolutely central to black culture's contribution to the "entertainment of the world," it is marginalized by the narrative of *Stormy Weather*—at least up to the film's finale. As far as entire numbers go, the riverboat jam is the only one that is narratively coded as improvisation. Other numbers referencing social dancing include the uncredited jazz tap solo mentioned above, the Cakewalk in the early part of the movie, and a mere 20 seconds of bluesy "1920s black American get-down social dancing,"[18] which quickly gives way to a more balletic style in Katherine Dunham and her Troupe's dance to the title song. All of these are clearly framed as professional performances in the diegetic showbiz world rather than as spontaneous improvisations. Furthermore, missing from the dance dictionary are the Charleston and the Black Bottom of the 1920s and the Lindy Hop (or Jitterbug) of the 30s and 40s. Considering the immense popularity of these styles that were not exclusively, but primarily, social dances, their omission from the movie is rather curious and well worth looking into.

On one level, the absence isn't surprising, given that *Stormy Weather* is a backstage musical with professional entertainment as its subject matter. However, most musical films of the period—including the backstage variety—went to great lengths to create their "myth of entertainment"[19] by making professionally produced performances appear to stem from spontaneous improvisations. In *Stormy Weather*, by contrast, the Hollywood musical's "myth of spontaneity"[20] is almost completely eclipsed as "none of the musical numbers happens solely as a natural outgrowth of feeling."[21] Thus, the genre only accounts for part of the picture, whereas a quick look at the (film) history of some social dances throws a different light on their exclusion from *Stormy Weather*.

The Charleston, although developed in small-town African American communities of the South and later popularized by the black stage musical *Runnin' Wild*,[22] subsequently became associated with the urban white flapper in the popular imagination. Considered downright revolutionary, it became symbolic of the New Woman's freedom and was featured in silent films with some of the era's most popular female white stars.[23] By ignoring the Charleston of the 20s, *Stormy Weather* thus turns a blind eye to the fact of the dance's usurpation by white Hollywood and at the same time it indirectly denies its liberating potential to African Americans.[24]

The case of the Lindy Hop is somewhat different. The partner dance of the big band era was also adopted and adapted by whites across the nation, many of whom cared little for its African American roots. At the same time, however, swing music and dancing offered one of the period's rare sites of racial integration: Harlem's largest dance venue, the Savoy Ballroom, was integrated, and in New York's most popular annual dance contest, the Harvest Moon Ball, blacks regularly competed and won against whites in the Lindy Hop section.[25] Although it was not perceived as equally revolutionary for African Americans as the Charleston had been for white women, the Lindy Hop and big band swing afforded a similar space for challenging the limits of the times. Furthermore, the Lindy Hop (unlike the Charleston) already had its black Hollywood history in 1943. It had been danced spectacularly by Whitey's Lindy Hoppers, a group from Harlem, in several Hollywood features, most notably *A Day at the Races* (1937) and *Hellzapoppin'* (1941). In the narrative and generic contexts of these slapstick-fraught anarcho-comedies, there is a note of subversion to the Lindy numbers that are staged as spontaneous outbursts, danced surreptitiously, beyond the control of whites.[26] The narrative of *Stormy Weather*, by contrast, allows for no such subversion, no breaking of white rules, because its black universe does not openly acknowledge the fact of white rule any more than it admits the possibility of racial integration.

Of course one might ask, then, why the Cakewalk—which sparked America's very first national and international dance craze long before the Charleston and the Lindy— is featured in *Stormy Weather*. With its origins in parody or "derision dancing,"[27] it might well be considered the most subversive of black social dances. The film's highly stylized version of the former plantation dance, though, contains no irony, no making fun of whites, however indirectly, and the number's minstrelisms are indeed hard to dismiss in the context of such a comparatively modern movie. Perhaps the dance's complex history of multiple and reciprocal imitations and appropriations had obscured its subversive origins to the point where they would pass unnoticed by Hollywood's "historians." Or, more likely, the historical distance—the number comes early, in the post–World War I segment of the story—permitted locating the offensive aspects of minstrelsy safely in the past. Moreover, the Cakewalk's appearances in film were pretty much limited to a few early documentary Biograph shorts that were hardly relevant in a 1940s Hollywood context.

These observations might seem somewhat far-fetched or speculative, given that decisions about what to include in the film were doubtless influenced by other factors, such as the availability of performers. Yet, just as awareness of the Cotton Club shows makes *Stormy Weather*'s jungle numbers appear in a different light, viewing the film's marginalization of African American social dancing in the context of dance history helps to account for the movie's seemingly random mix of styles and numbers. In *Stormy Weather*, as is often the case, history is told through what is missing as much as through what is shown.

Black Performance under Black Control

While throughout the first two-thirds of the movie white control of black entertainment is both invisible and inescapable, things change in the finale, when Cab Calloway takes over. Under the famous bandleader's "stage management,"[28] the film's final segment hints at a hidden truth about the heyday of black entertainment in white Hollywood, namely that of the relative creative freedom it afforded the performers. Often choreographed by the dancers themselves, with minimal intervention by (white) directors or choreographers, black dance acts, even more than purely musical numbers, functioned as sites of freedom in a system otherwise all too clearly dictating what African Americans could and couldn't do.

This becomes clear in the finale, where the entire spectrum of modern black dance is finally given its due. As has been noted repeatedly, the Nicholas Brothers' spectacular acrobatic tap is the film's climax, surpassing anything done by the aging protagonist. With their highly expressive, seemingly boundless physical prowess, the brothers have generally been seen as transgressing, at least symbolically, the limits imposed on black performers.[29] And indeed, as with all their film appearances, Fayard and Harold Nicholas were in charge of most of the actual choreography.[30] The same is obviously true of the blues ballet by Katherine Dunham, who had already made herself a name as an innovator in African American modern dance before ever appearing on the screen. Then there is the ensemble's

FIGURE 6.3 Modern urban outfits and contemporary jazz dancing in the film's final segment. Directed by bandleader Cab Calloway, the finale unites social dancers with professional performers, as well as the different generations of tap dancers represented by Bill Robinson and the Nicholas Brothers.

tap routine, where the dancers' distinctly modern urban outfits, rid of all minstrelsy or jungle associations, go hand in hand with their equally contemporary style of jazz dancing that includes moves such as the Shorty George, the Suzie Q, and the Falling-off-a-Log (Fig. 6.3).[31] And at the very end, as the audience joins the fun, the film finally hints at the close connection between professional performance and social dancing, exemplifying how the former is inspired by the latter: a slow tracking shot cuts through the dancing crowd in the foreground, and what we see along the way looks so convincingly improvised that it raises serious doubts about how much of it was rehearsed before shooting. Meanwhile, the ensemble's jazzy routine remains visible in the background, so that the two spheres are united in the same space, before the camera finally closes in on the stars. Bringing together this variety of modern black dance—jazz and ballet, social and professional—the finale is the movie's truly classy show. And what is more, Cab Calloway's singing and dancing bandleader functions as a stand-in director for the entire final sequence—which is, after all, rather self-reflexively set in present-day Hollywood—suggesting that there is no longer any need for white control of African American performance.

The Nicholas Brothers, outshining Robinson, make the most obvious case for the reappropriation of black performance by blacks. More than just replacing one dance style with another, their non-narrative number also supersedes the type of narrativized film performance associated with the older dancer. Despite the generational gap,[32] the film careers of Robinson and the Nicholas Brothers spanned roughly the same years, starting in the early thirties, and their casting in *Stormy Weather* continues in the vein of their previous careers: the young brothers were always cast as themselves, occasionally with a few lines of dialogue, but never playing any part other than that of the entertainers and dancers they were. Robinson, by contrast, was assigned acting parts combining the entertainer with the servant stereotype, most famously in his films with Shirley Temple, which earned him a comparatively large degree of fame, but also the reputation of an Uncle Tom. In *Stormy Weather* there is no direct reference to such servitude and Bill Williamson claims he went to Hollywood for the first time in 1936, that is, after the real Bill's most successful film appearances with Temple. The dancer's true Hollywood career as a white girl's servant is thus obscured in favor of an idealized tale set in an "all black" world where Bill achieves a good deal of success independently, with no white master to serve or blond girl to teach. Nevertheless, he appears as some-one who "has learned how to behave . . . for white audiences."[33] Earlier on, in the frame story, Bill teaches his trademark step to a little black girl, thereby symbolically passing on the tradition to the next generation. The new generation of tap dancers, however, is embodied by the Nicholas Brothers, who are obviously way past the point where they would have needed instruction from Robinson (or anyone else, for that matter). As Robinson's somewhat subdued performance persona is eventually eclipsed by the young brothers' expansive, exuberant, elegant appearance that seems to come out of nowhere, the celebration of black entertainment of the past 25 years turns into a fare-well to Robinson's performance style and—by extension—Hollywood's narrative con-trol over the black entertainer as servant. Unsurprisingly, what *does* remain of white control in the finale is the plot's resolution, that is, the reuniting of Bill and Selina in the most conventional of Hollywood happy endings imaginable. Yet narrative closure only makes for a shallow pretext for a full 25 minutes of contemporary black-controlled black performance.

In a sense, *Stormy Weather*'s lack of a noteworthy narrative is, of course, quite in line with the industry's customary ghettoization of blacks, indicating a degree of dis-dain for the performers, as if they didn't deserve a decent story in the same way as the white movie stars did. At the same time, the improbabilities of the plot with its ageless characters, the anachronisms with regard to costumes and hairstyles, and the gaps in the movie's cultural history can be read as part of an overall strategy of obscuring his-tory—including Hollywood's own history of the exploitation of black talent. *Stormy Weather* thus simultaneously—and paradoxically—emphasizes and downplays the historical significance of black entertainment. Though underscoring racial segregation in the industry, the explicit focus on "only entertainment" also makes this entertain-ment "speak for itself"—most eloquently in those performances that are least involved with the narrative. While the flimsy plot focuses on Bill and Selina, the cultural history told along the way often highlights artists with little or no relevance to the plot. With regard to dance, Dunham and her company, the Nicholas Brothers, and the uncred-ited dancer of the backstage jazz solo are the performers most completely disconnected from the narrative, without a line of dialogue or any other appearance outside their numbers. And it is also in these instances that black performance is most independent aesthetically, with no semblance of assimilation to white tastes. Robbed of its history and at the same time made all-important in its barely narrativized presence, the best of black entertainment, the film implies, doesn't *need* a story—in any case not one scripted by white Hollywood. And, devoting one-third of the film's total runtime to the finale's celebration of the present, it seems as if Hollywood reluctantly admits that black entertainment has come into its own. The fact that this is both the first and last explicit tribute to African American achievement during the studio era indicates that the film industry had no use for such black independence—not even in the symbolic space of the movie musical's dance floor.

NOTES

1. See Knight, Arthur: *Disintegrating the Musical: Black Performance and American Musical Film.* Durham, NC and London: Duke University Press, 2002, pp. 123–168.
2. Bogle, Donald: *Toms, Coons, Mulattoes, Mammies, and Bucks: An Interpretive History of Blacks in American Films.* Fourth Edition. New York and London: Continuum, 2006, p. 118. See also Dyer, Richard: "The Colour of Entertainment". In: *Only Entertainment.* Second Edition. London and New York: Routledge, 2002, pp. 36–45.
3. Massood, Paula J.: *Black City Cinema: African American Urban Experiences in Film.* Philadelphia: Temple University Press, 2003, p. 39.
4. Knight: *Disintegrating the Musical,* p. 248.
5. See also Knight: *Disintegrating the Musical,* pp. 118–119.
6. See Massood: *Black City Cinema,* p. 42; Knapp, Raymond: *The American Musical and the Performance of Personal Identity.* Princeton, NJ, and Oxford: Princeton University Press, 2006, p. 82; Knight: *Disintegrating the Musical,* pp. 157–158.
7. In terms of film history, the time from 1918 to 1943 can, of course, hardly be considered *one* period, as these years saw a wide variety of crucial developments including the coming-of-age of the Hollywood feature film industry, the establishment of the star system, the transition from silent to sound film (and, in its wake, the birth of the film musical), and the introduction of the Production Code.
8. See Clover, Carol J.: "Dancin' in the Rain". In: Cohan, Steven, ed.: *Hollywood Musicals: The Film Reader.* New York and London: Routledge, 2002, pp. 157–173; Dyer: "The Colour of Entertainment"; Gabbard, Krin: *Black Magic: White Hollywood and African American Culture.* New Brunswick, NJ, and London: Rutgers University Press, 2004; Knight, *Disintegrating the Musical*; Landay, Lori: "The Flapper Film: Comedy, Dance, and Jazz Age Kinaesthetics." In: Bean, Jennifer M. and Negra, Diane, eds.: *A Feminist Reader in Early Cinema.* Durham, NC, and London: Duke University Press, 2002, pp. 221–248; MacGillivray, Scott, and Okuda, Ted: *The Soundies Book. A Revised and Expanded Guide.* New York, Lincoln, NE, and Shanghai: iUniverse, Inc., 2007; Rogin, Michael: *Blackface, White Noise: Jewish Immigrants in the Hollywood Melting Pot.* Berkeley, Los Angeles and London: University of California Press, 1998.
9. Knapp: *The American Musical,* p. 85.
10. See, for instance, Dixon Gottschild, Brenda: *Digging the Africanist Presence in American Performance. Dance and Other Contexts.* Westport, CT, and London: Praeger, 1996, pp. 35–43.

11. See Haskins, Jim: *The Cotton Club*. New York: Hippocrene Books, 1994; Malone, Jacqui: *Steppin' on the Blues: The Visible Rhythms of African American Dance*. Urbana and Chicago: University of Illinois Press, 1996, pp. 87–88.

12. See Knight: *Disintegrating the Musical*, pp. 110–119, for a discussion of the blackface number.

13. See Massood: *Black City Cinema*, pp. 38–42, for a discussion of the film's spatiotemporal settings.

14. This association of Bojangles with Fred Astaire is, of course, particularly ironic given Astaire's highly problematic blackface "homage" to the older dancer in *Swing Time* (1936).

15. Clark, VéVé A.: „Performing the Memory of Difference in Afro-Caribbean Dance: Katherine Dunham's Choreography, 1938–1987." In: Clark, VèVè A., and Johnson, Sara E., eds.: *Kaiso! Writings by and about Katherine Dunham*. Madison: University of Wisconsin Press, 2005, p. 328.

16. See Malone: *Steppin' on the Blues*, pp. 70–110; Stearns, Marshall and Stearns, Jean: *Jazz Dance: The Story of American Vernacular Dance*. Cambridge, MA: Da Capo Press, 1994.

17. For the close connection between jazz music/musicians and rhythm tap/tap dancers and the centrality of improvisation to both see Malone: *Steppin' on the Blues*, pp. 94–99.

18. Clark: "Performing the Memory of Difference," p. 329.

19. Feuer, Jane: "The Self-Reflective Musical and the Myth of Entertainment". In: Cohan, Steve, ed.: *Hollywood Musicals: The Film Reader*. London and New York: Routledge, 2002, pp. 31–40.

20. Ibid., p. 32.

21. Knapp: *The American Musical*, p. 93.

22. See Stearns and Stearns: *Jazz Dance*, pp. 111–114.

23. See Landay: "The Flapper Film."

24. The one notable exception of a famous *black* woman dancing the Charleston is, of course, Josephine Baker, who appeared in a number of French, but not American films. See, for instance, Kalinak, Kathryn: "Disciplining Josephine Baker: Gender, Race, and the Limits of Disciplinarity." In Buhler, James, and Flinn, Caryl, and Neumeyer, David, eds.: *Music and Cinema*. Hanover, NH: Wesleyan University Press, 2000, pp. 316–335.

25. See Malone: *Steppin' on the Blues*, pp. 101–106; Manning, Frankie and Cynthia R. Millman: *Frankie Manning: Ambassador of Lindy Hop*. Philadelphia: Temple University Press, 2007, pp. 88–92, 164–166.

26. See Crease, Robert P.: "Divine Frivolity: Hollywood Representations of the Lindy Hop, 1937–1942." In Gabbard, Krin, ed.: *Representing Jazz*. Durham, NC, and London: Duke University Press, 1995, pp. 207–228.

27. Malone: *Steppin' on the Blues*, p. 18.

28. Knapp: *The American Musical*, p. 87, see also p. 89 for a discussion of Calloway's performance persona.

29. See Knapp: *The American Musical*, p. 92; Knight: *Disintegrating the Musical*, pp. 156–158.

30. See the interview with Fayard Nicholas in Berry, S. Torriano, and Berry, Venise T.: *The 50 Most Influential Black Films: A Celebration of African-American Talent, Determination, and Creativity*. New York: Kensington Publishing Corp., 2001, pp. 63–67.

31. See Knapp: *The American Musical*, pp. 91–92, for a comparative discussion of the earlier Cakewalk and the final numbers.

32. Robinson was born in 1878, Fayard and Harold Nicholas in 1914 and 1921, respectively.

33. Knapp: *The American Musical*, p. 86. Knapp also points out that it is a mistake to consider Robinson's character Bill Williamson as an only slightly different version of himself.

BIBLIOGRAPHY

Berry, S. Torriano, and Venise T. Berry. *The 50 Most Influential Black Films: A Celebration of African-American Talent, Determination, and Creativity.* New York: Kensington Publishing Corp., 2001.

Bogle, Donald. *Toms, Coons, Mulattoes, Mammies, and Bucks: An Interpretive History of Blacks in American Films.* Fourth Edition. New York and London: Continuum, 2006.

Clark, VéVé A. "Performing the Memory of Difference in Afro-Caribbean Dance: Katherine Dunham's Choreography, 1938–1987." In *Kaiso! Writings by and about Katherine Dunham*, edited by VéVé A. Clark and Sara E. Johnson, 320–340. Madison: University of Wisconsin Press, 2005.

Clover, Carol J. "Dancin' in the Rain" (1995). In *Hollywood Musicals: The Film Reader*, edited by Steven Cohan, 157–173. New York and London: Routledge, 2002.

Crease, Robert P. "Divine Frivolity: Hollywood Representations of the Lindy Hop, 1937–1942." In *Representing Jazz*, edited by Krin Gabbard, 207–228. Durham, NC, and London: Duke University Press, 1995.

Dixon Gottschild, Brenda. *Digging the Africanist Presence in American Performance. Dance and Other Contexts.* Westport, CT, and London: Praeger, 1996.

Dyer, Richard. "The Colour of Entertainment". In *Only Entertainment.* Second Edition, 36–45. London and New York: Routledge, 2002.

Feuer, Jane. "The Self-Reflective Musical and the Myth of Entertainment". In *Hollywood Musicals: The Film Reader*, edited by Steve Cohan, 31–40. London and New York: Routledge, 2002.

Gabbard, Krin. *Black Magic: White Hollywood and African American Culture.* New Brunswick, NJ, and London: Rutgers University Press, 2004.

Haskins, Jim. *The Cotton Club.* New York: Hippocrene Books, 1994.

Kalinak, Kathryn. "Disciplining Josephine Baker: Gender, Race, and the Limits of Disciplinarity." In *Music and Cinema*, edited by James Buhler, Caryl Flinn, and David Neumeyer, 316–355. Hanover, NH: Wesleyan University Press, 2000.

Knapp, Raymond. *The American Musical and the Performance of Personal Identity.* Princeton, NJ, and Oxford: Princeton University Press, 2006.

Knight, Arthur. *Disintegrating the Musical: Black Performance and American Musical Film.* Durham, NC, and London: Duke University Press, 2002.

Landay, Lori. "The Flapper Film: Comedy, Dance, and Jazz Age Kinaesthetics." In *A Feminist Reader in Early Cinema*, edited by Jennifer M. Bean and Diane Negra, 221–248. Durham, NC, and London: Duke University Press, 2002.

MacGillivray, Scott and Ted Okuda. *The Soundies Book. A Revised and Expanded Guide.* New York, Lincoln, NE, and Shanghai: iUniverse, Inc., 2007.

Malone, Jacqui. *Steppin' on the Blues: The Visible Rhythms of African American Dance.* Urbana and Chicago: University of Illinois Press, 1996.

Manning, Frankie and Cynthia R. Millman. *Frankie Manning: Ambassador of Lindy Hop.* Philadelphia: Temple University Press, 2007.

Massood, Paula J. *Black City Cinema: African American Urban Experiences in Film.* Philadelphia: Temple University Press, 2003.

Rogin, Michael. *Blackface, White Noise: Jewish Immigrants in the Hollywood Melting Pot.* Berkeley, Los Angeles, and London: University of California Press, 1998.

Stearns, Marshall, and Jean Stearns. *Jazz Dance: The Story of American Vernacular Dance.* Cambridge, MA: Da Capo Press, 1994.

CHAPTER 7

···

HIP-HOP IN HOLLYWOOD: ENCOUNTER, COMMUNITY, RESISTANCE

···

THOMAS F. DEFRANTZ[1]

THIS chapter constructs a genealogy of a "hip-hop body" in Hollywood films. We might note that media of the moving image has always encouraged the circulation of black social dances to a far-flung viewership. These film dances have transformed the terms of corporeal possibility for their audiences, no matter the historical era or location of the viewers. From the earliest Thomas A. Edison films of cakewalkers to the twenty-first-century Internet postings of California turf dancers, black social dances have been distributed via film to audiences eager to engage the physical possibilities of these dance and musical genres. The hip-hop body, though, raised an important capacity for dance in Hollywood to stand as a metaphor for community-based social engagement and neoliberal resistance to capital. The hip-hop body produced in Hollywood films stands as representative of racial and cultural exchange, indicates the possibility of progressive group politics, and restricts structures of hierarchical, old-guard authority.

Hip-hop dance found its way into Hollywood formulas very quickly. In the early 1980s, some Hollywood producers began to exploit hip-hop dance—especially breaking—to produce a limited series of movie musicals. These "breaksploitation" films set a standard of participation for young artists, and in particular, young artists of color, to enter the movie industry as laborers, and to enter the global imagination of film audiences as representative agents of change. As we consider the classic films of the breaksploitation era, predicted by *Fame* (1980) and *Flashdance* (1983), and including *Beat Street* (1984) and *Breakin'* (1984), we'll consider the material circumstances of filmmaking, the representational narratives and editing techniques common to their construction, and the ways in which these films produced a commodified hip-hop dancing body that became a standard representational practice for the form. Taken together, these films inspired a global audience for breakdancing, and are inextricably linked to the sweep and scale of young people's interest in these corporeal practices. We'll so pay special attention to the grounding assumptions of normative corporealities that breakdancers upset by practicing their dances in the context of Hollywood musicals. Finally, we consider an emergent global audience for hip-hop cultural manifestations, one inspired in large part by the dissemination of these few films that depicted b-boying and b-girling.

AFTER THE HAYS CODE

To frame a way of thinking about the arrival of hip-hop dance and young artists of color in Hollywood, we have to revisit the circumstances of mainstream filmmaking of the 1970s and 1980s. By the time Hollywood abandoned the Hays Code to install the MPAA film rating system in 1968,[2] the genre of movie musicals had plummeted from popularity. The golden era of unspeakably white narratives following a tri-part formula of [white] boy meets [white] girl, boy loses girl, and boy gets girl became impossibly old-fashioned for emerging American audiences, and Hollywood slowed its production of the form. The fewer Hollywood musicals of the 1970s accentuated emotionally complex, indeterminate narratives that employed music and dance as elements among many; these musicals include *Cabaret* (1972), *Saturday Night Fever* (1977), and *Sgt. Pepper's Lonely Hearts Club Band* (1978). Note that the latter two movies, constructed around popular music forms of disco, rock, and funk, included artists of color as supporting and background characters. In some ways, we can argue that disco, rock, and funk music, which had grown from African American musical sources, inspired the 'natural' inclusion of artists of color into Hollywood musical scenarios.[3]

Indeed, shifts in popular music that acknowledged African American wellsprings in the 1970s, including disco and funk music, arrived alongside activist gains of the civil rights era. These musical genres posed representational challenges for conservative mainstream Hollywood production, as the leading artists in these forms were mostly African American and often gay. *Car Wash* (1976), *Thank God It's Friday* (1978) and *Can't Stop the Music* (1980) presented working-class characters of color trying to find their way amid the rising consumer-conscious era that preceded neoliberal economic policies of the 1980s. While popular music and dance feature in each of these films, their production values and promotional profiles held little in common with the overwhelmingly white golden-age Hollywood musicals of the past.

Indeed, the rising visibility of African American musicality and African Americans in public life surely opened a space for characters of color to be at the center of Hollywood musicals. *Jesus Christ Superstar* (1973), *The Wiz* (1978), *Hair* (1979), and *Fame* (1980) featured African American and Latina protagonists and secondary characters. Excepting *The Wiz*, we might note that these films incorporated dance only occasionally, and typically as a reference to the capacity of music to inspire rhythmic motion, more than as a necessary outgrowth of emotional activity that could advance narrative or describe character. More importantly, none of the leading actors of color in *Superstar* or *Hair* danced much at all, or narrated themselves as dancers in the subsequent telling of their careers. As popular music shifted toward funk and hip-hop outside of the movie theater, Hollywood struggled for ways to incorporate the rising visibility of African American arts, including rapping and hip-hop dance, in the musical genre.

Fame (1980) offers an exceptional case in its presentation of young people of color, straight and gay, involved in then-contemporary music and dance. The protagonists of *Fame*—characters who hope to enjoy careers in the mainstream entertainment industry as creators and performers—aspire toward success marked by notoriety, rather than artistry. As the title of the film suggests, the young people here are encouraged to develop qualities of celebrity, and in this process, they are to learn the basic skills that mark the areas of artistry they engage—drama, music, and dance. But note that these skills are considered ancillary to the plot imperative to seek *fame* as its own reward. Surprisingly, the music and dance of the film do not refer to the emergence of hip-hop. The dance sequences of the film, created by Louis Falco, a former dancer with José Limón, employs a flowing, ballet-based modern dance mode popular in pre-professional dance training of the time. *Fame* intended to be of the world of young artists-in-training, but arrived more demonstrative of the world of a gritty, mainstream Hollywood and Broadway.

Fame trades in narrative tropes familiar to many Hollywood offerings that demean the aspirations of women; in the film, things end badly for all of the female characters. Jewish Doris Finsecker is impregnated, and by implication forced to abandon her dreams of acting stardom; wealthy WASP ballerina Hilary Van Doren, also impregnated, endures an abortion after a teary scene describing her ambivalence and disappointment at the turn of events that deter her from easy access to dancing stardom; and Latina singer and dancer Coco Hernandez ends the film in humiliation and degradation, topless and crying at an adult-film casting call that presumably ends her reach for musical and film stardom. These plot points, borne by characters stereotypically marked by flags of ethnic identity, demonstrate plot narratives that moved Hollywood musicals far from the previous golden era.[4] While those earlier films had traded in a nostalgia for innocent times of the past, as in *Singin' in the Rain* (1952); or in locations far away from contemporary urban diversity, as in *Mary Poppins* (1964), the new Hollywood musical focused on themes presumably relevant to urban youth of the time. Note, then, how the shift to Hollywood musicals that could be buoyed up by hip-hop culture seemed to require a drastic shift in the sort of stories that could be told, as well as the performers who could be cast in order to tell them.

HIP-HOP AND HOLLYWOOD

When hip-hop emerged as a cultural force in the 1970s and 1980s, it offered resistant aesthetic space for young people of color, especially in its originary neighborhoods of the South Bronx. Hip-hop proposed its organizational elements of writing (graphic arts), mc'ing (rapping), dj'ing (musical production), and corporeal activity (b-boying and b-girling) as creative foundation for a life well lived: life recognized to emerge on its own survivalist terms, resistant to existing structures of authority, and engaged with aesthetic and social concerns of the contemporary moment. Hip-hop emerged as profoundly concerned with the trope of the 'real;' the everyday valences of experience shared by young people far removed from the aspirational middle-class values proffered by Hollywood and other big media of the time. By their own accounts, few of the young artists affiliated with early hip-hop thought that its affiliated arts could become an avenue of economic advance.[5] In some ways, the incorporation of hip-hop into Hollywood systems of production surprised its practitioners as much as the audience who enjoyed their sudden appearances on the screen.

By 1982, writers and pundits already called the corporeal form of hip-hop "'breakdancing," with mainstream media following the lead of dance journalist Sally Banes's 1981 Village Voice article.[6] Hip-hop spread to California quickly in communities of young people of color, and in the early 1980s, some savvy Hollywood producers imagined possibility in hip-hop's aesthetic devices. The opening gambit toward exploiting these possibilities of an alignment of hip-hop and Hollywood came via a 75-second sequence of the breakout hit *Flashdance*. From a fleeting vision in this respectable, but predictable, Hollywood concoction, b-boying claimed an international audience and inspired global interest hip-hop's physicalities.

Flashdance (1983)

Flashdance deserves scrutiny for its many ambiguous delineations of class, ethnicity, and sexuality. Its story offers an obvious middle-class aspirational narrative, as steel-welder-by-day/exotic-dancer-by-night Alex enjoys a fantasy romance with her boss: middle-class, Porsche-driving plant manager Nick Hurley. Nick takes Alex to fancy restaurants and arranges her special audition for the Pittsburgh Conservatory of Dance. Alex is depicted as a free-floating, self-sufficient working-class cipher, a laborer who seems to enjoy her two careers as well as her huge downtown converted loft apartment. As portrayed by actress Jennifer Beals, Alex is visibly racially mixed but the film treats her as white by never making any reference to her ethnicity amid the blonde and visibly black women who work alongside her at Mawby's striptease bar. Alex seems to have few friends at her welding or dancing jobs; she acts as an emotional rudder for her white friend Jeanie, who suffers failed ambitions to become a professional ice skater. When Jeanie takes work as a dancer at the nude bar Zanzibar, Alex rescues her from the degradation. Despite its narrative sequences in stripclubs, sexuality in the film is strangely muted, without a hint of homoeroticism. Even scenes at Mawby's and the Zanzibar are presented as clean adult entertainment for heterosexual men. As the author of commonsensemedia.com points out, *Flashdance* is "largely a fairy tale, a glamorous wish-fulfillment pop fantasy for teen girls on what being an adult is like."[7]

Each of the dance sequences of *Flashdance* deserves its own analysis, but for our purposes the single "street dance" scene matters most. This scene acts as a set-up to grant Alex access to physical information she'll need in order to complete her narrative journey and successfully audition for the ballet school. The film presents its shots of the dancers here with an almost-documentary flourish, keeping the camera pulled back to a full-body distance for the bulk of its short duration. Most of the clips in this sequence last five seconds, and present solo movements performed by very young members of Rock Steady Crew. In the sequence, Alex and her friend Jeanie approach two b-boys who pop and pantomime in common moves of "wind-up toy" and "man walking with umbrella against the wind." Alex and Jeanie stop to watch the dancing, and, in a suggestive time-lapse sequence, become the center of a crowd gathered to witness the ever-more spectacular gestures of the dancers. Dancers demonstrate floorwork, freezes, and a well-timed suicide dive to the smiles of the gathered crowd. The sequence seems to have little narrative content, but we will learn at the end of the film that the movements Alex witnesses here play a large role in her final, make-it-or-break-it dance audition sequence.

Alex stays among the crowd witnessing the b-boys, smiling at the edges of the film frame. At one point actress Beals dances improvisationally in response to the b-boying, swinging her hips and clapping her hands with enthusiasm, and a semblance of funkiness appears in her embodiment of a complex back-beat rhythm. But in this brief sequence, Beals lays bare her dispersed energetic field as entirely distinct from the precise, controlled energy exuded by her dance double, Marine Jahan. Jahan famously performed Alex's dances, aided by an uncredited gymnast and b-boy Crazy Legs in the final dance sequence of the film; in this brief sequence, though, we note well that Beals is a different sort of social dancer than her doubles, including Jahan.[8]

In the culminating dance scene of the film, b-boying becomes Alex's trump card as she creates a spectacular performance to secure her place as a student in the ballet school. After turning on her stretched foot in an enhanced, multi-cut sequence, she dives through the air, rolls and flips, and then backspins to the delighted applause of the audition committee. Her incorporation of a b-boy move in the ballet studio confirms the Hollywoodization of both the spreadability, and accessibility, of b-boying.

Oddly, though, we never see Alex practice her b-girl moves. Early in the film, Film 7.1 Flashdance (1983) Ending Scene ⏵ we are invited to voyeuristically watch Alex perform her sweaty home workout in a famous sequence replete with many close-ups of feet pounding on the floor, hips gyrating in circular pulsation, and throbbing splay-legged stretches. But the backspin that culminates her audition scene arrives prepared only by the logic of the Hollywood fantasy. The implication of her ability at the end of the film is either that she practiced off-screen, as she had rehearsed the three dances that she (implausibly) performs in the Mawby's nightclub, or that she improvised her way into the movement sequence when the moment of the audition arrived. If we follow the logic of this latter implication, we note that b-girling is assumed to be entirely portable and obtainable, acquired and distributed by any dancers who happen to see it and then inhabit its contours. By no means is Alex to be considered a true b-girl, or even a nominal one; she simply performs a backspin. But, in that revolution on the ground, she confirms that b-girl corporealities belong within the Cinderella-story Hollywood frame of class mobility.

Style Wars (1983), Wild Style (1983), and Breakin' and Enterin' (1983)

Flashdance continued a trend of danc-ical films; movies built around sequences of dancing set to songs, or montages, but without the actual singing presence of its main characters. It might be important to note that the breaksploitation films that followed Flashdance similarly resisted singing by their leading characters. These are movies that expect dancing to stand in for the singing moments of earlier musicals, and as such, they arrive with a distinctive profile from the mainstream of Hollywood fare. Two documentaries and one fictional film that leaned toward cinéma vérité established camera angle tropes for hip-hop Hollywood and the hip-hop body. Style Wars, shot in New York in 1982 and released the next year, held huge implications regarding the place of the camera in the development of the form, the sensibility of documenting and transmitting dance to a larger audience than the immediate participants in the cipher, and the direction of an inevitable future for hip-hop Hollywood filmmaking.

Style Wars treats breaking as a part of a constellation of public art, even as it interrogates the legality and ethical dimensions of graffiti on New York City subway cars. Professionally produced, the film stabilizes the idioms of hip-hop with sequences that define its boundaries and confirm its participants' ambitions. A full-length documentary about then-established hip-hop culture, Style Wars includes several sequences of dancers demonstrating and playing with the form even as they offer evidence of its methods and its terms of engagement. In one sequence, a group, including youthful celebrity dancer Crazy Legs, defines and demonstrates steps from the "original breaking" vocabulary: categories of movement, including footwork, backbridge and headspin; and movements with names, including "the baby," "the turtle," a "dead freeze," the "headache," and "the hump. " As in Flashdance, a crowd gathers as he offers evidence of these dance achievements; these scenes are cut with sequences of competitive nightclub dancing by two New York crews, the Rock Steady Crew and the Dynamic Rockers. In these scenes, the camera explores two vantages: low to the ground, and high overhead. These two angles become the benchmark aesthetics of presenting hip-hop dance on film. The low angle allows the film audience to imagine itself as a participant/witness within the circle of the battle cipher. The overhead angle invites the viewer to note the spectacular, circular energy generated by breakdancing in floorwork and power moves. It is important to note that neither of these two preferred camera angles are practical in the live experience of breakdancing; participants are seldom able to view these movements from the ground or overhead in live performance circumstances. The two 'impossible' angles allow film audiences to feel 'in on' the activity of b-girling and b-boying in a hip-hop-inspired cipher; they also establish a mode of viewing for dance in hip-hop films, as they visually confirm a spectacularly powerful, heroic, and towering hip-hop body.

Wild Style (1983)

Many of the young dancers of *Style Wars* appear in the independent Charlie Ahearn film *Wild Style*. The entire film *Wild Style* can be seen as Hollywood-aspirational in its attempts to inflect the underdog-survivor genre with hip-hop sensibilities. The story follows Zoro (played by celebrity graffiti artist Lee Quinones) as he struggles with his family and love relationships. Several emerging hip-hop luminaries appear in the film as themselves, or gently cinematized versions of themselves, including rappers Busy Bee, DJ Grandmaster Flash, and b-boys Crazy Legs, Mr. Freeze, Frosty Freeze, Prince Ken Swift, and Mr. Wiggles.[9]

The film looks raw. Shot in the South Bronx, replete with real-world imagery of filth and decay, it demonstrates the wasteland feeling of decrepit buildings and burned-out neighborhoods strewn with garbage, but tempered by interiors of functional, sparse, and chilly working-class Bronx apartments. In all, the film generates a seething isolation of a neighborhood all-but-forgotten in public discourse. While the South Bronx of the 1980s had been represented by Hollywood in gruesome films such as *Fort Apache: The Bronx* (1981); *Wild Style* offered vistas without apology for grime, spatial disorganization, and general urban blight pierced by the creative energy of hip-hop as a vibrant emergent cultural constellation.

While the screenplay has a narrative arc, dance appears in the film as a necessary and situated companion to music in several nightclub scenes. Dancers, including the Rock Steady Crew, Pop-O-Matics, and Electric Force, demonstrate their dance style in various club sequences; these extended scenes bear no narrative responsibility, and largely exist to confirm the accuracy of the film as a representation of hip-hop culture. B-boys are generally shown performing popping and locking, or engaging floorwork as soloists surrounded by a group of interested witnesses. Editing in the film cuts the bodies into fragments in these sequences, focusing alternately on torsos, feet, or hands, and seldom provides full-body imagery that might locate the dancers in space.

In one nightclub sequence, white underground actor Patti Astor appears as herself, and smiling onlookers escort her into the dance circle to encourage her to perform. The crowd eggs her on, and also laughs at her efforts. The sequence effectively demonstrates white interest in black social dance, as well as the inevitable inclusion of white witnessing and participation in these dance forms. Notably, Astor does not dance well, and comes across as an outsider to the aesthetic properties of the dance circle. Film 7.02 Wild Style (1983) Club Scene ▶

Wild Style offers important evidence of burgeoning hip hop Hollywood, in its extended depictions of b-boys in motion, its rawness of production, the inclusion of young teenagers as performers, and most importantly, the deconstruction of aesthetic ideologies of finish and perfection proposed by earlier movie musicals. If *Fame* offered bulbous, free-form structure via choreographer Louis Falco's contact-improvisation inspired choreography, *Wild Style* featured no sole choreographic author, and no assumption of overarching control over the movements captured on film.

Breakin' and Enterin' (1983)

Directed by black film entrepreneur and producer Topper Carew, this hard-to-find documentary devotes a remarkable amount of time to California iterations of hip-hop dance and b-boying and b-girling. From its opening frames, the film features b-boys working on the ground in footwork, as soloists and in duets, and popping and locking toward the camera. The dances presented here are clearly street performances designed to attract attention from passing pedestrians who might contribute to a 'dancer's fund' by placing change and small bills into a passed hat. The dances arrive not as competition movements, as they had inevitably been in the New York films *Style Wars* and *Wild Style*. Instead, *Breakin' and Enterin'* offers viewers a spectator-centered form of hip-hop dance that will eventually lend itself directly to Hollywood production.

Like *Wild Style, Breakin' and Enterin'* seems raw, underdeveloped, and entirely of the furtive moment. Rappers and DJs narrate their methods directly to the camera; future celebrity rapper and actor Ice-T offers up rhymes that describe the creative gestures of the young artists documented here. The Radiohole—a Los Angeles-area club analogous to the New York Roxy—acts as site for demonstrations of hip-hop dance, including some sequences featuring b-girls. In all, though, the film feels like an advertisement or trailer for a longer film yet to be made. Note that many of the dancers chronicled in this documentary will become featured dancers in the breaksploitation film *Breakin'* just a year later. Film 07.03 Breakin' 'N' Enterin' (1983) Opening Sequence ▶

Breakin' and Enterin' has no particular story to tell about hip-hop culture in Southern California; rather it presents evidence of a hip-hop dance community without mobilizing that evidence toward any particular end. The film does offer documentation of the places and movements that hip-hop dancers engaged at the time. In addition to the Radiohole, we also encounter breakdancers dancing in the bright sunlight of Venice Beach, facing an inevitable crowd of onlookers cheering them on. As in *Style Wars*, young artists are called upon to narrate and demonstrate movements that they have devised and performed; in this film we get Boogaloo Shrimp explaining how to do "the helicopter" and end with a pose. Charismatic performer Shabba Doo offers a thumbnail history of pop and lock movements from the area that includes the "funky chicken," "the lock," the point," and the "Uncle Sam." Several dancers discuss the difference between street dancers and professional dancers, and the ways in which these dances are created, literally, on the streets, rather than in a dance studio or on a stage. This distinction arrives as a badge of honor for the dancers, who claim their 'outsiderness' to mainstream dance practice as a marker of their authenticity within hip-hop. Note, though, that Shabba Doo is willing to claim identity as a member of a Professional Street Dance crew, a company organized to consider hip-hop dancers as professional artists, responsible to the form and its professionalization. This claim sets the stage for a West Coast codification of hip-hop dance that can fit into emergent Hollywood aesthetic structures.

Unlike *Style Wars, Breakin' and Enterin'* trades in post-production effects to enhance dancer movements. In one sequence toward the end of the film, a dancer's movements are transformed into a vibrating outline of a body in motion. The image offers a graphically entertaining method to demonstrate the visual trace of breakdance. But this sequence, replete with movement screened forward and in reverse, with saturated colors, and the insertion of unexpected amorphous shapes, suggests dancing without reference to the people creating the dance. The psychedelic editing style here demonstrates what Hollywood hip-hop will come to value: the dancing labor of young people transformed by electronic effect for a sensational visual image. Here, viewers come to see breaking as decorative demonstration, rather than a potential realization of identity, or expressive personal communication. Film 07.04 Breakin' 'N' Enterin' (1983) Post-Production Scene ▶

These three films established a framework for thinking about the physical, aesthetic, and commercial locations of hip-hop dance in relation to Hollywood musical practices. In terms of physical location, hip-hop confirmed its capacity as a multiracial dance form, created and practiced by young artists, that lived outside of the dance studio, in venues of the outdoors and the dance club. Because hip-hop had grown up on concrete and cardboard, it offered a down and dirty, admittedly spectacular demonstration of physical capacity in dance that didn't require the special surfaces that tap dance, ballet, or modern dance often necessitated. In terms of aesthetic location, hip-hop arrived within newly articulated Africanist aesthetic structures noted by scholars, that (1) placed a high value on physical innovation and originality; (2) realized the importance of an individual's presence within a group dynamic; and (3) demonstrated a recognizable "flash of the spirit" in performance. In terms of commercial location, hip-hop arrived especially suited to the crucial marketing demographic of teenagers who saw the genre as generationally specific and as connected to the promise of a particular social life bounded by competitive events in idyllic urban nightclubs. Hip-hop routines were inevitably created by the performing artists, without recourse to the intervention of a professional choreographer. Thus, hip-hop required less production attention than other forms of Hollywood dance, as it could be rehearsed anywhere, its practitioners held themselves accountable to standards of quality that demonstrated their skill and virtuosity, and didn't require celebrity choreographic authority.

Beat Street (1984)

The 1984 film Beat Street offers hip-hop as its object and subject, in a family-friendly story that demonstrates the communal bonding, criminality, aesthetic innovation, and youthful exuberance endemic to the genre in its foundational elements. B-boying, Mc'ing, Dj'ing, and Writing (spray-can art) are each represented in the movie as central elements of the lives of its various young protagonists of color. The movie gives hip-hop a full Hollywood treatment, with star-crossed romance, adventure, tragedy, musical-dance interludes, and a grand finale that, in their total, entirely contain the unruly offscreen capacities of hip-hop. The story addresses class divisions, hints at the implications of racial profiling, and confirms an inevitable heterosexuality and homosociality that were perceived to underscore hip-hop as a genre.

This Harry Belafonte-produced film arrives quite near to *Wild Style* and *Style Wars* in its approach and effect. It contains several obvious Hollywood narrative tropes, including a love song montage and a finale performance that reconciles antagonistic forces; it features hip-hop culture as an oppositional possibility of expression for young people, set within a framework of familial tensions and aspirational personal growth. The film follows a multiracial group of young protagonists depicted as generational and class outsiders to the then-contemporary world of mainstream, middle-aged, moneyed [white] beneficiaries of Reagan and Thatcher-era neoliberal economic policies. Four friends, each interested in one of the foundational elements of hip-hop—graffiti, dj'ing, mc'ing, and b-boying—make their way through a series of small adventures. The film includes scenes shot on location in the gritty South Bronx as well as several New York City subway stations and nightclubs of the early 1980s and several dance sequences that bear special scrutiny for their contents and implications.

In a dance battle sequence filmed at the Roxy nightclub, *Beat Street* echoes camera perspectives from *Style Wars*, including high overhead and low-to-the-ground shots. The camera captures a circle of witnesses and competitors in a showcase sequence that highlights the individuality of each performer who enters the circle. Reaction shots add to the sense of an audience engaged in the construction of the performance, and the participation of the entire group to decide on the winner of the competition. These two important features of a hip-hop cipher—the engagement of a witnessing audience, and the individuality of each competitor—arrive in full measure here.

In a later sequence, leading b-boy character Lee goes to a college theater to audition for a television program. In this sequence, breakdancing appears alongside neo-African jazz dance, choreographed for the film by Lester Wilson, an outstanding artist who had acted as choreographer for John Travolta in *Saturday Night Fever*. In this scene, the camera cuts in and out incessantly from the jazz dance, so that we only see a movement or two at a time in a frontal, presentational arrangement toward the unblinking and unsmiling camera. But as Lee shares his b-boy movements for the group, the audience forms a circle, to smile and cheer him on; their reaction shots are integrated into the exuberance of the dance as a whole.

Diegetic structure allows actors in films to engage in their creative performance arts by playing characters who possess similar skills; this method has long served film musicals as a way to extend the suspension of disbelief necessary for audience identification with film narrative. Steven Hager's screenplay structures *Beat Street* as a hip-hop backstage musical. The characters of the film are artists engaged in being artists, allowing sequences of dancing to emerge from situations that call for dancing. For example, an audition sequence for acts who hope to perform at the Roxy club allows for extended performances by singers, djs, and b-boys—in this case, two young men who demonstrate their locking and waving abilities. A subway-station battle scene arrives in the film without much plot preparation, but its outcome holds consequence for the characters involved in the dancing. Note that this subway sequence includes elements of synchronized choreography that has the battlers walking toward and past each other, and executing spectacular handsprings simultaneously, as dancers might in any Hollywood musical. Film 7.05 Beat Street (1984) Subway Battle ⊙

In the film's final sequence, the breakdancers and the theatrical dancers come together in a spectacle cast as a tribute to a graffiti artist killed in a beef with a competitor. This number combines gospel singers with hip-hop dancers to suggest a transcendent possibility for hip-hop and breakdancing. In the logic of the film's narrative, the link of hip-hop to gospel intends to embed hip-hop within a larger framework of African American music and culture, and align it with acceptable modes of expression respondent to family values. The pairing of gospel and hip-hop responded to anxieties that hip-hop represented the anarchic displacement of black culture by the needs and desires of disconnected youth. But in the context of this final number, hip-hop becomes a corporeal expression of hope for young dancers who mourn their friend's passing.

In terms of filmmaking, though, random editing depreciates its value considerably, as three-second clips of b-boy floor work arrive among fleeting images of clapping gospel singers as well as turning and smiling musical theater dancers. B-boying arrives onstage here, without a participating audience encouraging its gestures, and in the process is rendered as a presentational genre, like jazz dance. The hip-hop body of the end of the film predicts a possibility for progressive group politics, as it connects to the needs of the community to mourn both inter-generationally and across musical cultures. But removed from its circle of participating witnesses, the hip-hop body succumbs to the authority of the presentational stage space, where b-boying might be interchangeable with theatrical jazz dance.

Breakin' (Breakdance: The Movie) (1984)—Centering White Womanhood

The earliest hip-hop films struggled with conventional wisdoms that assumed a limit to the capacity of a broad movie-going public to appreciate young men of color at the center of mainstream fare. Young men engaged in hip-hop culture could fit into conventional Hollywood narratives because they could be cast as outlaws to social norms or as criminals. For example, breakdancers worked without permits on the street and sometimes disrupted traffic in subway stations, and therefore they became eligible for arrest. The love story at the center of *Beat Street* arrived in slightly progressive terms, as it valued an emotional relationship between young people of color committed to their own choices as emerging artists amid a nuanced world that included contemporary classical music and dance as well as hip-hop culture. Rather than continue this line of possibility, though, the two most successful[10] breaksploitation films of the early 1980s featured a white woman protagonist who comes to her emotional and social maturity via her encounter with hip-hop practice in southern California.

Breakin', released as *Breakdance: The Movie* in some countries, arrived as a predictable tale of subjection, resistance, and ultimate triumph for its main white woman character, Kelly. Played by young dancer Lucinda Dickey, Kelly is cast as the star of the film from its first credits; she acts in the film as the physical embodiment of a Hollywood-scripted hybridity of theatrical jazz dance and street dance. Set in and around the venues of the earlier documentary *Breakin' and Enterin'*, the film follows Kelly's movement away from the narrow and limiting life of theatrical jazz dance to the discovery of her inner balance and freedom as a hip-hop-capable, breakdance competitor, embedded within a world of young men of color, one of whom almost functions as her romantic interest. The film follows Kelly's degradation and sexual harassment in her initially preferred theatrical dance studio environment; her encounter and discovery of a vibrant b-boy culture on the beaches of Venice, California; her fascination and training within the milieu of breaking; her disappointments and setbacks with her new-found friends; and her ultimate triumph as a hip-hop inflected performer who ends up headlining a spectacular—and utterly ridiculous—stage show extravaganza alongside her new breakdancing friends.

The film confirms the emergent music video aesthetics of dance representation of the time that focused on quick cuts and physical segmentation, with dances pasted together visually, while tied to a single, well-produced audio track. From its first frames, we see short cuts of three to five seconds duration, segmenting the body into a flash of footwork, or the precise movements of arms or hands, or the torso popping and locking. Discrepancies between the screen dance performance and the tempo and accents of the music quickly confer that the audio heard in the movie theater was not always heard by the dancing performers during filming.

The setup for the film is Kelly's desire to work as a dancer; hip-hop becomes a way for her to believe in her dancing and connect it to a world larger than just her own ambition. Kelly's dilemma appeals to adolescent females. She wonders, should she sleep with her favorite choreographer and teacher, Franco, or can she find her way as an artist interested in her own choices? We follow Kelly through her milieus: first as a star dancer in a theatrical jazz class, then traveling with her queer African American friend Adam to see the street dancers on Venice beach. The film makes striking difference between the dance class, which is proscenium-styled performance that uses the mirror (and the camera) as the audience for the dance, and the Venice street dancing circle, which includes a participating audience of witnesses, clapping and dancing along as individual artists enter the circle to offer movements to the disco-inspired song "Freakshow." Notably, the main two hip-hop dancers are Kelly's co-stars, Ozone (Adolfo Quiñones, also known as Shabba-Doo) and Turbo (Michael Chambers), who are depicted to be queer-friendly; they embrace Adam and his friend warmly in a meeting sequence at the beach.

The film depicts Kelly as naïve: someone who doesn't know anything about emerging hip-hop culture. She doesn't know language cues such as "fresh" or "bad," and her ignorance provides cues for the film viewers to learn about hip-hop at the same time as she does. When Turbo visits Kelly at her dance studio and joins into a contemporary jazz dance class, he opens the space from a frontal-oriented dance into a circle that calls and responds to his movements as he breaks on the studio dance floor. In this scene, and throughout the film, the tension between show dancing and street dancing represents tensions in Kelly's emotional life, as she has to choose between the forms.

The film has several dance set pieces, including Turbo's outstanding magical broom dance tribute to Fred Astaire, in which he performs with a broom that stands still, rises, and floats (with obvious wires) as he waves and pops through space to a hip-hop beat. Here, the camera stays at a distance for some time, to reveal the entirety of Turbo's body in motion, as it might have in an Astaire sequence. But note that the camera also moves in to provide segmented shots of Turbo's dancing ability that convey a sense of excitement. Throughout the film, Kelly's desires provide the impetus for dance representation: in another sequence, the main characters go to a nightclub to see hip-hop dance because Kelly is sad and needs to be cheered up. In this dance competition staged at the Radiotron, the camera moves in and out from the dancers in a balanced series of cuts generally timed with the movement and music, creating sequences that are exciting to watch and, thankfully, clear in terms of what's happening when and where.

The film narrative realizes ambitions to place hip-hop dance firmly within Hollywood tropes of adolescent self-discovery through white encounter with a munificent cultural other. Kelly is christened "Special K" by Ozone, in one of several memorable tag lines ("Every street dancer needs a street name"), and taken into the confidence of Ozone and Turbo so that they can do righteous battle with rivals the Electro Rock crew, Pop N' Taco (Bruno Falcon), Poppin' Pete (Timothy Solomon) and Lollipop (Ana Sánchez). Kelly has to learn how to be a street dancer, and during a two-minute Hollywood training montage of hand gestures and locking, she learns enough to compete convincingly. At the subsequent rematch with the Electro Rocks, Ozone offers up some wacking—a queer hip-hop dance style—before Special K is revealed as a surprise agent who wows the crowd with acrobatics and simple spins on her knees. The sequence tips its hat toward reality here: because Special K doesn't have much vocabulary as a b-girl yet, the trio can offer no unison dancing. Film 7.06 Breakin' (1984) Club Battle Rematch Scene ▶

The Hollywoodification of possibility forces the story into some awkward corners that are true to the musical/competition genre, but hard for hip-hop. An unfulfilled romance between Ozone and Kelly is exacerbated by Kelly's seeming flirtatiousness with professional manager James. James as the (white) 'professional' manager offers foil to (black queer) Adam as the 'play' manager; again, Kelly must convince the white establishment representatives that the cultural 'others' are worthwhile and valuable. Memorable quotes from the film along these lines include: "Street dancing won't get you to Broadway!" (James to Kelly); "They put more heart and soul into their work than anyone I know!" (Kelly to James); and "I don't dance for anybody but myself" (Ozone to Kelly, regarding James's scrutiny of the trio's dancing abilities in the nightclub). A "fish out of water" sequence at a Hollywood party pits Turbo and Ozone against upper-class white doyennes; an inspirational, "each-one-teach-one" sequence features Turbo teaching children locking and breaking in an alleyway. In this latter scene, a multiracial group of children are encouraged by Turbo, who calls directions to them: footwork, break, spin. The film adds layers to the cultural-encounter/opposites-attract narrative implications: Kelly must convince Ozone to participate in a stage dancing competition, and get over his fear of being "in the world." In turn, Ozone takes Kelly to the beach where the dancers include a disabled artist who offers up floorwork and headspins while on his crutches. The visual dissonance of the street forms as seen in the studio space, where trio Kelly, Ozone, and Turbo enjoy a playful montage of practicing in a white-walled, mirrored space created only for dance, confirms an oppositional narrative at work throughout the film.

For the final competition sequence, the heroic trio of dancers start in black tie, with a fake 'high-class' name as the "Allegro Vivace Dance Trio." When they are denied an opportunity to audition among the "professional dancers," Ozone walks to the table and tears his costume off, revealing himself as a rough-around-the-edges street dancer, and looks at each judge at the table, in the filmmaker's nod to the audition scene of *Flashdance*. The trio proceeds to dance without the sanction of the audition board, and, of course, they get the job headlining the ambiguous stage production that follows this scene. Here in the audition dance, and in the final show performance, the dance movements caught by the camera don't make any sense as a routine, and when the camera pulls away, the trio of artists popping, locking, and offering some floorwork, look small and insignificant on the large proscenium stage. When the camera moves in to frame the dancers at full body, or in close-up, though, their breaking and locking are revealed for their dynamic quality on film. Film 07.07 Breakin' (1984) Final Audition Scene.⊙ The final show that the dancers headline looks something like a cross between a music video and a fashion shoot; it arrives in a confusing and nonsensical manner that renders the actual dance movements to be irrelevant to the spectacle of fast cuts, camera movements, and extravagant costume and lighting shifts.

The final rhyme by Ice-T that leads into the credits extols "all of us have our dreams—you can make it with motivation hard, hard work and determination," and ends with a summary of what hip-hop tries to demonstrate in Hollywood: "colored people just like you trying to make their dreams come true." This lyric clarifies the 'insider-outsider' sensibility that surrounds these early hip-hop films; the performers and artists have little if any access to the technologies of reproduction and distribution that constitute Hollywood film production; these movies are the glimpse of celluloid celebrity available to an art form already ten years into its formation and practice.

Breakin' confirmed the Hollywood hip-hop body in its three important manifestations: as representative of racial and cultural exchange (in the encounters of Kelly, Ozone, Turbo, and other dancers), as an indicator of the possibility for progressive group politics (in the sequences of teaching youth and the formation of their dancing group), and as a method of resistance against structures of hierarchical, old-guard authority (represented by the jazz dance studio). Unfortunately, the producers of the film tried their luck in an unnecessary sequel that effectively undid any progressive possibilities present in their first offering.

Breakin' 2: Electric Boogaloo (1984)

This unexpected sequel, apparently filmed immediately after its progenitor, arrives more like an episode from a television series than a fleshed-out Hollywood production.

Directed by B-movie specialist Sam Firstenberg, the 94-minute exercise trades in feel-good, happy breakdancing, presented in the style of an extended-form music video targeted to a family-friendly, pre-pubescent audience. The film includes throngs of multi-generational, happy dancers in theatrical dance idioms; scores of smiling break-dancers who face toward the camera at every opportunity; and an obvious narrative of dance as a tool that can bring a community together to resist the efforts of evil developers who would tear down an important community center in the midst of a mostly people-of-color neighborhood.

The sequel retains the same trio of main characters from the first film, and seems to pick up about a year later. As it begins, we meet Kelly, now dancing in a Las Vegas-styled stage show, while Ozone and Turbo now teach dance to children at the community center. Kelly tussles with her disapproving rich family, who want to send her to Princeton and marry her off to a handsome and wealthy young white lawyer. But by the end of the film, Kelly dumps her boring boyfriend, helps her friends from the 'hood win a dance battle or two, and brings together the neighborhood for a massive block-party dance show that convinces the city to leave its community center in place. Following the logic of Hollywood happy-ending narratives, Kelly's wealthy parents provide the final installation of funds needed to resist the developers as they come to appreciate the good work that she does for others. Note that this plot is repeated with only slight variation 25 years later in *Step It Up: 3D (2010)*.

The film tries to stabilize hip-hop dance movement as central to the new form of Hollywood musicals by incorporating its gestures in every conceivable locale and circumstance. In a nod to classic musical films including *An American In Paris* (1951), an early sequence in the film depicts a happy multiracial neighborhood grooving and bouncing to a lightweight hip-hop beat. An overhead camera tracks through the scene to reveal the extent to which hip-hop dance has taken over the citizenry: everyone dances, and even a white policewoman giving tickets can bust a move to join in with a multiracial contingent of smiling church ladies who perform freezes and waves. Film 07.08 Breakin' 2 (1984) Street Scene ▶

In another sequence set in a hospital, "sexy nurses" perform MTV-esque music video dances, male patients breakdance in the hallways, doctors pop and freeze as they perform surgery, pregnant women perform unexpected acrobatics, and even patients in the midst of surgery awaken to join the dancing fray. As in the earlier large-scale Hollywood musicals, we see lots and lots of dancers, but very little actual dancing. Here, the bits and pieces of hip-hop dance that we see stand as a cipher of pleasant rhythmic motion available to all without any particular political valence. Film 07.09 Breakin' 2 (1984) Hospital Scene ▶

Perhaps in a nod to the grittier East Coast phenomenon of *Beat Street*, *Breakin' 2* includes surprising staged representations of physical violence. A dance battle sequence set underneath a freeway overpass turns violent with the introduction of Nunchucks, a double-stick weapon popular in the United States in the 1970s and 1980s. But the potentially serious issue of gang fighting becomes quickly undermined by the film's highly formulaic composition. Set pieces in the film include a fish out of water sequence for Turbo and Ozone visiting at Kelly's large suburban home, practically repeated from *Breakin'*; a montage in which Turbo learns how to romance a partner through coaching by Ozone; a montage of energetic fundraising activities for the community center; and a narrative dilemma of Kelly's choice between helping the center raise funds or dancing in a new show in Paris. Again, Turbo gets to pay homage to Fred Astaire, this time in a dancing on the ceiling sequence that allows him to pop, float, and wave across the walls and ceiling of his room as he imagines his burgeoning romantic feelings. Innovative in its conception but lacking in its technical realization, the disappointing sequence echoes a general sense of production malaise that plagued early hip-hop films.[11]

While *Breakin'* 2 nodded toward a nominally progressive narrative politic of the underdog rising up against corporate greed, as well as a multiracial alliance that might resist white hegemony, the film trivializes these possibilities by containing the hip-hop body within its strict Hollywood formula. By the end of this film, in the ultimate dance party production number, the hip-hop body is rendered interchangeable with other kinds of dancing bodies, no matter any political ambition of their movements or histories. This potential for Hollywood accommodation of a hip-hop body stuck, and virtually all films involving hip-hop or breaking after the millennium treat hip-hop as a weapon suited to answer a need to raise money and resist social ills, including *Honey* (2003), *You Got Served* (2004), and the *Step Up* series (2006, 2008, 2010, 2012).[12]

Several successful musicals emerged in the era alongside these breaksploitation films, most notably *Footloose* (1984) and *Purple Rain* (1984). While each of these Hollywood blockbusters concerned itself with the place of young male creative expression, neither bothered to explore hip-hop. Films from the next years, including the Sidney Poitier-directed *Fast Forward* (1985), Michael Schultz's *Krush Groove* (1985), and the Joel Silberg-directed *Rappin'* (1985) used hip-hop as a plot point to allow their protagonists to overcome social challenges presumably important to young audiences: staying current in dance (*Fast Forward*), building a successful business (*Krush Groove*), and, not surprisingly, saving a neighborhood from a greedy land developer (*Rappin'*). *Rappin'* arrived as an especially poor offering; it borrowed its narrative from *Breakin'* 2, and while it did include actor Ice-T repeating his role as an ostensible tour guide through hip-hop (as he had in both *Breakin' and Enterin'* and *Breakin'*), the film offers several weak demonstrations of dance neither fish nor fowl; not recognizable as breaking or b-boying, but rather, as poorly done Hollywood jazz dance. In all, the film arrives undercooked and hammy, and demonstrates minimal relationship to hip-hop culture. Perhaps it stands as the ultimate breaksploitation film, titled in relationship to an urgent cultural innovation, but offered as a low-cost talent show, poorly executed.

Briefly Upsetting the Norms of Hollywood Dancer Training

The early hip-hop films called for dancers capable of engaging b-girling and b-boying in recognizable, spectacular motion; this need created opportunities for dancers who had trained in peer-mentored local crews rather than dance studios. But this brief shift of access to work in the film industry abated quickly, as codified hip-hop and breakdancing classes sprouted up around the world. By the time that iconic Hollywood dancer Gene Kelly created on-screen narration for *That's Dancing!* (1985), a travelogue of dance on the silver screen, hip-hop was treated as the foundational dance technique of the present moment. In scenes immediately following the film's opening credits, Kelly narrates as a group of breakdancers demonstrate their moves on a piece of cardboard in a gritty outdoor street. In two short years, Hollywood had absorbed popping, locking, and breaking, and transformed an aesthetic constellation of physical practice that spoke to political and social circumstances, to deploy it largely as a containable, shorthand narrative marker of race, class, and upward-mobility aspiration. Film 07.10 That's Dancing (1985) Gene Kelly ⏵

In all, as the *Breakin'* movies unequivocally confirm, these early hip-hop films were fast to make, and responded to the bubble of interest in hip-hop by cultural outsiders. The distribution of the imagery contained by these films spread hip-hop corporealities toward an eager and interested global public, one which quickly copied its moves and embraced its physical ideologies.[13] Throughout the 1990s, a rise in hip-hop dance classes and studio-based training practices led to the codification of hip-hop as a form with a pyramidal structure—something that could be learned from a teacher, rather than developed by the artists involved, as had been the standard of transmission until that time. This shift in teaching and transmission restabilized hip-hop as a form that could be controlled by the marketplace; a form suitable for film production that could be organized and overseen by a hired choreographer or dance director. Hip-hop dance moves continued to trade in the individual innovation of its practitioners, but over time, young artists contributed fewer and fewer movements to the choreographic soup that became screen versions of hip-hop dance.

The hip-hop body produced by these early hip-hop films arrived consistently in encounter with young people of color, with an interest in the possibility of group work to produce social change, and a resistance to standing traditions of control and authority exerted by those outside the group. These three imperatives of a hip-hop real spoke to the dissident, resistant impulses that had inspired hip-hop as a cultural form in the neighborhoods of the urban United States. Remarkably, the Hollywood film industry managed to absorb these conditions of hip-hop affiliation even in treacly, hegemonic commercial productions of the twenty-first century. If nothing else, this constructed hip-hop body made way for young artists of color to be included in Hollywood musicals, even if they would still not become the central characters; it offered narrative strategies of collective cooperation to disenfranchised youth, even if those film-character youth seldom wanted more than to save the community center/program in order to fight big business another day; and it confirmed the ability of young people to create their own expressive forms of culture, even if hip-hop film choreographers became essential to latter-day production teams. These achievements may not have been obvious for the earliest b-boys and b-girls whose movements were committed to celluloid, but the breaking they began surely continues.

Notes

1 Many thanks to Melissa Blanco Borelli, and members of the IFTR Choreography and Corporeality Working Group, for comments and prodding that aided the development of this work.

2. The Motion Picture Production Code, also known as the Hays code, was adopted by the precursor to the Motion Picture Association of America (MPAA) in 1930 and remained in effect until 1968. The code allowed censorship of Hollywood productions according to guidelines of moral decency. See http://en.wikipedia.org/wiki/Motion_Picture_Production_Code.

3. See *Teenagers and Teenpics: The Juvenilization of American Movies in the 1950s* by Thomas Doherty (Boston: Unwin Hyman, 1988).

4. Several contemporary studies of race, gender, and sexuality in Hollywood musicals offer alternative renderings of their contents; see *The Musical: Race, Gender and Performance* by Susan Smith (London and New York: Wallflower, 2005); and *The Hollywood Film Musical (New Approaches to Film Genre)* by Barry Keith Grant (Chichester: Wiley-Blackwell, 2012).

5. This narrative is repeated in virtually all of the documentaries of hip-hop referred to in this chapter.

6. See Sally Banes, "Breaking," in *Fresh: Hip Hop Don't Stop*, edited by Nelson George, Sally Banes, Susan Flinker, and Patty Romanovsky. New York: Random House, 1985, 79–112.

7. See http://www.commonsensemedia.org/movie-reviews/flashdance; accessed January 12, 2012.

8. See http://en.wikipedia.org/wiki/Flashdance; http://www.people.com/people/archive/article/0,20087493,00.html; accessed January 12, 2012.

9. For full cast information, see http://www.imdb.com/title/tt0084904/fullcredits#cast and http://en.wikipedia.org/wiki/Wild_Style.

10. According to the website http://boxofficemojo.com/movies/?id=breakin.htm, *Breakin'* earned 38,602,707 in lifetime domestic release, *Breakin'* 2 earned 15,101,131, http://boxofficemojo.com/movies/?id=breakin2.htm/, and *Beat Street* earned 16,595,791 http://boxofficemojo.com/movies/?id=beatstreet.htm.

11. Sound effects for this sequence have not been "sweetened" in any fashion to provide anchoring into an everyday world of gravity. Instead, we hear a poor pop song playing that may or may not actually go along with any of the dancing that Turbo performs. The disconnection of sound and image renders the sequence much less powerful than Fred Astaire's dance in *Royal Wedding* (1951), which included Foley sound effects that tied the dancer's movement to a normative gravity.

12. Note that there are few, if any, hip-hop dance films from the 1990s; the exception to this trope might be the highly successful *Save the Last Dance* (2001), which updates *Flashdance* with a white female theatrical dancer learning hip-hop, and taking on a black boyfriend, in order to successfully audition for the Juilliard School.

13. Scholar Mary Fogarty has called the connections among hip-hop devotees linked by film "imagined affinities." See Mary Fogarty "Breaking Expectations: Imagined Affinities in Mediated Youthf Cultures," *Continuum: Journal of Media & Cultural Studies*, 26:3, 449–462, 2012.

BIBLIOGRAPHY

Banes, Sally. "Breaking." In *Fresh: Hip Hop Don't Stop*, edited by Nelson George, Sally Banes, Susan Flinker, and Patty Romanovsky, 79–112. New York: Random House, 1985.

Doherty, Thomas. *Teenagers and Teenpics: The Juvenilization of American Movies in the 1950s.* Boston: Unwin Hyman, 1988.

Fogarty, Mary. "Breaking Expectations: Imagined Affinities in Mediated Youth Cultures." *Continuum: Journal of Media & Cultural Studies* 26:3 (2012): 449–462.

Grant, Barry Keith. *The Hollywood Film Musical (New Approaches to Film Genre).* Chichester: Wiley-Blackwell, 2012.

Smith, Susan. *The Musical: Race, Gender and Performance.* London and New York: Wallflower, 2005.

PART II

THE COMMERCIAL BIG SCREEN

CHAPTER 8

....

DIRTY DANCING: DANCE, CLASS, AND RACE IN THE PURSUIT OF WOMANHOOD

....

COLLEEN DUNAGAN AND ROXANE FENTON

THE link between dance and romantic love in film goes back at least as far as the films of Fred Astaire and Ginger Rogers in the 1930s. In each film, Astaire's character would pursue Rogers, wooing and ultimately winning her over through dance. (The characters even argued in movement.) When *Dirty Dancing* was released in 1987, it renewed the fascination with falling in love through dance for another generation. *Dirty Dancing* is not a musical, but rather a dance film, a genre in which characters dance, but only within the logical and realistic space of the film narrative (or diegetic space). Nevertheless, dancing plays a major role in propelling the narrative, and its ending recalls some key elements of classic film musicals. Like the Astaire-Rogers films, *Dirty Dancing* presents and reinforces widely held cultural ideas about romantic love, sex, and dance and the relationship among all three. Thus the movie participates in the perpetuation of myths of femininity and romantic love, and specifically the role the body and dance play in those constructions.[1]

Set in the summer of 1963, *Dirty Dancing* presents the coming-of-age story of seventeen-year-old Francis "Baby" Houseman (Jennifer Grey), an upper-middle-class Jewish teenager who spends the summer with her family at a resort in the Catskills. There she meets working-class dance instructor Johnny Castle (Patrick Swayze) and his dance partner Penny Johnson (Cynthia Rhodes). When the idealistic but naive Baby learns of Penny's unplanned pregnancy and need for an illegal abortion, she tries to help, stepping in to learn Penny's role in a dance exhibition number and perform with Johnny. The training montage that follows provides a filmic, narrative, and danced space apart from the rest of the resort where Baby can cross temporarily and safely into the sexualized, working-class world of the Other in order to discover her sexuality.[2] For Johnny, the attraction built between the two of them while dancing provides a personal touchstone that leads to his individual rejection, through dance, of the class position into which he has been placed.[3]

Director Emile Ardolino has said that he viewed the role of dance in *Dirty Dancing* as a metaphor for the paradigm shifts in politics and sexuality that would take place in the 1960s.[4] The sexual suggestiveness of the dancing then would stand for the atmosphere of greater sexual openness and exploration made possible in part by the introduction of the birth control pill. The film is set as the Civil Rights Movement was moving to the center of national politics, yet the film narrative makes almost no reference to those changes. Instead, it presents a rather color-blind approach to race, more in keeping with the dominant neo-conservative ideology of the 1980s, the decade in which the film was made, an ideology that claimed that the aims of the civil rights struggle had been achieved.[5]

Within the world of the film itself (diegesis), the dancing serves to advance the film's narrative and to develop character, in part, through the differences between dancing bodies and the changes dance facilitates in Baby, her relationship to Johnny, and the community. At the core of the film lies Baby's transformation from girl to woman, which is achieved not only metaphorically but also literally through dance. Thus, dance plays a central role in the narrative. Effecting this transformation through dance relies upon long-standing ideologies that link sex with dancing, so that the film reveals Baby's blossoming sexuality as being brought on by learning to dance and the resulting new awareness of her body.[6] A naturalized view of gender and gender identity, one commonly presented in mainstream American film, would suggest that the process of learning to dance allowed Baby to get in touch with the femininity that was already an essential part of her by virtue of biology or nature. However, by linking Baby's development as a woman with her development as a dancer, the film opens the possibility of reading that femininity as something that must be learned, through sweat and struggle, like dancing.[7] This presentation of ballroom dance in the film is in contrast to other ideologies of dance as a natural and spontaneous expression.[8] Thus, we argue the film presents Baby's character learning and adopting normative notions of femininity as she learns to dance. Further, by changing her body, Baby moves from a state of idealistic naivety to one of mature, sexualized womanhood. In doing so, she leaves behind blissful ignorance of ethnic, class, and gender differences and becomes aware of her own gendered social position.

As we will show, the camerawork and editing reinforce this transformation and the role of dance by gradually shifting the way Baby is shown from wide and medium shots to close-ups that fragment her dancing body in ways that emphasize gender and sexuality. This shift in how she is filmed is complemented by changes in how she dresses and moves, as her clothing becomes more revealing and her dancing more skilled. The opening and closing scenes of the movie highlight the change in Baby's character. As the Housemans drive to the resort in the opening scene, the film presents a contrast between Baby and her older sister Lisa. Lisa is concerned with stereotypically feminine things—boys and her appearance. Baby is an intellectual tomboy who wears jeans and reads books. By the final scene, however, Baby has adopted a more feminine appearance. The finale is the first and only time the film viewer sees Baby both dressed as a woman and comfortable displaying markers of adult femininity. She wears a form-fitting dress with a scooped neckline, make-up, and high-heeled shoes. In the end, Baby replaces her sister as the ideal by demonstrating her ability to combine moral substance with womanly appearance.

The journey between these two versions of Baby, who is finally called Francis at the very end of the movie, happens through dance. First, her lack of dance skills, and similarly her lack of awareness of her own body, are established. Almost immediately after the Houseman's arrive at the resort, we learn that Baby is not a dancer, as we watch her stamping and bopping with little body awareness during a group Merengue lesson. This scene helps set the stage for her growth as a dancer and her ascendancy through dance into womanhood. In the rest of the film, dance scenes show the development of both Baby's character and her relationship with Johnny. We watch Baby learn to dance, see the growth of her physical intimacy with Johnny, and observe class distinctions and transgressions made visible through their relationship.

Mambo and "Dirty Dancing"

We next see Baby dancing several scenes later, as she makes small talk with the resort owner's grandson Neil (Lonny Price) while doing a stilted box step in the resort's ballroom. As they dance rigidly to the counts, they maintain a very "proper" ballroom embrace with ample distance between their torsos and minimal contact through the hands. Neil is clearly presented as a socially acceptable partner and potential boyfriend, one who might even share her social concerns. In the film's only direct mention of the Civil Rights Movement, he tells Baby of his plans to participate in a freedom ride to the south at the end of the summer. Neil and his dancing fail to hold Baby's attention, however, once Mambo music begins playing and resort dance instructors Penny and Johnny perform an exhibition Mambo number from within the crowd on the dance floor.[9]

Throughout the subsequent dancing scene, the distance between Neil and Baby, on one hand, and Johnny and Penny, on the other, is emphasized and highlighted through the camerawork. While Baby and Neil are mostly shown in medium-wide shots that cut them off at the knees, Penny and Johnny's dancing skill is highlighted by the use of wide shots that show both their bodies and the choreography in their entirety.[10] The camera also establishes Baby's fascination with skilled dancing and with Johnny. As the dance continues, she gradually stops dancing to simply watch. At the same time, the editing cuts back and forth between shots of Baby and Neil watching and Baby's view of Johnny and Penny as they dance. As camera angles alternate, the camera cuts in closer to Baby, edging Neil out of the frame and focusing in on Baby's reaction to the performance (Fig. 8.1). Her face reveals a kind of nervous desire. Or perhaps the expression indicates a new physically and sensually grounded form of desire awakening in the previously naive Baby.

FIGURE 8.1 Screen Capture of *Dirty Dancing,* director Emile Ardolino (1987): the camera edges Neil out of frame while Baby watches in awe as Johnny and Penny dance the mambo.

Penny and Johnny represent the professional ballroom industry and the glamour it promises.[11] Johnny's last name, "Castle," calls up the legendary Vernon and Irene Castle, dance instructors and performers who set the fashion in the early twentieth century and who popularized "cleaned up" versions of black social dances for white middle- and upper-class dancers.[12] Therefore, it is not surprising that Penny and Johnny's Mambo is that of professional ballroom dancers—indeed, Johnny is an Arthur Murray–trained instructor. While their performance involves more of the body and a wider variety of steps than that of the surrounding middle-class couples, their version does not derive its skill or complexity from its relationship to the musical rhythms.

The Mambo originated in Havana, Cuba, in the 1930s and 40s. Initially "Mambo" was used to identify a trend in the existing *danzón* style, rather than to a separate dance form. It was not until the second half of the 1940s that new music was being labeled as Mambo and teachers were advertising a new dance form called Mambo.[13] While historical records show that there was disagreement about the basic step pattern(s) that constituted the Mambo, two groups of dancers in New York City were simultaneously developing the form: professional white studio dancers and Latin dancers living in Manhattan. According to David Garcia's sources, the Latin dancers were "incorporating their entire body" and embodying the "specific arrangements and musical events such as breaks and brass punches," while the professional dancers were more concerned with "using the so-called 'correct' foot patterns."[14] This split, as Garcia points out, was supported by a racialized view of the dance that saw the Latin style through the lens of "African primitivism."[15]

Reaching back to the period of slavery, Euro-Americans both distanced themselves from and were fascinated with African American music and dance. The trope of the primitive identified particular characteristics that were in conflict with middle- and upper-class European social and religions norms, and associated them with Africans, African Americans, and their cultural forms. The trope included both negative and positive traits, including sensuality; promiscuous sexuality; loss of bodily control; natural expressiveness; athletic and dancerly prowess; and a childlike innocence prone to irrational, excited behavior. This trope of the primitive served as means of Othering Africans and African Americans, positioning them in opposition to Euro-Americans and American culture at large. When Latin American dance began to enter into the discourse of American popular culture it too was seen through this trope of primitivism.[16] Euro-American desire for the socially forbidden traits associated with "primitive" dance forms has drawn generations of dancers to those forms, even as the dances themselves were altered to better fit the norms of white society.[17]

The development of the Mambo and the different ways of approaching the dance that Garcia describes were part of a long history in American social dance, stretching back at least to the quadrilles and cakewalks of the 1800s. New social dance forms developed within smaller communities, ones often delimited by race or class, and then were appropriated and gradually integrated into white mainstream popular culture. As dances were widely appropriated, popularized, and spread to middle- and upper-class white communities, they were altered—often by professional dance teachers—in a process that removed some of the markers of racial difference and worked to make the dances fit hegemonic gender and etiquette rules, particularly rules about sexual propriety.[18]

In the European-based forms that were considered acceptable, partnered dance sequences included held torsos, a standard embrace with limited body contact, verticality, and an emphasis on the feet as the most active body part. In these dances contact between partners was concentrated in the hands and arms, while gender roles dictated that the woman follow the man's lead. In contrast, dances arising within African American communities and those imported from Latin American countries (such as Cuba) have involved action in more of the body, and have therefore been viewed as both more emotionally expressive and more sexual. These non-European dance forms tend to incorporate the movement of the torso, as well as the arms and legs, and articulate the body through isolations that correspond to the syncopated rhythms of the music. In addition, the partnering in these forms included closer stances and greater torso contact than in the Euro-American style. They also allowed partners a greater degree of independence within the dance.[19]

While in the film we never see the Latin New York version of Mambo, Baby's exposure to the staff's "dirty dancing" later that night introduces a dance form that breaks the rules of the Euro-American ballroom. It is (sexually) excessive in its bodily behaviors, and appears improvised, spontaneous, and both emotionally and sexually expressive. Baby's initial encounter with the Mambo leaves her in awe of Penny and Johnny's skills as movers, and her exposure to the staff's dirty dancing later that same night sets into motion her desire for dance, and Johnny (Fig. 8.2). She accompanies Johnny's younger cousin Billy Kostecki (Neal Jones) to a party in the staff quarters, a clear transgression of the class hierarchy of the resort. As they enter the room where numerous couples are

FIGURE 8.2 Screen capture of *Dirty Dancing*, director Emile Ardolino (1987): the staff dirty dancing.

dancing, the camera follows along and then cuts back and forth between the dancers and Baby's face as she watches them. As Billy leads her through the crowd, the camera (via Steadicam) moves through the room as well, suturing Baby's gaze to that of the audience such that the viewer shares Baby's experience. The camera presents her gaze in close-ups of exposed female thighs, couples dancing pelvis to pelvis, most often with the woman straddling the man's thigh, and hips grinding to the hard pulse of the song. The camera's gaze catches bodies in medium close-up shots and then lazily drifts up or down the bodies. When the film cuts back to Baby, we see her openly staring, eyes wide and mouth slightly open—somewhere between wonder and shock. She is clearly fascinated by the sexual (and we will argue, racial) Otherness she sees.

Baby's fascination peaks when Johnny and Penny return from the ballroom and join the dancing. As the song ends, Johnny breaks off and beckons Baby onto the dance floor, where he tries to teach her dirty dancing (Fig. 8.3). He first tries to get her to isolate her pelvis and circle it, scooping down and back and then up and forward. In her initial attempts she sticks her butt out, so that her pelvis is locked back and away from his. Then, when he attempts to move closer, she either doesn't move her hips or awkwardly moves them at the wrong moments, making the dance look too much like the sex that it implies. Eventually, he has her riding his thigh, arms around his shoulders, as he sways her from side to side and leads her into circling backbends. She looks enraptured and naively thrilled to be in his arms. Baby's awkwardness in this moment highlights her lack of knowledge about dance, sex, men, and, more importantly, her body. The scene solidifies the difference between Baby and Johnny on a bodily level.

The dancing in the film is clearly marked by class difference and helps to signal classed spaces in the movie. Ballroom dance, including the white professional version

FIGURE 8.3 Screen capture of *Dirty Dancing,* director Emile Ardolino (1987): Baby's first awkward attempts to learn dirty dancing from Johnny.

of the Mambo danced by Penny and Johnny (and later Baby and Johnny), represents the (upper) middle-class world of the adult resort guests. Dirty dancing, on the other hand, marks the youthful world of the working-class entertainment staff. None of the dancing is directly depicted as racially marked. However, Baby's gendered transformation through dance is made possible by the ideologies that link excess bodily movement with sexual expressiveness, non-white bodies, and social dance. And, in fact, the class distinctions made through dance are based on and intimately connected with racial ones. Thus it matters that both the Mambo and dirty dancing still bear the traces of racial difference as they have been represented through movement and cultural transmission. We argue that both the Mambo and dirty dancing represent a racialized and sexualized Other for Baby to embody.

We read the African American and Latin influences in dirty dancing in various movement elements. The articulated spines, mobile hips and chests, sustained movement, and extended full body contact suggest historical African American social dances, such as the Slow Drag. There are also Latin dance resonances. While Ortega's choreography and the film's title have sometimes been linked to the Brazilian Lambada, which quickly rose and faded in prominence on the international dance scene during the mid-to-late 1980s, his version of dirty dancing is slower, less rhythmically driven, and more stationary than the Lambada. However, Ortega's dance does contain hip articulations and side-to-side steps that bear some resemblance to Lambada, Merengue, and today's Bochata.[20]

We are concerned with ways in which the racialized lineage/influences of the dancing can be read. In promotional material and commentary on the DVD, Ortega and screenwriter Ellen Bergstein present claims about both the historical authenticity and choreographic originality. Ortega calls dirty dancing, "a really wonderful idea based on authentic dance style of the early sixties, of the period."[21] Both Ortega and Bergstein make references to dancing in their youth as inspiration for the dirty dancing in the film. Ortega recalls the dancing as well as adults' reactions to it. He reminisces about slow dancing with a partner of the opposite sex in ways that involved "too much contact" and were "sexually suggestive." He recalls adults perceiving dancing as something that could lead to "improper behavior."[22]

Ortega's recollections suggest the Grind, which was popular among African American teenagers in the late 1950s and early 1960s. In *Watch Me Move*, a 1986 documentary on African American social dance, Merald "Bubba" Knight, brother of Gladys Knight and a member of the Pips, describes the Grind as a combination of slow dragging and stationary pelvic movement. Dancer and actress Paula Kelly-Chaffey goes on to describe dancers pressed against one another, holding each other under the buttocks, which is illustrated as she speaks in a short black-and-white film clip. Kelly-Chaffey points out that this dance was as close as you could get to "being with" someone of the opposite sex with your parents' sanction.[23]

In further comments about his own dance experiences, Ortega reveals some of the racial meanings they conveyed for him, and, we argue, signal racial meanings embedded in the film's dirty dancing. Ortega remembers "beautiful black girls" who would ask him to dance and who were the most "soulful creatures on the planet." He says that they, "woke me up" on several levels, and when he danced with them he became a "hot Latin heartbreaker." He attributes his becoming popular to his being able to get into special places with the music and dance in these racially marked experiences.[24] With these comments, Ortega obliquely perpetuates the stereotype of black women as highly sexual and of African American dance forms as sensual and emotionally transformative.[25]

Although Baby's transformation takes place explicitly through the more sexually modest ballroom Mambo, these associations called up in her first experience dancing with Johnny help establish both Baby's and the audience's expectations of the kind of changes to follow. From this point forward, Baby's actions are strongly motivated by her interest in Johnny. Her discovery of Penny's unplanned pregnancy sets in motion events that give her an opportunity to get closer to him.

LEARNING TO DANCE

When Penny's abortion interferes with her ability to perform at the Sheldrake, a neighboring resort, Johnny sarcastically suggests that Baby could do it, since she's the only one who isn't already working during the day. Despite his reservations, the others talk him into teaching Baby how to dance so that she can perform the exhibition routine. This encounter kicks off the Baby-learning-to-dance montage. Baby's relationship to Johnny is her relationship to the Mambo, and this dance montage depicts her journey from non-dancer to dancer as well as her journey from child to woman and from idealistic upper-middle-class white female to class-conscious rule breaker. This same process takes Johnny from disgruntled member of the working class who prostitutes himself with female resort guests to a redeemed worker who once again believes in the potential of the system despite the way it has failed him. Baby's efforts to learn the Mambo and Johnny's desire to teach her take place in a context of conflict and desire; their class affiliations position them in opposition to each other with Johnny as Other and Baby as unmarked (despite her Jewish ethnicity). It is this opposition that fuels their desire and serves as a narrative tension that runs parallel to Baby's learning to dance. In turn, the camera shots and editing within the montage work to highlight and develop this pairing of conflict and desire.

The filming process organizes the dancing into shots that convey emotion, character development, sexuality, and the work of learning to dance. These shot motivations are conveyed through close-ups that fragment the body, medium-wide shots that provide detail while still revealing most of the choreography, and wide shots that show whole the entire body and its mastery of the choreography. Furthermore, Baby's increased dance skill is paired with changes in her clothing in order to link her transformation from tomboy to sexually aware woman with her mastery of dance. Although Baby's experience learning to dance the Mambo takes up a significant portion of the film and includes both a montage and more substantial scenes, our analysis summarizes these effects and looks at just three examples.[26]

In one scene, set in the resort's dance studio, Johnny and Penny work together to teach Baby to dance. According to assistant choreographer Miranda Garrison, she and Ortega drew upon her experience as an Arthur Murray instructor to bring authenticity to the both the dance sequences and to the education of Jennifer Grey as Baby. Grey was taught to dance in real time over the course of filming the movie, so that rather than watching someone pretend to learn to dance, audiences, in one sense, actually experienced Grey's dance education. They suggest this was intentional, designed to get the desired effect from her character.[27] The use of Arthur Murray teaching methods then furthers this sense of authenticity with regard to the "work" of learning to dance. In addition, the use of Murray techniques demonstrates the sexual politics of ballroom dance for the film's audience.

As Johnny teaches Baby the importance of keeping her arms firm (this is your dance space, this my dance space), he teaches her how to define her kinesphere and the importance of maintaining distance and control within the dance form. Murray's techniques also allow us to witness the physical transference of female sexuality from Penny to Baby. Per Garrison's instruction, the scene includes a shot of Baby and Johnny dancing while Penny shadows Baby (Fig. 8.4). She dances directly behind her with one hand on Baby's mid-back and one on her hip. Penny directs Baby, reinforcing verticality, control of the spine, and the hip isolations that facilitate the rhythmic pattern of the feet. It almost looks like Penny is holding Baby in place, cementing her into this new physicality.[28] Baby's clothing is shifting as well, becoming more revealing and more clearly feminine. In this scene, Baby wears a modest sixties-style lavender bikini with short-like bottoms. This is the most revealing of her outfits so far and is one step closer to Penny's dancewear (black tights, a black leotard, and a leopard print belt in this scene). As Penny

FIGURE 8.4 Screen capture of *Dirty Dancing*, director Emile Ardolino (1987): Penny assists Johnny in teaching Baby to dance.

dances with Baby and Johnny, "Hungry Eyes," a pop ballad written by Eric Carmen for the movie, takes over the soundtrack and all diegetic sounds. This song carries us into the next set of shots.

Our second example comprises two sequences of shots that appear to take place on a stage. These sequences are important because the shots are all close-ups that fragment their bodies into three parts: upper body, torso from chest to hips, and legs and feet. As Sherril Dodds notes in her book *Dance on Screen*, this kind of fragmentation creates and reinforces associations between body parts and specific values or meanings, linking them to dance. According to Dodds, shots of the feet reveal the work and specificity of the dance form, shots of the upper body convey emotional and intellectual effort, and shots of the torso and pelvis present sexual bodies and display the physical intimacy of the dance.[29] Rather than use dance doubles, as was the case in *Flashdance*, which Dodds analyzes, the creators of *Dirty Dancing* required all the actors to do their own dancing. Because director Ardolino did not need to choose shots in order to give the impression of one person dancing, we feel even more confident in reading these meanings into the close-up shots in the learning montage.

In the sequence with Baby and Johnny dancing on stage, the shots of their legs gradually reveal increasing sophistication in her performance of steps. At the beginning, Baby wears tennis shoes, drops her heels, and steps on the wrong counts (Fig. 8.5). As the shots of her feet change, she wears silver high heels, steps on relevé, and performs the correct rhythmic pattern and steps (Fig. 8.6). These shots of her feet reveal the way in which the labor of dance is tied to gendered behavior—tennis shoes are linked to her tomboyish nature and lack of skill, while high heels are symbolic of her successful embodiment of both dance and femininity. In a second sequence later in the montage,

FIGURE 8.5 Screen capture of *Dirty Dancing,* director Emile Ardolino (1987): Baby, in her tennis shoes, dancing with Johnny as he teaches her.

FIGURE 8.6 Screen capture of *Dirty Dancing,* director Emile Ardolino (1987): Baby's lessons progress, and she graduates to heels.

the use of body-fragmenting close-ups returns. Shots of their legs continue to reveal her efforts to master step patterns, and head shots show Johnny encouraging her and both of them concentrating. But this sequence begins with a close-up of Baby's torso, from breasts to upper thighs, moving with the steps as she dances. Culturally speaking, the shot focuses on the most sexualized parts of a woman's body and their articulation furthers this sexualisation. These torso shots emphasize the progress Baby has made in assuming more feminine (and objectifying) dress and show the results of her efforts to bring her behavior in line with her clothes. She now wears flesh-colored tights, leotard bottoms, and a white V-neck crop top that ends at the bra line.[30]

The efforts of the montage to depict Baby's gradual acceptance of and success at embodying this sexualized femininity culminate as "Hungry Eyes" comes to a close. The final sequence of shots involves her and Johnny's repeated attempts to master a bit of upper-body choreography. In this move they stand with her back against the front of his torso. He lifts her arm up to cradle his head and then teases his fingers down the inside of her arm and along the side of her torso to take her other hand at her waist. This shot is repeated. The first two times, she begins to giggle as he traces the line of her arm, so that he is forced to stop and start over. Once she manages to maintain her composure, the audience is rewarded with the completed sequence. As Baby masters her discomfort, the mood becomes more sensual. Her eyelids droop and she rests her head slightly against Johnny's bare chest. His hand lingers as it traces its path. The camera pans to follow this action in a close-up shot, emphasizing how daringly close his hand comes to her breast and allowing the viewer to revel in the intimacy of the choreography. The scene is a vivid example of how Baby is learning not only how to dance but also how to be a sexual being.

The remainder of the film presents the final stages of Baby's transformation from girl to woman through her eventual mastery of the exhibition ballroom dance, which only reaches its highest level once she has finally had sex with Johnny. The audience first sees the exhibition dance in its entirety when Johnny and Baby perform at the Sheldrake, but Baby is clearly nervous (Fig. 8.7), and she fails to complete the lift and performs other aspects of the choreography worse than we saw in the rehearsal montage. She also wears makeup and an adult dress publicly for the first time, but she does not appear comfortable in them. She has made progress in both her dance skill and her growth into

FIGURE 8.7 Screen capture of *Dirty Dancing*, director Emile Ardolino (1987): an awkward moment as Baby and Johnny perform at the Sheldrake.

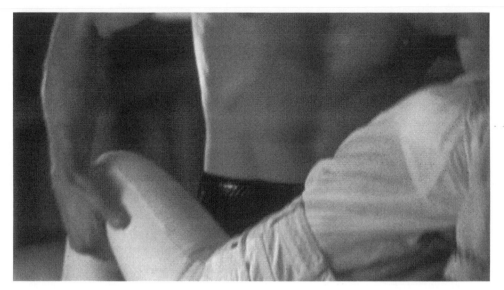

FIGURE 8.8 Screen capture of *Dirty Dancing,* director Emile Ardolino (1987): Baby masters dirty dancing with Johnny.

womanhood, but she is not yet proficient at either. This performance also provides the moment in which Johnny's feelings for Baby become solidified, which we discover when he peeps in the rearview mirror as she is changing in the backseat on the way back to the resort.

Baby never fully performs dirty dancing as the staff does it, but her earlier attempt with Johnny in the staff house lives up to its romantic and sexual promise when she goes to him in his cabin later that same night. As they dance to a record he has on, "Cry to Me" (Solomon Burke, 1962), there are a few allusions to the earlier dirty dancing (Fig. 8.8). In one, he dips her, and she allows herself to release her weight to him, trusting him as she smoothly and sexily arches backwards. The dancing this time leads up to sex.

We next see them dance together in the playful scene in the dance studio as they flirt to "Love is Strange" (Micky and Sylvia, 1957). Baby now appears comfortable both in her body and with sensual, flirtatious movement. We argue that on the surface, the film links spontaneous dancing with sex and sexualized body awareness. As we have pointed out, such awareness is also linked to class, and although it is not acknowledged in the film, to race, through cultural ideologies of sexualized racial marking. The transgressive nature of their now sexual relationship returns to the fore as further narrative events cast them both, temporarily, out their respective social positions.

THE FINALE

The idyll of Johnny and Baby's romance comes to an end when Johnny is accused of theft. Baby reveals their relationship in an effort to protect him, but he is fired anyway for their relationship (and the class transgression it represents). In the process, Baby is further distanced from her father. This turn of events sets the stage for the final scene of the movie when Johnny defies authority in order to come back to the resort and dance the final dance with Baby and the entertainment staff. It is the culminating moment in which the themes and actions of the narrative find their resolution in a utopia founded on dance. The now famous line, "Nobody puts Baby in a corner," captures the irony of this dance utopia. The line is delivered by working-class Johnny Castle to Baby's father, the upper-middle-class doctor, and signifies Johnny's decision to stand up for himself by standing up for Baby. At the same time, while the line suggests Baby's independence as a woman, the continued use of her nickname, with its diminutive nature, and the fact that it is Johnny (a man) who utters this statement sutures her into the "appropriate" heterosexual gender role. This action is somewhat redeemed or softened when Johnny introduces her to the audience as "Francis Houseman." The use of her given name acknowledges her growth and signals to the film viewers that what comes next is the last step in her transformation. However, the utopia promised by dance is one grounded in self-defeating contradictions. Johnny's power to overcome class differences really resides in Baby, who stays safely tucked inside her own class even as she performs Johnny's working-class, racially marked dancing. Ultimately, the independence and knowledge that Baby gains from Johnny (and dance) remain dependent upon her adoption of normative female gender characteristics.

As suits this utopic space, in the final dance we see the exhibition choreography as we imagine it is meant to be performed. There is an ease to Baby and Johnny's interactions and partnering—they seem at home with one another, and Baby appears comfortable with her body and the dance. The camera allows us to fully appreciate this transformation by capturing a significant portion of the performance in wide shots that show their full bodies as well as the stage space. In addition, the dance is shot in its entirety, though from more than one angle, and edited to maintain the continuity of the choreography— all of which serve to remind us of the cinematic aesthetic of Fred Astaire and Ginger Rogers's musical numbers and their emphasis on a fairy tale world of luxury in which dance unites the couple. However, unlike the Astaire-Rogers numbers, the camerawork highlights the emotional content of the scene by incorporating a number of medium shots of their upper bodies, allowing the audience to witness their connection while limiting our ability to see the totality of movement. Then, in a manner reminiscent of film musicals, the power of dance transforms the narrative space when Johnny leaps from the stage to lead the staff members onto the floor in the choreography that he has been working on, which they, of course, all seem to know even though he was not allowed to direct the last dance of the season.[31]

Film viewers are assured of their union and that Baby's transformation into dancer and woman is complete when she triumphantly completes the lift she had been unable to do at the Sheldrake (Fig. 8.9). She is literally elevated by Johnny in this moment; it is the choreographic embodiment of his relationship to her and her assimilation into her gender role. Furthermore, the lift is evidence that dance can lift all of us above or out of our problems, and the achievement of the lift transforms the narrative as the dancing

FIGURE 8.9 Screen capture of *Dirty Dancing,* director Emile Ardolino (1987): Baby takes flight in the final dance.

spreads throughout the audience and carries the film into an idyllic space. As the staff continues dancing, they clear the chairs out of the way and draw the audience up to dance with them. While the film never fully leaves the diegetic space, the spontaneous dance communion of staff and guests evokes the utopic space of the film musical number—a space in which anything can happen and dancing is a normal form of human expression.[32]

The final dance suggests that a new era is arriving. *Dirty Dancing* shares with the golden age of film musicals the evocation of nostalgia for mythic cultural elements as a means to ushering in or making us at ease with contemporary cultural values. As a result, the utopic image always carries unresolved contradictions within itself. Max Kellerman and his bandleader Tito Suarez discuss this in terms of the resort's business and generational change. In turn, the dance style introduced by Johnny seems to offer a glimmer of new life to the resort through youth culture, but leaves class differences unresolved. Furthermore, the achievement of utopia through dance is undercut by the film viewer's knowledge that the reunion of Johnny and Baby is temporary.

This final dance offers contradictions for Johnny's character too. With its blending of ballroom and staff dance styles, it seems to provide Johnny with a chance to escape the failed promise of the ballroom dance industry and present his own choreography and new approach to dance. In the commentary, Garrison frames this as an escape from the restrictions of the Arthur Murray dance style and business model.[33] However, it is not clear what substantive career opportunities this new dance offers him.

In a final contradiction, the film's narrative relies on the association of dance with sex, but the final utopia achieved as a result of dance's transformative power is one based on

FIGURE 8.10 Screen capture of *Dirty Dancing,* director Emile Ardolino (1987): two older female resort patrons throw off their furs and join the staff in a final dance.

escaping the bounds of class, ethnicity, and perhaps race. The film's viewers may think of the turmoil of the 1960s and the Civil Rights Movement. Instead, the film presents a color-blind vision of race relations fully representative of the dominant attitudes toward race in the Reagan years of the 1980s. In the finale, a multicultural world of equality is presented through the dancing, as elderly white women toss off their furs to adopt torso and pelvic articulations that exceed the boundaries of the Euro-American ballroom's confined center (Fig. 8.10).

NOTES

1. We mean myth in the sense used by Roland Barthes, as a naturalized and widely held cultural belief. Roland Barthes, *Mythologies*, trans. Annete Lavers (New York: Hill and Wang, 1972).
2. For an account of the construction of otherness as based on class, race, and gender within the context of the tango, see Marta E. Savigliano, *Tango and the Political Economy of Passion* (San Francisco: Westview Press, 1995).
3. The core of our argument regarding the intersections of class and sex in the transformation of Baby corresponds to the reading of the film's narrative provided by Juliet McMains. In her book on the ballroom industry in America, McMains uses Baby's character development and discovery of dance as an example of the "layering of sexual and class transgression" that lies within the concept of "Glamour" at work within DanceSport. Juliet McMains, *Glamour Addiction: Inside the American Ballroom Dance Industry* (Middletown, CT: Wesleyan University Press, 2006), 8–9.

4. Quoted in Larry Billman, *Film Choreographers and Dance Directors: An Illustrated Biographical Encyclopedia with a History and Filmographies, 1893 through 1995* (Jefferson, NC: McFarland & Co., 1997), 160.

5. For a discussion of neo-conservative ideologies of race in 1980s America, see Michael Omi and Howard Winant, *Racial Formation in the United States from the 1960s to the 1990s* (New York: Routledge, 1994).

6. Dancing's association with sex has been analyzed by a number of scholars. Two notable examples are Susan Leigh Foster, "The Ballerina's Phallic Pointe," in *Corporealities*, ed. Susan Leigh Foster (New York: Routledge, 1996) and Linda J. Tomko, *Dancing Class: Gender, Ethnicity, and Social Divides in American Dance* (Bloomington: Indiana University Press, 1999). Tomko's text is particularly relevant to the dynamic at work in the film, as she looks at social dance during the early part of the twentieth century and its role in gender, ethnicity, and class formations.

7. A great deal has been written across many fields about the social construction of gender. Two authors who write about the issue in different ways are Judith Butler and Iris Marion Young. Judith Butler, *Gender Trouble: Feminism and the Subversion of Identity*, 2nd. ed. (New York: Routledge, 1999) and Iris Marion Young, "Lived Body vs. Gender: Reflections on Social Structure and Subjectivity," *Ratio (new series)* 15, no. 4 (2002).

8. Often, this understanding of dance is linked to race. Two accounts of the consequences for African America dancers are Brenda Dixon Gottschild, *Waltzing in the Dark: African American Vaudeville and Race Politics in the Swing Era* (New York: St. Martin's Press, 2000) and Julia L. Foulkes, *Modern Bodies: Dance and American Modernism from Martha Graham to Alvin Ailey* (Chapel Hill: University of North Carolina Press, 2002).

9. There is some rupture in the film's continuity regarding this dance and the one Johnny and Baby perform at the Sheldrake and in the final show. All three dances are choreographically similar (though not identical), and both Penny and Johnny's original dance and the exhibition at the Sheldrake are identified by characters as the Mambo. Further, the chapter title for the learning montage on the DVD is "Mambo 101." However, the montage is interrupted by a scene in which Johnny tells Baby, "It's not on the one; it's not the Mambo." We interpret this statement as an error in continuity, because we argue that all three of these dances are built upon the ballroom form of the Mambo and any variations in the choreography are driven by narrative concerns.

10. Some of the major aesthetic shifts in the camera-choreography relationship throughout the film musical genre in the twentieth century and the effect this relationship has on dance's position within the film as a whole are discussed in greater depth in Jerome Delamater, *Dance in the Hollywood Musical* (Ann Arbor, MI: UMI Research Press, 1981).

11. McMains, *Glamour Addiction*.

12. A number of scholars have examined the careers of the Castles and other professional dancers and instructors who "cleaned up" African American and other dances for white ballrooms. We list three who have written about this practice in the early twentieth century. Susan Cook, "Passionless Dancing and Passionate Reform: Respectability, Modernism, and the Social Dancing of Vernon and Irene Castle," in *The Passion of Music and Dance: Body, Gender, and Sexuality*, ed. William Washbaugh (New York: Berg, 1998). Julie Malnig, *Dancing Till Dawn: A Century of Exhibition Ballroom Dance* (New York: New York University Press, 1992). Danielle Robinson, "Performing American: Ragtime Dancing as Participatory Minstrelsy," *Dance Chronicle* 32 (2009).

13. David F. Garcia, "Embodying Music/Disciplining Dance: The Mambo Body in Havana and New York City," in *Ballroom, Boogie, Shimmy Sham, Shake: A Social and Popular Dance Reader*, ed. Julie Malnig (Urbana: Univeristy of Ilinois Press, 2009).
14. Garcia, "Embodying Music," 172.
15. Garcia, "Embodying Music," 175.
16. See Brenda Dixon Gottschild, *Digging the Africanist Presence in American Performance: Dance and Other Contexts* (Westport, CT: Greenwood Press, 1996), 21–46. Foulkes, *Modern Bodies*, 51–78.
17. Homi Bhaba has theorized this dual rejection and fascination as part of colonialism. Homi K. Bhabha, *The Location of Culture* (New York: Routledge, 1994). Eric Lott has written about a similar dynamic within the audiences for early minstrel shows. Eric Lott, *Love and Theft: Blackface Minstrelsy and the American Working Class* (New York: Oxford University Press, 1993).
18. Cook, "Passionless Dancing." Malnig, *Dancing Till Dawn*.
19. Gottschild, *Digging the Africanist Presence*, 1–10. Robinson, "Performing American," 101–105. McMains, *Glamour Addiction*, 109–131.
20. Anuradha Muralidharan, "Lambada: Not Really Dirty Dancing!," 2007, Suite 101.com, http://worlddance.suite101.com/article.cfm/lambada (accessed July 15, 2010).
21. This is from a "making-of" promotional spot from the 1980s, which is included on the special features disc, under interviews. It is not titled, but can be reached by clicking on the unlabeled dancing couple icon. Eleanor Bergstein, "Dirty Dancing: Ultimate Edition," ed. Emile Ardolino (Lionsgate, 1997 (1987)).
22. Commentary track, Bergstein, "Dirty Dancing."
23. Arthur Cromwell, producer, W. E. Baker, director. *Watch Me Move*. Los Angeles: KCET-TV, 1986.
24. Commentary track, Bergstein, "Dirty Dancing."
25. On stereotypes of women of color see Ananya Chatterjea, *Butting Out: Reading Resistive Choreographies through Works by Jawole Willa Jo Zollar and Chandralekha* (Middletown, CT: Wesleyan University Press, 2004).
26. Lesley Vize's analysis has created a detailed chart of shots, music, and dance in the training montage. Our analysis has a different focus but covers some similar ground. Lesley Vize, "Music and the Body in Dance Film," in *Popular Music and Film*, ed. Ian Inglis (London: Wallflower Press, 2003).
27. Commentary track. Bergstein, "Dirty Dancing."
28. On constructions of traditional female physicality, see Iris Marion Young, *Throwing Like a Girl and Other Essays in Feminist Philosophy and Social Theory* (Bloomington: Indiana University Press, 1990), 141–159.
29. Sherril Dodds, *Dance on Screen: Genres and Media from Hollywood to Experimental Art*, 2nd ed. (New York: Palgrave, Macmillan, 2004), 37–44.
30. This treatment of the female body as sexual object through dress and camera has a long history within the film musical genre. Dance Director Busby Berkeley is notable for his extreme use of this element—see Lucy Fischer, "The Image of Women as Image: The Optical Politics of Dames," in *Genre: The Musical—A Reader*, ed. Rick Altman (New York: Routledge & Kegan Paul, 1981).
31. Two texts that provide more detailed analyses of the film musical genre and the narrative-to-number relationship are Rick Altman, *The American Film Musical* (Bloomington: Indiana University Press, 1987) and Martin Rubin, *Showstoppers: Busby Berkeley and the Tradition of Spectacle* (New York: Columbia University Press, 1993).

32. Richard Dyer, *Only Entertainment* (New York: Routledge, 1992). Altman, *American Film Musical*.

33. In the commentary, Ortega notes that he drew on his Cuban and Spanish heritage to incorporate Latin rhythm steps, blending the ballroom and the "world of dirty dancing" to create what he calls "dirty Mambo." Bergstein, "Dirty Dancing."

BIBLIOGRAPHY

Altman, Rick. *The American Film Musical*. Bloomington: Indiana University Press, 1987.

Barthes, Roland. *Mythologies*. Translated by Annete Lavers. New York: Hill and Wang, 1972.

Bergstein, Eleanor. "Dirty Dancing: Ultimate Edition." Edited by Emile Ardolino. DVD Lionsgate, 1997.

Bhabha, Homi K. *The Location of Culture*. New York: Routledge, 1994.

Billman, Larry. *Film Choreographers and Dance Directors: An Illustrated Biographical Encyclopedia with a History and Filmographies, 1893 through 1995*. Jefferson, NC: McFarland & Co., 1997.

Butler, Judith. *Gender Trouble: Feminism and the Subversion of Identity*. Second edition. New York: Routledge, 1999.

Chatterjea, Ananya. *Butting Out: Reading Resistive Choreographies through Works by Jawole Willa Jo Zollar and Chandralekha*. Middletown, CT: Wesleyan University Press, 2004.

Cook, Susan. "Passionless Dancing and Passionate Reform: Respectability, Modernism, and the Social Dancing of Vernon and Irene Castle." In *The Passion of Music and Dance: Body, Gender, and Sexuality*, edited by William Washbaugh, 133–150. New York: Berg, 1998.

Cromwell, Arthur, producer. W.E. Baker, director. *Watch Me Move*. TV broadcast. Los Angeles: KCET-TV, 1986.

Delamater, Jerome. *Dance in the Hollywood Musical*. Ann Arbor: UMI Research Press, 1981.

Dodds, Sherril. *Dance on Screen: Genres and Media from Hollywood to Experimental Art*. Second edition. New York: Palgrave, Macmillan, 2004.

Dyer, Richard. *Only Entertainment*. New York: Routledge, 1992.

Fischer, Lucy. "The Image of Women as Image: The Optical Politics of Dames." In *Genre: The Musical—A Reader*, edited by Rick Altman, 70–84. New York: Routledge & Kegan Paul, 1981.

Foster, Susan Leigh. "The Ballerina's Phallic Pointe." In *Corporealities*, edited by Susan Leigh Foster, 1–24. New York: Routledge, 1996.

Foulkes, Julia L. *Modern Bodies: Dance and American Modernism from Martha Graham to Alvin Ailey*. Chapel Hill: University of North Carolina Press, 2002.

Garcia, David F. "Embodying Music/Disciplining Dance: The Mambo Body in Havana and New York City." In *Ballroom, Boogie, Shimmy Sham, Shake: A Social and Popular Dance Reader*, edited by Julie Malnig, 165–181. Urbana: University of Illinois Press, 2009.

Gottschild, Brenda Dixon. *Digging the Africanist Presence in American Performance: Dance and Other Contexts*. Westport, CT: Greenwood Press, 1996.

Gottschild, Brenda Dixon. *Waltzing in the Dark: African American Vaudeville and Race Politics in the Swing Era*. New York: St. Martin's Press, 2000.

Lott, Eric. *Love and Theft: Blackface Minstrelsy and the American Working Class*. New York: Oxford University Press, 1993.

Malnig, Julie. *Dancing Till Dawn: A Century of Exhibition Ballroom Dance*. New York: New York University Press, 1992.

McMains, Juliet. *Glamour Addiction: Inside the American Ballroom Dance Industry.* Middletown, CT: Wesleyan University Press, 2006.

Muralidharan, Anuradha. "Lambada: Not Really Dirty Dancing!" Accessed July 15, 2010. http://worlddance.suite101.com/article.cfm/lambada.

Omi, Michael, and Howard Winant. *Racial Formation in the United States from the 1960s to the 1990s.* New York: Routledge, 1994.

Robinson, Danielle. "Performing American: Ragtime Dancing as Participatory Minstrelsy." *Dance Chronicle* 32 (2009): 89–126.

Rubin, Martin. *Showstoppers: Busby Berkeley and the Tradition of Spectacle.* New York: Columbia University Press, 1993.

Savigliano, Marta E. *Tango and the Political Economy of Passion.* San Francisco: Westview Press, 1995.

Tomko, Linda J. *Dancing Class: Gender, Ethnicity, and Social Divides in American Dance.* Bloomington: Indiana University Press, 1999.

Vize, Lesley. "Music and the Body in Dance Film." In *Popular Music and Film*, edited by Ian Inglis, 22–38. London: Wallflower Press, 2003.

Young, Iris Marion. "Lived Body vs. Gender: Reflections on Social Structure and Subjectivity." *Ratio (new series)* 15, no. 4 (2002): 410–428.

Young, Iris Marion. *Throwing Like a Girl and Other Essays in Feminist Philosophy and Social Theory.* Bloomington: Indiana University Press, 1990.

CHAPTER 9

···

DISPLACE AND BE QUEEN: GENDER AND INTERCULTURALISM IN *DIRTY DANCING: HAVANA NIGHTS* (2004)

···

CINDY GARCÍA

POSTCARD PROJECTIONS

···

In the opening of *Dirty Dancing: Havana Nights*,[1] protagonist Katey Miller[2] reconstructs the memory of her unexpected and undesired relocation to a prerevolutionary Cuba in November 1958.[3] Interrupting the trajectory of Katey's senior year of high school and her plans to go to college, her father follows his career with Ford Motor Company and moves his white, upper-middle-class family to Cuba. Cityscapes of Havana, through the sound and flash of a camera shot, turn into postcards—with captions that read "Visit the Isle of Romance" and "Holiday Isle of the Tropics"—and then change back into live action shots (Fig. 9.1). The images freeze the U.S. imagination of Cuba as a playground for U.S. Americans. Popping in and out of this colorful opening collage, snapshots of Katey and other girls from her U.S. high school yearbook black-and-whitely fuel the binary opposition between the modest upper-middle-class femininity of a rational, stable United States and the uncontained, sexualized femininity of a volatile Cuba. The postcard image of a smiling Cubana dancing beneath a palm tree, swirling the white ruffles of her skirt, contrasts severely with Katey in a somber black sweater, withdrawn in the backseat, as she rolls into Havana. The visual dissimilarities in the first minute of the movie between her still, lost-in-thought body and the bodies of dancing Cuban women not only distinguish the bodies of the women from each other in terms of race,

FIGURE 9.1 Katey's (Romola Garai) body displaces the image of a dancing Cuban woman on a postcard in the opening of *Dirty Dancing: Havana Nights* (2004). (DVD capture from *Dirty Dancing: Havana Nights*, directed by Guy Ferland, produced by Lions Gate Films, Miramax Films, Lawrence Bender Productions).

class, and nation, but also foreshadow Katey's thirst to learn mambo in the "land of fiestas and siestas."

In these brief opening seconds, the film captures the story of Katey's sexual awakening. Cinematic portrayals of women in dance films often produce scenarios in which Anglo leading ladies displace women of color who are featured extras or supporting actresses on the dance floor. Such is the case in *Dirty Dancing: Havana Nights* as Katey begins to discover her sexuality while learning to dance with Javier Suarez,[4] a young Cuban waiter at her hotel. I argue that Katey's intercultural coming-of-age happens at the expense of and through the dispensing of the Cuban women in the film.

Dirty Dancing: Havana Nights follows the Hollywood trend of foregrounding the heterosexual romances in films about Latin American, Latino, and Caribbean-based popular partner dance genres. Within this lineage, *Dirty Dancing* (1987)[5] highlights class tensions between the "proper" ballroom mambo and the underground "dirty" social dancing of the resort workers in the Catskill Mountains; *Salsa—The Motion Picture* (1988)[6] features the nightclub salsa of East L.A.; and *Dance With Me* (1998)[7] contrasts the dance competitions of Latin ballroom with the social practice of Cuban casino and rumba in Houston. The story of *Havana Nights* takes place in Cuba[8] and depicts the opposition between the Americanized ballroom mambo and the "dirty" hypersexualized moves of nightclub partner dance. In this dance film genre, *Havana Nights* continues to consume Caribbean-based Latina/o-ness through the eroticized heterosexual dance practices. With this analysis, however, I find that the consumption and displacement of Latina-ness, in this case, Cubana-ness, drives the euphoric intercultur-alism of this dance romance. *Havana Nights* reflects that the gendered costs of intercul-turalism become naturalized within Latino/Caribbean dance in the U.S. imaginary.

In this chapter, I examine how blond (United States of) American teen Katey Miller's transition to life in Havana and her emergent fascination with Cuban dance practices can be understood by closely reading her relationships with Cuban women. I trace the representation of American and Cuban femininities in this Hollywood production to elucidate how the themes of difference, fear, and fascination projected onto the Cubana dancing body legitimate Katey's ultimate choreographic displacement of Cuban women on the dance floor. Through such a reading that pays attention to the relationship of women and of the main character's interactions with peripheral characters, I follow a well-established practice in film analytical reading practice that focuses on characters in the margins. Such an analytical practice can offer insight into the ways that the film configures relations of race and gender within the context of U.S. popular culture.[9] My main interest here, however, is to take this periphery-to-center reading practice fur-ther through my attention to the contrasting corporealities of American and Cuban women. How does attention to the relationships between Katey and the Cuban women in the film shed light on understandings of interculturalism? What does an analysis of moving bodies bring to understandings of American and Cuban femininities? While mainstream films such as *Havana Nights* might "direct" us to identify with the hetero-sexual spectacle of Katey's sexual awakening in Javier's mambo embrace, my intention is to offer an alternate reading based on the homosocial interactions that occur in the periphery.

"THIS IS CUBA: NOBODY CARES WHAT YOU DO HERE"

Havana Nights gives insight into the attitudes of the United States toward Cuba and Cubans in the 1950s, which is when the story is set, as well as in the 1990s, when the film was made. In 1950s Cuba, many U.S. businesses advertised and sold products in Cuba. Ford Motor Company, who transfers Katey's father to Havana in the narrative, operated 35 dealerships across the country (Pérez: 336). Fulgencio Batista was the U.S.-backed dic-tator of Cuba who allowed the U.S. Mafia to open and control casinos and U.S. corpora-tions to profit. As Carlos,[10] Javier's brother, tells Katey, "You Yankees, you come here and you pour money into the casinos, into the pockets of the gangsters who run this coun-try." At this time in Cuba's prerevolutionary history, U.S. Americans took advantage of Cuba as a tourist destination where they could gamble and engage in prostitution freely. Sheila, one of the high school girls smoking a cigarette poolside at Katey's hotel sum-marizes, "This is Cuba. Nobody cares what you do here." With the Cuban Revolution in 1959, however, Fidel Castro nationalized the land that American companies had bought, and he shut down the prostitution and gambling rings. *Havana Nights* does not explicitly deal with the politics and particulars of the revolution or the U.S. postrevolutionary fear and loathing of Fidel Castro and the perceived threat of communism. Instead, the film focuses on the melodrama of the revolution as it comes between Katey and Javier's passionate dance relationship.

Yet, even though the film is about dance, the production is also not concerned with historically accurate representations of dance and music from 1950s Cuba. Some of the dance moves in the film, such as the drop performed by couple number two at the Latin Ballroom competition finals, appear to anachronistically come from salsa practices associated with Los Angeles of the late 1990s. The music played at La Rosa Negra is salsa or salsa infused with hip-hop sounds by artists like Wyclef Jean ("Dance Like This"), Mya ("Do You Only Wanna Dance"), and Orishas ("Represent, Cuba"). I do not highlight these anachronisms in order to critique the film for its inaccuracies, but rather to show how the production employs these more contemporary moves and artists to create a heightened sense of racialized eroticism for film audiences of the new millennium.

Released in 2004, the film appears after the Buena Vista Social Club, the legendary Cuban musicians with a prerevolutionary sound, instigated a new appreciation/consumption of Cuban music in the United States in the 1990s (Keach: 114). Cuban dance genres such as casino started to more widely circulate in U.S. salsa spaces, exoticized and incorporated as legitimate along with the popular social dance practices associated with Puerto Rico, New York, and Los Angeles. Much of the movement performed at La Rosa Negra, however, consists of rhythmic bumping and grinding, unidentifiable with any particular Latino/Caribbean dance genre.

FEMININITIES IN CONTENTION

In the introductory narrative, Katey establishes her own rational, educated femininity through voice-over. She identifies herself as more studious and less frivolous than the other girls at her high school—they want to talk about prom, she wants to read Jane Austen—and implies that her intellectual goals will not be achieved while living in a place like Cuba. Fifty-seven seconds into the opening sequence, the film continues to represent Katey's femininity as associated with the intellect in sharp contrast to Cuban femininity as associated with a hypersexualized body.[11] Katey and a Cuban woman briefly partner each other, though not in the same frame. Katey stands stiff and uncertain before a life-sized postcard of Havana. The scene cuts to a blurred image that gains focus as the camera pulls away and the music from the background gains volume. The blur where Katey once stood takes the shape of a Cubana filmed from behind, wearing tight pants that accentuate the rhythmic wiggle of her hips as she dances with a crowd of happy Cuban men and women in the street. Cinematically, Katey's body becomes a Cuban body.

This leads into a series of shots of black Cuban bodies writhing against each other glistening with sweat in a Havana nightclub we come to know as La Rosa Negra.[12] The words

"*Dirty Dancing: Havana Nights*, Based on True Events" emerge over the bodies, situating their moves as dancing, as dirty, as black, Cuban, and in the realm of the factual. Back in the car, Katey continues in voice-over, "I was really scared." Though she speaks of her transition to Cuba in general, her statement of fear also frames the visual representation of the black dancing bodies—bodies that perform an exotic sexuality that both frightens and fascinates.[13]

An uncritical multicultural analysis might conclude that Katey is open-minded because she embraces difference—a dance practice (and dance partner) that the other Americans in Cuba consider too vulgar, sexy, and racialized as black. She refuses to let the American racist attitudes influence her. Instead, she commits herself to learning the local partner dance moves with such sophistication that she moves up the dance club social hierarchy to become Queen of Night at La Rosa Negra, *Dirty Dancing's* Havana hot spot. This reading of the narrative would fit in with the discourse of multicultural-ism of the 1990s that Hamid and Gabriel (1993) critique as attempting to "capture ideo-logically and economically both the threat and the allure of the other" by rendering difference as a "style" to be consumed (Hamid and Gabriel: x). In the case of *Havana Nights*, Katey's coming-of-age consumption of Javier's "different" dance style depoliti-cizes Katey's queenly achievement at the end of the movie.

Following Hamid and Gabriel's apt critique of this seemingly benign multicultural-ism, I suggest that attention to Katey's relationship with Cuban women along her way to the top, rather than solely the center stage heterosexual dance partnership between Katey and Javier, disturbs this success story. Through an analysis of the interactions among the women, I find that American Katey displaces her Cubana foils on her way to becoming Queen.

THE RED DRESS AND VIOLENCE

The themes of difference, fear, and fascination persist as Katey befriends the hotel waiter, Javier. She happens to catch him dancing rumba in the same happy crowd that briefly appeared on the street at the beginning of the movie. Recall that the earlier cuts to this scene replaced one of the dancing Cuban women's bodies with Katey's. At this point, the displacement of the Cuban women dancers begins to happen narratively as well as visually. Javier leaves the crowd to walk Katey back to the hotel, where he later catches her solo in the dance studio awkwardly emulating the smooth rotations of the hips per-formed by the women dancing on the street. "For an American, you move well," he eval-uates. The implication is that Katey does not measure up to the "real dancers" whom he tells her can be found Saturday nights at La Rosa Negra.

La Rosa Negra literally translates as "The Black Rose," the "authentic" Cuban night-club where the film conflates black, sweaty bodies with mambo, sex, and roses. Within the symbolism of the movie, La Rosa Negra is the realm of the Cuban dance practices associated with blackness. This is Javier's space and we've already gotten a glimpse of it in the initial seconds of the movie. On Saturday, Katey shows up there with her date, James,[14] the boss's son, in a form-fitting red dress with spaghetti straps that lightly rest on the shoulders. It is the kind of dress the Cuban women at La Rosa Negra might wear.

It is also the kind of red dress that the American teen girls at the country club, Katey and James' first stop that night, find shockingly revealing. Katey feels so embarrassed to be seen in the dress that she is reluctant to remove her sweater. James is surprised by this dress that seems so out of character, but the dress seems to legitimate his sexual advances toward Katey later in the night. Where did Katey get such a dress that disrupts her peers' constructs of white American country club femininity?

She gets it from her hotel maid, Yolanda,[15] who seems to understand that Katey's femininity has begun to morph. In her hotel room, Katey is no longer satisfied with the prim pastel party dress she is supposed to wear this evening. She asks Yolanda if the dress looks square. Yolanda agrees that it does, but then offers her own red dress to the American teen. The film cuts away from Yolanda to direct our attention to Katey, who holds the dress up and imagines herself in it. I'm watching Katey, but I'm wondering about the maid and trying to fill in the gaps. Has she lent Katey the dress she uses for going out dancing on her nights off? Why does she not resent that Katey gets to go out while she stays behind to clean up after her? Why does she rescue Katey from an inevitable fashion faux pas? Most importantly, Yolanda has symbolically transferred her own Cubana femininity to Katey. Why? The film does not answer these questions but rather veers away to focus on Katey's relationship with Javier. A character on the periphery, Yolanda the maid becomes an extension of Katey and her desires, contributing to the romanticism of Katey's sexual awakening.

I suggest that the maid demonstrates that her labor exceeds that of making beds and scrubbing washbasin as she serves as a facilitator of white bourgeois Katey's transformation. Kathleen McHugh, in her analysis of domesticity and white bourgeois femininity in Hollywood melodramas, writes that white women's "housework is rendered invisibilized as labor and transformed into emotional, sentimental acts saturated with pathos" (McHugh: 6). In this story, however, Katey does not perform housework, which is racialized as black. What calls my attention is that, despite their racial, class, and cultural differences and the hierarchical relationship between the women, the film portrays the maid as inexplicably yet unproblematically empathetic to Katey. By accepting the red dress, Katey effectively displaces the maid from her nighttime femininity and leaves her to remain in the background as a hotel worker. The affective labor of a black Cuban domestic woman is depicted as a seamless, unrecognizable extension of services she renders as a hotel maid.

Yet, why does Yolanda volunteer to give Katey her dress? Judith Rollins theorizes the psychologically exploitative relationship between American bourgeois white women and domestic servants as one that relies on servant deference to her employer. "The psychological exploitation of domestics [...] has the two essential functions of affording the employers the self-enhancing satisfactions that emanate from having the presence of an inferior and the employers' lifestyle, ideology, and social world, from their familial interrelationships to the economically and racially stratified system in which they live"

(Rollins: 156). Of course, this understanding sheds light not precisely on the character of the maid, but on the way she is imagined in this film—as a vague benevolent presence who helps to justify Katey's entrance into the world of La Rosa Negra.

When Javier spots her in the red dress, he leaves his partner on the dance floor to go speak to Katey. "You look so Cuban," he tells her. He asks her to dance right away but tones down the moves he had been performing earlier, sticking with some basic steps and turns. Nervous at first, Katey begins to relax when Javier does not try to lead her in the same way he leads his other partners. When the song changes, everyone steps back, forming a circle around Raoul and Esmerelda,[16] The King and Queen of La Rosa Negra. "When they dance, the floor is theirs," Javier explains to Katey.

James has been the only other American at the club, and he has been not only observing Katey's enthusiastic dance with Javier, but also her nascent Cubana femininity. From his perspective, the red dress and Katey's willingness to dance with Javier in this space of blackness are his invitations to make unwanted sexual advances toward her. Even as Katey only lukewarmly inhabits a Cubana femininity, James finds that this legitimates his move to take advantage of Katey in his car outside the club. When Katey pushes him away, he rips the dress.

I find this rip to be a critical moment in the film. James literally rips the dress to violate Katey. As I have been suggesting, Katey's absorption of Yolanda's femininity through the dress is highlighted in this critical scene. In the ripping of the dress, several layers of violence become apparent. James's sexual threat poses a danger to Katey. Ripping the dress is a violent act that also marks an interruption to James's further physical violation of Katey. Even as the scene cuts to the next, I remain pondering yet another site of the assault. As I have been arguing, Katey in the red dress has taken on the femininity of women at La Rosa Negra. The rip, then, symbolically violates the black Cuban women who inhabit this kind of femininity. While Katey can remove the dress, men such as the boss's son regard Cuban women, no matter what they wear, as objects of their sexual desire.[17] The film does not address what happens when Katey returns the ripped dress to the maid.

THE COMPETITION

When Katey inadvertently gets Javier fired for socializing with a hotel guest, she immediately feels guilty to discover that Javier has found work as a mechanic, an apparently lower-paying job. That's when Katey learns about an upcoming "Latin Ballroom" dance contest from the hotel's dance instructor. "You mean dance with you?" Javier asks Katey, because he does not think her dancing compares to that of his Cuban dance partners. The grand prize is $5,000. "The winners get to go to America," Katey tells Javier. This seems to seal the deal. But neither Katey nor Javier dances Latin Ballroom. Their plan: If they mix a little bit of her ballroom training (we learn that she already knows the foxtrot) with his knowledge of popular local dance practices, Katey can help Javier earn money for his family. He has aspirations of taking them all to the United States.

Her formal ballroom training collides with his "natural/sexual" way of "feeling" the music as they quibble over technique. She criticizes him for his weak frame. He complains that they could fit another couple between them and that her hips move too much like a box. "It's like dancing with my mother's ironing board," he says as she tries to get him to sweep across the floor. In this daytime dance lesson, which takes place at La Rosa Negra, they both attempt to teach each other their contrasting dance knowledges—a continuation of the Katey-as-mind/Cuban-as-eroticized-body juxtaposition. La Rosa Negra by day is a fairly comfortable space for Katey to explore her relationship with Cuban femininity as Javier's partner. They are the only two people dancing in the empty space. They dance outside of the nighttime setting in which Katey's femininity-in-transition would be compared to that of the Cuban women present.

By the time they return to La Rosa Negra by night, Katey has on a black halter dress, not unlike the one previously worn by Esmerelda. The dress marks her continued transition as she and Javier begin to dance. Javier still maintains a comfortable distance from Katey as she maneuvers under their arms, unwinding to face him. He draws her close, breaking the frame. At first Katey seems to relax and feel the music as she circles her shoulders with large awkward-yet-exuberant rotations. But then, Javier reaches his hand down her hip and pulls her close, a common La Rosa Negra setup for a dip that arches back from the pelvis-to-pelvis point of stability. Unable to work through her fear of dancing so closely with Javier, Katey suddenly pushes him away. Javier, caught up in the moment and unable to waste good music (he later explains), seizes a nearby dancing Cubana who gratifies his dance urges: he pulls her hips to his as she arches her back into the dip, then easily shimmies her shoulders as the two of them press against each other, up and down in time with the music. Katey observes the Cuban woman who smoothly follows Javier's lead without any apparent need for practice. Javier seems to make the point that dancing is natural for Cubans and that an American like Katey will never be able to dance like a Cubana no matter how much she practices, no matter what she wears—because, Javier accuses, she is afraid.

QUEEN FOR A NIGHT, QUEEN FOREVER

Even with all of her dance lessons from Javier, the field trip to La Rosa Negra, and new wardrobe, Katey finds that she still cannot successfully perform Cubana femininity. She had closely observed Javier's replacement dance partner performing in a manner she simply cannot bring herself to do. Without a frame, the gyrating hips, pelvic thrusts, and orgasmic dips make Katey nervous.

Back in the safety of the hotel dance hall, Katey consults with the American instructor of "Latin Ballroom," played by Patrick Swayze,[18] denying she feels any fear while dancing with Javier. Through their discussion of dance, Swayze acts as Katey's American patriarchal moral compass and regulator of femininity. He gives her a lesson on how to perform Cubana femininity without losing her respectability as an upper-middle-class

American teen; how to perform exoticism without bodily risk. He tells her that she should be afraid of dancing with Javier, but that she must work through her fear in order to connect with him. In an impromptu dance lesson, he validates Katey's ballroom frame, but he also teaches her to perform the same backbending dip that the featured extra did with Javier. He thus disciplines Katey to allow Javier to have access to her body, but still keep him at a distance with a strengthened frame. He authorizes the manner in which Katey should engage with the exotic, liberating her from the perceived confines of American upper-middle-class femininity while polishing and incorporating the dance techniques of La Cubana.

By the end of the movie, Katey displaces Esmerelda from her queenly position. On the day after the Cuban Revolution and the day before the Americans return to the United States, Katey and Javier successfully attain the status of King and Queen of the Night at La Rosa Negra. Katey allows Javier to lead her into an arching dip, but she also takes the advice of Patrick Swayze and maintains her frame. As implied in the narrative, without the ballroom technique of keeping a strong frame, dancing would be too much like sex. Consider again the black sweaty bodies dancing without employing such a ballroom frame at the beginning of the film. Their bodies appear eroticized, their dance practices uncontained. Symbolically, Katey has become not simply Cubana, outperforming the Cuban women at their own contest, but a "better" Cubana, one who performs her passion as contained by a frame. What I am suggesting here is that after Katey learns to "let go" to perform Cubana femininity, she must "whiten" her moves with ballroom techniques. The film depicts Esmerelda and Raoul and all the other dancers graciously conceding the floor to Katey and Javier. While Katey may be the queen for one night, she does not occupy the political position of Cubans by day. The revolution curtails Katey's reign at La Rosa Negra. With her U.S. passport, she returns to the United States as Javier, the maid, and the Cuban women at La Rosa Negra stay put to deal with the everyday realities of the Revolution. Katey's displacement of La Cubana at the club may be temporary, but it establishes the triumph of a white liberal bourgeois American ballroom femininity over a static, hypersexualized Cuban femininity, unchanged by revolutions on or off the dance floor.

CONCLUSION

Katey and Yolanda appear dancing together for eight seconds in Katey's hotel room, during a montage that features Katey and Javier at rehearsal. A couple of feet apart from each other, Katey and Yolanda each lift their hair with their fingers and let it fall back down as they spin joyfully. Is Yolanda teaching Katey some of her moves or is Katey now teaching Yolanda some of what she has been learning? What is clear is that the two of them seem to perform the same moves in a similar manner, meaning that Katey's training is paying off. Once we have a chance to make the comparison, the camera shifts to focus on Katey. Yolanda disappears from the frame. Over and over again the filmic techniques contribute to a narrative that asks us to identify with Katey's transformation, to dismiss Yolanda's subsequent disappearance and Esmerelda's graceful relinquishment of her title as queen. In Latino/Caribbean-based dance movies such as *Havana Nights*, heterosexual couplings define the basis of interculturalism on the dance floor in the U.S. American imaginary. Does the consumption of Latina bodies and the disavowal of this consumption drive conceptions of U.S. American–Latino interculturalism? To what extent to current theories of interculturalism take relationships among women into account? In proposing an analytical practice against the directed gaze of identification, in this case the romance between Katey and Javier, and turning to peripheral relations between Katey and the Cuban women, I've sought to rethink notions of interculturalism outside of a heterosexualized framework.

Notes

1. Directed by Guy Ferland; produced by Lions Gate Films, Miramax Films, and Lawrence Bender Productions.
2. Played by Romola Garai.
3. For their generous and insightful comments on this chapter, I thank Lucy Burns and Melissa Blanco Borelli.
4. Played by Diego Luna.
5. Directed by Emile Ardolino; produced by Vestron Pictures and Great American Films Limited Partnership.
6. Directed by Boaz Davidson; produced by Golan-Globus Productions.
7. Directed by Randa Haines; produced by Mandalay Entertainment and Ballroom Dancer.
8. The movie was filmed in Puerto Rico.
9. Fatimah Tobing Rony addresses cinema not as an object, but as the social practice of cinema-*making*, one that can naturalize categories of race and gender (8–9) and in which can facilitate the viewer's fascinated cannibalistic consumption of racial Others (10).
10. Played by René Lavan.
11. Dance scholar Susan Leigh Foster (1998) challenges ideas of the mind/body split which have often historically been used to equate racialized (and classed and/or gendered) Third World Others with the body and First Worlders with intellect, serving as a rationale for oppressive laws and racist practices. Foster brings together mind and body in her theory of choreography—an intellectual plan for movement done by thinking bodies. Foster's theory assists in the denaturalization of racialized, classed, and gendered hierarchies.
12. Translation: The Black Rose. The name presents the club as a space of blackness. Javier, played by Mexican actor Diego Luna, is not actually black but more of a light brown. Luna-as-Javier's performance of Cuban popular dance in the film associates him with a black Cubanness. Hence, the film depicts him as legitimately occupying space as an accomplished and desirable dancer at La Rosa Negra. The film does not address the racial politics among Cubans.
13. See Ana López on Hollywood representations of Latinas as sexualized in film.
14. Played by Jonathan Jackson.
15. Played by Marisol Padilla Sánchez.
16. Played by César Detrés and Yessenia Benavides.

17. For more on representations of black women as sexualized in popular culture, see Patricia Hill Collins (2004).
18. Swayze stars in *Dirty Dancing* (1987).

BIBLIOGRAPHY

Collins, Patricia Hill. 2004. *Black Sexual Politics: African Americans, Gender, and the New Racism.* New York: Routledge.

Foster, Susan Leigh. "Choreographies of Gender." *Signs* 24, no. 2 (Autumn, 1998): 1.

Hamid, Naficy, and Teshome H. Gabriel. 1993. *Otherness and the Media: Ethnography of the Imagined and the Imaged.* Chur, Switzerland: Harwood Academic Publishers.

Keach, William. 2001. "Cuba on Our Minds (Review)." *Raritan* 21, no. 2 (2001): 114–126.

López, Ana. 1997. Of Rhythms and Borders. In *Everynight Life: Culture and Dance in Latin/o America.* Durham & London: Duke University Press, 310–343.

McHugh, Kathleen Anne. 1999. *American Domesticity: From How-To Manual to Hollywood Melodrama.* New York: Oxford University Press.

Pérez, Louis A. 1999. *On Becoming Cuban: Identity, Nationality, and Culture.* Chapel Hill: University of North Carolina Press.

Roberts, Chadwick. "Lily 'White': Commodity Racism and the Construction of Female Domesticity in the Incredible Shrinking Woman." *Journal of Popular Culture* 43, no. 4 (2010): 801–819.

Rony, Fatimah Tobing. 1996. *Third Eye: Race, Cinema, and Ethnographic Spectacle.* Durham, NC: Duke University Press.

CHAPTER 10

"IT'S SORT OF 'MEMBERS ONLY' ": TRANSGRESSION AND BODY POLITICS IN *SAVE THE LAST DANCE*

INNA ARZUMANOVA

SAVE THE LAST DANCE

THE lights in the club are dim. The dance floor is crowded, with the voice of Ice Cube radiating through the DJ's speakers: "You can do it, put your back into it." The club, a multiracial mecca of hip-hop kids, pulsates with energy as Sara (Julia Stiles) and Derek (Sean Patrick Thomas), the protagonists and central lovers in *Save the Last Dance*, make their way onto the dance floor spotlight. The couple's choreographed and learned dance imagines the club space as a multiracial utopia, siphoned off from the structural realities of race.

Like many films in its cohort, director Thomas Carter's 2001 film *Save the Last Dance* is determined to embrace multiracialism through the depiction of an interracial romance. Sara, who is white and a newcomer to Chicago, falls in love with Derek, who is African American. The two bond primarily over their mutual love of dance and after facing racially charged opposition to their relationship, persevere, and, in the film's last scene, symbolically secure their romance on the dance floor. In an ode to what is rendered as racial progress and transcendence, reifying America's exceptionally progressive and forward-thinking treatment of race, the dramatic dance finale is a familiar convention in contemporary teen dance films. These films are one of the most common channels of multiracial philosophy in American pop culture. Always set to a hip-hop soundtrack, the narratives fetishize race as an embodied category and affix its signification in their portrayals of dance crews and interracial romance. Dance is positioned as an equalizing medium, allowing mastery to smooth out otherwise fragmented and intersectional identities and managing to exaltedly transcend what figures as traditional identity politics. The de-racializing of bodies that these narratives allege assumes a deliberate reduction of identity to a moment that produces a pure corporeal meritocracy for the audience's marvel. This moment promises to render race an insignificant and passé category, judging bodies based on their mastery of dance choreography instead. Dance, then, is imagined as a vehicle through which bodies are no longer constrained by racial categories; a vehicle that operates on a system of equality and meritocracy. One need only master the right moves and race disappears as an impediment.

Here, dance becomes a mechanism that allows for an ideological shift toward a multiracial ethos through the representation of interracial coupling. Historically, mainstream dramas about cross-racial relationships have tended to draw on the familiar motifs of forbidden attraction, social tension, and doomed love, ultimately positioning the plot in the cautionary capacity (Wartenberg, 1999). In non-genre dramas, it is a well-worn narrative, in which the interracial couple either transcends all negative stereotypes, standing bravely (but futilely) against their corrupt context (as in *West Side Story, Mississippi Masala,* and in some measure, *Guess Who's Coming to Dinner*), or else embraces every destructive fantasy, simultaneously confirming fear and fascination (as in *Jungle Fever, The Rich Man's Wife, Hancock*).[1] In dance films, however, the canon looks considerably more mixed.

While dance—specifically, dances like the mambo, the cakewalk, the twist, and hip-hop—have long been at the center of conversations about race in popular culture, contemporary dance films seem to uniformly favor over-simplified multiracialism in their handling of racial relations and the multiplicity of its realities. In addition to *Save the Last Dance,* films like *Feel the Noise, Honey,* and *Step-Up,* to name just a few, have rejected perhaps the most significant narrative convention of their well-documented predecessor storylines—the tragic end. In these stories, interracial love does not corrupt under the weight of undefeatable racial tension. On the contrary, in testament to performative triumph, racially embodied love, articulated and narrativized through dance choreography, conquers all.

It is this rigid adherence to the previously intractable narrative of transcendence that sets the contemporary dance films apart from their predecessors. As a body of knowledge, these teen dance films are both legitimated by and reproductive of the contemporary historical moment, in which socio-cultural, political, and economic conditions conspire to validate a previously impossible narrative. Films like *Save the Last Dance* stand to reimagine (to the extent that pop products work to constitute reality) the histories of racism and Eurocentric notions of racial mobility by severing its actors, the storytellers, from their varied and conflicting trajectories of racial struggle in favor of multiracialism. In narrating the nation as a utopia of racial harmony and easy social and racial mobility, the film deflects from the current realities plaguing interracial coupling, obscuring subtle but mainstream racist discourse and the sustained effort to mark, identify, and contain difference at all costs. As such, the racial morality advocated in *Save the Last Dance* resonates with what James Carey (1989) calls "happy pastorals of progress," which are appeals to our collective bright destiny, progressing past preoccupations with historical oppression and entering a better, shining future (p. 9). Furthermore, films like *Save the Last Dance* render the problems of race as individual ones, staging the conditions for an easy, equally individualized, solution in the finale.

Reading the teen dance film *Save the Last* Dance as exemplary of its cohort, this chapter explores why dance seems to be so conducive to utopian narratives of racial progress, to narratives that lay claim to racial transcendence in order to validate U.S. exceptionalism and applaud American commitment to diversity. Specifically, I focus here on the narratives of racial transformation and "becoming" that are enabled through dance choreography but ultimately foreclosed by the film's governing multiracial discourse and its attendant antiblackness. Examining the ways in which the trope of blackness is fixed through the body of the black male figure, I seek to complicate the traditional "appropriation" argument that is often leveled at films like *Save the Last Dance*, to show the way antiblackness constitutes the core of the film's multiracialism.

Why Dance? Transgression and Radical Possibility

An examination of choreographed racial transformation in *Save the Last Dance* must first address the question of dance: why dance is so attractive to the multiracial project and parade-style celebration of difference. In *Save the Last Dance,* dance is a learning ritual and corporeal meritocracy, and a flattening out of difference through embodiment seems to be the lesson. Sara and Derek's romantic relationship grows in the dance studio, as they learn to blend Sara's ballet background with Derek's hip-hop dance moves to produce dance choreography that empties the historical and racialized legacies of each dance style in favor of corporeal mastery. The bulk of Derek's hip-hop tutelage, in fact, consists of teaching Sara to control her body, to relax it, to police its formal precision, to sway her limbs in line with hip-hop attitude, reducing that moment of potentially productive disruption, of clash and rich racial conversation through heavily racialized dance styles, to a kind of meritocracy that is measured through the successful disciplining of the body.

In dance, this type of universalizing mastery has a longer history yet. Traditional ballet, for example was a vehicle of westernization during colonialism, spread across the globe in an attempt to "civilize" the newly colonized (Foster, 2003). In contrast to the freedom of form valued in later political lobbyists like modern dance (along with jazz and avant-garde art), however, the logic behind ballet's advocacy relied on the dance style's emphasis on order, pedagogy, and universal custom. According to Foster (2003), ballet "promise[d] a homogenizing medium for the expression of cultural difference" (p. 435). Forbidden-love narratives also figured heavily in traditional ballet, both sanitizing and fetishizing the "other," often slipping into the genre of spectacle (Foster, 2003). As in *Save the Last Dance,* as well as other recent teen dance films, dance performance is a useful cinematic tool because physical discipline and the mastery attributed to dancers allows a presumed shedding of racial otherness, a multiracial agenda used explicitly in these films as material, marketable coolness in service of commercial ends (Mazzarella, 2006).

The choice of dance is a particularly interesting one because corporeal performance has the potential to be a site of more than just flattening difference, but also of transgression for the normative holds of race, gender, and sexuality. Many dance scholars have argued for the subversive potential of dance as a performance that offers the possibility of inhabiting more fluid racial, sexual, and gendered subjectivities (Adair, 1992; Boyd, 2004; Martin, 1998; Ward, 1997; Wolff, 2003). Dance can be seen as a space of latent radical possibility, with bodies gesturing toward an unscripted subjectivity. The very process implicit in the notion of performance suggests potential sites of intervention, a threat of becoming. I'm relying here on a conflation of Judith Butler's (1990) rendering of identity performance, where embodied performance constitutes gender, sexuality, and race, and the notion of dance as a literal translation of performativity. For Butler, performance hinges on the process of "becoming," wherein the body and its corollary identity undergo transformation (Butler, 1990). In this formulation, identity is maintained through constant performance, suggesting that a rupture in the ordered continuation of this performance constitutes a likewise rupture in the normative modes of gender, sexuality, and race (Butler, 1990). In the context of daily identity performances, dance is a literalization of performance—a kind of performance *as* performance—producing a spillover that can create the conditions of possibility for subversive movement and occupation of space.

Referring to this potential for spillover, Janet Wolff (2003) declares that dance can be "political as well as aesthetic transgression" (p. 423). Thanks to choreographers and dancers like Isadora Duncan, Martha Graham, and Doris Humphreys, modern dance specifically has traditionally been seen as a breakthrough for women, writing a new language of the body, allowing a shift in authorial perspective and the haunting masculine gaze that usually accompanies it (Wolff, 2003). According to Elizabeth Dempster (1998), the modern female body in dance is "dynamic, even convulsive" (p. 224). Dempster's notion of the body becoming a site of struggle is entirely conducive to Butler's prescription of "becoming" in the course of performance. The body, as a site of political transgression is, to borrow from Susan Bordo (1993), "shaped by histories and practices of containment and control" (p. 21).

Yet, this is not at all to suggest that dance's function or its significance as a site of performance is restricted to radical political expression. Dance can be as much about locating joy and pleasure in one's body as it can be about transgressive potential. Wendy Perron of *Dance Magazine* demonstrates this well in her review of The Trey McIntyre Project. McIntyre's dance company "is all about pleasure," she begins. "It comes from the music, the nifty, puzzle-like choreography, and the sheer joy of the dancers themselves. Trey's ballets are entertaining and challenging in just the right ratio" (Perron, 2011, p. 1). Inasmuch as Perron's observation articulates the multiple modes of affect—pleasure, challenge, joy, etc.—that bodies can choreographically inhabit, this chapter explores

FIGURE 10.1 Screen capture of *Save the Last Dance*, director Thomas Carter (2001). Derek teaches Sara how to relax her body in hip-hop and how to sway with rhythm.

how the dance choreography in films like *Save the Last Dance* both trades on the promise of transgression and simultaneously removes its political possibility.

Hip-hop dance, which dominates the landscape of teen dance films and serves as the soundtrack to *Save the Last Dance*, wields exactly that potential for transgression.[2] During their first dance lesson, Derek instructs Sara to shake off the sharp edges of what we later learn is her ballet training. Instead of the rond de jambe attitude she showcases in this scene, he teaches her to slouch, to relax the strict convention of bodily comportment (Fig. 10.1).

By virtue of aggressively breaking with the refined, restrained movements attributed to properly disciplined ballet bodies, and especially female bodies, hip-hop can offer dancing transgression. Here, the body accomplishes something akin to the carnivalesque performance of hysterics: using the female body "in public, in extravagant ways, [with] latitude of movement and attitude [that] [is] not permitted . . . without negative consequences" (Russo, 1986, p. 222). With the drop of every beat, the body stakes out a language of transgression, rendering a moment of productive spectacle, of the carnivalesque body, set loose on possibility.

Narrating the history of the African American dancer Aida Overton Walker, Daphne Brooks (2006) writes that Walker "yoke[d] her modern dance choreography with New Negro revisionist racial and gender ideologies" (p. 4). Brooks looks to the bodies of those like Walker to find performances that objected the "powerful stillness," which, to return to Butler again, implies a lack of becoming through dispossession, imposed onto their bodies in the post-bellum south (Brooks, 2006, p. 5). In racial melodrama (Brooks deals primarily with post-bellum black musical theater) it is the body, not the form of storytelling that "speak[s] the unspeakable" (Brooks, 2006, p. 40). "Excessive bodies . . . reign in the excess they produce" and, by "critically defamiliarizing their own bodies by way of performance...yield alternative racial and gender epistemologies" (Brooks, 2006, p. 40, 5). Brooks's point is partly about the function of affect and its ability to pluck political possibility from the shape of performance. That is, any radical possibility that bodies can seek to inhabit in dance performance is routed through the affective register, which is both intangible and central to dance's capacity for transformation.[3]

That transformation and an activation of a "becoming" are critical to the transgressive work of dance performance is easily summed up in Randy Martin's (1998) notion of mobilization. For Martin, mobilization refers to the articulations that bodies manage to stake out through movement and is therefore contingent on some kind of transformation. In fact, mobilization is the paradigm through which a dance performance's political dimension becomes readable because it is through mobilization that the subject is constituted and reconstituted (Martin, 1998).

The works of some dance scholars have been unpacked here in order to highlight that transgression and political possibility in dance lie in the concurrent movements of body and subjectivity—movement and transformation of the subject through the movement of the body. Bodies move in order to render fluid subjectivities, in order to carve out subversive presences. Significantly, stillness and fixity, in this configuration, amount to both material and symbolic dispossession.

Dancing Subjects and Stillness in *Save the Last Dance*

"I can't work like this...with you dictating to me," pleads Sara in the film's fourth private lesson between the couple. She is practicing a crossover with kicks in the mirror as Derek stands by, watching (Fig. 10.2). Sara struggles, trying to smooth out the transitions between the crossovers, heel-toe digs, crossbacks, and arm waves that the routine calls for. Frustrated, she slides back and forth across the screen, attempting to synchronize her traveling slides to her arm waves, as Derek observes, a still dictator in the back of the room. This scene, in fact, captures the choreographic trajectory of the film, which, as the plot progresses, immobilizes Derek. That is, his dancing skills are on display in the first two private lessons of the film, modeling hip-hop dance moves and attitude to the traditional ballet dancer. In the first lesson, he is the central focus as he teaches her to bounce right to left, to bend her rigid knees and make her arms elastic. The second lesson is already a more collaborative affair, as Derek teaches Sara how to charge in a choreographed battle, requiring their bodies to move in sync, leaning and dipping into each other's spaces. By the third lesson, Sara takes over: she practices basic pirouettes and arabesques with a ballet class as Derek watches, seated in a corner of the studio, mesmerized by her skill (Fig. 10.3). In fact, by the time Sara accuses Derek of being a dictator in their fourth lesson, he has been largely phased out as a dancer. He is, as she suggests, a dictator, an immobile one, whose presence is only necessary as a reminder of what her choreographic and racial transformations are meant to resemble.

The contradictory, still presence that Derek comes to embody is brought to the fore in the fifth lesson, where Sara practices alone, unable to nail her moves without

FIGURE 10.2 Screen capture of *Save the Last Dance*, director Thomas Carter (2001). Sara practices her dance routine in the mirror as Derek stands by, instructing but not participating.

FIGURE 10.3 Screen captures of *Save the Last Dance*, director Thomas Carter (2001). In the third lesson sequence of the film, Sara practices with a ballet class while Derek sits in the corner of the studio, watching.

her hovering referent point, her dictator. Derek is useful, this last lesson seems to suggest, but only as a mechanism of immobilized support. By the completion of these lessons, Sara has quite literally delivered on her joking promise to "dance circles around" Derek. She is now the dancer. Derek's movement as a dancer has served its purpose and has consequently, ceased. In the first debut of her newfound dance skills, at the Stepps Nightclub, they begin as a couple, but as the crowd forms around them, Derek quickly fades to the background. As Sara confidently throws her hands up and begins to roll her hips more confidently and aggressively, the adoring crowd chants "Go Sara! Go Sara" (Fig. 10.4). Derek, still visible in the shot, barely sways nearby, mostly watching. Her mobility, narrativized through choreography, has rendered him still.

FIGURE 10.4 Screen capture of *Save the Last Dance*, director Thomas Carter (2001). Sara debuts her dance moves at Stepps Nightclub, as the crowd surrounding the couple shouts "Go Sara! Go Sara!"

Given that *Save the Last Dance* makes both implicit and explicit use of dialogues on racial relations, interracial sex, and racialized bodies in motion, the dance scenes in the film house that potential to perform the racialized and gendered body in transformative ways, to constitute the racial body through transgressive modes of becoming. However, as the representational and ideological codes of the film are so closely wedded to reifying a multiracial reality that traffics in racial transcendence and renders structural racism obsolete, the corporeal transformation that makes dance an inherently political project is doled out in rather conservative ways. As the film's dance scenes demonstrate, mobility and subjective becoming are granted to the white female protagonist alone, revealing the trope of antiblackness that structures the core of multiracial narratives of progress and transcendence.

The film's narrative arc adheres to the strict narrative convention of its cohort: the non-black female lead learns blackness through dance—hip-hop choreography, to be specific—and ultimately secures her new identity through sex with her black male partner. For the white female protagonist, hip-hop lessons are always also lessons on a deeply racially coded "swagger." Dance is pedagogical here and the lesson is always an essentialist blackness, with successfully choreographed racial passing made salient by way of hip-hop mastery. While Sara passes both racially and literally, as she gains a sort of mobility, moving into club spaces previously foreclosed to her because of racial divisions, Derek, her black partner, remains in no more than a pedagogical capacity. Derek's purpose, in fact, is to enable Sara's transformation by choreographing her new identity, helping her don all the necessary racial accoutrements to complete her passing performance. For Sara, this transformation into an essentialized and commodified blackness is achieved through dance and the romantic love for which dance becomes a proxy, with a successful relationship as the official inauguration into hip-hopdom. This

FIGURE 10.5 Screen capture of *Save the Last Dance*, director Thomas Carter (2001). In the beginning of the film, Chenille transforms Sara's clothing and lends her accessories to make the white ballet dancer more hip-hop-appropriate.

hip-hopdom, in the tradition of lifestyle politics, becomes a substitute for blackness. As is customary in multiracial narratives that fetishize difference and commodify race, hip-hop dance, music, dress, and in some cases, swagger are all unmistakable signs of commodified, MTV blackness (Fig. 10.5).

In *Save the Last Dance*, then, the mobility and transformative capacity of the white subject (Sara) is only possible at the expense of the black subject (Derek)'s guaranteed immobility. Perhaps the most telling culmination of the couple's lessons and journeys in (im)mobility is Sara's contemporary piece for her second (and successful) Juilliard audition. This scene is undoubtedly the climax of the film, the choreographed product of numerous dance lessons and lived, racial transformations. Sara combines strong elevés and rond de jambes with various traveling slides, a dramatic drop-and-pop, and finally, a hip-hop chair routine. Derek, who co-authored this choreography and the identity Sara now confidently inhabits, watches from behind a curtain, emerging only for a moment to reassure her (Fig. 10.6). Here too, Sara's success relies on Derek's presence—unlike her ballet routine, the contemporary piece, full of hip-hop moves and taught swagger, seems to fail without Derek's body of reference. Her mastery, however, requires that he is denied mobility, unable to engage in the dance performance that he helped engineer. Derek, in fact, underscores his own position of passive watching in this scene's pep talk: "Ain't nobody watching you but me," he says to Sara.

This scene is a good reminder that the film's ideological commitment to celebration of difference and multiracial agendas dictates that a static antiblackness must constitute the key condition of possibility for the fluidity and mobility of non-black, and often

FIGURE 10.6 Screen captures of *Save the Last Dance*, director Thomas Carter (2001). As Sara auditions for Julliard, Derek stands off-stage. The scene moves between shots of her performance and shots of him watching. His immobile presence is necessary to her success and transformation.

specifically white, bodies. Derek's body must be a fixed signifier of blackness in order for Sara to choreographically manage any kind of racial or gendered masquerade. It is this arrangement that the Juilliard audition scene demonstrates. Sara's audition for The Juilliard School serves as evidence of her personal journey of discovery throughout the film. By this performance, she is no longer a rigid ballerina, naive and unfamiliar with "urban" realities. Here, her choreography, a fusion, as previously described, of hip-hop and ballet, signals what she has become through her tutelage: an enlightened, hybrid subject, who moves easily in and out of cultures and racialized subject positions. Derek, on the other hand, has seen no such transformation. Having choreographed and pedagogically facilitated Sara's journey through self-discovery, at the end of the film he is exactly who he is at the beginning: a "good-boy," as Chenille (Derek's sister, played by Kerry Washington) observes, who still wants to be a doctor but significantly, no longer dances, only watches. Derek's body, in fact, cannot be a site of becoming because it is burdened with the task of being a site of negation, a vessel that enables antiblackness.

Antiblackness and the "Specter of Rape"

To demonstrate the ways in which the film's explicit antiblackness articulates itself by denying any kind of *becoming* to black masculinity, it is worth mentioning that the specifically black man/white woman coupling that *Save the Last Dance*, as well as most contemporary teen dance films, are so eager to see proliferate on multiracial terms, is traditionally haunted by what Valerie Smith (1998) calls the "specter of rape." Smith observes that interracial rape is an intersection of uniquely American race and gender discourses, wherein the construct of rape has been understood simply: black man rapes white woman. This unofficial definition validated the lynching of black men during the period of Reconstruction, solidified white male status as both owner and protector, and paradoxically rendered violence against black women impossible and unimportant (Smith, 1998). To abstract away from *Save the Last Dance* specifically for a moment, one of the racial standards for coupling in recent teen dance films is that the male lead must be readable as black. While the female leads are sometimes white, as in the case of *Save the Last Dance*, sometimes Latina, the male figure is always fixed in an essentializing rendering of cinematic blackness. This fixity that's required of blackness is only exacerbated when the female partner is Latina or Afro-Latina, in films like *Honey* or *Feel the Noise*, for example. In these Romeo-and-Juliet plots, which all the films adhere to, the romance drama necessitates that the lovers be rendered opposites, leading various articulations of Latina identity to align with whiteness always in opposition to blackness.

In fact, the function of fixed blackness in *Save the Last Dance* is in line with Jared Sexton's (2008) argument, which asserts that at the heart of multiracial utopias is an explicit antiblackness, a fear of what is represented as a threatening and looming black nationalism. To mitigate that fear, in these utopic spaces, blackness is always rendered as an immobile signifier, laboring on behalf of white mobile *becoming* as well as its own vilification. Sexton proposes that this is not simply the traditional boundary between blackness and whiteness. Rather, multiracial narratives, seeking to redeem what they posit as interracial sexuality, position blackness as regressively policing the boundary between itself "and everything else" (Sexton, 2008, p. 13). It is blackness that is narrated as the impediment to a neoliberal teleology of progress. Whiteness, on the other hand, emerges as devoted to racial transcendence.

In *Save the Last Dance*, the only characters that challenge Sara and Derek's romantic relationship are African American. Chenille, Malakai (Derek's best friend, played by Fredro Starr), and Nikki (Derek's ex-girlfriend, played by Bianca Lawson) are the only ones in the film who oppose the interracial coupling, openly citing race as the reason. In the image of these "typecast, two-dimensional characters . . . blackness is reduced to one more obstacle to be overcome" (Boyd, 2001, p. 75). Meanwhile, Sara's father Roy (Terry Kinney) seems to have no serious problem with the relationship and neither does Diggy (Elisabeth Oas), who is Chenille's friend and the only other young white character in the film. In stark opposition to what Sexton would call the depiction of the black characters' racialized nationalism, both Roy and Diggy are positioned as multiracial and racially progressive. Not only does neither one of them oppose the relationship, each one has already gained entry into a version of commodified blackness by the time the audience is introduced to them. Roy is, after all, a trumpet player in a Chicago jazz band, which wraps him in the coolness traditionally ascribed to white jazz musicians, while Diggy is repeatedly described as "down," a linguistic shorthand used to suggest that she has shed corny whiteness, in favor of cool, essentialized blackness. In fact, Diggy's status as "down," like Sara's, is also routed through hip-hop choreography. She repeatedly show-cases her dance moves at Stepps, always with black male partners, having secured access to what she tells Sara is a "sort of 'members only'" club.

Not only, then, have these white subjects performed feats of racial mobility, leaving their black counterparts to signify a form of static blackness, but, paralleling Sexton's argument, the film's deployment of dance suggests that black characters constitute the only impediment to interracial coupling and transcendence, while white characters embody a commitment to diversity and progress. As such, *Save the Last Dance* is a clear articulation of a rather specific multiracial ideology that ultimately uses bodies that signify blackness in order to secure the privileges of what is rendered innocent whiteness. Sara stands in perfect testament to the innocence that whiteness claims with regard to racial tensions. After Chenille explains the problems Nikki may have with interracial relationships, Sara naively proclaims, "Well, we like each other. What is the big damn deal? It's me and him, not us and other people" (Fig. 10.7). Sara's disingenuous ignorance

FIGURE 10.7 Screen capture of *Save the Last Dance*, director Thomas Carter (2001). In her conversation with Chenille, Sara is bewildered about the role of racial construction in inter-racial relationships.

of the historical privileges of whiteness and the racist structures of domination that complicate interracial coupling allows the film's narrative to applaud white commitment to civil-rights era politics of inclusion and therefore re-inscribe whiteness as the subjectivity laboring on behalf of a progressive, racially just future. It is the kind of colorblind morality that, according to Robyn Wiegman (1995), characterizes today's American pop cultural sphere, disaffiliating whiteness from its position of power and history of racial privilege, only to reassert that very same advantage. Additionally, the innocence that Sara performs as proxy of progressive whiteness speaks to the ways in which the discourses of multiracial progress treat race as a project of the individual alone.

Dancing Alone: Individualism and Dance Crews *in Save the Last Dance*

This notion that the topic of race is an individual one is a central trope both in multiracial discourse in general (Dean, 2009; Hong, 2006; Sexton, 2008) as well as *Save the Last Dance* in particular. Mirroring neoliberal discourse's exaltation of individual rights and agency, political struggle is relegated to the realm of expressive individualism and personal morality as well as individual responsibility (Hong, 2006). Writing about what she calls "communicative capitalism," Jodi Dean (2009) argues that inside the structures of neoliberalism, agendas that position themselves as left-leaning mistakenly cast structural problems as individual ones, to be corrected on equally individual terms, through affect and exhaustive communication.[4] Likewise, *Save the Last Dance*, a narrative that certainly imagines itself as leftist and progressive, positions problems of race as individual, rather than institutionalized, structural, and regenerating ones, and uses dance to articulate this ethos. In the scene mentioned above, where Sara is baffled as to why interracial coupling might ignite discourses of violence and privilege, her point is a telling one. She doesn't understand why it's anyone else's business. After all, for her, their relationship and their struggles are theirs alone—personal and individual—to be resolved through affect, expression, and of course dancing.

In the film, in fact, the struggles between Sara and Derek play out exclusively through dance; through their personal duets, private lessons, and couples' performances in the club. Here, not only is it an exceptional (*exceptional* in that they demonstrate performative mastery) couple that is granted cinematic validation as an on-screen romance worthy of the audience's sympathy, but also exceptional individuals. Individual women accomplish racial passing via mastery of hip-hop, managing to dance their way into exclusive clubs, into "urban" acceptance and commodified cache. Dance crews exist only in the background, with uncertain and uninterrogated fates. Despite the traditional and contemporary prevalence of dance crews in hip-hop, *Save the Last Dance* eschews this issue altogether. In fact, the film ends with the proverbial narrative close-up of the leading love story, with Sara and Derek's fracturing off from their respective crews (their friends and families) heavily implied. Again, dance narrativizes this hinted plot point.

FIGURE 10.8 Screen capture of *Save the Last Dance*, director Thomas Carter (2001). In the film's last scene, Derek and Sara triumph on the Stepps dance floor.

Sara's second Juilliard audition finishes with her leaping triumphantly into the air into a powerful grand jeté. As the scene moves into a slow-motion shot, focusing on her nearly horizontal, suspended split, the scene is cut with the image of two trains, approximating the same horizontal motion, high above the ground, poignantly moving in opposite directions. This juxtaposition reminds the viewer that Sara's transformative success and Derek's immobile contribution to it are antithetical to the life and people they leave behind.

In context of Sexton's argument about the threat that black nationalism poses to multiracialism, this absence of dance crews and suggested future fracturing makes some sense. As the closest image of coalition politics, of collective mobilization and group identity enactment, dance crews approximate the very threat of black nationalism that multiracial discourse imagines. In fact, at the end of the film, Sara and Derek's acceptance as a couple, it seems, depends entirely on their shedding of group affiliation. The film's plot ends with Sara's acceptance into Juilliard and Derek's acceptance into Georgetown University, with both plot points suggesting impending relocation from Chicago. Furthermore, the very last scene of the film finds Sara and Derek finally performing their choreographed couple's dance at the nightclub, Stepps. While the rest of the well-meaning friends are undoubtedly present, they fade into the background. The focus and lighting is on the couple, gesturing to the ultimate triumph of individual will over the problems of race (Fig. 10.8).

CONCLUSION

Per Jared Sexton's argument about the explicit antiblackness that resides at the core of multiracial narratives, the representational and ideological codes of the film *Save the Last Dance* wage a politics of racial progress and transcendence at the expense of the film's imaginary of a stable, fixed, and threatening blackness (Sexton, 2008). Derek's black male body becomes the point of negation, the axis off which happy difference proliferates and pivots. That is, while Sara's racial identity can afford more fluidity, Derek's subjectivity must not escape the limitations of a legible, essentialized blackness, as a not-so-subtle reminder that multiracialism serves to mitigate the threat of black masculinity and its political implications. For dance performance to labor toward constituting a multiracial utopia in *Save the Last Dance*, blackness, and the threat of coalition it always suggests, must be marked, made still and constant, and depoliticized. The depoliticization happens through dance, which commodifies blackness, allowing non-blacks passing entry, dismantles crews, and makes sure the black male lead serves as fixed accessory, always dancing in place rather than reaching toward the transformation that his white partner is granted. The coherent, unwavering signification that is asked of black bodies in *Save the Last Dance* works to sustain a multiracial narrative of progress, where whiteness is exceptionally progressive—both innocent and well meaning—and blackness is a militant impediment to progress. In the end, dance, with all its transformative potential, choreographically facilitates the project, allowing the illusion of bodies moving in a space of pure embodiment and physical meritocracy, allowing hip-hop to stand in for blackness, and ushering in Sara's personal, racialized transformation. In the film, it is dance that endows Sara with mobility, leaving Derek fixed permanently in place. Through her lessons in hip-hop, she is allowed free movement, to shed or don new identity, to choreographically pass as a different race, and to remain attached to the privileges of racial centrality and normativity. Derek, her black male partner, makes no figurative leaps across race or class, sacrificing his body to multiracial ideology of racial progress and the neoliberal cause it shores up.

Notes

1. Nadia Ramoutar's (2006) study of the top-grossing (non-genre specific) films from 1967 (*Guess Who's Coming to Dinner*) to 2005 (*Hitch*) found that 42 percent of female characters in interracial relationships were victims of violence, and that most had no discernible occupation, other than spy, sex worker, or entertainer. The reliance on these conventions is in fact so prominent that interracial couples "have a greater statistical probability of dying than of getting married or dating seriously" in film (Keen, 2006; Ramoutar, 2006).
2. The "harlem shake" is a useful example of hip-hop choreography enabling the body to inhabit potentially transgressive movements. In this dance, the body shakes uncontrollably, as in a ritual hysteria, shaking off inhibition and convention, highlighting its liminal possibilities and tapping into affective registers.
3. Expressing similar sentiment about the role of affect in dance, Lucy Fisher (2004) discusses Sally Potter's 1997 film *The Tango Lesson*. Fisher quotes Potter as saying that one "can't really film the experience of dancing, at least not directly. You may get the surface of it, but you don't get anything that resembles the incredible feeling in the body that dance gives you" (p. 47). Here again, the "feeling" of dance is critical but elusive.
4. Jodi Dean sees this failure as the price of waging leftist politics on the terrain of neoliberalism, which is itself founded in individualism.

References

Adair, C. (1992). *Women and Dance: Sylphs and Sirens.* New York: New York University Press.

Bordo, S. (1993). *Unbearable Weight: Feminism, Western Culture, and the Body.* Berkeley: University of California Press.

Boyd, J. (2004). Dance, Culture, and Popular Film: Considering Representations in *Save the Last Dance. Feminist Media Studies* 4, 1.

Brooks, D. (2006). *Bodies in Dissent: Spectacular Performances of Race and Freedom, 1850-1910.* Durham, NC: Duke University Press.

Butler, J. (1990). *Gender Trouble.* New York: Routledge.

Carey, J. (1989). *Communication as Culture: Essays on Media and Society.* Boston, MA: Unwin Hyman.

Dean, J. (2009). *Democracy and Other Neoliberal Fantasies: Communicative Capitalism and Left Politics.* Durham, NC: Duke University Press.

Dempster, E. (1998). "Women Writing the Body: Let's Watch a Little How She Dances." In A. Carter (Ed.), *The Routledge Dance Studies Reader.* New York: Routledge.

Fischer, L. (2004). "Dancing through the Minefield: Passion, Pedagogy, Politics, and Production in 'The Tango Lesson.'" *Cinema Journal* 43 (3), 42.

Foster, S. L. (2003). "The Ballerina's Phallic Pointe." In A. Jones (Ed.), *The Feminism and Visual Culture Reader.* New York: Routledge.

Hong, G. K. (2006). *The Ruptures of American Capital.* Minneapolis: University of Minnesota Press.

Keen, C. (2006). "Hollywood Films Portray Biracial Couple Negatively if Shown at All." *University of Florida News.* Retrieved from http://news.ufl.edu/2006/10/11/couples/.

Martin, R. (1998). *Critical Moves: Dance Studies in Theory and Politics.* Durham, NC: Duke University Press.

Mazzarella, S. R. (2006). "Constructing Youth: Media, Youth, and the Politics of Representation." In A. N. Valdivia (Ed.), *A Companion to Media Studies.* Malden, MA: Blackwell Publishing.

Perron, W. (2011). "Curtain Up." *Dance Magazine, August 2011.* Retrieved from http://www.dancemagazine.com/issues/August-2011.

Ramoutar, N. (2006). "The Color of Love on the Big Screen: The Portrayal of Women in Hollywood Films in Interracial Relationships From 1967 to 2005" (Doctoral dissertation). Retrieved from University of Florida/ProQuest database. (Pub. No. AAT 3224611).

Russo, M. (1986). "Female Grotesques: Carnival and Theory." In T. de Lauretis (Ed.), *Feminist Studies, Critical Studies* (pp. 213–229). Bloomington: Indiana University Press.

Sexton, J. (2008). *Amalgamation Schemes: Antiblackness and the Critique of Multiracialism.* Minneapolis: University of Minnesota Press.

Smith, V. (1998). *Not Just Race, Not Just Gender.* New York: Routledge.

Ward, A. (1997). "Dancing Around Meaning (and the Meaning Around Dance)." In H. Thomas (Ed.), *Dance in the City.* New York: St. Martin's Press.

Wartenberg, T. E. (1999). *Unlikely Couples: Movie Romance as Social Criticism.* Boulder, CO: Westview Press.

Wiegman, R. (1995). *American Anatomies: Theorizing Race and Gender.* Durham, NC: Duke University Press.

Wolff, J. (2003). "Reinstating Corporeality." In A. Jones (Ed.), *The Feminism and Visual Culture Reader.* New York: Routledge.

CHAPTER 11

"THE WHITE GIRL IN THE MIDDLE": THE PERFORMATIVITY OF RACE, CLASS, AND GENDER IN *STEP UP 2: THE STREETS*

RAQUEL L. MONROE

THE 1983 dance film *Flashdance* introduced the dancers' leg warmers, cut-up sweat-shirts, and "tees" into mainstream fashion fare. Youth around the country sported dance studio garb to emulate the fashion in the movie. While the fashion was trendy, the toprockin', footwork, and power moves briefly performed in the film by the Rock Steady Crew propelled the b-boy's signature steps from New York City's inner city enclaves into the throes of popular culture, where it still remains. American youth, and eventually youth globally, danced to imitate the b-boy swagger performed in the film and the slew of other films it inspired in the 1980s. Golan-Globus Production's 1984 film *Breakin'* was one such film (Fig. 11.1).

Breakin', the first major motion picture dedicated solely to "street dance" forms, con-flated black and Latino street dances under the generic term "breakdancing" which erased particular differences within the style and started the trend of homogenizing street dance movement vocabulaires. As a result, breakdancing is now globally accepted as a form of yet another homogenizing term "hip-hop."[1] The film also initiated another trend that continues to define the narratives of hip-hop dance films: the white female protagonist as the dancing body that helps audiences navigate through the form. Although *Breakin'* touted breakdancing as its selling point, it was through jazz dancer Kelly (Lucinda Dickey) that the audience came to know Ozone (Adolfo "Shabba-Doo" Quiñones), Turbo (Michael "Boogaloo-Shrimp" Chambers), and their lifestyle as street dancers in Los Angeles's inner city.

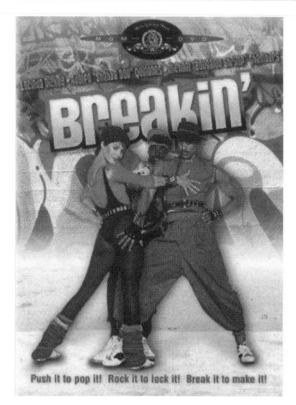

FIGURE 11.1 Screen capture of *Breakin',* director Joel Silberg, 1984, the movie poster.

Internet Movie Database provides a telling summary: "A struggling young jazz dancer (Lucinda Dickey) meets up with two breakdancers. Together they become the sensation of the street crowd."[2] This description situates Dickey as the main protagonist with Quiñones and Chambers as her sidekicks. As the film develops, Dickey and Quiñones venture into an interracial love affair. Their race and class differences cause tension, but their love for dance conquers all. Dickey's appearance in the film made the movie and the nascent dance form of breakdancing palpable to white audiences both locally and globally, and it was with great anticipation that audiences eagerly awaited the 1984 release of the sequel *Breakin' 2: Electric Boogaloo.*

Breakin' (and to some extent its sequel *Breakin 2: Electric Boogaloo)* established the cliché narratives that continue to construct mainstream hip-hop dance films: dance, typically in a community center of some sort, saves disenfranchised youth from the violence of the inner city; dance is the multicultural panacea that homogenizes difference and makes us all one. A recurring theme in both narratives is the use of the white or racially ambiguous female to navigate and introduce the audience to urban life where black and brown b-boys and b-girls dance to survive.

While scholars from various fields have dutifully documented the rampant commodification and consumption of what we now call hip-hop,[3] the attention paid to women in hip-hop primarily focuses on the denigration of black women by misogynist rap lyrics[4] or the successful female MCs who have blazed trails in the hyper-masculine space that is hip-hop.[5] The "don't stop, get it, get it" male and female bodies that freeze with cheeks on floors and knees propped on elbows are largely absent from scholarly discourse. Perhaps the ephemerality of the dancing body discourages the pen. Or, audiences find the music and personas that rap the lyrics far more intriguing and accessible than the dancers who rock the beats. However, since these early breakdancing films introduced hip-hop dance forms to the world with a white woman sandwiched between two black and brown males—a continuous trend—the implications of this practice and the performance of black expressive culture by diverse raced, classed, and gendered bodies deserves further discussion.

In order to enrich such a discussion, I choose to focus on *Step Up 2: The Streets* *(2008)* as my primary text for analysis. Yet, the narratives in all of the films I enumerate throughout this chapter clearly illustrate how a white female dancer's success weighs on her ability to infiltrate a masculine space and perform "black" performativity equal to or better than her black counterparts. I define black performativity as does dance theorist Thomas F. DeFrantz "to be gestures of black expressive culture, including music and dance, that perform actionable assertions."[6] DeFrantz theorizes how black social dances exemplify his notion of *corporeal orature*, where movement aligns with speech to "incite action."[7] As a foundational aspect of black expressive culture, hip-hop dance forms allow the black body to move beyond mere physical prowess to communicate and embody power and liberation from systemic oppression.[8] Hence, the "dance as savior" theme present in hip-hop dance films speaks to DeFrantz's theorizations. "Breaking" does save the community center in *Breakin' 2: Electric Boogaloo.* Popping and locking does create the space for Kelly and Ozone's illicit interracial and class-clashing love affair. I contend, however, that the ability of the white dancing body to emulate the "physical prowess" of her black counterpart deters the overthrow of "systemic oppression." Instead, the power of the black dancing bodies in hip-hop dance films serves to highlight and authenticate the exceptionality of the white female dancer. Moreover, to ensure white middle-class consumption and comfort, the filmic representations of hip-hop dance continually construct the white female dancer as an object of desire and cast her black and brown counterparts as contrary, aggressive opponents or hypersexual helpmates.

For example, in 2001, *Save the Last Dance* continues the white-girl-as-navigator premise that *Breakin'* set up (Fig. 11.2). Subsequent films about hip-hop dance and its variations (e.g., step, krumping) feature black and/or brown main characters, thereby turning them into cultural insiders.[9] In *Honey* (2003)[10] Jessica Alba uses her dance skills to save her fledgling community center. *You Got Served* (2004) features black and brown male dance crews battling for prize money. The feature documentary *Rize* (2005) depicts black youth in South Central Los Angeles who use "krumping" as a catalyst for emancipation. 2007's *Stomp the Yard* and *How She Move* focus on stepping, a rhythmic dance form where performers rhythmically slap their hands against their bodies and stomp their feet to create beats. Although stepping is its own art form, it is easily subsumed under the hip-hop dance category. Noticeably missing from this list of dance films is the *Step Up* series, the only hip-hop dance films to have four movies released in theaters.[11]

FIGURE 11.2 Screen capture of *Save the Last Dance,* director Thomas Carter, 2001, the movie poster.

The *Step Up* franchise manages to maintain its reliance on a white lead and it is the second film that becomes the focus of my argument.

STEP UP

Both *Step Up* (2006) and *Step Up 2: The Streets* (2008) (Fig. 11.3) take place in Baltimore, a predominately black city[12] notorious for its high crime rate.[13] In *Step Up*, Channing Tatum plays a white hip-hop dancer forced to do community service at Maryland School for the Arts (MSA) after a run-in with the law. While there, he falls in love with the lead dancer and proves that street dance has a place inside the legitimate, educational, concert dance space. Its sequel, *Step Up 2: The Streets*, the focus of my analysis, narrates the experience of Andie (Briana Evigan), a white female hip-hop dancer, whose black female guardian threatens to send her to Texas to live with her aunt if she does not

FIGURE 11.3 Screen capture of *Step Up 2: The Streets*, director Jon M. Chu, 2008, the movie poster.

stop consorting with those "criminals," the mostly black b-boy and b-girl dance crew "The 410." MSA will be her saving grace as well.

STEP UP TO BLACK PERFORMATIVITY

A melancholic tune plays in the background. Sneaker-clad feet quickly rotate around each other. The camera pans to reveal a b-boy cipher. Two b-boys battle upside down confidently balancing on their hands. The expertise with which they rotate their torsos and rapidly twist their legs inspires awe in the members of the cipher, and possibly in those of us viewing in theaters or our homes. In sepia tones, the camera cuts to a series of similar ciphers on street corners, inside gymnasiums or dance clubs. The dancers and the crowd are always a diverse group of men, save the occasional female dancer. The camera then travels across a bridge through a graffiti-laden neighborhood, taking the audience through what we will later learn are the rough streets of Baltimore. Andie's voiceover offers nostalgic memories of growing up as a dancer. She narrates as the visuals provide a trip through Baltimore's ghetto:

> I remember the first time I saw someone move like they were from another planet, couldn't keep my eyes away. When I was little, my mom took me to watch a jam session in the neighborhood; started out small but word spread. Soon some of the best dancers around were showing up to compete and something they eventually called "The Streets" became the hub, and I got a front row seat to history. I wanted to glide and spin and fly like they did but it didn't come easy. My mom would tell me "don't give up, just be you.' Cause life's too short to be anybody else." She was right. When I was 16 my mom got sick [and] in a couple months she was gone and everything changed, including the streets.[14]

Step Up 2: The Streets departs from the typical narrative hip-hop dance film in which dance emerges triumphant. Indeed, dance will be triumphant but this time the white lead is not an outsider who infiltrates the neighborhood yet seems to not really belong. In *Step Up 2*, Andie is *from* the neighborhood. She lives *there*, her closest friends are black and Latina/o, and her whiteness frames her as the minority. The film's departure from racial binaries highlights class as the differentiating factor. *Step Up 2* successfully illustrates how "epidermic-reality" does not determine which dancing bodies can make the beat visible in the global hip-hop nation.[15] Yet, the film still relies on black performativity to authenticate and legitimize white participation in an African American form.

Cultural theorists Mickey Hess[16] and Todd Fraley[17] thoroughly interrogate the performativity of race and the need for white authenticity in hip-hop. In his analysis of white rapper Eminem, Hess explains how the artist learned from the Vanilla Ice debacle[18] that he should not attempt to align his identity with that of poor black youth. Instead, Eminem turns his personal experience into material for his lyrics, ultimately presenting "a new model of white hip-hop authenticity in which being true to yourself and to your lived experiences can eclipse notions of hip-hop as explicitly black-owned."[19] A direct geographical connection to "black urban neighborhoods," however, is crucial for audience consumption and acceptance of a white rapper's authenticity, writes Fraley.[20]

While *Step Up 2* is not about rappers, the analysis still applies. The establishing scene in *Step Up 2* firmly situates Andie as a legitimate resident of Baltimore, thereby affirming her authentic relationship to a black space. "The 410" crew uses Baltimore's area code as their name specifically to "rep" their turf. Furthermore, her deceased mother instilled in her the importance of "being true to herself." The opening scene then simultaneously negates "blackness," and deploys it as a legitimizing agent. Even if the audience does not recognize Baltimore as a predominately black city, historically, images of run-down streets, graffiti, and breakdancing become synonymous with the inner city and thus signify "blackness." The audience assumes black bodies move in these spaces without the predominance of their visual presence. Andie's whiteness and the diverse bodies dancing in the cipher are situated within this black setting, yet her mother's reminder to "just be you," communicates the irrelevancy of race and gender. This dismissal yet a reliance on blackness reveals how hip-hop "renders visible" the performative nature of race while still relying on essentialized notions of black performativity.[21] The negation of blackness also interrogates notions of whiteness in the cultural imaginary.

In his seminal article on whiteness, Richard Dyer argues that we have to work to make whiteness visible, since the filmic apparatus establishes whiteness as a pervasive norm by which all non-white bodies are defined.[22] However, this is not the case in any aspect of hip-hop: b-girls/boys, MCing, DJing, or graffiti writing. Whiteness is hyper-visible in hip-hop, as are women in this notably masculine form, originated and performed primarily by Latino and African American males. But race, like gender, is socially constructed through a series of embodied repetitive acts defined and reinforced by specific cultural codes.[23] That is, what it means to be a man, woman, or a member of a particular race is embedded in our cultural practices of these codes and reinforced by our repetitive performance of these practices. The b-boy/girl cipher, however, destabilizes the performative constructs of race and gender. In the cipher, diverse raced, classed, and gendered bodies riff off of one another to inform new ways of moving. To center its narrative around race as its filmic predecessors have would negate the lived diversity of the global hip-hop nation. Hence, when a white male body strikes a b-boy stance, Middle America no longer gasps in surprise. His body can still signify blackness, but the commodification of hip-hop and other black cultural expressions ensures comfort with this particular performance of blackness by young white males. The white b-boy's performance once again reveals race as a performative construct and illustrates that bodies can learn gestures or the "corporeal orature" involved. In contrast, a woman's embodiment of a form defined as masculine however, can still read as transgressive to audiences adhering to normative ideas of masculinity and femininity.

Playground Aesthetics or "Dancing Like a Black Girl?"

Feminist scholar bell hooks reminds us that white male slave owners constructed black women as "masculinized, domineering, amazonic creatures" to explain their ability to endure hardships no "lady" was supposedly capable of enduring (...). [24] In contrast, white women represent grace, civility, chastity, and ideals of beauty, reminiscent of the nineteenth-century's cult of true womanhood.[25] But the construction of feminine whiteness counters this narrow representation of womanhood. Thus, a white woman performs a serious transgression when she participates in an aggressive, competitive, physically demanding dance form like breakdancing. This transgression marks the appeal in films like *Step Up 2: The Streets*. Andie's performance in the film, however, is anything but masculine, in fact her clothes and choreography work together to make her the central object of desire. Throughout the film, Andie mostly

FIGURE 11.4 Screen capture of *Step Up 2: The Streets*, director Jon M. Chu, 2008, Andie improvises for the class.

wears revealing mid-drift tank tops and her signature move is not a b-girl power move but her ability to execute choreographed steps, and jiggle her buttocks. Dare I say, "like a black girl?"

In "Making New Friends," the fifth scene of the film, Andie sits on the dance floor with her new classmates uncomfortably waiting for her turn to improvise. "Listen and interpret" the teacher (Will Kemp) commands. He then plays a lyrical song to which Andie responds, "Are you serious?" and then dances to illustrate her command of street forms. Andie's performance ends in rapid stutter steps and, with her arms extended forward and bent at the elbows, her hands in loose fists, she arches her back, looks over her shoulder and watches her buttocks jiggle (Fig. 11.4). Kemp abruptly stops the music, pulls her aside and scolds her. The scene cuts to Andie walking out of the building and down the front stairs while the sound of little girls chanting a rhythmic game drones in the background. Andie leans against a pillar and longingly looks toward the sound. The camera reveals a group of four little black girls playing doubleDutch (Fig. 11.5). Her future love interest in the film, dancer/choreographer Robert Hoffman, interrupts her melancholy. The two flirt cynically with one another as the camera cuts back and forth between them and the double-Dutch crew.

The doubleDutchers consist of ten black youth—nine females and one male. They appear to range from elementary school- to high school-aged youth. The original four jumpers and turners sit along a chain-linked fence waiting for their turn with the rest of the participants. A girl and boy turn the ropes while one girl jumps, and her rapid consecutive steps and slightly arched back causes her buttocks to vibrate and jiggle, reminding the audience about Andie's performance from the previous classroom improvisation scene. The girl does not look over her shoulder to watch her shaking behind as did Andie. Instead, she is playing a game, not performing or directing the audience where

FIGURE 11.5 Screen capture of *Step Up 2: The Streets*, director Jon M. Chu, 2008, children jumping double Dutch.

to gaze. Unaware of how the filmic apparatus choreographs black women's "butts" as excessive, lewd, and hypersexual, the little girl drives pleasure out of the physicality of her moving body.

In *The Black Dancing Body*, dance scholar Brenda Dixon-Gottschild devotes an entire chapter to the "butt" to narrate its contested participation in American dance history. I present a quote from her writing on Josephine Baker to surmise the power and influence attached to jiggling black behinds: "In the white-supremacist view this butt was the degenerate sign and symbol of a black wave sweeping over Europe and threatening Aryan hegemony—a war of the races raged on the battlefield of Baker's black behind, so to speak."[26] In *Step Up 2*, however, Andie's butt rages no wars; instead, the film constructs it as a spectacle exclusive to her white body in order to illustrate her aptitude and connection to black social dance expression. A corporeal fluency acquired on the playground with (other) little black girls, who were her playmates.

DoubleDutch as a childhood game has specific implications for African American women and their participation in hip-hop, affirms Kyra D. Grant. Categorizing doubleDutch as a musical game played by black girls, Grant theorizes, the rhythmic chants, jumping, and rope-turning are later reflected in African American "musical activities" and dance."[27] In 1982 *the Double Dutch Girls* accompanied the breakdancing Rocky Steady Crew, and graffiti artists on a European tour featuring "subculture expressions from New York City."[28] DoubleDutch was an integral part of the development of hip-hop aesthetics but the continual masculinization of hip-hop culture rendered invisible the participation of black girls.[29] Grant notes, however, that hip-hop choreographer Leslie Segar acknowledged in a 1993 interview "that double-dutch represented an 'old school' influence that contributes to hip-hop choreography."[30]

And, we see this contribution in *Step Up 2: The Streets* the minute we recognize from where Andie learned her particular butt reverberation step. This moment in the film does not strive to pay tribute to the influence of double Dutch on hip-hop choreography so much as it is yet another opportunity to establish Andie as an authentic dancing body in hip-hop. The filmic apparatus choreographs Andie's dancing as an integral part of her embodied cultural experience, yet shrouds the labor of the young black bodies with which she aligns herself. Taken from the playground and placed in other contexts, black girls' jiggling flesh transgresses, while Andie elevates her white flesh as an accomplished, aesthetically pleasing spectacle. She may be a white girl but black cultural expression is as much hers as it is the black girls' playing double Dutch. Yet another example of how hip-hop aesthetics toggle back and forth between a dependence on identifiable black performance aesthetics yet problematizes the expectations of which bodies can perform these aesthetics.

Andie's gender performance also relies on the gendered performances of the other female characters in the film. Andie's relationship to other women in the movie is shaky at best. Here, the movie depends on stereotypes of black women and Latinas. Initially, her best friends include a black woman, Felicia (Telisha Shaw), and a Latina, Missy (Danielle Polanco) who are also members of "The 410" crew (Fig. 11.6). Andie's acceptance into MSA compromises her relationship with the two women. She will no longer be able to regularly rehearse with the crew. Felicia, who in the beginning is a friendly, supportive friend "who has Andie's back" and would cover for her when she missed rehearsals, quickly turns into the mean, aggressive, sharp-tongued black woman over-represented in popular culture. Missy performs as the boy-crazy "spicy" Latina,

FIGURE 11.6 Screen capture of *Step Up 2: The Streets*, director Jon M. Chu, 2008, Andie sits with Felicia and Missy during rehearsal with "The 410."

FIGURE 11.7 Screen capture of *Step Up 2: The Streets*, director Jon M. Chu, 2008, Andie and the "MSA Misfits" head to Missy's party.

another trite representation. She also turns against Andie but has a change of heart after "The 410" humiliates Andie and her crew of MSA misfits at a battle (Fig. 11.7). Aside from Andie, the MSA crew has two other women, an Asian foreign exchange student (Mari Koda) who expertly performs old school hip-hop, and a black girl (Janelle Cambridge), who is "too tall to partner." Multiracial pop songstress Cassie Ventura plays the high school's triple threat Sophie (she sings, acts, and dances) and is a direct antagonist to Andie. They desire the same white man.

Situating Andie as the one "white girl" amongst all women of color accomplishes two specific goals at once. First, it further demonstrates that race does not determine which female bodies can and should dance which styles; this is determined by specific class distinctions. Sophie (Ventura) is the privileged middle-class girl whose parents can afford to provide ballet lessons and the tuition to MSA, while Andie whose whiteness positons her as the assumed body for concert dance forms fails miserably in her private ballet lessons with the head teacher. Sophie displays her elitism when she turns up her nose when asked to help with the garbage at Missy's house party. Koda, who is a foreign exchange student, quickly jumps in and saves her from performing the demeaning task. At Missy's home we also witness Andie's expertise in salsa, demonstrating once again the ease she feels among black and brown people and their dance forms, an ease not felt in the assumed white, elite space of MSA.

The second function of the multiracial female cast is to highlight Andie's femininity. Andie's clothing is far more feminine and revealing than the other female dancers in the MSA crew. Koda always wears a Kangol hat, tank tops, and baggy pants, or a sweat suit,

FIGURE 11.8 Screen capture of *Step Up 2: The Streets*, director Jon M. Chu, 2008, Final battle scene with Andie, Missy, and Koda.

reflecting her affinity to old-school hip-hop à la Run–D.M.C, as well as LL Cool J before his illustrious acting career. Cambridge, the tall black girl character, wears unattractive bifocals and dresses in frumpy baggy clothes. The distinction between Andie and the MSA female misfits actualizes in the final battle scene of the movie. Andie dons her signature red bra top, while the rest of the women are dressed in the same drab, baggy clothes similar to the men (Fig. 11.8). Aside from Andie, it is difficult to make gender distinctions based on apparel.

Andie is not as hypersexualized, however, as Missy's spicy Latina, who always sports outfits to highlight her feminine assets. At her party, she forces Andie to change into a dress before she meets Missy's cousin, declaring, "Latin men like their girls to look like women, not boys." Once Andie emerges in Missy's white spaghetti-strap sundress, Missy gasps, "Miss thing, you got titties!" Dressed in white, with her brunette hair released from its ponytail to flow down her back, Andie enacts feminine beauty, indirect contrast to her asexual MSA crew counterparts and the hypersexual Latina (Fig. 11.9). Andie's whiteness affords her the opportunity to navigate various aspects of her femininity. She can be the sexy yet tough b-girl, the soft, feminine innocent, and in the final scene of the movie, the hypersexual focus of desire. This then is the constructed power of whiteness. Andie's ability to shift between assumed static boundaries reifies whiteness as a privileged state of being, while the women of color remain stuck in old media constructs of their identities.

FIGURE 11.9 Screen capture of *Step Up 2: The Streets*, director Jon M. Chu, 2008, Andie salsa dances with Chase.

CONCLUSION: PARADOXICAL CIPHERS

Admittedly my initial response to *Step Up 2* was not that of a dance scholar, but of an African American woman who as a budding teen witnessed the commercial birth of "breakdancing" through *Flashdance* and later *Breakin'*. I remember wondering why there were no women that looked like me in these movies. Although I am not a b-girl, I can still (kind of) execute black social dances with relative skill and swag. I remain deeply impacted by the absence of women who look like me in the lead roles of films that rely on black dancing bodies for authenticity. However, as a dance scholar I read and interpret the significance of this absence from the films of the past and presently from *Step Up 2*, with what black feminist scholar bell hooks refers to as the black female's oppositional gaze. She contends that, with the possible exception of early race movies, black female

> spectators have had to develop looking relations within a cinematic context that constructs our presence as absence, that denies the "body" of the black female so as

to perpetuate white supremacy and with it a phallocentric spectatorship where the woman to be looked at and desired is "white."[31]

Thus my analysis works to illustrate how the filmic apparatus appropriates the labor of black female bodies on playgrounds and dance floors to buttress the performance of white female hip-hop dancers. I wish to render visible all of the bodies that laid the foundation for the dancing hip-hop nation. To this end, I return to *Step Up 2: The Streets*, when Andie and the MSA misfits prepare to battle "The 410," at the local hang out "The Streets." The host, however, will not let Andie's crew battle, claiming they are not from "here." Andie chastises the crowd for forgetting the history of "The Streets" and delivers a rousing speech asserting the diversity of the hip-hop cipher:

> Some of you guys think that we don't belong here, but it doesn't matter where we're from. The Streets are supposed to be about different people coming together. We call this a battle but what are we fighting for? We're all here because we have this thing we do. We dance. Right? Being a part of the Streets used to mean much more than just turf or power. It was about bringing something new to the floor. And it shouldn't matter what we wear, what school or what neighborhood we're from, because the best part about the Streets is that it's not about what you got but what you make of what you got. So If the 410's too scared to defend their title against us then hell, we'll be outside doing our thing where the Streets started.[32]

Andie's final speech and *Step Up 2: The Streets* reiterate dichotomous narratives in hip-hop dance films that are both relevant and frightening. The film, like hip-hop, destabilizes essentialized notions of race but reifies trite representations of gender. Diverse raced, classed, and gendered bodies can all join the b-girl/b-boy cipher but the filmic apparatus still casts notions of desirably femininity on white female bodies to the detriment of women of color. Hip-hop dance forms render whiteness hyper-visible, but the white performance of black performativity becomes the selling point for films where black performers are cast as ancillary characters to authenticate the white protagonists. The theme of universal belonging expressed in this final scene washes over real issues of racism, classism, and sexism evident by casting practices that objectify white women as marketing tools, or by narratives that exploit inner-city poverty and violence to sell films. As dance scholars we must work to illuminate the dancing bodies wedged "in the middle" between the politics of filmic representations, production, and audience consumption.

NOTES

1. Jorge "Popmaster Fabel" Pabon, an original member of the Rock Steady Crew, insists that the media coverage in the 1980s grouped New York's b-boying and b-girling with the popping and locking of the West Coast "funk" movement, referring to them collectively as

"breakdancing." See "Physical Graffiti: The History of Hip-Hop Dance," in *Total Chaos*, ed. Jeff Chang (New York: Basic Civitas, 2006), 18.

2. *Breakin'*, IMDb, Internet Movie Database, accessed January 8, 2011. http://www.imdb.com/title/tt0086998/.

3. For a discussion on the globalization of hip-hop in dance studies, please see Halifu Osumare, *The Africanist Aesthetic in Global Hip-Hop: Power Moves* (New York: Palgrave Macmillan), 2008.

4. Shanara R. Reid-Brinkley. "The Essence of Res(ex)pectability: Black Women's Negotiation of Black Femininity in Rap Music and Music Video," in *Meridians: Feminism, Race, Transnationalism* 8, no. 1 (2008): 236–260.

5. The *Hip-Hop Studies Reader* contains an entire section dedicated to the role of black women in hip-hop. See Murray Forman and Mark Anthony Neal, eds., "I'll Be Nina Simone Defecating on Your Microphone: Hip Hop and Gender," in *That's the Joint: The Hip-Hop Studies Reader* (New York: Routledge), 247–306.

6. Thomas F. DeFrantz, "The Black Beat Made Visible: Hip Hop Dance and Body Power," in *Of the Presence of the Body: Essays on Dance and Performance Theory*, ed. André Lepecki (Middletown, CT: Wesleyan University Press, 2004), 67.

7. Ibid.

8. Ibid., 71

9. Dance scholar Marta Savigliano argues that the filmic representations of other cultures provide contemporary audiences with the allusion of an ethnographic experience from the comfort of their living rooms. See Marta Savigliano, *Angora Matta: Fatal Acts of North-South Translations* (Middletown, CT: Wesleyan University Press, 2003), 209–224.

10. See Blanco Borelli's article in this volume.

11. *Step Up* (2006); *Step Up 2: The Streets* (2008); *Step Up3D* (2010); *Step Up Revolution* (2012).

12. According to the 2011 census, 63.6 percent of Baltimore residents identify as black. For a brief review of census data please see, "Baltimore city QuickFacts from the US Census Bureau," accessed August 29, 2012. thttp://quickfacts.census.gov/qfd/states/24/24510.html.

13. Ezra Klein, "How Dangerous is Baltimore," *Washington Post*, November 12, 2009. http://voices.washingtonpost.com/ezra-klein/2009/11/how_dangerous_is_baltimore.html.

14. *Step Up 2: The Streets*, directed by Jon Chu, choreography by Jamal Sims, Nadine "Hi Hat" Ruffin, and Dave Scott (2008; Burbank, CA: Touchstone/Disney, 2009), DVD.

15. Here I reference DeFrantz's "The Black Beat Made Visible" and Osumare's *The Africanist Aesthetics in Global Hip-Hop*.

16. Mickey Hess, "Hip-Hop Realness and the White Performer," *Critical Studies in Media Communication* 22, no. 5 (December 2005): 372–389.

17. Todd Fraley, "I Got a Natural Skill . . .: Hip-Hop, Authenticity, and Whiteness," *Howard Journal of Communication* 20, no. 1 (2009): 37–54.

18. Rapper Vanilla Ice falsely marketed himself as having grown up in the ghetto with a criminal record to align him with the "rap rhetoric." See Mickey Hess, "Hip-Hop Realness," 374.

19. Mickey Hess, "Hip-Hop Realness," 373.

20. Todd Fraley, "I Got a Natural Skill," 43.

21. Ibid., 39.

22. Richard Dyer, *White* (London: Routledge, 1997).

23. For a full discussion on performativity, see Judith Butler, *Bodies that Matter: On the Discursive Limits of Sex* (New York: Routledge, 1993).

24. See bell hooks, *Ain't I A Woman: Black Women and Feminism* (Boston: South End Press, 1981), 81–82.
25. See Evelynn M. Hammond, "Toward a Genealogy of Black Female Sexuality: The Problematic of Silence," in *Feminist Genealogies, Colonial Legacies, Democratic Future*, ed. Jacqui Alexander and Achandra Talpade Mohanty (New York: Routledge, 1997), 93–104.
26. Brenda Dixon-Gottschild, *The Black Dancing Body: A Geography From Coon to Cool"* (New York: Palgrave Macmillan, 2003), 156.
27. Kyra D. Grant, "Translating Double-Dutch to Hip-Hop: The Musical Vernacular of Black Girls' Play," in *That's the Joint! The Hip-Hop Studies Reader*, ed. Murray Forman and Mark Anthony Neal (New York: Routledge, 2004), 251.
28. Ibid., 260.
29. Ibid.
30. Ibid.
31. bell hooks, *Reel to Real: Race Sex and Class at the Movies* (New York: Routledge, 1996), 199.
32. *Step Up 2: The Streets*, directed by Jon Chu.

BIBLIOGRAPHY

"Baltimore City QuickFacts From the US Census Bureau." Accessed August 29, 2012. thttp://quickfacts.census.gov/qfd/states/24/24510.html.

Breakin'. IMDb. The Internet Movie Database. Accessed January 8, 2011. http://www.imdb.com/title/tt0086998/.

Brinkley, Shanara R. Reid. "The Essence of Res(ex)pectability: Black Women's Negotiation of Black Femininity in Rap Music and Music Video." In *Meridians: Feminism, Race, Transnationalism* 8, no. 1 (2008): 236–260.

Butler, Judith. *Bodies That Matter: On the Discursive Limits of Sex*. New York: Routledge, 1993.

DeFrantz, Thomas F. "The Black Beat Made Visible: Hip Hop Dance and Body Power." In *Of the Presence of the Body: Essays on Dance and Performance Theory*, edited by André Lepecki, 64–81. Middletown, CT: Wesleyan University Press, 2004.

Dyer, Richard. *White*. London, Routledge, 1997.

Forman, Murray, and Mark Anthony Neal, eds. *That's the Joint! The Hip-Hop Studies Reader*. New York: Routledge, 2004.

Fraley, Todd. "I Got a Natural Skill . . .: Hip-Hop, Authenticity, and Whiteness." *Howard Journal of Communication* 20 (2009): 37–54.

Grant, Kyra D. "Translating Double-Dutch to Hip-Hop: The Musical Vernacular of Black Girls' Play." In *That's the Joint! The Hip-Hop Studies Reader*, edited by Murray Forman and Mark Anthony Neal, 251–263. New York: Routledge, 2004.

Gottschild, Brenda Dixon. *The Black Dancing Body: A Geography From Coon to Cool*. New York: Palgrave Macmillan, 2003.

Hammonds, Evelynn M. "Toward a Genealogy of Black Female Sexuality: The Problematic of Silence." In *Feminist Genealogies, Colonial Legacies, Democratic Future*, edited by Jacqui Alexander and Achandra Talpade Mohanty, 93–104. New York: Routledge, 1997.

Hess, Mickey. "Hip-hop Realness and the White Performer." *Critical Studies in Media Communication* 22, no. 5 (December 2005): 372–389.

hooks, bell. *Ain't I A Woman: Black Women and Feminism*. Boston: South End Press, 1981.

——. *Reel to Real: Race Sex and Class at the Movies.* New York: Routledge, 1996.

Klein, Ezra. "How Dangerous is Baltimore." *Washington Post*, November 12, 2009. http://voices. washingtonpost.com/ezra-klein/2009/11/how_dangerous_is_baltimore.html

Osumare, Halifu. *The Africanist Aesthetic in Global Hip-hop: Power Moves.* New York: Palgrave Macmillan, 2008.

Pabon, Jorge, "Popmaster Fabel." "Physical Graffiti: The History of Hip-Hop Dance." In *Total Chaos*, edited by Jeff Chang, 18–26. New York: Basic Civitas, 2006, 18.

Savigliano, Marta. *Angora Matta: Fatal Acts of North-South Translation.* Middletown, CT: Wesleyan University Press, 2003.

Step Up 2: The Streets. Directed by Jon Chu. Choreographed by Jamal Sims, Nadine "Hi Hat" Ruffin, and Dave Scott. 2008. Burbank, CA: Touchstone/Disney, 2009. DVD.

CHAPTER 12

....

AFFECT-IVE MOVES: SPACE, VIOLENCE, AND THE BODY IN *RIZE*'S KRUMP DANCING

....

STEPHANIE L. BATISTE[*]

KRUMP dancing, as envisioned in the rousing documentary film *RIZE* (David LaChapelle, 2005), seems to conjure concepts outside of itself. Beyond the movements, paces, and faces, the documentary positions the dance form and its dance communities as responses to violence, dispossession, and urban alienation. Far beyond negotiating such oppressive context, however, the creative acts of krump and clown dancing express young L.A. dancers' sense of self and community through kinetic affect, that is, through a complex expressive matrix of joy, disappointment, ownership, ecstasy, and danger that they embed in the dance. Affect refers to internal sensations that we translate into feelings. The performance and cultural expression constituted by krump and clown dance emerge as a affective mode of engagement with experiences of home, space, and the city. This dance practice defines a space of home as a system of feeling in millennial Los Angeles. As such, kinetic affect defines space through dance as a relationship between community and the body. Home here is not so much a material edifice as a set of spaces where one embodies community. The body and dance animate and theorize concepts of violence and belonging, rather than serve as a defense against the proliferation of one and lack of another. Via the milieus and scenarios represented in *RIZE*, krump dancing reveals a rich world of love and pain through which dancers characterize life in black urban space.[1] The scenario is a moment in which performers in "the act" inherently engage participants, the present, the past, and perhaps the future. Following Sara Ahmed's proposition that far from individual, affect is a social process that defines and binds particular groups of people, I contend that these dancers re-imagine individuality and black racial identity via affect and in the process refuse external applications of self and community definition.[2] The range of krump's affective performance confounds any sense of how black subjects are supposed to feel, as dancers define and defy the limits of affective circumscription or stereotype. Physical movement permits the embodied

FIGURE 12.1 Screen capture of *RIZE*, director David LaChapelle, (2005), Social group of dancers describing their practice in agreement and casual support.

subject, the dancing agent, to take over, to create meaning and craft theory beyond words, and to enforce kinetic bonds of resonating communal connection.

The dance form demonstrates kinetic control and flawless rhythmic precision demonstrated in profound speed almost too rapid for the eye to absorb that gets broken by pauses and real-time slow motion. This freestyle, hip-hop dance is improvised within a broad spectrum of "jabs, arm swings, chest pops, and stomps" and most often takes place within a circle, or cipher, of participant spectators.[3] Forceful swinging and pulsing of the arms from the shoulders and elbows accompanies and alternates with intense concave and convex contractions and extensions of the torso, lifting of the chest, and quick patterns and rhythms displayed by the feet. Arms often gesture forward, out, and up. Multi-directional rotation of the torso from the hips and through the thighs includes vertical, horizontal, and diagonal swings. In some instances dancers bounce and extend the butt, but more often in krump the pelvis is neutral or jabs forward via extreme abdominal contraction. Dancers move the arms, feet, legs, and torso simultaneously or in quick succession. Incorporating influences of 1980s breakdancing, krumpers perform flips, handstands, drops, and spins that are oriented toward and across the ground.

Over and over again in the scenarios offered by the documentary film, dancers display these infectious moves in ways not seen before. Heavy dramatic bass beats provide the sonic environment for most krump dancing. The intensity, speed, and physical risk of the dancing projects self-assurance, performative control, and power.

The documentary film attempts to trace the development of two related forms of dance in young black communities that began in South Central Los Angeles around the turn of the millennium—clowning and krumping. Clowning as a widespread practice was initiated by Thomas Johnson, "Tommy the Clown," as an act for party entertainment. Johnson would dress in full clown attire and provide humor, music, and participatory dancing at events.[4] Clowning maintains an entertainment ethos in its investments in pleasure and play. This includes a playful, overt sensuality rooted in a bouncing of the gluteus that some call the stripper dance. The colorful clown appearance and its individual appropriations characterize its practitioners. Krump dancing is aggressive and aggressively abstract, resists the production of commercial pleasure, draws and uses audience response while not pursuing or pandering to it, and eschews approval, so that even though it is also a community practice it is even more internally focused, and demonstrates a sensuality rooted in forceful provocation rather than ironic seduction. Krump aesthetics revise and reject the clown in specific face painting practices and dress.

This chapter focuses predominantly on the in situ representations of krump dancing that *RIZE* archives. The film and the dance form constitute different artistic genres that reinforce and contradict each other in various ways. Some tension exists between the two, in that LaChapelle's film perpetrates some of the classic nativizing characteristics of ethnographic film.[5] It interviews subjects without recognition of the presence and shaping influence of the researcher; it presents self-revealing informants; its informants narrate anthropology's most basic form of "primitive" culture, dance; it uses panoramic views as a shorthand for locational difference; and it intersperses unidentified, de-contextualized and de-historicized, color-faded film footage—late twentieth-century footage visually cast as older, de-historicized, and thus timeless--overlaid with decidedly ritual drums—of "tribal" "African" dancers' limber bodies[6] (hear/see the primitive) as a homogenizing collapsing of and visual shorthand for complex connections of black diaspora. For these reasons, neither the film nor its thesis about black urban life can be taken at face value. These techniques proffer the simple, almost banal, thesis that then seems to be proposed by the youth themselves: urban black life is brutal and dance serves as an outlet. The banality of this statement rests implicitly on the primitivist connection between black bodies and dance that undermines more serious consideration of the significance and complexity of black dance forms. Further, the film narrative makes a direct connection between violence, misery, and dance as escape or consolation offering a stereotypical, elementary idea about art-making. Anyone who has heard of Picasso or Basquiat or ever watched *Behind the Music* knows that it is not always misery that breeds art and has seen that the process of creativity itself, along with the difficulties of life that inspire or disrupt it, does not always amount to healing or triumph. In fact, *RIZE*'s own exposure of some dancers' economic or artistic motivations to dance and of others' continued struggles with life despite dance undermines the facile claim that art stems from and provides a release from oppression. Fortunately, the dance form itself reveals a more complicated story, whereby performers critique and transform, rather than merely respond to their environment. To the extent that *RIZE* positions violence as a determining contextual element in the development of its thesis, this chapter takes up krump's engagement with violence to reveal dancers' complicated relationship to this aspect of urban life. To some extent "rizing" above generic boundaries and the formulaic heritage of ethnographic film history that bears heavily upon *RIZE*, the subjects use the kinetic control offered by the very mode of the dance presented to shake the boundaries of the ethnographic frame. The dancers' commando-style ownership of the physical spaces, content, and presentation of the performance challenges the confining space of ethnographic film.[7]

Navigating the ever-present frame of LaChapelle's ethnographic lens, this chapter attends to elements of the dance preserved in *RIZE* for their significance in the community that performs them. Important here is the educational function through which *RIZE* as a popular documentary film shifted a local practice to a mass market and rightly identified the producers of a form that had begun to appear in mass mediated spaces. The exposure increased dancers' opportunities for public and mediated performance and in some cases for employment as artists. Anna B. Scott observes that black dance and black film developed together as recordings became one of the ways dancers experienced each other's performance and choreographic work.[8] Although filmic frames in the United States have often been racist and stereotyping, film, video, and television became communicative spaces where dance has been preserved and traded across distances of geography and time. Dancers' own interactive, navigational practices in using film serve as a model for my own excavation of meaning in *RIZE*'s dance milieus.

KRUMP DANCE AS KINETIC AFFECT

Krumping reveals a connection between affect, community, and the body. In multiple moments ecstatic krumpers fall or cast themselves into the bodies or hands of others on the cipher who lift and throw them back into its center. An exchange occurs between dancers, participants, and gazers in these moments that exemplify intense exchanges of feeling present in the dance. Meanings of "affect" as something experienced include "an inner disposition or feeling; the capacity for willing or desiring; a mental state, mood, or emotion; a desire or appetite; the outward display of emotion or mood, as manifested by facial expression, posture, gestures, tone of voice, etc.; senses relating to the body; an abnormal state of the body; a disease or disorder (*n*)."[9] Meanings of affect as something done include "to have an effect on the mind or feelings of (a person); to impress or influence emotionally; to move, touch; to aim at, aspire to; to seek to obtain or attain; to assume or display (a quality, etc.) for effect (*v¹*)."[10] Affect is embodied as impression, sensibility, or sensation and also finds or is defined by expression. In this sense affect can be personal and transmissible—transmissible in linking souls specifically through means often termed "inexpressible" or "beyond words." The character of being beyond words seems to heighten inversely with the depth of feeling—affording wordless dance the capacity to capture and transmit intense affective power in its very gestures. Affect is internal and external and often powerfully involved in the constitution of the self and the impact of others.[11] To liken affect to disease means to insist upon its total penetration of the body and it's inextricability from the flesh as well as its power to bring change. The "disease" or proliferating impact here is created by an infection of love and communal support. As a community-oriented social dance practice, krumping defines itself through the possibility of a total embodiment as a physical goal. Extension beyond the self as a spiritual goal in the dance practice achieves resonance between the individual and the group, the body and the environment, the internal and the external. Performers, as such, can be said to trade in accessing, perhaps producing, and distributing affect as feeling or emotion. Krump's kinetic affective communication evokes dancers' enactments of feeling on a level that is personal and internal, the possibility and projection of sensation and sensibility in a manner transmissible and interpersonal, and the crafted display of emotion as a practice of intentional (and sincere) artifice. Each part of the body moves in idiosyncratic rhythm, improvisationally coordinated with all the others parts in thousands of beats per minute, each beat hitting like a blow delivered to the surrounding space. This force of movement from a particular part of the body, say a fist, combined with a facial grimace, or a swing of the head and arm combined with some choreographic "wink" in the overlapping ciphers, that is, in the communities and spaces of krump performance, communicates joy, belonging, release, frustration, rejection, humor, desire, etc.[12] Since hip-hop dance performance operates like the speech act "I dare you," it poses to its audience an open challenge for response that manifests the transitive nature of affect.[13] My analysis identifies that response as a spectrum of feelings that inhabits networks of interpersonal connections. Krumpers theorize the power of kinetic affect in their dance's infectious exciting character, especially since they accomplish it by focusing inward to achieve "personal transcendence" as much as by projecting outward to the audience.[14]

Dancers and dance communities display a broad range of rich emotions in different scenarios throughout the documentary. A calmness and contentment characterizes young folks, including La Nina, Baby Tight Eyez, and others who have allowed the filmmakers into their home spaces for interviews. After a public "Battlezone," dancers reveal vulnerability in their sharing of disappointment, frustration, and anger about losing the competition. One dancer's expression of rage manifests itself in his insistence on his own proficiency and the value of his particular methods. After unknown perpetrators rob community leader Tommy-the-Clown's home, his friends empathize and comfort him in his sadness and sense of betrayal and loss. A young "Tight Eyez" describes acting as a surrogate father for a younger dancer, "Baby Tight Eyez," who has been named after him. Networks of close relationships and fictive kin that form the substance of clown and krump dance communities show dancing to be much more than a linear response to random external stimuli. In dance spaces, performers watch, encourage, celebrate, and exhort. The affective diversity of krump scenarios undermines the film's somewhat simplistic thesis that black people have tough lives so they

FIGURE 12.2 Screen capture of *RIZE*, director David LaChapelle, (2005), Dancers and witnesses on cipher encourage and cajole the dancer.

"Dance!"[15] as some manifestation of instinct or nature. Rather, dancing responds to and stimulates complicated relationships between people and their surroundings. Performers reveal joy, anger, love, sorrow, pain, disappointment, despair, excitement, thrills, consolation, and empathy in an exposure of the personal risk and trust involved in working together via kinetic art.

The dancers experience a pleasure derived from their own bodies. The motion is transcendent and sensual in its total embodiment. This embodied pleasure operates as physically and psychically invigorating motion, because, like any creative practice, the dancing is both an opportunity for release—venting, letting go, exercise, and for production—creativity, skill, improvement, commitment, making and doing something meaningful. Dancers boldly confess their feelings and strive to enact them. In this sense, the culture of dancing permits (or reveals) intense emotional interaction. Dancers demonstrate a strong sense of emotional honesty and empathy so commonplace that they take it for granted; yet that accrues little notice when urbanites are represented as tough, as survivors, or as victims. The community formed in the tight-knit groups shown in *RIZE* project affect in the substance of the dance and in dancers' interactions with one another.

A close reading of some uses of the body in krump dance reveals krump's own kinetic creation of affect, as well as maintenance of an affective matrix in, and extending beyond, the cipher. Dancers repeat a motion in which they extend their full torsos forward from the low top of the hips and up, breastbone reaching impossibly skyward. This move is often accompanied by a horizontal or downward extension and/or retraction of the arms. This lifting renders the heart and core of the body both exposed and elevated, thrust forth with power and intention. Despite the careful grimaces that characterize krump performance, this heart-centered, lung-thrust-lifting manifests the core of the joy that I see embedded in the dance. A concave retraction of the torso often eventually resolves in a return to a version of the lifted torso position. This heart-breath-lifting often precedes and follows the falls where dancers are caught, lifted, and patted or slapped by the hands of other dancers in the cipher. The patting is a life-touch that resurrects the spirit after the fall—a communication, an affirmation of community and recognition. The aggression of the chest lift, simplistically read as anger, strikes me as a physicalized rebellion against anger, against death and reclamation of a heart- and breath-centered life. Through its concrete-defying acrobatics and hyperspeed limb contractions and extensions, as well as its rotations of the spine, the core of the krumper's body returns and returns again to the lifted chest and abdomen with straight, concave, or hyper-extended back. Even the twists and vibrations of the hips or shoulders seem masterfully disarticulated from a stable, strong, and forceful torso. The vibrant energy of the chest thrust animates a resurrection from the self, the group, the street, and the city that precipitated, necessarily ironically, in the communal nature of the cipher. This sharing and affirmation, extension, response, and lifting and response again produce joy in the cipher. The satisfaction of mastery in the dancer and her crew produces joy in technique and virtuosity, sublimeness and transcendence in "buckness"—a spiritual state of solitude

FIGURE 12.3 Screen capture of *RIZE*, director David LaChapelle, (2005), Lil' C performance of krump's iconic chest thrust in the cipher with dancers.

and power that characterizes krump proficiency. The power of this stasis and control of the core provides a consistency and stability through krump's frenetic changes such that the other gesticulating parts of the body can also be in humorous, sensual, aggressive, or tragic juxtaposition to the torso. The torso from hips to shoulders provides a home space in krump practice.

RETHINKING "VIOLENCE" AND HOME

Violence takes many external forms in millennial Los Angeles, including gang violence, police brutality, the LA uprising, and gunshot wound deaths so common that folk wisdom accuses the LA coroner's office of calling them death by "natural causes." Both violence and creativity buffer the space between the pained embodiment of the dead and the mournful embodiment of the living in Central and South Central Los Angeles. The social violence of unemployment, underfunded schools, and incarceration enacts an emotional violence that families, friends, leaders, and organizations hustle to stem.[16] Some of *RIZE*'s featured youth report deeply personal, social experiences with drug-use, abandonment, and family-members' suicide. They declare the dangers of gang activity and potential victimization. One young dancer becomes a victim of a random shooting during RIZE's filming. The proximity of death and violence fosters a melee of fear and love in dancers' relationship to home. What is demonized as violent city space is also personal home space for young people. An unnamed dancer shares reveals of the random gun violence, "It makes me feel like I don't want to be in this place anymore, but you just can't leave. This is my home."

The City of Los Angeles in ever-widening circles of publicness, from the front sidewalk to mass meeting spaces, constitutes a space of home and citizenship, both personal and communal—a shared political commercial racial landscape. People tend to speak about home with a nostalgia that reveals its affective capacities of desire, maintenance, identification, and protection. The sense of longing with which it is represented associates home with safety, comfort, and solace, even if that home offers turmoil and unrest—depending on the circumstances. The geographical space of a personally normal home in Central Los Angeles offers comfort and solace for young people alongside threats of violence. Urban dance practice asserts home in the midst of poverty and unrest, excitement and play, the quotidian and mundane. Visualization of the dance in *RIZE* challenges viewers to see home from the perspective of young people whose lives don't necessarily match ideals of anything middle, average, or white. Krump's map of young black life captures a space of feeling of people among other people in houses and apartments couched between the roaring planes and the silent asphalt, glass, and concrete. Given the dominance of notions of violence in thinking about the 'hood, the neighborhood, the ghetto, and the inner city, clowning and krumping as dance practices re-form the notions of home and the city through the body by appropriating and interpreting "violence" in movement.

> *A dancer acts out gestural blows with extended feet and fists.*
> *A dancer delivers blows to another in punctuated slaps*
> *on theshoulder, side, and back.*
> *A dancer leaps in the air with fists punching while forcefully pumping his chest upwards and pelvis back simultaneously in full extension*
> *His chest's contraction happens fast as he grimaces indiscriminately and twists jaggedly, redirecting his torso to repeat, with arms out, in another direction*
> *A dancer slams to the ground catching his weight with his shoulder . . .*

The dancing looks like fighting with its hard pushing, shoving, and grabbing. Dancers embody a kinesthetic fervor in the forceful rapid full-body pulsing that claims space and crafts community. They capture and aestheticize "violence" as a mode through which to project feeling.

The nature of violence, real violence, stereotypical violence, and performed violence, in the environments and representations of the dancers looms large RIZE's treatment of krump. Dancers performance of violence or "violent" performance does not only or even necessarily directly respond to and negotiate these levels of violence, however. So-called violence or responses to it that manifest in krump dance are themselves symbolic, metaphorical, and productive of new systems of knowledge and community. The prologue of the film links the history of violence in the city to vernacular dance

FIGURE 12.4 Screen capture of *RIZE*, director David LaChapelle, (2005), Miss Prissy vigorously transitioning through a chest extension and contraction in the process of her performance.

forms, using historical images, urban montage, and the words of Dragon. Dragon offers a retrospective speech coincident with footage of the "1965, Watts Riots" and the "1992, Rodney King Riots" [*sic*]. Over a panorama of smoke rising from a flat cityscape Dragon explains, "This is our neighborhood. This is where we grew up. We were all kids back then when this happened [the LA Rebellion] and we managed to grow from these ashes. [Long pause.] And this is where we still live…" The visual series positions a krump session labeled "2002, Los Angeles" as a third version of the violence—redeemed as binary reversal by the stirring soprano overlay of the classic gospel song "Seek Ye the Lord." The song positions the dance session as salvation, editorially linking Dragon's life-raft metaphor, black spirituals, and urban violence. The implication is that the relationship is necessary, the conditions extreme, and the dance practice magical. While the dancing is undeniably fantastic, my argument disarticulates the *necessary*, assumed character of these relationships to imagine how the dance expresses other embodied stories and histories that resist official records or knowledge. Even the linguistic move from "LA riots" to "Rodney King riots" to "LA rebellion," all of which can be simultaneously dramatized in krump performance, seems charted by the body as each arrives closer to a subject—from an object enacting rage, to a symbolic victim, to communities rejecting violent stereotypes, police brutality, and poverty amidst abundance. This shifting history allows for multivalent theorizations of place, community, and history through the body.

In *RIZE*, violence serves as part of the frame that distinguishes its "remarkable" artistic practice. The dancers, however, surpass the frame, as they communicate, through truly remarkable dance, a story more nuanced than one of exceptional kids overcoming the deprivations of the ghetto. The introductory footage of the Watts Riots and LA rebellion segues into a millennial scene of a trio of girls near a car dancing out a beating reminiscent of Rodney King's beating by the Los Angeles police.[17]

> *One girl leans forward over a white car as the two others pretend to deliver blows to theback and head. From a rhythmic fake pounding all three rise to a simultaneous vertical bouncing while pumping their fists into the air in a gesture of resistance or triumph.*

Without the dramatic montage, this dance could refer to any police beating and almost any gang jump-in or stomp-down. Its visual contextualization makes the dance serve specific narrative purposes connecting dance to large-scale urban violence. The dancing shown in the next scenario, the first official krump session we see, features a similar trio suggesting yet another dramatization of a beat-down.

> *One dancer in the center of a crowd kneels with his hands on the pavement. He encourages the slaps that make contact with his arms and back by two other dancers. The blows land and the performer absorbs the slaps as encouragement bouncing upright to his feet, quickly extending his hips only to wrap his arm dangerously, precariouslyaround a fellow dancers neck...*

The montage creates a linear connection to the girls' dancing and the history of violence depicted in the film's introductory footage. Neither the urban uprisings, nor the girls, however, are direct historical or narrative precursors to this form that follows. Important gaps exist in the visual shift between these two dances and between the practice of krumping and the history it is positioned to represent. While the dancing girls may enact the history of structural and physical brutality in the city through improvisation and representational choreography, the subsequent dancers that appear performing at night encircled by an audience of participants do not depict the violence of the past in such a direct and narrative way. Though structurally similar to the montage of the girls at the car, with people standing in similar positions, the moves of this group, that introduces krumping, per se, do not fake physical contact, but actually slap and push. Frenetic, precise, and improvisational, krumping is violent in its energy and intensity. The energy in this scene, however, does not narrativize literal violence associated with black bodies as a result of LA's torrid past. The setup of this visual sequence creates an echo of the representational dance of the three girls. Closer scrutiny reveals its operation as an ironic reversal of a beat-down. While gestural metaphors of physical violence and resistance to brutality still obtain in the way krumping makes meaning, these dancers neither represent a fight, per se, nor narrativize anything near interpersonal or social attack as intimated in the film's editorial sequencing. Instead, they are

FIGURE 12.5 Screen capture of *RIZE*, director David LaChapelle, (2005), Lil' C encourages slaps from fellow dancers.

engaged in a significantly different improvisational communal practice where the physical interaction, the blows and "beating" between the participants constitutes support, affirmation, congratulations, and encouragement. Rather than violence, the standing over and touching of one another through grabbing the arms and slapping the shoulders and back is a structure of love, not one of hurt and destruction. This distinction reveals the dance to be not some binary mode of reaction or, even, protest, but instead a mode of creation and innovation.

CREATIVITY, COMMUNITY, AND SPACE

The visual narrative, however compelling and dramatic, and however relevant historically in understanding the cultures of young black urbanites, ultimately misleads and simplifies. Youth engagement with violence and city space in krump dancing resonates much more broadly than a linear reaction to white racism and urban decay. Certainly the dance practice fulfills some of the needs expressed by young dancers related to poverty and a lack of opportunity. Just as important, however, the dance practice delineates communities of people in control of their creative potential and activating their power of expression to fulfill intangible social and personal desires. The dancers interviewed speak plainly about the meaning of their own subculture. Dancers readily share the meaning they bring to dancing. These performers are hip to the significance of their work and its relationship to themselves and world around them. One dancer explains, "krumpness is the closed chapter of your life. Of hurt, sorrow, anguish that people don't know about." This consciousness renders the young dancers as artists and critics who decide the direction and nature of their work. As improvisation, krumping remains constantly creative. Dancers explain that daily practice encodes rapid changes in technique and style. A krump session provides creative improvisational repetition and functions as something more like a jam session than a rehearsal.

> *At a session, krumpers take turns performing in the cipher while dancers in the cipher encourage, cajole, and admire with words and pats. Individuals on the cipher move in resonance with the performer, adding a supporting beat or playing an improvisatory kinetic riff on the solo artist's contribution.*

Someone who misses a krump session immediately reveals their recalcitrance in their stale style. The vigilance and dedication required to master the dancing and its communal changes reveals krump mastery to be much more labor-intensive than an eruption of movement in response to pain or difficulty. The dance itself becomes not authentic to down-and-out yet spectatorial blackness, that is, so-called "real" black identity, poverty, oppression, but, instead, a testament to the will to master and the will to perform.

RIZE visually hijacks this performative agency by reductively connecting krump practices to undocumented ethnographic footage suggesting past-less, present-less painted "natives" dancing in an unmarked venue, location, and time. The filmic effect connects *RIZE* to the nativizing gaze of ethnographic recording by filmically supporting homogenized "blacks'" "natural" almost biological ability to dance and connecting this to an image of a pure, unchanging, recognizable "Africa." The visual primitivism, a classic example of traditional ethnography, oversimplifies black dance history, the processes of diasporic cultural transmission, and homogenizes significant choreographic and ethnic difference. The random, decontextualized connection as a nativizing gesture consequently "tribalizes" young dancers' anti- and trans-gang organizational and social practices. It implies a reductive violence that the dancers themselves, in contrast, actually re-direct and re-imagine.

For krumpers, dance and the body serve as sites for processing, absorbing, deflecting, and claiming urban space, not, reductively, resisting victimization to it. The dance practice carves out social space. Dancers practice krumping in private, public, and commandeered urban spaces. These include homes, garages, backyards, recreation rooms, neighborhood streets, elementary school yards, alleys, abandoned buildings, The Forum, and the LA River. Through these choices performers lay claim to private spaces and diverse public ones. They deploy spatial creativity in using the physical environment and provide for themselves varied inspiration for use of the body interacting with a range of external stimuli. The space then influences the movement in an improvisational interaction between the environment and the thinking, creating dancer.[18]

As a group activity, krumping requires diverse participation of spectators—dancers perform in the center of a standing audience. It requires room for the movement *and* for the crowd. The social space created is a space for sonic and kinetic communication, the establishment of community and various levels of activity, connection, and belonging. An enormous amount of touching occurs for a dance form so much about the individual strutting their stuff. The great deal of platonic grabbing, hugging, and lifting of bodies characterizes the interpersonal, physical interaction of the social group and supports the dancer. Sometimes when it seems a dancer will fall out of the circle they fall against a spectator participant who catches and throws them back in. The catch provides physical encouragement through touching and tossing. The dancer reconnects with human touchstones of safety in the midst of the performance. The spirituality of krump in part exists in the groups' witness of this experience and in the communal catch of cipher, where the flailing body is surrounded and helped by the community, where friends watch, lead the body off, prevent injury, and provide a safety net. Overwhelmingly not *group dancing*, however, dancers still perform solo or, at least, singularly. Krumping becomes an opportunity for claiming the literal physical space of one's own body, one's own person, and for using that space to turn inward, to rebel, to create, and to theorize the urban experience in an encouraging social environment of affirming witnesses.

As rigorous and intense exercise, krumping can be seen as physically preserving, particularly when one considers the dangerous physical ailments that statistically plague blacks in the 'hood. Hypertension, high blood pressure, high cholesterol, heart disease, diabetes, and stress abound. In opposition to these, young and, sometimes, old folks work out.

> *Corpulent men and women from teen to middle age bounce their glutes and swing their arms for the crowd...*
> *A girl and boy of about eight compete in a public competition flexibly snaking aross the floorin a straddle, defying gravity in acrobatic leaps and vibrating their limbs over the stage...*

The physical demands of mastery and competition discourage physically deteriorating drug use. The relatively democratic nature of black dance culture shown in *RIZE* admits Asians, whites, heavy and slim, children and adults—whoever can bring the energy and skill to perform. All sweat and tone and tire in a performance culture not so much concerned with authenticity, but with action and commitment.

Krump's individualistic nature provides an opportunity for self-expression. Styles are often very personal and closely associated with one dancer's particular rhythms or another's personality. Dancers' unique names like Dragon, Tight Eyez, Miss Prissy, El Nino, etc., reflect this individual potential. The space also exists for sharing and using others' moves in an ecstatic embodiment of community and mutual respect. At the same time that movement is individual, dancers are expected to keep up with a pace of development and transformation in the culture that mimics the pace of the style. Performers compete with each other as well as with the very pace of change to display proficiency. Dancers connect with one another and commune with themselves in the presence of others who recognize and affirm them.

Elaborate practices of face painting bear out the total engagement of the dancers with their environments. Face painting, seen throughout and especially at the battlezone event chronicled in *RIZE*, emerges as a parallel art form signifying a total embodied commitment of self to the dance. Taking up precise and time-consuming work, dancers apply structured, sharp lines, and brightly colored divisions to their faces. The paint encapsulates the self in a mask that mediates and represents the environment. Kaleidoscopic face paint represents individuality even as it fully or partially obscures the face of the dancer. The style of paint and degree of facial coverage identifies dancers to some extent with their dance crew and style of dancing—clown or krump. In that sense, the face paint underscores social inclusion. Dancers' own highly idiosyncratic masks, however, whether partial or full, render the wearer of the paint unmistakable. Clown paint displays fearless irony of the "clown." Dance originator Tommy-the-Clown's makeup reflects the traditional white-faced clown with cherry red exaggerated smile, lifted brows, cheeks as red balloons, and even a characteristic rainbow wig. Other dancers wear blue and black flames outlined in white, black zigzags and arcs forming elaborate designs featuring greens and purples. Clown

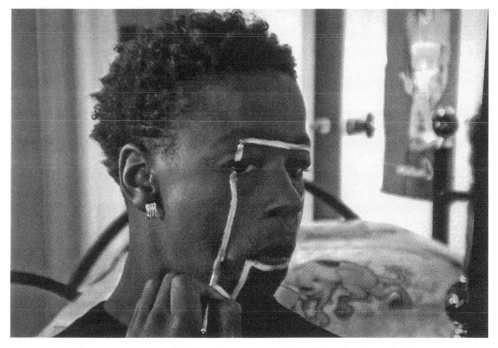

FIGURE 12.6 Screen capture of RIZE, director David LaChapelle, (2005), Dancer painting his face.

paint defies sambo stereotypes of black masculinity, appropriating the clown mask as a "serious" expression of a hip and fun black identity. The "clown" paint bridges the gap between children's entertainment (the basis of clown dancing) and grown-folks' dance practices, infusing the dance culture with the whimsicality and sardonic gravity of youth and adult play. Clown-like face paint exhibits a sheer whiteness of a fully covered face as an "in-your-face" deflection of white racial identity—a structure that becomes irrelevant in the conduct of clown and krump dancing. Some of this use of white appears in krump dancers' slightly different face painting practices. Krumpers' face paint resembles clown-face in its impulse to decorate the face. Krump face painters tend to use abstract lines that typically cover smaller portions of skin. One sees fewer and simpler lines in the application of vibrant colors and designs. The designs of sharp lines and swoops reflect and interpret the city landscape and external environment as well as dancers' personal style. Dancers' face paint achieves emphasis and erasure. The masks operate as windows mediating agenic subjects' view of the world— "veiling" while accentuating the self, interpreting external space and external gazes on the skin. For some the masking negotiates shyness and provides freedom. For others, it ascribes power. A layered, fully engaged nexus of self, surface, and external world exists in the paint.

Spirit, Ecstasy, and Danger

Krumpers engage in traditional gestures of mourning like the rending of clothes and pouring libations.

> *Dragon, Lil' C, and Miss Prissy rend their shirts to punctuate their moves in the process of the dance...*
> *Dancers pour water, restorative libations over their torsos without slowing their pace...*

The suggestion of death in these movements and in a long sequence in the film about a girl dancer's murder illustrates the proximity of fatal violence and loss to young people's lives. A 15-year-old clown dancer, Quinesha Dunford, is randomly shot and killed during RIZE's filming.[19] The child's family and friends mourn her loss and struggle with its senselessness.[20] Autobiographical confession reveals the suicide of krump master Lil' C's father. Phases of the dance and ritual gestures suggest death, resurrection, and liminality—all states of transition that foster a recreation of the self. These conditions appear in the performers' shift between self-consciousness, sociality, and "buckness" or spiritual release. The falling, contact, and re-animation that occur during dancers' performance in the cipher dramatize a form of resurrection where physical contact and force restore the dancers' collapse or expiration. The touch constitutes the space between the potential for death and the persistence of life. The precise physical control of the body to achieve virtuosity and the communality

FIGURE 12.7 Screen capture of RIZE, director David LaChapelle, (2005), Tight Eyez rends shirt in the process of dancing.

of the cipher indicates a submission to forces greater than the self—the surrender present in each "re-creation." Forces of hope and renewal created within the individual dancing alone and within the connections between participants in the cipher challenge the presence of death. Critique and transformation of death and danger are embedded in the movement, that is, in the promise of continued dancing and in its vivacity.

The progress of the dance and its improvisational repetitions constitute an evolution of emotion toward freedom and the sublime. Dragon explains, "in the midst of krumpness, there's a spirit there." Violence as context and content becomes negated and superseded by krumping's ethos of ecstasy and danger—danger of precarious gesture, pain, physical victimization, and death; ecstasy of proximity to the spiritual world and physical transcendence. Krumping requires physical intrepidness to master the rigorous moves, to face the high expectations for performance, and to take on the physical space with one's body. It takes "heart," a vernacular combination of commitment, boldness, and love. The cipher reproduces an environment of physical danger given its solid elements with which dancers collide. Krumping recrafts and claims space by using the body to disrespect physical boundaries. The dance ignores or overcomes the concrete, asphalt, fences, light posts, benches, and other bodies accepting the pain that accompanies collision.

FIGURE 12.8 Screen capture of RIZE, director David LaChapelle, (2005), Dancer mounts electric pole before he drops to the concrete below to dance flat on his back from knees folded beneath him.

> *Performers fling themselves off walls, up electrical posts, over link fences,   and back.*
> *They throw themselves against the ground and push it out of the way to become*
> *upright hard return.*

One gets the sense that the air steps aside in order to make space for movement. At the same time the performer ignores or overcomes the physical danger to the body offered by trumped obstacles. Both ignoring and overcoming danger are acts of defiance. The violence of the urban environment no longer seems an uncontrolled threat but a set of specific conditions of danger that can be overcome. In this sense the actions of the body in the dance and performance environment become a metaphor of the defiance of physical, emotional, economic, political, and spiritual dangers of being young and black in the city. It also performs a physical expansiveness that exudes spirit in each contraction and extension of trunk and limb. The body makes theory.

The dance space also offers the opportunity to appropriate and opt out of an environment of danger, in a sense by fulfilling it in the body through extreme *introspection* coupled with the extreme literal *acting out* of movement.

> *Dancers make limited eye contact with the spectators, mostly looking down or*
> *around, gazing at their own bodies or at no one in particular.*

Even in battles when the dance is presented for public display and entertainment, krump dancers gaze primarily at their opponents and look past the audience. Meanwhile, krump dancers "mean-mug"—grimacing, scowling, and extending their tongues as a challenge to onlookers and as a mode of alienation. The dance isn't pretty. It doesn't pander. And although it is highly social, it doesn't make friends. Krumpers' aggressive glare carves personal space and sustains distance between the self and others except to the extent that fellow dancers identify with the look and its significance. When the glare becomes introspective, dancers' countenance projects ugliness as a marker of the dance's intensity. Ms. Prissy explains that they "may not have the prettiest smile" but she is "krump"—"this is what makes us krump." Dancers report going into themselves spiritually to find the source of their work.[21] The resultant combustion of kinetic energy and skill achieves physical, emotional, and spiritual ecstasy—a possession summoned from within.

At one point after a young woman called Daisy has exhausted herself in the dance her friends carry her bodily out of the cipher. A 20-second segment of the film, the name of which echoes a dancer appropriating the classical, called "Our Ghetto Ballet," shows Daisy dancing in a closed school playground at night.

> *Daisy is commanded to hop off a bench to the asphalt below. She steps forward as quickly as her contracting and extending arms and lifting and vibrating shoulders allow. As her friends watch and cheer, subtly keeping the rhythm with their shoulders, necks, and upper bodies, Daisy stomps, jerks, and tosses herself into a welcome exhaustion.*[22]

A breathless witness, Baby Tight Eyes explains, "She just struck. This is what we all been waiting on. This is what all of us been waiting on." A proud girl in the background shouts out in congratulations, calling her "cousin." A young man declares, "She has reached the inevitable." One can see Daisy's release of performative self-consciousness as she ceases checking for others' approval and focuses completely on her own execution. The young woman accomplishes a social crossing over with participant spectators hoping and waiting for her to succeed. The community offers physical aid, affirmation, and relief throughout and in the aftermath. When she has "struck," she experiences total possession by the dance, an ecstatic total forgetting and simultaneous actualizing of the performative self. The young woman "getting krump" or "buck" renders the dance an apprehension of the sublime, of freedom in the dance through its intensity. This experience obtains for others as well. In a resonant image Lil' C performs at the water's edge couched between a space of play, the Santa Monica Pier, a space of renewal, the ocean with its saline ability to wash the spirit clean, and a space a possibility, the open sky at purple dusk.[23]

Dancers who describe the process of getting "buck" liken the ultimate total release of the self to a holy-spirit possession—to oneness with a force beyond the self.[24] Getting buck becomes a goal of the dance and the province of only the most skilled practitioners. Divorced from a "base" sexuality that some identify as the "stripper dance," the sensuality, power, and commitment of krumping fuse into a sublime state. In krump's diasporic

FIGURE 12.9 Continued

FIGURE 12.9 Screen capture of RIZE, director David LaChapelle, (2005), (a) Daisy dancing. (b) Daisy "has struck" or reached a buck state. She pauses after her display, overwhelmed. (c) Baby Tight Eyez leads eruption of the group's celebration at Daisy's accomplishment. (d) Dancers on the cipher catch Daisy, embrace her, and lift her out of its center.

resonances with identifiable, geographically specific contemporary sacred West Indian dances' sensual movements of the body, we can see krump's physical connections with god(s) and godliness.[25] Buckness resolves the secular oxymoron of what by evangelical Christian standards appears to be a sensual, worldly dance with the practitioners' self-professed Christianity. It reconciles traditional Christianity's distance between the sexual and the sacred, closing any distance between the body and the spirit.

Ms. Prissy confesses that her ironic moniker, in full hip-hop contradiction, misnames her fervor and demeanor as a dancer. In krump cultures women appear and lead, dance and participate in the center and on the rim of the cipher. In her self-naming, Ms. Prissy narrates a liminal self, poised between beauty and grace and ugliness and roughness. Similarly, tension exists for Ms. Prissy between krump culture, modern dance, and Christianity. She maintains a balance between them in her simultaneous existence in multiple landscapes of ciphers, krump sessions, dance studios in Hollywood, and her small Pentecostal church. The connection between dance traditions and locations for Ms. Prissy seems to reside in a spiritual space where dance forms and contexts in tension resolve at the altar.[26] Although Miss Prissy and Dragon's comparatively stolid liturgical modern movement before celebrants in church differs greatly from what they manifest on secular stages, it is not surprising that many dancers report that they krump for Christ or that they praise and seek Jesus in the action of the dance—within their own selves and in an effort to celebrate and spread the gospel in church and other public spaces.[27]

Because the dance resists a simplistic narrative of progress or existential escape that implies that the urban world is somehow left behind or below, dancers take on and trounce the environment of danger instead of *"rize-ing"* above it as offered by the title. Krumping as form repudiates this manner of romance. Even Dragon, who insists, "we will rise," implies not an escaping out or away, but a collective reckoning and a collective lifting. The dance form *takes on* the urban environment in terms of both enrobing oneself within it and challenging it. Dancers appear fully clothed in the circumstances of one's personal life, one's own vernacular style and circumstances of living in the city. Dancers' ugly mug, aggressive gestures, and punishing speed call out the problems of violence, dispossession, crime, murder, and unemployment in the city. The film's recounting of the deep sense of despair at the loss of a "competition," of absent parents, a shooting, robbery, and fear of gang activity demonstrate the punishments of the city. Performers bring them into proximity, beat the hell out of them, and throw them back again. Likewise, dancers krump out their friendship, excitement of competition, spiritual responsibility, and creativity in the city. Spaces of the urban and of the body become spaces of home, of communal ownership, and recognition.

ARTIST FINALE

As the dancers report, they become ciphers—conduits, translators, critics—of urban experience and of personal expression. The cipher—surrounding circles of participants and audience—supports the way they make meaning and also protects the dancer as artist. By processing violence through movement and encoding its dangers within it, krump dancers actively define the metaphorical social, personal, and physical spaces of the city, home, and the body. Like most black cultural forms its adaptability accommodates opportunity, allowing practitioners to allow *RIZE* to make public an inwardly focused subculture. This same *public*-ity offers dancers paid creative work and celebrity for their talent. In the hot high-color high-definition finale of oiled slow-motion krump bodies, impeccably muscled professional dancers play confidently to the camera with challenging closed expressions and controlled physical power. The performance takes on an emotional power that saturates the audience. The multivalent affective power of the dance—of joy, rage, compassion, love, praise, frustration—transfers to us not even in a live circulation of performative fervor, but from the screen. It is impossible to watch the dancers and listen to the beats they animate without wanting yourself to dance. Our desire to dance—itself a feeling, a wish to make something happen in the world—signifies the potential for human connection and freedom animated in krumpness. Its affective power becomes kinetic. The dancers' commitment to their craft, to the representations of the city, and investments in their lives forces our hearts to beat to their rhythms, to feel expansive with the power of their dance, positively, to want to "get krump."

NOTES

* I'm especially thankful to Marlon Bailey, who shared the kinetic contagion and danced with me in our dramatic analysis of *RIZE* at BPT in 2007. I owe special thanks to Hershini Bhana Young, Tommy DeFrantz, and Omi Osun Joni L. Jones, Julie Carlson, Stephanie LeMenager, and Melissa Blanco-Borelli for their comments, support, and inspiration.

1. The "scenario" is a "set up that relies on live participants, is structured round a schematic plot, and has a foreseeable (though adaptable) end." Diana Taylor, "Translating Performance," *Profession* (2002), 47–48. The schematic plot can include sets of identities, histories, and politics that bear on the scenario.

2. Sara Ahmed, *The Cultural Politics of Emotion* (New York: Routledge, 2004), 1–6.

3. This description of four "basic" krump moves appears in *The Heart of Krump*. [DVD]. [Shiri Nassim (producer), Los Angeles: Ardustry Home Entertainment, Krump Kings Inc. (2005).] Several scholars explore the aesthetic of improvisation that pervades the history and substance of black performing arts. See Thomas F. DeFrantz, "African American Dance—Philosophy, Aesthetics, and 'Beauty,'" *Topoi* 24, no. 1, (2005): 93–103; Fred Moten, *In the Break: The Aesthetics of the Black Radical Tradition* (Minneapolis: University of Minnesota Press, 2003); Robert F. Thompson, *Flash of the Spirit: African and Afro-American Art and Philosophy* (New York: Random House, 1983).

4. Please see http://www.tommytheclown.com/index.html for Tommy the Clown's professional website.

5. Fatimah Tobing Rony, *The Third Eye: Race, Cinema and Ethnographic Spectacle* (Durham, NC: Duke University Press, 1996), 7, 9–10.

6. RIZE's credits identify the "Footage from 'The Nuba Material' courtesy of Reifenstahl-Produktion." Leni Reifenstahl was a remarkable, celebrated twentieth-century female filmmaker who gained fame and notoriety through her propaganda work for the Nazi Party and her close friendship with Adolf Hitler. The footage is most likely from the 1960s, an interesting time to document primitive Africanisms, given the decade's black revolutions. The Nuba people live in the Sudan.

7. Though little scholarly work has been published on *RIZE*, reviews and commentaries on the film consistently note some of its more obvious shortcomings, including its primitivism, essentialist homogenization of diasporic people and dance forms, and exploitation of a spectacularity of the black dancing body. See Kim Hewitt, Review, *Rize*. Dir. David LaChapelle. Lionsgate films, 2005, *Journal of Popular Music Studies* 17, no. 3, (2005): 345–352. Brenda Smaill's focus on documentary pain and the possibility of social justice addresses affect through the notion of pain or injury. Unfortunately, she takes the "self-reportage" of pain and urban oppression in *RIZE* at face value, which facilitates her article's inappropriate lumping of Los Angeles's black youth with Vancouver's drug addicts in documentaries about "minoritarian" populations. Smaill, "Injured Identities: Pain, Politics and Documentary," *Studies in Documentary Film* 1, no. 2, (October 2007): 151–163.

8. Anna Scott, Black Performance Theory National Convening, Northwestern University, 2007. I am grateful to Anna Scott, Thomas DeFrantz, and Tavia Nyong'o for their comments following a presentation by myself and Marlon Bailey at this meeting.

9. "affect, *n.*" *Oxford English Dictionary Online.*

10. "affect, v^1." *Oxford English Dictionary Online.*

11. See Teresa Brennan, *The Transmission of Affect* (Ithaca: Cornell University Press, 2004), 3–9.

12. Thomas DeFrantz analogizes dance to spoken language in his canonical analysis of black social dance. In this way he asserts the capacity of black dance to communicate via gesture, rhythm, etc. Thomas F. DeFrantz, "The Black Beat Made Visible: Hip Hop Dance and Body Power," in *Of the Presence of the Body: Essays on Dance and Performance Theory*, ed. André Lepecki (Middletown, CT: Wesleyan University Press, 2004).

13. DeFrantz, 2004, 6.

14. DeFrantz, 2004, 3.

15. I am grateful to scholar, ethnographer, and filmmaker John Jackson Jr. for his trenchant work on post-modern ethnographic film and his thoughts about this slide between experience and dance in *RIZE*.

16. See Jeff Chang, *Can't Stop, Won't Stop: A History of the Hip Hop Generation* (New York: St. Martin's Press, 2005). Chang chronicles the economic, social, and political circumstances that accompanied and helped to determine the creative and political directions of "the Hip Hop Generation," born between 1965 and 1984.

17. *RIZE* (2005), Ch. 1, Main Titles/The Riots, 1:40–4:30.

18. The "subject" is an individual both responding to her/his environment and to her/his own being, wishes, and desires. That is s/he is the subject of his or her own life and also subject/ed to the forces around her/him in the world.

19. *RIZE* is dedicated to Quinisha "Lil' Dimples" Dunford.

20. *RIZE* (2005), Ch. 17, Amazing Grace, 1:04:38–1:06:27.

21. Author interviews with Southern California Krump dancers Bashir "The Professor" Hassan, Miriam "Ace" Burnett, and Dominic King, February, 2010. These dancers consider

themselves krump dancers even though they have trained with "clown" dancers and in Tommy's clown studio. A 2010 dance culture demonstrates that the forms have further influenced one another.

22. *RIZE* (2005), Ch. 8, Our Ghetto Ballet, 33:02–33:25.

23. *RIZE* (2005), Ch. 11, Don't Hold Back, 41:00–42:30.

24. Author interviews with Southern California Krump dancer Bashir "The Professor" Hassan, November, 2010.

25. For a discussion of the residence of Yoruba and vodun gods in specific parts of the body see Yvonne Daniel, *Dancing Wisdom: Embodied Knowledge in Haitian Vodou, Cuban Yoruba, and Bahian Candomblé* (Urbana: University of Illinois Press, 2005), 74.

26. *RIZE* (2005), Ch. 18, God's Gift, 1:12:00–1:14:33

27. Author interviews with Southern California Krump dancers Bashir "The Professor" Hassan, Miriam "Ace" Burnett, and Dominic King, February, 2010.

BIBLIOGRAPHY

Ahmed, Sara. *The Cultural Politics of Emotion*. New York: Routledge, 2004.

Author interviews with Southern California Krump dancers Bashir "The Professor" Hassan, Miriam "Ace" Burnett, and Dominic King, February 2010.

Author interviews with Southern California Krump dancer Bashir "The Professor" Hassan, November 2010.

Brennan, Teresa. *The Transmission of Affect*. Ithaca: Cornell University Press, 2004.

Chang, Jeff. *Can't Stop, Won't Stop: A History of the Hip Hop Generation*. New York: St. Martin's Press, 2005.

Daniel, Yvonne. *Dancing Wisdom: Embodied Knowledge in Haitian Vodou, Cuban Yoruba, and Bahian Candomblé*. Urbana: University of Illinois Press, 2005.

DeFrantz, Thomas F. "African American Dance—Philosophy, Aesthetics, and 'Beauty.' " *Topoi* 24 (January 2005): 93–103.

DeFrantz, Thomas F. "The Black Beat Made Visible: Hip Hop Dance and Body Power." In *Of the Presence of the Body: Essays on Dance and Performance Theory*, edited by André Lepecki, 64–81. Middletown, CT: Wesleyan University Press, 2004.

Gottschild, Brenda Dixon. *Digging The Africanist Presence in American Performance and other contexts*. Westport, CT: Greenwood Press, 1996.

Hewitt, Kim. Review of *Rize*, directed by David LaChapelle. *Journal of Popular Music Studies* 17 (2005): 345–352.

LaChapelle, David (director). *RIZE*. Los Angeles: Lions Gate Films, 2005.

Moten, Fred. *In the Break: The Aesthetics of the Black Radical Tradition*. Minneapolis: University of Minnesota Press, 2003.

Nassim, Shiri (producer.) *The Heart of Krump*. Los Angeles: Ardustry Home Entertainment, Krump Kings Inc. 2005.

Rony, Fatimah Tobing. *The Third Eye: Race, Cinema and Ethnographic Spectacle*. Durham, NC: Duke University Press, 1996.

Scott, Anna. Black Performance Theory National Convening, Northwestern University, 2007.

Smaill, Brenda. "Injured Identities: Pain, Politics and Documentary." *Studies in Documentary Film* 1 (October 2007): 151–163.

Taylor, Diana. "Translating Performance." *Profession 2000* (2002): 47–48.

Thompson, Robert F. *Flash of the Spirit: African and Afro-American Art and Philosophy.* New York: Random House, 1983.

CHAPTER 13

A TASTE OF HONEY: CHOREOGRAPHING MULATTA IN THE HOLLYWOOD DANCE FILM

MELISSA BLANCO BORELLI*

THE figure of the mulatta colors many cultural imaginaries with her specific narratives. One such narrative, the trope of the "tragic mulatta" appears prominently, often obfuscating any other type of representation possible. As Hazel Carby writes, "the figure of the mulatt[a] should be understood and analysed as a narrative device of mediation" (1987:88), mediating between the white and black worlds said figure straddles. Couched in Enlightenment ideologies of race, the mulatta emerges as a tragic figure in that her genesis occurs from a violent union between two races—a "dominant white" one, and a "subservient black" one. Werner Sollors explains the etymology of the word mulatto:

> of sixteenth century Spanish origin, documented in English since 1595, and designating a child of a black and a white parent, was long considered etymologically derived from 'mule'; yet it may also come from the Arabic word muwallad (meaning "Mestizo" or mixed) (1999:128).

Even with skin that approximates "whiteness," the proverbial "taint" or "drop" of impure African blood condemns her and her value to be less than human, despite the fascination with her representation of ambiguity and varying skin color gradations. The undervalued "figment of [the concept of] pigment" (1998:16) as DeVere Brody calls it, conversely added to her value as a popular sexual commodity for heterosexual male desire. As a filmic presence, the mulatta first appeared in D. W. Griffith's *Birth of a Nation* (1915). Lydia, the mulatta mistress of the white abolitionist carpetbagger, appears independent, powerful, threatening, yet desirable. Film historian Donald Bogle attributes this connection between "the light-skinned Negress" (2001:15) and desirability to a closer proximity to a white aesthetic ideal which gave "cinnamon-colored gals" (2001:15) a chance at lead parts. Other films such as *Imitation of Life* (l934; 1959), *Pinky* (1949), *Shadows* (1959), and *Devil in a Blue Dress* (1995) utilize the trope of the mulatta and render her full of regret, emotionally unfulfilled, or sad and alone due to each film's respective circumstances. As Charles Scruggs states, "the mulatta is a visible expression of the broken taboo, a figure bearing witness to the interconnection of the races, and the 'site of the hybridity of histories'" (2004:327). Fraught between desire, melancholy, and despair, the mulatta usually encounters a tragic fate, unable to escape these pre-scripted choreographies of her race. These characterizations prevent more complex representations of this racialized and gendered body primarily by constricting the notion of mulatta into narratives based on textual discursive practices. As a result, the mulatta figure suffers from rather limited representations unable to acknowledge her potentiality as something other than tragic.

In this article, I seek to vivify and corpo-realize mulatta representations by particularly focusing on films where mulattas use their bodies, specifically their hips, in active mobilizations as performers, dancers, or choreographers. As I have argued elsewhere, my theory of hip(g)nosis exposes the contours of the hip as a site of cultural production, produced and deployed by historically racialized mulatta bodies in their negotiation of "blackness," "whiteness," the political economy of pleasure, and becoming.[1] As a result, the excesses of the hip's choreography, its existence as a product that can dazzle, dodge, divert, and, of course, hip-notize, locates it as/in a space where the enacting mulatta body achieves some agency through the different values imposed on it.

Thinking through and moving with the mulatta's hip, I will examine the filmic representations of the mulatta body in the Hollywood film *Honey* (2003), starring Jessica Alba. More specifically, this chapter aims to unravel how the Hollywood filmic apparatus engages with signifiers of raced sexuality and hierarchies of dance styles to enforce and reify mythic narratives about dance, dancing raced bodies, and dance-making. In order to frame the discussion of how the mulatta body operates through the visual economy, I will establish a genealogy of this body in a U.S. context through two other dance/performance films: *Sparkle* (1976) and *Flashdance* (1983). These juxtapositions illustrate how the mulatta subject develops from a tragic figure (in *Sparkle*) to independent and self-reliant (in *Honey*) with dance acting as the analytical framework by focusing on particular choreographed and "improvised" dance sequences performed by each film's respective mulatta protagonist.

SPARKLE

Sparkle tells the story of three sisters in late 1950s Harlem who aspire to a singing career. As the all-female group, Sister and the Sisters, the lead singer, Sister (played by Lonette McKee) becomes their corporeal calling card.[2] It is her mulatta body that enables their first "big-time" gig. Her character's narrative lies within the trope of the "tragic mulatta" as evidenced by her demise through drug addiction and an abusive man. Despite the corporeal vivacity she demonstrates early on, Sister's mulatta body cannot escape the tragedy pre-scripted onto it. As a result, the mulatta body rests within the confines of its familiar narrative trope, ravaged and unable to be anything but a victim.

When the film opens, an image of Jesus with his outstretched hands invites us in. We are in a church and a gospel choir sings "Precious Lord." As the camera pans down, Sparkle (Irene Cara) and Stix (Philip Michael Thomas) sway and clap as they sing with ebullience. Next to them stand Delores (Dwan King), Levi (Dorian Haywood), and finally, Sister. Bogle historically situates the character of Sister as such:

> McKee [...] gives the 1970s definitive portrayal of the likable, haughty, "hincty," high-yeller black girl who thinks she's got all the answers (and who usually has more than most). Her portrait of a black woman ready to take life on without fear or foolish constraints is similar to what past actresses [...] attempted to present. She chews gum, shakes her hips, and talks trash with forceful abandon. Ambition, drive, and survival are written all over this tall, curvy, jivey, sexy, hip sister. (2001:256)

When a neighbor warns Effie, Sister's mother, to "keep an eye out on your oldest gal [Sister], she is busting at the seams," Effie describes her as being "high-spirited." These descriptive monikers signal the lack of containment Sister's body represents. She is uncontrollable and immune to convention or discipline. A brief moment during a rehearsal illustrates this point.

One evening, the group goes over a song and dance routine for the talent competition. The camera frames Sister in the center, sitting in an armchair nonchalantly flipping through a magazine. To her left and right are the out-of-focus mid-sections of Sparkle and Stix. When asked if she plans on joining the rehearsal, Sister does not bother to raise her face or to make eye contact. She merely replies, "Uh-uh, I already know it," and continues looking through her magazine. Her speech act asserts her embodied knowledge. In this short exchange, Sister's character suggests a confidence that becomes associated with representations of the mulatta performing body. In other words, the expected rhythmic quality of its racialized connections with "blackness" coupled with the mulatta's aesthetic appeal render the act of rehearsal unnecessary as she just needs to perform. The mere appearance of her mulatta corporeality silently labors in this instance. Here, the embedded histories of how to interpret, watch, and make legible the mulatta body assist the viewer. As Aisha D. Bastiaans asserts, "the habituated visual and narrative logics of race [...] rely upon a viewer's careful observation of clues" (2008:224) or what I refer to as tropes of mulatta narratives. A "literate" audience would understand Sister's refusal to rehearse, since its labor of discernment would already have provided the tools to read her corporeality properly, or to see how her body becomes readable through its multiple deployments of raced and gendered signifiers. Thus, the notion of corporeality comes with a physically embedded movement and gestural vocabulary that enables visual-kinesthetic coherence. Even her bodily refusal to rehearse signals a rebellious corporeality, one that prefers to articulate itself outside the group's specific choreography. This next analysis attests to how Sister's mulatta corporeality demonstrates its subversive potential through her moving hips.

The Hearts (the first incarnation of the singing group) wait backstage; all of them wear red sweaters except Sister, who dons a figure-enhancing black dress. Her hair hangs loose, one side pulled up and adorned with a single red flower. This outfit can be read as an aesthetic homage to Dorothy Dandridge (a mulatta film actress). In the film musical *Carmen Jones*, Dandridge wears a similar outfit (her skirt was red), also accented by a red flower she holds in her hand and later wears. As *Carmen Jones* opened in 1954 and *Sparkle* takes place in 1958, Sister's reference to the film historically coincides. Sister's style, swagger, and seductive stare work as simulacrum of the filmic mulatta body. Additionally, Dorothy Dandridge's fate as a "tragic mulatta" in both the film and her life, haunt Sister's filmic image.[3] In this context, the "tragic mulatta" acts as a filmic commodity, a spectral presence. Borrowing from Derrida's notion of the specter that both inhabits and haunts, Dandridge's ghost moves through and on Sister's image. However, a spectator must be present to mediate and ascertain the value of the mulatta commodity. The haunting of the mulatta flesh by itself is not what solely constructs it as a commodity for "the commodity is even very complicated; it is blurred, tangled, paralyzing, aporetic, perhaps undecidable" (Derrida 1994:150), yet, it provides an understanding of the cultural work that film, race, and gender representations do, in order to make mulatta corporeality legible.

At the talent competition, The Hearts sing and perform a synchronized choreography—their arms bend at the elbows and swing side to side, they clap to the beat, and sway left to right. Sister's interpretation, however, contains different gestural excesses or bodily flourishes. For example, she shimmies her shoulders, changes level, and bends her knees to swing her hips downward. Eventually, Sister breaks from the line and steps forward, her arms lifted in the air, languorously moving them down her hair and resting them behind her head, looking out into the audience, purposefully seducing. She pauses, one hand behind her head, elbow cocked, while she pulses her hips subtly in place, accentuating the music's downbeat. Hers is an "actionable assertion" (DeFrantz 2004:66) that demonstrates the relationship between body, rhythm, beat, and pleasure in black social dance. She turns around with an exaggerated twirl and slowly rejoins the line. The performance continues with the camera operating as a disembodied spectator who tries to watch their performance through the moving shoulders, backs, and heads of the audience. After the camera has panned across each one of them in a mid-shot, Sister returns as the main focus. Once again, she steps away from the group and improvises her solo routine—seductive arm gestures, poses, hair flipping, and intimated hip swinging, as the screen only displays her from her waist up. Shoulder shimmies and a hair toss, gestures of sexuality and pleasurable enjoyment, lead her back to the line. When the song comes to an end, all five of them rest their arms on one another's shoulders, bouncing to the music. Sister's refusal to rehearse has rendered her performance a solo one, distinct from the group, thereby asserting how she stands out. The audience applauds vigorously, as shouts and hollers overpower the fading strains of the song. The Hearts perform a collective bow and exit the stage. Sister detaches herself from the group and remains on the stage, relishing the applause and attention. The camera is now behind Sister, facing out to the audience. Sister encourages her audience with poses, placing her

FIGURE 13.1 Screen capture from *Sparkle*, (1976), dir. Sam O'Steen. Sister spreads her arms wide toward the audience.

hands on her hips and then opening her arms out wide (Fig. 13.1). She not only invites further applause but also beckons male desire into her corporeal space. Two large men begin to approach and enter the space her arms have opened up, just as Stix returns to pull her off the stage.

This scene not only constructs Sister as having "natural" talent and improvisational skill but also solidifies her distinct corporeal presence within the group. Furthermore, the reaction to her dancing and enticing heightens the allure and aesthetic capital Sister contributes. Stix, desperate to get another music gig for the group, changes the composition of the group to just women. At the Shan Doo Club, Stix tries to convince its owner that Sister and the Sisters are worth hiring. Levi shows the owner a picture of Sister and claims "you've never seen girls like this before." The camera cuts to a close-up of a black-and-white headshot of Sister, flower in her air, a faint, seductive smile on her lips. Stix uses her aesthetic capital further, and tempts the owner by claiming that "they call her the ugly one." The club owner immediately concedes and offers them one opportunity to impress him later that week. This act of witnessing and judging the beauty of the mulatta works twofold: it is both a visual labor based on historical processes, and it enables mulatta corporeality to have perceived aesthetic power and, in turn to be beautiful and adored.[4] However, just as the visual labors and defines the "beauty" associated with the mulatta body, I want to affirm dance scholar Thomas DeFrantz's critical disturbance of beauty. He challenges the notion of beauty "as something visually apprehended, toward 'beauty' as a performed gesture felt by a witnessing audience [. W]e must be willing to resist the primacy of sight as truth, and allow for the possibility of an aesthetic sensibility concerned with spirit" (2005: 98). In this way, Sister's image, and the idea of a hybridized and "beautiful" body are not just visually stimulating, but require other forms of acknowledged sensation—touch, taste (in the Bourdieu sense), veneration, and kin-aesthesia—in order to make them significant and ultimately beautiful. This is how the mulatta body offers an understanding of the processes involved in rendering "beauty," not as an a priori artifact, but as the culmination of historical, discursive, intellectual, and sensual labors. It must perform, dance, or move in order to set these nodes into play.

Now, back to the Shan Doo Club. Dim stage lights leave Sparkle, Sister, and Delores in shadows, with hints of light reflecting off of their shoulders and the red of their dresses. Sister stands in the middle, with Sparkle and Delores on either side of her. The camera captures them in a medium shot from their mid-thigh up. They face stage right and they swing their hips in unison to the music. When they turn to face the audience and the light brightens, we see them dressed in identical red gowns, with matching long red gloves, and a red flower in Sister's hair. As they continue to sing, their bodies execute choreography reminiscent of classic Motown female groups. From the waist down, they softly sway their hips back and forth, while the arms lift, bend, curve, pause, pose, and move through the air, articulating a lyric through a hand gesture, or tracing the sinuous curves of their hip movements through the space. At the start of the chorus (an interrogative asking "What can I do with this feeling?"), they angle themselves toward stage left, the upstage arm outstretched perpendicularly to their bodies, while the downstage arm quickly swings vertically up at the first part of the chorus lyric—"what can I do" (Fig. 13.2). Two steady downbeats immediately follow these words, and their bodies articulate the two beats with two hip pulses to the side.

FIGURE 13.2 Screen capture from *Sparkle* (1976), dir. Sam O'Steen. Sister and the Sisters perform "Hooked on Your Love."

Sparkle (HQ) Hooked on your Love

FIGURE 13.3 Screen capture from *Sparkle* (1976), dir. Sam O'Steen. Satin's transfixed stare.

Sister purses her lips seductively while finishing the rest of the chorus's choreography; the hips continually swing, and the elevated arm comes down and subtly glides up the opposite arm, pausing on the shoulder. The camera cuts to Satin, a dark-skinned black man watching the performance, finger resting on his chin (Fig. 13.3). His stoic expression and blink-less stare belie his desire, as his gaze serves metonymically as that of the universalized male gaze. Furthermore, his hip-notized stare validates the corporeal and aesthetic capital of Sister's swinging hips and appearance. A reaction shot of Levi, who had already demonstrated his desire for Sister in previous scenes, serves as further proof of the heterosexual male gaze witnessing the spectacle of Sister.

When the camera finally returns to the action on the stage, Delores and Sparkle begin switching positions behind Sister, who, through filmic devices such as the close-up, remains in (as) the center (of attention). Although they all perform the same choreography, Sister's interpretation becomes the only one visually available. The hip swings and sways continue as do the sinewy arm movements, as the camera slowly begins its close-up of Sister. It frames her from her chest up, until, toward the end of the song, only her face encapsulates the screen. With her face showing visible expressions of sensuality, self-pleasure, and joy, Delores and Sparkle's bodies literally become fragmented as only their red-gloved arms or hands invade the screen in the background.

After this successful performance, Satin arrives at their dressing room and invites Sister to a party. Satin, a neighborhood gangster, possesses some accoutrements of financial success: flashy clothes, an expensive car, and gifts of fur coats for his lady friends. Sister's ambition for "the big time" leads her to begin a relationship with him, despite his violent ways and her mother's warning that he "will drag you down into the gutter." She begins to arrive at performances with a bruised face and starts to use cocaine, claiming, "Sister can't fly with just one wing." Drugs, Satin, and her brash desire to be different exacerbate Sister's demise. As a reminder of her wasted potential but aesthetic value, the last image of Sister shows her lying in her coffin with the ubiquitous red flower in her hair. It is Sparkle who eventually obtains the successful singing career. Although Sister's proximity to "whiteness" may have promised some mainstream success, the film celebrates Sparkle, the brown(er) girl, with the last scene taking place at her concert in New York City's prestigious Carnegie Hall. *Sparkle* can thus be perceived as a cautionary tale against a powerful, performing mulatta body since she will always be doomed to a tragic fate.

FLASHDANCE

Adrian Lyne's *Flashdance* (1983) focuses on Alex, the mulatta protagonist who works as both a welder and an erotic dancer in order to save money to attend a ballet conservatory. *Flashdance*, *Sparkle*, and later, *Honey*, locate the mulatta body within a nocturnal libidinal economy. Her dancing body achieves recognition in the space of a nightclub, a site where the narrative function of the mulatta partners alongside vernacular or popular dance forms with dance vocabularies that can sustain the excesses of her hip and its corporeal utterances. These filmic nocturnal diversions clandestinely mask the issue of race in *Flashdance*, since its main character is never confirmed as mulatta. As Harryette Mullen states, "because [Alex] lives alone, works with whites, and dates an affluent white man, the deracinated black character (or generic white American) that Jennifer Beals plays is probably presumed to be white" (1994: 86). In contrast, I suggest that the social situations, narrative devices, and the lead actress Beals's corporeality within the film enable a reading of her as not white, not ambiguously "other," but as specifically mulatta with its accompanying set of narratives. *Flashdance's* mulatta narrative includes: mulatta as deracinated figure; mulatta possessing both a highly sexualized body and insatiable sexual desire; and, mulatta as recipient of white male patronage. My reading concurs with Scruggs's statement about the mulatto figure in that "even when no 'mark' of blackness can be seen, the mulatto yet functions as hidden history" (2004:327). Alex's hidden history thus appears through these mulatta narratives. Although Alex's race suffers from narrative elision, her body is coded as "other" through markers of class and her embodied dance practice. As no genealogical or family connections appear, we are left to read the character of Alex through the actress's ambiguously raced body, constructing the "hidden history" that lies behind her epidermal reality.[5]

Beals, who happens to be "mulatta" (she is African-American and Italian-American) innocuously plays Alex "without any racial features [...as] clearly the tan Other. [...] The film shrewdly graces her with a white mother surrogate who serves as the emotional foundation for her life, the woman who encourages her to pursue her dream of dancing" (Bogle 2001:291). Beals's mulatta corporeality tinges these narrative devices by enacting a remembrance of other historical narratives this corporeality experiences. Beals-as-Alex operates as what Joseph Roach calls "a body possessed of its social memory" (1996: 209). In *Sparkle, Flashdance,* and *Honey* the performance of "mulatta" con-figures a circum-Atlantic memory. Just as Sister's sassy ways, red flower, and black dress allude to Dorothy Dandridge and stir up a re-membering of this particular mulatta, Beals-as-Alex continues to recall the historical mulatta body for those witnessing it. Notably, their filmic presences corporealize "mulatta-ness," demonstrating what Roach argues when he states, "the mutually interdependent performances of circum-Atlantic memory remain visible, audible, and kinesthetically palpable to those who walk in the cities along its historic rim" (1996:30). Roach's performance theory of surrogation as a process of culture's reproduction and recreation relies on the relationship between performance, memory, and substitution. For Roach this process of surrogation persists; it has neither end nor beginning, but operates on a continuum needing constant substitutes to take the place of the cultural artifact so that the "thing" might exist to facilitate the circum-Atlantic memory and by default maintain the cultural memory. Film, as a cultural artifact, engages and does cultural remembrance work, using familiar narrative devices, situations, and corporeal (re)iterations to reify racial and gendered ways of being, irrespective of the complex corporealities specific to multiple raced and gendered subjectivities.

Alex's relationship with her boss becomes another example of how the filmic apparatus deploys or re-inscribes mulatta narratives. Her boss, Nick, first notices her when she dances and strips in the first dance sequence of the film. She performs various jerky, angular movements before she begins her disrobing. She points to a chair that has been placed on the stage, and moves toward it through a turn. She leans back into the chair, arching her back, legs outstretched, a lithe feminine silhouette against the white background. The camera moves into a close-up on her face looking out into the audience. A quick reaction shot shows Nick staring at her enraptured. The juxtaposition of these two shots establishes the connection between her performance and its fomentation of desire in him.

A second act of disrobing follows and Alex now wears a small, revealing red teddy. This garment becomes further eroticized when she leans back into the chair, pulls a chain and unleashes a torrent of water onto her body. Dance scholar Sherril Dodds aptly analyzes this moment as a metaphor for ejaculation (2001:39). Alex's damp, moving, and gesticulating body further entices her audience by running close to the front of the stage and, with quick hand gestures, invites them into her corporeal space. At one particular moment in the choreography, she turns to face away from her audience and presents them her almost bare buttocks, hips shifting side to side, flesh jiggling and wiggling in response to her movements. Her movement vocabulary ranges from jazz spins and leg kicks to more languid poses that display the curves and arches of her body. Presumably, Alex has created this choreography and it serves its purpose within the nightclub setting: to excite, entice, and entertain the male bodies that sit around the stage and stare up at her wet moving one. Nick, like Satin in *Sparkle*, cannot take his eyes from her as she pulses to the remaining beats of the song. He looks even more satisfied when he finds out that this nearly naked, dancing body is one of his employees. A power and gender dynamic emerges from this three-minute scene that affects how Alex's body and agency operate throughout the rest of the film.

By having her boss become her lover and subsequently use his connections to procure an audition spot for her at the conservatory, Alex connects with a genealogy of mulatta concubinage for the improvement of socio-economic status. New World colonial histories are rife with tales about such sexual liaisons that involved mulatta mistresses, wealthy landed aristocrats, and sentimental abolitionist love stories.[6] In *Flashdance's* "post-modern" mulatta narrative, Alex's dependence on a patron ensures her future dance career and happiness. Thus, despite Alex's strong desire to, and talent for, dance, her choreographic labor as displayed in the audition scene, which features a hybridized movement vocabulary ranging from ballet, jazz, breakdancing, and gymnastics, and her economic self-reliance, the racialized and sexualized power dynamic serves to not only undermine her dance skills, but her own agency as well.[7] Would she ever have had a chance to audition without having provided her white lover with, what we can assume by her sexual appetite and physical stamina, nights of frenetic love-making? One need only remember the scene when they kiss for the first time and she hungrily attacks his lips. Unfortunately, this representation of mulatta sexuality, liberated and liberating to be sure, barely moves her away from the trope of the unfulfilled mulatta. Without his help, she may have continued to dance at the erotic club, still dreaming of a ballet career.

HONEY

In contrast to *Flashdance, Honey's* depiction of an independent and ambitious mulatta does not specifically rely on male patronage—white or black. Like Alex, Honey longs to be a dancer, but a screen body in music videos, not a ballerina. Honey's mother (played by Lonette McKee from *Sparkle*) wants her to study ballet, but Honey prefers to dance and teach hip-hop. Mary C. Beltrán reads Jessica Alba's Honey as "a brash Puerto Rican dancer from the Bronx" (2009:164). Arguably, the casting of Lonette McKee as Honey's mother undermines such a reading. Not because Puerto Ricans cannot be mulatto, but because McKee's presence and filmic history, specifically for African-American audiences, clearly mark her and as a result, her screen daughter, as mulattas. Honey-as-mulatta thus allows Lonette McKee's filmic bodily presence to labor and continue the process of surrogation and re-creating a circum-Atlantic memory of the mulatta body.

Honey demonstrates her dance skills at the nightclub where she works as a bartender. Once more, we find the mulatta dancing body primarily situated and garnering recognition in a club through vernacular dance. Sister's dancing serves as accompaniment to her group's singing and as a means to an end ("the big time"). Alex's dancing body functions as a spectacle and she, like Sister, performs onstage in a working-class club. Although Honey works at an urban nightclub, she dances *after* her bartending shift finishes. Her dancing is for personal enjoyment, as evidenced by the first dance sequence of the film.[8] As the film's opening credits finish, Honey closes down the bar and proceeds to the dance floor. When the DJ sees her, he changes the music and her "improvisation" begins. She walks around a male partner, swinging her hips in an exaggerated manner. They do not necessarily partner, as hip-hop dance tends to be a solo endeavor, but she uses him for quick support, one hand resting on his shoulder as she marks a circular path around him. She walks away and stops behind a female dancer, both of them bending forcibly and pumping their bodies upward for three pulsating counts. Honey then positions herself in the middle of two other female dancers; with hands on hip, she hip-pops to the left, back, right, front, one arm outstretched, then hip-shakes. With their legs wider than hip distance apart, they do a quick dip of the pelvis downward and quickly propel their torsos upward, leading with the hip. Two pronounced hip thrusts to the right and left conclude their unison routine. Their hipped enunciations make the rhythm of the music visible—a hybridized sonic landscape of Indian *bhangra* and hip-hop. Honey continues to dance alone inside a small circle of space opened out for her by the dancing crowd. Jumps, arm locks, torso undulations, level changes, and breakdancing vocabulary combine and culminate in pirouette turns that propels her around four times to ultimately land, spread out, knees bent supine on the floor. The crowd goes wild with applause and shouts of approval while she continues to dance on her own among them. In this context, I want to consider Thomas DeFrantz's writing about how the black beat is indeed made visible through hip-hop. In black social dance, orality, drum (beat or rhythm), and the body exist as a cohesive expressive unit. Furthermore, the call-and-response structure between Honey's moves and the crowd's reaction inflect her performance with an Africanist aesthetic. When Honey continues to dance on her own, to corporealize the music with her own interpretive skill she embodies DeFrantz's explanation: "to dance hip hop, the body is held 'tight'; that is, focused, with strong weight, and capable of an explosive suddenness [...] these performed accents help to ground alternative rhythmic conceptions of the beat; to keep it fresh; to allow a dancer to reenter the same beat in many different ways." (2004:74). Like *Sparkle* and *Flashdance*, this dance sequence serves to show the mulatta's physical dexterity in a popular dance style, or more precisely a "natural" ability to dance for pleasurable displays or inner transcendence. They appear as "untrained" dancer bodies capable of virtuosic or mesmerizing physical feats prone to induce hip-notism, spectacle, or banal desire because of their body's affiliation with notions of rhythmicity and aspects of "blackness."

Unknown to Honey, a video of her dancing at the club ends up in the hands of a white music-video producer, Michael Ellis. He shows up at the nightclub, gives her his card and asks her to call him because he can offer her dance work in music videos. Whereas for her, dance functions as a form of physicalized self-expression, for Michael, her dancing body becomes a commodity redolent with the attributes of her racialized gender and thus, exploitable. Honey is skeptical of Michael at first, but at her friend's insistence, she calls him and gets invited to be a "video dancing body" for the hip-hop group Jadakiss. When Honey arrives at the video shoot, Michael is displeased with the existing choreography. He stops the filming and asks Honey to imagine being at the club, to just "feel the music" and see what she physically conjures up. She closes her eyes, bounces to the music for several counts, opens her eyes and turns to one of the male dancers, calling him over with a wave of her hand. She appears to mumble something inaudible, lifts her arm to give him a brief glimpse of what she will do; he nods, theirs is an embodied choreographic exchange, and their mini-routine begins. Her upstage arm lifts while her downstage leg hooks itself onto his waist. She thrusts her hips up-down, up-down, quickly turns to face away from him with legs spread widely apart and bends forward, her buttocks squarely placed by his waist. She reaches down to the floor, slides across on one knee, gets up, one arm raised, and pumps her hips to the side before she undulates her torso and continues to improvise. Michael interrupts, the music stops and he states approvingly, "*That* is sexy…Everybody else, follow what she is doing." Again, the filmic apparatus continues its process of reification as it constructs Honey's mulatta dancing body as "sexy." The verbal declaration inhibits Honey's laboring body from being the different expressive bodies she physically demonstrates throughout the film: a choreographing body, hired body, video dancing body, and finally an instructional body.[9]

In addition to becoming a screen dancing body, Honey also teaches hip-hop at a community center. During class, she breaks down the choreography into counts, goes over it slowly, adds the music, and even incorporates one of her student's accidental falls into the routine. In contrast, *Flashdance* exclusively showcases the end-result of Alex's "maniacal" workouts. The film audience has no insight as to where she creates her solo-striptease performances. The layout of her apartment—a converted warehouse—with its mirrors and ballet-barres, demarcate her home as a space where danced bodily labor occurs, but other than the excerpt of her working out and stretching, her choreographic labor is absent. In *Honey*, however, the choreographic labor remains visible. Spared a dissection by the camera of Honey's dancing body into rippling buttocks, pounding feet, or an undulating torso (as in *Flashdance*), her body engages in repetition, rehearsal, and corporeal pedagogical exchanges.

Another compositional moment occurs when Michael asks Honey to change some choreography over a lunch-time video-shoot break. She finds an isolated spot that happens to look out onto a basketball court. As she rehearses the existing choreography she becomes increasingly frustrated; no new choreographic ideas seem to work. She happens to look over at the court across the way and begins carefully to watch the players' movements: their criss-crossing arms, wide stances, pivots, and jump shots. Honey incorporates this movement vocabulary and develops a phrase to replace the old one. In this instance, I am reminded of introductory dance composition assignments where students are asked to make a dance using everyday or pedestrian movements. When she returns to show and teach the new and improved choreography, Michael approves and Honey cements her success, albeit briefly.

Michael's sexual desire for Honey becomes evident in the second half of the film. He makes sexual advances toward her and expects reciprocation as gratitude for the opportunities he has offered her. Honey rejects his advances and he blacklists her in the music video industry. The mulatta narrative that sets up relationships with white male patrons as being or becoming sexual ones thus appears in the film, but Honey's control over her own body and its multiple labors renders it obsolete. Ultimately, Michael's actions prove inconsequential, having no bearing on Honey's reputation, talent, or ambition. She helps raise money for her mother's dilapidated community center through a fundraising performance featuring her dance students. The filmic apparatus erases the choreographic labor of the fundraiser by only showing the performance through slick edits, jump cuts, and close-ups on virtuosic displays of hip-hop dancing. Meanwhile, hip hop star Missy Elliott shows up at Michael's offices, demanding Honey as her choreographer and threatening to fire him. Michael's attempted sabotage clearly fails, since the last shot of the film shows Missy Elliott arriving at the fundraiser and quickly scurrying in, implying Honey's successful future as a video dancer and choreographer.

Dance studies and performance theory offer ways of removing the tragedy inscribed on mulatta narratives by focusing on how the body read or coded as mulatta uses its very physicality to subvert, contest, or engage with its limited representations. *Honey's* choreographer, Laurie Ann Gibson, another mulatta body, has had a successful career as a dancer, film/video choreographer, and dance teacher.[10] If *Honey* can be read as a case of art imitating life, then perhaps the "tragic mulatta" will eventually be erased by an ensemble of dancing mulattas working through ways to choreograph her, once and for all, off the stage.

NOTES

* Originally Published in *International Journal of Performance and Digital Media*, December 2009.
1. See Blanco Borelli, 2008.
2. After *Sparkle*, Lonette McKee has had a consistent and successful career as an actress, singer, producer, and composer. She has been nominated for a Tony for her portrayal of "Julie," the tragic mulatta in *Showboat*. Ironically, she was the first African American woman to play the role and in reality, McKee has been far from the tragic mulattas she often has played. http://www.lonettemckee.com, accessed September 7, 2009.
3. Dandridge was a glamorous mid-twentieth-century actress and singer. She was the first African American to be nominated for an Academy Award for Best Actress in 1955. She faced casting difficulties given her "ambiguous" appearance and died of an overdose in 1965 at the age of 42.
4. The word "adore" comes from the Latin *adorare* "to worship," from *ad-* "to" + *orare* "speak, pray"(*Oxford English Dictionary*). Within "colorstruck" epistemologies the mulatta or more specifically the "yellow skin" is desired and venerated.
5. When casting for the film, producers wanted an unknown. Two white actresses, Demi Moore and Leslie Wing, were considered for the role before Beals was cast. One wonders how a white body would have functioned in this role and how it may have affected the narrative.
6. For literary analysis of the role of the mulatta concubine, see Jenny Sharpe's *Ghosts of Slavery: A Literary Archaeology of Black Women's Lives*. (Minneapolis: University of Minnesota Press, 2003).

7. Alex willingly becomes romantically involved with her boss, unlike eighteenth- or nineteenth-century mulatta/white male liaisons, which were often coerced relationships due to the power dynamics inherent in slavery.
8. This does not mean that Alex's dancing cannot be analyzed through a feminist lens of dancing for empowerment and self-pleasure, but the economic motives behind Alex's erotic dancing are made clear in *Flashdance*. Honey also has economic motives, but she works at the club as a bartender. She need not remain there after her shift is over, yet she does so in order to dance.
9. Dance scholar Susan Foster captures the expressive potential of these different types of bodies in her chapter "Dancing Bodies."
10. See http://en.wikipedia.org/wiki/Laurie_Ann_Gibson and http://www.myspace.com/laurieanngibson (accessed on September 11, 2009).

BIBLIOGRAPHY

Bastiaans, Aisha D. (2008) "Detecting Difference in Devil in a Blue Dress: The Mulata Figure, Noir, and the Cinematic Reification of Race," in *Mixed Race Hollywood*, edited by M. Beltrán and C. Fojas, 223–247. New York: New York University Press.

Beltrán, M. and Fojas, C. (2008) *Mixed Race Hollywood*. New York: New York University Press.

Beltrán, M. C. (2009). *Latina/o Stars in U.S. Eyes The Making and Meanings of Film and TV Stardom*. Chicago: University of Illinois Press.

Blanco Borelli, M. (2008). "Y ahora qué vas a hacer, mulata? Hip Choreographies in the Mexican Cabaretera Film Mulata (1954)." *Women & Performance: A Journal of Feminist Theory*. Volume 18, Number 3, pp. 215–233.

Carby, H. (1987) *Reconstructing Womanhood: The Emergence of the Afro-American Woman Novelist*. Oxford: Oxford University Press.

DeFrantz, T. (2004) "The Black Beat Made Visible: Hip Hop Dance and Body Power," in *Of the Presence of the Body: Essays on Dance and Performance Theory*, edited by Andre Lepecki, 64–81. Middletown, CT: Wesleyan University Press.

DeFrantz, T. (2005) "African American Dance: Philosophy, Aesthetics and 'Beauty'" *Topoi* 24:1, 93–102.

Derrida, J. (1994) *Specters of Marx: The State of the Debt, the Work of Mourning, and the New International*. New York: Routledge.

DeVere Brody, J. (1998) *Impossible Purities: Blackness, Femininity and Victorian Culture*. Durham, NC: Duke University Press.

Dodds, S. (2001). *Dance on Screen: Genres and Media from Hollywood to Experimental Art*. London: Palgrave MacMillan.

Foster, S. (1997). "Dancing Bodies," in *Meaning in Motion: New Cultural Studies of Dance*, edited by J. Desmond, 235–257. Durham, NC: Duke University Press.

Lyne, A. (1983). *Flashdance*, Paramount Pictures.

McRobbie, A. (1998). "Fame, Flashdance and Fantasies of Achievement," in *Fabrications: Costume and the Female Body*, edited by J. Gaines and C. Herzog. London: Routledge. pp. 39–58.

Mullen, H. (1994). "Optic White: Blackness and the Production of Whiteness," *Diacritics* 24, No. 2/3, Critical Crossings, 71–89.

O' Steen, S. (1976). *Sparkle*, Warner Bros. Pictures

Roach, J. (1996). *Cities of the Dead: Circum-Atlantic Performance.* New York: Columbia University Press.

Scruggs, C. (2004). "The Pastoral and the City in Carl Franklin's 'One False Move,'" *African American Review* 38:2, 323–334.

Sollors, W. (1999) *Neither White nor Black but Both: Thematic Explorations of Interracial Literature.* Cambridge: Harvard University Press.

Woodruff, B. (2003). *Honey.* Universal Studios.

CHAPTER 14

"HE'S DOING HIS SUPERMAN THING AGAIN": MOVING BODIES IN *THE MATRIX*

DEREK A. BURRILL

> ...if seeing and knowing were, until now, the great quests at once ethical and aesthetic, ever since the eighteenth century with its Enlightenment, seeing and being able have become the great quests of our twenty-first century, with the outstripping of the politically correct by the optically correct—this correction that is no longer the ocular correction of the glass lenses in our spectacles but the societal correction of our view of the world, in the age of planetary globalization.[1]

I recently asked a friend what she remembered first and foremost about the *Matrix* films. She fired back without hesitation, "the dodging bullets scene." Our conversation then moved to the standard philosophical/epistemological questions that seem to always circulate around the films and their analysis: alternate universes, the contexts of reality, simulation, the ends and means of violence, revolution and technology, identity, etc. But, at root, our conversation still seemed to gravitate toward that one moment, that one haptic blaze of balletic embodiment. Afterward, I returned to my screen and watched the scene again through a download from somewhere on the Internet. What struck me this time was the subtle sophistication of the camera movement. The spectator literally sees Neo's body from all angles, as if watching from an omniscient point of view, a kind of simultaneity akin to Marcel Duchamp's seminal painting, *Nude Descending a Staircase, No. 2* (1912). The Cubists (with whom Duchamp was loosely associated) sought to capture a viewpoint as if the painter and viewer were viewing the world at the speed of light, seeing all sides of all objects, all at once. Their technique was an attempt to represent the pace of technological "progress" and the changes in our perceptive apparatus that it entailed. In a similar sense, the directors configured this scene as a means of mapping the body's attitudes regarding digital technologies and the complexities they foster. Of course, the film has made "bullet-time" cinematography famous, to the point that it has been widely parodied in popular culture (the *Max Payne* videogame series, as well as *Max Payne*, the film). But, intrinsically, when Neo (Latin for "new") bends over backward in his attempt to dodge the bullets (a part of his quest to hone his skills as an extension of his "One-ness"), the CGI (Computer Generated Images) and cinematographic book was rewritten. The Warchowskis—the team responsible for the franchise's inception and the directors, writers, and executive producers of the films—imagined, created, and utilized a new technological system that could properly capture what the rest of us sensed in our daily lives, the increasing creep of digital technology and the mild schizophrenia that accompanies it. When Neo bends over backward, it is a signal that the greater culture is feeling equally strained. But, at the same time, the attendant excitement is equally palpable. It is as if we are relearning our bodies in our collision with the digital and the virtual. Considering that Neo dodges all the bullets save one, the scene is also a potent reminder that our bodies will always be subject to growing pains, mistakes, and obsolescence, no matter how virtuosic our digital or real performance is or how seductive the mode of representation may be.

However, it's the otherworldly sense of embodied power—whether from the digital posse's (Neo, Trinity, Morpheus, etc.) transport mechanism from the virtual world to the real world through landlines (vortexed into the digital and back out again into the analog), or from their ability to download massive amounts of information and objects into their projected-cognitive world ("I know Kung-fu")—that remains so integral to our fascination with the franchise. So, in this anthology regarding dance and the popular screen, this chapter situates itself as a means of theorizing how the bodies in motion in the *Matrix* films (hereafter referred to as *M3* as a means of differentiating them from the many other tie-ins inspired by the films) are an important resource in understanding how bodies on screen are imagined and choreographed, but also how they are rehearsed, captured, digitized, reproduced, bought, sold, presented, and commodified. This chapter also asks how critical interventions that question and stretch notions of dance on screen serve not only to question the parameters of dance, but also how they can show how dance on screen is itself a technology, one formed of tool, technology and technique. Finally, I will perform a close inspection of two scenes from the franchise, showing that the way the bodies are imagined and staged in the films signals how cyber-citizens imagine and stage their own bodies and what kinds of symptoms we can expect from this constant exposure.

Genre and the Body

First, there a few things that should to be said about the science fiction (SF) genre of film. The genre, at root, often operates based on a central dialectic: utopia vs. dystopia. Anyone that has seen, or is a fan of, science fiction films is well aware of this tension, well played out in *M3*; technology will save us (humans, the environment, other species, the ozone, etc.) vs. technology will be the ruin of us. Represented in films such as

Blade Runner (1982) and later crystallized with the rise of cyberpunk films (often based on the novels of Phillip K. Dick) such as *Minority Report* (2002) or *Strange Days* (1995), *The Matrix* trilogy, and more recently, *Inception* (2010), Looper (2012), or Oblivion (2013). The basic premise is usually the same: innate "human-ness" is "always-already" threatened by our technological inventions and their inevitable complicated complexification. The always-already is written into our DNA.[2] We were always-already (technologically at least) equipped to sow the seeds of our own destruction. Now, the human race must see if we can develop an equitable understanding of control, progress, development, and consciousness. And so the always-already (present) possibility of self-annihilation transfers from our DNA to our digital code, a closed-off, naturalized form of techno-scientific determinism. We are, indeed, our ends to our own means. What do we do about it? These digital SF films offer us insight into a solution, no matter how dystopic it may seem. Somehow, some way, the body always returns as a useful force, a form and enunciation that manages to usurp the prevailing wisdom that bodies have become useless, "dead meat" on the other side of the screen.[3] However, with the crushing popularity and questionable utility-value of Massive Multiplayer Online Role Playing Games, social networking sites, YouTube, etc., the tether linking the body to the virtual has become that much more intrinsic and "essential." Cyberspace is so often hailed as a superior, sexier, and more exciting place than the "regular" world. As Edward Castronova writes, in his book *Synthetic Worlds*:

> Synthetic worlds have the potential to become permanent homes for the conscious self. Millions upon millions may decide that moving into cyberspace is the best thing to do. Yet once they are there, do we know that they will retain their initial set of desires and hopes in unchanged form? Do we know that they will remain fully informed about other options for living their lives, which may range from other synthetic worlds to the outer world in all its rough-edged glory?[4]

And, so, the point here is that the flesh, the body, the mechanics, training, ideas, and emotions of the working, struggling body always seems to creep into the equation. It is the ghost in the machine, but also the essence of the machine, for all machines are built in the eyes of their maker.[5]

In their introduction to the text *Science Fiction Cinema*, editors Geoff King and Tanya Krzywinska suggest that a good way to describe how we all live in postmodern, sci-fi society is by way of "schizophrenia." To their ends, schizophrenia is a fragmented existence, where the self is broken into multiple selves as a means of navigating the complex and confusing world of modern and postmodern technologies. The schizophrenic lives in a "perpetual present," with no clear sense of the past or the future. They have a sense of the world with heightened intensity, but a clear sense of "true" reality is lost, so that the subject is unmoored from traditional cultural structures—family, work, play, ethics. They find that our contemporary world looks a lot like most sci-fi, a paraspace (or alternate space), a schizophrenic state that is pure spectacle but can unsettle our sense of reality, so much that science fiction narrative, concept, theme, and design has in fact determined what our reality really looks like. William Gibson, famous for coining the term "cyberspace" in his seminal cyberpunk work *Neuromancer* (1984), is widely acknowledged, through his prose, as the "imaginer" of what we now know as the Internet, the World Wide Web, and virtual reality. The fictional has served to form the real, and so the subject responds with the strategy of schizophrenia. We can see this throughout *M3*—the characters seem to have a core self, but are perfectly comfortable inhabiting a constructed skin to get the job done.

Although there is a great deal of popular and academic writing on the *Matrix* franchise, very little seems to be written about how (other than through special effects) the bodies in the films actually function and make meaning, However, there is a fair amount written on Hong Kong action cinema's influences on the fight choreography, particularly the choreography and wire work created and staged by Yuen Woo-ping for the films. For this chapter, I will not perform an analysis of the bodies as product of fight choreography and training. Instead, I aim to develop a vocabulary and theory of bodies written into a digital imaginary captured on screen, and to explore how the technologies themselves configure how we make sense of it all. In short, when bodies are choreographed and captured in *M3*, how does the technology itself reflect, contend with, and alter our own sense of embodiment? Also, since the body itself is a form of technology, how does it imagine (and therefore change) itself in relation to virtual technologies, technologies that do the imagining for it? Movement on screen, in the traditional sense, has largely been analyzed in two ways: (1) How is movement on screen a product of the mode of production? And, (2) How is the movement captured? In this chapter, I also ask another question: How do virtual technologies, and digitization in general, alter both of these questions? In order to tease the answers out, I would like to focus on two scenes from the second film, *Matrix: Reloaded* (2003), where we see a vocabulary of movement instituted by the first film and its extension through further technological invention and development, as well as the use of an *aesthetics of excess* as a means of crystallizing how movement on screen creates pleasure and desire.

BREAK IT DOWN: RELOADED

Matrix: Reloaded (2003) begins with the familiar green and black symphony of digital alphanumerics, scrolling and swirling to suggest our (the viewers') presence in the code, inside some machine, somewhere. This slowly fades, from the shape of the face of a clock in green/black code, to the face of an analog time clock. Someone punches their timecard, signaling the labor-centered drudgery that pervades the lives of those caught in the matrix (the virtual world fed to the human batteries under the subjugation of the sentient machines). So, we know right away what these bodies in the matrix are for: work, and boring work at that. These digital dupes live and die in an existentially hollow world, never knowing that their endless toil serves a much more basic function. Without knowing it, the inhabitants of this world suffer the ultimate form of oppression, subjugation, and exploitation;—they are fuel cells with an invented consciousness.[6] While the questions here beg theoretical attention, particularly Marxist and poststructuralist theory, I want instead to focus on the bodies and their labor as signifiers in the films. In this scene we see an example of labor (security guard) that the Warchowskis cast as boring, listless, and repetitive. In short, analog. When Trinity explodes on the scene, catapulting off of a roof on a motorcycle, we watch as she executes a perfect backward swan dive flip, landing squarely and on balance, her right leg extended outward, her left arm serving as an elegant counterbalance, reminiscent of Janet Jackson and Anthony Thomas's choreography in Jackson's seminal video, *Rhythm Nation* [1989]). Trinity's right hand is squarely planted, palm down, as if to signal a particular knowledge of the earth and gravity itself, a tricked-out, digital Martha Graham moment. She quickly and effortlessly dispatches the security guards that attempt to stop her, performing flips, twists, and spins gracefully, in an almost detached manner. This is reminiscent of the Chinese martial art known as Wing Chun, made famous in the West by Bruce Lee, although the movement in this scene is more highly stylized and acrobatic. Central to Wing Chun is balance, so that the artist is akin to a bamboo shaft, flexible but stable, malleable but firm. Using a relaxed, centerline-focused technique allows the user to deflect or redirect forces within a short range, thus the emphasis in Wing Chun on close-quarters attacks and defense.[7] Trinity uses one weapon—her helmet. It's a clever reversal to so obviously misuse this safety device, but it also signals that her main weapons are her head and brain, the computer of the Body. That Trinity is dominatrix-sexy, clad in black patent leather (or rubber), and powerfully technical in her combat techniques, also signals that she is *not* analog; she is digital, a projection of an idealized, powerful, sexual self. This is the first of many body dichotomies that are set up by the films. In this case, the cyberpunk heroes of the film are the ultimate body fetish: lithe, graceful, technically controlled, clad in cyber-cool threads, able to travel and move through the "game" in ways the everyday citizens cannot.

A second important and telling scene, a fight scene between Neo and Seraph (Colin Chou, a Taiwanese-born stuntman, actor, and martial artist), features more traditional fight choreography and martial arts filming and editing techniques. Rather than relying on CGI or heavy wire-work, this fight scene is shot using more familiar angles, shots, edits, and camera movement and in doing so emphasizes the physicality of the actors *themselves*, rather than the characters as avatars in the Matrix (although Seraph is a computer generated entity who lives entirely in the Matrix). In what appears to be a generic dojo made from plain blond wood beams and walls, non-diegetic rumbling Taiko drums and other percussion instruments organically and rhythmically buttress opaque rice-paper windows and a generally Buddhist-ascetic design concept. The scene begins with oscillating standard medium close-up shots of both Neo and Seraph, focusing on the actor speaking. This sets the tone and mood of the space, as well as physical and emotional motivation for each character. Comprising most of the scene are three main angles: (a) medium shots from the torso up, emphasizing the upper-body balance and flexibility of each actor/artist; (b) full body shots featuring both actors from a 90-degree side-angle, emphasizing full body articulation, including kicks, spins, and leaps; and (c) crane and tracking shots that follow individual bodies from the side or above. The odd thing about this whole scene is it's utter lack of artistry or affect. It feels as if it's a demo clip for a particular fight choreographer, presumably searching for work. In this sense, the scene functions as a literal and figurative reminder that there are *real* bodies in this film that do perform *real* stunts (although one of two shots do feature obvious quick wire-work). What is most striking, however, is how transparent this ploy seems, as if the Warchowskis were worried that they didn't have enough *real* stuff for *real* action/martial arts buffs (presumably boys and men). So, in the end, it seems more like a rehearsal for the scene itself, as a marketing strategy for men in crisis, or as a level in a videogame that the player must finish in order to move forward. And, in fact, Seraph ends the fight sequence, gently raising his hand:

SERAPH
Good. The Oracle has many enemies. I had to be sure.
NEO
Of what?
SERAPH
That you are the One.
NEO
Could've just asked.
SERAPH
No. You do not truly know someone until you fight them.

So, what we have here is a form of essentialist authentication in the midst of a CGI dream world, a scene where the directors seem to be hedging their bets on the power of digital effects, while appealing to our commodity-driven sense of "specialness" as actual owners of our bodies and their movements (to *know* someone is to *fight* them). We may not be able to dodge bullets, but good old Kung Fu still works. In the end, the dull physical actuality of Neo and Seraph's routine, along with the hygienic cinematography and editing, results in an uneasy binary made up of real bodies and virtual selves, where here specifically, the real bodies are on show and are recorded as markers of (detached) authenticity, even though in this scene they are in the Matrix, representations built on digital code.

This scene, Trinity's first scene, and the following "bullet time" scene (where she plummets out of a building while firing at and being fired upon by agents), are excellent examples of what Paul Virilio, in the epigram introducing this chapter, means by "... seeing and being able." Whereas previous (Western) cultures have put a premium on seeing and knowing, Virilio finds that our digitized culture lionizes seeing and *being able*. *Knowledge* as power has effectively been replaced by *ability* as power, and this is nowhere more obvious than in digital culture. We consume bits of knowledge, fragments and clumps through blogs, Twitter, and Facebook, so that traditional knowledge streams (information contextualized and extended beyond fragments into sedentary groupings) become irrelevant, or simply too difficult to parse.[8] Instead, what is essential is access and ability. The user has to know *how* to use the software and hardware, and greater familiarity and facility with both confers power. Similarly, in *M3*, the cyberheroes are specially abled, their bodies work (to a certain extent) without gravitational, biological, and physical constraints. This film, as a representative of a particular mode of representation—science fiction cinema—celebrates excessive bodily ability, what I call the *aesthetics of excess*. The Warchowskis created a design/thematic, conceptual world (a future within a future, a cyberspace of sleek and labyrinthine structure, a robotic, oppressive, artificially intelligent, apocalyptic global surface, the future-primitive underground city of Zion, etc.) so complete and complex that the bodies and their movement in these worlds must follow suit. The structures of the average, the virtuosic, and the virtual are enunciated through choreography, movement, and body politics so that the cinematic tools (cinematography, special effects, narrative, character, etc.) and the tools of cinema (bodies) follow the same logic: the aesthetics of excess. During one of several scenes where Neo flies ("He's doing his Superman thing"), he bolts through the sky and then swoops upward, completing an elegant pirouette, seemingly without purpose. He then comes to a hovering rest, arms and legs in a curvilinear set of arcs. The effect is dazzling. But, why the pirouette? Is this a necessity of flying? A way to actually stop? Again, according to *M3*'s concept/theme, this gratuitous technical flair is a logic unto itself—it is pure "being ableness," pure excess for (presumably) the viewer's pleasure and power, and as a means of reflecting and fulfilling our viewing desires.

In order to capture and record these kinds of movement, CGI are essential. In preparation for the first film, the directors and their technical crew developed and devised several novel techniques, both analog and digital. The first was wire-work and ropes attached to harnesses around the actors. With these the directors could defy the laws of gravity while using and filming actual bodies. And while these technologies are rather old contraptions invented in the theater centuries ago, they also have a long history in film, particularly in Hong Kong action cinema. Recent examples include the bamboo-top fight scene in *Crouching Tiger, Hidden Dragon* (2000), where the combatants perch and hop from the tops of bamboo reeds and stalks, as if their body weight has evaporated into air. In *M3*, physics and gravity becomes even more negligible, where a punch can send someone 30 feet into a wall, crushing the tile and cement as if it were cardboard. Second, they developed a method of photography, where (initially) 124 cameras were positioned around the subject (for the first "bullet-time" scene in the first film), firing at intervals of 1/30 of a second. The actors were surrounded by blue screens that would be filled with digital detail in post-production. Creating a 360-degree view of Neo, the camera exposure intervals created a space where time and space could be controlled, thus slowing or speeding up what the viewer sees and how quickly the POV could be adjusted. By shooting at approximately 12,000 frames per second (FPS), certain camera "angles" could be frozen, slowed, extended, and reversed.[9] The Cubists would have been jealous. However, in order to up the ante in the aesthetics of excess, the directors and their crew came up with image-based rendering, a process where actual photographs of skyscrapers and cityscapes were taken, downloaded into a computer, given three-dimensional characteristics including relative volume and scale, and then reconstituted as a background for Neo's building-top battle. So, while Keanu Reeves's actual body forms the centerpiece of the scene, its construction and "worlding" are an act of digital artistry, an invented occurrence in a simulated world. At the center of this, however, is still a real body, suspended by real ropes, fighting against real gravity.

Putting the film in historical context, it is no surprise that despite all of the complex technology that made this scene and others possible, bodies are still at the center of the fight. Fulminating in a kind of economic sublimation (and subsequent crash), the dot-com "revolution" of the late 1990s (particularly in North America and Europe) similarly imagined itself as a period of unbridled economic, social, and cultural expansion. Yet, despite the mantras spouted by the cyber-prophets about the technology itself, it was real-world bodies that fueled this dizzying spiral. Programmers, designers, inventors, venture capitalists—and most importantly, users—formed the backbone of the first wave (will there not be many?) of digital culture. So while the digital imaginary often seems to threaten escape velocity, disappearing from our view and eluding our control, in the case of the dot-com revolution, it came crashing down on the people and the markets that fueled its inflated distention. Central to the *aesthetics of excess* is the *passion for control*. It is the same in the matrix: Neo, Trinity, Morpheus, and the rebels are always in search of sneakier ways to get the better of the machines, on "our" turf as well as on "theirs." However, one senses that the digital posse has a secret crush (much like the audience) on these weapons of mass digitization, a fetish disavowed by their cool, detached pose.

THE PEOPLE WANT TO PARTY

In the first third of *Matrix: Reloaded*, the rebels meet for a night of revelry and revolution in their underground cavernous city in order to psychically (and physically) combat the coming storm of machines threatening to wipe them out, presumably for just existing outside the carefully controlled matrix. The scene begins with Morpheus (Laurence Fishburne doing his best Shakespearean vocal histrionics) drumming up support for the coming war. After he has brought them to a suitable frenzy, the rave begins. I use the term "rave" because all of the requisite components of an underground dance party are present: pulsing techno music, "multi-culti" elements (taiko drums, an ethnically diverse population, a druggy hypnotic logic), and a seething sexuality. In this case, the population is *actually* underground, living in caves far below the surface (a place uninhabitable to humans). Or, as Morpheus calls it, "the desert of the real."[10] Regardless, everyone seems pretty happy to let it all go and have a night of freedom and flagrancy. However, the scene is telling for a number of reasons, and in particular it enunciates the tropes central to the body-machine dialectic. During the scene, the cinematography is varied, moving from establishing shots to extreme close-ups, using slow motion and tracking shots to capture the crowd's elemental ecstasy and the intimacy of their embodied embraces.[11] Taiko drummers populate one of the first shots, setting the mood as a primal, rhythmic experience, albeit with stereotypical "future primitive" elements: the contemporary caveman costumes, the sexual and erotic nature of the group/couple dancing, etc. Of course, when we do see bodies writhing together, they are ostensibly heterosexual, often with the darker male in back of a lighter-skinned female, grinding in slow motion to diegetic (and non-diegetic) soundtrack. Interspersed with this are scenes of Neo and Trinity, both on shore leave, coupled in a tangled embrace, practicing missionary, white lovemaking while the colored masses grind in the cavern. These are familiar erotics of popular dance as a sexually charged erotics of embodiment, where dancing is a "last chance" to really "let loose." The parallel editing here juxtaposes the filthy (perhaps "othered") masses bumping and grinding in the face of destruction, with a serene and pristine white couple copulating in an effort to continue the "best" parts of the new society. At the zenith of this we see Neo and Trinity in mid-orgasm, when suddenly we are thrust into Trinity's falling scene, again swathed in black leather/rubber, firing rapidly at an Agent in pursuit. Like the French term *le petit mort*, it seems that even in the imagined techo-future, an orgasm is still "a little death," a space where the female body is suddenly out of control. Here, Trinity plummets toward the ground, the physical space where the patriarchal unconscious waits to subsume the "messy" sexuality of femininity. So, is the essence of embodiment in *M3* the cavernous underground where the feral masses slink and slide into oblivion, with a devil-may-care attitude about the machines that are coming? Or is it the relative physical stability of the Neo/Trinity coupling, where the digital unconscious is the marker of a much more perilous conflict, that of the efficacy of the body in an imagined space, within the matrix?

In *Dance On Screen*, Sherril Dodds performs a complex and substantial analysis of the modes and themes of how bodies on screen are captured, and how technologies of representation alter our perceptions and readings of said bodies. The book covers how bodies on film, television, and video make meaning, particularly in regards to cinematographic conventions such as framing, shot choice, camera movement, and POV. A particularly useful chapter focuses on music videos and their relationship to popular dance films. One of her targets is the 1983 dance film, *Flashdance*. She astutely points out how the camera tends to focus (in certain scenes—music video segments, really) on individual body parts, thus drawing attention to how these body parts signify discretely, instead of treating the body as a whole. This cinematographic strategy, Dodds argues, tends to make the female body into a series of parts, an objectified collection of sexual and physical stereotypes. In the end, the differentiation (and, again, objectification) of the female dancing body's parts results in a breakdown of the identity the dancing body performs. The feet are the grounding mechanism, the hips and torso the sexual center, the face and head the "project manager," etc. The concern here is that if the body is considered as an object instead of as a subject, it is prone to exploitation and subjugation. A similar situation exists in *Matrix: Reloaded* during the cavernous rave scene. What we see of the masses are mixed-race faces in exaltation, feet festooned with jewelry twisting in the dirt, diaphanously clad pelvises gyrating against other similarly coded (pro)portions. They are a steamy mass of sweaty sex, instead of a collective of individuated bodies, each with dreams, hopes, and needs. However, what we see of Neo and Trinity during their sex scene are either full-body shots (two sublime white corpses entwined) or their loving faces staring at each other in captive embrace. This is the *passion for control*, the sustaining myths we perpetuate in order to glorify embodiment, particularly in reaction to digital disembodiment. So, while certain technologies were created to capture the matrixial[12] bodies in combat (the moving virtual camera, wires, CGI), the directors turned toward more traditional methods in order to record bodies in more "traditional" pursuits: dancing and fucking. This differentiation speaks worlds. It seems that the technology that is dance, and similarly (but not always) that is sex, still has the power to transport us (in the real, and as viewers of film) into "virtual" worlds. But when it comes to combat, the actual laws of physics, time, and space are still so firmly in place that the camera and its technological apparatuses must do the inventing/meaning-making for us (the viewer).

All of this describes a kind of schizophrenic, excessive, and erotic visual and perceptive mode of address. What seems an aid for us in the navigation of our new technological phantasmagoria, the digital imaginary—may simply be another trick of the eye, a subtle ideological means of winning the argument between human and machine. Regardless, however technology seeks to cloak, erase, or take advantage of factors of identity (often through stereotypes) by more and more seductive means of mode and technique, it becomes that much more significant to apply careful analysis to the ways and means of reproduction and what kinds of meaning they foster. In short, the camera and its apparatus are never neutral. The obviousness of this statement seems pedantic. However, when we pay careful attention to how special effects trick us into thinking that bodies can do anything, we should always remind ourselves that real bodies hurt, fail, and feel pain—and in doing so—reveal our obsessions and anxieties that remain so tightly focused on alleviating, even erasing the evidence.

Postscript

In the summer of 2010, I went with the same Matrix-question friend to see *Inception* (2010). We both marveled at the scenes where the physics engine seemed to run out of batteries, characters floating in a subconscious haze while Joseph Gordon-Levitt wrangled them into a "way out" of the virtual dream-world, what they referred to as the "kick." We agreed that none of what we saw would be possible without *M3*. But, we also agreed that we each had the sneaking suspicion that the technology would have been developed regardless, that our sense of embodiment was always-already compromised by the much more mundane technologies of the everyday. Additionally, the haphazard nature of the bodies moving in these scenes from *Inception* signaled a much different problem: in the subconscious space created within the film's narrative, the bodies can't do "anything," and, even more so, they seem to be subject to "everything," including the slipperiness of dream worlds, marauding psychic projections and others' roles in the dream narratives. This is a definitively different conceptualization of the Big Digital Question that *M3* posed a decade before. Now, perhaps, we are acknowledging that the fever pitch of our digital dreams hasn't quite panned out, that these incursions into cyberspace have costs and don't always work out. *M3* showed us that everything is available for download, our virtual selves are better than the everyday meat, and most importantly, that our technological selves are our better halves. It seems, however, that our technological selves have become such good salespeople that we are fated to buy into faulty goods (identities, ideas, positions, prosthetics), hardware packaged with software coded with it's own obsolescence (and I'm not just talking about iPhones here). In other words, while we may be able to change software—even operating systems—the hardware is always destined to wear out. However, this less than ideal reality is ameliorated by the software (and sometimes hardware) upgrades that are always available, a notion itself predicated on a kind of positivist upward mobility, even semi-immortal transcendence. The trick then is to acknowledge that while the hardware must fail eventually, every bit of code, every software package and upgrade is built by bodies in the world, by way of the movement modes that substantiate physical knowledge and knowing. To acknowledge this won't decouple the digital dialectic between real world bodies and their virtual selves. But it is a potent reminder that when we (as individuals and groups) favor one side of the binary, a core epistemological and ontological bias presents itself. This is key, as all forms of political, social, and cultural discourse always stem from the body's lived realities, as well from the fantasies our bodies manufacture for its escape.

NOTES

1. Paul Virilio, *Art as Far as the Eye Can See* (Berg: Oxford, 2007), 118–119.
2. See *Cyber-Marx*, by Mark Dyer-Witheford, for a compelling discussion of socialist and communist visions of technology and alternate futures for telecommunications and connectivity.
3. I take the term "dead meat" from the quintessential cyberpunk novel, William Gibson's *Neuromancer* (Ace Books, 1984).
4. From *Synthetic Worlds: The Business and Culture of Online Games*, by Edward Castranova (Chicago: University of Chicago Press, 2005), 238.
5. See the Fritz Lang film, *Metropolis*, and R. L. Rutsky's excellent analysis in his book *High Techné*.
6. Since there is a great deal written on this aspect of the Matrix franchise, this is a cursory treatment of this topic. For more in-depth analysis, see *The "Matrix" and Philosophy: Welcome to the Desert of the Real*, by William Irwin (Open Court, 2002), and *More Matrix and Philosophy* by William Irwin (Chicago: Open Court, 2005). Also, see Chapter 4 of my book, *Die Tryin': Videogames, Masculinity, Culture* (New York: Peter Lang, 2008).
7. So, a general note here on fight choreography for those more accustomed to dance or performance: many of the choreographic, technical, and training emphases in martial arts can be the analog, cousin, or shadow to much of dance technique and performance. Formulate your analysis by: viewing the framed movements, techniques, and expressions of particular bodies in individual scenes, as well by performing a cursory background check on the particular martial art discipline in use, and then complete a careful analysis of filmic technique and digital effects. Attending to all of these factors will then present further physical, cultural, and ideological questions and problems.

8. At the time of this writing (2013), these were some of the primary social and cultural digital forms. I am interested in, if this book is still indeed "read" in, say, five years, how silly or outdated (or disappeared) these technologies will seem, a signal of the pace of digital cultural obsolescence.

9. Compare this to the general standard of projection rate in a film theatre of 24 FPS. Filming at incredibly high FPS produces material that is so complete in its capture of objects and space, it is akin to seeing more than is possible with the naked eye and in such great detail that the effect can be unsettling. This happened when *The Hobbit* (2012) was shot at 48 FPS and in some cases projected at 48 FPS. Yet, once the film stock is edited and printed, it still must be projected at a rate comfortable for the human eye.

10. This line from the film was used by the techno-theorist par example, Jean Baudrillard, in his essay on the ends of simulation, "Welcome to the Desert of the Real," as well as the title for the text, *The "Matrix" and Philosophy: Welcome to the Desert of the Real* by William Irwin (Chicago: Open Court, 2002).

11. It is interesting to note that the entire rave scene was filmed on a real set, although the upper half of the caverns used CGI. It is one of the rare large-scale sets to have been built for the films—perhaps to give the real bodies something *real* to react to and with.

12. See Bracha L. Ettinger ("Matrixial Trans-Subjectivity Theory")—*The Matrixial Borderspace*, (Essays from 1994–1999), (Minneapolis: University of Minnesota Press, 2006), or "Matrixial Gaze and Screen: Other Than Phallic and Beyond the Late Lacan," in *Bodies of Resistance*, edited by Laura Doyle, 103–143 (Evanston, IL: Northwestern University Press, 2001).

BIBLIOGRAPHY

Castranova, Edward. *Synthetic Worlds: The Business and Culture of Online Games.* Chicago: University of Chicago Press, 2005.

Challiyil, Pradheep. *Journey to the Source: Decoding Matrix Trilogy.* Chennai: Sakthi Books, 2004.

Couch, Steve. *Matrix Revelations: A Thinking Fan's Guide to the Matrix Trilogy.* Southampton: Damaris, 2003.

Dodds, Sheryl. *Dance on Screen: Genres and Media from Hollywood to Experimental Art.* Basingstoke: Palgrave MacMillan, 2005.

Dyer-Witheford, Mark. *Cyber-Marx: Cycles and Circuits of Struggle in High Technology Capitalism.* Chicago: University of Illinois Press, 1999

Ettinger, Bracha L. "Matrixial Gaze and Screen: Other Than Phallic and Beyond the Late Lacan." In *Bodies of Resistance*, edited by Laura Doyle, 103–143. Evanston, IL: Northwestern University Press, 2001.

——. "Matrixial Trans-Subjectivity Theory," in *The Matrixial Borderspace* (Essays from 1994–1999). Minneapolis: University of Minnesota Press, 2006.

Faller, Stephen. *Beyond the Matrix: Revolutions and Revelations.* Altanta: Chalice Press, 2004.

Garret, Seay. *The Gospel Reloaded.* Colorado Springs, CO: Pinon Press, 2003.

Gillis, Stacy. *The "Matrix" Trilogy: Cyberpunk Reloaded.* London: Wallflower Press, 2005.

Gray, Christopher. *Philosophers Explore The Matrix.* Oxford: Oxford University Press, 2005.

Haber, Karen. *Exploring the Matrix: Visions of the Cyber Present.* New York: St. Martin's Press, 2003.

Horsley, Jake. *Matrix Warrior: Being the One.* New York: St. Martin's Griffin 2003.

Irwin, William. *The "Matrix" and Philosophy: Welcome to the Desert of the Real.* Chicago: Open Court, 2002.

——. *More Matrix and Philosophy.* Chicago: Open Court, 2005.

Kapell, Matthew, and William G. Doty. *Jacking In to the Matrix Franchise: Cultural Reception and Interpretation.* London: Continuum International, 2004.

King, Geoff, and Tanya Krzywinska. *Science Fiction Cinema: From Outerspace to Cyberspace.* London, Wallflower, 2001.

Lawrence, Matt. *Like a Splinter in Your Mind: The Philosophy Behind the "Matrix" Trilogy.* Oxford: Blackwell, 2004.

Marriot, Michel. *The Matrix Cultural Revolution.* New York: Thunder's Mouth Press, 2003.

Rutsky, R. L. *High-Techné.* Minneapolis: University of Minnesota Press, 1999.

Virilio, Paul. *Art as Far as the Eye Can See.* Oxford: Berg, 2007.

Yefeth, Glenn. *Taking the Red Pill: Science, Philosophy and Religion in "The Matrix."* Chichester: Summersdale, 2003.

PART III

MUSIC VIDEO AND TELEVISUAL BODIES

CHAPTER 15

GIRL POWER, REAL POLITICS: DIS/RESPECTABILITY, POST-RACIALITY, AND THE POLITICS OF INCLUSION

TAKIYAH NUR AMIN

At its core, politics isn't just about government, political parties or the actions of elected officials. Fundamentally, politics is about relationships among people and how they intersect with and are informed by dominant ideologies and systems of authority in the real world. This broader understanding requires an engagement with the power of ideas and how they "govern" our actions as they circulate in the public sphere and serve as a context for performance. In this chapter, I argue that performance acts as a site where the power to extend, reaffirm and complicate political ideas is enacted through embodied expression. I explicate the ways in which Beyoncé's danced performance and video for the pop hit "Run The World (Girls)" circulates in a context that is informed by ideas about black women's femininity and sexuality and how it "talks back" to those ideals. First, I introduce the enduring legacy of negative stereotypes about black women's femininity and sexuality, using the pernicious depictions of and commentary about First Lady Michelle Obama as evidence of the palpable presence of these ideas in contemporary life. Second, I explain how black women's historical marginalization and dehumanization, undergirded by the aforementioned stereotypes, gave rise to a "politics of respectability" that constrained and policed black women's bodies and voices. These two perspectives converge to argue that Beyoncé's video and danced performance for her pop hit "Run The World (Girls)" suggests on its face that women can exercise leadership, power, and dominance by deploying heteronormative femininity, and that such ideas are fraught for black women in particular given the aforementioned history. While the international pop star seems to celebrate the image of women in power and presents a tacit challenge to gendered power dynamics in her lyrics, the message of the accompanying video—and the dancing in it in particular—does little to address or unsettle long-standing pejorative ideas about the supposed hypersexual nature of black women, an idea that has and continues to be invoked as evidence of their unsuitability to function as both citizens and leaders.[1] Moreover, I assert that the mutual admiration between Beyoncé and the First Lady has been criticized in the popular media precisely because it complicates long-standing ideals articulated by black women's respectability politics and its preoccupation with the sexuality and public deportment of black women. The video, with its apparent pronouncement and celebration of women's empowerment, circulates in a public sphere that is contextualized by long-standing historical discourses that render its message ironic and inert, especially when considered in relationship to the real business of "runnin' the world." I argue that while this girl power anthem and accompanying video suggests a politics of inclusion and affirms post-racial ideals, this sense of collectivity is undermined through its re-presentation of traditional, "normal" female bodies and is further complicated by the persistent specter of gendered racial inequality in the real world. The pronouncements and demonstrations of inclusion put forth in "Run The World (Girls)" are both confounded and, ultimately, diminished, given the political context in which this performance circulates.

Emerging in the nineteenth century, negative portrayals of black people were depicted in "art and popular imagery [that] served to both reflect and establish racist ideas and to reiterate the social order; images of blacks most often iterated limiting and derogatory perceptions held by whites and helped create a "visual iconography for black representation."[2] As stereotypical and damning images of blacks in general—as lazy and childlike, for example[3]—circulated within popular American consciousness, particular ideas about black womanhood as failed and black female sexuality as abject, deviant, and deranged emerged as well. Stereotypical images of black womanhood during the slavery and post-slavery era circulated to suggest that black women were in fact, fundamentally immoral and sexually loose. These depictions were often juxtaposed with the idea that black women were essentially unable to enact femininity because their physical strength (a byproduct of forced labor) didn't fall in line with notions of the Victorian feminine ideal; *real* women were not only white but also small, soft, and unsuitable for manual labor or work because of their "enviable" frailty. While it is true that post-enslavement, many black people embraced a newfound sexual freedom (i.e., the freedom to choose one's own sexual partners) it is overreaching to assume that emancipation exacerbated some kind of inherently deviant sexuality that resided within the very personhood of black women. While it is accurate that, "some manumitted black women exercised their newfound sexual mobility by engaging freely in sexual relationships with black men," it was problematic that "whites saw the sexual activity and newfound independence of the manumitted female slave as further evidence to support their claim that black women were sexually loose and innately morally depraved."[4]

Consider that since First Lady Michelle Obama emerged in the public sphere, pejorative comments about her body have been commonplace. When Wisconsin Republican Congressman Jim Sesenbrenner made inappropriate comments about the size of Mrs. Obama's backside in 2011, it was just the most recent at that time in public commentary about her physicality.[5] The obsession on the part of the public with the First Lady's

FIGURE 15.1 Screen capture of Michelle Obama, showcasing her bare arms.

choice to wear sleeveless dresses and tops (Fig. 15.1) and her open dislike for wearing pantyhose (Fig. 15.2)[6] immediately garnered criticism about her inappropriate style choices, suggesting that she was unsuitable for the role of First Lady.[7] I assert that comments about the size of her backside were in fact rooted in the same kind of rhetoric that produced the stereotype of black women as hypersexual—as if the size of her derriere was evidence of a lascivious nature—reinscribing the notion that black women's bodies are "ground zero for promiscuity."[8] Mrs. Obama's public persona as an intelligent woman, wife, and mother is juxtaposed with the public's obsession with dissecting her body and fixating on her bare limbs. Her physical being is read as both unfeminine and inappropriate, harkening back to the desexualization of black women in the nineteenth century. Consider the 2008 cover of *The New Yorker* magazine, which depicted Mrs. Obama as a gun-toting, afro-wearing, frowning militant and the 2012 cover of Spain's *Fuere de Serie* magazine, which featured the First Lady's face airbrushed onto the body of Marie Guillemine Benoist's bare-breasted slave woman from the 1800 painting, *Portrait d'une Negresse*.[9] Taken together, the comments and images referenced here suggest both enduring and pernicious stereotypes about black women, rooted in nineteenth-century ideas, that continue to circulate in popular consciousness.

In a May 2012 interview with *People* magazine, the First Lady set off a firestorm when she shared with reporters that if she could switch places with anyone, it would be international pop and film star, Beyoncé.[10] In response, journalists penned op-eds sharing

FIGURE 15.2 Screen capture of Michelle Obama and her un-clad legs.

their dismay and concern about what they saw as Mrs. Obama desiring to be a woman who trades on a gendered, super-sexy identity as the key to her success. By way of example, contributing editor for *TheRoot.com* and author Demetria L. Lucas wrote:

> For a woman of Michelle Obama's caliber to uplift [Beyoncé] as a role model, and to speak of swapping lives with her, sends a damaging, demeaning and dangerous message to women and girls. It says that despite education and intellect, grace and power, what really matters is our looks, our willingness to submit and our ability to swivel our hips to sexually satisfy the opposite sex. We hear that message loud and clear every time a reality show airs. We don't need to hear it from our first lady, too.

This response to the First Lady's candid admission suggests that into this twenty-first century moment, preoccupations about the appropriateness of black women expressing (or perhaps *desiring* to express) a frank sexuality persist, especially if the woman is to be considered respectable and proper. *After all, how could it possibly be appropriate for a First Lady—a black one at that—to express herself (or desire to express herself) in that way?* According to Lucas, the "love affair" between Mrs. Obama and Beyoncé is both highly problematic and dangerous. While Mrs. Obama's articulated desire might have been merely the expression of a fantasy or desire to perform or be a "superstar," it was read as a real failing on the part of the First Lady. Why would she want to be a woman who is for all of her glamour and stardom, "lacking" a formal education? Why would Mrs. Obama want to be a woman who uses her super sexy image to make a living in pop music and video? Why would she want to be a woman who seems to intentionally play on the notions of female manipulation through overt sexuality in order to assert power? While the admiration between these two global icons seems to be mutual, the public outcry has not been against the idea that Beyoncé would admire Mrs. Obama and want her daughter to be like *her*.[11] Of course the pop diva *should* desire to be educated, circumspect, and sober, in keeping with the accepted behavior modes for African American women under the banner of respectability politics. Moreover, Lucas's response demonstrates how contemporary preoccupations around black women's respectability continue to persist in contemporary life and as such, complicate readings of Beyoncé's artistry, particularly in the realm of music video performance.

In April of 2011, Beyoncé released to American audiences the song and accompanying video for "Run The World (Girls)" as the lead single for her then upcoming fourth studio album, *4*. While the song has garnered intense popularity, it is the accompanying music video for the single that receives this chapter's attention. With over 148 million hits on YouTube,[12] the video features Beyoncé, clad at various points in armor, lingerie, and a multiplicity of figure-revealing couture gowns,[13] in the Mojave Desert with an attendant "army" of (presumably) all women (Fig. 15.3). Beyoncé and her company of *girls* perform a hyper-stylized routine to the synth-pop tune, including dances derived from contemporary African movement vocabularies,[14] juxtaposed with intense hip-rolling, crawling, and isolated shoulder-thrusting, torso, and hip movements. The "girls," with Beyoncé as their leader, approach an opposing, truculent male army and confront them

FIGURE 15.3 Screen capture of Beyoncé and her all-girl army from the video, "Run The World (Girls)."

FIGURE 15.4 Screen Capture of Beyonce approaching the male army.

(Fig. 15.4)—both vocally and through dance—with the message that it is they who are in charge. In the song Beyoncé highlights this triumph of female authority by stating:

> Some of them men think they freak this like we do
> But no they don't
> Make your cheques come at they neck,
> Disrespect us? No they won't!

Beyoncé proceeds to give a "shout-out" to women who are financially self-sufficient:

> This goes out to all my girls
> That's in the club rocking the latest
> Who will buy it for themselves
> and get more money later

Beyoncé meditatively croons that her "persuasion"—in this case, women—can "build a nation," before reminding listeners that through the "endless power" of herself and the "girl" army, others (presumably men) can be positioned to "do anything" for her and by extension, women. This pronouncement precedes the infectious call-and-response chorus of the song:

> Who run the world? Girls! (x4)
> Who run this motha? Girls! (x4)
> Who run the world? Girls! (x4)

The song proceeds with Beyoncé giving recognition to women who are college graduates and celebrating those women who are adept at both making money and being mothers, before repeating the chorus of the tune.

Interestingly, while Beyoncé extols the virtues of female empowerment and global authority, the accompanying physical performance suggests that the "power" and "persuasion" to which Beyoncé is verbally referring is derived in part from her sexual identity

FIGURE 15.5 Screen capture of military style movement in the video.

and that of the other dancing "girls." While not all of the movement choices function in this manner (there is much saluting and other references to classic military formations for example) (Fig. 15.5), many of the dance moves executed in this clip have a hyper-stylized, sexually frank quality that is expressed by Beyoncé and her "girls." By way of example, consider that while intoning the repetitive chorus, Beyoncé is seen revealing her undergarments and adjusting her breasts (Fig. 15.6) in time with the music. The first time we see the "army" of women dance in the video, the majority of them are clad in tube tops, briefs, garters, thigh-highs, and capes as they execute deep hip isolations and booty-shake movements for the camera (Fig. 15.7). Later, Beyoncé rolls and contorts her body on the sand-covered ground while intoning the lyrics that precede the chorus, before she is joined again by the army, who performs seductive full-body rolls and hair flips for the viewer, juxtaposed with the driving bass line of the chorus. When the movements are "read" together with the attire and parallel to the lyrics, it is clear that an emphasis on heteronormativity and the frank expression of sexual identity undergirds Beyoncé's pronouncement of female empowerment and that the embodied performance in the video "talks back" to enduring notions of black women's respectability politics.

As bell hooks points out, the majority of black men and women post-enslavement and into the era of reconstruction strived to adopt the values, behaviors, and attitudes of whites in order to be deemed socially acceptable; black women in particular strived to dispel the myth that they were sexually loose by emulating the (public) conduct and mannerisms of white women.[15] As a response to these pervasive negative characterizations, black women in the late nineteenth and into the early part of the twentieth century adopted what sociologist Patricia Hill Collins refers to as a "politics of respectability." As black women strived to refute the notion of their sexuality as morally depraved, black middle-class women in particular rejected the "controlling image[16] of the Jezebel"—the wild, devious sexually brazen woman—by adopting a way of life that was "characterized by cleanliness of person and property, temperance, thrift, polite manners and sexual purity."[17] Black women across class lines were striving to reject a racist and false image

FIGURE 15.6 Screen capture of Beyonce adjusting her breasts.

FIGURE 15.7 Screen capture of the all girl army in their burlesque-style costumes.

of sexual depravity that had been projected onto their bodies for hundreds of years by enacting this informal politic.

As a consequence of America's complex history, Beyoncé's video emerges—for better of for worse—in a context that has been shaped by negative stereotypes and derogatory controlling images about black female sexuality that continue to persist into the present.[18] The danced performance in the video for "Run The World (Girls)" in particular, taken along with enduring ideas about black women's sexuality and respectability politics, create a unique tension that raises the question: how does this performance complicate persistent notions of "proper" or "correct" black female identity, when Beyoncé, invokes a stance of female global authority while referencing an apparent and frank sexuality? While one might consider why Beyoncé (who herself was approaching her 30th birthday when the video was released) might refer to herself and her army of attendants as "girls" instead of "women" or question the validity of invoking sexuality vis-à-vis dance vocabulary as the core of female power in the video performance, it is key here to acknowledge that images, including popular music videos, do not exist or emerge in a world or context wholly unto themselves. This popular performance emerges within a larger discourse of racialized and gendered representations, oft-circulating ideas concerning black women's respectability politics and notions of black female sexuality. As such, it is both useful and important to consider how this performance responds to competing contemporary ideas about black female identity, respectability and power.

It may very well be that Beyoncé herself and her creative team didn't consider or were not concerned with whether or not the visual representation of the artist and dancing army of "girls" would circulate in a context that has been shaped by notions of black female sexual depravity, in direct conflict with a politics of respectability. Intent aside, the video, with its invocation of global female authority, rubs against historical ideas about what a black woman in particular might need to *do* or *be* or *avoid* in order to be seen as someone who could in fact, *run the world*. Pursuant to respectability politics, historically, it was most often those black women who chose to portray themselves as proper and upright "ladies" that received the most disdain, abuse, and derision at the hands of whites[19]— not those women whose public deportment was considered socially unacceptable (but in-keeping with the supposed "natural state" of black women as morally depraved). The popular criticisms of Mrs. Obama exemplify this contradiction. Consequently, the danced performance in Beyoncé's video complicates ideas of what correct or appropriate black female identity should be by invoking a personal strength and external authority while at the same time acknowledging a sexual identity that can and should be deployed at the behest of a woman who *runs the world*. What is being proposed here is that the fully self-possessed woman, imbued with the potential for leadership, is one who derives her authority to make others "do anything" at her command—at least in part—through the overt expression of herself as a sexual being. As such, the video enters into conversation with long-standing discussions about black female sexual identity and respectability politics. Specifically, the danced performance in this video resonates with long-held ideas on the part of some black women about the need to proclaim and celebrate one's own sexual identity as a place of power and as a place from which authority emerges. The video does in fact talk back to cloistered notions suggesting that for black women in particular to claim authority, the denial of oneself as a sexual, sensual being (in favor of a more "respectable" image) is perhaps not the road to take. While as a pop icon, Beyoncé can invoke her alter ego—Sasha Fierce"—to distance herself from her real identity and thus from the super-sexy image she employs in her work, most women leading in the world do not have the option to invoke a doppelganger upon whom negative stereotypes may be shifted. Beyoncé's real-world image, as

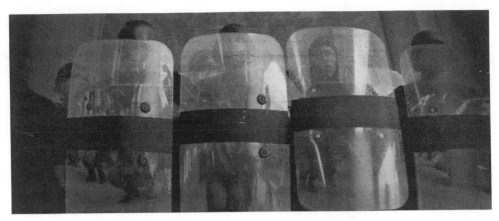

FIGURE 15.8 Screen capture of the "opposition," fully clad in riot gear.

ingénue, wife, and dedicated mother is separate from the "Sasha Fierce" persona, a remix of the hypersexual "Jezebel" stereotype of black female sexuality, who uses her cunning and sexual manipulation to extract money from and exert power over men. While one might argue the extent to which this particular pronouncement of self-possessed black female identity and authority has an impact on how black women in positions of considerable power construct their public personas, the video presents a perspective that is both ironic and provocative, given the historical context which frames its emergence.

Notably, in the video when Beyoncé advances her all-female army, the men do not retreat. In the heat of the Mojave Desert where this post-apocalyptic scene takes place, the men seem to represent state or official power—at one point, they are attired in riot gear and helmets and are wielding large shields (Fig. 15.8). Interestingly, the women are not in army gear or police uniform but instead are dressed in lingerie and burlesque-style costume, as noted in Fig. 15.9. The women reference their power through the dance—using their bodies to suggest that they run the world by wielding traditional femininity and sexuality and by suggesting that in so doing, they can take charge of an apparently hostile situation. Interestingly, not only does the all-male opposition in the video stand their ground, they tend to gaze at the women with expressions that range from anger to amusement to confusion. The irony is that the very power that the video seems to be invoking on the behalf of women is framed as being viable against a very tangible kind of threat—the power of the state. Beyoncé's invoking of heteronormative behavior and socially acceptable femininity is not only fraught because such definitions and ascriptions have often been denied black women in real life, but because the confrontation of the two groups in the video remains unresolved through the deployment of the "weaponry" that she invokes.

Some might argue that the message of the song and accompanying video is one of female empowerment, intended to encourage women to feel strong and/or capable in a presumably male-dominated world. Still, the video's superficial politics of inclusion, as embodied in the all-female army, is necessarily complicated by both the re-presentation of normative bodies and the homage to racial egalitarianism. First, the centerpiece of

FIGURE 15.9 Screen capture of Beyonce and her "Girls" showcasing their impressive movement skills and lithe bodies.

the video is Beyoncé and her army of equally able-bodied *girls*, all of whom are able to execute the complex and demanding choreography while wearing tightly fitted costumes, whipping their archetypical long female hair and displaying their lithe, sinewy bodies (Fig. 15.9). We see no members of Beyoncé's army who are differently abled or who have short hair or who seem to be of advanced age or who have bodies that are heavy or especially plump. What of the solidarity invoked in this girl power anthem and subsequent video? Is the message that only particular kinds of *girls* can run the world and that all others are somehow unqualified? Are only gender-conforming *girls* who are willing to derive their power from an overtly (heteronormative) sexual identity able to access the "right" kind of power that results in some kind of leadership? The song's invocation of motherhood, formal education, and intimate relationships with men as the basis for power suggests a very narrow framing for women's authority that arguably creates a space where more women are excluded from it than included within its confines.

Similarly troubling is Beyoncé's current claiming of a multi-racial/multi-ethnic identity (given her association with black music and culture for the entirety of her career) and her presentation of the *girls* from (seemingly) a variety of different racial backgrounds. Plainly, simply presenting multi-racial bodies or invoking a multi-racial/multi-ethnic identity does not change the historical context that frames this popular performance; the video itself does not constitute a wholesale erasure by which years of history are washed away and replaced by autonomous bodies or benign images, uninformed by stereotypes of the past. Beyoncé's politics of inclusion as demonstrated by the presence of her multi-racial army is contextualized by the political notion of post-raciality, an idea that suggests that racial preference, disparities based on race, and the ongoing salience of race in public life is no more. If we are, in fact, post-racial, then identity politics are inert—necessarily mute and a vestige of a past. Unfortunately, the video circulates embedded in a history where race has and continues to matter in every area that mitigates the life chances of women (i.e., health, education, economic empowerment, career attainment, etc.). The ongoing salience of race in the twenty-first century as it intersects with the lives of women suggests that access to the necessary resources and power to *run the world*—both tangible and abstruse—are not equally accessible across race. As such, the video enters into conversation, through this singular performance, with long-standing discussions about black female sexual identity and respectability politics in particular and larger questions about the many ways in which race functions as a real barrier to accessing power and authority, despite a shared gendered identity.

Music video performances inhabit a location in the popular consciousness that is framed by words, concepts, and meanings that have been re-presented time and again. By extension, historical ideas—about race, gender, and sexuality, in this case—remain as an appropriate lens through which to engage and raise questions about danced performance and our engagement with visual culture. Here the tension between what one might read as a small-screen fantasy and the historical ideas that frame and inform real life collide and collude to create a site where one can meaningfully engage contemporary visual culture through the consideration and "reading" of popular performance. We see then that even contemporarily, old ways of thinking, being, and doing persist. The visual realm gives rise to media that circulates within multiple contexts that complicate any dance performance, even in a four-minute music video.

Notes

1. See bibliographic entry for Harris-Perry.
2. Harris, *Colored Pictures: Race and Visual Representation*, p. 40.
3. Harris, p. 45.
4. hooks, *Ain't I a Woman: Black Women and Feminism*, pp. 54–55.
5. Fuller, "*Republican Congressman Jim Sesenbrenner Insults Michelle Obama's 'Big Butt!*,'" p. 1
6. Sweet, "*On 'The View,' Michelle Obama Makes a Pantyhose Confession*," p. 1.
7. Harris-Perry, *Sister Citizen: Shame, Stereotypes and Black Women in America*, pp. 279–280.
8. Collins, *Black Sexual Politics*, p. 151
9. Peck, "Michelle Obama Pictured as Nude Slave in Spanish Magazine *Fuera de Serie*: Is it Offensive?," p.1
10. See bibliographic entry for *People*.
11. McDevitt, "Beyoncé Writes a Note to Michelle Obama," p.1
12. Information accurate as of August 31, 2012.
13. For details on attire worn in the video, see bibliographic entry for *The Independent*.
14. The creative team for this video included Tofo Tofo, a male duo from Mozambique who was hired to teach Beyoncé their style of African contemporary dance. For more information, see bibliographic entry for Vena, Jocelyn.
15. hooks, p. 55.
16. Collins defines controlling images as "the gender-specific depiction of people of African descent within Western scholarship and popular culture," p. 350.
17. Collins, *Black Sexual Politics: African Americans, Gender and the New Racism*, p. 71.
18. For an extended discussion on this issue see bibliographic entry for Harris-Perry.
19. hooks, p. 55.

BIBLIOGRAPHY

Brannigan, Erin. *Dancefilm: Choreography and the Moving Image*. New York: Oxford University Press, 2011.

Collins, Patricia Hill. *Black Sexual Politics: African Americans, Gender and the New Racism*. New York: Routledge, 2005.

Fuller, Bonnie. "Republican Congressman Jim Sesenbrenner Insults Michelle Obama's 'Big Butt!'" *Huffington Post Politics*, December 23, 2011.

Harris, Michael D. *Colored Pictures: Race and Visual Representation*. North Carolina: The University of North Carolina Press, 2003. http://www.huffingtonpost.com/bonnie-fuller/republican-congressman-ji_b_1167394.html

Harris-Perry, Melissa V. *Sister Citizen: Shame, Stereotypes and Black Women in America*. New Haven, CT: Yale University Press, 2011.

hooks, bell. *Ain't I a Woman: Black Women and Feminism*. Massachusetts: Southend Press, 1981.

Lucas, Demetria L. "Mrs. O and Beyoncé: A Problematic Love Fest?" *The Root*, May 30, 2012. Accessed June 1, 2012. http://www.theroot.com/articles/culture/2012/05/michelle_obama_and_beyonce_a_problematic_love_fest.html

McDevitt, Caitlin. "Beyoncé Writes a Note to Michelle Obama." *Politico*, April 12, 2012. Accessed June 1, 2012. http://www.politico.com/blogs/click/2012/04/beyonce-praises-first-lady-in-handwritten-note-120332.html

McPherson, Katrina. *Making Video Dance: A Step-By-Step Guide to Creating Dance for the Screen*. New York: Routledge, 2006.

"Michelle Obama Takes Sasha & Malia to Beyoncé Concert." *People*, May 27, 2011. Accessed June 6, 2012. http://www.people.com/people/article/0,,20599156,00.html.

Mirzoeff, Nicholas. *The Visual Culture Reader*. New York: Routledge, 1998.

Peck, Patrice. "Michelle Obama Pictured As Nude Slave in Spanish Magazine Fuera de Serie: Is It Offensive?" *Huffington Post Politics*, August 28, 2012. Accessed August 30, 2012. http://www.huffingtonpost.com/bonnie-fuller/republican-congressman-ji_b_1167394.html

Sweet, Lynn. "On 'The View,' Michelle Obama Makes Pantyhose Confession." *The Chicago Sun Times*, June 18, 2008.

Vena, Jocelyn. "Beyoncé 'Nailed It' in 'Girls' Video, Choreographer Says." MTV News (MTV Networks), May 19, 2011. Accessed December 21, 2011. http://www.mtv.com/news/articles/1664223/beyonce-run-the-world-girls.jhtml

"Which Haute Couture Looks Did Beyoncé Wear in Her 'Run the World' Video?" *The Independent* (London: Independent Print Limited), May 19, 2011. Accessed December 15, 2011. http://www.independent.co.uk/life-style/fashion/which-haute-couture-looks-did-beyonc-wear-in-her-run-the-world-video-2286395.html

DENATURALIZING COCO'S "SEXY" HIPS: CONTRADICTIONS AND REVERSALS OF THE DANCING BODY OF A CHINESE AMERICAN SUPERSTAR IN MANDARIN POP

CHIH-CHIEH LIU

INTRODUCTION

ZAX WANG: We used to say that it is very difficult for a *Chinese ("hua-ren") body* to deliver such a powerful body "feel" like Jennifer Lopez, but when we see your dance, whoa, who says that a *Chinese ("hua-ren") body* can't achieve such a result? It actually can.

COCO LEE: I think that there are many talented dance stars these days...

A-WEI CHANG: But some of them spend lots of time practicing! Your dance looks so *natural* as if you move like this every day. (A-Wei begins to shake his hips in a reserved manner).

ZAX WANG: Yes, that's right. Unlike other stars who follow the choreography to precision, Coco performs a *"free style"* and delivers a sense of *"freeness,"* as if she can dance like this anytime...[1] (Zax too begins to twist his shoulder and hips).

(*Showbiz* [完全娛樂] 2005, my emphases)

Broadcast nationally on a Taiwanese television channel in 2005, the above interview, pivoting on dance in the music videos, comes from an evening entertainment program, *Showbiz*, which features a sexy Chinese American superstar in Mandarin pop, Coco Lee (hereafter Coco). Mandarin pop, as one of the most lucrative music genres in East Asia, is transcultural in construction, with its musical features, performance styles, and modes of production strongly influenced by various Asian, American, and European countries, as well as Chinese diasporic cultures (Moskowitz 2010, 1–15); all of these features are traceable in Coco's image and dance style. Reflecting a shared perception toward Coco's dancing body in contemporary Taiwan, the two male hosts—Zax and A-Wei—show an intense fascination toward her dance, paying special attention to her rocking hips. This dance style is, in Taiwan, widely understood to "naturally" embody the idea of "sexiness," and is often compared to various American stars, such as Jennifer Lopez, leading to a curious cultural myth—that Coco is argued to have achieved "what a Chinese body can hardly achieve." The above interview was followed by Coco's joking imitation of walking across a street demonstrating her rocking hips. This fun-making incident immediately captivated the two hosts. Both of them tried to imitate her, to openly demonstrate their inability to achieve the same standard. Coco was later twice requested to perform again, receiving a large amount of admiration each time. Coco's rocking bottom, in this sense, is perceived as an awe-inspiring corporeal spectacle which "naturally" epitomizes her Chinese American identity and the idea of "sexiness."

Presented as almost a "natural" fact, cultural discourses pivoting on Coco's twisting bottom are, however, arguably anything but "natural." In this chapter, what I aim to demonstrate is that what appears to be a "natural" articulation of the dancing body is neither "natural" nor straightforward. Rather, situated in a multimedial context, I set out to argue that Coco's dancing body is a symbolic battlefield: it is context- and media-specifically constructed according to Mandarin pop's logic of spectacle. This process is marked by a constant negotiation, resulting in a paradoxical formation that is full of contradictions. Her dancing body is eroticized in the music video while at the same time being desexualized in "real" life; she stresses "American-ness" while at the same time emphasizing "Chinese-ness," and the meaning of "Chinese-ness" continues to shift according to local cultural and political sensibilities. In other words, what I try to achieve in this chapter is to denaturalize the "natural" bodily configuration and to reveal its contradictions and reversals in the process of formation.

This continuous negotiation is foregrounded by the expansion of media and cultural space. The fact that contemporary popular culture is multimedial and transnational contributes to the space in which the process of arbitration can take place. Richard Dyer, in his groundbreaking works—*Stars* (1979) and *Heavenly Bodies* (1986)—states that stars are constructed of "a complex configuration of visual, verbal and aural signs" (1979, 34), consisting of "everything that is publicly available" and therefore is always "extensive, multimedia, intertextual" (1986, 2–3). With the dominance of visuality in the contemporary world (Hall 1991; Jameson 1998; S. Shih 2007), music video has arguably become one of the main media in the construction of star image. According to Roger Beebe and Jason Middleton, music video is now enjoying "a major renaissance" (2007, 2–3), as it is distributed, viewed, and downloaded across different forms of medial and national boundaries. In this sense, contemporary star image is decidedly transnational and multimedial, with music video taking the lead. In the *Showbiz* interview, the discussion of Coco's rocking hips is generated from her dance in the music video. Therefore, to investigate the multiple and shifting meaning of Coco's dancing body, this chapter will first delineate one of the most pronounced meanings of Coco's image—an "Americanized" and eroticized body—through a detailed music video analysis using film studies (Bordwell and Thompson 2004), dance studies (Dodds 2002; 2009) and music video studies (Dickinson 2007; Vernallis 2007). I will then move into other forms of media in different times and locations to analyze the process of negotiation as a means to demonstrate the co-existence of contradictory meanings.

This chapter is divided into five sections. In the first section, a theoretical foundation will be established to denaturalize the dancing body. I then, in the second section, introduce Coco and the genre of Mandarin pop. Starting from a methodological introduction on music video analysis, the third section is followed by a detailed analysis of *Hip Hop Tonight* (2007). Moving outside a single visual medium, the last two sections will individually analyze the tension between "American-ness" and "Chinese-ness" and the shifting meaning embedded in the term "Chinese-ness." In the end, I will point out the contradictions and reversals of Coco's "sexy" hips as a means to denaturalize her performing body.

DE-NATURALIZING THE DANCING BODY: A THEORETICAL PERSPECTIVE

In contemporary cultural and aesthetic theories, the artificiality embedded in various social, cultural, and corporeal "facts" has been eloquently argued and meticulously examined by many scholars working in the cultural- and arts-related fields. From the perspective of gender studies, Judith Butler (1990), arguably one of the most influential contemporary cultural theorists, states that there is no ontological foundation for gender; she avers that gendered bodies are many "styles of the flesh" that are performatively constructed through various cultural "acts." Butler argues that performative practice suggests "a dramatic and contingent construction of meaning" (1990, 177), which naturalizes gender identity through "stylized repetition" (1990, 179). In other words, what seems to be "natural," in Butler's understanding, is a successful result of a repetitive and performative process through which ideologies are naturalized. When Roland Barthes analyzes the construction of myth, he argues that myth has the ability to "transform history into nature" (1972, 129), and it can be argued that, in many ways, Butler's understanding of body and identity functions almost identically.

Similarly, from the perspective of dance studies, corporeality, as Susan Leigh Foster asserts, is not "as natural or absolute given" but is "a tangible and substantial category of cultural experience" (1996, xi). The dancing body is thus "a site of discourse and of social control" (Thomas 1995, 20) in that "ideologies are systematically deposited and constructed on an anatomical plane" (Dempster 1995, 23). Moreover, in the dancing body, cultural discourses are not "merely inscribed upon it" but are "both enacted and produced through the body" (Desmond 1997, 33). Using Ann Cooper Albright's words, the dancing body has the ability to "mobilise cultural identity" (1997, xiii). In this sense, dance contributes to the performative practice of the body, producing ideologies and cultural identities while at the same time naturalizing the process of production. As a result, the dancing body has become "so 'naturalised'" that it remains one of the under-studied academic fields (Desmond 1997, 31). Reverting to Barthes's theory, the dancing body is not merely an embodied form of myth, but the very place in which myth is created, animated, and distributed.

In Coco's case, the fact that her rocking hips remain widely to be perceived as a "natural" dancing body, although carrying complicated gendered and cultural codes, indicates the existence of a major corporeal myth in contemporary Taiwan. It is operated as common sense in everyday life and, for this reason, its academic significance has not been recognized in existing scholarly work. The misconception toward the dancing body in Mandarin pop is aptly reflected in Marc Moskowitz's insightful statement that the genre "has surprisingly complex cultural implications for such a seemingly superficial genre" (2010, 1). In this statement, Moskowitz seems to note Mandarin pop's inclination to create myth, i.e., to naturalize "complex cultural implications" and give it a "superficial" appearance. As one of the superstars in this genre, Coco, it can be argued, naturalizes cultural complications through dance; her body smoothes the embedded contradictions so successfully that gendered and cultural codes can be instantly delivered, resulting in physical responses from Zax and A-Wei in an almost simultaneous manner. Therefore, in order to excavate the embedded cultural assumptions of Coco's rocking hips, it is necessary to contextualize her star image in Mandarin pop and to understand the genre's logic of spectacle.

MANDARIN POP, ITS LOGIC OF SPECTACLE, AND COCO THE DANCE SUPERSTAR

Mandarin pop is one of the most vibrant and lucrative music genres in East Asia. The genre is transcultural in construction and, with Taipei forming one of its key centers, its success has led to foreign investment by major international companies such as EMI (the United Kingdom), Polygram (Netherlands), Sony BMG (Japan and Germany), Universal (Netherlands) and Warner Brothers (the United States) (Moskowitz 2010, 6–7). Michael Keane, a media scholar, argues that "it is now the developed 'Western' media economies that are talking of catching up with East Asia" (2006, 848).

Mandarin pop originates from the 1920s jazz era in Shanghai. As a music genre, its history is strongly marked by the political entanglement between China and Taiwan in that the genre "migrates" with the current Taiwanese authority via Hong Kong during the Civil War in the first half of the twentieth century (Moskowitz 2010, 16–29). With the Western imperialist presence in Shanghai at the time, the jazz movement's music features and performing styles are characterized by strong foreign influences and are linked with the elite class (Moskowitz 2010, 16–18). This historical context indicates that Mandarin pop is characterized by the ideas of foreignness, glamour, and high class. Indeed, in a recent study, Jeremy Taylor compares the advertisements of the two major music genres in Taiwan—Mandarin pop and Hokkien pop—and points out the contrast of their embedded cultural discourses: while Mandarin pop advertises "foreign whisky," featuring "international stars of Hong Kong cinema," Hokkien pop is linked with "local stars" and advertises "Taiwanese beer" (Taylor 2008, 64). When Douglas Kellner, in his reading of Guy Debord's *The Society of the Spectacle* (1967), argues that the society needs to be comprehended as a combination of spectacles, rather than the society of *the* spectacle, he highlights the importance of an interpretive and interrogatory approach (2004, 10–11). In his theory, each spectacle needs to be context-specifically analyzed in order to highlight its contradictions and reversals (2004, 10–11). In the case of Mandarin pop, its history and contemporary modes of representation indicate that the ideas of foreignness, glamour, and high class lie at the core of its logic of spectacle.

Under this logic, Coco seems to be easily considered by the audience to have embodied the idea of spectacle, both culturally and corporeally. Culturally, Coco is a Chinese American with a hybrid background: she was born in Hong Kong to a China-educated mother, grew up in the United States, began her career as a pop star in Hong Kong, yet achieved stardom in Taiwan and crossed over to the United States in 1999. She has released more than 20 albums since 1993, including many award-winning chart-toppers, in Mandarin, Cantonese, and English in various Asian, American, and European countries. Her crossover album, *Just No Other Ways* achieved the 49th place in the Billboard chart (2000) and she became the first Chinese American singer to reach such a position (Ho 2003, 327). Another highlight in her career was her performance at the 2001 Oscar Awards Ceremony in which she sang the theme, *A Love Before Time*, for the Oscar-winning film *Crouching Tiger and Hidden Dragon* (Drake 2001).

Corporeally, Coco's star image is marked with the idea of "sexiness." As the media scholar Josephine Ho puts it, Coco in Taiwan is "perhaps better known among the local crowd as the sexiest body in the sexiest outfits, on top of her Rickie-Martin-style butt movements" (Ho 2003, 327). Coco's "sexiness," in many ways, is presented through the lens of internationalism with an asymmetrical focus on "American-ness." This attention is reflected in her bill-matter (the recognized description of the star), which include "Mariah Carey of Taiwan / Asia," "the Asian Jennifer Lopez" and "International Superstar" (Craine 2000; *Showbiz* 2005; Hsu 2006). However, despite "sexiness" being widely used as one of the features of Coco's star image, the term, as I set out to demonstrate, is context-specifically used, constructed, and understood, reflecting Joke Hermes's observation that "sexiness" in popular culture appears, "not to be related to an older Platonic ideal" of "the beautiful, the good and the truthful," but follows "a Foucauldian disciplinary system that is structured around a central norm" (2006, 89). In order to compare the meaning of "sexiness" in the United States and in Taiwan, I draw upon *Merriam-Webster Dictionary Online* to form my working definition in that "sexy" is defined as "sexually suggestive or stimulating: erotic" (2011, n.p.).

In this chapter, I will focus on Coco's 2006 release, *Hip Hop Tonight*, the first single of her complete album *Just Want You*. Following *Promise* (2001), *Just Want You* is Coco's first major release in Taiwan in five years, an unusually lengthy break in Mandarin pop. The introductory advertising attempts to justify this gap by highlighting that the album is "Coco's most satisfying work," produced in her "busy schedule in different international fields of pop music" (Sony BMG 2006a, n.p.). Despite the subsequent results, in which *Just Want You* was not a commercial success, and *Hip Hop Tonight* did not achieve any musical awards, the timing of its release after a five-year period still attracted intense attention from audiences and therefore gave it a defining status in the development of her star image in Taiwan.

Hip Hop Tonight is a collaboration between Coco and a Taiwan-based Chinese American male star, Vanness. Musically, the song is officially described as "fusing hip-hop and funky styles" (Sony BMG 2006b, n.p.),[2] featuring a duet between Coco's ballad, mainly sung in Chinese, and Vanness's fast and slang-laden rap in English against heavy musical beats and a dance-driven soundscape. Visually, the video is characterized by their dance performance in an urban warehouse context, suggesting a New York ghetto. In the next section, the video will be analyzed and special attention will be paid to the interplay between different gendered, nationalized, and racial signs in the junction between sound and image. This analysis will be further expanded against publicly available data, including television interviews, news articles, online discussions, etc.

"HIP HOP TONIGHT" (2007): AN ANALYSIS

The studies of music video, in recent years, have altered from a one-sided emphasis—either a sound-centered (e.g., Goodwin 1992) or an image-centered approach (e.g., Kaplan 1987)—to highlight the interaction between different media. In this new direction, Kay Dickinson, in Beebe and Middleton's groundbreaking volume *Medium Cool* (2007), asserts that music videos are "media hybrids" in that there is "a thoroughfare with two-way traffic" between sound and image and that different parameters "waver opportunistically between states of separation and attachment" (2007, 13–15). Conversely, Carol Vernallis, in the same volume, also states that there is a constant "give and take between sound and image" (2007, 112). From the perspective of dance studies, attentions are given to the meaning-creating processes in the interplay between different media, paying special attention to the dancing body. According to Sherril Dodds, the sound-image relationship is "never arbitrary" (2009, 250–251); it seeks to create "a sensory experience that reflects the character of the singer/band" to "construct performing bodies inscribed by promotion" (2002, 243). Based on the above methodological foundation, Coco's dancing body will be regarded as the center in the interactive process between sound and image. I focus on the way her body generates cultural meanings in this multimedial interplay by thematically focusing on her twisting waist, her rocking hips, her display of "American-ness" and her construction of eroticism.

Visually, *Hip Hop Tonight*[3] begins with a close-up of a ghetto blaster on the floor with, musically, booming bass sounds echoing in the background, constructing the inner-city context that is often linked with the genre of hip-hop. With the scene quickly cutting to a long shot, Coco is shown, through a sepia filter, in a warehouse, walking casually and confidently toward the far side. Styled in a maroon bikini top and a pair of military-green low-rise trousers, Coco exposes a large part of her torso, which gives an indication of her torso-related dance style. With the beats growing stronger, Coco begins her exercises in synchronization to the musical rhythm: she slowly extends her limbs in a lazy, yet rhythmic, way; she casually runs on the spot to exercise her feet and bends forward in a relaxed manner to stretch her arms. These exercises, with the development of the rhythm, gradually incorporate into a sped-up, powerful, full-bodied corporeal articulation: she elongates her arms and rocks her hips and, against the window in a profile shot, the light glitters on her naked torso, forming a visual highlight (Fig. 16.1). Her twisting body is quickly cut into a zoomed-in, face-on, shot to focus on her bosom, torso, and hips; her twists speed up and her dance is now bursting with energy, forming a visual highlight against the dark background (Fig. 16.2). These two scenes appear in synchronization with the emergence of Coco and Vanness's names in a scintillating golden font, giving her twisting torso and her rocking hips a defining status.

Indeed, Coco's waist and hip movements are a repeating theme throughout the music video, and are always presented in conjunction with musical rhythms. Toward the end of the video in the instrumental part, where the tempo gradually develops into a musical climax featuring intensive drum beats and Coco's voicing of "oh" (2.27–2.45), the camera, against various cuts, gradually stabilizes on her rocking hips. Her speed of twisting and rocking increases, and the momentum of her hips is sustained against the highest musical pitch, strengthening the physical and musical tension (Fig. 16.3). At the end of this musical phase, there is a sudden alteration of the soundscape from intense beating

FIGURE 16.1 Screen capture of Coco Lee's *Hip Hop Tonight*, Sony BMG Music Entertainment, 2006, Coco's waistline (0.11).

FIGURE 16.2 Screen capture of Coco Lee's *Hip Hop Tonight*, Sony BMG Music Entertainment, 2006, the camera highlights Coco's waist (0.12).

FIGURE 16.3 Screen capture of Coco Lee's *Hip Hop Tonight*, Sony BMG Music Entertainment, 2006, the intensification: Coco's waist and hip movements (2.45).

to gentle chanting and, visually, the camera cuts to a facial close-up of Coco, showing her crooning tenderly to deliver a sense of relaxation (Fig. 16.4). The circle between intensification and relaxation constructs a sense of orgasm, and her twisting waist and rocking hips are now becoming the sites through which potential sexual implications are articulated.

FIGURE 16.4 Screen capture of Coco Lee's *Hip Hop Tonight*, Sony BMG Music Entertainment, 2006, the relaxation: Coco's facial close-up.

Throughout the music video, there is an intense interplay between sound and image that focuses on Coco's dancing body, highlighting the rotation of her waist and hips. The interaction between sound and image is carefully synchronized and, taking into account what Kay Dickinson calls "a thoroughfare with two-way traffic" (2007, 15), *Hip Hop Tonight* produces a musically enhanced body in that Coco's dancing body assumes the weight of the beats and the speed of camera cuts in the "give and take" between sound and image. This specific body configuration, in the introductory advertising, is termed "sexy hip hop": her waist is described as "serpentine," and her hips are referred to as being an "electric motor" (Sony BMG 2006c). Reverting to the interview in which Zax and A-Wei exclaim that Coco's dancing body is "so natural" and regard it as a corporeal spectacle, it can be argued that her body is produced in the sound-image conjunction, tacitly appropriating the weight of musical beats and speed of cuts to embody sexual meanings and to assume the momentum of sound and image, constructing a dancing body that is widely regarded as a corporeal spectacle.

Most importantly, Coco's "sexy" waist twisting and hip rocking are specifically constructed to be an "American" style. In *Hip Hop Tonight*, this is presented through referencing to "American" superstars. In one of the scenes in the video, this dance style is performed in an outfit with a black bra on top of a small white shirt. This outfit is highlighted by a medium close-up in which Coco's upper body occupies the shot (Fig. 16.5). In this scene, Coco energetically pumps her arms up and down to produce a "squeezed" effect to her chest, enhancing the visibility of her black bra through body motion. The visibility of her chest is further highlighted when the camera cuts into a group dance scene: Coco is shown in the center, rocking her body vehemently (Fig. 16.6). In this

FIGURE 16.5 Screen capture of Coco Lee's *Hip Hop Tonight*, Sony BMG Music Entertainment, 2006, Coco's Madonna style (1.50).

scene, her waist-and-hips dance style is again articulated, in an outfit which is mostly identified with Madonna, the contemporary sex icon in the United States.

In this scene, Coco's skin color, through makeup and lighting, also conforms to Madonna's racial identity as a "white" American. This scene is in sharp contrast to her warm-up exercise scene (Figs. 16.1 and 16.2), in which the makeup and lighting reflect her bill-matter as "the Asian Jennifer Lopez," encouraging a link between Coco's "sexiness" and a Latina image. Moreover, similarities between the exercise sequence in *Hip Hop Tonight* and Cassie's "Me and You" (2006), a music video of an African American star, have been observed among Coco's audiences (Smiling Orange [ID] 2006), inserting a subtext of "black-ness" to Coco's "sexiness."

Through the construction of the mise-en-scène, *Hip Hop Tonight* seems to refer to Madonna, Jennifer Lopez, and Cassie in a superficial and hybridized way, rendering the use of signs into a color confusion, in that transcultural flows seem to deposit different "colors" onto Coco's skin: she is "genuinely" "white," "brown," and "black." Coco signifies, on the one hand, Madonna's style, constructing a sense of "whiteness"; on the other hand, she is described as one with an innate sense of rhythm in performing hip-hop, stereotypically regarded as an attribute of "black-ness." In addition, her waist and hip movements are often compared with Jennifer Lopez, contributing to a superficial construction of "brown-ness." In this process, racialization—be it to "whiten" or "darken"—is used as a strategy to sexualize Coco's dancing body.

Apart from the issue of race, national identity is also used in this process to construct a hypersexualized performing style. In studying the relationship between racial, national, and sexual boundaries, Joane Nagel argues that sexual stereotypes often overlap with race- or class-based boundaries in that African Americans and Latinos are

FIGURE 16.6 Screen capture of Coco Lee's *Hip Hop Tonight*, Sony BMG Music Entertainment, 2006, Coco's waist movement (1.51).

often described in the United States as being "hypersexual" (2003, 9–10). In Coco's case, with the emphasis of "American-ness," the racialized stereotypes that Negal described are performatively re-articulated into Asia through music video. This process propels a new set of gender representations of femininity in Taiwan, with the United States utilized as a hypersexualized sign. In this process, discourses are naturalized; history, power relationships, and processes of transmission are obscured. "American-ness" is, now, factually "sexy"; Coco, as a Chinese American, earns the credibility to convey the "Americanized" "sexiness" in performance to achieve, according to Zax, "what a *Chinese* (*"hua-ren"*) *body* can't achieve."

The meaning of "sexiness" constructed in *Hip Hop Tonight* denotes sex-oriented eroticism, a phenomenon that is particularly noticeable in Vanness's performance, both in lyrics and in gesture. From a lyrical perspective, the rap makes many direct references to sex, often at high speed and in slang, such as "open dem legs and let me in," "stopping hunnies with my magic stick," and "makin' 'em shoot a dirty flick subtext rated X," etc. In "subtext rated X," the video is presented, visually, with Vanness's portrait in a medium close-up, in which his upper arm and chest are visible. He crosses his arms in a fast and jerky manner with his left arm placed horizontally in front of his chest and the other arm flicking forcefully upward, forming an "X gesture" (Fig. 16.7), which, in American and European contexts, denotes "fuck" or "fuck off." This gesture is performed with intense strength and speed so that his right arm "penetrates" the upper camera frame, encouraging a reading of sexual penetration. Moreover, as Patricia Hill Collins noticed, the theme of the "materialistic, sexualized black woman has become the icon within hip-hop culture" (2004, 126), and the use of the genre has already presupposed (hyper) sexual politics which are particularly "Americanized." Performed by a Chinese

FIGURE 16.7 Screen capture of Coco Lee's *Hip Hop Tonight*, Sony BMG Music Entertainment, 2006, the 'X' gesture (1.43).

American star rapping inner-city English slang on sex, Vanness's performance in *Hip Hop Tonight* seems to follow Taiwanese cultural assumptions of "genuine" hip-hop, and thus continues to highlight the "Americanized" and eroticized presentation of "sexiness" as spectacle.

LOCALIZING THE "AMERICANIZED," "SEXY" DANCING BODY IN TAIWAN

Despite the fact that Coco's corporeal articulation of an "Americanized" "sexy" dancing body reaffirms Mandarin pop's logic of spectacle, there is an apparent "danger": the idea of eroticism has a potential to collide with post-war cultural logic of the "Chinese tradition" in that overtly sexualized representations in public are closely related to the idea of immorality and therefore can trigger a counter discourse to spectacle. Against this context, there is a noticeable attempt in Coco's image to "desexualize" and "Sinocize" cultural and corporeal codes constructed in the music video. This tendency can be seen in the lyrics and the introductory advertising. In the lyrics, references to sex are narrated at high speed in English slang, difficult to understand by non-English-native speakers, while Chinese parts merely suggest a party event. Moreover, the sexual subtext in Vanness's "X gesture" is mostly recognized in American and European contexts, and could easily be understood as a mere punch in East Asia. Furthermore, in the introductory advertising, *Hip Hop Tonight* is described as expressing "party ambience" because "music is for *happiness* and dance is for *enjoyment*" (Sony BMG 2006b, my emphases).[4] In this remark, the connotations of eroticism, so pronounced in the music video, have been replaced by ideas such as happiness, enjoyment, and partying.

From a wider scope in the construction of Coco's star image outside the music video medium, "Chinese-ness," "tradition," and a desexualized image are further articulated as a means to balance presentations of eroticized "American-ness." This phenomenon is demonstrated in the construction of "mummy's little girl," an important and prolonged theme in the development of Coco's image. Coco's mother is depicted as a hard taskmaster, devising draconian diets in preparation for Coco's performances (H. Shih 2001) and controlling her possible sexual encounters. According to Coco in a 2002 interview, "my mother is a very traditional Chinese" and, for that reason, "I was banned from having boyfriends. I was eighteen the first time when I spoke to any boy on phone" (Yang 2002, n. p.).[5] To the present day, Coco continues to state that she is willing to end any romantic relationship should her mother disapprove (Chiang 2010). From the acceptance of telephone censorship to the willingness to end relationships, Coco's filial obedience is demonstrated and the notion of a "traditional" "Chinese" family bond is emphasized. By highlighting her mother, Coco Sinocizes "American-ness" and desexualizes possible connections to eroticism.

However, there is a significant change in Coco's star image toward the end of the 1990s, the time when she attempted to cross over to the "international" stage, that is, the market of the United States. This resulted in the release of two albums: *Just No Other Way* (1999) and *Exposed* (2005). In *Exposed* (2005), eroticism is stressed to such an extent that three of her music videos—"No Doubt," "So Good," and "Touch"—were banned in China; "So Good" was also prohibited from being broadcasted in Taiwan (Now News 2005). After this album, the idea of sex was approached differently. On the official introductory advertising, she states that "I think I *have the right* to be sexy since I'm already 29" (Now News 2005, n. p., my emphasis).[6] In this comment, Coco tacitly acknowledges the potentially significant, and possibly negative, impact of the idea of sex in a "Chinese" context and she tries to avoid counter-discourse of spectacle by using the idea of individualism. The embedded assumption is that the display of "sexiness," if not in disguise, needs to be justified. In Coco's case, her age is clearly stated as a means to construct this license and the idea of nationality seems to be implicitly deployed since the notion of having the "right" is one of the key foundations of Western philosophy and political discourses. Moreover, apart from this comment, Coco seldom talks about sex in front of the media unless questioned. Coco's "sexiness" is, therefore, constructed through her dancing body in the music video to convey a meaning of spectacular eroticism. However, outside this realm, "American-ness" is paradoxically Sinocized as a means to desexualize "sexiness." From the music video to other media, Coco demonstrates a localizing process of the dancing body. In this process, a second meaning, which contradicts the previous definition, is created. "Sexiness," in this vein, has embedded tension in a Taiwanese context and has to be continuously Sinocized and desexualized in order to comply with local cultural sensibilities.

Negotiating "Chinese-ness"

While there exists a constant attempt to highlight Coco's "Chinese-ness" as a means to balance her overtly "Americanized" "sexiness," it is necessary to note that "Chinese-ness" is also context-specifically constructed and vacillatingly deployed in different locales. Different from her presentation of "American-ness," which is superficially constructed yet widely accepted as an "authentic" representation in East Asia, Coco's "Chinese-ness" is confronted by different, and often politicized, usages. This is the direct result of various ways through which the term "Chinese" can be translated as an identity and as a language. From the perspective of identity, the two most common translations of "Chinese" are *zhong-guo-ren* (中國人), a politicized term closely linked with China as a nation-state, and *hua-ren* (華人), a term to group "Chinese" from a cultural perspective, implying, according to Ien Ang, "the unity of overseas Chinese communities as one people and their unbroken ties with the Chinese homeland" (2001, 81). Due to political tensions existing between China and Taiwan and the rise of Taiwanese nativist sensibility during the 1990s, there is a tendency in contemporary Taiwan to use *tai-wan-ren* ("Taiwanese"; 臺灣人) and, sometimes, *hua-ren* (華人) in preference to *zhong-guo-ren* (中國人). From the perspective of language, the split embedded in identity naming is also apparent. While "Chinese" means *pu-tong-hua* (普通話), or *zhong-guo-hua* (中國話), in China, it denotes *kuo-yu* (國語) in Taiwan. Other translations including *zhong-wen* (中文) and *hua-yu* (華語), both of which encompass different forms of Chinese, both in Taiwan and in China.

Across the national boundaries, linguistic differentiations, and political tensions mentioned above, there is a significant phenomenon in the media representations of Coco in China and Taiwan, both of which regard her as their *own* star. Her bill-matter includes "Mariah Carey *of Taiwan*" and at the same time "the queen of voluptuous bottom *of China*" (Zhang 2009, my emphases). She is categorized under "female star of Taiwan" in the prominent Taiwanese news website *UDN*, while one of Coco's interviews on the famous China-based news website *Sina* was entitled "Coco Lee: I am proud of being *zhong-guo-ren*" (Hsu 2006). The keen interest in Coco displayed in both China and Taiwan is surprising against the conflicting political sentiments prevailing in East Asia. In the field of popular culture, Taiwanese performers who pursue a career in China are often enmeshed in identity interrogations, with the potential consequence of boycott.[7] These negative backlashes are often justified in China by an argument that the Taiwanese performers "refused to be *zhong-guo-ren*".[8] In this media comment, the trinity of *zhong-guo* ("China"; 中國), *zhong-guo-hua* ("Chinese"; 中國話), and *zhong-guo-ren* ("Chinese (politicized)" 中國人) is emphasized, which not only shows how *zhong-guo*, as a hegemonic term, is built into the terminology of popular cultural discourses, but also demonstrates its embedded ideological struggles. In this context, the consistent acceptance of Coco in both places is an extraordinary phenomenon.

This acceptance is, arguably, a result of Coco's careful deployment of identity categories in different contexts, translating "Chinese" to comply with local political sentiments. To investigate the strategic switching of these potentially politicized terms, I will compare two individual events that took place in Taiwan and in China. In Taiwan, the official advertising of *Just Want You* (2006) reads,

> Away from the *hua-yu* music field for four years, the new *hua-yu* album of the *international queen*, Coco's *Just Want You*, has finally been released after repeated calls! [...] She has been busy in the *international music field* and, with her growing *international fame*, becomes stricter towards herself [in the pursuit of quality for her musical products]. This *kuo-yu* album is especially dedicated to her *hua-ren* fans, who have been with her all the time during her growth.[9]
>
> (Sony BMG 2006a, n. p., my emphases)

In this example, the text uses "*kuo-yu* album" to describe the language while at the same time deploying a large amount of terms connected with the idea of "*hua*"—"*hua-yu* music field," "*hua-yu* album," and "*hua-ren*" (Taiwanese)—as a means to construct a sense of internationalism. Since the logic of spectacle in Mandarin pop resides in foreignness, it can be argued that the use of "*hua*" is an active construction of the idea of spectacle. Possibly for this reason, Coco, in Taiwan, is mostly associated with this term; her body, in the *Showbiz* interview, is termed as a "*hua-ren*" *body* by Zax and A-Wei. Moreover, the embedded international assumptions in "*hua*" has the potential to dissolve regional struggles, creating what Homi K. Bhabha terms "the third space," a place where "new structures of authority" can be constructed (1990, 211). Situated in between "Chinese-ness" and "American-ness," Coco's hybrid identity allows internationalism to be convincingly enounced in an "odor-free" manner, constructing a spectacle which is untouched by political tensions.

In China, the meaning of "Chinese" significantly switches. In an interview published on the China-based news website *sina.com*—titled "Coco Lee: I am proud of being *zhong-guo-ren*"—the term *zhong-guo-ren* ("Chinese [political]") repeatedly appears. This interview is intriguingly non-existent in any news website in Taiwan apart from a small reference to the Oscar night and is often subject to revision in the transmission process.

> KELLY HSU: You must be the first *hua-ren* to sing at the Oscars!
> COCO: Yes, [...] this is certainly an important breakthrough in my career. Up to now, there is no *hua-ren* singer who can stand in front of the international stage. I am *zhong-guo-ren* and I step onto the Oscar stage with my identity as *zhong-guo-ren*. [...] *My hair is black and my skin is yellow.* [...] I am proud to be *zhong-guo-ren*.[10]
>
> (Hsu 2006, n. p., my emphases)

Similar to the first case, ideas of "*hua-ren*" and internationalism are constantly highlighted. Among these claims, Coco politically emphasizes herself as *zhong-guo-ren* with "Chinese features," including black hair and yellow skin, despite, ironically, these features being the least noticeable parts of her star image in Asian contexts[11] and it is not until the Oscar night that her hair appears to be black, as described by the news media, to reassure her "Chinese-ness" (Hsu 2006).[12] The trinity of "race," culture, and skin color (hair color in this case) is therefore revealed as a myth: "my hair *is* black," as a statement, can only be achieved through a performative event of hair-dying. Moreover, the China-centered identity category, *zhong-guo-ren*, is repeatedly emphasized to construct a sense of national pride. Therefore, Coco's "self-defined" *zhong-guo-ren* in this interview demonstrates a performative construction with recognition of nationalism in China. Compared with her media representations in Taiwan where *hua-ren*, rather than *zhong-guo-ren*, is most commonly used, it can be argued that Coco's use of "Chinese-ness" is vacillatingly articulated in different contexts. It is in a constant process of localization, where different terms are strategically and site-specifically deployed.

Although Coco's nationalistic claim to be *zhong-guo-ren* facilitates her popularity in China, the term is questioned and is given a nonchalant response by her Taiwanese audiences. However, Coco seems to enjoy an exception through her "American-ness." For example, a Taiwanese blogger compares Coco to Jay Chow, a Taiwan-born male superstar, as they both identify as being Chinese, yet exempts Coco by stating that "they can speak differently because one is Taiwanese while the other is American" (annapsyche [ID] 2007, n. p.).[13] Coco's use of a politically China-centered identity category is, in this blogger's opinion, justified and accepted, demonstrating the power of hybridity in that she possesses what Bhabha (1994) termed the "third space of enunciation." In this in-between space, even the same signs "can be appropriated, translated, rehistoricized and read anew" (1994, 55); Coco is able to transcend internal power struggles between two antagonistic powers by interpreting "Chinese" differently from a diasporic viewpoint: the conflict between *zhong-guo-ren* ("Chinese [political]") and *tai-wan-ren* ("Taiwanese") is dissolved into the new term *hua-ren*, while *pu-tong-hua*, *kuo-yu* and *zhong-guo-hua* (different words that connote "Chinese" in China and Taiwan) become *zhong-wen*, or more commonly, *hua-yu*. Coco's use of "Chinese-ness" is, therefore, in constant negotiation in different Asian contexts: it reinterprets *hua* to demonstrate that its meanings have "no primordial unity or fixity" (Bhabha 1994, 55), producing a new space in-between antagonistic powers.

CONCLUSION

Starting from a television interview where Coco's "sexy" dancing body is collectively understood to be a "natural" style, I have argued that her rocking hips and twisting waist, in which "sexiness" is embodied, are never "natural" or self-evident. Rather, with the crucial role the music video plays in the formative process of the contemporary star image, Coco's dancing body is tacitly and performatively constructed in music video in the conjunction between sound and image, re-articulating various racialized, nationalized, and gendered signs into a spectacular configuration. In this process, "sexiness" denotes a sense of "Americanized" eroticism that mobilizes, performatively, Coco's cultural identity. Through the Internet and television entertaining programs (*Showbiz* for example), cultural identity and corporeality are repeatedly linked up. The co-emphases of the body and of identity produce a naturalizing effect to obfuscate the process of construction. Coco's "Americanized" and eroticized dancing body becomes *truly* and *naturally* spectacular; it is a corporeal version of what Barthes terms the "myth."

In the historical context in Taiwan, however, public displays of eroticism are considered low class and can trigger possible counter-discourses on the logic of spectacle. Coco's "sexy" dancing body, therefore, is constantly in negotiation in a localized context outside the medium of music video. In this process, Coco's "American-ness" is Sinocized and eroticism is desexualized, resulting in a context-specific meaning of a desexualized "sexiness." In addition, Coco's use of "Chinese-ness," as the counterbalance to her "American-ness" in the localizing process, is also localized, shuttling between China-centered usages, Taiwan-focused parlances, and the culturally Chinese phrase—"*hua*"—which transcend different political categories. Therefore, Coco's "sexy" dancing body is in a continuous process of negotiation: it is constructed to be an "Americanized," "eroticized" dancing body in "Hip Hop Tonight," while at the same time having a Sinocized and desexualized connotation outside the context of music video, and the meaning of "Chinese-ness" continues to shift in different locales.

Performatively and vacillatingly constructed, the dancing body is an important analytical point where different, often contradictory, cultural meanings intersect in the contemporary world. Departing from an event—Coco's "sexy" hips—in the lucrative and transcultural music genre of Mandarin pop, the undertone of this chapter is to address the significance and richness of East Asian popular culture. It is a genre with a strong tendency of naturalization, where the contradictions embedded in the dancing bodies are often smoothed out, constructing a mode of communication that appears to be self-evident. It reflects Moskowitz's observation that Mandarin pop "has surprisingly complex cultural implications for such a seemingly superficial genre" (2010, 1). In other words, this force has a tendency to trivialize the complexity, wrapping profundity with a coat of superficiality. By pointing out this feature and providing an examination of a major corporeal spectacle, I hope this chapter will lead to a new research route toward the dancing body in music video, in popular culture, and in East Asia in the future.

Notes

1. Author's translation: "王仁甫:"所以其實我們之前在說華人的肢體比較難跳到像J Lo那種很有power的舞,可是我們這一次在看到Coco的時候發現:哇賽!誰說華人跳不出來?明明就跳的出來!"李玟:"沒有我覺得現在其實很多女歌手都非常的優秀啊!"張善為:"可是有些人是要花很多時間去練.我覺得在妳的身上看出來他是渾然天成的,好像妳平常就是這樣子."王仁甫:"對對對!其實Coco的舞蹈你不會覺得她是排舞,像一般歌手大部分舞蹈是排舞,這個地方要跳什麼,但是Coco的好像是很free的free style直接就..."

2. Author's translation: "首支單曲「Hip Hop Tonight」就是最新之作，融合了Hip Hop與Funky曲風，整首歌充滿Party的感覺。"

3. "Coco Lee—Hip Hop Tonight," [n.d.], video clip, accessed August 15, 2012, *YouTube*, http://www.youtube.com/watch?v=s35V1r7MzEo.

4. Author's translation: "首支單曲「Hip Hop Tonight」就是最新之作，融合了Hip Hop 與Funky曲風，整首歌充滿Party的感覺。音樂就是要快樂，跳舞就是要過癮。[...]"

5. Author's translation: "「我妈妈是非常传统的中国人」、「不能交男朋友」、「我第一次和男孩子正式讲电话是18岁的时候」"

6. Author's translation: "嗯，我已經29歲了，我想我有權利表現的性感一點。"

7. In 2003, for example, Rainie Young (楊丞琳), a Taiwanese female singer widely known for her fondness for Japan, mistook the eight-year Sino-Japanese War (1937-1945) as eleven years, and replied, "Oh! It is *only* eight years!" when she was corrected (Yu 2007, n. p., my emphasis). This faux pas was considered as a serious offense: she was elected as the most-hated singer in China; boycotted for the next four years; and was only re-accepted in 2007 after various public apologies (Yu 2007). In 2004, Hui-Mei Chang (張惠妹) was boycotted in China for singing for the President's inaugural ceremony in Taiwan (Ho 2003; Tsai 2007; Yu 2007).

8. In the case of F4, a pop group of four boys, media in China criticized the group for regarding Taiwan as a country because, in this sense, F4 refused to be *zhong-guo-ren*, and, "why do you speak *zhong-guo-hua* [...] if you disdain to be *zhong-guo-ren*?" Author's translation: "既然你那麼不屑當中國人，幹嗎講中國話、寫中國字？" (Yu 2007).

9. Author's translation: "暌違華語樂壇四年，國際天后Coco李玟最新華語大碟「要定你」，千呼萬喚終於全新出爐！[...]四年來忙碌於全球流行樂壇間，日漸高漲的國際聲望讓她對自己的要求更加嚴格，尤其是要獻給讓她成長茁壯的華人歌迷們的國語專輯，為了不辜負大家對她的期待回報歌迷的支持，她更是傾盡全力用盡全力的準備，也就這樣子《ㄍㄧㄥ了近四年，「堅持給你最好的」讓我們等了那麼久！"

10. Original in Chinese: "彼岸：「你是第一個在奧斯卡頒獎禮上演唱的華人歌手吧！」李玟：「是啊，[...] 這是我事業上的一次重大突破。一直以來，從來沒有一位華人歌手可以立足國際樂壇。我是中國人，我以中國人的身份登上奧斯卡的舞台[...]。我的頭髮是黑色的，我的皮膚是黃色的，[...] 我很驕傲我是中國人。」"

11. Her skin color seems to vary through the use of the lighting and makeup, ranging from "white," "brown," to "black" to emphasize her "American-ness," as demonstrated in *Hip Hop Tonight*. Coco's hair color also has a tendency to take on dramatic colors, ranging from brunette, to blond, to red and purple. For example, in *Coco's Party* in 1996, she had purple hair with a red hat; and in *DiDaDi* in 1998, she had flamboyant red hair that resembled a fire hydrant. Apart from these two examples, she generally kept her hair in different shades of brown, and sometimes it was closer to blond than brunette.

12. Coco stated in the interview, "my hair is black; my skin is yellow; and I am a Chinese." Author's translation: "我得頭髮是黑色的，我的皮膚是黃色的，我就是一個中國人。"

13. There were two pieces of news recently: Jay Chow refers to China as "our own country" [...], while Coco Lee says "Beijing Olympic is the pride of *hua-ren* in the world" [...]. They can speak differently because one is Taiwanese while the other is American. Author's translation: "前一陣子還有兩個新聞，就是周杰倫針對奧運歌曲說中國是「自己國家」。李玟受邀演唱奧運歌曲，則說「北京奧運是全世界華人的

驕傲」。一個台灣人，一個美國人，可以說出邏輯不一樣的話（沒有邏輯的當然是台灣那一個，請問他拿哪一個國家護照？）"

Works Cited

Ang, Ien. *On Not Speaking Chinese: Living Between Asia and the West*. London and New York: Routledge, 2001.

annapsyche [ID]. "Paradox in Some Taiwanese Stars (某些泛綠台灣人的矛盾與無奈)." *Pixnet Blog*, December 19, 2007. Accessed October 18, 2010. http://annapsyche.pixnet.net/blog/post/12022154.

Barthes, Roland. *Mythologies*. New York: Hill and Wang, 1972.

Beebe, Roger, and Jason Middleton, eds. *Medium Cool: Music Videos from Soundies to Cellphones*. Durham, NC: Duke University Press, 2007.

Bhabha, Homi K. "The Third Space (an Interview)." In *Identity: Community, Culture, Difference*, edited by Jonathan Rutherford, 207–221. London: Lawrence & Wishart, 1990.

Bhabha, Homi K. *The Location of Culture*. London and New York: Routledge, 1994.

Bordwell, David and Kristin Thompson. *Film Art: An Introduction*. Boston, MA: McGraw-Hill, 2004.

Butler, Judith. *Gender Trouble: Feminism and the Subversion of Identity*. London and New York: Routledge, 1990.

Chiang, Chi-Ling (江芷稜). "Coco Worries only Her Mum in a Love Relationship (李玟談戀愛就怕媽媽搖頭)." *ETS News* (華視新聞), January 30, 2010.

Coco Lee—Hip Hop Tonight," [n.d.], video clip, accessed August 15, 2012, *YouTube*, http://www.youtube.com/watch?v=s35V1r7MzEo.

Collins, Patricia Hill. *Black Sexual Politics: African Americans, Gender, and the New Racism*. London and New York: Routledge, 2004.

Cooper Albright, Ann. *Choreographing Difference: The Body and Identity in Contemporary Dance*. Middletown, CT: Wesleyan University Press, 1997.

Craine, Charlie. "Coco Lee—Interview." *Hip Online*, February 28, 2000. Accessed December 30, 2010. http://www.hiponline.com/1935/coco-lee-interview.html.

Debord, Guy. *The Society of the Spectacle*. London: Rebel Press, 1967.

Dempster, Elizabeth. "Women Writing the Body." In *Bodies of the Text: Dance as Theory, Literature as Dance*, edited by Ellen W. Goellner and Jacqueline Shea Murphy, 21–38. New Brunswick, NJ: Rutgers University Press, 1995.

Desmond, Jane. "Embodying Difference: Issues in Dance." In *Meaning in Motion: New Cultural Studies of Dance*, edited by Jane Desmond, 29–54. Durham, NC and London: Duke University Press, 1997.

Dickinson, Kay. "Music Video and Synaesthetic Possibility." In *Medium Cool: Music Videos from Soundies to Cellphones*, edited by Roger Beebe and Jason Middleton, 13–29. Durham, NC: Duke University Press, 2007.

Dodds, Sherril. "Sensational, Performing, and Promotional Bodies." In *Music, Sensation, and Sensuality*, edited by Linda Phyllis Austern, 231–244. London and New York: Routledge, 2002.

Dodds, Sherril. "From Busby Berkeley to Madonna / Music Video and Popular Dance." In *Ballroom, Boogie, Shimmy Sham, Shake: a Social and Popular Dance Reader*, edited by Julie Malnig, 247–260. Urbana: University of Illinois Press, 2009.

Drake, Kate. "Coco Pops." *Time*, April 2, 2001. Accessed March 15, 2011. http://www.time.com/time/magazine/article/0,9171,103842,00.html.

Dyer, Richard. *Stars*. London: BFI Publishing, 1979.

Dyer, Richard. *Heavenly Bodies: Film Stars and Society*. London and New York: Routledge, 1986.

Foster, Susan Leigh. *Reading Dancing: Bodies and Subjects in Contemporary American Dance*. Berkeley and Los Angeles: University of California Press, 1986.

Goodwin, Andrew. *Dancing in the Distraction Factory: Music Television and Popular Culture*. Minneapolis: University of Minnesota Press, 1992.

Hall, Stuart. "The Local and the Global: Globalization and Ethnicity." In *Culture, Globalization and the World-System: Contemporary Conditions for the Representation of Identity*, edited by Anthony D. King, 19–40. Minneapolis: University of Minnesota Press, 1991.

Hermes, Joke. "'Ally McBeal,' 'Sex and the City' and the Tragic Success of Feminism." In *Feminism in Popular Culture*, edited by Joanne Hollows and Rachel Moseley, 79–96. Oxford and New York: Berg Publishers, 2006.

Hip Hop Tonight. Music video. Performed by Coco Lee. Taipei: Sony BMG, 2006.

Ho, Josephine. "From Spice Girls to Enjo Kosai: Formations of Teenage Girls' Sexualities in Taiwan." *Inter-Asia Cultural Studies* 4/2 (2003): 325–336.

Hsu, Kelly. "Coco: I am Proud to be Chinese (李玟：我驕傲我是中國人)." *Coastide (彼岸杂志)*, October 31, 2006. Accessed October 1, 2007. http://magazine.sina.com.tw/coastide/200610/2006-10-31/ba22623.shtml.

Jameson, Fredric. *The Cultural Turn: Selected Writings on the Postmodern, 1983–1998*. London and New York: Verso, 1998.

Kaplan, E. Ann. *Rocking Around the Clock: Music Television, Postmodernism, and Consumer Culture*. New York: Methuen, 1987.

Keane, Michael. "Once Were Peripheral: Creating Media Capacity in East Asia." *Media, Culture & Society* 28/6 (2006): 835–855.

Kellner, Douglas. "Media Culture and the Triumph of the Spectacle." (2004). Accessed March 15, 2011. http://gseis.ucla.edu/faculty/kellner/essays/mediaculturetriumphspectacle.pdf

Moskowitz, Marc L. *Cries of Joy, Songs of Sorrow: Chinese Pop Music and its Cultural Connotations*. Honolulu: University of Hawaii Press, 2010.

Nagel, Joane. *Race, Ethnicity, and Sexuality: Intimate Intersections, Forbidden Frontiers*. New York: Oxford University Press, 2003.

Now News. "China Cannot 'Touch' 'So Good': The Banning of Coco's Four Songs ('So Good'中國無法'Touch'：4歌被禁登陸CoCo遺憾)." *Now News (今日新聞)*, March 28, 2005. Accessed March 15, 2011. http://www.nownews.com/2005/03/28/91-1770439.htm.

"Sexy." In *Merriam-Webster Dictionary*. Accessed March 15, 2011. http://www.merriam-webster.com/dictionary/sexy.

Shih, Hsin-Yuan (施心媛). "The Shadow of Kung Fu (俠影重重)." *The People's Livelihood Newspaper (民生報)*, March 27, 2001.

Shih, Shumei. *Visuality and Identity: Sinophone Articulations across the Pacific*. Berkeley and Los Angeles: University of California Press, 2007.

Showbiz (完全娛樂). Taipei: SET Metro (三立都會台). Broadcasted on March 20, 2005.

Smiling Orange [ID]. "OMG! The Music Video of Hip Hop Tonight is an Imitation (天哪~Hip Hop Tonight MTV居然是模仿別人的！)." *Cocobbs Online Forum*, November 2, 2006. Accessed February 14, 2008. http://www.cocobbs.com/archiver/?tid-84432-page-1.html.

Sony BMG. "Coco: Just Want You." 2006a. Accessed October 18, 2010. http://stars.udn.com/star/StarsContent/Content9941/

Sony BMG. "Coco: Just Want You." 2006b. Accessed October 18, 2010. http://www.g-music. com.tw/GMusicProduct.aspx?ProductID=0828768698426

Sony BMG. "When Coco Meets Vanness: (當舞后CoCo遇上舞王Vanness，性感尬舞 火辣又養眼！)." 2006c. Accessed October 18, 2010. Available: http://www1.iwant-song. com/d-c0001/?sn=d-c0001_20060905_08.

Taylor, Jeremy E. "From Transnationalism to Nativism? The Rise, Decline and Reinvention of a Regional Hokkien Entertainment Industry." *Inter-Asia Cultural Studies* 9/1 (2008): 62–81.

Thomas, Helen. *Dance, Modernity, and Culture: Explorations in the Sociology of Dance*. London and New York: Routledge, 1995.

Tsai, Eva. "Caught in the Terrains: An Inter-Referential Inquiry of Trans-Border Stardom and Fandom." *Inter-Asia Cultural Studies* 8/1 (2007): 137–156.

Vernallis, Carol. "Strange People, Weird Objects: The Nature of Narrativity, Character, and Editing in Music Videos." In *Medium Cool: Music Videos from Soundies to Cellphones*, edited by Roger Beebe and Jason Middleton, 111–151. Durham, NC: Duke University Press, 2007.

Yang, Wen-Chieh (杨文杰). "The Coco Off Stage (李玟透露「玟」所未闻的生活)." *Beijing Youth* (北京青年报), September 23, 2002. Accessed October 28, 2010. http://www.southcn. com/ent/celeb/coco/gallery/200403150569.htm.

Yu, Wei-Ching (余惟靜). "The Trap of Nationalism: the Case of Taiwanese Pop Star in China (台湾艺人掉进「台独」陷阱)." *World News Journal* (世界新闻报), August 22, 2007. Accessed March 15, 2011. http://gb.cri.cn/12764/2007/08/22/2905@1728044.htm.

Zhang, Xiao-Mei (张晓梅). "Top Ten Voluptuous Bottoms in China (中国「十大电臀天后」最新排行榜)." *Sina* (新浪), 21 April, 2009. Accessed October 18, 2010. http://eladies.sina.com.cn/zc/p/2009/0421/0800855660.shtml.

CHAPTER 17

SINGLE LADIES, PLURAL: RACISM, SCANDAL, AND "AUTHENTICITY" WITHIN THE MULTIPLICATION AND CIRCULATION OF ONLINE DANCE DISCOURSES

PHILIPPA THOMAS

INTRODUCTION

> The public is an examiner, but an absent-minded one.
>
> Walter Benjamin (1968)

In his classic thesis *From Work to Text*, Roland Barthes outlines what he sees as the difference between a "work," which "can be held in the hand," and a "text," which "only exists in the movement of a discourse" (1977b, 157). As such, the text is produced relationally between the viewer/reader/listener and the material work. If a text's being is inseparable from its action, one never sees, reads or hears the same text twice (Genette 1997, xvii). As Barthes exclaims: "the Text cannot stop…its constitutive movement is that of cutting across" (1977b, 157).

Visually distinctive, catchy, stylish and fun, the music video accompanying Beyoncé Knowles's 2008 hit *Single Ladies (Put a Ring on It)*[1] quickly became an Internet phenomenon, spawning numerous homages, parodies, and reinterpretations, which I shall refer to here for the sake of clarity as *editions* of the *Single Ladies* text. Additionally, the first edition was the subject of a media scandal invoking issues of race, "authenticity," and appropriation. This chapter seeks to explore how cultural texts disseminated online are made and remade, challenged and championed, with the mutability inherent to all texts becoming literally visible in this specific environment.

It is not the Internet that transforms "works" into "texts"; we do that every time we engage with them. However, the Internet brings the traces of others' readings visibly before us, in the comments beneath postings, "likes," re-posts and other practices of marking our passage through online material. So, how can one negotiate the layers of information generated in response to online material? These fragments of text, which bookend a work, re-positioning and perhaps interrogating it, are what literary theorist Gérard Genette calls "paratexts" (1997). Theorizing literary paratexts such as book covers, prefaces, reviews, and afterwords, Genette casts the paratext as a "threshold"; "an airlock which helps the reader pass without too much respiratory difficulty from one world to another" (1997, 408). Arguing that "a text without a paratext does not exist" (1997, 3), Genette claims that conversely, paratexts can exist without the texts they refer to, thus, it is possible to claim to *know Single Ladies* through rumors, reviews, and comments without having seen the video. Further, it is possible to know only the scandal and *be* scandalized without recourse to the disputed works.

It is important to recognize that readers of texts do not see the illusive "whole picture," rather, we select from "a complex of interrelated meanings," tending to interpret these as a "discrete, unified whole" (Couldry 2000, 70-71). I posit that this partiality is what allows discourses of "authenticity" back into a space of fracturing and mutability. Similarly, the Internet encourages multiple viewing positions and distances: of the +276 million[2] viewings of *Single Ladies* on YouTube alone, some will be accounted for by viewers who've watched it repeatedly; some viewers will watch only once or a snippet out of curiosity, some because it was featured on a friend's social media page or a blog they subscribe to, some because they want to listen to the song, some because they are conspiracy theorists hunting for occult symbolism,[3] or even some so that they can debate the gender of a performer.[4] As Les Back points out, the Internet has no inherent ideological orientation, rather "the relationship between form and content is to be found at the interface between particular technologies and their utilization" (2002, 633).

In order to think about how online texts are shared and invested in by diverse groups, I use the term "public" throughout this text in preference to "audience" or "viewers" to denote Michael Warner's conception of "a social space created by the reflexive circulation of discourse" (2002, 62). A "public" is a group that is self-organizing, and has a way of being "interpolated" (Althusser 1970) or hailed, by which you become part of that group through recognizing yourself as the subject of address. So, a public (unlike a group, or audience) does not exist apart from this discourse, they are in a constant relation with each other only by virtue of their relationship to the text (Warner 2002, 51). This relationality engenders a more active notion of audience, and one that can be split rather than presumed to be in unison and acted on, for example the bored-public or fan-public (although these can still overlap). Warner argues persuasively that "counterpublic" claims made for subordinate or marginal groups should not assume that these counterpublics have ways of organizing their knowledges that would necessarily be seen as oppositional to the dominant publics.

The website YouTube.com is central to the development of this textual narrative, so it is important to consider it as co-producer of these editions of *Single Ladies*. YouTube is an independent subsidiary of Google.com. In 2008, the website was not a broadcaster; it framed and packaged content, but did not produce any content of its own.[5] Third parties (both individuals and corporations) provide this content for free, either directly for use on YouTube or recycled from existing media content. YouTube videos are stored on central servers rather than operating as a peer-to-peer network, it is partly for this reason that Robert Gehl refers to YouTube as an archive, a digital "wunderkammer" ("closet of wonders") (2009, 45). Gehl's figuration helps us think about the ways that YouTube manages its flows of visitors, who move through much as they would any other archive or collection, their paths varying widely, their intentions equally so (Gehl 2009, 45-46). In conceptualizing YouTube as an archive, one is able to appropriate the problematic concerns addressed to paper archives; the labor involved in creating and maintaining the archive, and how this labor is then exploited by those who mine the archive in order to display the objects for their own profit (Gehl 2009, 46). At the time of writing,[6] in addition to the search bar my YouTube home page (www.youtube.com) offers grouped suggestions on what to watch based on my location and search history such as "Popular on YouTube – United Kingdom," "Gaming," "Movies," "Music," "Sports,". Once you have chosen a video or entered a search term, the next page on display will offer up "Related Videos" to the user. The ranking system is based on hits on Internet search engines (primarily Google) and the deft use of "tags" to signal content.

There is nothing democratic about the way that YouTube arranges its content for view. As in a paper archive, some artifacts will never be seen, with claims that approximately 30 percent of uploaded videos account for 99 percent of views on the site (Zern 2011). As Michel Foucault famously argued, there is nothing neutral about the archive (1972). Ultimately, power comes not from the act of collecting, but from the act of arranging archival objects into "facts" about the world.

Barthes characterizes the text as *metonymic*, a sort of symbol "concerned with the activity of associations, contiguities and carryings-over" (1977, 158). As such, the text poses problems for systems of classification, hierarchy, and summarization, and this flurry of ceaseless activity is where texts draw their energy from—the explosion of irreducible plurality. It is in this spirit of opening-out and embracing the irreconcilable that I shall explore the work *Single Ladies* as a text throughout my paper. I would also advise that this text be read alongside the videos to which I refer; links are provided in the endnotes.

Single Ladies First Edition: The Original Single Lady

The video for *Single Ladies* was directed by Jake Nava and conceived in collaboration with Knowles.[7] Filmed in monochrome, Knowles and her two female backing dancers are presented in simple black leotards in an empty studio, dramatically lit but otherwise free of distractions, which firmly signals that the dance is the central feature of this work. Similarly there are relatively few close-ups and primarily seamless edits, the screen generously allowing space around all three bodies, which are presented in a triangular formation (Knowles center stage). The camera follows the continuous up-tempo routine to the end, finishing with a medium close-up of the three performers looking triumphant, breathing audibly from their exertion. The video was shot in tandem with the video for her single *If I Were a Boy*, and its minimalist form was the creative solution for the expenditure on this prior video (Cairns 2009). *Single Ladies* straddles the two prevailing formats of music video as both a "performance" and "concept" work (Austerlitz 2006, 1). As such, the video is equally dependent on Knowles's commanding performance and on the concept that underpins it and distances it from the sphere of live performance. In the video's renunciation of montage as the highest form of communication, it is part of a continuum of music videos that address the medium's visual excesses.[8]

As a work it also foregrounds one of the key aspects of Knowles's star persona: the hyper-visibility of her (often dancing), laboring body. Beyoncé always "works it," this is what Richard Dyer might term the "coherent continuousness" (1986, 11) of her self-presentation, which becomes the popular public conception of who Beyoncé Knowles *really* is. Knowles rose to international public awareness first as a member of the successful girl group *Destiny's Child*, which was managed by her father, Matthew Knowles, a university-educated businessman and entrepreneur. Via this child-star trajectory, her image has been protected from the start, progressing from talent shows, to a wholesome girl-group member, to a well-respected solo artist. Advantaged by the knowledge of the fraught route negotiated by African American girl groups from *The Ronettes* to *En Vogue*, she has not ascended via the teeth-and-nails glamour-girl route or that of the backing dancer catching the eye of a producer. Interestingly the "well-brought up" middle-classness of Knowles might have endangered her chances of popular appeal were it not for her famously puritan work ethic. This work ethic, grace, and desire for perfection of her art, places her within the group of "professional" stars complicit in the production of their own stardom (Dyer 1986, 14). The star image is then in Marxist terms both "congealed labour" used in the creation of each new song, album, or related cultural product, and the *thing* that their labor produces (Dyer 1986, 7).

Marx wrote that "labour is the worker's own life-activity, the manifestation of his life" (in Wayne 2003, 33). As such, labor is not only the thing that transforms the world, an essential practical creativity, but it is utterly vulnerable to capture by the capitalist system. Stars both "play out the way that work is lived in capitalist society" (Dyer 1986, 7) and are massively lucrative commodities themselves, tacked onto the bodies of living human beings. Although this corporeal link makes us seek moments of the "real" human within, stars tend to guard their privacy unless the real (i.e., vulnerable) version of themselves might help sell their product. Michel de Certeau writes that statistics can only "grasp the material used by consumer practices—a material which is obviously imposed on everyone by production—and not . . . their surreptitious and guileful 'movement', that is, the very activity of 'making do'" (1984, 35). Fans "make do" with the images they have of their stars, subverting and embellishing to suit their own purposes.

Contemporary racism dictates that black artists come under much more scrutiny than their white counterparts for their involvement in, and appropriation by, the culture industry (Cashmere 1997). The implied assumption is that it is somehow more distasteful for a black artist to realize the market potential of their artistry. Derek Conrad Murray argues that although hip hop is no longer revolutionary in the main, it is still transgressive in its facilitation and celebration of black achievement in the global economic arena (Murray 2004, 5). Indeed, it attained its legitimacy not through assimilation but through rugged individualism and "guerrilla capitalism" (Murray 2004, 8). As Matthew Knowles grew up during the 1960s and 70s, he could not have been unaware of President Nixon's call for African Americans to create a mainstream enterprise culture that would yield "Black Capitalism," and have the added advantage of decapitating the civil rights movement (Cashmere 1997, 153). This call is echoed throughout the pseudo-equality of the developed world, the fantasy of "don't dream it, be it" within an enterprise culture wherein if you don't succeed, it is only because you just didn't *want* it enough, and not attributable to social inequity.

Single Ladies Second Edition: *Single Ladies* vs. *Mexican Breakfast*

Single Ladies posting on YouTube was quickly followed by a user version created by painstakingly editing together parts of the footage of Beyoncé's single with footage from legendary choreographer Bob Fosse's *Mexican Breakfast* (1969) as performed on *The Ed Sullivan Show*.[9] The motivation and message of the user who created this edited version was one of extreme consternation; he claimed Knowles had no right to sample Fosse's movement in her work. The comments posted beneath were similarly outraged, calling Fosse a genius and Knowles a thief. The story was picked up by the international press, despite the fact that at the video's debut on public television Knowles had explicitly credited Fosse's piece, which, ironically, she first saw on YouTube, as the inspiration for the *Single Ladies* routine.[10]

As Ralph Ellison noted, "usually when you find some assertion of purity, you are dealing with historical, if not cultural ignorance" (in Dixon Gottschild 2003, 284). This outraged "counterpublic" is indicative of the online democratization of "specialization" and its attendant problems. For example, if the YouTube user who denounced the video as theft had any specialist knowledge beyond an intimate knowledge of Fosse's repertoire, he would have understood that Knowles is utilizing jazz, a dance form in which historically whites have emulated the stylistics of African American social dance without giving due credit or renouncing their "white privilege." White privilege, it should be emphasized, comprises of psychological privileges as well as material benefits. Fosse brought an affected coolness,[11] polyrhythm, and articulated torso to jazz dance that was deeply indebted to African American vernacular movement forms. However, this being America in the 1950s, he was neither obliged nor expected to credit his inspiration;

racial segregation and prejudice allowed for cultural ignorance or amnesia in support of a fantasy of white innovation and genius. Fosse used black vernacular movement with the explicit purpose of unlocking the sensuality of his dancers' own bodies, albeit in a tamed and titillating version, which would appeal to white audiences (Dixon Gottschild 2003, 46). The legacy of this puritan attitude about appropriate ways to articulate the body endures in the complaints of YouTube viewers who deride performers of dance hall moves for "dancing like sluts."

Barthes's final approach to the challenge of the text is that of pleasure (1977, 164). Crucially for Barthes, part of the bittersweet pleasure in reading is acknowledging that one cannot rewrite the very text one is reading. One can write something else that speaks to it, attempt a copy or homage, but this will always be different, because the context is different. As the text itself is a network, a combinatory system, Barthes argues that there is no vital "respect" due to the text; it can be "broken." Moreover it can be read without recourse to the authority of the "Author" (1977b, 161), a sentiment he prefigures in his famous text *The Death of the Author* (1977a). This is not to suggest that the figure of the author may not resurface in the text, but Barthes argues that when this occurs it is as a "guest" (1977b, 161) and as such "his life is no longer the origin of his fictions but a fiction contributing to his work" (1977b, 161).

So, what is at stake if we consider Bob Fosse as the Author of his choreographic style, or as the "true" author of *Single Ladies*? Fosse was an exceptionally famous choreographer, who substantially contributed to the fiction of his own creative genius. This was thanks in part to his prolific output in varied roles as choreographer, film director, actor, and dancer. He even directed a fantasy-biopic of himself entitled *All that Jazz* (1979). There have been numerous homages to Fosse's aesthetic[12] and much of the material has been absorbed into "cultural memory."

However, what separates Knowles's performance is that she doesn't set Fosse's material in a familiar setting, reminiscent of his own works. Instead she carries the movement away from the reference, creating a new artistic work in its own right. The works under consideration are very different. Her fellow performers are powerfully built women, technically excellent and formidably fierce. The routine skillfully fuses Fosse's vintage material with contemporary urban dance hall and gay club craze waacking, bringing an athleticism and power to her performance totally absent from Fosse's cute, soft-core jazz. The formal structure of the movement is performed either with all three dancers moving simultaneously or with an Africanist j-setting format with Knowles leading the others—and by proxy, the video's public—into a community of movement.

I read a cultural coup here, in the way in which Knowles has accentuated the Africanist underpinnings of jazz dance, an art form that had been sanitized and standardized by artists like Fosse. To borrow from Cornel West's elegant phraseology, she "pull(s) from past and present, innovatively producing a heterogeneous product" (West in Storey 1998, 391). This is the same method of revolt that Charlie Parker used against the white artists who had colonized jazz and turned it into the middle-class "jazz of the museum" (West in Storey 1998, 389).

Jean Baudrillard suggested that in our contemporary moment we are powerfully drawn to simulacra (1994), alternatively, one could highlight our contemporary search for origins or roots, and our fetishistic fabrication of them if none are apparent. A key feature of vernacular culture is its Authorlessness, its blatant delight in textual "poaching" (de Certeau 1984, xxi). Similarly, popular culture engenders an emotionally resonant and often thrilling sense of shared ownership: "I love that song!" "Me too!" It is important to establish that my concern in this chapter is not to establish the "truth" of the cultural origins of *Single Ladies*. Rather my criticism is of the drive toward fixedness inherent to that approach. However, it is equally important to address the historical, cultural politics of reification of white male genius and inspiration, and to continually trouble the canon. In seeking to emphasize Fosse's "genius" and damn Knowles's "copying," I can't help but be reminded of the Cartesian duality that still haunts readings of raced, sexed, and dancing bodies. That in this narrative of authenticity Fosse represents the head—as white, male, genius—and Beyoncé the body—as black, female, cipher, is depressingly familiar. That this scandal even occurred attests to the inequality in the social exchange of appropriation-approximation-assimilation (Dixon Gottschild 2003, 21) by dominant cultures. Expressed differently, if online media artifacts function as "prosthetic cultural memories" (Landsberg in Gehl 2004, 48), then they are as faulty and partial as real memories, and additionally only as rich as what is selected and uploaded.

SINGLE LADIES THIRD EDITION: WE ARE SASHA FIERCE (IN COMPETITION)

In 2009, Knowles's label, Columbia Records, launched an online competition for fan dance video versions of *Single Ladies*, with a prize of $2,500 and inclusion in Knowles's "I Am" World Tour (2009). Participants had to adhere strictly to the rules of the competition, including the stipulation that "Contestants should adhere precisely to the iconic *Single Ladies* dance routine performed by Beyoncé and her two dancers in the original clip—no new choreography should be added."[13] This stipulation has the effect of "fixing" the choreography of *Single Ladies* as an (iconic) object to be replicated rather than embellished. The resulting effect is what Harmony Bench terms a "viral choreography," as distinct from a "dance craze" in which one learns a few basic steps with which to improvise. The fan-editions of Single Ladies are faithful copies of the entire routine (Bench 2010).

As well as profiting Columbia, Knowles, and YouTube, user-generation creates free content for television chat shows in the form of human-interest stories and pre-generated media buzz. Not only do publics want to *know* stars, we also want to know those who achieve a kind of supplementary fame. For example, the queer re-imagining of *Single Ladies* undertaken by Shane Mercado catapulted him into minor celebrity with interviews and performances on talk shows such as *The Bonnie Hunt Show*. Stars operate by making us yearn for the *real* person behind the star image, the hints of a stable personality behind each vehicle. In a sense we look for clues in each new work produced, stars personifying Marx's adage that "It is not the consciousness of men that determines their existence, but, on the contrary, it is their social existence that determines their consciousness" (Marx 1904, 11). Further, identity is constituted not outside but within representation (Hall 2006, 19). Perhaps there is an act of substitution involved in our fascination with those made momentarily famous—they are just like us (and therefore knowable), but suddenly illuminated through relation to the unknowable, "auratic" star. These user editions of *Single Ladies* are judged and filtered by other users on a number of indexes of value: the skill in execution (often aided by the use of split-screen to watch the new version against the original); fidelity and commitment in learning the routine to performance standard; the bravery to make it public; adoration of Beyoncé; voyeuristic pleasure in grotesque or unusual bodies; or mockability. It is interesting that there were both queer male performances and heteronormative drag interpretations, of the latter notably a *Saturday Night Live* skit featuring Knowles herself, and a version by tween heartthrob Joe Jonas of the Jonas Brothers.

The necessary process of learning the routine for the competition through repeated viewings of the online video also ensured that the original would be at the top of the viewing tree. In addition, competitors would watch the videos uploaded by their competition and would keep checking back to read comments on their interpretation. One could argue that what we are currently participating in is a marketization of our online practices, part of what David Harvey describes as a neoliberal endeavor to "bring all human activity into the domain of the market" via technologies of information creation, accumulation, and storage, which then guide decisions in the global marketplace (Harvey in Dean 2009, 26). For this capture of consumer desire to be effective, we all need to feel that our personal opinions count, and interact with the Internet as producers rather than just users/consumers (Dean 2009, 24). In other words, we need to subscribe to the belief that "enhanced communications facilitates democracy" (Dean 2009, 25), although in this superabundance of comment and content it becomes even easier for messages to get lost, to disintegrate and warp like the secret in a game of Telephone. The marketing textbook *The Soul of the New Consumer* argues that the central obsession of today's information-bombarded consumers of non-essential items is for "authenticity" and "difference" and a search for quality that fascinates, rather than simple value for money (Lewis and Bridger 2001, 10). Lewis and Bridger are characterizing a type of developed-world, middle-class, concerned, ethical consumer with the required Internet access to fully participate online. Perhaps there are links between our online participation and our consumer behavior within "the discovery of difference, the establishment of difference and the appropriation of difference" (Yiannis Gabriel and Tim Lang in Lewis and Bridger 2001, 15). It is important to state that the flip side of this is the search to expose copying, inauthenticity, or cheating.

At the start of the twentieth century, Walter Benjamin wrote of the urge of the masses to "bring things 'closer' spatially and humanly...everyday the urge grows stronger to get hold of an object at very close range by way of its likeness, its reproduction" (1968,

223). Ironically, in the endless consumer-led uploading of fan-versions of cultural events like *Single Ladies*, while bringing the self into a relationship with the "original," the copy only enhances the "auratic" status of the original. Myriad *Single Ladies* do not circulate "unmarked" by their status as copies. The original is marked by several features, notably the presence of Knowles herself, the superior quality of production, quality of sound, number of views, and its position firmly at the top of the YouTube viewing tree. In other words, there is an underlying modal specificity to the Web life of *Single Ladies* and subsequent editions.

Single Ladies Fourth Edition: *Single Ladies* of Piccadilly Circus

I was hugely excited when a friend sent me the link to a video[14] that seemed to show a flash mob in Piccadilly Circus "spontaneously" enacting the *Single Ladies* dance. However, on closer inspection one realizes that the participants are all female, all dressed uniformly, and all proficient enough dancers to perform the routine. In fact, this event was staged in order to inspire audience delight, be captured on mobile phones, and disseminated as cheap viral advertising for Trident Gum, who was sponsoring a Beyoncé concert in the O2 arena at that time.[15] The campaign certainly performed, as the video debuted on the weekly Visible Measures Viral Video Chart as the second-most-watched video on the Internet, with 373,706 hits in its debut week.[16]

Although cautious notes have sounded of late, much of the initial, influential discourse on the Internet focused on its utopian potential,[17] its promise of disembodied democracy, new forms of learning, and knowledge production. In these narratives, the Internet is imbued with uncanny powers of representation, as if it were a magical glass that preserved and presented the voices of those not powerful enough to speak the language of official power. However, Henry Jenkins draws attention to the (often overlooked) paradox inherent in the continuing development of Web 2.0, as although the user is able to "archive, annotate, appropriate and re-circulate media content in powerful new ways" (2004, 33), there is an ever-shrinking pool of conglomerated media corporations that produces a huge amount of this content. This process of media convergence "alters the relationship between existing technologies, industries, markets, genres and audiences" (Jenkins 2004, 34). For example, a Beyoncé fan might look at the star's dedicated YouTube channel and find ads for her clothing venture *House of Dereon*, teasers for her new videos and album, charity appeals, the trailer for her 2008 film *Cadillac Records*, etc.

Why do Internet users re-edit, re-frame, and create paratexts for the cultural texts they consume? James Lull suggests that today we are all net-savvy "cultural programmers," who busily construct our own "customized clusters, grids and networks of personal relevance" (2001, 132). Lull calls this the individual constructing of "supercultures" (2001,

132), in which the "multi-accentuality" (Volosinov 1973, 23) of cultural texts becomes submerged in the narrative of that particular "programmer." Lull seems rather myopic in arguing that these supercultures "promote self-understanding, belonging, and identity while they grant opportunities for personal growth, pleasure and social influence" (2001, 132). It is vital to add here that all "supercultures" are not created equal. For example, what kind or level of "social influence" does participation ensure? What are the consequences of non-participation—a furtherance of the stratification of haves and have-nots in the world? Jodi Dean cautions: "what if the so-called facts circulate tribally, consolidating communities of the like-minded even as they fail to impress or even register to anyone else?" (2009, 147).[18] The Internet does seem to be enabling new forms of community that cut across localities and mobilities to coalesce around common intellectual, ideological, spiritual, or emotional investments. These knowledge cultures, however tactical or momentary, are held together and reaffirmed through co-production and knowledge exchange (Jenkins 2004, 35). However, research conducted into the directedness of online browsing suggests that the Web is broken into four major "virtual continents" each with their own navigational priorities. It is therefore totally possible that following links in one continent may never bring you into contact with data from another (Dean 2009, 43). This means that actually what happens online is further segmentation and isolation, rather than an opening up to other spaces and perspectives.

CONCLUSION: A HEDONIST AESTHETICS?

One must be careful when making claims for dance as a tool for political self-empowerment. Dance may well provide a kinaesthetic kick and make you "feel good," but in its muted representation it is an especially fertile area for cultural and political misrecognition. Black musicians and artists historically have used their bodies because it was often the only cultural capital they had (Stuart Hall in McClary 1994, 79). Obviously this is no longer the case, but black sports stars and entertainers live with the burden of a powerful and indelible archive of images of blackness. Moreover, for a black artist, dance's emphasis on physicality doesn't counter the suggestion that in negotiations between blacks and whites, the black "culture of expressivity" has been seen as their most valuable resource (Houston Baker in Cashmere 1997, 2), with the workable, desirable black body as commodity. Ironically, one significant value of black culture may be in providing whites with (premature) "proof" of the end of racism, that is, black culture is allowed to flourish while we retain the racial hierarchy intact (Cashmere 1997, 2)—something Paul Gilroy refers to as "redemptive diversity" (2002, 1). If it is true that whites are eager to employ and assimilate black language and culture, yet they fear black bodies and their experiences, what a complex set of entanglements for a pop star to negotiate.

Beyoncé doesn't neatly resolve the contradictions of her star-image, but rather appears to revel in it. Reflecting on the polarized and passionate feminist readings of

Knowles's work in the press and blogosphere, I posit that her critics might be looking for the wrong kind of political affirmation and failing to acknowledge the complexity of her subject position. Perhaps one should consider her fully as a Forbes feted African American capitalist icon[19] first, before considering how this clashes and intersects with other political readings. For example, a woman's assertion that she is financially independent and further, cannot be bought, has a doubly powerful meaning when spoken by a woman whose ancestors were literally enslaved. In an un-nuanced discourse, Knowles is trapped in a "double-bind" (Bateson 2000, 201), figured either as a conflicted woman, a victim of patriarchy and insufficiently feminist, or as a Diva, Bitch, or "disturbingly manly." These are problems that have always beset African American female stars attempting to work out a place in a cultural industry that still privileges and accepts ambiguity primarily from white stars. As bell hooks observes, "it is only as one imagines 'woman' in the abstract, when woman becomes fiction or fantasy, can race not be seen as significant" (hooks 1999, 124). Knowles's ability to employ a knowing irony, a predicate of much positive feminist analysis of white female stars like Madonna and Lady Gaga, is never suggested; instead, her canon is taken at face value.

I am reminded of Raymond Williams's call for a "cultural revolution (which) extend(ed) the active process of learning, with the skills of literary and other advanced communication, to all people rather than to limited groups" (1961 in Couldry 2000, 26). What are the limits of this online "participating democracy" (1961 in Couldry 2000, 26), if we do not similarly widen access to critical thinking about our increasingly net-mediated culture?

There are hundreds of websites and blogs devoted to processing and scrutinizing the moment's media events, with an emphasis on criticizing the official account and discerning "hidden patterns" across stories. Additionally, there are numerous gossip, spiritual, and occult websites with large numbers of participants discussing Knowles and other entertainers' demonic possession. Sites like vigilantcitizen.com combine media analysis with gossip and conspiracy theory; such sites are rampantly popular. Titles like *The 2009 VMAs: The Occult Mega-Ritual* might seem amusing at first glance, but the socio-political conclusions to draw are depressing. On answers.yahoo.com one young Canadian girl writes: "everyone is saying that Beyoncé and Jay Z are devil worshipers, is it true?" A respondent affirms, "you can tell they are because all her dreams have come true." No possibility, then, of success due to effort, ambition, or talent for this "counter-public." Although these confused fears bespeak a healthy suspicion of the media industry, one should be wary of overly positive accounts of this kind of popular knowledge; after all, these cohesive conspiracy beliefs show a woeful naivety concerning the creation of cultural artifacts (e.g., the suggestion that Knowles is signaling that she is a Satanist via a video she did not style, direct, or solely author), and more importantly mistake the inequalities that are integral to the capitalist system. Dean suggests that the international appeal of the 9/11 Truth Movement "manifests a shift in conspiracy thinking...from questioning to certainty" (Dean 2009, 148), which will have important implications for questions of knowledge and power. The Internet makes more transparent than ever the plurality of conceptions of what constitutes both "reality" and "truth," further dismantling Universalist claims.

Expounding on the plethora of user-led blogs, Jenkins argues that cultural theorists need to abandon our romance with the idea of audience resistance, and acknowledge that "contemporary consumers may gain power through the assertion of new kinds of economic and legal relations and not simply through making (resistant) meanings" (Jenkins 2004, 36). However, what are the limits to this empowerment if we are still primarily providing free labor for the corporations that are the infrastructure of the Internet? The ease with which media and information circulate on the Internet ironically means it is easier than ever for things to lose their specificity and merge with larger flows of data (Dean 2009, 26)—or as in the case of *Mexican Breakfast*, to be suddenly pulled out of the stream by the corporate owner, leaving all the paratexts floating adrift without reference to an "original."

Although the generations who have grown up with Internet access are highly sophisticated in the use of interface technologies, they often seem totally ignorant of how their own online activities market products and operate as free-labor, making enormous profits for companies offering "free" products, such as Facebook, YouTube, etc. This issue is at the heart of my concern with conspiracy readings of contemporary culture-making; they act as a veil to the real ideology at play in the culture industry. We may be seduced by the compelling image of our stars as "Illuminati Puppets," attending secret meetings, making pacts with the devil, and so forth; but behind the curtain are groups of workers, making deals, creating stars, and manufacturing popular culture.

NOTES

1. The song first debuted on the radio on 10/08/08, and the video debuted on MTV's *Total Request Live Show* on 10/13/08. *Single Ladies* is a double A-side lead single with *If I Were a Boy*, from the 2008 album *I Am...Sasha Fierce*, released by Columbia Records.
2. 276,290,651 recorded views at 02/10/14, +75 million views within the first year online.
3. Many of Knowles's recent music videos have been obsessively analyzed for "clues" to her satanic possession on the website www.vigilantcitizen.com, among others.
4. There were numerous postings, wiki questions, blogs, and so forth about the video that suggested one of the backing dancers was a man in drag, for example: http://www.mediatakeout. com/2010/27818-investigative_report_is_one_of_the_dancers_in_beyonces_single_ ladies_video_actually_a_dude_details__and_close_ups_inside.html
5. Since 2011, YouTube have been experimenting with the provision of original content.
6. Accurate at 02/10/14.
7. Choreographed by JaQuel Knight and Frank Gatson Jr.; the dancers are Ebony Williams and Ashley Everett.
8. For example, *Nothing Compares to You*, by Sinead O'Connor (1990), directed by John Mayberry; *Untitled*, by D'Angelo (2000), directed by Paul Hunter and Dominique Trenier; *Cold War*, by Janelle Monáe (2010), directed by Wendy Morgan.

9. Frustratingly, the original user-uploaded video of *Mexican Breakfast* spliced with *Single Ladies* has been removed by SOFA Entertainment (the owners of *The Ed Sullivan Show*), as has the video of *Mexican Breakfast*, however, periodically new versions emerge such as this one: http://www.youtube.com/watch?v=kjm8Wr22i3k

10. Knowles made this public announcement on the television shows *106 & Park* (*I Am! Season 2010*), the flagship show of the Black Entertainment Network (BET). In the vlog below a fan attempts to counter the Beyoncé "haters" with video evidence recorded from this show: http://www.youtube.com/watch?v=e-SlfHHd3qI&feature=related

11. Commentators have emphasized that behind the appearance of Coolness is the politics of disaffection (Cashmere (1997), 44) and (Dixon Gottschild 2003, 44).

12. For example: *Billie Jean* (1982), Michael Jackson, directed by Steve Barron; *Maybe* (2004), Emma Bunting, directed by Harvey and Carolyn, *Get Me Bodied* (2007), Beyoncé Knowles, directed by Knowles and Anthony Mandler.

13. http://www.beyonceonline.com/us/news/beyoncé-announces-official-single-ladies-dance-video-contest

14. This is the official recording uploaded by Trident/ Pretty Green, but other versions circulate.: http://www.youtube.com/watch?v=OLj5zphusLw

15. Trident Gum is a brand of Cadbury, the stunt was created by Pretty Green, and the concept by Initials Marketing.

16. http://adage.com/article/viral-video-charts/viral-video-trident-s-beyonce-dance-debuts-2/136473/

17. For example: Castells (2000), Coleman (2006), Trier (2007), Harroway (1991).

18. A charge that can similarly be leveled at this chapter in this academic volume.

19. See Beyoncé Knowles's profile on Forbes "Rich List": http://www.forbes.com/profile/beyonce-knowles/

BIBLIOGRAPHY

Althusser, Louis. "Ideology and Ideological State Apparatus." In *Mapping Ideology*, edited by Slavoj Žižek, 100–140. London: Verso, 1994.

Austerlitz, Saul. *Money for Nothing: A History of the Music Video from the Beatles to the White Stripes*. New York: Continuum, 2006.

Back, Les. "Aryans Reading Adorno." *Ethnic and Racial Studies*, 25 no. 4 (2002): 628–651.

Barthes, Roland. "The Death of the Author." In *Image, Music, Text*. Edited and translated by Stephen Heath. 142–148. London: Fontana Press, 1977a.

——. "From Work to Text." In *Image, Music, Text*. Edited and translated by Stephen Heath. 155–164. London: Fontana Press, 1977b.

Bateson, Gregory. *Steps to an Ecology of Mind*. Chicago: University of Chicago Press, 2000.

Bench, Harmony. "Screendance 2.0: Social Dance-Media." *Participations* 7, Issue 2 (2010). http://www.participations.org/Volume%207/Issue%202/special/bench.htm.

Benjamin, Walter. "The Work of Art in the Age of Mechanical Reproduction." In *Illuminations*. Translated by Harry Zohn. New York: Schocken Books, 1968.

Baudrillard, Jean. *Simulacra and Simulation*. Translated by Sheila Faria Glaser. Ann Arbor: The University of Michigan Press, 1994.

Cairns, Dan. "YouTube Plays Part in Beyoncé Knowles' Life" *The Sunday Times*, May 10, 2009.

Cashmere, Ellis. *The Black Culture Industry*. London: Routledge, 1997.

Couldry, Nick. *Inside Culture: Re-Imagining the Method of Cultural Studies*. London: Sage, 2000.

Dean, Jodi. *Democracy and Other Neoliberal Fantasies: Communicative Capitalism and Left Politics*. Durham, NC: Duke University Press, 2009.

de Certeau, Michel. *The Practice of Everyday Life*. Translated by Steven Rendall. Berkeley: University of California Press, 1984.

Dixon Gottschild, Brenda. *The Black Dancing Body*. New York: Palgrave McMillan, 2003.

Dyer, Richard. *Heavenly Bodies*. London: Macmillan Press, 1986.

Foucault, Michel. *The Archaeology of Knowledge*. London: Routledge, 1972.

Gehl, Robert. "YouTube as Archive: Who Will Curate This Digital Wunderkammer?" *International Journal of Cultural Studies* 12, no.1 (2009): 43–60.

Genette, Gérard. *Paratexts: Thresholds of Interpretation*. Translated by Jane E. Lewin. Cambridge: Cambridge University Press, 1997.

Gilroy, Paul. "'After the Love Has Gone': Bio-Politics and Etho-Poetics in the Black Public Sphere." *Public Culture* 7 (1994): 49–76.

——. "Ali G and the Oscars." *Open Democracy*. April 3, 2002. http://www.opendemocracy.net/faith-Film/article_459.jsp

Hall, Stuart. "Black Diaspora Artists in Britain: Three 'Moments' in Post-War History." *History Workshop Journal* 61 (2006): 1–24.

hooks, bell. *Black Looks: Race and Representation*. New York: South End Press, 1999.

Jenkins, Henry. "The Cultural Logic of Media Convergence." *International Journal of Cultural Studies* 7, no.1 (2004): 33–43.

Lewis, David, and Darren Bridger. *The Soul of the New Consumer*. London: Nicholas Brealey Publishing, 2001.

Lull, James. *Culture in the Communication Age*. London: Routledge, 2001.

Marx, Karl. *A Contribution to the Critique of Political Economy*. Translated by N. I. Stone. Chicago: Charles H. Kerr and Company, 1904.

McClary, Susan and Robert Walser. "Theorising the Body in African-American Music." *Black Music Research Journal* 14, no.1 (1994): 75–84.

Murray, Derek Conrad. "Hip-Hop vs. High Art: Notes on Race as Spectacle." *Art Journal* 63, no. 2 (2004): 4–19.

West, Cornel. "Black Postmodern Practices." In *Cultural Theory and Popular Culture, 2nd Edition*, edited by John Storey, 387–391. Harlow: Pearson Prentice Hall, 1998.

Wayne, Mike. *Marxism and Media Studies*. London: Pluto Press, 2003.

Warner, Michael. "Publics and Counterpublics." *Public Culture* 14, no.1 (2002): 49–90.

Volosinov, V. N. *Marxism and the Philosophy of Language*. Translated by Ladislav Matejka and I. R. Titunik. Cambridge, MA: Harvard University Press, 1973.

Websites and Hyperlinks

Adage.com: Viral Chart Figures for the week of April 27, 2009 http://adage.com/article/viral-video-charts/viral-video-trident-s-beyonce-dance-debuts-2/136473/

Beyonceonline.com: Columbia Records announces dance video competition.

Forbes.com: Knowles's profile on Forbes "Rich List" http://www.forbes.com/profile/beyonce-knowles

Mediatakeout.com: Gender trouble http://www.mediatakeout.com/2010/27818-investigative_report_is_one_of_the_dancers_in_beyonces_single_ladies_video_actually_a_dude_details__and_close_ups_inside.html

YouTubevideo:*SingleLadies(originalvideo)*http://www.youtube.com/watch?v=4m1EFMoRFvY

YouTube video: Beyoncé confirmed that *Single Ladies* video was indeed inspired by Broadway choreographer Bob Fosse (a fan addressing the scandal) http://www.youtube.com/watch?v=e-SlfHHd3qI&feature=related

YouTube video: Shane Mercado http://www.youtube.com/watch?v=IoRjc7HStoE

YouTube video: Shane Mercado on The Bonnie Hunt Show (11/18/08).

YouTube video: Saturday Night Live parody (11/15/08) http://www.youtube.com/watch?v=YFUQcG72130

YouTube video: *Single Ladies* flash mob (this is the official recording uploaded by Trident) http://www.youtube.com/watch?v=OLj5zphusLw

YouTube Global Blogspot: Zern, James (2011) *Mmm Mmm Good—YouTube Videos Now Served in WebM* http://youtube-global.blogspot.com/2011/04/mmm-mmm-good-youtube-videos-now-served.html, posted on 4/19/11, retrieved 5/26/11.

CHAPTER 18

THE DANCE FACTOR: HIP-HOP, SPECTACLE, AND REALITY TELEVISION

LAURA ROBINSON

"Sheer and utter perfection"
—*Simon Cowell*
"You have rendered me speechless"
—*Amanda Holden*
"Scintillating"

—*Piers Morgan*

ON Saturday, May 30, 2009, 18.5 million people sat down in front of their televisions and watched an eleven-piece all-male London street dance crew called Diversity compete against fellow London dance crew Flawless in the final of *Britain's Got Talent*, a U.K. ITV televised talent show that offers winners £100,000 and the opportunity to perform at the Royal Variety Show. Both crews' high-octane performances fused body popping, waving, and Nu-Skool hip-hop choreography with tight robotic unison, symmetrical group formations, virtuosic athletic stunts, comedic narrative, and popular intertextual references.

Alongside their ability to excite and entertain, these two-minute performances are steeped in meaning and require an interdisciplinary analytical approach, drawing upon the theoretical frameworks of popular dance, dance on screen, musicology, identity politics, television studies, and semiotics. Adding in the complex and fast-paced relationship between choreography, camera, and production, these tightly packed texts are also framed within the wider codified format of the televised talent show: a glossy, pre-packaged small-screen experience where backstage interviews, judge's comments, rehearsal footage, and personal accounts of the contestants' progressive journeys all expand the boundaries of performance beyond that of the staged choreographed material.[1] Coupled with the wider debates regarding celebrity culture and the commodification of dance practice, these street dance performances present an interesting challenge for the dance researcher in both their complexity and significance in popular culture. Drawing upon a textual analysis of Diversity's and Flawless's 2009 final performances, this chapter aims to equip the reader with the critical methods for exploring meaning within male group urban dance performances on the U.K. popular screen.

Guy Redden (2008) situates the contemporary revival of the televised talent show against popular British talent show programs from the 1970s and 1980s, including *New Faces* and *Opportunity Knocks*.[2] These programs showcased talent acts and relied on the studio audience to clap the loudest for their favorite act and for viewers to send in their winning choices on a postcard. The shift toward a virtual interactive relationship between audience and talent show began with *Popstars*, a televised contest to discover a new singing group, which gave power to the home viewer through the rapid processing of telephone, text, and online voting.[3] This format has evolved through other televised talent shows, including *X-Factor* and *Britain's Got Talent*, which combine "elements of lifestyle and reality with the classical talent search" (Redden, 2008, p. 3).[4] McMains (2010) analysis of the U.S. celebrity ballroom series, *Dancing with the Stars*, also highlights the importance of technological advances in production, with prior rehearsal and careful choices in camera angles and shots giving the home viewer a two-dimensional experience of televised dance.

Since the launch of *Come Dancing* in 1949, popular dance forms have become a major component of U.K. reality television broadcasting and advertising, and have been featured in large-scale media events, including viral flash mobs, televised world record attempts, 3D films, and prime-time competitive television programs (Fiske and Hartley, 1993). Adding to the contemporary televised competitive ballroom experience of *Strictly Come Dancing*, the popularity and media attention surrounding popular dance styles carved a space for other interactive televised talent show dance competitions, including BBC3's 2009 *Move like Michael Jackson* competition, and the 2010 launch of both Sky 1's *Got to Dance* and the U.K. version of *So You Think You Can Dance*, closely followed by BBC1's *Alesha's Street Dance Stars* in 2011.

Considering the burgeoning popularity of framing popular dance, and specifically hip-hop choreography, within a sensational and competitive televised format away from its traditional vernacular origins, it is surprising that televised talent show competitions remain an under-researched area of academic inquiry within popular dance studies. Juliet McMain's (2009) research frames ballroom dancing within American culture in *Dancing with the Stars*, but does not specifically focus on hip-hop dance within the reality format. In addition, Alexis Weisbrod's (2011) doctoral research situates the stereotypical presentation of the African American male hip-hop dancer within the U.S. version of *So You Think You Can Dance*, but does not consider the importance of production techniques or the dynamics of group performance.

Consequently, this chapter sets out to examine the importance of the connection between hip-hop performances and the remote voting audience through an influx of dynamic corporeal images and intertextual references to popular culture. Specifically, this chapter will consider the use of hip-hop dance vocabulary, the relationship between soundtrack and dance, the construction of a black masculine identity, and the importance of competition and commercialization within the two dance performances. While this research focuses on male street dance crews, it should be noted that mixed sex and all female urban dance groups do also compete, but to date they have not been given the equivalent presence and "air time" as their male counterparts, and consequently have not achieved the same level of notoriety within the televised format.

FROM STREET TO SCREEN

The populist history of hip-hop culture positions breakdance or b-boying as the founding stylistic pastime of the urban dance movement; an improvised form of physical graffiti that incorporates footwork, floor work, and end poses known as freezes (Fricke and Ahearn, 2002; Toop, 2000; Chang, 2005; Schloss, 2009). The dance itself was a physical manifestation of the hip-hop sound, and was performed in a circle in the break of the music. It incorporated top rock, a rhythmic stepping pattern that allowed the dancer to enter the circle and find the beat of the music, and floor work that included six steps (a series of six fast steps performed low to the ground) leading to power moves that incorporated improvised acrobatics, spins, and flips and ended in a freeze. In October 1982, the Rock Steady Crew, a famous U.S. East Coast b-boy group, appeared in the film *Flashdance* (1983), thus fueling the transnational spread of breakdance and other dance styles that sit under the banner of hip-hop, including West Coast funk dance styles and Chicago house dance. Young people across the globe began to copy the iconic and athletic shapes of the dancers (Osumare, 2007; Toop, 2000).[5]

In line with both the technological advances in music videos and the birth of MTV youth culture, late 1980s U.S. popular music artists, including MC Hammer, Michael Jackson, and Janet Jackson introduced hip-hop dance styles to new audiences away from the dance's vernacular origins and re-presented the styles in a choreographed and codified format (Goodwin, 1992). The popularity and visibility of these dances led to the media-generated umbrella term "street dance"—a dance genre with an urban aesthetic, incorporating hip-hop dance styles, jazz dance spatial formations, and gymnastics. In both Diversity's and Flawless's performances, hip-hop dance styles such as body popping, tutting, waving, and house dance steps are weaved into the pieces through group ensemble effects and merged with other dance styles and gymnastic stunts. Ashley Banjo, Diversity's choreographer, uses fluid waving through the body to smoothly morph the group into a three-tier robot (Fig. 18.1), while Flawless choreographer, Marlon Wallen, merges body popping with slow-motion isolations to travel backward in tight unison (Fig. 18.2).

Despite the recontextualization of the dance, the aesthetics of black social dance practice are still apparent within the performances. Brenda Dixon Gottschild's (1998) concept of the "Africanist aesthetic" provides a useful framework to describe the visual properties inherent in African-inspired dance forms, which include the qualities of polycentrism and polyrhythm, high-affect juxtaposition, ephebism, and the aesthetic of cool. Within these five themes, Gottschild (1998) observes other familiar traits of Africanist qualities, including asymmetricality, looseness, the valuing of repetition,

FIGURE 18.1 Diversity builds their three-tier robot.

FIGURE 18.2 Flawless uses isolated body popping to travel backwards.

Diversity: Dance Group - Britain's Got Talent 2009 - The Final   Like   share   More info

FIGURE 18.3 Diversity's upright and vertical stance performed in unison.

the grounded nature of the movement, and the importance of weight within the dance. Within both crew performances, the grounded quality of the movement is rooted in the loose nature of the wide-legged stance of the dancers, juxtaposed against the multiple rhythms and fast angular arm gestures released from this low center of gravity. In particular, Flawless's unison routine to the remixed soundtrack of heavy breathing incorporates polyrhythms across the body, with fast footwork contrasted against asymmetrical arm patterns and changes of direction. In addition, the nonchalant and relaxed performance quality of the dancers' movements contrasts against the intense power and effort of the dancers, titled the "aesthetic of cool" (Hazzard-Gordon, 1992; Gottschild, 1998). Diversity's oversized baseball caps hide their faces from the viewers, maintaining their calm exterior (Fig. 18.3), while the Flawless dancers actively use their comical facial expressions and eye contact with the audience to contradict the effort in their movements (Fig. 18.4). This performance strategy maintains a relaxed and laid-back manner to the choreography, and in turn heightens the spectacle of the dance.

Diversity's dancers remain far more vertical and centered throughout their performance, whereas Flawless's dancers inhabit a much lower center of gravity, with a wide stance, bent knees, and crossed arms. However, both performances demonstrate control and linearity through their rapid arm sequences and spatial positioning. Moving on then from Gottschild's Afrocentric model of cultural ownership, these physical variations in U.K. hip-hop dance style can be better understood through Halifu Osumare's concept of the "transnational body": hip-hop aesthetics exported globally though commercialization and subcultural networks and subsequently recontextualized and adapted with localized articulation (2007, pp. 16–17). By adapting their choreography

FIGURE 18.4 An example of Flawless's use of facial expressions.

to incorporate a higher center of gravity, comedic narrative, and a rapid fluctuation of images, the crews demonstrate a transnational body and in addition create an emotional connection between themselves and the voting audience.

THE MUSICOLOGY OF THE IMAGE

In their analysis of hip-hop dance, both Jonathan Jackson (2001) and Thomas DeFrantz (2002) highlight the important fusion between sound and movement, acknowledging how both black social dance and music utilize the same processes of experimentation and invention. In the case of the crew's choreographed performances, both groups compose fractured soundtracks consisting of spliced sound effects, spoken word, samples of film theme tunes and popular music tracks, electronic dance beats, and orchestral pieces to enhance the drama of the choreography.

In terms of a framework of analysis for these musical works, I draw upon Andrew Goodwin's (1992) study of MTV music video culture and his concept of the musicology of the image. Goodwin (1992) argues that moving bodies within music videos create a visual rhetoric through the underscoring of tempo, the mimicking of gestural rhythm and movement, the emphasis of accents, the visualization of lyrics and the corporeal display of dynamics. This synthesis between movement and music equates to a visual pleasure for the reader, and makes musical of the television image. Diversity's directional and rhythmic bodily visualization of the rap style superman quote, "Hold up, look

Diversity: Dance Group - Britain's Got Talent 2009 - The Final   Like   share   More info

FIGURE 18.5 Diversity's corporeal visualization of "Hold up, look up in the sky, is a bird, is a plane, nope."

up in the sky, is a bird, is a plane, nope," is an example of the soundtrack influencing the choreography, and the visualization of the music (Fig. 18.5).

I would maintain, however, that while the relationship between music and dance is closely linked in the context of televised talent show competitions, the change of context has reversed the emphasis from the visual images supporting the soundtrack to the oral accompaniment rating secondary to the spectacular choreography. For example, as the Diversity three-tier robot marches and strikes out to the side with its six arms, five heavy, rhythmic mechanical beats are layered on top of the choreography to enhance the robotic intertextual reference. In addition, the sharp cutting of camera shots from a wide shot to a medium close-up in unison with sound effects, lighting, and pyrotechnics all enhance the dynamic effect of the choreography.

Interestingly, then, Flawless's appropriation of Michael Jackson songs and dance motifs acts as both an homage to the late popular music icon, as well as a vehicle to allow a wider audience to access Flawless's style of street dance. Throughout their performance, the group utilizes several famous Jackson movement motifs, including angular knee flicks, tipped trilby hats and pelvis thrusts, and their soundtrack consists of Jackson tracks including "Smooth Criminal" (1988) and "Wanna Be Starting Something" (1983) in both their original and remixed format (Fig. 18.6). These popular intertextual references instantly create recognizable images and generate a visual connection between the remote audience and performer. When the songs are presented in a remixed format, though, Flawless's choreography shifts to Nu-Skool choreography: complex arm and step patterns mixed with gymnastic stunts. Here, the soundtrack is used to not only

FIGURE 18.6 Flawless appropriates Michael Jackson's iconic hip thrusting stance.

create a link with the popularity of the Michael Jackson images but also demonstrate the evolution and creativity apparent in the crew's choreography.

Breakin' Identity

One of the main values of analyzing male urban dance competitive performances lies in the consideration of these texts as sites of knowledge formation, Afro-diasporic cultural expression, and construction of individual young black male identity. Tricia Rose (1994), Katrina Hazzard-Gordon (1996), and Sally Banes's (2004) historical analyses of breakdance concur that in the style's early development, the projection of male dominance can be viewed as a reaction to the hostility of the socio-economic climate, as crews battled on street corners to claim territory through the inscription of personal identity onto city surfaces, with freezes acting as metaphorical graffiti tags.

Though televised crew performances are far removed from the street corner battles, I would maintain that the need to project a strong and masculine presence through urban dance styles and the claiming of space is still apparent in the televised performances of Flawless and Diversity. In particular, the extensive use of strict symmetrical unison within both pieces creates the impression of a single, strong male unit moving as one. This uniform approach to the choreography is coupled with the regimented costume, stationary camera shots capturing the action across the entire stage, and the aural accompaniment of the audience's positive elation. By performing complicated

FIGURE 18.7 Diversity's jet plane formation.

polyrhythmic sequences in tight unison, the dancers are presented as a strong community unit—a collective whose success is only determined by the individual performances of its counterparts.

Furthermore, Banjo creates a series of popular intertextual references within Diversity's performance by using the bodies of the crew to create the image of transformer robots, machine guns, and aliens. As the group forms the shape of a jet plane, a young dancer runs from upstage and front-flips over the plane toward the audience while light effects shoot forward from the back display screen to create the effect of a launch. All these choices signify popular pastimes for young boys and males alike, and create an important shared popular reference between audience and performer. I would also maintain, though, that these group formations also resonate a phallic symbolism,[6] with both groups performing choreography and group freezes within spatially formed pointed diamonds toward the audience (Fig. 18.7). While this shape allows heightened visibility of all group members, it also presents the male dancers within a powerful and dominant spatial pattern.

Despite these overtly masculine and potentially imposing images, both groups remain accessible to the television audience by incorporating parody and fun into their routines. Diversity creatively mocks the talent show contest they are competing in by recreating the image of a bad singer and three judges (Fig. 18.8). In comparison with the sharp angles and wide-open stances of the previous choreography, the group's movements are far more expressive, using large circular arm gestures, tilted front knees, and nodding head gestures, accompanied by C&C music factory's "Gonna Make You Sweat (Everybody Dance Now)" (1990). I would argue that Banjo uses this clever parody not

Diversity: Dance Group - Britain's Got Talent 2009 - The Final   Like   share   More info

FIGURE 18.8 Diversity's parody of the *Britain's Got Talent* judging panel.

only to provide a comical intertextual reference for the audience, but also to reaffirm the group's strong and dominant presence in the rest of their choreography.

Additionally, Flawless frames its routines within the narrative of a journalist trying to take a photograph of the winning talent show group. The photographer catches the group with wide leg stances, bent knees, crossed arms while performing repetitive isolated hip thrusts toward the camera, accompanied by rhythmic drumbeats (Fig. 18.9). While this overtly sexualized and masculine image is potentially alarming to the family audience, the speed of the image is swallowed up within the fast moving pace of the dance and swiftly balanced out by a light-hearted, funk-inspired homage to James Brown's "I Feel Good" (1965). In addition, the photographer's shocked face mimics the potential audience's reaction, suggesting that the group is making a tongue-in-cheek reference to the potency and significance of the image.

Another display of masculine presence is constructed through the use of virtuosity and athleticism within the dances. DeFrantz comments that virtuosity is achieved in hip-hop dance through the physical tightness of the body combined with the visualization of sharp rhythmic phrases and polyrhythms and accents, which equates to an "outwardly-explosive directness of precision" (2004, p. 74). In both Diversity's and Flawless's performances, this explosiveness is pre-choreographed using breakdance power moves, including one-handed freezes and head spins, as well as virtuosic back flips and perfectly timed aerial tumbles over other dancers (Fig. 18.10). These tricks are intensified through the use of camerawork, with shots cutting from a very wide angle to capture the beginning of the front flip, and then cutting into a close-up of the dancer mid-air to heighten the athleticism of the movement. Similar to Juliet McMains's

FIGURE 18.9 Flawless performs their repetitive hip thrusts to the camera, looked on by the shocked photographer.

observations of the heightened melodrama apparent within the "picture-perfect poses" of ballroom dancing in the U.S. television show, *Dancing with the Stars,* Diversity's and Flawless's stunts and tricks incite screams and cheers from the studio audience, requiring the tricks to become more impressive as the dance progresses (2010, p. 263).

While these physical stunts are visually impressive, Ken Mcleod's (2009) analysis of African American sports and music practices links the need for dominance and athleticism within hip-hop dance with the black male experience, asserting that the impressive and spectacular performances in fact reaffirm the stereotypical constructed image of the black male as a symbol of manliness and aggression, and in turn endorses the African American man's seclusion from the mainstream. Alexis Weisbrod's doctoral research into American competition dance also reveals that in the U.S. version of *So You Think You Can Dance,* the program categorizes the hip-hop dancer as having no formal training, as the style is learned "from the streets," reaffirming the stereotype of the oppressed African American male by constructing an urban identity (Weisbrod, 2010, p. 166).

While I would agree that a dominant and masculine identity is constructed through the use of hip-hop vocabulary, sound track, and an aggressive dynamic, I would also argue that these virtuosic displays of athleticism are linked with the tight temporal framework of the televised competition, as the performers must engage and impress the judges and audience in under two minutes, requiring an intensity and compression of the choreography. This intensity is also heightened through the episodic structure of the pieces, the fast cutting of the sound track, and the constant shift in camera angles to reflect the fast-paced nature of the pieces. Consequently, I contend that the textual

Flawless: Dance Group - Britain's Got Talent 2009 - The Final   Like   share   More info.

FIGURE 18.10 Flawless ends its performance with a downstage two-man aerial acrobatic tumble.

analysis of these performances cannot be situated within the choreography alone, and must therefore take into account the encompassing televised competitive framework.

"Chase the Dream, Not the Competition"

Guy Redden (2008) situates the genre of the talent show within a long history of competition on television, including sports, quizzes, and game shows, and argues that it would be incorrect to dismiss the make-over television formats as purely entertainment, as the themes of risk and opportunity are reflective of broader society.[7] He comments though, that unlike other reality television shows, such as quiz shows, the talent show rewards "deserved fame"—artistic achievement that is far more complex to appreciate and classify in a competitive framework (2008, pp. 11–12). While Flawless's and Diversity's performances take place in the theatricalized environment of the proscenium arch stage, the codes and conventions of the televised competition are ever-present and frame the dances within the wider performance of the television program. The audience is dually presented in the visual representation of the studio audience and the acknowledged virtual community around the U.K. and beyond, who consume the program in the private sphere. The background noise of the screaming audience is present throughout the performances, reacting with excitement to moments of virtuosity, while the heads of the judges remain ominously present in the very wide camera shots.

Both Redden (2008) and McMains (2010) comment on how the panel of judges in televised talent show competitions not only provide scores and feedback, but also provide the home audience with the relevant vocabulary required to discuss and debate the performances and potentially shape the result of the interactive voting. McMains (2006) observes, though, that in these competitions, judgment and evaluation occur without the advertised formal structure of rules and criteria, and this allows for human influence and discrepancy. Redden (2008) comments that these debates provide a vital source of entertainment due to conflicting decisions, and that the dramatic tension of the program merges with the spectacular and intense choreography to heighten the themes of risk, opportunity, and chance. In their prerecorded interviews shown immediately prior to their performances, both Flawless and Diversity crews reiterate this drama, with comments including, "there's a lot of expectations on us tonight, so we've got to go out and do everything we can, you know, who dares wins," and, "as soon as we step on that stage, it's going to be the biggest moment of our lives." Such dramatic statements heighten the tension in the performances, making the viewing experience even more engaging and adding to the televisually constructed narrative of competition.

McMains observes that in ballroom dancing competitions, the mechanisms of competition are in full view, and that "the physical proximity of desired objects (including people, costumes, money, and dance skill) and that which they symbolize (fame, power, recognition, and intimacy) intensifies the promise of eventual accessibility" (2006, p. 4). This close geographical proximity of desired prizes is also apparent within *Britain's Got Talent*; the opportunity to perform in front of 18 million people, as well as media exposure and fame already encountered by participating on the program heightens the desire to win. Both Redden (2008) and McMains (2006) comment, though, that while the desire to succeed drives the dancer to master his or her own body, the process is unfulfilling, as the desire for fame and social transformation is very rarely achieved.

Redden extends this observation, stating that by coupling ordinariness with a dramatic emphasis upon the reality of the contestant's experiences, the producers carefully build a notion of a contestant's journey and progression through the program. Despite their gravity-defying choreography and ability to perform in perfect unison, Flawless members describe themselves as "just a group of mates from North London," while Diversity members emphasize the importance of community over the desire to win, stating, "to be doing this with my brother and my best mates; it's just the best feeling in the world you know." These individual interview accounts of the urban dancers normalize their experiences and background, creating a vital link between the viewer's everyday experience and those of the performer. Consequently, Redden (2008) argues that these programs are reflective of an aspirational society that desires a life away from the ordinary, and this is exaggerated by the ecstatic and dream-like portrayal of winning. By celebrating those contestants who prove themselves to be special, the programs re-present working-class life as something from which to escape, which in turn marks ordinary contestants as inferior.

I would, however, extend Redden's argument to include the visual construction of a community unit. Despite their differences in background and age, both crews place emphasis on the value of community and friendship by presenting themselves as a close-knit family in their interviews and their choreography, and this is a positive message that will appeal to a wide audience. When receiving their final comments from the judges, both crews demonstrated a united front by holding onto each other, with the implied message of "whatever happens, we've got each other." This sense of community reflects the original ethos of hip-hop culture and at the same time contests the media-generated images of egocentric gangster culture observed in rap music, neutralizing the dance form so that it's accessible for the talent show audience.[8]

DANCING THE COMMERCIAL

Finally, it is vital to consider the capitalist modes of production and dissemination apparent in televised talent show competitions. Interestingly, street dance is commonly referred to as "commercial dance": a firm nod toward the dance's presence as a commodity within modes of capitalist production, including television advertisements, music videos, concerts, and television appearances.[9]

Redden (2008) comments on how access to the life-changing opportunities offered by televised talent shows is unrestricted in that anyone is welcome to audition, although success remains limited. This process mirrors capitalism in that success is only available to the few, which also reflects the broader economy in that the value of people is determined by the controlling markets (Redden, 2008). Contestants must modify their behavior and work hard in order to achieve, as success in the entertainment industry equates to financial gain, celebrity social status, and opportunity. This work ethic is reflected in the crew's interviews: Flawless members stress how they have practiced through the night and battled through injury and tiredness, while Diversity members state that "they are gonna dance harder than they've ever danced before." Since their appearances on the show, both crews have experienced celebrity status and opportunity through theater and stadium tours and television appearances. In addition, Ashley Banjo from Diversity became a judge on a televised talent show, Sky 1's *Got to Dance*. In terms of financial wealth, though, neither crew has experienced the level of economic success equivalent to that of fellow singing finalist Susan Boyle, who in 2010 was estimated to be worth £11 million.[10] Consequently, it can be argued that regardless of the level of effort and opportunity, popular dance still remains a financially undervalued practice within contemporary society, specifically when linked to racialized bodies that can be regarded as expendable commodities in and of themselves.

Similar to McMain's (2006) analysis of Dancesport, it can be argued that street dance represents the celebration of the "cult of surfaces": the increasing desire for the false commodities of fame, power, and social mobility. This acute consciousness of the externalization of shapes and positions of the body resonates with DeFrantz's (2004) argument regarding the communicative meanings apparent in hip-hop dance, and how the "subsequent reproduction of the dances by people looking only from the outside leads to the flat, militaristic repetition commonly viewed in the commercial music video sphere" (DeFrantz, 2004, p. 68). While these arguments are important in understanding the commodification of urban dance practice, I would also argue that the formal and codified competitive structure of televised talent show competitions re-present street dance practice as both a way of maintaining positive social identity and as a physical device to advance social status. When observing the complete package of choreography, competitive structure, and televised production, I contend that the rapid changing of virtuosic and spectacular images is in fact reflective of the fast-paced and mediated nature of contemporary society and creates a renewed communal link between the performer and the virtual audience.

NOTES

1. Juliet McMains (2010) argues that the talent contest is judged by the viewer on the extensive "backstage" coverage and biographical attention just as much as on the performances themselves.
2. *New Faces* was a British talent show that ran from 1973 to 1988. *Opportunity Knocks* was a series of programs in which variety and musical performers are judged by the studio and TV audience (British Film Institute Database, 3/8/11).
3. *Popstars* was first aired in New Zealand in 1999 (Redden, 2008).
4. *The X-Factor* is a televised competition to find singing talent (http://xfactor.itv.com/).
5. *Flashdance* (1983) tells the story of Alex, a Pittsburgh woman who works as a welder and an exotic dancer, and who wants to get into ballet school. The Rock Steady Crew was featured in a small scene within the film, where Alex and her friend are walking through the city and stop to watch the breakdancers.
6. Here I am drawing a parallel between the role of the phallus as a symbol of power and the imposing masculinity of the group formation.
7. For further reading on the importance of entertainment, see Richard Dyer, 1992.
8. For further reading regarding hip-hop music culture, see Tricia Rose, 2008.
9. For further reading about dance as a commodity, see Sherril Dodds, 2005.
10. Susan Boyle Net Worth. www.therichest.org [January 27, 2012].

WORKS CITED

Banes, Sally. "Breaking." In *That's the Joint!: The Hip-hop Studies Reader*, edited by Murrey Forman and Anthony Marc Neal, 13–20. London and New York: Routledge, 2004.
British Film Institute Database. "Opportunity Knocks." Accessed August 3, 2011. http://ftvdb.bfi.org.uk/sift/title/410764.
British Film Institute Database. "New Faces." Accessed August 3, 2011. http://ftvdb.bfi.org.uk/sift/series/343.

Chang, Jeff. *Can't Stop Won't Stop: A History of the Hip Hop Generation.* New York: St. Martin's Press, 2005.

DeFrantz, Thomas. "The Black Beat Made Visible: Body Power in Hip hop Dance." In *Of the Presence of the Body: Essays on Dance and Performance Theory,* edited by Andre Lepecki, 64–81. Middletown, CT: Wesleyan University Press, 2004.

Dodds, Sherril. *Dance on Screen: Genres and Media from Hollywood to Experimental Art.* New York: Palgrave MacMillan, 2004.

Dyer, Richard. *Only Entertainment.* 2nd ed.. New York: Routledge, 2002.

Fiske, J and J. Hartley. "Dance as Light Entertainment." In *Parallel lines: Media Representations of Dance,* edited by Stephanie Jordan and Dave Allen, 37–50. London: J. Libbey and Co. Ltd, 1993.

Fricke, Jim, and Charlie Ahearn. *Yes Yes Y'all: the Experience Music Project Oral History of Hip-Hop's First Decade.* Cambridge, MA: Da Capo Press, 2002.

Goodwin, Andrew. *Dancing in the Distraction Factory: Music Television and Popular Culture.* Minneapolis: University of Minnesota Press, 1992.

Gottschild, Brenda Dixon. *Digging the Africanist Presence in American Performance: Dance and other Contexts.* Westport, CT: Praeger, 1998.

Hazzard-Gordon, Katrina. "Dance in Hip Hop culture." In *Droppin' Science: Critical Essays on Rap music and Hip Hop Culture,* edited by William Eric Perkins, 220–237. Philadelphia: Temple University Press, 1996.

ITV. "X-Factor Official Site." Accessed January 4, 2012. http://xfactor.itv.com/2011/news/.

Jackson, Jonathan David. "Improvisation in African-American Vernacular Dancing." *Dance Research Journal* 33 (2001), 2: 40–53.

McLeod, Ken. "The Construction of Masculinity in African American Music and Sports." *American Music* 27 (2009) 2: 204–226.

McMains, Juliet. *Glamour Addiction: Inside the American Ballroom Dance Industry.* Middletown, CT: Wesleyan University Press, 2006.

——. "Reality Check: Dancing with the Stars and the American Dream." In *The Routledge Dance Studies Reader,* 2nd ed., edited by Alexandra Carter and Janet O'Shea, 261–272. London and New York: Routledge, 2010.

Osumare, *Halifu. The Africanist Aesthetic in Global Hip-Hop: Power Moves.* New York: Palgrave Macmillan, 2007.

Redden, Guy. "Making over the Talent Show." In *Exposing Lifestyle Television: The Big Reveal,* edited by Gareth Palmer, 129–143. Aldershot and Burlington: Ashgate, 2008.

Rose, Tricia. *Black Noise: Rap Music and Black Culture in Contemporary America.* Hanover, NH: University Press of New England, 1994.

——. *The Hip Hop Wars: What We Talk about When We Talk about Hip Hop—and Why It Matters.* New York: Basic Civitas, 2008.

Schloss, Joseph, G. *Foundation: B-boys, B-girls, and Hip-Hop Culture in New York.* New York: Oxford University Press, 2009.

Toop, D. *Rap Attack 3: African Rap to Global Hip Hop.* 3rd ed. London: Serpent's Tail, 2000.

Weisbrod, A. "Competition Dance: Redefining Dance in the United States." PhD diss., University of California, Riverside, 2010.

YouTube. "Diversity Final Britain's Got Talent—Grand Final HQ HD Original Full 2009." Accessed January 4, 2012. http://www.youtube.com/watch?v=B-08egEWiZE.

YouTube. "Flawless (HQ) FINAL BGT 2009." Accessed January 4, 2012. http://www.youtube.com/watch?v=1tQcHDWlSP0.

CHAPTER 19

....

DEFINING DANCE, CREATING COMMODITY: THE RHETORIC OF *SO YOU THINK YOU CAN DANCE*

....

ALEXIS A. WEISBROD

As a vehicle that presents dance to millions of American viewers, as well as international audiences through various incarnations, *So You Think You Can Dance* (SYTYCD) can be credited with increasing the accessibility of dance by bringing different dance styles directly into the audiences' homes. One of several recent pop culture phenomena that have removed the financial costs generally associated with American concert dance, *SYTYCD* auditions thousands of dancers in search of "America's Favorite Dancer" and makes the entire experience widely available through network television. In an era of reality television, *SYTYCD* successfully connects Americans across the country with a structure of dance performance that allows them to be viewers *and* participants. The show gives its audience a greater sense of familiarity with dance, empowering audience members to dialogue with and about the practice in greater detail or, possibly, for the first time. However, the resulting discourse is one that is influenced by the distinct framework provided by the show's producers.

So You Think You Can Dance has foregrounded many forms of dance in media and popular culture. In an effort to legitimize dance as a form of art and communication worthy of a greater cultural status than it is currently afforded within the United States, the show alters and recontextualizes dancing bodies in order to make its images accessible for a wide audience. The result is not a legitimization of a preexisting form of dance but, instead, a popularization of a new practice, a carefully constructed bricolage of dance that spectacularizes white and non-white bodies alike through a particular rhetoric. This piece examines how *SYTYCD* juxtaposes dancing bodies deemed traditional—those trained in a studio—and non-traditional bodies—including those trained in non-normative spaces (i.e., urban)—through its unique construction of dance created by the show's producers. I consider how the show's lexicon, specifically the words and rhetoric used by the judges, creates bodies and racially marks dance movement and genres as a tool for audience use as they read dance in the mediated space of *SYTYCD*.

With viewers voting to determine the winner, the show's producers, judges, and choreographers frame dance and dancing bodies for ease of accessibility and understanding. In her text *Dance on Screen* Sherril Dodds writes, dance "on film and television is influenced by... economic, political, technical and aesthetic components and, in turn, the images that are screened shape the spectator's perception of dance."[1] *SYTYCD* shapes audience perception in several ways. As with any mediated version of dance, the apparatus capturing the images establishes limitations on audience reading, which is the result of multiple cameras, various angles, and shots. Much like the music video, dances consist of multiple edits, with shots varying in length but always changing in relation to beats or accents in the music. However, unlike the music video, which often switches between scenes and ideas in order to give the audience lots of information quickly, *SYTYCD* displays only the dance and its bodies. Filmic dance, which works to convey character development as well as storyline, generally cuts between segments of the body, such as the legs, buttocks, or face, the body as a whole dancing image, and other images, including additional characters, whereas *SYTYCD* frames the dance as an almost complete image. Using various angles, the show's producers retain a sense of the proscenium stage, only filming from the front portions of the performance space.[2] With exception of the occasional brief close-up of a contestant's face, the camera keeps the dancing body/ies centered in the frame, allowing the television audience to see the dance as a single entity.[3] Although this frame provided by the apparatus is crucial, it is not the only one shaping audience perceptions.

The structure of the show works to integrate audiences into a particular understanding of dance, creating a collective viewing experience, regardless of an individual's previous knowledge of dance. John Fiske, in *Reading Television*, suggests that dance on television functions to manage "the tensions inherent in our social structure and activity."[4] *SYTYCD* incorporates both sets of codes defined by Fiske—1. "Sport as ritualized social conflict" and 2. "Dance as ritualized social coherence"—as it uses competition and conflict to merge an audience under a singular dance viewing practice.[5] Moreover, it uses "code of sport" such as "signs of comparison and evaluation of performance," while also uniting bodies through similar and shared performances. Relying on a familiar structure of competition, which creates alliances and conflicts, audiences are instructed to read dance through a unifying framework presented by the show. Utilizing a familiar competitive structure, *SYTYCD* foregrounds dance as entertainment, shaping dancing bodies into commodities for consumption by mainstream media and popular culture as dancers lose subjectivity and become an object created through the agenda of the show.

Judge and producer Nigel Lythgoe defines dance's role during the show's first season when he notes: "It is unfair to ask [viewers] to understand the technicalities of dance. They want to be entertained."[6] In this statement, Lythgoe establishes the parameters within which he expects the audience to be knowledgeable, while also situating *what* dance should be and *how* audiences should perceive it. Lythgoe is suggesting that if the audience is "bored" they can discern that the dance and/or dancers must have some-how failed.[7] To avoid this, dances and dancers must conform to expectations of popular culture, including ideas and aesthetics that are readily accepted into mainstream cul-ture. Lythgoe also effectively indicates the judges' position as mediators, translating the necessary information (including the physical technique of different dance forms) for voting audiences. This positioning is reinforced for audiences in host Cat Deeley's com-mon introduction of the judges as "experts" there to "help [the audience] make [their] decisions."

The initial stage of the show consists of auditions in various locations across the United States, during which the notion of the dancing body as commodity begins to be established. Most often dancers perform a brief solo, although ballroom dancers typically audition in partners. From this solo dancers are labeled according to genres, such as hip-hop, contemporary, Latin ballroom, tap, krump, etc. This label both leads and follows dancers in to further stages of the show, becoming the primary descriptor for each dancing body. Based on this audition, judges Nigel Lythgoe, Mary Murphy, a rotating third judge, and the occasional fourth judge,[8] a seat usually occupied by one of the show's popular choreographers, either reject the dancer, send them "directly to Vegas" with the presentation of a plane ticket, or ask them to stay for "Choreography," at which point they are taught a short dance phrase of partner work and then eliminated or sent to Vegas.[9] Although the audition phase works to introduce viewers to participants, it also assists in giving viewers a point of comparison in order to gauge the talent and use-value[10] of dancing bodies, a necessary ability when the voting process begins.

The dancers who make it to "Vegas Week" continue through multiple waves of auditions over the course of several days. Each wave is defined by a different style of dance—hip-hop, ballroom, contemporary, Broadway, etc.—and a different choreogra-pher, in order to gauge which dancers are able to successfully traverse the multitude of dance styles that they will have to perform during the competition portion of the show. In Season 2, Lythgoe makes sure to remind the dancers that if he does not feel they are capable of performing on the show he "will overrule everyone at this [judges'] table, [he] will not have [them] on the show."[11] In this brief moment Lythgoe makes the actual authority of the producers transparent, partially removing the power instilled in dancers as skilled bodies and that of the audience as active participant. The factors of Lythgoe's determination of who can be on the show can only be assumed. Physical appearance, personality, and the overall complexion of the final Top 20 must surely play a role. Regardless, Lythgoe asserts his power as the final determinate of who is worthy of being commodified, giving the commodified bodies even greater cultural status as a result of achieving this elite role.

Vegas Week concludes with the determination of the Top 20 dancers and the interac-tive audience's options predetermined.[12] Each week dancers, in heterosexual couplings, randomly pick genres such as hip-hop, krumping, *Paso Doble*, quickstep, contempo-rary, jazz, Broadway, and *cha cha* to perform.[13] Because the competition portion of the show relies on audience votes to determine the bottom three couples, from which the judges eliminate one female and one male (later these votes eliminate dancers directly), situating each dance and dancer within the codes and context of each genre is vital in adequately framing the performance for the audience, specifying and limiting their reading of and understanding of these dance genres.[14] As a result, it is critical that the labels of dancing bodies as well as the history and technique of each dance form, as conceived by the show's producers and judges, be successfully conveyed to the audience. The rhetoric used by judges to define each dancer since their arrival on the show becomes central to the audiences' voting process.

As judges critique dancers, the labels attributed to each become attached to a *conceived body* that informs the dancer's performance for the benefit of the viewer. Modifying Susan Foster's notion of the "perceived body," which is the physical body the dancer observes in his/her reflection that is composed of "skeletal, muscular, and nervous systems and any fat tissue of the biological body," I define the conceived body as the one created for and imagined by the audience *in relation* to the label initially attributed to the dancer.[15] This body exists in the reflection of the audience as they create ideas of who the physical body *should* look like within a certain dance form and in relation to the label of the dancing body. While the individual dancer/contestant may envision a different, perceived body, the one offered to and conceived of by the interactive audience is the most important to her/his overall role on the show. A contestant's label and conceived body suggests her/his training background, which is necessary in determining how successful she/he is on the show. For example, it is assumed that the dancer labeled "ballroom" is able to perform partnered movements and footwork with skill but that traditional (i.e., ballet) upper-body carriage found in lyrical and contemporary or the quick isolations and "funky" attitude of hip-hop will not be easily adapted by the ballroom dancing body. Therefore, if s/he performs a genre beyond her/his label well, beyond the skills of her/his conceived body, she is praised for her ability to do the unexpected, elevating her status on the show.

Without identifying the label as a *specialty*, it becomes the primary mode for defining and commodifying these dancing bodies. *SYTYCD*'s judges and producers present each dancer as if they are only trained in a single form of dance. Not since the first season, when some dancers were described with multiple genres (i.e., "hip-hop/jazz" or "lyrical/gymnastics") has it been suggested that any dancer is trained in multiple forms. With every season these labels have become more codified and have shifted away from multi-discipline labels, illustrating the show's creation of strict one-dimensional dancing bodies. For example, Season 4's Joshua Allen who auditioned with hip-hop choreography (Fig. 19.1) Ultimately, each of these labels and genres is made familiar for the audience based upon the rhetoric of the judges that is produced as they response to each performance. Although it did not become a label until Season 2, the show's most popular label, "contemporary," was used to classify twelve of the Top 20 dancers in Season 4, ten in Season 5, and never any less than seven in later seasons.[16] By Season 5 "contemporary" appeared every week in a choreographed duet and twice in Season 8. Throughout Season 1, bodies that would later be tagged contemporary were known as lyrical dancers. Originating in the industry of dance studios and competitions, the term "lyrical," with the exception of its use early on in *SYTYCD*, remains only in these amateur spaces.

FIGURE 19.1 Screen capture of Joshua Allen at his Dallas, Texas Audition. Season 4, Episode 2, original air date, May 28, 2008.

Most likely to validate its production of dance, *SYTYCD's* evolution from lyrical to contemporary marks a shift away from amateur stages and a move toward traditional Euro-American concert dance production. In contrast to lyrical, contemporary holds a long-standing role in Western concert dance. Choreographers such as Deborah Hay, Cunningham, and Balanchine are commonly regarded as "contemporary" American choreographers. For example, in her 1997 text *Choreographing Difference*, Ann Cooper Albright defines contemporary dance as "the experimental dance that has taken place over the past decade...rooted in Euro-American modern and postmodern dance, much of this work takes on the hybridity of contemporary culture, at once deconstructionist and visionary," separating it from the postmodern genre.[17] However, the "contemporary" presented on *SYTYCD* does not resemble that created by contemporary concert choreographers nor does it fit Albright's definition.

In this attempt to identify with traditional concert dance, the show creates a new version of "contemporary" that is distinct from that of the concert dance genre that Albright defines. This new "contemporary" dancer, having evolved from the "lyrical dancer," enters *SYTYCD* with a physical practice trained through the structure of corporate competitions. Lyrical dancers such as Melody Lacayanga and Nick Lazzarini (both Season 1), and contemporary dancers such as Season 3's runner-up Danny Tidwell; Season 4's Top Female Katee Shean, Season 5 winner Jeanine Mason, Season 6 runner-up Jakob

Karr, and Season 8's Jordan Casanova and winner Melanie Moore have considerable dance training within the circuit of dance competitions.[18] As dancers who fit into this newly defined version of contemporary, they are distinct from previous versions in that they do not exceed what has come before them.[19] By this I suggest that the performance and training of these contemporary bodies centralizes entertainment and popular culture over visionary or experimental artistic practices. In shying away from "lyrical" and foregrounding contemporary, *SYTYCD*'s producers not only disengage these bodies from their competition background but also work to situate them within a more elite professional dance community. Indisputably diverging from the standard practices of modern, post-modern, and contemporary concert dance, this "contemporary" body is a competition dancer disguised by the rhetoric employed on *SYTYCD*.

Those dancers labeled contemporary by the show often gain acclaim for skills that they don't attain on the show. Most often praised for their "lines" (the length and position of legs and arms in various movements) and "technique" (specifically referring to ballet and jazz techniques), the contemporary dancer is often able to perform multiple dance styles with seeming ease and skill. (See Fig. 19.2 for a clear articulation of the contemporary dancer as exemplified by Miranda Maleski.) A characteristic of their competition training, the contemporary dancer's versatility is one of the reasons they were able

FIGURE 19.2 Screen capture of Miranda Maleski's solo performance. Season 8, Episode 11, original air date, June 30, 2011.

to succeed through so many waves of auditions.[20] Successful performances in "unfamiliar" styles are an impressive feat. Instances such as Katee Shean's successful hip-hop routine with Joshua Allen during the performance of the Top 20 in Season 4, wherein she was praised by judge Dan Karatye for her ability to "hold her own," or Lythgoe identifying Miranda Maleski's hip-hop performance early in the season, as seen in Fig. 19.3, as "the best contemporary dancer that [he] has seen do hip-hop,"[21] would be considerably less impressive for viewing audience if the breadth of their training was articulated. Although the conceived body attributed to contemporary dancers suggests that they are trained in a single form of dance, specifically affiliated with elite, high-art practices of dance, in fact their bodies are composed of multiple dance forms, including ballet, jazz, and lyrical, among others.

In working to equate its "contemporary" dancers with traditional Euro-American concert dancers the show ultimately associates these dancers with the normative racial construction and identity that has dominated high-art spaces for so many years. Ballet's upright lift of the body, central to the iconic Euro-American dance form, is evident in the bodily alignment of *SYTYCD's* contemporary label. The genre of lyrical, which has been adapted and has become this notion of contemporary, fuses ballet with a particular evolution of jazz dance that removes the Africanist aesthetics. While the training behind these competition-trained "contemporary" dancers embeds these Euro-American characteristics in their bodies, the false notion of these dancers as "concert" bodies also enforces this understanding and reading by audiences.[22] More specifically, the use of a

FIGURE 19.3 Screen capture of Miranda Maleski and partner, Robert Taylor Jr., performing a hip-hop routine choreographed by Nappytabs (Tabitha and Napoleon D'umo). Season 8, Episode 6, original air date, June 22, 2011.

concert term in relation to these contestants removes the complex training of these bodies and simplifies it so that they are read as *only* trained in traditional Euro-American concert dance practices. This framing disengages the social and popular forms of dance that also train these bodies and suggests a fictitious relationship to high-art practices, when in fact these bodies are the result of a unique site of dance as competition merges high with "low" art practices in a site of popular culture.

The construction of the conceived body of Season 4 winner Joshua Allen revealed a clear juxtaposition between "traditional" dancers and non-traditional dancers.[23] The first hip-hop dancer to win the title of "America's Favorite Dancer," throughout the competition Allen was constantly praised by the judges for his ability to master each of the forms he was asked to perform despite being "untrained." Judge and producer Nigel Lythgoe commented on Allen's "natural" Samba ability.[24] (See Fig. 19.4) And in a Broadway performance Lythgoe commended Allen not merely because he felt it was a strong performance but because its strength lay in contrast to Allen's label of "hip-hop," specifically "popper."[25] As the show progressed, the judges continued to admire Allen's work while often repeating the claim that he is "untrained."

This inference about hip-hop dancers was established in the first season when Jamile McGee was the only hip-hop dancer to make it into the Top 4 (with 3 lyrical dancers). In an early episode judge Mia Michaels said to McGee, "You bring authenticity to this competition, that's the real deal," implying that *SYTYCD* is intended to find "undiscovered"

FIGURE 19.4 Screen capture of Joshua Allen and Katee Shean performing a Samba routine choreographed by Tony Meredith. Season 4, Episode 10, original air date, June 25, 2008.

talent, and later she tells him not to "over-train."[26] Despite the fact that many of the show's hip-hop *choreographers* teach in professional dance studios such as Millennium Dance Complex and Debbie Allen Dance Academy, it is assumed that the show's hip-hop *dancers* lack formal training experience. In one episode Michaels positively affirms the hip-hop style of krumping as "dirty," "raw," and "ugly," words that continue to be used with regard to hip-hop and related styles.[27] Even after Michael's departure from the show following Season 7, this language continues through others on the judging panel, including Lythgoe. This lexicon suggests that the hip-hop presented on the show is the consequence of dancers trained at, and choreography created in, urban spaces similar to that of the genre's origin.

Hip-hop, which originated in the Bronx during the 1970s, has been a part of mainstream culture for over two decades. Although it was originally produced by disenfranchised African American and Puerto Rican youth, it has long been a part of popular culture. It is now a dance practice with many variations, representing a range from marginalized, urban bodies to commercialized, affluent ones. The sites available for hip-hop extend far beyond the communities in which it originated in the 1970s. However, presenting hip-hop without acknowledging the multiple constructs that currently define it as a genre controls its framing on the show. The language used by the judges clearly draws upon the transgressive racial identity that hip-hop dance signifies. As bodies whose dominance is reflected in both their role of power and of affluence, the show's judges (and producers) exploit the marginalized and racially marked practice of hip-hop, which they identify with an oppressed or underprivileged body.

Although Allen *did* have prior experience with other forms of dance, including modern, ballet, and jazz, the producers portrayed it as no less than miraculous when he successfully traversed different dance forms. Not only is this visible immediately after his audition when, after receiving his ticket to Vegas he did an à *la seconde* ballet turn for the camera, but he also clarified this idea in an article in "Natural Muscle Magazine," stating that he took modern, ballet, and jazz classes (although he did not believe himself to be as "technically trained" as other contestants).[28] There was even a moment on the show when a picture of Allen as a young boy at a ballet barre was shown. Even if Allen had not trained in dance forms other than hip-hop, to consider him "untrained" is a false representation of the physical experience that informs his work on the show. This rhetorical framing insinuates that hip-hop dancers—who rehearse extensively in spaces that do not always resemble traditional privatized spaces—simply inexplicably produce skilled dance movement. This characterization establishes a tension that distinguishes between the formal Euro-American training of traditional bodies and the non-traditional work of hip-hop bodies, invisibilizing the labor of non-traditional bodies.

This framing of bodies like Allen's disempowers them from potential transgression through the stereotypical character Sambo. Made popular by the minstrel shows of the mid-nineteenth century, this particular characterization of African American males depicts them as lazy and buffoonish, incapable of having or acquiring skill. Moreover, the normative role of privilege for the African American male based upon physical talent, in which talent is assumed to be an inborn gift rather than achieved through intensive labor, is also at play in this characterization of the hip-hop dancer. By falsifying Allen's training and simplifying the labor of his body to a "natural" talent the audience has no choice but to read his body with a colonial gaze. In his text *Appropriating Blackness*, Patrick E. Johnson, in a discussion of the work of Patricia Williams, writes, "The position of the voyeur's "zoom lens" is necessarily predicated on his or her power and privilege."[29] And in the case of *SYTYCD*'s audience, its power is limited to that provided to them by the framing of dancers through the structure of the show. Johnson writes that "Black performance…becomes the site at which people and behavior are construed as 'spectacles of primitivism' to justify the colonial and racist gaze."[30] While the contemporary body is understood as "formally" and "technically" trained, which implies extensive physical labor, the hip-hop dancer is coded as the "other," lacking its own laborious training system and in *need* of "formal" training. Moreover, it is those hip-hop dancers that conform easily and quickly to these traditional styles that are the most successful on the show.

Maintaining racist productions of the body, the gaze constructed by the show's rhetoric situates the hip-hop dancer as "Other." As a common mode of production in mainstream culture, hip-hop is no longer situated on the margins and is highlighted by many commercial outlets. Often used in capitalist modes of production such as advertising, hip-hop has a complex relationship with both financial and cultural capital that assures its centrality in American culture. Meanwhile, the rhetoric of *SYTYCD*'s judges' utilizes archaic perceptions of hip-hop bodies in order to develop and present a character that represents marginalized bodies through socially embedded stereotypes of these racially marked bodies.

The juxtaposition of the "contemporary" dancer and the "hip-hop" dancer creates a binary relationship that allows each to inform the other. The "rawness" of the hip-hop dancer becomes more visible for the audience as the classically technical capacities of the contemporary dancer are highlighted and discussed. Drawing upon a standard racial binary of white/black and Euro-American/African American, these labels of dancing bodies are created into and used because they are sellable, consumable identities. The simplicity with which both these dancing bodies are characterized draws upon the standard impoverished, urban identity attributed to African American bodies and the affluent, suburban identity of Caucasian bodies. And both mute the complexities behind these dancing bodies as subjects, such as the competition dancer who has trained in a variety of forms or the hip-hop dancer who has taken years of ballet class.

In order to evolve dance's role as capital and as a vehicle for other forms of capital, *SYTYCD* uses language to falsify the training history of bodies it presents. As a result, the spectacle of the dance performance is intensified. Most often associated with the formal performance setting of high art, dance in the United States is always already a spectacle. The inclusion of the practice in a structure of competition heightens this spectacle significantly by associating dance with sport practices and competitive behavior. This too is intensified when placed in as an interactive media experience for a national (and international) audience.

Guy Debord defines spectacle as "a social relation between people that is mediated by images" and states, "the spectacle is *capital* accumulated to the point that it becomes images."[31] As a bricolage of many different images of commodities, dancing bodies on *SYTYCD* become commodities and spectacle as they integrate many other elements from popular culture, including music, fashion, and performance. Relying on the spectacle of the competition body and the spectacle of race, among others, *SYTYCD* incorporates many already socially embedded commodity fetishes in order to construct a new desired commodity. These bodily commodities, as they are quantified through competition, create a social relation between viewers, between dancers, and between dancers and viewers. According to Debord, "the spectacle is the stage at which the commodity has succeeded in totally colonizing social life."[32] These dancing bodies gain broad celebrity status in American culture and a more specified celebrity status in a particular community of competitive dance. Whether it is the addition of Season 4's Chelsie Hightower to the roster of resident ballroom dancers on ABC's *Dancing With the Stars*; Katee Shean, Danny Tidwell, and Sabra Johnson modeling for Capezio; or Blake McGrath (Season 1) appearing in MTV's *Dance Life* (2007) and choreographing for *SYTYCD Canada*, these dancing bodies, through increased credibility and visibility as a result of the show, become commodities *because* of their unique spectacle. Most recently, *SYTYCD* has capitalized on this commodification of dancing bodies; beginning in Season 7, they have partnered with Gatorade, signing the winning dancers as featured athletes for the sports drink brand.[33]

These bodies-as-spectacle rely on their ability to materialize race. Using the dance style with which the dancers audition, racial configurations are placed on each dancing body. When looking at the Top 4 dancers from each season the standard relationship of Caucasian bodies as contemporary dancers and African American bodies as hip-hop dancers is upheld. The rare exceptions to this include Katee Shean and Melody Lacayanga, who both appear to be of Asian descent, as well as African Americans Brandon Bryant and AdéChiké Torbert. Although Season 3's Danny Tidwell phenotypically appears to have African American heritage, he is quickly associated with Travis Wall and adoptive mother Denise Wall, both appearing distinctly Caucasian, which allows him to "pass" regardless of his skin tone. While other African American dancers have made it into the Top 4, these performers have either been hip-hop dancers or labeled as "modern," a rare term on the show, or "jazz," a descriptor that was removed in early seasons and has begun to make its own complex return into the lexicon of the show. The judges' rhetoric applied to the show's dancing bodies sustains a paradigm of race that has an extensive history in American culture, which ensures that these bodies fit into an established system of discipline and racial discourse.

The bodies of dancers on *SYTYCD* are attributed differing sets of codes, which function to limit and survey these bodies, based upon the dance form through which they are labeled. A dancer such as Allen is turned into spectacle as his labor is underestimated; he is also kept from the possibility of Euro-American sensibilities and training. Meanwhile, the labor of the contemporary dancer is shifted as her training is resituated through a play on language. The structures through which each of these dancing bodies trains and performs are reframed in order to exacerbate the spectacle of their performance. The recontextualization of these bodies is largely to benefit the acting panopticon,[34] the viewing audience.

The undisputed value of *SYTYCD* is its ability to bring dance to millions of viewers with great ease of access. However, as it does so it utilizes simplistic constructions of dancing bodies/identities that rely on a relationship of comparison in which the labor of certain bodies is masked or muted. Rather than displaying the complex dancing bodies that are actually present, *SYTYCD* uses language to present one-dimensional dancing identities that are racial stereotypes based upon particular dance forms and styles. |In simplifying the subjectivity of these dancing bodies, the show's producers not only create commodifiable objects from them but also ensure simplicity for audience reception. This ultimately works to assist in the formation of alliances and attachments to dancers as the audience becomes involved and invested in the competition of these dancing bodies.

Although the frames of viewing established by the apparatuses capturing the dance are central for audience reception, it is the frames of rhetoric that construct each dancer that have the greatest effect on audience perception. Through the unique work of *SYTYCD*, the rhetoric of the judges trains its interactive audience to read dancing bodies through racialized identities. And the weight of the words and labels attributed to the contestants is immeasurable as national and international audiences become acquainted to dance through the show's platform. Without dividing the image of the dancing body and isolating elements for the sake of consumer appeal, *SYTYCD* presents a whole dancing body, which is made into spectacle by the incomplete picture of its training and experience as presented by the language used by the show's judges and producers. This lexicon teaches viewers how to read the dance and in turn determines how the audience votes and, therefore, which dancers are successful. *SYTYCD*, in its effort to re-value dance in the United States, does so by invisibilizing the labor of its contestants and repackages these bodies for the show's audience as well as for their consumption by consumer culture after their time on the show.

NOTES

1. Dodds, Sherril. *Dance on Screen: Genres and Media from Hollywood to Experimental Art.* London and New York: Palgrave, 2001, p. 4.
2. This was an interesting choice in the first five seasons when the stage was almost entirely round, with audiences surrounding all but a small back portion. As a result the live audience was experiencing the performance in the round. However, in the final episodes of the fifth season a new traditional, proscenium stage was introduced, only allowing live audiences to view from the front.
3. Around the same time the new stage was introduced the close-up shot was replaced with a 360-degree pan, which allowed the television audience to experience portions of the dances in the round.
4. Fiske, John. *Reading Television.* New York: Routledge, 2003, p. 101.

5. Fiske, *Reading Television*, 102–103.

6. "Episode #1.7." *So You Think You Can Dance*. Fox: 11/30/2006. Television.

7. This concept is reiterated in the fifth season when contestants Jeannine Mason and Phillip Chbeeb performed a Russian folkdance that was not well received by Lythgoe, who responded by saying that he felt it wasn't the dancers' skills that might result in lower votes that week but the dance, which he felt was not carefully chosen for the show and its audience. As a result this performance was not well received by the audience and was even intentionally mocked by the show's producers, as it became a recurring comical theme during that season's live national tour.

8. A former dancer, Lythgoe is the producer and co-creator of *So You Think You Can Dance*. Mary Murphy, known for her success in ballroom dance, is a judge and choreographer on the show. Murphy was not affiliated with the show during its seventh season. The use of a celebrity judge has become common in recent seasons and is particularly prevalent in Season 8.

9. During the first season, dancers were sent to Hollywood. Additionally, there was a limited number of spots, fifty, for each audition city. The number of dancers sent through in later seasons has never been disclosed.

10. Here I am harkening directly to Marx's use of this term in order to highlight the complexities of these dancing bodies embedded within a capitalist system. Specifically, I am alluding to the value and significance of these dancers within the experience of viewers.

11. "Las Vegas Callbacks." *So You Think You Can Dance*. Fox: 6/2006. Television.

12. The first season only sent sixteen dancers through to the competition while the seventh season, because of a format change, accepted eleven, who were then paired up with previous contestants known as "All Stars."

13. Although it is not excavated in this piece it is important to note that in using heterosexual couplings *SYTYCD* is able to draw upon normative gender relationships in order to avoid potentially transgressive readings of dances performed in same sex couplings. It is particularly interesting when these heterosexual couples are juxtaposed with same-sex couplings during the performances of the Top 4. The addition of these couplings is so that dancers have a wide variety of performances to execute in the final episode when the voting for the winner takes place.

14. Foster, Susan Leigh C. "Dancing Bodies." In *Meaning in Motion New Cultural Studies of Dance (Post-Contemporary Interventions)*. Ed. Jane C. Desmond. New York: Duke University Press, 1997, p. 236-241.

15. Foster, "Dancing Bodies," p. 237.

16. The only exception to this is Season 7, where a format change resulted in only eleven Top Dancers moving on from Vegas Week. Of these eleven, six were labeled "contemporary."

17. Albright, Ann Cooper. *Choreographing Difference*. Hanover, NH: University of New England Press 1997, p. 191.

18. Online results from Showstopper's 2002 San Mateo regional competition list Melody Lacayanga as the 1st Overall Soloist in the 15 & Over category. Though it is not the target audience, it is common for high school dance teams to attend these types of competitions; Shean's high school dance team is one such group. Although Tidwell was an extremely skilled and popular dancer on the show he first gained notoriety as the adopted brother of Travis Wall, Season 2 runner-up. The adoptive mother, Denise Wall, is nationally known for her strong competition studio, Denise Wall's Dance Energy, which has been featured in several industry magazines, including on the cover of the October 2008 issue of *Dance Teacher*. The visibility of competitively trained dancers has increased in later seasons with

dancers such as Mason, who has an extensive background in competition, having won many solo and group titles at many corporate competition events. Similarly Karr, prior to his time on the show, won national solo titles at several well-regarded competition events. Moore also won titles during her time training at a competitive studio in her home town. Meanwhile Casanova trained with Dellos Dance and Performing Arts as well as Dance Precisions, two studios renowned for their continued success on the competition circuit.

19. In my larger work I examine the practice of dance competition in the United States, defining the dancing body created through the structure of corporate competitions. In this work I examine how these bodies are all similarly designed through a site of dance that does not privilege original choreographic or physical productions.

20. Competition dancers train and compete in a multitude of dance genres ranging from jazz, lyrical, contemporary, ballet, and hip-hop, among others, in order to remain successful within the industry.

21. "Top 20 Perform Again." *So You Think You Can Dance.* Fox: 6/22/2011.

22. In my larger work I argue that the competition body is primarily composed of ballet and an appropriated version of jazz that masks many of the Africanist elements of the practice.

23. A similar narrative was constructed for Season 6 winner Russell Ferguson, a krumper who had attended University of the Arts for dance prior to his time on the show.

24. Season 4, Episode 10

25. Season 4, Episode 8

26. "Episode #1.5." *So You Think You Can Dance.* Fox: 8/17/2005.
     "Episode #1.11." *So You Think You Can Dance.* Fox: 9/28/2005.

27. "Episode #1.8." *So You Think You Can Dance.* Fox: 9/7/2005.

28. Pz. "He's So Much More Than Dancing." *Natural Muscle Magazine.*

29. Johnson, E. Patrick. *Appropriating Blackness.* Durham, NC: Duke University Press, 2003, p 8.

30. Johnson, *Appropriating Blackness,* p. 7.

31. Debord, Guy. *Society of the Spectacle,* translated by Ken Knabb. Wellington: Rebel Press, 2004, p. 17.

32. Debord, *Society of the Spectacle,* p. 21.

33. In a campaign to market dancers as athletes, those that sign with Gatorade join an elite group of professional and Olympic athletes.

34. Foucault, Michel. *Discipline and Punish, the Birth of the Prison.* New York: Vintage, 1995.

BIBLIOGRAPHY

Albright, Ann Cooper. *Choreographing Difference.* Hanover, NH: University of New England Press 1997.

Debord, Guy. *Society of the Spectacle.* Translated by Ken Knabb. Rebel Press, 2004.

Dodds, Sherril. *Dance on Screen: Genres and Media from Hollywood to Experimental Art.* London and New York: Palgrave, 2001.

Fiske, John. *Reading Television.* New York: Routledge, 2003.

Foster, Susan Leigh C. "Dancing Bodies." In *Meaning in Motion New Cultural Studies of Dance (Post-Contemporary Interventions),* edited by Jane C. Desmond. New York: Duke University Press, 1997.

Foucault, Michel. *Discipline and Punish, the Birth of the Prison*. New York: Vintage, 1995.

Johnson, E. Patrick. *Appropriating Blackness*. Durham, NC: Duke University Press, 2003.

Pz. "He's So Much More Than Dancing." *Natural Muscle Magazine*. http://www.naturalmuscle. net/joshua_allen_feature

Episodes Cited

"Episode #1.7." *So You Think You Can Dance*. Fox: 11/30/2006. Television.

"Las Vegas Callbacks." *So You Think You Can Dance*. Fox: 6/2006. Television.

"Top 20 Perform Again." *So You Think You Can Dance*. Fox: 6/22/2011.

"Top 16 Perform." *So You Think You Can Dance*. Fox: 6/25/2008.

"Top 28 Perform." *So You Think You Can Dance*. Fox: 6/18/2008.

"Episode #1.5." *So You Think You Can Dance*. Fox: 8/17/2005.

"Episode #1.11." *So You Think You Can Dance*. Fox: 9/28/2005.

"Episode #1.8." *So You Think You Can Dance*. Fox: 9/7/2005.

PART IV

SCREENING
NATIONHOOD

CHAPTER 20

HATCHETS AND HAIRBRUSHES: DANCE, GENDER, AND IMPROVISATIONAL INGENUITY IN COLD WAR WESTERN MUSICALS

KATHALEEN BOCHE

WHEN director Stanley Donan asked Michael Kidd to be the choreographer for *Seven Brides for Seven Brothers*, Kidd hesitated at first. For him, the dancing had to make sense within the plot. Kidd explained his concerns as follows:

> So, I said to Stanley and Saul Chaplin, "I can't see any dancing in this picture. You've got these seven slobs living out in the country. They've got horse manure on the floor. They're unwashed. They're unshaven. They look terrible." I said, "These people are going to get up and dance? We'll be booted out of the theater. It doesn't make any sense to me." (*Sobbin' Women* 1997)

Kidd accepted the role of choreographer on one condition: that there would be "no dancing, per se" (*Sobbin' Women* 1997). Of course, that stipulation depends on how one defines "dancing." There is plenty of choreographed rhythmic movement in *Seven Brides*, but Kidd was reluctant to call the movement dance. The movement was in fact choreographed dancing, but Kidd wanted it to look spontaneous and plausible for a bunch of burly unrefined woodsmen. He insisted that the choreography look like the kind of movements that Oregon woodsmen might do—no dream ballets for this musical.[1] Kidd used hand tools and ranch paraphernalia to create dance sequences for the movie—items that would logically be a part of everyday life in 1850 Oregon (Fig. 20.1). In order for the musical numbers to be believable, the movement had to stem from everyday actions of the woodsman brothers.

FIGURE 20.1 Screen Capture of *Seven Brides for Seven Brothers*, director Stanley Donen, 1954, during the "Lonesome Polecat" number.

From the end of World War II through the 1950s, Hollywood movie studios produced many musicals that focused on iconic figures of American identity, especially the cowboy and the frontiersman. Popular western-themed musicals from this period include *Annie Get Your Gun* (1950), *Calamity Jane* (1953), *Seven Brides for Seven Brothers* (1954), and *Oklahoma!* (1955). Through dance, song, costume, and dialogue, the cowboy and frontiersman characters express elements of the American national identity. Such qualities include rugged individualism, patriotism, expansionism, the provider/protector ideal, and improvisational ingenuity. What I term "improvisational ingenuity" is the ability to use the materials at hand in creative, inventive ways that serve a useful purpose. This chapter focuses on how improvisational ingenuity serves as a vehicle to express these elements of American post-war whiteness through the dancing bodies of the frontiersmen and women in these films. The idea that necessity breeds creativity is not a new one, and it is also not a uniquely American one, yet this chapter seeks to demonstrate how these qualities manifested in the choreographies created and used in the musicals such as *Annie Get Your Gun* and *Seven Brides for Seven Brothers*.

Gender Role Anxiety

Created during the early years of the Cold War, these western musical films addressed social anxiety by focusing on positive aspects of post-war white American-ness. Offering an ideal for American society in a time of insecurity, the cultural work of these films and iconic characters was to reinforce dominant conservative post-war values. As women left their wartime jobs to return to the domestic world, these musicals promoted a return to strict gender roles that had relaxed somewhat during World War II. By calling on elements of American-ness that had been established long before the Cold War, these musicals helped to reconcile the struggle between individualism and conformity that characterized these years.

Mythologized as the quintessential American, the man of the West is a hero who takes matters into his own hands. Rather than brooding, the cowboy/frontiersman takes action; he refuses to be a victim. He tames nature, animals, and even people. His kind of dancing is raw, close to the earth, and full of abandon.[2] The cowboy/frontiersman is a romantic figure who evokes a longing for a simpler time and more natural place.[3] The maverick, do-it-yourself spirit of American-ness reflects the lineage of cowboys as they are constructed in and by American culture.

By looking back on an earlier period in American history through a manufacturing of nostalgia, these western musicals reminded audiences in the early 1950s of a time when gender roles were supposedly well defined and procreation was a duty, a responsibility necessary for building and expanding the nation. These films romanticize the heyday of the Old West, a period ranging from the mid-nineteenth century to the early twentieth century. While the Progressive Era was gaining momentum in the early twentieth century, the ideology of separate spheres still dominated white middle- and upper-class American society. This nineteenth-century ideology contended that there were two domains in life—one public and one private. The public sphere was physically and intellectually demanding, dangerous, and full of temptation; as men were thought to be the stronger sex, they dominated public life. Women were thought to be mentally inferior and physically fragile—too vulnerable to withstand the trials of life outside the home (Murray 2004, 18). So, woman was the keeper of hearth, home, and family. Women who worked outside the home usually did so out of financial necessity and often were subjected to abysmal working conditions; however, they were still responsible for home and family. Many gender historians today argue that separate spheres never really existed— women have always participated in the public world, though sometimes in indirect ways (Meyerowitz 1994). During the Progressive Era, reformers challenged strict gender roles. It should be noted that reformers were concerned with improving conditions for white women, generally not for African Americans or other marginalized groups.

With the post–World War II baby boom and focus on the nuclear family, social ideals returned to the separate spheres worldview. American women had taken over traditionally male occupations during the war but were expected to return to the domestic sphere afterwards. Not all women were happy to relinquish their newfound place in the professional world (Hunter 2008, 336). According to Marilyn Hegarty's research of wartime propaganda, the financial and sexual independence of women threatened the dominant gender dichotomy. Hegarty explains, "As wartime women necessarily crossed established gender boundaries by responding to their prescribed civic obligations, in both factory and dance hall, they became suspicious individuals," (1998, 112). After the war, part of the pressure for women to stay contained within the home had to do with Cold War anxiety and competition with the Soviet Union to become the dominant world power.[4] Popular culture often conflated anti-communism with other commonly perceived threats to the American way of life. "Perhaps the most striking aspect of anti-Communist rhetoric is how often it became a vehicle for criticizing internal weaknesses within the United States itself" (Hendershot 2003, 4). Women could contribute to the Cold War indirectly through their role as caregivers, but not as scientists or engineers. In charge of raising children, women imparted religious and social values and generally ensured that children would become good, productive American citizens.[5]

Against this backdrop of anxiety, film musicals provided the ultimate heightened interpretation of reality, where the iconic larger-than-life cowboy and frontiersman were right at home. The genre of movie musicals is a codified, formulaic one, and also one that was immensely popular during the 1940s and 1950s. This period is often referred to as the "Golden Age" of musicals. Full of swaggering hyper-masculine men, lush music, and high-energy group dances, these movie musicals deliver messages, in an attractive package, about a specific type of American identity and the ideal community. They work on a subconscious level.[6] As the musicals discussed here were box-office hits when released, vast numbers of Americans saw these films and were potentially affected by them.

It is important to note that the creators of these popular films may not have necessarily or consciously intended for their work to reinforce the gender dichotomy. Rather, the redressive qualities of these film musicals grew out of the dominant hegemonic worldview of the time. Yet, since the filmic apparatus reinforces ideological beliefs, one can argue that gender dichotomies function within this sphere. According to cultural studies theorist Dick Hebdige, individuals can only experience social relations and processes "…through the forms in which they are represented to those individuals. These forms are, as we have seen, by no means transparent. They are shrouded in a 'common sense' which simultaneously validates and mystifies them" (1988, 13). Operating under the assumption that the audience would accept the ideas they presented as common sense, the films' creators assumed that no one would question the ideas they expressed on the screen.

COLD WAR SOCIAL DRAMA

As a conceptual underpinning, Victor Turner's theory of social drama provides insight into how these musicals functioned within the context of the Cold War (1974). Turner describes social dramas as occurring in four phases: breach, crises, redressive action, and either reintegration or schism. The Cold War can be considered as a social drama that occurred simultaneously on two levels—one internationally between the United States and the Soviet Union, and the other nationally between men and women. Internationally, the breach phase in the social drama of the Cold War was World War II. During World War II, the Soviets became allies of the United States; this alliance was actually a breach of prior relations. The crises phase began as World War II was ending and European war-ravaged countries were left vulnerable to the spread of communism. With programs like the Marshall Plan, which gave aid to Western European countries weakened by the war, and the Truman Doctrine, which gave aid to countries bordering the USSR, the United States attempted to contain communism and prevent the USSR from expanding its borders (Dunbabin 2008, 134; Barson and Heller 2001, 41).

Redressive action occurred in the form of the Red Scare of the late 1940s and 1950s, including anti-communist propaganda and various forms of popular culture (Barson and Heller 2001; Hendershot 2003). In the final phase of Turner's theory of social drama, there is either a reintegration and return to the former state of affairs before the breach, or a schism in which a group separates and creates a new model of operation. During the 1950s, the anti-communist propaganda and reinforcement of strict gender roles in popular culture resulted in an intense pressure to conform. As previously mentioned, World War II was also a breach of gender roles, as many women went to work outside the home. The crisis occurred when men returned from the war and women were expected to give up their jobs and return to the domestic sphere.

This is where the western musicals come into play during the Cold War. Representing American ideals, the cowboy and frontiersman figures presented audiences with a model for how they should behave in post-World War II society. Each movie presents a particular social drama, and as a subgenre, they play out a national American social drama. The social drama occurs in these musicals with many couples rather than only one. While *Annie Get Your Gun* ends with only one romantic partnership, it is the exception. *Calamity Jane* finishes with a double wedding, and *Seven Brides for Seven Brothers* ends with the marriage of six couples. *Oklahoma* culminates with the wedding of Curly and Laurey, as well as the eminent marriage of the peripheral couples of Will and Ado Annie, and Ali Hakim and Gertie. This multi-coupling suggests that the primary protagonists are not an exceptional couple, but rather how *society* should be thus reinforcing the significance of the heterosexual marriage plot in post-war white middle-class American society.

As an element of American-ness that is closely associated with the iconic images of the cowboy and the frontiersman, improvisational ingenuity was essential to the redressive action of Cold War era western film musicals. As stated earlier, in the dancing, improvisational ingenuity commonly manifests itself in the innovative use of the props at hand. This is a favorite choreographic tool used in these musicals, ostensibly because it makes the dancing seem more organic to the story. Often, the characters are performing an everyday task or creatively solving a problem.

DANCING IMPROVISATIONAL INGENUITY

Through the animation of everyday items or props at hand, this "do-it-yourself" spirit appears in the dancing in Hollywood musicals. The items are used out of their ordinary context, becoming dance partners for the characters. Or, the characters use the items as tools to enable movements that would not otherwise be possible. Jane Feuer applies anthropologist Claude Levi-Strauss's term bricolage to the sort of improvisational ingenuity that occurs in these prop dances (1982, 4). In French, the term literally means tinkering, fiddling, or pottering. Describing the anthropological use of the term bricolage, Feuer says, "In creating his cultural and intellectual artifacts, primitive man makes use of materials at hand which may not bear any relationship to the intended project but which appear to be all he has to work with" (1982, 4). It relates to an improvisational do-it-yourself mode of thinking and creating. Seen in opposition to modern industrial thought, with its scientific planning and engineering of projects, bricolage does not require the right tool for the right job. While choreographers of these musical numbers intend for bricolage to seem spontaneous and natural, the way that they achieve the appearance of spontaneity is painstakingly engineered; choreography is a laborious task that conventions of film, such as editing and camera angle, can erase. According to Feuer, "The *bricolage* number attempts to cancel engineering (a characteristic of mass production) by substituting *bricolage* (a characteristic of folk production)" (1982, 5). Musicals attempt to hide engineering, or choreography with props, behind the impressive improvisational ingenuity of the characters.

There are several reasons why choreographers worked so hard to make the dancing in musicals during the late 1940s and 1950s look like spontaneous American folkdance. First, it was a general goal of musicals at that time to help the audience suspend their disbelief, or at least to avoid jarringly obvious breaks between the storyline and the musical numbers. This concept that the singing and dancing should assist in the progression of the story had not always been the goal of Hollywood musicals. For example, Busby Berkeley's grand, surreal musical numbers of the 1930s were not meant to aid in the development of the plots of his films—they were just meant to be impressively spectacular (Rubin 1993, 39-40). Many choreographers of the 1940s and 1950s musicals believed that making the dancing a logical part of the storyline helped the audience to accept the idea that ordinary people in everyday situations would get up and dance at that moment. The choreographers hoped that this contrived logic would help the audience make the all-important leap of faith—to accept that meticulously choreographed numbers could happen on the spur of the moment with no rehearsal, and to make the dance, body, and (white) American-ness seem an effortless yet virtuosic ideal.

Second, making the dances look simple and effortless allowed the audience to believe that they might be able to dance like that too. "By cancelling choreography as a calculated dance strategy, non-choreography implies that dancing is utterly natural and that dancing is easy" (Feuer 1982, 9). The audience could identify with the dancers and their perspective, even imagining themselves in the bodies of the dancers. Third, the kind of dancing they did was uniquely "American"—a hybrid of American folk dance, tap, ballroom, ballet, and modern dance. *Oklahoma!* choreographer Agnes de Mille attributed the success of the original stage musical to the fact that it had patriotic appeal—it was distinctly American in setting and style, and the country was engaged in World War II (De Mille 1980, 188). The western musicals of the Cold War era were about celebrating "Americana," and improvisational ingenuity figures into this trope. Reinforcing the idea that Americans need not look to other countries for dance, these musical numbers affirmed that the United States was an inventive, creative world power.

DANCING FRONTIERSMEN

While both male and female characters in Cold War western musicals portray improvisational ingenuity in their dancing, they do so in different ways. Frontiersmen and cowboys generally display improvisation ingenuity in outdoor venues, dancing with tools and other found objects. For example, in the *Seven Brides* number "Lonesome Polecat," Kidd turned stylized ranch chores into dance. The everyday activities of chopping wood, sawing, sharpening axes, and tending sheep—all ingredients of self-sufficiency and rugged individualism—are slowed down to an adagio tempo so that the gracefulness of the movement is made visible. Matt Mattox slices through the air with his hatchet as he spins around wistfully (Fig. 20.2). The fact that the mountain men are lonesome is a result of their steadfast rugged individualism. According to the logic of the film, acting on one's own individual interests and behaving with socially unacceptable manners makes for a proud but lonely life. The frontiersmen express their loneliness by turning their tools into dance partners as they move through their chores. This could be interpreted in a few different ways—it might suggest that the men think of women as objects or tools, or that the men wish women were as uncomplicated as simple tools.

The most spectacular exhibition of improvisational ingenuity in *Seven Brides* occurs in the barn-raising dance. When Kidd started choreographing the number, he told a prop man to "go down to the prop shop, find anything you can that would be lying around when they build a barn: bring planks of lumber, bring sawhorses, bring an axe, bring anything you can that would apply" (*Sobbin' Women* 1997). Kidd began tinkering with the items, starting to create gymnastic choreography on the sawhorse and an axe-jumping bit (*Sobbin' Women* 1997). The barn-raising number began with bricolage, as Kidd improvised with what the movie studio prop shop had on hand. Kidd crafted his improvisations into set choreography, and then, ironically, the dancers painstakingly

FIGURE 20.2 Screen Capture of *Seven Brides for Seven Brothers*, director Stanley Donen, 1954, Caleb (Matt Mattox) dancing with a hatchet during the "Lonesome Polecat" number.

rehearsed for weeks so that the number could look natural and spontaneous. Although Kidd intended for the dancing to look improvised, it was actually choreographed, set, and rehearsed.

In the barn-raising scene, the mountain men have a pressing personal need to improvise; they are engaged in a competition with the local townsmen over the affections of the lovely town ladies. The brothers' seemingly improvised dance with nearby objects (which Kidd choreographed) begins when three of the brothers step up and pivot on picnic tables, and then lift their dance partners up and down from the tables. Two of the townsmen jump up on the edge of a water well and perform a few jig-like steps, showing off. Elbowing his brother Daniel (Marc Platt) and winking at him, Frank (Tommy Rall) has a spontaneous idea to outdo the townsmen. Showing off his log rolling skills, Frank runs on the spinning crossbar of the well as Daniel cranks the handle faster and faster. Frank descends from the well with an aerial cartwheel (no hands). One of the townsmen tries to best Frank by jumping up on a plank of wood laid across two sawhorses. Turning the plank into a balance beam, the townsman performs over-the-logs (also known as over-the-top), shooting one leg out across the other and jumping over it with his standing leg. Caleb (Matt Mattox) rises to the challenge, performing a running step on the plank. Three townsmen attempt to beat Caleb, but each one loses his balance and falls. Taking advantage of the flexibility of the plank, Caleb executes two toe-touches before alighting from the makeshift balance beam. Inspired by a nearby hatchet, a townsman jumps up on the planks, holding the hatchet sideways in front of his body. He successfully jumps over it, but his movement looks rather clumsy. Realizing that jumping continuously backward and forward over the hatchet would look much smoother, Gideon (Russ Tamblyn) shows up the townsman (Fig. 20.3). He finishes by hurling the hatchet at a tree stump, which it hits like a bull's-eye.

Gideon motions for Caleb and Daniel to join him, and the three execute a dive-roll off the plank into the arms of their dance partners. When Daniel accidently pushes

FIGURE 20.3 Screen Capture of *Seven Brides for Seven Brothers*, director Stanley Donen, 1954, Gideon (Russ Tamblyn) hatchet-jumping on a sawhorse during the "Dueling Dancers" barn-raising dance.

one of the townsmen, the townsman challenges him to an arm-wrestling match on two parallel planks stretched across sawhorses. The townsman bests Daniel and Caleb, but he is no match for hot-blooded Frank. Engaging in a succession of highly stylized arm-wrestling dances with the townsmen, Frank emerges as the winner. Caleb, Ephraim (Jacques d'Amboise), and Daniel join Frank on the planks, and they perform a celebratory dance of unison kicks and jumps. They clear the way for Gideon, who performs show-stopping acrobatics, including a back flip. Three of the brothers cartwheel across the boards toward one another, creating the visual effect of a kaleidoscope of legs. Frank then impresses the crowd with aerial cartwheels on the double planks. Noticing that the ladies are unoccupied, the townsmen dance them back into the proper dance space, the barn foundation. However, in the end, the ladies jump into the brothers' arms, preferring them to the townsmen. Both the townsmen and the brothers show improvisational ingenuity; the backwoodsmen are just more creative and strong enough to be better at all things physical. As outdoorsmen, the brothers supposedly possess a raw masculinity that the refined townsmen cannot match. In contrast, the townsmen's sedate, indoor lifestyles dull their capacity for ingenuity.

DOMESTICATED COWGIRLS

In *Annie Get Your Gun,* the musical number "Anything You Can Do" seems to address women's power roles in a post-World War II era. If a woman can do anything better than her man, then why should she abstain from doing these things? Apparently, the price a woman pays for professional success is a lack of husband and family, as evidenced by the number "You Can't Get a Man with a Gun." In the musical, Annie only secures her man's love when she misses a shot and lets him win a competition. This is actually a change that the creators of the musical made from the real life story of Annie Oakley. Oakley's love interest and professional rival Frank Butler realized that she was more talented than he, and willingly became her devoted husband and manager. The fact that the creators of the musical changed this important detail is telling. On the surface, it might seem that representations of strong-willed frontierswomen in musicals like *Annie Get Your Gun* and *Calamity Jane* encouraged women's independence. But, actually, they reinforced the idea that even a strong woman must submit to a man's will in order to find love and happiness. Improvisational ingenuity is only acceptable for women inside the domestic sphere. This is a recurring theme in most of the western film musicals of the era.

In *Calamity Jane*, another musical about a strong-willed frontierswoman, the musical number "A Woman's Touch" shows improvisational ingenuity. Calamity and her new roommate Katie make do with the items on hand in Calamity's filthy, dilapidated cabin to give the place a thorough cleaning. In the number, cleaning becomes dancing. Singing and dancing are often used to make cleaning less laborious and boring, particularly in Disney films such as the number "Whistle While You Work" from *Snow White and the Seven Dwarfs*. The movement in "A Woman's Touch" also suggests an indomitable optimism, which is essential to improvisational ingenuity. Katie just happens to be a maid by profession, so she conveniently has a maid's uniform with her. The women turn sweeping and dusting into a buoyant stepping and spinning. Katie uses an old can of yellow paint found in the cabin to dress up the front door. She indicates to Calamity to cut the bedposts of her loft bed so that they can create a second bed out of the wood.

"A Woman's Touch" functions paradoxically in its social message. On the one hand, the musical number praises women and exhorts the magic they seem to create in the domestic sphere. On the other hand, it reinforces the idea that cleaning is women's work, and that women should only display improvisational ingenuity inside the home. The lyrics of the song literally suggest that women have an inborn aptitude for housework, baking, and interior design. The fact that Calamity is not an expert in these areas would seem to imply that these are learned skills that are not actually instinctual to women. However, according to the logic of the movie, she has the instincts, but just never developed them. Here, the filmic apparatus reinforces and further cements essentialist notions of gender and the supposed skills women possess.

Through the course of this number, Katie also makes over Calamity, both in dress and manner. While Katie searches through her trunks of clothes for something that will look becoming on Calamity, Calamity tinkers with the pieces she casts aside. Calamity tries on a hat, but she puts it on backward. Putting her arms through the pant legs, she turns a pair of pantaloons into a shrug sweater (Fig. 20.4). As a masculinized woman, Calamity

FIGURE 20.4 Screen Capture of *Calamity Jane*, director David Butler, 1953, Calamity (Doris Day) wears pantaloons as a shrug sweater during "A Woman's Touch."

FIGURE 20.5 Screen Capture of *Oklahoma*, director Fred Zinnemann, 1955, during the "Many a New Day" number.

is dysfunctional within the domestic sphere, but Katie helps feminize and reform her. For women, primping and dressing up for men was presented as a patriotic activity, since the sight of beautiful women boosted heterosexual men's morale in this time of anxiety. This was part of courtship and creating ideal couples and families. Again, women's improvisational ingenuity occurs within the domestic sphere as represented in these films.

Women also make use of female attire and beauty aids in the number "Many a New Day" from *Oklahoma!* Dressing and primping become dancing as the young women in the number dance with hairbrushes, mirrors, fans, and petticoats. Choreographer Agnes de Mille incorporated pantomime and ballet into this number, as she did with many of the numbers in the musical. The girls seem to be inspired by the process of grooming and preening for a party, making up a dance on the spur of the moment based on their beauty regimen. As she sings, lead character Laurey tightens another girl's corset for her. As Laurey adjusts the laces, the girl pulls toward and away from her in time with the music. The girls smooth their hair, fan themselves, and primp before the mirror as they sing the chorus. Near the end of the song, Laurey hears the laugh of her rival, and the girls arm themselves with their beauty paraphernalia (Fig. 20.5). They turn fans into shields and hairbrushes into potential weapons against the powerful structure of patriarchy, thus showing improvisational ingenuity's ability to offer minor moments of respite from such limited gender roles.

CONCLUSION

While both male and female characters express improvisational ingenuity in the western film musicals, they do so in separate spheres. This reinforced the gender dichotomy and implied that men and women had a patriotic duty to use their improvisational ingenuity within their separate domains. Ostensibly, this was supposed to aid in the competition against the Soviets and the general fight against communism. However, reinforcing the ideology of separate spheres also had the effect of excluding most women from the workplace. Acting as a check against women's newfound independence in the workforce during World War II, these western film musicals presented an ideal social model in which men practiced improvisational ingenuity outside the home and women put their creativity to use in the domestic sphere.

Offering up a model for a society in crisis, Cold War western film musicals reinforced the dominant patriarchal social values regarding gender and family in the United States. Expressing elements of American identity that are sources of nationalistic pride, the iconic cowboy and frontiersman figures in these films act as behavioral models. Feminine characters in these films also express elements of American identity, but they do this only within the confines of the domestic world. While the masculinized women in these films display some elements of American identity in the public sphere, in order to become accepted as a part of society, they must become feminized, get married, and be incorporated into the domestic sphere. By glorifying the iconic American figures of the cowboy and frontiersman, these films elicited patriotic pride in audiences. During a period of anxiety and uncertainty, western film musicals offered reassurance. These films associated patriotism with a return to conservative social models such as gendered separate spheres and the nuclear family. While focusing on the American character may have been a conscious choice on the part of filmmakers and choreographers, it is unlikely that they purposefully intended to set up ideal models to reinforce the gender dichotomy and rationalize the politics of the Cold War. However, these films were purveyors of the popular culture of the era, which reinforced dominant social values in subtle, yet effective ways.

In this time of anxiety, these film musicals offered a nostalgic vision of a romanticized American-ness, one that was not threatened by the burgeoning Civil Rights movement or the rise of Cold War international antagonisms. However, this idyllic vision is one that never really came to fruition. "The extent to which American identities existed in an uneasy state of renegotiation is revealed in a range of contemporary texts, whether from the perspective of female dissatisfaction in Betty Friedan's *The Feminine Mystique* or the middle-class male's readjustment crisis in *The Man in the Gray Flannel Suit*. This state of flux was represented nowhere more than in Hollywood cinema" (McNally 2008, 5). As historians have pointed out in recent years, not all women were housewives in the 1950s. The idealized gender roles presented on screen countered the reality that some women worked outside the home. Yet, these films showcase the ability for choreography and its use in representing a fragile American-ness, one that was soon to be destabilized by bodies seeking to engage in new understandings of improvisational ingenuity: lunch counter sit-ins, pow-wows, and political marches.

Notes

1. The stagemusical *Oklahoma!* (1943) featured a dream ballet choreographed by Agnes de Mille. In this sequence, the main character Laurey's feelings about her love interest get

translated into choreography. This musical demonstrated how a dance sequence alone could further the action of the narrative.

2. Improvisational ingenuity was common in the dancing of mid-nineteenth century frontiersmen. Referring to dances as "fandangos," California miners danced in improvised settings such as saloons, church meeting halls, and brush arbors. Because women were scarce in the early years, men danced both the lead and follow roles, with the "female" sometimes denoted by a handkerchief or other bit of women's attire, such as a hoop skirt. See Gretchen Schneider, "Pigeon Wings and Polkas: The Dance of the California Miners." *Dance Perspectives* 39 (Winter 1969): 1–57.

3. See Michael L. Johnson, *Hunger for the Wild: America's Obsession with the Untamed West* (Lawrence: University Press of Kansas, 2007); Cathy Luchetti, *Men of the West: Life on the American Frontier* (New York: W.W. Norton & Co., 2004); Bart McDowell, *The American Cowboy in Life and Legend* (Washington, D.C.: National Geographic Society, 1972).

4. See Elaine Tyler May, *Homeward Bound: American Families in the Cold War Era* (New York: Basic Books, 1988).

5. This is a concept from classical antiquity that has reappeared throughout the centuries—women contribute to society by raising virtuous citizens who participate in government. In the United States, the idea was popular during the Revolutionary Era, as well as subsequent periods. Historian Linda Kerber introduced the term "Republican Mother," a concept that subsequently occupied the research and writing of Revolutionary Era gender historians for many years. See Linda K. Kerber, "The Republican Mother: Women and the Enlightenment—An American Perspective," *American Quarterly* 28, no. 2 (Summer 1976): 187–205.

6. According to Marxist theorists Max Horkheimer and Theodor W. Adorno, Hollywood films work on a subconscious level that encourages viewers to accept the status quo (1947). One of the ways that Hollywood films achieve popular success is by making it seem as though the star could be just like the viewer; or, to put it another way, anyone could be the star. But, at the same time, a tension exists because the viewer knows he or she could never really be the star. Film has a way of washing over the viewer, of encouraging him or her to be a passive spectator who need not question the content put before him or her.

BIBLIOGRAPHY

Barson, Michael, and Steven Heller. *Red Scared! The Commie Menace in Propaganda and Popular Culture.* San Francisco: Chronicle Books, 2001.

Braudy, Leo. *The World in a Frame: What We See in Films.* Garden City, NY: Anchor Press, 1976.

De Mille, Agnes. *America Dances.* New York: Macmillan Publishing, 1980.

Dunbabin, J. P. D. *The Cold War: The Great Powers and Their Allies.* Harlow, England: Pearson Education Limited, 2008.

Feuer, Jane. *The Hollywood Musical.* Bloomington: Indiana University Press, 1982.

Heale, M.J. *McCarthy's Americans: Red Scare Politics in State and Nation, 1935–1965.* Athens, GA: The University of Georgia Press, 1998.

Hebdige, Dick. *Subculture: The Meaning of Style* (1979). Reprint, London: Routledge, 1988.

Hegarty, Marilyn. "Patriot or Prostitute?: Sexual Discourses, Print Media, and American Women during World War II." *Journal of Women's History* 10 (Summer 1998): 112–136.

Hendershot, Cyndy. *Anti-Communism and Popular Culture in Mid-Century America*. Jefferson, NC, and London: McFarland & Co., Inc., 2003.

Horkheimer, Max and Theodor Adorno. "The Culture Industry: Enlightenment as Mass Deception." In *Dialectic of Enlightenment* (1947). Edited by Gunzelin Schmid Norr. Translated by Edmond Jephcott, 94–136. Stanford, CA: Stanford University Press, 2002.

Hunter, Jane H. "Gender and Sexuality." In *A Companion to American Cultural History*, edited by Karen Halttunen. Malden, MA: Blackwell Publishing, 2008.

Kennedy, John F. "Some Elements of the American Character." Independence Day Oration 1946. Available from http://www.jfklibrary.org/Historical+Resources/Archives/Archives+and+Manuscripts/Kennedy.John+F/jfk_pre-pres/subcoll_1_HoR/02.+Speeches/; Internet; accessed February 2009.

May, Elaine Tyler. *Homeward Bound: American Families in the Cold War Era*. New York: Basic Books, 1988.

McNally, Karen. *When Frankie Went to Hollywood: Frank Sinatra and American Male Identity*. Urbana: University of Illinois Press, 2008.

Murray, Marcy M. "Strong Women and Cross-Dressed Men: Representation of Gender by Circus Performers During the Golden Age of the American Circus, 1860–1930." *Bandwagon: The Journal of the Circus Historical Society, Inc* (May–June 2004): 18–23.

Meyerowitz, Joanne, ed. *Not June Cleaver: Women and Gender in Postwar America, 1945–1960*. Philadelphia: Temple University Press, 1994.

Rubin, Martin. *Showstoppers: Busby Berkeley and the Tradition of Spectacle*. New York: Columbia University Press, 1993.

Siegel, Marcia B. *The Shapes of Change: Images of American Dance*. Boston: Houghton Mifflin, 1979.

Stiles, T. J., ed. *In Their Own Words: Warriors and Pioneers*. New York: The Berkley Publishing Group, 1996.

Turner, Victor. *Dramas, Fields, and Metaphors: Symbolic Action in Human Society*. Ithaca and London: Cornell University Press, 1974.

——. *The Anthropology of Performance*. New York: PAJ Publications, 1986.

VIDEOGRAPHY

Annie Get Your Gun. Dir. George Sidney. DVD. Metro-Goldwyn-Mayer. 1950. 107 minutes.

Calamity Jane. Dir. David Butler. Warner Bros. Pictures. 1953. 101 minutes.

Oklahoma! Dir. Fred Zinnemann. DVD. Magna Theatre Corporation. 1955. 145 minutes.

Seven Brides for Seven Brothers. Dir. Stanley Donen. DVD. Metro-Goldwyn-Mayer. 1954. 102 minutes.

Sobbin' Women: The Making of Seven Brides for Seven Brothers. Dir. Scott Benson. DVD. Turner Entertainment Co. 1997. 35 minutes.

CHAPTER 21

SOME DANCE SCENES FROM CUBAN CINEMA, 1959–2012

VICTOR FOWLER

TRANSLATED BY TOM PHILLIPS

THANKS to the archive of cultural images generated by cinema, television, radio, and the music industry, the island of Cuba is now identified with its music and social dances. It is the land of the rumba, the conga, the mambo, the cha cha chá and the son (which has now evolved into salsa). Film and television have spread images of Mickey Mouse dancing the conga, Desi Arnaz playing the drums in a rumba, President Kennedy dancing a cha cha chá and Chayanne dancing salsa. As the political scientist Rafael Hernández states:

> To dance, naturally, the Cubans, the kings and queens of the mambo or the Havana son follow the path towards success and fame in New York, Paris, Mexico City or Madrid. Desi Arnaz is the paradigm of this type of film playing himself in Cuban Pete ("Con rumbo a Cuba," 1946), although the character of the "rumbero cubano" had been established by Carmen Miranda and César Romero (Weekend in Havana, 1941), whose legacy in stylized ballroom choreographies of Cuban dances would include authentic *criollos* like Armand Assante, Diego Luna and the Frenchman Vincent Lecouer.[1]

DANCE, THE UNBRIDLED PASSION OF THE *CRIOLLO*

In a classic piece of Cuban costumbrista literature Emilio Roig de Leuchsenring, the official historian of the City of Havana for almost three decades, wrote: "dance impassioned our great-great-grandparents, great-grandparents and grandparents far more than it impassions their great-great-grandchildren, great-grandchildren and grandchildren today."[2] Although it is only a short piece that appeared in the journal *Carteles* under the title "El baile, desenfrenada pasión del criollo," the text still identifies several meanings of dance in Cuban culture, in particular, as the title itself and the examples quoted show, the act of identifying dance with the figure that personifies the self-image that members of Cuba's hegemonic white culture regard as their identity: the *criollo*. It is this which explains why the examples used—quotations from books of memoirs, a historical study of Havana's rise, an article from the early days of Cuba's press in 1792, costumbrista articles from nineteenth-century Cuba and the testimony of a nineteenth-century French traveler to the island—primarily refer to the formal dance of drawing rooms, and not to the popular spaces of dancing.

CUBAN FILM AND DANCE

Historians and critics agree that, with a few honorable exceptions, the aim of Cuban film producers before 1959 was to offer a pleasing and "beautiful" image of the country. To achieve this, a combination of popular forms of music and dance was ideal, and so the cinema became a major vehicle for promoting the most renowned exponents of the country's popular music and dance, albeit filtered through criteria that excluded spaces of poverty. Examples of this type of film include such works as: *Romance del palmar* (1938); *Cancionero cubano* (1939); *¡Qué suerte tiene el cubano!* (1950); *Bella la salvaje* (1953); and *Sandra, la mujer de fuego* (1953), among others. Several of these films have plots so weak that they border on the ridiculous and even the nonsensical.[3]

POPULAR DANCE AND ENTERING HISTORY: *CUBA BAILA*

Fidel Castro's Cuban Revolution triumphed on January 1, 1959, and a few months later, on March 24, established the Instituto Cubano del Arte y de la Industria Cinematográfica (ICAIC). Established though a law emphasizing the value of film as an art form, the ICAIC was the first cultural institute founded by the new government. In 1960 Julio García Espinosa, a young filmmaker who in 1955 had directed a short film, similar in style to Italian neorealism, the content of which was influenced by critical realism, directed one of the first feature-length fiction films of Cuba's new cinema following the triumph of the Revolution: *Cuba baila*. The film uses a portrayal of a *quinceañera* party—the Cuban equivalent of the "sweet sixteen"—to explore the worries of a lower-middle-class family in pre-revolutionary Cuba as the mother tries to use the event to help her daughter climb the social ladder. As Michael Channan writes in his well-known study, *Cuban Cinema*:

> The mother of the protagonist family is keenly aware of the importance the music at her daughter's fiesta will play. Although the cost is almost prohibitive, she wants an orchestra like the one that impresses them as minor guests among the upper bourgeoisie. Musically, such an orchestra means the Viennese waltz and North American hits, instead of the popular Cuban dances preferred by the daughter herself and her local boyfriend, whom her mother slights. To obtain a loan to pay for it, the father has to ingratiate himself with his superiors at the office by attending a political meeting in a local square.[4]

In the closing minutes, the mother's failure is symbolically represented by the change from the waltz the guests are dancing ("Blue Danube") to the danzón—a typically Cuban style of music—"Tres lindas cubanas," by the composer Antonio María Romeu, which closes the film and which is the very same piece that opened the film.

Dancing an Old Conflict: The People and *Un día en el solar*

The 1965 completion of the feature-length fiction film *Un día en el solar* (directed by Eduardo Manet, with a script by Lisandro Otero based on a ballet by the choreographer Alberto Alonso and with choreography by Alonso himself) was an important moment in contemporary Cuban cinema for a number of reasons: it was the first color film made by the ICAIC, it was the first musical made by the ICAIC, and it was the first occasion in which the *solar* (the typical large, shared house of Havana's working-class neighborhoods), with its popular characters and habits, was the setting of a feature-length film. The plot, a rewriting of a ballet conceived years earlier by Alonso, is an attempt to respond to an old concern of his: how to represent the lives of the people through dance? How can you combine the tradition, education, and abilities of classical dancers and their spectacle—which are a privileged part of the consumption and definitions of distinction of elite sectors—with popular dance and spectacle?

Along with his brother Fernando, Alberto Alonso had trained as a classical dancer in the Academia de Ballet of the Sociedad Pro-Arte Musical in Havana with the Soviet teacher Nicolas Yavorsky and had spent six years as a character dancer with the Ballet Ruse de Monte Carlo (between 1935 and 1941). In 1941 he took charge of the ballet school of the Pro-Arte and went on to produce an important body of work as a choreographer, as can be seen in the following quote from Alonso's obituary, written by the Cuban ballet critic Roberto Méndez:

> In 1943 Alberto created several of his noteworthy pieces of work: *Concerto*, an "abstract" ballet based on the music in a Vivaldi concerto, recreated by Johann

Sebastian Bach; *Forma*, a very ambitious work based on a score by José Ardévol and a poem by José Lezama Lima and with the direct participation of the Coral de la Habana, directed by María Muñoz. Neither should we forget his *Icaro*, which is a free version of Sergio Lifar's original, which he cubanized with the help of the young composer Harold Gramatges, who devised a complex percussion arrangement for the masculine solo.[5]

Alonso's next choreographic work, the ballet *Antes del alba* (1947), caused something of a scandal in Havana's elegant society as—apart from being set in a Havana *solar*—the protagonist, danced by Alicia Alonso, "abandoned by the man she loves, commits suicide by setting fire to herself."[6] As Méndez goes on to note:

> Hilario González's score [...] integrated popular rhythms from the rumba to the bolero and the "botecito". Alberto's choreography obliged the ballerinas to step outside of academic rectitude and to move with the sensuality of Cuban dance. It was the first time on the island that ballet had been linked to the most pressing social problems.[7]

A similar social focus runs through the story of *Un día en el solar*, as the events narrated clearly show the marks of the new Cuba inaugurated by the Revolution; examples of this include the relations between the couple who appear in the opening sequence (she is a white student, he is a black athlete), the love story between Sonia and Tomás (he appears not only studying chemical formulas, but in the final minutes we also see him taking part in political tasks with the revolutionary authorities) and, finally, the sequence where the *dirigente de barrio* (a representative of the new government charged with monitoring the political views of the people in the neighborhood, dressed in militia clothing) gathers the people of the *solar* to practice military marching (in reality they carry out a series of gymnastic movements imitating soldiers with rifles) (66:55). At this point it is interesting to note that the film was made in 1965, just three years after the infamous missile crisis.

Following this, and as a conclusion to the film, the people of the *solar* dance one last time, but now the music we hear is a rumba (a style originating in the Havana *solares*); as a surprising sign of the new unity, the *dirigente político* (now wearing the white *guayabera* that was the national dress at that time) also dances to the beat of the drum as part of the group, closing the circle on the focus or message that the filmmakers want to transmit to the viewer; the country's deep truth or essence is born and is to be found in these popular spaces where races, musical forms, and styles of dancing are mixed together.

A LITTLE DECLARATION OF LOVE AND WAR: *LOS DEL BAILE*

Also in 1965 the documentary maker Nicolás "Nicolasito" Guillén Landrián directed *Los del baile*, (http://youtube/fGSks2IE6R8) a short film that focuses on the dancers at a party where the musician Pedro Izquierdo is playing. Known in Cuba as "Pello, el afrocán," Izquierdo was the creator of the rhythm known as the "mozambique," combining twelve congas, two bass drums, three cowbells, a frying pan, four trumpets, and three trombones.[8] From a musical history perspective, Izquierdo described the mozambique as: "a combination of beats from different rhythms: rumba abierta, columbia, bambú, seis por ocho, the bonkó enchemiyá, the kuchí yeremá, the ekón of the Abakuá people, and the side-drum of the conga."[9]

After the success of the Revolution, one immediate impact on the field of music of the escalating conflict between Cuba and the United States was the isolation of Cuban music from those musical circles and sectors of the music business relying directly or indirectly on capital investment from the United States. In parallel with this, a considerable number of dancers and musicians left the country, which had a significant effect. It was within this panorama that the rise and rapid acceptance of the mozambique rhythm among dancers became an important cultural phenomenon—the type of event that mixes the dialectic development of music in a country and its links with tradition, national pride, and political instrumentalization.

Nicolasito Guillén's short documentary is most notable for three points: capturing "Pello, el afrocán" in his moment of greatest glory and showing a wide variety of ordinary people attending the party where we see "Pello" playing; displaying images of the home lives of these dancers as counterpoints to the dance; and establishing a subtle dialogue with history through the careful composition of shots, the skillful capturing of symbolic markers of the era, and a montage that takes advantage of a highly expressive soundtrack.

The dancers, the great majority of whom are of African descent, bring us face to face with those people who have traditionally lived in the conditions of greatest poverty, but who also, in the process of cultural resistance, have created rhythms and dances (like the rumba and the conga) which—after passing through a long process of "refinement"—attain universal fame. As a consequence of this process, which the Cuban anthropologist Fernando Ortiz described as "the social whitening of the drums,"[10] Cuba for the first time danced en masse to something that was essentially black music; remember that the mozambique was little more than a combination of metal instruments (trumpets, trombones, cowbells, and pans) and a crushing percussion (two bass drums and twelve congas). Of all this, the twelve congas were the sonic and visual evidence of a sort of triumphant revenge by the African element of Cuban popular culture; furthermore, in a deliberate contrast within the spectacle, an attractive young white woman danced each piece on stage (00:20). In this context the Cuban poet, ethnologist, musician and folklorist Rogelio Martínez Furé wrote that the mozambique represented "the definitive consecration of percussion on skins and metal"[11] and the triumph of the drum, "the most hunted and most revered of our instruments."[12]

As a result of these factors it is not unreasonable to see this short documentary by "Nicolasito" Guillén, a black filmmaker himself, as a declaration of love and war: an attempt to foreground that special moment in which the country was conquered by the music of Pedro Izquierdo. *Los del baile* is a short piece that begins with "Pello" directing his musicians as the mozambique bursts thunderously into life on the soundtrack. It then shows several dancers, the action is cut, and the viewer is unexpectedly taken into the house of a young woman of African descent (whose presence only makes sense if she was at the dance). The film then cuts between brief images of this woman in her home (she is seated in a regal manner) and images of the dance; the key thing here is that both the soundtrack and the dance are no longer examples of the mozambique, but instead the couples are doing the moves of a slow dance which seems to be a danzón. Indeed this is the music, played on a clavinet, that can be heard on the soundtrack. With this contrapuntal use of montage the director suggests that the people we saw dancing to the rhythm of the drums are also part of the dance rhythm in which Cuba's Spanish and African heritages are synthesized.

Having reached this point (2:53), in a surprising scene, the young woman of African descent appears, brushing her hair in a cracked mirror that is blurred by age, giving way seconds later (3:06) to images of women of African descent having their hair styled and straightened and the unexpected image of a drawing of an eye placed in the center of the shot, on a small table. In the Yoruba religion this eye, which can also be placed behind the door, in the entrance to the house, or another visible location, serves to warn that the place is protected. If the blurred and broken mirror represents the difficulty of finding one's self image, the straightening of the women's hair connects this difficulty with being black and the search for an imitative and inauthentic standard of beauty. Within this sequence, the presence of the drawing of the eye symbolizes control, self-vigilance, and worldview. From our viewpoint, the return to the dance happens once this blurred condition has been overcome, when the subject comes to know itself and reaffirms its values and identity. For this reason, when we see the sudden shot of a wall with three posters showing political propaganda behind the dancers (3:50), the director makes a deep political declaration: just as the poster in the center shows a photo of Fidel Castro above a phrase taken from one of his speeches ("If they want peace there will be peace; but if they want war we are not afraid of war!"),[13] *Los del baile*—the people of the dance—turn out to be the same as *los de la guerra*—the people of the war. To confirm the symbolic content of the shot, in the poster on the left the phrase "Eternal revolution" ("Revolución eterna") stands out, and the one on the right shows a photo of a smiling black soldier and the phrase "Parade and rally" ("Desfile y concentración") underneath. At this point the documentary shows couples dancing to the rhythm of the mozambique and finally completes the important synthesis when, seconds from the end (5:54), we see the couples dancing the moves of the mozambique but on the soundtrack we hear the clavinet of a danzón.

DANCE AND RESISTANCE: *MEMORIAS DEL SUBDESARROLLO*

Memorias del subdesarrollo primarily conveys its meaning by using dance as a symbolic signifier of national identity. This film, which was directed by Tomás Gutiérrez Alea in 1969, is considered the best work in the history of Cuban cinema and in 2009 was voted the best Latin American film of all time in the first global survey of the 100 best films in Latin American cinema; the survey was organized by the film website NOTICINE.com.

The film's action takes place in 1962, during the days preceding the missile crisis, and revolves around the figure of Sergio, a member of the petit-bourgeoisie who hates his class and has never felt comfortable in it.

Sergio passes through the different scenes like an anthropologist taking notes. He is an observer who constantly questions the condition of underdevelopment but without contributing toward its transformation; his only connection is a deeply critical gaze which, while stripping away the charm of what surrounds him, also removes any connection with his surroundings. This character's tragedy is that if his discomfort (or hatred) enables him to distance himself from his social class—even at the cost of choosing to remain in Cuba when the rest of his family leave for the United States—the limits of his bourgeois concept of the people and the nation stop him from becoming a true part of the new society. It is interesting that, in order to illustrate the protagonist's alienation from the space around him, the director chooses a dance sequence that he places at the opening of the story and which he repeats later on, a few minutes from the story's ending.

In this establishing sequence (inserted as a way into the plot) the camera places us, without explanation, in a public dance, packed with ordinary people (most of whom are of African descent). We hear shots and a man falls murdered (0:41). After this surprise there is a commotion around the dead man, but the music continues and the dancers return to their revelry while, in a brutal counterpoint, the police carry the body out on their shoulders above the crowd (1:10). The camera films the scene from above and the empty circle that opens up when the dead man falls is followed by this vision of a body lifted up and the people who close the space around him as though it were a symbolic wound. It is very important to note that only the professional actors knew what was going to happen in this scene, so the reaction of the crowd was not acted but "real." That these are people who can absorb suffering and continue with their pleasure is isolated by the camera in the form of a young woman of African descent dancing with her partner; the camera approaches, focusing on the woman's eyes, but she in turn returns the camera's gaze, which then becomes frozen in a still of her face until the scene fades to black.

On one side we see an intellectual who attempts to become part of and understand the masses who have become a new actor in the country's history (this intellectual is both Sergio the story's protagonist and Alea the director); on the other side we find the energy emanating from the people and the idea that it is not by intellectualizing existence that the nature of the people can be revealed, but rather by entering into their pain, resistance, and resilience. This is precisely what is foregrounded by the joy-death-joy combination during the dance.

Fragments of this scene are repeated, albeit from a different viewpoint, later on when Sergio walks down a street where a political demonstration is being held, accompanied by drums. He says to himself, "Everything comes to me too early or too late. In another time maybe I could have understood what is happening here. Today I can't anymore."[14] The Sergio of the repeated scene is accompanied by a young woman and drinks beer from a paper cup in the middle of the crowd of dancers. In this variation on what could have been, the shooting scene is repeated and a man falls dead to the ground, but this time the camera concentrates on an isolated Sergio who is alienated from his surroundings, an intruder. One especially interesting element here is that the music on the soundtrack and which the dancers enjoy is by "Pello, el afrocán" who—to the rhythm of a mozambique—plays a piece called "Teresa."

In light of this, to fully understand *Memorias del subdesarrollo* it is important to recall our earlier comments on the rhythm of the mozambique created by "Pello, el afrocán"; as Sergio, the protagonist of the film, is abandoned by the camera for the last two minutes of the story, we are obliged to provide the introduction and epilogue, and when the camera focuses on Sergio for the last time he is shut in his house, consumed by panic after hearing on the radio that the missile crisis has begun (93:42). From here the camera passes between two rows of anti-aircraft guns and the dozens of soldiers and volunteer militia who operate them. It is clear that these militia are the same members of the masses who appear in the dance scene that opens the narration and who practice military exercises in *Un día en el solar* or appear in the political poster of *Los del baile*; in this manner the absurd death in the opening scene of *Memorias del subdesarrollo* acquires meaning within political history.

Son o no Son, or "Dance, Humanism, and Emancipation"

Son o no son is a feature-length fiction film with elements of documentary and film essay structured as a series of costumbrista sketches; it is an experimental film in which a director of musicals (played by the choreographer Alberto Alonso) tries to stage a show paying homage to traditional Cuban music. The director encounters all manner of difficulties, at the same time as he starts to question the meaning of art, the relationship between elite and popular forms, the relationship between the Western norm and peripheral national cultures, comedy, cultural consumption, and banality, among other issues. Given that the director of this strange film is Julio García Espinosa, we can assume that this film continues the path opened by Espinosa and Alonso in their earlier films *Cuba baila* and *Un día en el solar*.

After linking various scenes from the film essay, lightened with jokes between them, in the middle of a performance by a double-bassist, the director inserts an intertitle that reads "how hard it is to make a musical" ("qué difícil es hacer un musical") (24:15); shortly afterward (27:21) the intertitle gives way to a film critic's weighty discourse about the relationship between musical cinema, social class, cultural consumption, and ideology (31:54). The most radically experimental moment occurs when García Espinosa uses the screen of the very film he is making to send a letter to the Bolivian director Jorge Sanjinés: "I think we have dedicated too much time to analyzing the quality films that are screened in empty cinemas and too little to analyzing those bad films that fill cinemas all over the world every day."[15]

Son o no son proposes a fascinating game of mirrors and superimpositions as it shows a great classical composer, performer, and orchestral-director (the Cuban maestro Leo Brower) directing a classic from the repertory of the traditional Cuban trova (60:56); to make the joke more cutting—or the invitation to think more pointed—the song has previously been arranged with all rules of a neo-classical orchestration, reminiscent of Mozart's symphonies.

The final section of the film treats us to a brilliant performance of "El carbonero" by the members of Félix Chapottín's band and the singer Miguelito Cuní. This song is a classic piece by these Cuban musicians and, in broader terms, from the repertoire of the Cuban son. At the same time, dozens of couples dance, enjoying the rhythm, but—and this is of key importance—they do so in a variety of ways, some respecting the tradition or canon of the *son* dancer which is similar to the *danzón* (straight-backed, marking the beat with slow movements) and others with a freedom that approaches the style known in Cuba as the casino (with more relaxed movement of the arms, which make shapes and following the beat); at the same time, and also within the group, others introduce variations as the dance incorporates "imported" moves that became popular in the 1970s when the film was made (such as hip pulses), some move simply following the rhythm (as they do not "know how to dance") and a third person even takes the improvisation to the extreme of descending until he touches his partner's ankles with his forehead. This diversity and creativity that unfold before our eyes and that takes place in any popular dance space is what makes the choreographer Alberto say:

> We must understand that the people have created fine choreographies over the years from the danzón to the son, from the mambo to the cha cha chá, and they continue creating. [...] I will not stop until we overcome this division between a minority art and a popular art![16]

It is here that, closing the game of mirrors and time-periods, García Espinosa has the inspired idea of inserting an intertext on a blue background that reads, "the son has been danced in all periods, everywhere and by everyone"[17] and then, while the soundtrack reproduces a classic Cuban *son* ("Castellanos, qué bueno baila usted," with the voice of Benny Moré accompanied by his orchestra), he shows a montage of seven short film clips containing scenes of dancing from various cultures: popular dances from Spain, Central Europe, Slavic regions, Polynesia, and South East Asia.

Consequently, this montage closes the film by leading the viewer, through dance, toward an essential unity of human experience in order to remind us that: "this is not really a film about the son."[18]

RESISTING AND SURVIVING AMONG THE RUINS: *HABANA SOLO*

I will finish by analyzing a short piece by the photographer and videoartist Juan Carlos Alom: *Habana Solo* (2000). This short film of just 15 minutes in length offers a powerful portrait of Havana as a city in ruins, an image that contemporary photography has made into a sort of cliché for considering Cuba. Alom's piece is divided into four sections, which the viewer must assemble like a jigsaw. The opening sequence establishes a counterpoint between images of the famous Cuban jazz pianist Frank Emiliano playing Latin jazz and images of poverty in the city. The second section starts with a hand-held camera that wanders through the streets of poor neighborhoods, focusing on scenes from daily life. A third part shows the world of work and its principal appeal is scenes of workers (working, resting, or posing for the camera) and images of beautiful Cuban women in the street. The fourth section, however, contains a sudden cut given that the action takes place on a rooftop in a poor neighborhood: a young man of African descent dances a rumba, but the soundtrack is totally silent.

In a film muting the soundtrack is an act of authorial violence that contrasts with the "conventional" (never absolute) silence of the spaces portrayed and which, as such, obliges the viewer to examine the film in search of the meaning proposed by the director. From this point of view, the backdrop for this strange dance (the buildings of el Vedado, present in our imaginary as an architectonic metaphor of "modern" Havana and of the middle class in the distance) is a reminder of a silent tension between two lifestyles, two versions of the Cuban past-present: the former bourgeois areas and areas of continuing poverty.

In order to fully understand this soundless dance, whose duration—in a 15-minute work—is 90 seconds in which we must look back to an earlier moment: the image of a political slogan which, next to a photo of an aging Fidel Castro, hangs from a wire fence (6:30'). The phrase on the poster ("Here we are standing and proud," "Aquí estamo de pie y firmes")not only contains a strange syntactical construction but also a spelling mistake that is characteristic of people with a low level of education; this shows that we are in the heart of the poorly educated class, where the poorest sectors of society with the fewest opportunities can be found. Despite this, politics are a part of life here and people feel engaged with it.

Alom refuses to offer picturesque images of the city or to introduce any false glamour, and so the beautiful Cuban women that the camera shows are dressed in poor-quality clothing. The solitary dance on the roof is a gesture without spectators whose main meaning is the tension established between the dancer and the buildings in the distance. There is no music and his movements, as the seconds pass, become mysterious and almost frenzied.

If, as Espinosa's film reminds us, when we talk about the *son* we are not talking about the *son*, then as we study the insistence of a solitary body, working, dancing on a roof, we also talk of something different. This could be a discourse on the people, their ability to resist, and their stubborn hope.

NOTES

1. "Para bailar, naturalmente, los cubanos. Los reyes y las reinas del mambo o del son habaneros toman el camino del éxito y la fama hacia Nueva York, París, México o Madrid. Desi Arnaz es el paradigma de este cine, interpretándose a sí mismo en Cuban Pete (Con rumbo

a Cuba, 1946), aunque ya el personaje del «rumbero cubano» había sido fijado por Carmen Miranda y César Romero (Weekend in Havana, 1941), cuya descendencia en coreografías de salón estilizadas de bailes cubanos, incluiría a criollos reyoyos como Armand Assante, Diego Luna y el francés Vincent Lecoeur," (Hernández: 2005).

2. "el baile enloquecía a nuestros tatarabuelos, bisabuelos y abuelos, mucho más que hoy entusiasma a sus tataranietos, bisnietos y nietos" "El baile, desenfrenada pasión del criollo," *Carteles* (1950: 82–83).

3. (Cumaná: 2011: I, 322–323).

4. (Channan 2004: 151).

5. En 1943 crea Alberto algunas de sus obras notables: *Concerto*, un ballet "abstracto" basado en la música de un concierto de Vivaldi, recreado por Juan Sebastián Bach; *Forma*, obra muy ambiciosa, apoyada en una partitura de José Ardévol y en un poema de José Lezama Lima y con la participación directa de la Coral de La Habana, dirigida por María Muñoz. No hay que olvidar tampoco su *Icaro*, que es una libre versión del original del Sergio Lifar, que él cubanizó con el apoyo del joven compositor Harold Gramatges, quien concibió todo un complejo acompañamiento de percusión para el solo masculino (Méndez: 2008).

6. "abandonada por el hombre que ama, se suicida prendiéndose fuego" (IDEM).

7. "la partitura de Hilario González [...] integraba ritmos populares desde la rumba, hasta el bolero y el "botecito." La coreografía del Alberto obligaba a los bailarines a salir del envaramiento académico, a moverse con la sensualidad del baile cubano. Era la primera vez que en la Isla el ballet se vinculaba a los más urgentes problemas sociales" (IDEM).

8. (Orejuela 2006: 255).

9. "una combinación de golpes de distintos ritmos: rumba abierta, columbia, bambú, seis por ocho, el bonkó enchemiyá, el kuchí yeremá, el ekón de los abakuá y el redoblante de la conga" (Orejuela 2006: 256).

10. "el blanqueamiento social de los tambores" (Ortiz 1952: 98).

11. "la consagración definitiva de la percusión en cueros y metales" (Orejuela 2006: 258).

12. "el más perseguido y el más reverenciado de nuestros instrumentos" (Orejuela 2006: 258).

13. "Si quieren paz, habrá paz; pero si quieren guerra, ¡no tenemos miedo a la guerra!"

14. "Todo me llega demasiado temprano o demasiado tarde. En otra época tal vez hubiera podido entender lo que está pasando aquí. Hoy ya no puedo" (1, 16:24').

15. "Creo que hemos dedicado demasiado tiempo al análisis de las buenas películas que son proyectadas en salas vacías y demasiado poco al análisis de aquellas películas malas que a diario llenan las salas de cine en el mundo entero" (39:57').

16. Tenemos que entender que el pueblo ha creado todo una coreografía en estos años, desde el danzón al son, al mambo, al *cha cha chá* y sigue creando. [...] ¡Yo no paro hasta que no se supere esa división entre un arte de minorías y un arte popular! (1, 12:46').

17. "el son se ha bailado en todas las épocas en todas las partes y por todo el mundo" (1, 16:10').

18. "en realidad esta no es una película sobre el son" (1, 17:10').

BIBLIOGRAPHY

Castillo, Luciano. "Julio García Espinosa y el largo camino de Cuba baila." *La Jiribilla* (online journal) (Havana). Vol. 10. September 17–23, 2011. http://www.lajiribilla.cu/2011/n541_09/541_03.html.

Channan, Michael. *Cuban Cinema*. Minneapolis: University of Minnesota Press, 2004.

Cumaná González, María Caridad. *Film: 1931–1959*. In West Durán, Alan (editor). *Cuba*. Farmington Hills: Gale Cengage Learning, 2012.

Fowler Calzada, Víctor. *Conversaciones con un cineasta incómodo: Julio García Espinosa*. Havana: Centro de Investigación y Desarrollo de la Cultura Juan Marinello-Ediciones ICAIC, Havana, 2004, p. 37.

Giró, Radamés. *Diccionario enciclopédico de la música en Cuba (4 volúmenes)*. La Habana: Editorial Letras Cubanas, 2007.

Hernández, Rafael. "La imagen de Cuba en el cine. El making de un canon." *Cine Cubano* (online journal) (Havana). No. 2, 2005. http://www.cubacine.cult.cu/revistacinecubano/digital02/centrocap63.htm.

Méndez Martínez, Roberto. *Alberto Alonso, la muerte de un Fundador. La Jiribilla* (online journal) (Havana). Vol. 6. December 29–January 4, 2008. http://www.lajiribilla.cu/2007/n347_12/347_35.html.

Noguer, Eduardo G. *Cien años de cine cubano*. Miami: Librería Impresión Corp., 1998.

Orejuela Martínez, Adriana. *El son no se fue de Cuba. Claves para una historia 1959–1973*. Havana: Editorial Letras Cubanas, 2006.

Ortiz, Fernando. *Los instrumentos de la música afrocubana*. Havana: Publicaciones de la Dirección de Cultura del Ministerio de Educación, 1952. Vol. 3. p. 98.

Roig de Leuchsenring, Emilio. "El baile, desenfrenada pasión del criollo." *Revista Opus Habana* (online journal). Havana. July 13, 2010. http://www.opushabana.cu/index.php?option=com_content&task=blogsection&id=9&Itemid=43 originally published in: *Carteles*, 31(17): 82–83; April 23, 1950.

West Durán, Alan, ed. *Cuba*. Farmington Hills, MI: Gale Cengage Learning, 2012.

Films discussed

Original title: *Cuba baila*
Director: Julio García Espinosa
Country: Cuba
Original language: Spanish
Format: 35 mm
Genre: Fiction
Type: B/W
Length: 81 min.
Year of production: 1960
Production company: ICAIC
Distributor: Distribuidora Internacional de Películas ICAIC
Script: Julio García Espinosa with the collaboration of Alfredo Guevara and Manuel Barbachano Ponce
Producer: José Fraga
Cinematography: Sergio Véjar
Film editing: Mario González
Music: Música Popular
Sound: Eugenio Vesa Figueras
Cast: Raquel Revuelta, Alfredo Perojo, Vivian Gude, Humberto García Espinosa

Original title: *Los del baile*
Director: Nicolás Guillén Landrián
Country: Cuba
Original language: Spanish
Format: 35 mm
Genre: Documentary
Type: B/W
Length: 6 min.
Year of production: 1965
Production company: ICAIC
Script: Nicolás Guillén Landrián
Producer: Eduardo Valdés
Cinematography: Luis García
Film editing: Justo Vega, María Esther Valdés
Music: Pedro Izquierdo, "Pello el Afrocán"
Sound: Raúl García

Original title: *Un día en el solar*
Director: Eduardo Manet
Country: Cuba
Original language: Spanish
Format: 35 mm
Genre: Fiction
Type: Color
Length: 86 min.
Year of production: 1965
Production company: ICAIC
Script: Eduardo Manet, Julio García Espinosa
Producer: Miguel Mendoza
Cinematography: Ramón F. Suárez
Film editing: Nelson Rodríguez
Sound: Eugenio Vesa, Germinal Hernández
Cast: Sonia Calero, Tomás Morales, Roberto Rodríguez, Asenneh Rodríguez, Regla Becerra, Alicia Bustamante
Script: Eduardo Manet, Julio García Espinosa

Original title: *Memorias del subdesarrollo*
Director: Tomás Gutiérrez Alea (Titón)
Country: Cuba
Original language: Spanish
Format: 35 mm
Genre: Fiction
Type: B/W
Length: 97 min.
Year of production: 1968
Production company: ICAIC
Distributor: Distribuidora Internacional de películas ICAIC

Script: Tomás Gutiérrez Alea, Edmundo Desnoes
Producer: Miguel Mendoza
Cinematography: Ramón F. Suárez
Film editing: Nelson Rodríguez
Music: Leo Brouwer
Sound: Eugenio Vesa Figueras, Carlos Fernández, Germinal Hernández
Cast: Sergio Corrieri, Daisy Granados, Eslinda Núñez, Beatriz Ponchora, Gilda Hernández, René de la Cruz, Omar Valdés

Original title: *Son... o no son*
Director: Julio García Espinosa
Country: Cuba
Original language: Spanish
Format: 35 mm
Genre: Fiction
Type: Color
Length: 84 min.
Year of production: 1980
Production company: ICAIC
Script: Julio García Espinosa
Producer: Guillermo García
Cinematography: Jorge Haydú
Film editing: Justo Pastor Vega
Sound: Ricardo Istueta
Cast: Enrique Arredondo, Centurión, Wilfredo Fernández, Daisy Granados, Eslinda Núñez, Carlos Ruiz de la Tejera, Sonia Calero, Leo Brouwer, Miguelito Cuní.
With the participation of: Cuerpo de Baile del Cabaret Tropicana and Orquesta Chapotín
(the details of the films analyzed are from the Portal del Cine y el Audiovisual Latinoamericano y Caribeño, of the Fundación del Nuevo Cine Latinoamericano. Available: http://www. cinelatinoamericano.cult.cu).

Original Title: *Habana solo*
Director: Juan Carlos Alom
Country: Cuba
Original language: Spanish
Format: 16 mm
Genre: Documentary
Type: B/W
Length: 15 min.
Year of production: 2000
Production company: ICAIC

CHAPTER 22

....

"SHINE YOUR LIGHT ON THE WORLD": THE UTOPIAN BODIES OF *DAVE CHAPPELLE'S BLOCK PARTY*

....

ROSEMARY CANDELARIO

A block party evokes bodies in the street, camaraderie, and friendly neighbors.[1] The block party is a phenomenon that celebrates local culture and functions as a tactic to build or reinforce community on the street where one lives. How-to websites suggest block parties as a way to get to know your neighbors, have fun, and even promote home(land) security by identifying who belongs on the block and who does not. Block parties are also revered as the fertile ground on which hip-hop music and culture first grew. The film *Dave Chappelle's Block Party*, directed by acclaimed French movie and alternative music video director Michel Gondry, endeavors to create the intimacy of a neighborhood by bringing people from the five boroughs of New York City and the greater Dayton, Ohio area to the corner of Quincy and Downing Streets in Bedford-Stuyvesant, Brooklyn, for an outdoor concert featuring comedian Chappelle's favorite hip-hop and neo-soul performers. The event (September 18, 2004) and the film of the event (released March 2006) both seek to construct a new vision of community, perhaps even a utopian one, through the intentional selection of the location of the event, the bodies who will be at the party, and how those bodies will interact, as audience members in the street and performers on the stage.

In what follows, I employ the methods of a dance scholar to analyze a non-dance event. By doing so, I do not mean to suggest that the block party/*Block Party* should be regarded as a dance. Instead, I want to consider how using dance studies methodologies to read the bodies and their actions in particular locations can add to our understanding of an event that would typically be approached from a music, filmic, or even ethnographic framework. What does an attention to the corporeality of the performers and audience members contribute to scholarship on this film? More broadly, what can it contribute to research in the humanities? Addressing the latter question has become increasingly urgent as Dance Studies' theories, methods, and areas of concern have begun to spread across the disciplines, but without an agreed-upon sense of what Dance Studies is or how it may be useful to other fields. Susan Leigh Foster's groundbreaking essay, "Choreographies of Protest," lists a series of questions that may prove helpful in homing in on what dance scholars have to offer the academy.

> [W]hat are these bodies doing?; what and how do their motions signify?; what choreography, whether spontaneous or pre-determined, do they enact?; what kind of significance and impact does the collection of bodies make in the midst of its social surround?; how does the choreography theorize corporeal, individual, and social identity?; how does it construct ethnicity, gender, class, and sexuality?; how have these bodies been trained, and how has that training mastered, cultivated, or facilitated their impulses?; what do they share that allows them to move with one another?; what kind of relationship do they establish with those who are watching their actions?[2]

Embedded in these questions is the rejection of centuries of devaluation of the body as mere vessel for the mind and a concomitant equation of body with pure emotion. On the contrary, bodies here are understood as signifying entities, on their own and in relationship with others, engaged in articulate and legible movements that evidence political agency. This sort of inquiry opens up the possibility that bodies—fundamentally inscribed by their culture(s)—are capable of intelligently enacting, resisting, and (re)creating those cultures.

To return to *Dave Chappelle's Block Party,* questions such as those Foster articulated enable us to tease out the multiple ways the concert-goers and performers may signify, individually and as a group, and to suggest what their coordinated and unrehearsed actions theorize. For example, as I will discuss, the performers and audience members from Brooklyn, Yellow Springs, Ohio, and other places are all racialized and gendered in particular ways that impact how they participate in and signify ideology, power, and the nation, all issues of particular concern to the event and the film. Such an examination aims to shed light on how these bodies and their actions enable—or not—the utopian community, a sort of alternative America, that *Dave Chappelle's Block Party* endeavored to construct, however temporarily, on a block in Brooklyn.

Site-ing the Block

Growing up, Chappelle split his time between living with his mother in Washington DC and spending summers in Yellow Springs, Ohio, with his father, who was a professor at Antioch College. Chappelle moved to New York after graduating from high school to pursue a career in comedy. Even after his father passed away in 1998 and his burgeoning career took him to Hollywood, Chappelle maintained contact with Yellow Springs, and he lives there on a ranch with his wife and three children. These biographical details about Chappelle are important to the conception and presentation of *Block Party*, which is located alternately in Yellow Springs, Ohio, and Bed-Stuy, Brooklyn, both of which are specifically local and specifically not Hollywood. Of Bed-Stuy he says, "Some of it look like when *The Cosby Show* comes back from commercial break, and some of it look like when *Good Times* came back from the commercial break, but in the same block."[3] In light of Chappelle's subsequent departure from the set of his Comedy Central show eight months after the block party, we could read his emphasis on the local as a reaction to the pressures of international success and the sense that everyone around him was changing.[4] Just as Jennifer Lopez needed to insist that she was still "Jenny from the Block,"[5] Chappelle seemed to need to manufacture a block where he could locate his body as black as well as a "real" person, just another body in a group of "some folks from Ohio." Indeed, the movie poster, replicated on the DVD cover, depicts a rainbow vision that encompasses both the rural and the urban, and evokes 1960s and 1970s imagery of peace and love on the one hand, and Black Power on the other. The front cover places Dave's body in (front of) a context of black musicians and performers whose microphones and raised arms signify both a musical and an activist performance, while the back cover places him alongside (yet more prominent than) "some folks from Ohio" and Brooklyn residents. A megaphone in Chappelle's hand signifies him as in charge: a coach, or a speaker at a rally. Rays of sunshine permeate the images, despite the hurricane that threatened the actual block party with rain.[6] These bodies are brought together symbolically and materially at the L-shaped intersection of Downing and Quincy Streets, Brooklyn, a residential neighborhood that also includes a chair factory, a Salvation Army warehouse, a day-care center, and the eccentric Broken Angel building.

Yellow Springs is positioned as Chappelle's hometown in *Block Party*, while Ohio is located as the "heartland" of the United States, and therefore as a place that is quintessentially "America." We wander the town with Chappelle, meeting people on the street and in businesses he frequents: an African American probation officer, barbershop owners and clientele, the young men who are astounded to meet the famous comedian and are equally astounded to report they've just been called the N-word on the local golf course, and the elderly white owner of the shop where Chappelle buys his cigarettes. We also travel with the film crew to Central State University (CSU) in nearby Wilberforce, Ohio, to meet the marching band, the Invincible Marching Marauders. CSU is one of 105 Historically Black Colleges and Universities in the United States, and the only one in Ohio.[7] By locating black bodies (including his own) and black culture firmly in the "heartland," Chappelle makes a claim for black bodies as American bodies.

Bed-Stuy, Brooklyn, on the other hand, is constructed as a site of black bodies, and as a birthplace of black culture. Spike Lee films such as *Do the Right Thing* (1989) and *Crooklyn* (1994) portray racial strife and Lee's own family history in the neighborhood. In Chappelle's film, Mos Def talks about growing up in the neighborhood, and how hip-hop itself grew up in Brooklyn, at block parties. In one scene Lil' Cease names all the rappers who are from the area, including Lil' Kim, Jay-Z, Junior M.A.F.I.A., and The Notorious B.I.G., who, as a child, attended the day-care center on the very block where the concert was held. When concert-day rain forced the organizers to move the performers' green room from the roof inside to the day-care center, famous musicians circulated in the same rooms and halls where Biggie Smalls once ran and played as a child.

In thinking about the block as a site of production of a particular type of American body, it is helpful to consider how Anna Scott theorized the *bloco afro Carnaval* groups in Bahia, Brazil, where she identified cultural production as a form of labor and cultural enactment as a commodity. In this context, the "epidermal reality" of the blackness of bodies forms a kind of space, which must be performed to exist. This space then "becomes both a location and a commodity, a site within which to generate community and distribute meaning."[8] Because the performance of blackness is occurring within white hegemony, the public space is not truly public. Sound and motion are employed, not to create space, but to enact alterity in order to justify the presence of black bodies in civic spaces. This enactment through sound and motion can re-choreograph a space, and in the process disrupt panoptic control, opening up room for change. This represents a complex re-theorizing of blackness in relation to space, sound, and motion. Thus, if we add Scott's understanding of space to Foster's insistence on corporeality, we will have a strong framework with which to analyze the work that *Block Party* does to construct a utopian community in which to place a new (African) American body.

STAGING THE BLOCK, CHOREOGRAPHING THE PARTY

Dave Chappelle and Michel Gondry worked together to choreograph the block party and *Block Party*. Chappelle had the idea to organize a concert and asked Gondry to film it, despite the director's lack of experience with hip-hop artists or African American culture. In fact, Gondry remarked that he felt "a little guilty of being white and doing it. Maybe I took the job of an African-American director, I don't know. But Dave asked me, so I would have been stupid to not do it."[9] In the documentary featured on the *Block Party* DVD, *September in Brooklyn: The Making of* Block Party, Chappelle indicates that his choice of Gondry reflects his desire to do something outside the mainstream, something that could evoke the spirit of the jazz community as well as hip-hop history. Gondry suggested that the concert be held not in Central Park as planned, but in Brooklyn, where the music came from originally. Chappelle then had the idea that the event should take the form of a block party. While Chappelle chose the acts, Gondry is the one who insisted that there be a "house band" for the concert to provide the connection to jazz culture that Chappelle desired, a role The Roots took on well before they became the house band on *Late Night with Jimmy Fallon*.

While Chappelle is omnipresent in *Block Party*, Gondry is physically absent, save his off-screen voice in two brief scenes with Cindy Wood of the Broken Angel building and with Jill Scott. His gaze, however, is ubiquitous, and defines how viewers of the movie experience the event. In *September in Brooklyn*, he describes how he specifically asked his camera crew to avoid "typical MTV video stuff,"[10] instead asking each of the nine camera/sound teams to function as independent documentary units, taking longer shots of the action and providing a visual context for performers and interviewees. In short, Gondry wanted to make a documentary rather than a concert film or a typical music video. Instead of following a chronological order during the editing process, Gondry chose to interweave concert footage, Ohio scenes, and shots from the rehearsal studio throughout the movie, until the arrival of the buses from Ohio integrates them into the concert. Even still, Gondry moves the film back and forth from the stage to the green room, the street to the roof, and the block party to the rehearsal studio, once even delivering the punch line to a joke told on stage from rehearsal footage, making plain the discipline required by performers, even at a party.

In a curious editing choice, Gondry twice includes a scene in the Broken Angel house in which Cindy Wood talks about why she doesn't like rap. The first appearance of the scene comes as we are taking a tour of the house, the second near the end of the film, after we see Cindy leaning out a window, enjoying the concert. Both times she says, "I don't like rap music because rap music composes a lot of foul language, and I don't think it's proper for children. I don't even think it's proper for adults either, to be using that type of language."[11] The scene is clearly important to Gondry and/or Chappelle, otherwise why include it twice? As the most visible white woman in the film, one might think she is meant to represent older white America's relationship to hip-hop. However, Cindy is clearly well outside the white American mainstream herself, as an eccentric artist living in a beautiful, soaring pile of trash in Brooklyn. Perhaps the repetition of the scene is meant to indicate that even those who profess not to like the music are welcome in the marginal community created through the block party.

The concert organizers and performers spoke multiple times of "bringing the concert to the people rather than the people to the concert,"[12] and it is true that holding the event in Bed-Stuy and controlling who found out about it ensured a very different audience than would have been present at a Central Park concert. Still, the people were literally brought to the concert on buses. Even those coming from New York City were required to register online, and were given a location in Chinatown to get on buses. As was evident in the film, they did not know where the event would be held, or who would be performing.[13] The bus as mode of transportation to the concert was significant on many levels, the most prominent being the key role bus segregation and bus boycotts played in the Civil Rights movement. Buses also evoke communities such as schools and churches, suggesting that even the process of getting to the block party was part of a construction of an African American community. The fact that the community was built in Bed-Stuy says, in particular to the movie audience, that it is a "block" with meaning and potential beyond its negative image.

THE CORPOREALITY OF PARTY GOERS

More than five thousand bodies came to the block party, as fans, performers, and crew. At its center was a politically engaged group of hip-hop and neo-soul musicians hailing from New York and Philadelphia, many of whom performed on *Chappelle's Show* (2003–2006). According to Questlove of The Roots, most of the participating artists used to jam together before they were famous, so the concert is in one sense a (re)enactment of a pre-existing community. The bodies on the stage were ideological, protesting, racialized and (for the most part) masculine. Layered over all of these inscriptions was power: the individual power of celebrity and money and access, yes, but also a collective power that the performers attempted to create with the audience and which the filmmakers attempted to share with an even wider audience. The crowd itself was composed of racialized (predominantly African American) bodies who became protesting bodies in response to the movements and lyrics of the performers. Eyes were fixed on the stage, lips sang along, heads and hands pumped the beat, bodies swayed under the direction of the performers. In this way, the performers on the stage were like the CSU marching band director and drum majors, conducting synchronized movements of individual bodies and musical harmony of many instruments to produce a powerful collective identity.

During one of his comedy sets in between musical acts, Chappelle, accompanying himself on conga drums, chanted, "5,000 black people chilling in the rain, 19 white people peppering the crowd. Everyone is welcome. Trying to find a Mexican. Very hard to find a Mexican."[14] Indeed the racialized bodies at the party were predominantly black and white, accepting and reflecting the limitation of the national American body to white or black. The group dead prez did attempt to challenge this narrow inscription, and establish cross-racial and cross-ethnic solidarity in the following scene of the movie.

> M-1: Throwing up my gang sign. [makes gesture with his right hand, palm forward, middle finger and thumb straight, pointer, ring finger, and pinky bent] It's bad. Well no, really, it means something. It means *ya basta*. Know what I'm saying? It's Mexican. For all my *compañeros and compañeras*. This means *ya basta*. Enough is enough.
> DAVE: Is that some Mexican shit?
> M-1: Yeah.
> DAVE: So if I see some Mexicans and I throw this up [makes sign], and this means...
> M-1: *Ya basta.*
> DAVE: *Ya basta.* And they'll be like, "All right."
> M-1: Oh well you know, I never really...
> STIC.MAN: Check with them first.
> M-1: Yeah, I don't wanna...
> DAVE: Don't have me doing this. Don't just walk up to a Mexican and start doing this shit.
> M-1: Enough is enough.
> DAVE: *Ya basta* [both making sign]. (Fig. 22.1).
> M-1: We had enough here. We're ready for better.
> STIC.MAN: Any way... [throws up sign, turns it around with back of hand facing forward to give the finger, turns hand back and forth].
> DAVE: Next time my wife is feeding me too much... "Would you like some more potatoes?" [throws sign] *Ya basta!* I've had enough [both members of dead prez bent over laughing].[15]

FIGURE 22.1 Screen capture of *Dave Chappelle's Block Party*, director Michel Gondry (2006), "Enough is enough."

Though the sign is turned into a joke (as is the absence of Mexicans at the concert in Chappelle's skit), with M-1 admitting he doesn't really know if the sign signifies what he thinks it does, dead prez are actually quite serious about the gesture, using it prominently on their website at the time.[16] Later in the film M-1 introduces himself in Spanish as "eme uno," continuing his attempts at linguistic solidarity with absent Latinos. Along with Chairman Fred Hampton Jr., who makes an appearance on stage with Mos Def, dead prez are perhaps the most ideological bodies at the block party. Along with many of the other musicians participating in the block party, dead prez engages in what Teresa de Lauretis calls a "movement between the (represented) discursive space of the positions made available by hegemonic discourses and the space-off, the elsewhere, of those discourses."[17] They know that they are inside the dominant American ideology and also mainstream hip-hop culture, but they are challenging it every step of the way. Much of this movement between hegemonic space and the elsewhere is textual in the case of dead prez, as they position themselves through their lyrics on the margins of hip-hop. Sometimes their bodies are implicated, however, as when Dave Chappelle, standing on the roof of the day-care center in a quiet moment in the days before the block party, spoke of the absence of dead prez from the airwaves:

> I think the more you say with it, the less airplay your get. You know, guys like dead prez, they say it all. But you hardly ever hear them on the radio. Because they say things like, [putting megaphone to his mouth] "Who shot Biggie Smalls? If we don't get them, they gonna get us all. I'm up for running up on them crackers in their city hall" [puts down megaphone, walks away from the edge of the roof]. You'll never hear that shit on the radio. Never in a million years will you hear somebody say on the radio, "I'm up for running up on some crackers in city hall." And people have

stopped asking who killed Biggie Smalls. But if you in show business and black, you'll wonder about that every day. 'Cause they might get you, too [ambling across roof, megaphone at side].[18]

Onstage at the block party, dead prez put their hip-hop and Black Power bodies into motion, addressing the commodification of cultural production in their song "It's Bigger Than Hip-Hop:"

> These record labels sling our tapes like dope.
> You can be next in line and signed and still be writing rhymes and broke.
> You rather have a Lexus or justice?
> A dream or some substance?
> A Beemer, a necklace or freedom?[19]

As M-1 and stic.man draw out the word freeeeee-dommmmm, they throw their fists in the air; the crowd responds in kind, singing along as the song ascends into its last verse. In this way, dead prez, like other performers that day, choreograph the protest of the audience, performers and crowd alike "display[ing] a physical relationship ... to the oppression they suffered."[20]

As the first featured woman performer on the stage (previously women were present only as backup singers), Erykah Badu brings a female gendered body to the stage. But along with her female body, she brings an intentional performance of an African (American) body through her huge hair. Questlove from the Roots sports an afro, as does Jill Scott, but Badu's hair is bigger than anyone else's, impossibly big, announcing not only her presence, but also her status as an undeniable Black Power body, which is reinforced by a Black Panther button on the lapel of her plaid jacket. Just as Frances Negrón-Muntaner has used "Jennifer's Butt" to talk about the racialized bodies of Latinas,[21] hair has long been used to talk about the racialized bodies of African Americans, and to indicate membership in particular political communities. The dance company Urban Bush Women even created a performance called *HairStories*, in conjunction with which they held Hair Parties as an opportunity for dialogue about the relationship of nappy hair to ideas of heritage and beauty.[22]

When partway into her set the wind kicks up and starts blowing her hair back, Badu herself removes what turns out to be a wig, revealing her own short locks underneath. In the process, Badu exposes her own manipulation—or is it play?—of the image of the African American body. This intentional creation of a body double is reinforced by a voiceover by Chappelle in which he opines that "It's always more interesting to look at the person behind the image. Everyone's got a difference between their personal life and their public life. You kind of have to. Not every part of you can be for sale, right?"[23] In other concert performances, Badu has worn an exaggeratedly tall African-inspired headdress, which she ultimately removes to reveal her own bald head. Although her removal of the wig at the block party seemed unplanned—between the time the wind blows the wig and she removes it, there is a moment of indecision on her face—she has clearly used similar tactics before to indicate an ability to move back and forth between different stereotyped bodies, in the process revealing the constructed nature of each of those bodies. Her ability to strategically move between different bodies at different times demonstrates her agency despite the fact that she, like everyone, exists within larger hegemonic discourses that attempt to hold her in one place. (Interestingly, when she returns to the stage later in the evening to sing backup with Jill Scott, the wig is firmly back in place.)

At the end of her set, wig nowhere in sight, jacket removed to reveal a black T-shirt that cryptically reads "coroner," Badu walks to the front of the stage. Holding a nearby musician's arm, she gingerly steps over something on the edge of the stage, where she pauses like an uncertain swimmer on the edge of the pool. Mary Hall, the elderly storeowner from Ohio invited personally by Chappelle to come to the event, narrates what happened next: "She jumped off into the crowd's arms [laughs delightedly]. That was exciting!"[24] (Fig. 22.2). In fact, this moment is the one time in *Block Party* when we see the performing body join the spectator bodies. Many of the performers throughout the film, including Chappelle, insist that they are there as fans and spectators, and indeed we see them watching other acts. The performers also continuously connect with the audience visually, kinesthetically, and aurally, but Badu is the only one to connect with them physically, and the joy of her body is palpable.

The (em)power(ed) body in *Block Party* is of course Dave Chappelle himself. At one point in the film, while talking about the connection between comedy and music, Chappelle suggests that it is his will to power that got him where he is, saying "I am mediocre at both, but have managed to talk my way into a fortune."[25] A concrete symbol of his power is the megaphone that he carries with him in the days leading up to the block party, though he switches to the more standard microphone the day of the concert.

FIGURE 22.2 Screen capture of *Dave Chappelle's Block Party*, director Michel Gondry (2006), "She jumped off into the crowd's arms."

FIGURE 22.3 Screen capture of *Dave Chappelle's Block Party*, director Michel Gondry (2006), Dave Chappelle's megaphone.

A megaphone amplifies the voice, suggesting someone giving orders, or attempting to make their voice heard above the crowd. He drives down the streets of Brooklyn, megaphone out the window of his car, announcing the block party. He also uses it to indicate when he is switching between speaking as himself and reciting lyrics, such as in the rooftop scene described above (Fig. 22.3). As a comedian, Chappelle uses the megaphone to garner laughs as well, using it to communicate between two men trying to fix a car when the CSU marching band makes it impossible for them to hear each other in the opening scene. Yet the megaphone also indicates the limits of his power, which extends only so far as his distinctive voice can be heard. In a way, the film *Block Party* becomes an extension of the physical device, a metaphorical megaphone spreading his voice to movie theaters and video stores across the globe.

"WE SHOOK UP THE WORLD"

Many film critics recognized the utopian vision of *Block Party*, calling it "a celebration of harmony" (Colin Covert of the *Minneapolis Star Tribune*) and "a blissful buzz...that can restore your faith!" (Owen Gleiberman, *Entertainment Weekly*). Some critics, such as Jami Bernard from the *New York Daily News*, universalized the local block party, saying that the movie "make[s] you feel so good about America and the people in it—you just want to climb in the screen and live there." Karen Durbin, writing for *Elle* magazine, went even further to say that the movie "makes you...ridiculously hopeful for the human race."[26] Frantz Fanon pre-saged the moves of these white writers to claim black experience and culture as their own when he wrote "The presence of the Negroes beside the whites is in a way an insurance policy on humanness. When the whites feel that they have become too mechanized, they turn to the men of color and ask them for a little human sustenance."[27] Questlove from the Roots addresses precisely this dilemma when he talks in the film about the fact that their audience, like Dave Chappelle's, for the most part does not look like them. The fact is that mainstream hip-hop culture has become a national American culture, consumed and practiced by white youth (and adults) along-side African American, Latino, and Asian American youth.

What is the relationship between national culture and the national body? Is the body that of the producers or the consumers of culture? Of course, there can be multiple national bodies for each nation, and who constitutes an acceptable national body is constantly in flux. In contrast to the construction of a singular national body (often offered up for export), individuals are constantly being inscribed as members of a nation. This process is not a one-way street, however; individuals have agency within the national body to accept, exploit, or resist what is written upon them. In the case of *Block Party*, Chappelle and the bodies he and Michel Gondry have assembled are doing more than just making do with their inscribed roles. Addressing the commodi-fication of their bodies and their culture, the attendees of the block party enact alterity, and in the process offer up a vision of a (utopian) national body as young, black, pre-dominantly male, and significantly both urban and rural. This vision is perhaps best represented by one of the drum majors from the Central State University Marching Marauders.

We never learn the CSU drum major's name, and the few times we see him on the screen he is usually facing the camera, strongly corpo-real, even when he is just stand-ing and speaking. The night of the concert, we see him interviewed in the green room. He says, "It's great being out here in New York for my first time. I feel kind of like I'm at home. Seeing all these people out here with locks [touches hair], it's comfortable." His identification with the musicians and New Yorkers is a material one. The next day, as the CSU band boards the bus to head back to Southwestern Ohio, he stands, holding his uniform hat in a box, and observes, "it doesn't matter who you are, what you are, what you've come from, you can do what you want. 'Cause all those people out here, they're celebrities, they're in high places, but they're regular, just like me [film cuts to scene of the three drum majors leading the band] (Fig. 22.4). They was happy to see me doing my work like I'm happy to see them doing theirs."[28] Thus, he sees himself as part of a com-munity of laborers whose physical work is to perform music.

Although I have written about the partygoers as protesting bodies, they did not set out to attend a protest. Yet, to paraphrase Foster,[29] their very presence at the block party is evidence of their belief in the possibility of instigating change. The space of alterity created on September 18, 2004—acknowledged in Chappelle's joyous assertion at the end of the concert, "We shook up the world!"[30]—becomes through the film *Block Party* a utopic vision of community, in which the margins demonstrate their "theoretical con-dition of possibility,"[31] and in which black bodies (both urban and rural) have become American bodies.

FIGURE 22.4 Screen capture of *Dave Chappelle's Block Party*, director Michel Gondry (2006), "They was [*sic*] happy to see me doing my work like I'm happy to see them doing theirs."

NOTES

1. The lyric in the chapter title is from Mos Def's "Umi Says," performed as part of the block party.
2. Susan Leigh Foster, "Choreographies of Protest," *Theatre Journal* 55, no. 3 (2003): 397.
3. *Dave Chappelle's Block Party*, DVD, directed by Michel Gondry (Burbank, CA: Universal Studios Home Entertainment, 2006).
4. Robinson, Simon. "On the Beach with Dave Chappelle." *Time Magazine*, May 15, 2005. http://www.time.com/time/arts/article/0,8599,1061415,00.html, accessed June 19, 2007.
5. Single from her 2002 album *This is Me . . . Then*.
6. On the DVD cover, "some folks from Ohio" have second billing, under Dave Chappelle but above Kanye West and the other performers.
7. "The CSU Legacy." Central State University. http://www.centralstate.edu/prospects/about/index.php, accessed March 5, 2012. Chappelle's mother once taught at CSU, and participated there in the creation of the first PhD program in Black Studies in the United States.
8. Anna B. Scott, "Articulations of Blackness in Salvador Bahia, Brasil" (Presentation at Blackness in Global Contexts: Reflections on Experiences of Blackness from a Transnational Perspective, Davis, CA, 2002): 6.
9. Ross, Matthew. "Bring That Beat Back." *Filmmaker*. Winter 2006. http://www.filmmaker-magazine.com/winter2006/features/beat_back.php, accessed June 20, 2007.
10. *September in Brooklyn: The Making of* Block Party, DVD, directed by Lance Bangs and Jeff Buchanan (Burbank, CA: Universal Studios Home Entertainment, 2006).
11. *Dave Chappelle's Block Party.*
12. Ibid.
13. "Trivia for *Block Party* (2005)." IMDB. http://www.imdb.com/title/tt0425598/trivia, accessed June 19, 2007.
14. *Dave Chappelle's Block Party.*

15. Ibid.
16. http://www.deadprez.com/, accessed June 19, 2007.
17. Teresa De Lauretis, "The Technology of Gender," in *Technologies of Gender: Essays on Theory, Film, and Fiction* (Bloomington: Indiana University Press, 1987), 26.
18. *Dave Chappelle's Block Party.*
19. Ibid.
20. Foster, "Choreographies of Protest," 411.
21. Frances Negrón-Muntaner, "Jennifer's Butt." *Aztlán* 22, no. 2 (1997).
22. Atlas, Caron. "The Hair Parties Project: Case Study: Urban Bush Women." Animating Democracy.   http://www.artsusa.org/animatingdemocracy/pdf/labs/urban_bush_ women_case_study.pdf, accessed June 21, 2007.
23. *Dave Chappelle's Block Party.*
24. Ibid.
25. Ibid.
26. All of these quotes are displayed on the *Block Party* website: http://www.chappellesblock-party.com/home.html, accessed June 19, 2007.
27. Frantz Fanon, "The Fact of Blackness," in *Black Skin, White Masks*, translated by Charles Lam Markmann (New York: Grove Press, Inc., 1964), 129.
28. *Dave Chappelle's Block Party.*
29. Foster, "Choreographies of Protest."
30. Ibid.
31. De Lauretis, "Technology of Gender," 26.

BIBLIOGRAPHY

Dave Chappelle's Block Party. DVD. Directed by Michel Gondry. Burbank, CA: Universal Studios Home Entertainment, 2006.

De Lauretis, Teresa. "The Technology of Gender." In *Technologies of Gender: Essays on Theory, Film, and Fiction*, 1–30. Bloomington: Indiana University Press, 1987.

Fanon, Frantz. "The Fact of Blackness." In *Black Skin, White Masks*, 108–140. Translated by Charles Lam Markmann. New York: Grove Press, Inc., 1964.

Foster, Susan Leigh. "Choreographies of Protest" *Theatre Journal* 55, no. 3 (2003): 395–412.

Negrón-Muntaner, Frances. "Jennifer's Butt." *Aztlán* 22, no. 2 (1997): 181–195.

Scott, Anna B. "Articulations of Blackness in Salvador Bahia, Brasil." Presentation at Blackness in Global Contexts: Reflections on Experiences of Blackness from a Transnational Perspective, Davis, CA, 2002.

CHAPTER 23

OF SNAKE DANCES, OVERSEAS BRIDES, AND MISS WORLD PAGEANTS

Frolicking Through Gurinder Chadha's Bride and Prejudice

AMITA NIJHAWAN

IN her 2004 film, *Bride and Prejudice*, director Gurinder Chadha neatly translates current-day global economic relations onto nineteenth-century British class politics. Her film, an adaptation of Jane Austen's *Pride and Prejudice* (1813), suggests that today's relationship between India and the United States is not that different from the class politics that existed in nineteenth-century England, between a middle-class country gentleman and an estate-owning aristocrat. While North America is equivalent to landed gentry in this translation, India is the country gentleman that teeters between genteel poverty and an insecure, middle-class desire to please its betters.

Austen's much-sighed-after tale, in which a middle-class woman snags the upper-class bridegroom-of-the-season because of her manners, her decency, and her "good breeding," travels to Amritsar, India. Here, in its orientalist avatar, Lalita Bakshi (who corresponds to Austen's character Elizabeth Bennet) ignores the rival claims of a Non-Resident Indian man (Indian expatriates are known as NRIs, or colloquially, *desi*) as well as a second-generation British immigrant to catch an American bridegroom. In the hierarchy of today's global-political economics, for a fast-developing, booming economy like India's where the middle classes have more pocket money than they know what to do with, an American hotel owner William Darcy (who corresponds to Austen's character Fitzwilliam Darcy) is economically superior to all others, and therefore, he is the most eligible bachelor and only the fairest can win his hand.

Chadha tells the classic tale using not the simplicity and realism of her earlier fare like *Bend it Like Beckham* (2002), but by calling *Bride and Prejudice* a Bollywood musical. In true Bollywood style, the characters in the film break into song-and-dance sequences as metaphors for joy, dreams and longings, heartbreak, and romance.[1] The pomp and colors of the film, too, are suited more to the Bollywood palette than to an indie film like *Bend it like Beckham.*

In this essay, I argue that the dance sequences in *Bride and Prejudice* are not just glamorous interludes or a time for a "loo break." Instead, they are an essential tactic that delineates class structures within India, as well as between India and its economic others. Just like manners figure in Austen's novel to distinguish between the worth of various characters, in the film, dance sequences, bodily movement, and comportment demarcate lines of breeding, morality, and economic worth. It is the dancing bodies that tell us the difference between who is worthy and who is less so. In other words, the dances construct the class and moral hierarchy of the film.

This prompts the question: What moral and economic hierarchy does the film construct? The answer lies in Mrs. Bakshi's (who corresponds to Austen's Mrs. Bennet's) pyramid of what constitutes the most eligible bachelor for her beautiful daughters. For Mrs. Bennet in the book, annual income seems to be the best measure of a bridegroom's worth. However, when all is said and done, for Mrs. Bennet, if there is not much in the way of annual income or property to be had, then *a* bridegroom is better than no bridegroom at all. For Mrs. Bakshi, however, it is not just a man's annual income that is a measure of his worth. It is also political and geographical location, or rather his placement in global-political economics. So, while an Indian bridegroom may suffice, an NRI living in Los Angeles ranks higher. A second-generation immigrant in Britain, perhaps, stands higher still. But the political and romantic hierarchy of the film suggests that a Caucasian North American hotel-owner is the top prize of all. And just as in the book, in the film, it is the woman who ranks highest in the combined virtues of wit, sense, and beauty that can win this prize. Mrs. Bakshi, like Mrs. Bennet, longs not just to find bridegrooms for her daughters, but her desires are heightened by what various sons-in-law can bring to her own life in terms of economic advantage and international travel.

Chadha, through the narrative and the dance numbers in the film, shows us Indian longings for the "West"—an imaginary place of whiteness and wealth whose cleanliness, coolness, consumption, and glamour can be adopted by migration. And if migration is not possible, then Indians can attain a global luxurious lifestyle by consuming international brands and labels like Gap, Clairol hair color, and Pizza Hut, which exist right in India, inside Indian doors through foreign investment.

While the film, through this apparent consciousness of Indian desires, and through various antagonistic conversations between Darcy and Lalita, seems critical of Western economic imperialism and exploitation of developing countries, I argue that the film, in fact, masks the workings of imperialism and sends an open-legged invitation to imperialism to enter Indian doors. The Bakshi daughters serve as tokens of exchange[2] between India and North America. What better way to seduce the United States than by offering a tourist haven, a Mecca for foreign investment, and a bride with the combined virtues of modern sensibility and Indian family values?

CONSTRUCTING THE NATION-STATE

In the original story, the Bennets are a middle-class family who live in the English countryside in Hertfordshire. Mrs. Bennet's raison d'etre is to find suitable husbands for her five daughters. Much to the embarrassment of some of her family, she goes about attaining her aims without discretion or apology. Her husband Mr. Bennet's main goal in life, on the other hand, is to remove himself from the bustling demands of his household and the hysterics of his wife, and absorb himself in his books and his lofty ideas. While their two eldest daughters, Elizabeth and Jane, are blessed with that elusive and much-desired thing—breeding—that gives them discretion, decorum, and an elevation of thought and character, the other Bennet girls are often thoughtless and giddy.

When Elizabeth first meets Mr. Darcy, there is mutual hostility. He is prejudiced against her for being from a middle-class, under-bred family like the Bennets, and she is cautious of him because of his arrogance and class snobbery. Their growing, albeit reluctant, regard for each other, as well as a sense of each one's character is, throughout the book, demonstrated by the wit and sense in their conversation and the manner of carrying themselves in society. Similar strategies are used to show Elizabeth's suitor Mr. Collins's grasping, anti-intellectual nature; army-man and philanderer Wickham's cowardly and mercenary disposition; and the difference in character between the sisters, various neighbors, and sundry relatives.

Bride and Prejudice constructs similar lines of difference in class and nature between the characters. While Darcy, his friends, and the two older Bakshi sisters show superior understanding, others in the film display varying degrees of decorum. I argue that these differences in character are deployed in the film to show the distance between an old India and a new, modern, post-globalization India, which is an India with doors open to its diasporas and its foreign investors—a sexy, cool nation, not bogged down with its post-colonial need for duty, responsible citizenship, and an insular economic policy. The various characters in the film stand for an old and new India, India and its European and North American diaspora, India and its tourists and investors. The film, then, is not just a romance between a modern Indian woman and an American hotel owner, but it is India's successful wooing of the United States.

In order to understand this, it is important to look at the recent changes in the Indian national economy. The historic national budget of 1991, championed and introduced by the Congress Party (that currently forms the national government), opened India's economic doors to private and foreign investment, thereby overturning post-colonial Indian economic policies established in the 1950s.[3]

Since then, Bollywood, mirroring Indian political-economic policy, as well as in an attempt to compete with Hollywood and the global pop that raided Indian television post-1991,[4] has actively claimed audiences in the Indian diaspora. This is done through narratives that revolve around cool, young NRI characters, more-exotic-than-ever foreign locales, and cool hip-hop-inspired dance moves. I argue that *Bride and Prejudice* carries on this new Bollywood tradition. While using global pop as inspiration for Bollywood songs and dances is certainly not a new facet of Bollywood, the economic policies of the last twenty years have heightened this proclivity. Gopalan argues that these dance sequences and narratives that highlight India's relationships with NRIs "acknowledge a loyal audience abroad that wishes to see its own stories of migration and displacement written into these films. A number of Hindi films—*Pardes* (1997), *Dilwale Dulhaniya Le Jayenge* (1995), *Dil To Pagal Hai* (1998), *Kuch Kuch Hota Hai* (1998)—index an audience straggling between national identities, harboring longings for an original home, or possessing the capital for tourism" (6). The wooing of the Indian diaspora, and indeed international audiences, then, is an important aspect of recent Bollywood cinema.

In this chapter, I will mainly analyze four song-and-dance sequences, with references to some other dances and scenes from the film. The first sequence, "Balle Balle," is the opening dance number in the film, where Balraj (or Mr. Bingley) first sets eyes on Jaya Bakshi (Jane Bennet), and Darcy sees Lalita for the first time. The second sequence, "No Life without Wife" displays the difference between Lalita's dreams for a husband and the shortcomings of Kohli (or Mr. Collins) as a suitor. The third sequence "My Lips Are Waiting," performed by Ashanti in party-town Goa, displays India as an attractive destination for tourists, hippies, and investors alike. And the fourth dance number, the "Snake Dance," performed by Maya (Mary Bennet) for guests of the Bennets, reiterates the difference between an old India given to superstitions, snake charmers, and temple dancers, and a new India that is embarrassed by such excesses. All of the dance numbers highlight the anxiety of a fast-developing economy in its relationships with the Indian diaspora and its economic others.

"Balle Balle," and the Multifarious Attractions of the Indian Bride

Not only does Bollywood adore a good Punjabi wedding as a ready-made excuse to display courtship rituals and elaborate song-and-dance sequences, but ever since the runaway success of Sooraj Barjatya's Bollywood film *Hum Apke Hain Kaun* (1994) that is rumored to have grossed Rs155 million in just its overseas markets, and of *Monsoon Wedding* (2001), a diasporic offering by director Mira Nair, wedding sequences have more or less become a sign of India's outpourings of joy, exuberance, and hospitality.

Bride and Prejudice opens with a Punjabi wedding. A friend of the Bakshi family's is getting married, and it is the eve of the wedding, traditionally known as the ladies' *sangeet*, now often simply referred to as the *sangeet* in its modern avatar. While traditionally this event is an opportunity for the bride's female relatives to sing Punjabi folk tunes and dance *gidda* and *bhangra* in an informal, cozy setting, and for the older women to tease and prepare the bride for her wedding night, today's version is almost as lavish as the wedding itself. In recent *sangeets* that I have visited in middle- and upper-class Punjabi families, the music is no longer played on simple hand drums, but mixed by a DJ or a band; dance sequences frequently involve elaborately choreographed routines; and this is followed by a lavish spread for dinner, and dancing for all the guests.

"Balle Balle," the opening dance sequence in *Bride and Prejudice*, displays Balraj's prowess as a dancer, and his willingness to dance with the wedding party. While Darcy, as well as Balraj's sister Kiran (Caroline Bingley), show their snobbery by refusing to dance or to be charmed by the overwhelming hospitality of the hosts, and by complaining about the provincials, the noise, the pollution, the traffic, the turning off of the electricity at acute junctures, and even "Delhi belly," Balraj, (the Bingley character), dives in to the fray. In true Bollywood style, he dances a perfectly choreographed, high-energy, *bhangra*-inspired dance with a chorus of synchronized dancers. The young women of the wedding party, following traditional courtship rituals, giggle from a distance, till adjured into the dance hall, where, showing their good breeding and modesty, they only reluctantly agree to dance. Once they do, however, the two older Bakshi sisters shine in their beauty and their dance skill, both of which are highly prized attributes of Indian femininity. Luckily for all, Aishwarya Rai (who plays Lalita Bakshi), and Namrata Shirodkar (who plays Jaya Bakshi) are both former Miss India winners. While Rai was crowned Miss World in 1994, Shirodkar finished in the final five in Miss Universe 1993. Their respective victories as Miss India specifically demonstrate their skill in performances of Indian femininity.

The main dance vocabulary in this opening sequence is inspired by *bhangra*, yet spiced with a modern twist. *Bhangra* is a Punjabi folk dance, traditionally danced at celebrations, harvests, and weddings as an outpouring of joy. The dancing involves a pulsating beat, high-octane jumps, shoulder jiggles, and energetic choreography. Balraj, though a second-generation British immigrant, displays his Indian roots by participating with full prowess in this folk dance, while the Bakshi sisters display their coy charms. Mrs. Bakshi, in the meantime, breaks into a solo song and dance, making her family cringe for her. She calls attention to herself and sings in the tradition of the ladies' *sangeet*, which marks her as recklessly old-fashioned and under-bred—or at least, we are given to believe that this is an embarrassing display by the dismayed looks and adjurations of Mr. Bakshi and his daughters. While Mrs. Bakshi is a marker of an older India, the interactions between the various characters suggest that the Bakshi sisters are harbingers of a new India. It is the contrast between the two that is highlighted as important.

Instead of the more hip-hop-oriented or clubby dance vocabulary that has become popular is Bollywood, the use of *bhangra* points to the Bakshis' true Indian agricultural roots. Not only does the dance sequence allow for courtship rituals to be played out between Balraj and Jaya, who dance together, and show the snobbery of Darcy, who walks off in a huff after dancing for a few minutes with Lalita, but it also displays Indian farming roots—a true, essential, real India that maintains its hospitality, innocence, and sense of joy and morality, versus the modern India of high commerce, global telecommunications, and a less innocent outlook. This makes the Bakshis truly middle-class, the backbone of India, in the same way the Bennets of the original novel represent the British middle class. This demarcates them from the aristocracy, and suggests that despite being middle class, and therefore not as wealthy as the aristocracy, it is the middle classes that display true national spirit by being hard-working, upstanding, and moral citizens.[5]

No Life without Wife, and the Untenable Indian Bridegroom

Just as Jaya and Balraj's romance is playing out, and Mrs. Bakshi is starting to dream that her eldest daughter will soon be off her hands, Kohli, a family friend, makes a play for Lalita's hand. Kohli is a Silicon-Valley-based NRI, full of glorious stories of his California life. Tales of swimming pools; fast cars; a mansion; and a steady, well-paying, software-oriented job all give Mrs. Bakshi sleepless nights. Which of her daughters can snag this new prize, and catapult Mrs. Bakshi into the land of her dreams—California?

Just as in the book, in which Mr. Collins's rise to a position of prominence in a neighboring county is enough to satisfy Mrs. Bennet, and allow her to ignore his crudeness, pompousness, and his lack of good manners, so is the promise of future visits to Hollywood sufficient for Mrs. Bakshi. She dreams of American-style consumption, global fashion brands, cosmetics, and consumer goods galore, all at her feet through the route of a willing son-in-law. However—and this displays the difference in her and her daughter Lalita's character—this promise of diasporic riches and a wealthy lifestyle are not enough to tempt Lalita Bakshi. She, like her sisters and father, look down on Kohli for his crude manners, and his lack of discretion in boasting about his wealth. The Indian bridegroom may be a mercenary, under-bred character, addicted to acquiring more and more wealth and consumer goods, but the Indian bride is someone who demands more than material wealth from life.

In "No Life Without Wife," Lalita's sisters dance in their innocent white-silk pajamas and tease Lalita about Kohli's attentions, while Lalita explains why she is not interested in Kohli's suit. While dancing playfully, she skips, jumps, and twists around the room, and sings that she does not want a husband who will tie her down, who is crude and loud, and who will expect her to be the epitome of the traditional Indian wife who cooks for her husband and massages his feet, while he brings home the bacon. Unlike Bollywood heroines of the past, Lalita does not necessarily aspire to be a good Indian wife, but through the song she conveys her willingness for sex and romance. She refuses to put up with Kohli's grasping ways, his balding head or expanding waistline, and maintains that she wants a bridegroom who is attractive and well bred.

Partha Chatterjee, in his analysis of nationalist male-female roles at the turn of the century, explains the post-colonial Indian demarcation of man and woman, work and home, where the newly independent Indian man was aligned with commerce, science, and technology, and the good Indian woman was wife and mother of the nation, and a keeper of its spiritual values. In this post-colonial version of the Indian nation, says Chatterjee (131), "the new construct of "woman" (stands) as a sign of "nation," namely, the spiritual qualities of self-sacrifice, benevolence, devotion, religiosity, and so on...." In Bollywood, I would argue that female characters have often stood in for various travails of the Indian nation, and its relationships with its various others. The Bollywood film heroine is not just an individual, but also someone who represents the nation-state and its anxieties. Romance in Bollywood, similarly, is not between individuals, but between the nation and its others.

Lalita, through her longing for her kind of husband, reveals that the Indian woman—and hence, the Indian nation-state—has evolved from one that was traditionally acquiescent, dependent, willing to please and put up with the demands of its others. Instead, neo-liberated India has a mind of its own, longings and desires that are not just about accumulating wealth and doing its duty for the nation-state, but about fun, pleasure, romance, sex, and consumption. Lalita, as the new Indian consumer, wants the product she buys—in this case a husband—to give her pleasure. The product is not just a functional, consumer durable. It is not a washing machine, or a family car, but it is the equivalent of cosmetics, designer couture, and other signs of a booming economy.

My Lips Are Waiting, in Sexy, Sexy India

Ashanti's hot dance number is set in the hippie-tourist Mecca Goa. The dance number follows the tradition of item numbers in Bollywood films, where an often-random-seeming high-budget dance number—sometimes performed by the heroine of the film, but often by someone not otherwise in the film—is injected into the narrative. The dance number often has nothing whatsoever to do with the plot, but allows for a young woman to perform a sexy dance number without the added confusion of having to fit her into the storyline of the film.

In *Bride and Prejudice*, the two older Bakshi sisters, Jaya and Lalita, accompany Balraj, Kiran, and Darcy on a short visit to Goa, and this is where Lalita first meets Wickham. It is also the stage for many of Darcy and Lalita's conversations about India and about North American economic imperialism, in which Lalita accuses Darcy of wanting India to give him all the comforts that he is accustomed to in the United States, but with the added benefit of a little bit of exotic culture.

"You think this is India?" Lalita asks, pointing out to Darcy that Goa is not the real India, but simply a party town. "You want people to come to India without having to deal with Indians. Isn't that what all tourists want here? Five-star comfort with a bit of culture thrown in?" While film director Chadha makes a point of marking out Goa as not really India, she takes full advantage of Darcy's brief sojourn there to show off this tourist haven, to point out the beaches and the cheap alcohol, the sexy cabaret singer, and the constant opportunity to party. So much so that this segment of the film may as well be an advertisement sponsored by the Indian government to attract tourists to the country.

While the two Bakshi sisters, through their modest though modern dress, their eloquent but decorous conversation, their beauty and discretion, are established as nice girls from a good, middle-class Indian family, this stint in Goa, along with Ashanti's dance number, suggest that India is not just a place to find nice brides, but a destination for investors and for tourists looking for a good time. Ashanti performs a dance number on a small stage, accompanied by male backup dancers. In her sequined bikini and filmy sarong, she gyrates, rubs herself up and down, gently bites her lip, and through her words and many suggestive glances says that, "India sets you free." Her body is a burning bed of embers, she sings, and she promises satisfaction of your every longing. The camera, in the meantime, catches close shots of her lips, her bosom, and her hips. This performance is in marked contrast to Lalita, in her tank tops and long skirts, and her simple Punjabi *salwar*-suits. The camera does not follow Lalita's body parts or hug her curves or words in the same way as Ashanti's. Here we witness how another brown woman becomes sexualized in order to establish distinctions among the available femininities that appear in the film.

There is a tradition in Bollywood films to use foreign, or at least foreign-looking, women for item songs, thereby allowing a more seductive display of female flesh than has been traditionally allowed for the Bollywood heroine. The dancing is more suggestive, and borrows more from global pop. Helen—the ultimate item girl[6]—performed many such item songs, and in recent years, Malaysian pop sensation Tata Young swayed and gyrated her way through the theme song for the runaway hit *Dhoom* (2004). However, in recent years, and indeed going back to the disco years of the 1980s, the Bollywood leading lady has increasingly taken over the role of under-dressed, sexy siren, and often performs her own item numbers. Esha Deol's item number Dhoom Machale in *Dhoom* is just as sexy and suggestive as any vaguely blond item girl's.

However, it is important to remember that, despite its title, *Bride and Prejudice: A Bollywood Musical* is not a Bollywood film. It is a film from the diaspora. While Bollywood may have relaxed censorship norms and evolved to a point where leading ladies can gyrate and sway like the best of them, diasporic women are often subject to a whole other set of middle-class sensibilities. They are expected, says Yasmin Hussain in her analysis of various diasporic films and texts, to "reproduce their ethnic identity. Women not only need to bear children but need to reproduce the community's own culture" (123). Diasporic women are often given the responsibility of performing and reiterating the home culture, through their dress, behavior, and social mores. Says Hussain, "There is a commitment by women to the duties ascribed by culture, for instance, their willingness to submit to the demands of the family, which makes them vulnerable to control" (29). While the multitude of pressures often experienced by second- and third-generation diasporic women and the manner in which women rebel against such codes are too complex for the scope of this chapter, this analysis is important in order to point out that while Lalita Bakshi is supposedly an Indian woman, the context, production, and writing of the film is diasporic. It is a diasporic director's version of an Indian love story.

Further, while Chadha, herself a Nairobi-born Brit, in her earlier film *Bend it ... does* not shy away from tackling the complexity of growing up as a second-generation woman in Britain, with British sensibilities and sometimes-conflicting demands from the family, in *Bride and Prejudice*, the director falls prey to the error of imagining her "homeland" and its women in simplistic terms as more traditional than women in Indian diasporas. So the double context of the film—its Indian setting, but British production—is an important point to remember in its analysis. The imagination that pitches nice-girl Lalita and hence the true nature of the Indian-nation, against not-so-nice Ashanti and the illicit pleasures to be had in the country, emerge from Chadha, a diasporic director.

The second interesting feature of the stint in Goa, besides the opportunity to display a tourist Mecca, is that this is the setting where Lalita first finds herself attracted to Wickham, as Darcy watches their growing connection from a distance. Wickham, in sharp contrast to the suave Darcy, is the quintessential Goan tourist—on the lookout for an ongoing party, replete with a surfeit of drugs, cheap booze, and the promise of nirvana.

Upon their return to Amritsar, however, it is not Lalita, but Lakhi Bakshi (based on Austen's Lydia Bennet), who runs away with Wickham. While in Austen's narrative, this hasty match has somewhat tragic consequences for Lydia, in that her giddiness and general thoughtlessness lead her into penury and an eventually loveless marriage, Lakhi and Wickham in *Bride and Prejudice* simply run away—oddly enough—to an amusement park—partaking, it seems, in quite innocent, even childlike pleasure. The scenes between the two that follow make it clear that while Lakhi enjoys Wickham's company and the freedom that it promises, she is not thrilled with his physical advances. She shies away from them.

Lakhi and Wickham seem only to make their way through various amusement-park rides before Lalita and Darcy catch them up. Phew. That's a relief. Lakhi returns to the bosom of her good, middle-class family a virgin. In this plotline lies the biggest plot shift from Austen's book. While in most particulars the film mirrors the book's narrative and the inter-connections and class politics evident between various characters, Chadha balks at corrupting Lakhi, or indeed, compelling her into marriage with a low-life Goa-bound junkie. She keeps the middle-class Indian woman respectable.

Dances ... and India Is Cool Now

Finally, Mrs. Bakshi gets her wish, and Darcy, Balraj, and Kiran agree to come to dinner at the Bakshi residence. Here, Maya Bakshi, the youngest Bakshi daughter, entertains the company with a snake dance. She dresses in folk costume, in a short green-and-gold sari. She makes up her eyes with the deepest, darkest of kohl, and her hair, too, is pulled back in an old-fashioned bun. To the music of a *beena* (a snake-charmer's flute), Maya regales the company with a series of elaborate lunges with her hooded, snake-like hands, and deep stares through her unnervingly unswerving eyes. Toward the end of the dance, which she performs in the living room of the Bakshi house, the two-handed lunges turn into fast, one-handed jabs at the assorted company. Poor Mary Bennet's earnest organ-playing in Austen's narrative does not hold a candle to Maya's contortions. Similar to the book, the sisters and their father are heavily embarrassed by the youngest sister's belief in her prowess and her cringe-worthy performances. The guests are politely appalled, while Mrs. Bakshi is proud of her daughter's accomplishments.

The choice of a snake dance is telling. There is a post-colonial history of sending respectable middle-class daughters to dance gurus so that they can learn classical dance forms like *bharatanatyam* and turn into cultured daughters of the nation. As Janet O'Shea points out, even women in the diaspora have the responsibility of "intentional cultural reproduction, and thus, for the reiteration of their homeland's culture in diaspora" (3). Parents, both in India and its diaspora, thus encourage their daughters to learn classical Indian dancing not so that they can become professional classical dancers, says O'Shea, but as an entry into a middle-class community. This tradition of connecting classical Indian dance with middle- and upper-class respectability goes back to nationalist movements of the late-nineteenth and early-twentieth century. Caught between colonial and nationalist demands for women's reform, traditional dance practices like temple and court dancing began to be considered illicit and connected to prostitution. In order to preserve some of these dance practices but detach them from allusions of prostitution, a cleansed version of these practices was placed on the concert stage, and upper-class Hindu families were encouraged to send their daughters to dance gurus for education in teaching, manners, and etiquette.[7]

So, if anything, guests to an Indian household may be regaled by soulful singing, or even the rendition of a classical dance piece. A snake dance, however, places Maya and Mrs. Bakshi in an older, illicit, possibly non-existent India, full of superstition and a lack of modern thinking, an India given to hedonistic pleasure, where courtesans dance in the street, brothels, and temples. It suggests that Maya has little sense and even less sensibility. Mr. Bakshi and the older Bakshi sisters' embarrassment at this display, on the other hand, firmly places them in the realm of the modern, and therefore, in the context of a newer India that has apparently adopted modern values, while retaining their spiritual and family values.

CONCLUSION

At the end of the film, Darcy is converted. He is seduced not just by Lalita's charms but by the lure of a real, hospitable, attractive India, modern in its outlook, yet maintaining its family and cultural values. Through conversations with Lalita in which she compares his family's ambitions to arrange Darcy's wedding as a means to developing their own business interests with traditional Indian arranged marriage rituals that Darcy scorns, and in which she taunts him for being egotistical, Darcy's mind is opened to his own prejudices, and he reconciles to the idea that he is in love with Lalita.

By the end of the film, he is in fact so enamored by Indian rituals and values that at Balraj and Jaya's wedding he plays the Indian *dholak* or drum, dressed in an Indian *kurta*, as part of the bridegroom's procession known as the *barat*. His participation in this ritual—in the song and dance of India—signifies the overturning of his prejudice, and again, this transformation is signified by his participation in a physical and ritualistic practice, rather than through conversation. North America, then, has been won over and can be invited in, an invitation that serves, as luck would have it, to bring in jobs, tourists, and foreign investment into the country. If women are indeed tokens of economic exchange between men, then Lalita Bakshi carries out a successful coup in *Bride and Prejudice*. She is transferred from an Indian middle-class man to a wealthy North American one. And it is through her personal and cultural values, as signified through her body movements, dress, comportment, and participation in certain and not other dance practices that this ambition is realized.

NOTES

1. In her analysis of the structure of Bollywood films, Gopalan argues that dance sequences interrupt the flow of the narrative in ways that highlight plotlines and narrative expectations. She suggests that the songs rupture the flow of the narrative at key, disruptive times rather than at arbitrary moments. She says that the interruptions serve the purpose of "delaying the development of the plot, distracting us from the other scenes through spatial and temporal disjunctions..." (19).

2. Rubin argues that kinship systems turn the woman into a "gift" to be exchanged between men and this aspect of society is the central feature in the oppression of women. She suggests that the sexual division of labor between men and women (configured differently in different societies) is maintained and in fact exaggerated in order to ensure mutual dependence, so that male-female relationships are orchestrated around heterosexist-nationalist ideals. In addition, societies depend upon an exchange of goods between men, where women are currency to be exchanged, sold, and given to other men in exchange for wealth, goods, status, and power, or simply protection.

3. Though globalization is an inevitably gradual process (and in fact has always existed in some or the other form) in India, in economic terms, globalization or liberalization arrived in 1991, when the Congress Party unveiled its liberalization budget that opened India's economic doors to foreign investment and easier trade. This budget allowed for a large increase in privatization of Indian industries, a larger share in local industries for multinationals, as well as many changes in foreign trade policies. In everyday life, these economic developments allowed for huge amounts of change in media content and style, as well as fashion, and styling of bodies that had begun to burgeon before this policy change. For more on Indian economic policies since independence, refer to the edited volume by Choudhury, Ghamkar, and Ghosh, and by Kaushik Basu.

4. For more on the influence of global pop and music television on Indian media, refer to Juluri.

5. Chakravarty in her book on national identity in Indian cinema highlights the construction of the Indian farmer as being the rightful Indian citizen, especially in early-independence India, and of Indian agriculture as being the backbone of Indian economy and freedom. To this end, she analyzes Bollywood cinema of the 1950s to trace themes of farming and nationalism.

6. Refer to my article on item girls for more on this tradition, as well as on Helen's life and roles.

7. Many important theorists give a detailed analysis of this history of Indian classical dance practices and their placement on the concert stage. For a summary of these theories and histories, refer to O'Shea.

BIBLIOGRAPHY

Austen, Jane. *Pride and Prejudice*. New York: The Modern Library. 1995.

Basu, Kaushik, ed. *India's Emerging Economy: Performance and Prospects in 1990s and Beyond*. Cambridge; London: MIT Press. 2004.

Bend It Like Beckham. Gurinder Chadha. 2002.

Bride and Prejudice. Gurinder Chadha. 2004. Miramax.

Chakravarty, Sumita. *National Identity in Indian Popular Cinema: 1947-1987*. Austin: University of Texas Press. 1993.

Chatterjee, Partha. *The Partha Chatterjee Omnibus*. New Delhi; New York: Oxford University Press. 1999.

Choudhury, R. A., Ghamkar, Shama, and Ghosh, Aurobindo, eds. *The Indian Economy and Its Performance Since Independence*. Delhi; Oxford: Oxford University Press. 1990.

Dhoom. Sanjay Gadhvi. 2004. Yash Raj films.

Dil To Pagal Hai. Yash Chopra. 1997. Yash Raj Films.

Dilwale Dulhaniya Le Jayenge. Aditya Chopra. 1995. Yash Chopra.

Gopalan, Lalitha. *Cinema of Interruptions: Action Genres in Contemporary Indian Cinema*. London: British Film Institute. 2002.

Hum Apke Hain Kaun. Sooraj Barjatya. 1994. Rajshri Productions.

Hussain, Yasmin. *Writing Diaspora: South Asian Women, Culture and Ethnicity*. Burlington: Ashgate. 2005.

Juluri, Vamsee. *Becoming a Global Audience: Longing and Belonging in India Music Television*. New York: P. Lang. 2003.

Nijhawan, Amita. "Excusing the Female Dancer: Tradition and Transgression in Bollywood Dancing." *South Asian Popular Culture*. Vol. 7, Number 2. July 2009.

O'Shea, Janet. *At Home in the World: Bharatha Natyam on the Global Stage*. Middletown, CT: Wesleyan University Press. 2007.

Pardes. Subhash Ghai. 1997. Mukta Arts Ltd.

Rubin, Gayle. "Traffic of Women." In *Second Wave: A Reader in Feminist Theory*, edited by Linda Nicholson. New York: Routledge. 1997.

PART V

CYBER SCREENS

CHAPTER 24

....

MONSTROUS BELONGING: PERFORMING "THRILLER" AFTER 9/11

....

HARMONY BENCH

As I was doing research for this essay, I was astonished to realize that, although some scholars have written on Michael Jackson as a public figure whose changing physical features made him an exemplar of identity after deconstruction,[1] few theorists in any discipline have written on Michael Jackson's work. In Dance Studies, is this neglect due to an anti-popular bias in the field that has only recently begun to shift? Is it because, as Joan Acocella remarked after Jackson's death, in spite of his success as a dancer/performer, "he didn't have a lot of moves" (76)? Or is it a matter of him being a musician first, better left to music scholars who might also comment on his dancing?[2] Or indeed, was my own generation of dance scholars, many of whom grew up with Jackson on radio and television, so thoroughly fatigued by the scandal-plagued star by the time they embarked on careers contemplating the social and cultural histories of dance and its creative labor that few of us thought to write about Jackson's work and influence? For my own part, I can track a history of loving Jackson in the eighties, dismissing him in the nineties, and loving him again in the aughts. Certainly there were fans around the globe who remained loyal to Jackson throughout his career, but as I look around, I note that I am not the only thirty- or forty-something who re-embraced Jackson in the 2000s.

This recuperation of Jackson was, no doubt, part of a generation's blissful remembrance of youth, fed by the 2003 release of *Number Ones*, a DVD with fifteen of Jackson's music videos and an album featuring Jackson's chart-topping songs; the 2008 *Thriller 25*, which celebrated the 25th anniversary of Jackson's original *Thriller* album; and the well-publicized preparations for *This Is It*, which was to have been Jackson's "come-back" tour. Hollywood films, advertising, and fans all supported these music industry marketing campaigns to re-popularize Jackson after an extended hiatus. For example, 2004 saw the premier of *13 Going on 30*, a Hollywood movie starring Jennifer Garner, which was geared toward the teen and tween set. The film opens with the main character,

Jenna, facing her television set and dancing with the "Michael Jackson's Thriller"[3] music video as it plays onscreen. Some 20 years later, Jenna once again dances to "Thriller," this time at a party with friends and coworkers who, remarkably, remember (a modified form of) the choreography. In 2006, a YouTube video of a wedding party performing the "Thriller" choreography—starring a very enthusiastic and spot-on groom—was viewed by millions. In 2007, another "Thriller" video, featuring incarcerated Filipinos, went viral. Although Byron F. Garcia, the director of the Cebu Provincial Detention and Rehabilitation Center, has overseen the staging of many music video and other choreographies on his imprisoned population, "Thriller" is by far the most frequently viewed.[4] In 2008, a week before the release of *Thriller 25*, Naomi Campbell and some animated dancing lizards performed the "Thriller" choreography in a Sobe Life Water commercial that aired during the Super Bowl. In 2009, amid preparations for *This Is It*, Jackson suddenly died, and innumerable mourners the world over took to the streets as dancing flash mobs performing "Thriller" and "Beat It," among other works. Fueled by the inevitable nostalgia of adults in their 30s and 40s remembering their childhoods and the cyclical return of generational fashions, such events have enabled "Thriller" to reemerge as a work as relevant to the 2000s as it was to the 1980s. But it is not just fad that keeps the piece in circulation; I find that "Thriller" 's flirtation with monstrosity proves instrumental in encouraging the piece's adaptation. As a metaphor for difference and the threat it poses to community cohesiveness, the mythological figure of the monster proves germane to any era.

In this chapter, my interest is in the importance of "Thriller' in the 2000s, specifically the way dancers asserted a collective ownership over the choreography, which they deployed in both private and public settings and circulated online. In particular, I argue that as a shared cultural artifact, "Thriller" became a privileged site for articulating a collective sense of belonging that pushed against pervasive discourses of threat after September 11, 2001, and of insecurity amidst a euphemistically labeled "global economic downturn." Further, through the rupturing effects of flash mobs, "Thriller" also offered a way to resignify public spaces that had given themselves over to the fear and suspicion of a population caught up in the "War on Terror." Admittedly, my premise is highly speculative, grounded in my own felt sense and experience as an American who has spent a good deal of the last decade watching dance videos on YouTube. But mine is also an informed speculation, as the sheer number of "Michael Jackson" videos by fans, critics, and satirists alike demonstrate a renewed popular interest in Jackson in the first decade of the twenty-first century.

Recognizing a paucity of critical attention, I begin this chapter with a discussion of Jackson's music videos for songs on the *Thriller* album, paying particular attention to the music video "Michael Jackson's Thriller," after which I turn to more recent performances of "Thriller" that circulate through social media sites, where they become a part of the contemporary popular cultural landscape. What are the implications of Jackson's monster and those who follow in his/its footsteps by performing the "Thriller" choreography? What diagnosis, prognostication, or condemnation is present in this dance of death?

"MICHAEL JACKSON'S THRILLER"

Epic Records released the album *Thriller* in late 1982, and music videos for songs from the album appeared on MTV in 1983, beginning with "Billie Jean" (dir. Steve Barron) and "Beat It" (dir. Bob Giraldi) in March followed by "Michael Jackson's Thriller" (dir. John Landis), which finally premiered in December. As a group, they shifted the visual aesthetic of music videos, which, prior to that point, had been understood as little more than a way to market albums. All three videos borrow their narrative structures and overall look from cinematic conventions, including film noir, dance musicals, and horror film, and with each subsequent music video, Jackson included more of the dancing for which he was becoming famous. In the music video for "Billie Jean," he mostly walks along a studio set or dances in place—a dance floor aesthetic he retained from earlier videos such as "Don't Stop 'Til You Get Enough" and "Rock with You." Jackson's freestyle dancing is minimal and somewhat subdued, hampered, perhaps, by the awkwardness of keeping one hand in his pocket (so as not to grab his crotch?). He keeps a steady rock that migrates throughout his body from pelvis to shoulders and knees, accentuated occasionally by stomps, spins, toe-stands, hip-thrusts, and kicks.[5] But if his dancing is understated in "Billie Jean," that did not prevent the video from moving the genre forward via its narrative component, in this case a paparazzo trying (unsuccessfully) to snap pictures of Jackson as the latter makes his way to a hotel and into an already occupied bed.

Michael Peters's choreography for "Beat It" introduces much more detailed dance movement for Jackson, who is joined by a chorus of dancers. In the music video, news spreads of an impending fight and rival gangs gather while Jackson, alone in his bedroom, laments the pull to "be bad," to prove oneself as a man even if it results in one's own death. Leaving his bedroom, Jackson goes to a diner but finds it empty of patrons. It's the same at the pool hall. He is too late, but it is difficult to tell from the song's ambivalent tension between wanting to be a man and wanting to stay alive whether Jackson hopes to prevent trouble or be a part of it.[6] He finally arrives in a warehouse where the fight has already begun—two men are facing off to the wail of Eddie Van Halen's electric guitar. As they strike at one another with their knives, Jackson enters and interrupts the fight. Singing "It doesn't matter who's wrong or right," he places himself between the opponents. As Jackson steps forward, snapping his fingers, the group of dancers/gang members moves into formation behind him. Jackson emerges as a new leader, unifying the rival groups, and they follow him through Peters's choreography: displacing their pelvises and stepping backward while grasping the space in front of them, flinging their arms upward and snaking down through their bodies, and tracing semi-circles with their hips while keeping snapping right fingers close to their torsos. They are still dancing as the camera pulls back and the screen fades to black. While the "Beat It" music video seems to neatly resolve the conflict between the two opposing groups, even as it leaves open the question of what comes after the choreographed truce, the lyrics are unable to offer closure. Jackson continues to plead with his unnamed audience to "beat it," but whereas we can guess that young men fighting over territory will eventually meet their demise, it is not clear what the consequences might be if Jackson's call is heeded, or even if abstention from violence remains a tangible possibility in such a situation.

The dancing in "Michael Jackson's Thriller" is not troubled by the same dubious premise and promise as "Beat It," since it is already set in the realm of fantasy as a horror comedy film. Also choreographed by Peters, the film further extends the range of dance in Jackson's music videos while retaining the same choreographic structure as "Beat It": a chorus of dancers in triangular formation led through mostly unison movement by Jackson, who stands at its apex. This choreographic convention, which is also observable in Broadway and Hollywood dance musicals, can be seen in later music videos by Jackson and remains something of an industry standard for musicians who incorporate dance into their music videos and concert performances.

Like Broadway and Hollywood dance musicals, "Billie Jean," "Beat It," and "Michael Jackson's Thriller" offer visual narratives that play with and against the songs' lyrics. Each music video creates a coherent visual story alongside the song, but none literally depicts the contents of the lyrics. "Michael Jackson's Thriller," which was directed by filmmaker John Landis, develops the narrative element even further than the other two videos, and is more properly a short film than a music video per se.[7] Landis directed the 1981 horror comedy film *An American Werewolf in London*, the residual influences of which are readily seen in his collaboration with Jackson. In addition to including spoken text alongside sung lyrics, "Michael Jackson's Thriller" employs narrative devices such as foreshadowing and, like Landis's previous film, pokes fun at the horror genre itself.

"Michael Jackson's Thriller" opens with a statement from Jackson denying any endorsement "of the occult" (at the time, Jackson was a Jehovah's Witness), after which a familiar horror film scenario plays out: a teenage couple on a romantic nighttime drive gets caught up in a supernatural world. In this case, a full moon causes the letterman-jacketed "Michael" to transform into a werecat, courtesy of Richard Baker's special effects makeup.[8] This scene turns out to be a film-within-a-film, a movie that Jackson and his date are watching in a theater. Afraid, Ola Ray—Jackson's female companion and the only other named onscreen performer[9]—leaves the movie theater. Though he would clearly prefer to watch the rest of the film, Jackson follows. Teasing his "girlfriend," Jackson begins singing "Thriller" and imitating various creatures of the night as they walk down the street. Unbeknownst to them, they pass a cemetery just as its inhabitants begin to awaken with the late hour. The undead emerge to the sound of Vincent Price, a man who starred in horror films from the 1950s on, and whose distinctive voice was synonymous with the genre. Rotting corpses surround the couple, closing in on them. When Ray turns to face Jackson, she realizes that he has turned into a zombie (Fig. 24.1)—recalling his previous onscreen transformation into a werecat—and he begins leading the grotesque characters through a dance sequence while she remains frozen in place, just as the song's lyrics had earlier predicted:

> You try to scream, but terror takes the sound before you make it
> You start to freeze as horror looks you right between the eyes
> You're paralyzed

FIGURE 24.1 Screen shot, "Michael Jackson's Thriller." Original music video from 1983, uploaded to Vevo 2009.

In the video's musical arrangement, which is substantively different from the album version, the lyrics and instrumentation drop out except for a sole electric guitar that maintains a rhythm for the dancing monsters.

In Peters's choreography, the triangular ensemble twitches their right shoulders toward their ears, shrugging off the stiffness of death. Turning sideways but continuing to step toward the camera, they thrust their pelvises, holding one arm forward and one back to frame the movement of their hips. With his wiggling hips, curly hair, and red jacket, Jackson manages to be a rather sexy zombie, collapsing the thrills of horror and pleasure ("Girl, I can thrill you more than any ghoul would ever dare try..."). Throwing their heads back, the dancing nasties claw their cobwebby fingers in front of them, creating a space for them to move into. They clap their hands overhead, sink deep into a *plié* that glides them sideways while their heads rapidly slide back and forth atop their hunched shoulders. Elbows in and "jazz" hands spread outward, they *chassé* the ensemble forward with stiff legs and a shimmy. In what seems to be "Thriller's" best-remembered gesture, the dark creatures raise their clawed hands, cock their elbows, and march to one side and then the other. They windmill their arms, rock out on air guitars, and wave one arm overhead like fans at a rock concert. Right feet forming axes around which to rotate, they shuffle their left feet until, facing away from the camera, they take large bent-kneed steps upstage. Shedding his zombie appearance, Jackson turns around to resume singing and continues to lead the other dancers through a few more syncopated steps and pelvic thrusts. In this section, we see Jackson perform more of his signature moves: balancing on the tips of his toes, a multiple revolution spin, and a sudden inward and outward rotating half-kick—a bit of flash that always catches me by surprise.

Transformed once again into his zombie persona, Jackson spots Ray running to a nearby house. Clumsy but persistent when not dancing, the ghoulish clan breaks through the doors and windows, inching toward Ray, surrounding her until Jackson reaches out to touch/grab her and she screams. Suddenly, the forbidding haunted house turns into a welcoming living room, the undead have disappeared, and Jackson has returned to his human state. Surprised by the scream, he asks Ray what's wrong and offers to take her home. It appears that she had fallen asleep on the couch and had a nightmare brought on by the horror film she and Jackson had watched earlier. As they leave the house, Jackson turns back toward the camera; his eyes are yellow and he has a Cheshire cat grin. The image freezes as Price's evil cackle fills the air, leaving open the question of the young woman's future. Will she meet the same end as the girl who appeared opposite "Michael" in the opening horror movie?

When "Thriller" began playing on the radio and then television in the 1980s, monsters abounded in the political landscape. The Cold War, still going strong, made communism its enemy, and then-U.S. President Ronald Reagan concentrated much of his effort on preventing its spread abroad and promoting neoliberal economic policies at home. Developing nations turned to the assistance of the World Bank and International Monetary Fund to weather a global debt crisis. In the United States, the savings and loan industry was faced with the threat of widespread collapse; deregulation in 1980, which was intended to aid the industry's recovery, resulted in an accumulation of risky investments insured by the federal government, which plagued the U.S. economy throughout the 1980s and into the 1990s and ultimately cost American taxpayers billions of dollars. Additionally, the first cases of AIDS were detected and documented in the early 1980s. Though the disease was initially associated with gay men, it soon became clear that other populations were susceptible to HIV/AIDS. Misinformation borne of inadequate research into the disease's transmission and prevention contributed to wide-spread public anxiety and led to persecution of those found to be HIV-positive.[10] Each of these threats seemed to hover just around the corner. One never knew by what means communism might threaten democracy with its spread, in what new population HIV/AIDS might be detected and by what means one might become infected, or if regional or global financial collapse was imminent.

Though "Michael Jackson's Thriller" did not directly address these themes, it foregrounded threat and gave fear a starring role. As feminist horror film scholar Cynthia Freeland notes, the appeals of horror films lie in "addressing human fears and limitations, forcing confrontations with monsters who overturn the natural order—of life and death, natural/unnatural, or human/nonhuman. [Horror films] depict vivid threats to our values and concepts, our very bodily and mental integrity [and] provide visions of a world where action may or may not have a meaning, where a monster may or may not be sympathetic, where evil people may or may not win out in the end" (273–274). Working within the horror film genre, but in a comedic vein, Jackson upsets the natural order by incarnating three monstrous characters, only two of which are redressed in the film. The first, Jackson-as-werecat, is ultimately "just a movie," while the second, Jackson-as-zombie, is "just a dream." The third appearance of a monstrous Michael Jackson, however, remains without narrative closure. It is a final disruption that leaves the onscreen community and, by proxy, offscreen audiences perpetually under threat of attack by the unknown passing as "one of us." Ola Ray also embodies three victims over the course of the film: the first is assaulted and likely killed by Jackson's werecat, and the second awakens from her nightmare moments before some unspeakable act of violence is about to befall her. Escorted by Jackson, the third victim walks into an unimaginable future, all the more awful because it exists only as a threat on the horizon and not as identifiable action in the present.

Yet, because "Michael Jackson's Thriller" is as farcical as it is frightening, audiences are given a monster with whom they are encouraged to identify: the dancing zombie. Unlike the werecat in the beginning of the film and the ambiguous but nonhuman figure at the end—each of which alludes to horror films' "thrilling" combination of sex and violence—humor domesticates Jackson's troupe of dancing ghoulies through the ludicrous juxtaposition of masked terror and stylish movement. Such a character, provocatively toying with fear and playing at harmlessness, easily offers itself for emulation, and MTV, which made its television debut in 1981, provided an excellent support structure for imitation. As Will Straw argues in "Popular Music and Postmodernism in the 1980s," a crucial aspect of MTV's entrée into the American musical landscape was its ability to reach across the nation—from urban centers to suburban communities and small towns with access to cable television (8). The fourteen-minute "Michael Jackson's Thriller" played on television sets in homes across the United States simultaneously, thereby enabling American youths to learn the movie's key two-minute dance sequence.[11] It is this very activity of learning and dancing "Thriller" with a television that we see portrayed in *13 Going on 30*, mentioned earlier. Emulating the zombies on television and incorporating their movement, 1980s youths (as represented in the film by 13-year old Jenna) rehearsed an aestheticized version of monstrosity in the safety and comfort of their living rooms. Their encounter was thus controlled through the domestic site of its occurrence, where in some small way mastering monstrous choreography enabled the young dancers to vicariously master the monstrosity that surrounded them.

MONSTROSITY AND BELONGING, 2001–2009

Flash forward.[12] The children of the 80s are all grown up. They are getting married and having families. They worry about their jobs, their mortgages, the federal deficit, the stock market. Following the tumultuous 1990s (Gulf War, Los Angeles riots,[13] Bosnian

War, Rwandan genocide), the first decade of the twenty-first century brought the events of September 11, a global recession, anthrax scares,[14] suicide bombings, airport pat-downs, avian flu, swine flu, the War on Terror,[15] tainted food, carcinogenic plastics, terror alerts, the Indian Ocean tsunami and Hurricane Katrina, weapons of mass destruction (WMDs) and improvised explosive devices (IEDs), credit default swaps,[16] the shooting at Fort Hood,[17] the death of Saddam Hussein[18] and the hunt for Osama bin Laden,[19] the scandals at Abu Ghraib[20] and Guantánamo,[21] armed soldiers in the subways, "If you see something, say something,"[22] embedded journalists, 10 percent unemployment, the rising cost of everything and the increased pressure to buy it, shoe bombers,[23] Lehman Brothers,[24] WikiLeaks,[25] and so on.

In the face of their uncertain safety and economic insecurity, American communities began closing ranks, increasingly identifying and (verbally or physically) attacking perceived threats coded as "foreign"—Muslims, immigrants, even U.S. President Barack Obama[26]—and the nation began cultivating shared feelings of fear and paranoia. The monsters were closing in. At the same time that national rhetoric in the early 2000s encouraged citizens to be vigilant about identifying threats (abandoned luggage, people in turbans, undocumented workers, liquids in containers larger than three ounces), there were increasing revelations of American atrocities at home and abroad: illegal wiretapping of American citizens, an astonishing number of non-combatants and children killed in Afghanistan and Iraq, the sexual humiliation and abuse of prisoners at Abu Ghraib, the tortured confessions of inmates at Guantánamo, among others. This isn't us, we told ourselves, just "a few bad apples."[27] Or, alternately, we consoled ourselves saying we are not monsters, but we have a duty to protect our own and to ensure that the *real* monsters don't get us.

It is with the proliferation of monstrous acts that accompany wartime that "Thriller" reemerged in the 2000s, not as a film so much as a choreography,[28] a two-minute excerpt performed across the nation (and the globe) that contains within it all the ambivalence of the film and of the political situation in which Americans found themselves. As Judith Hamera suggests in her poignant talk "The Labors of Michael Jackson: Virtuosity, Deindustrialization, and Performing Work," "By the time of his passing, [Jackson's] American audiences were already consigned to a neoliberal Neverland, left to the tender mercies of some very smooth criminals" (n.p.).[29] The monsters were closing in, but how could we be sure who the monster was—how could we be sure we were not ourselves the monsters, as Jackson thrice reveals himself to be in "Michael Jackson's Thriller"? How better to process and publicly comment on the monstrosity of events from September 11, 2001, to Abu Ghraib and Guantánamo, or to the commercially criminal oligarchies to which Hamera subtly refers, than with Jackson's dance macabre?

Public and online performances of "Thriller" in the 2000s could be dismissed as a simple case of a generation longing for their youth. On their surface, they appear to be forms of apolitical escapism—fun and meaningless (or meaningful in an apolitical way, e.g., dancing to honor Jackson after his death). Hamera notes that Jackson too, particularly the Jackson of "Thriller," "was an object of nostalgic longing" (n.p.). But if the recycled popularity of "Thriller" is fueled by longing for one's own youth or for an era represented by Jackson in that iconic red jacket, it is a timely nostalgia. Twenty-plus years after its release, "Thriller" resonates and circulates within new socio-historical circumstances. It is therefore worth examining how such public and online performances reverberate within a politically conscious realm, contributing to a polyphonic patriotism and expression of cultural belonging. As performance theorist David Román claims of performance practices generally, reworkings and re-presentations of "Thriller" in the 2000s do "more than simply recuperate" "Thriller," they shape "the contemporary as a critical space invoking a cultural repository of alternative sites of knowledge production and collective belonging" (136). In the face of monstrous acts of violence undertaken on false pretenses or in defiance of (Geneva) convention, contemporary performances of "Thriller" return to the recent past to make sense of the present. Regardless of the political persuasions or party affiliations of the performers themselves, the performances of "Thriller" circulating online offer a way to resist and to tame—to a certain extent—the monsters that terrorize us now, whether those monsters are Others whom we fear or those we fear we have become.

The events of September 11, 2001, helped to forge and then galvanize an "American public" around fear. As queer and cultural theorist Michael Warner suggests, however, publics as such are not reducible to a sense of patriotism or national belonging, nor is a shared historical moment enough by itself to create the conditions of belonging—even as individuals form connections through memories, experiences, and interpretations of significant events. Nevertheless, in the wake of September 11, the nation and its publics were promoted as being one and the same. A certain brand of patriotism grounded in American exceptionalism permeated national rhetoric and seemed to overshadow all other means of contributing to the collective imagining of the nation.[30] Blindsided, it seems, by acts of real and symbolic violence against the United States and its globally representative institutions, many Americans resorted to xenophobia and jingoism, separating "us" from "them" as if to organize an otherwise incomprehensible threat. In the words of then-President George W. Bush, directed at the international community but addressed to an American audience, "Either you are with us, or you are with the terrorists."[31] In the months following September 11, challenging the terms of the national conversation around Islam, weapons of mass destruction, Iraq and Afghanistan, or the role of the United States as a global superpower was perceived by many (particularly those on the far right of the political spectrum) as traitorous. To engage in such speech was not to be included in the many publics from which America is constructed as a country and concept, but was to fall outside the singular "American public" as a betrayer of national interests.

Warner explains that a public—as distinct from a crowd, group, or audience—comes into being in relation to texts (including audio and visual texts) and their circulation. For Warner, a public is primarily a discursive entity: "It exists by virtue of being addressed" (67). In other words, a public exists by being spoken to or about, by having products directed at it as a group of consumers, by circulating through formal media channels and informal networks, and otherwise remaining a fluid but identifiable collection of people. Publics are social; they are poetic in their world-making, and they act historically—their longevity is determined by their continued promotion and/or the propagation of their discourses. Furthermore, according to Warner, a public is a relation among strangers, a "stranger sociability" contingent upon members' participation. A public cannot exist if no one answers the call of belonging, but those who include themselves as members of a public do not, as a result, have an intimate connection with one another. The stranger sociability of which Warner speaks is a mediated relationality, it is a sociability that must be continuously formulated in relation to something held in common—an event, object, sentiment, place, individual, etc. Participants in a public generate or participate in the dissemination of discourses that reinforce the identity of the public around the shared object; it is against the backdrop of an object held in common that a public emerges and participants articulate their belonging.[32]

In the case of the "American public," post-9/11 rhetoric mobilized national(ist) sentiment to restructure American belonging along the lines of paranoid patriotism rather than, for example, U.S. citizenship, or shared ideals of participatory democracy. Thus the "American people," an ostensibly inclusive category of U.S. citizens and longtime residents, was reduced to a singular "American public" that circulated through signs and especially affects in the wake of September 11.[33] Those Americans (broadly construed) who did not want to participate in the public being fashioned in their name worked to re-diversify national belonging and formed alternate publics adjacent to those cultivated through official political or commercial channels. Some protested the war in Iraq. A few travelled to New Orleans to help residents recover after Hurricane Katrina. Others campaigned for Barack Obama in the name of hope to combat the national(ist) affects of fear and paranoia. Whatever the action undertaken, and whatever their political affiliation, Americans of all stripes were compelled to articulate monstrous forms of belonging in identifying with the nation in times of war and federal and corporate malfeasance.

The performing arts offered yet another site through which to assert belonging. For example, Americans participated in the transformation of democracy into a genre of television, voting for their favorite singers and dancers on such reality competition shows as *American Idol* and *So You Think You Can Dance*. Less cynically, they took to the streets and to the Web to perform their own Americanness. Social media platforms were crucial for the fashioning and development of alternative performances and the publics and counter-publics those performances fostered and instantiated. YouTube in particular, what choreographer d. Sabela Grimes calls "The People's Archive,"[34] houses and circulates these performances for the creation and maintenance of diverse publics: it supports the temporary feeling of belonging to a group of strangers oriented around an event or object like an online video. Thus YouTube and other online venues facilitated the stranger sociability Warner describes as constitutive of a public.

In *Performance in America*, David Román argues that the performing arts are central to the U.S. national imaginary. In particular, he suggests that the ability of performance to bring performers and audiences together as a "provisional collective" (1) offers a way of thinking through belonging that does not reduce itself to nationalist sentiments or subcultural affiliations. Performance, he argues, is capable of cultural critique through its positing of new social modalities and formations and through its creative reworking of the past to better make sense of the present. Performers and audiences, Román argues, "may or may not share the same history or future, but in the moment during which they compose a group, they enact and perform a temporary and conditional we...that offers both respite and change from normative structures of being and belonging assumed both in the national culture and in the subcultural worlds that form a part of it" (1–2). If we take "Thriller" as an example of a work that allows for such a provisional "we" to emerge through its performance, we see that its importance lies not only in the chart-topping sales of the album, the popularity of the song, or the film's place in the history of music video. Performances of "Thriller" fashion a collective "we" through a poetics of recognition[35] that delves into territory much deeper than knowledge of Michael Jackson the icon or "Thriller" the pop song.

The "fellow feeling" cultivated by "Thriller" as a shared cultural object is bolstered by the physical and performative claim of "Thriller" as a shared choreographic object—an object that circulates through bodily as well as cultural memories.[36] Although the "Thriller" choreography itself, which is to say, the sequence of steps and bodily movements of which the dance is composed, does not appear to contain within it specific political intent, its affective relationship to its public is a political relationship. As a work, "Thriller" has woven itself into the fabric of American popular culture. But its continued importance lies in its ability to return time and again through reperformance, or what performance theorist Rebecca Schneider describes as reenactment: performances that attempt to render an event "in some way, ongoing, even preserved" (37). Schneider notes, "An action repeated again and again and again and again, however fractured or partial or incomplete, has a kind of staying power—persists through time—and even, in a sense, serves as a fleshy kind of 'document' of its own recurrence" (37). Through their reperformances and restagings for audiences onsite and online, dancers keep "Thriller"'s public alive; they reestablish "Thriller" as a shared object that accrues and deploys affect as it circulates and invites or interpellates[37] viewers into a public organized around it.[38] The public or "we" affectively aligned with "Thriller" establishes a sense of American belonging outside of quibbles between political parties and independent of larger existential concerns and crises spawned by the War on Terror and widespread financial uncertainty. In other words, "Thriller" continues to circulate among American audiences with just as much persistence and impact as other nation-defining discourses, but it does so without invoking nationalism in order to do so. The national-cultural belonging "Thriller" fosters is all the more powerful for the absence of the nation; its "we," provisional though it remains, is not likely to diminish as a result of differences in political ideology among its many performers.

Haunted by the film's visual imagery, performances of the dance segment in the 2000s allow "Thriller" to take on political import in ways that Jackson (or even contemporary performers) might not have imagined.[39] Corpses rising from their graves, the dancers offer a warning—reflecting not only their own monstrous being, but also the doom of repeating history. YouTube users—Filipino prisoners, flash mob dancers, and others—deploy "Thriller" as a past work that can comment on the present and affectively interpellate[40] audiences with whom the performers share a (global) history and a (popular) culture. The "we" created by performances of "Thriller" stands against the rhetorics of nationalism aggressively pursued throughout the 2000s, even as it offers its own mechanism of responses to the violence of the era. "Thriller" thus creates a public—a public of expert, amateur, and unwitting performers, a public of online spectators and viral media aficionados, a public of Michael Jackson fans and "haters" alike—that intersected with the "American public" as it was increasingly globally defined by the War on Terror.

"Michael Jackson's Thriller," Redux

How, then, does the "Thriller" choreography read against the political landscape of the 2000s? Foregrounding the shifting nature and location of monstrosity in "Thriller," Jackson personifies the slippery and changing faces of our collective contemporary uncertainties—whether they be predatory and rapacious, soulless or deadening; whether they are concrete realities or vague threats crafted primarily through their anticipation; whether they be oriented toward political, economic, ecological, techno-scientific, or socio-cultural domains. Like the horror film genre to which it alludes, "Michael Jackson's Thriller" offers viewers a way to confront terrifying forms and all imaginable threats while remaining within the relative safety of fiction. "Thriller" puts forward a domesticated version of terror, and for audiences in the fearful 2000s, "Thriller" extends the hand of humor. That we can ridicule and defiantly challenge monsters may be empowering, but too often it does not diminish the power they wield. Worldwide protests against the U.S. invasion of Iraq were not effective in halting the incursion, and mockery of the confused logic of financial gurus who led the U.S. economy into the Great Recession could not repair the damage. Yet the popularity of satirical television news programs such as those of John Stewart and Stephen Colbert suggests that humor remains a weapon of the weak. As Robert Stam and Ella Shohat offer in "Patriotism, Fear, and Artistic Citizenship," the power of humor and satire rests in laughter, which reminds us that we are not alone (130–131). This is, in essence, the function of "Thriller"'s many reenactments: to resolve the "us vs. them" battle depicted in the film with a "we" that is able to maintain its diversity, and to confront and diffuse monstrosity by humorously embodying it.

Although generally framed as fun, unexpected for the context, and meaningless except as entertainment, performances of "Thriller" nevertheless always comment on the situations of their performance. For example, when integrated into a wedding reception, as can be seen in the YouTube videos "Wedding Thriller Dance" (Brian and Sandy Lundmark/Rockwoodcomic, Fig. 24.2), "Wedding Thriller" (Drew/cbu377), "Thriller Wedding Dance" (biomedraul), "Thriller Wedding Dance 2008" (susi/indybrewd—unusual for being all female dancers), among innumerable others, the dance not only presents itself as entertainment for the gathered guests, but it also takes on the sexual overtones of "Thriller." Together, the wedding dancers perform the "Thriller" choreography as if playing monster—recalling Jackson and Ray's dangerous onscreen encounter

FIGURE 24.2 Screen shot, "Wedding Thriller Dance," by Rockwoodcomic / Brian and Sandy Lundmark and their wedding party, uploaded to YouTube 2006.

serves as its own kind of aphrodisiac. Bringing courtship to a conclusion, the groom in particular performs his ability to retain the "thrill" of a "bad" boy and remain deserving of the bride's romantic/sexual attentions. In contrast, when Filipino prisoners dance the choreography in "Thriller (original upload)" (byronfgarcia), their performance seems to comment on the predatory nature of the prison system, which preys on the economically vulnerable in the name of social order (Fig. 24.3). Danced by the incarcerated and framed by prison walls, the performance amplifies a sense of zombification among the imprisoned. The zombie becomes a figuration of lost freedom of movement, of feeling oneself to be among the living dead, forgotten by (and kept hidden from) the people on the outside. When performed in public as a flash mob in cities from New York City to Seattle to Tulsa (Fig. 24.4) (as well as a number of international locations), the dance reads dually as a performance in memoriam or in honor of Jackson, as well as a reappropriation of public space.[41] As the latter, attempts to recuperate or rescue public spaces from fearfulness or to ease residual tensions through the spectacularization and theatricalization of surprise (rendering surprise less threatening after having been usurped by shootings, bombings, and other acts of violence) help to symbolically cleanse that space. Flash mobs are structured such that participants disperse right after the performance, leaving no trace except in the viewer's mind (and videos circulating online), which allows a renewed experience of a venue in its normal state.[42]

Obviously, there is a significant difference between "Michael Jackson's Thriller" as a film and "Thriller" as an excerpted choreography performed onsite and circulated online. The film leaves the performers' fates unresolved, lingering in the space of rupture

FIGURE 24.3 Screen shot, "'Thriller' (original upload)," by Byron F. Garcia and residents of the Cebu Provincial Detention and Rehabilitation Center, uploaded to YouTube 2007.

FIGURE 24.4 Screen shot, "'Thriller' Flash Mob in Tulsa," by Heather Hall and the dancers of Studio One, uploaded to YouTube 2010.

within the social fabric that the horror genre affords. In contrast, performers bring the "Thriller" dance to a close with a final formation/pose or by dispersing in conventional flash mob fashion. That public and online performances of the "Thriller" choreography bring to a close what the music video/film leaves open does not, however, undermine the validity of reading the former through a politicized lens. As dance theorist Mark

Franko suggests, "It is justifiable and necessary to speak of dance as political in circumstances that are *conjunctural*, that is, in circumstances where forms of movement and socio-political life take shape simultaneously if apparently independently" (12, emphasis in orig.) He continues: "The dancing body has rhetorical, persuasive, and deconstructive force in the social field of the audience, which is a variant of the public sphere.... The way in which dance alters public space by occupying it is full of political innuendos, as is any unprecedented use of public space for the circulation of bodies" (15). Where scholars have approached Jackson as a postmodern conundrum, Jackson's dancing fans seem to favor the socio-spatial interruptions afforded by dancing to his music in unexpected venues—at weddings, on beaches, in shopping centers, and even in prisons.

Groups perform the "Thriller" choreography for many reasons. Read individually, each situation offers its own reworking of the "Thriller" text. Taken as a whole, they reveal "Thriller" to be much bigger than any single iteration—even Jackson's "original." Given the time of their occurrence, these reperformances of "Thriller" circulating in social media—wherever on the globe they were performed and recorded—offered American audiences a counter-discourse to the War on Terror and a failing economy, one that incorporated the monstrous in order to exorcise fear and promoted a mode of collective and affective belonging through performance. With its uncertain ending, however, "Michael Jackson's Thriller" does not diminish the threat it playfully frames. While some threats may have been put to bed (like the zombies, WMD were "just a dream"—although that dream had very real consequences), other threats—supposed, anticipated, imagined, unknown—hang in the future. Though we perform our belonging-together, we, like Ola Ray, do not know what lies ahead and in whose arms we might find ourselves. Emerging from the bad dream of the 2000s, what new monsters await? Will they, like Jackson's final monster, appear as wolves in sheep's clothing, showing themselves only after we have been duped? And then where will we be, and how will we perform our belonging?[43]

NOTES

1. In "Monster Metaphors: Notes on Michael Jackson's 'Thriller,'" Kobena Mercer describes Jackson as a postmodern conundrum, "a 'social hieroglyph'... which demands, yet defies, decoding" (29). In *The Monster Show: A Cultural History of Horror*, David J. Skal compares the transformations of Jackson's face via makeup in "Thriller" to those effected off-screen by plastic surgery. Following feminist philosopher Donna Haraway's theorization of the cyborg, Linda Badley suggests in *Film, Horror, and Body Fantastic* that Jackson's shifting identity demonstrates a desire to transcend "the limitations of gender, race, species, age, and class. Morphing is becoming—the subject choosing identity in change" (31). In "Reclaiming the Freak: Michael Jackson and the Spectacle of Identity," Racquel J. Gates suggests that underlying the ridicule of Jackson by comedians there "has always been a righteous indignation at Jackson's willful traipsing across racial and gender lines.... [He found] a loophole in the racial contract, one that allowed him to switch among various categories of identity at his convenience" (4).

2. See, for example, "Theorizing the Body in African American Music," Susan McClary and Robert Walser, *Black Music Research Journal* 14.1 (1994) 75–84. Many thanks to Ryan Skinner for this reference.

3. Because I address iterations of "Thriller" across media, I use *Thriller* to refer to the album of the same name, "Michael Jackson's Thriller" to refer to the short film/music video, and "Thriller" to refer to the song and/or dance.

4. As of May 23, 2011, "'Thriller' (original upload)" had almost 48 million views on YouTube.

5. Jackson premiered the moonwalk, which would thereafter be his signature step, when he performed "Billie Jean" for *Motown 25* in March 1983. That move is not in the song's video.

6. This same ambivalence is played out in the 1987 music video for "Bad" (dir. Martin Scorsese).

7. "Michael Jackson's Thriller" set the stage for Jackson's later collaborations with such luminaries as Martin Scorsese ("Bad," 1987) and Spike Lee ("They Don't Care About Us," Brazil and Prison versions, 1996) on music videos that explored the possibilities of narrative short film.

8. Baker also did the makeup for Landis's *An American Werewolf in London*.

9. The film's credits do not include any of the dancers in the ensemble.

10. Take, for example, the case of Ryan White, an Indiana teenager who contracted the AIDS virus from a blood transfusion that was to treat his hemophilia. After diagnosis, he was denied admittance to school; when he was finally allowed to return, many parents kept their children home out of fear that White posed a danger to their health. White, his family, and supporters were subjected to anti-gay taunts and death threats.

11. "The Making of 'Thriller'" (1983), a documentary containing rehearsal footage as well as the "Thriller" film in its entirety, was sold for home viewing on videotape and was also crucial to the spread of the "Thriller" choreography.

12. Although the 10th anniversary of September 11 is approaching as I write, Jackson's death in 2009 was met with an increase in "Thriller" performances documented and posted online. After 2009, there was a significant decline in these performances, and the contours of the political landscape had changed sufficiently enough that the eight years between 2001 and 2009 proved more appropriate for this chapter's argument than the 10 years between 2001 and 2011.

13. The Los Angeles riots were a response to the acquittal of three out of four LAPD officers charged with beating motorist Rodney King, a beating that had been caught on videotape. During the riots, in addition to extensive damage to public and private property, more than 50 people were killed and over 4,000 injured.

14. One week after the terrorist attacks of September 11, anthrax-laced letters were mailed to several news media offices and two U.S. Senators, resulting in the deaths of five people and the sickness of 17 more.

15. The phrase "War on Terror" was first used by U.S. President George W. Bush in the days following the September 11 attacks to describe an international military campaign against al-Qaeda and other militant Islamic groups.

16. "A process that allows the owner of risky credit to transfer the risk to someone else who is willing to assume the credit and get paid a premium for doing so" (Peter Newcomb, "Derivatives for Dummies," *Vanity Fair*, Mar. 24, 2008 Web, Jul. 5, 2011).

17. On November 5, 2009, Army psychiatrist Maj. Nidal Malik Hasan opened fire at Fort Hood, Texas, killing 13 people and wounding 29 others.

18. Hussein was convicted of crimes against humanity by the Iraqi Special Tribunal and executed on December 30, 2006.

19. Bin Ladin was ultimately found on a compound in Pakistan and killed in a raid by United Sates Navy Seals on May 2, 2011.

20. From October to December 2003, this penal compound west of Baghdad was the site of abuse and sexual humiliation of Iraqi prisoners by American soldiers, 11 of whom were later found guilty of maltreatment, aggravated assault, and battery.

21. The Guantánamo Bay detention camp, located at a U.S. Naval base in Cuba, was established in 2002 to house detainees with alleged terrorist ties from Afghanistan and Iraq. Reports indicate that prisoners there have not been treated in accord with the Geneva Convention and have been subjected to ill treatment, abuse, and torture.

22. A public awareness campaign launched in 2010 by Secretary of Homeland Security Janet Napolitano to encourage U.S. citizens to be aware of and report indicators of terrorism and violent crime to proper authorities.

23. In December 2001, Richard Reid attempted to blow up American Airlines Flight 63 with explosives he had hidden in the soles of his shoes. This led to the requirement that all airline passengers remove their shoes for inspection before boarding any flight leaving the United States.

24. Lehman Brothers, the fourth largest investment bank in the United States, declared bankruptcy in 2008 because of major losses due to the subprime mortgage crisis. The bankruptcy likely contributed to the worldwide economic recession.

25. WikiLeaks describes itself as a "non-profit media organization dedicated to bringing important news and information to the public" by providing "an anonymous way for independent sources around the world to leak information to [their] journalists" ("WikiLeaks," Wikileaks.org, Web, Jun. 30, 2011). Intended as a whistleblowing site, "information dumps" on WikiLeaks have included sensitive government documents, as well as videos incriminating the U.S. military in the indiscriminate killing of Iraqi civilians.

26. The so-called Birthers have claimed that, despite ample evidence, U.S. President Obama was born in Kenya, thus disqualifying him from the presidency.

27. When asked if the Abu Ghraib scandal would affect U.S. efforts in Iraq, Deputy Secretary of Defense Paul Wolfowitz replied, "Of course it has a negative effect. That's why it's such a disservice to everyone else that a few bad apples can create some large problems for everybody" ("Deputy Secretary Wolfowitz Interview on the Pentagon Channel, May 4, 2004," *U.S. Department of Defense*, Web, Jul. 1, 2011. <http://www.defense.gov/transcripts/transcript.aspx?transcriptid=2970>.)

28. To be sure, "Michael Jackson's Thriller" was remade in its entirety by fans in a variety of media, from Thomas the Train mashups to Lego stop-motion animations. These also contributed to and provide evidence of the overall resurgence of "Thriller" enthusiasm in the 2000s.

29. Hamera here refers both to Jackson's song "Smooth Criminal" and, presumably, to those in the financial industry who pursued risky and possibly illegal modes of self-enrichment that led, in part, to the onset of the Great Recession in late 2008.

30. See Robert Stam and Ella Shohat's polemic "Patriotism, Fear, and Artistic Citizenship" in Campbell and Martin, eds., 115–135.

31. President Bush made this declaration in his "Address to a Joint Session of Congress and the American People" delivered on Sept. 20, 2001. It is noteworthy that in this speech, even though President Bush takes a "with us or against us" position, he also cautions his audience to remain respectful of difference: "We are in a fight for our principles, and our first responsibility is to live by them. No one should be singled out for unfair treatment or unkind words because of their ethnic background or religious faith." ("President Declares 'Freedom at War with Fear,'" georgewbush-whitehouse.archives.gov, Aug. 17, 2011).

32. Fan cultures are an excellent example of this phenomenon: a group of people brought together by a shared interest and, moreover, engagement in creative acts alongside the object of fandom, whether that object is a television series, animated character, pop star or band, video game, or something/someone else.

33. Following the use of the term in contemporary cultural theory, affect here refers to emotion, sentiment, or feeling.

34. "The People's Archive," *Social *Dance* Media*, Aug. 28, 2008, Web, Jun. 7, 2011. <http://socialdancemedia.blogspot.com/2008/08/peoples-archive.html>.

35. Many thanks to Ryan Skinner for this insight.

36. For a discussion of shared choreographic objects circulating through viral media, see my essay "'Single Ladies' is Gay: Queer Performances and Mediated Masculinities on YouTube" in Melanie Bales and Karen Eliot, eds. *Where Is the Dance? From the Inside, Reaching Out: Recent Scholarship in Dance*, Oxford University Press, 2013. 127–151.

37. Interpellation is a concept developed by Marxist theorist Louis Althusser, which models how an individual becomes a subject for the state. Briefly, interpellation is the process whereby the state or its institutional representatives "hail" a person who, by recognizing him/herself as the one addressed, becomes imbricated with and implicated in the state's social and political functions. See "Ideology and Ideological State Apparatuses (Notes Towards an Investigation)."

38. As dance theorist Susan Leigh Foster argues in her book *Choreographing Empathy*, "any notion of choreography contains, embodied within it, a kinesthesis…that…summons other bodies into a specific way of feeling towards it" (2).

39. Jackson's commitment to social justice issues suggests, however, that while he may not have anticipated the specific socio-political circumstances in which "Thriller" would continue to circulate, the themes of fear and monstrosity and the adaptability of the song and choreography are not coincidental.

40. With the term "affective interpellation," I intend to convey a manner in which audiences are hailed not by ideology as Althusser understands it, but by sentiment and empathy as Foster describes in *Choreographing Empathy*.

41. "Thriller" flash mobs also function as part of Halloween celebrations, but I find that the performances of "Thriller" disconnected from Halloween demonstrate the relevance of the choreography beyond the annual opportunity to embody ghosts and gremlins.

42. In my estimation, it is no coincidence that commercial interests took up the flash mob/flash dance/flash choreography form as part of their marketing campaigns. If consumers are afraid of terrorism, they are less likely to travel or to linger in shopping centers, thus hurting businesses. If anyone had an interest in normalizing public spaces after September 11, 2001, it was brick and mortar businesses.

43. Many thanks to Ryan Skinner for his helpful comments and to Sheree Bench, Mair Culbreth, and Paige Phillips for their research assistance.

Works Cited

Acocella, Joan. "Walking on the Moon." *The New Yorker*. July 27, 2009. 76.

Althusser, Louis. "Ideology and Ideological State Apparatuses (Notes Towards an Investigation)." In *Lenin and Philosophy and Other Essays*. Translated by Ben Brewster. New York: Monthly Review Press, 1971. 127–186.

Badley, Linda. *Film, Horror, and Body Fantastic*. Westport, CT: Greenwood Press, 1995.

Campbell, Mary Schmidt, and Randy Martin, eds. *Artistic Citizenship: A Public Voice for the Arts*. New York: Routledge, 2006.

Foster, Susan Leigh. *Choreographing Empathy: Kinesthesia in Performance*. New York: Routledge, 2010.

Franko, Mark. "Dance and the Political: States of Exception." In *Dance Discourses: Keywords in Dance Research*. Edited by Susanne Franco and Marina Nordera. London: Routledge, 2007.

Freeland, Cynthia A. *The Naked and the Undead: Evil and the Appeal of Horror*. Boulder: Westview Press, 2000.

Gates, Racquel J. "Reclaiming the Freak: Michael Jackson and the Spectacle of Identity," *The Velvet Light Trap* 65 (Spring 2010): 3–4.

Hamera, Judith. "The Labors of Michael Jackson: Virtuosity, Deindustrialization, and Performing Work." Talk delivered at joint ASTR and CORD conference. Seattle, WA. Nov. 2010.

The Making of "Thriller." Dir. Jerry Kramer. Perf. Michael Jackson, John Landis, Rick Baker. Optimum Productions, 1983. VHS.

Mercer, Kobena. "Monster Metaphors: Notes on Michael Jackson's 'Thriller.'" *Screen* 27.1 (1986): 26–43.

"Michael Jackson's Thriller." Dir. John Landis. Chor. Michael Peters. Perf. Michael Jackson, Ola Ray. Narr. Vincent Price. Epic, 1983. Music video.

Román, David. *Performance in America: Contemporary U.S. Culture and the Performing Arts*. Durham, NC: Duke University Press, 2005.

Schneider, Rebecca. *Performing Remains: Art and War in Times of Theatrical Reenactment*. London: Routledge, 2011.

Skal, David J. "Scar Wars." *The Monster Show: A Cultural History of Horror*. Revised ed. New York: Faber and Faber, 2001. 307–332.

Straw, Will. "Popular Music and Postmodernism in the 1980s." *Sound and Vision: The Music Video Reader*. London: Routledge, 1993. 3–21.

"'Thriller' (original upload)." YouTube. Byronfgarcia, Jul. 17, 2007. Web. Jun. 15, 2011. http://www.youtube.com/watch?v=hMnk7lh9M30.

"'Thriller' Flash Mob in Tulsa." YouTube. IdaRedTulsa, Nov. 5, 2010. Web. Jun. 15, 2011. http://www.youtube.com/watch?v=tai8wuLcNLg.

"Thriller Wedding Dance." YouTube. Biomedraul, Jan. 14, 2009. Web. Jun. 15, 2011. http://www.youtube.com/watch?v=cbOvuSljiBQ.

"Thriller Wedding Dance 2008." YouTube. Indybrewd, Feb. 19, 2008. Web. Jun. 15, 2011. http://www.youtube.com/watch?v=q-vKvL9rd_k.

Warner, Michael. *Publics and Counterpublics*. New York: Zone Books, 2002.

"Wedding Thriller." YouTube. Cbu377, Aug. 7, 2007. Web. Jun. 15, 2011. http://www.youtube.com/watch?v=YT6InvLJUzA.

"Wedding Thriller Dance." YouTube. Rockwoodcomic, Aug. 30, 2006. Web. Jun. 15, 2011. http://www.youtube.com/watch?v=OPmYbPoF4Zw.

CHAPTER 25

....

DANCING "BETWEEN THE BREAK BEATS": CONTEMPORARY INDIGENOUS THOUGHT AND CULTURAL EXPRESSION THROUGH HIP-HOP

....

KARYN T.D. RECOLLET

> Aboriginal artists have taken hip hop influences and Indigenized them to fit Aboriginal experiences: The roots of hip hop are there but they have been ghost-danced by young Native artists who use hip hop culture's artistic forms and combine them with Aboriginal story, experience and aesthetics.
>
> Willard, T., 2009

THIS article explores the contributions of hip-hop art forms to contemporary Indigenous urban thought. B-boying and b-girling practices produce a rich visual culture that contours urban cultural landscapes and expresses unique urban identities that challenge stereotypical representations of "the Indian" and "the other" projected on the popular screen.[1] I provide a contextual framework suggesting that b-boying/b-girling and other hip-hop art forms arose out of a space of struggle and a need for a movement that represented social transformation. I also discuss the appeal of hip-hop for Native youth, resonating with similar experiences of social dislocation and erasure. I discuss the history of b-boying in relationship to Native cultural expressions. Hip-hop contributes to contemporary Indigenous thought, specifically the significance of "Indigenous motion" as a practice of a central nervous system shooting out pulsations to connect Native people within cities. I explore the significance of dancing "between the break beats," where, between spaces, are portals to creativity and the life force that connects us all. Finally, I look at the hip-hop crew as an important site for the reconfiguration of rich and complex Native identities and express how embodiment functions to transcend colonialism. I particularly examine the work that A Tribe Called Red, a Native American music and video collective, does via YouTube in order to create virtual fan communities. Through the aural and visual dissemination of Native sounds and images, I assert how A Tribe Called Red positions Indian-ness/indigeneity in a between-space of mobility and possibility.

There have been an abundance of youth organizations, websites, b-boy/b-girl crews, and radio shows that have formulated the backbone of Native hip-hop cultural expression in Canada. Youth organizations include Vancouver-based Redwire Native Youth Media[2] and KAYA, Knowledgeable Aboriginal Youth Association's "Song Weaver's Studio Program."[3] Such organizations support young Native artists engaging in hip-hop and offer collective spaces for young people to voice their collective experience. RPM (Revolutions Per Minute),[4] is an entire website dedicated to Indigenous music culture, housing artist profiles and interviews with artists in contemporary Native hip-hop culture. Canada is also host to Native hip-hop troupes such as Red Power Squad, founded by Conway Kootenay (Cree/Nakota Sioux) in 1998 and based in Edmonton, Alberta. Featured b-boy James Jones (Cree), aka B-boy Caution, and Angela Gladue (Cree), aka B-girl Lunacee, also belong to Urban Spirits Dance Crew, based in Edmonton. Numerous radio shows broadcast Native urban hip-hop cultural expressions all across Canada. These shows include Think NDN 102.7fm[5]; AB-ORIGINALS CBC Radio 3; and Streetz FM, just to mention a few. Further, organizations such as Blueprint for Life[6] offer hip-hop programming geared toward teaching Native youth hip-hop as a strategy for healthy communities.

BACKGROUND

A common thread within the literature on the historical emergence of hip-hop refers to the relationship between the civil rights movement and the new languages, ideas, and ideologies embraced by the hip-hop generation.[7] According to Alridge (2005), hip-hop brought about a new social critique through incorporating and expanding upon the ideas and ideology of the civil rights generation. Some scholars have argued that the civil rights movement had a more oppositional influence on the creation of the hip-hop movement's origins, claiming that hip-hop represented an outward rejection of the tenets of the civil rights movement. Boyd (2003) affirms that the civil rights movement foreshadowed the struggles of black people who weren't included in the middle-class or upper-class focus of the integrationist movement. Boyd (2003) claimed that "hip-hop replaced the pious, sanctimonious nature of civil rights as the defining moment of Blackness" (p. xxi). In an insightful discussion on the nature of the practices and policies formed through the civil rights movement, Collins (2006) identified that its racial integrationist policies specifically re-produced a system that "failed large numbers of working-class and poor African Americans who continue to deal with higher unemployment rates than whites, poorer housing, bad schools, and disparate health outcomes" (p. 9).

Essentially, the economic and political tactics employed by the civil rights movement failed to adequately address the economic tensions that urban black people experienced in the late 1970s. In a similar manner to the exclusionary political strategies geared toward Native peoples in the cities, Collins (2006) suggests that "integrationist projects advise young African Americans to assimilate into a social system that repeatedly signals that they are not welcome" (p. 9). Further, Native peoples in the cities here in Canada experienced similar tensions surrounding a perceived deficiency created through early urban integrationist policies. Native people in Canadian cities were also experiencing the effects of systematically ingrained economic and social inequalities that included poor housing, over-crowded conditions, substandard access to health care and education, and intense poverty. Peters (2004) identified that a common theme within the literature on Aboriginal urbanization during that time period was the belief that Aboriginal culture presented a major barrier to successful adjustment to urban society. Oftentimes the cities were represented as places of loss for Aboriginal peoples. The tensions that Aboriginal peoples experienced in the cities reflected those that were being experienced by African Americans south of the border, constituting the birthplaces of hip-hop. For these communities, similar tensions arose as a result of urban renewal programs and a heavy economic recession.

Hip-hop became the vehicle of expression for urban youth, particularly in the South Bronx, to voice their responses to the changes that were starting to take hold. Early on in the movement, there were those who foresaw the transformative potential of an embrace of hip-hop. Lipsitz suggests that one of hip-hop's founding fathers, Afrika Bambaataa, created the Zulu Nation in attempt to "channel the anger of young people in the South Bronx away from fighting and into music, dance, and graffiti" (as cited in Bennett, 1999, p. 78). Rose (1994) claims,

> Hip-hop gives voice to the tensions and contradictions in the public urban landscape during a period of substantial transformation in New York and attempts to seize the shifting urban terrain, to make it work on behalf of the dispossessed. (p. 22)

The uncensored, underground nature of hip-hop was enticing to those who failed to fit the mold. As an art form, hip-hop encapsulates five elements, which include the emcee, b-girl/b-boy, the D.J., the graffiti artist, and the knowledge/consciousness of hip-hop. In other words, it has a history of being an intensely visual culture rooted in the aesthetic of the city, and it stems from a particular perspective of urban eyes. This visual/ aural culture has appealed to the senses through the integration of layering and fusion—and as a consequence, has produced Native identities through a similar process of layering.

In addressing the rap component of hip-hop, Dyson (2004) speaks of the influence of hip-hop creating a space "for cultural resistance and personal agency, losing the strictures of the tyrannizing surveillance and demoralizing condemnation of mainstream society and encouraging relatively autonomous, often enabling forms of self-expression and cultural creativity" (p. 62). This cultural creativity is expressed most honestly through this layering of visual, aural, and embodied forms of expression. As it gets played out in Native communities, hip-hop's relationship with layering is manifest in the connection that modern-day storytelling has with the historical memory of Native foremother and forefathers.

For instance, Ernie Paniccioli[8] (2010) succinctly states "we need to create a new energy and that energy is predicated on respect for those that came before us and those ideas that worked." Within the movement, Native artists from a variety of Nations are accessing the visual world of pictures, oral stories, and mythological beings from our histories, and combining them with lyrical beats to produce videos that are part of the larger youth movement of decolonization. Blending rap lyrics with other styles that stem from hip-hop cultural life, young artists are creating and disseminating their storylines through social media such as YouTube. For example, Unconquered Media's *The Storm* has used this form of social media to circulate a video documentary that translates their message of strength and solidarity for Indigenous people, particularly in the decolonization struggle of the Seminole Nation. The creation of a Kiowa/ Choctaw director, the video for *The Storm* fuses Seminole language, lyricism relayed in the English language by Seminole artists, layered with black-and-white images of prominent historical figures of tribal members and their families as ancestral knowledge holders and keepers of the land. The visual imagery flows with the lyricism to produce a collage of voicings centered on the decolonization struggle. *The Storm* was filmed entirely on Seminole land and in historic tribal locations.

> Tradition flows like the blood in our veins, we'll never forget from where we came, unconquered and even today and you can tell by the smile on my face that I'm a warrior upholding the mic giving you a little history so you can get it right <yeah> with an army of 3000 strong we'll forever be together it don't matter the storm. (Battiest, Z., & Battiest, S. 2011)

Rooted in history, many young Native artists are identifying their forefathers and foremothers to include Big Bear, Annie Mae Aquash, Afrika Bambaataa, and Master Flash. These artists see themselves as born into a movement that responds to social injustice and inequality. The visual culture includes the embodiment of the dance form in re-claiming urban landscapes. B-girling/b-boying represented another cultural element that claimed urban space in resistance to the oppressive economic and social circumstances of the late 1970s. Like rap, it also had its origins among black and Hispanic youth from the Harlem, Bronx, Brooklyn, and Queens neighborhoods in New York City. It originated at a time when youth gangs expanded in the cities, creating a movement where young people themselves were trying to control their own destiny outside of that prescribed by a gang-style social mentality. Toronto-based Anishinaabe/Haida b-boy QRock suggests that b-boying and b-girling represented a street cultural approach to bringing together the synergy that each borough in New York represented (QRock, personal communication, January 20, 2012). An "urban vernacular dance," breaking acts as a discourse through which youth express their style, skill, and uniqueness via a series of dance moves, contortions and freezes. B-boys or break boys was the designation given to those early mid-seventies free-stylists who danced in the breaks of funk and disco records. B-boys were drawn to the funk that was coming out of the 60s and 70s. Basically, the term "break dancing" arose because of the expressive movements that took place in the breaks in the music.

Like rap, breaking in the late 70s and early 80s experienced a cross-cultural sharing within the boroughs of New York. After the break dancing of the 70s (which was predominantly picked up by black communities in New York), Puerto Rican youth started to adopt this art form and incorporate acrobatics and gymnastic moves. In this way, black youth passed it on and inspired the next generation of break dancers who were Puerto Rican. Today, its practitioners include an internationally diverse membership of creative, uniquely styled artists and can be considered a unique expression of Indigenous poetics. As pointed out during my interview with b-boy QRock, one of the original styles of b-boying was influenced by Native fancy dancers. Among the first generation of b-boys within the Mighty Zulu Kingz crew (est.1973),[9] Pow Wow and Sundance were influenced by film footage of a Native fancy dancer.[10] In seeking an original style, Pow Wow and Sundance mimicked moves and popularized the Indian Step, which is now acknowledged among b-girls and b-boys as a foundational movement within the art form.

From the beginning, breaking functioned as a way to claim public spaces, where places such as schools became ideal environments for early breakers to perform. However, according to dance historian, writer, and critic Banes (2004) there was also a strong underground component, since it would take place outside of the public eye. Hip-hop has a history as an underground practice that gave crews the opportunity to develop hidden languages that contained alternatives to dominant narratives. Sally Banes's insight into the underground nature of breaking highlights the importance of the practice whereby (before the onslaught of the media hype) breaking was self-generated and invisible to the adult world.

Hip-Hop Contributions to Contemporary Indigenous Thought

Hip-hop represents an exciting realm where new ideas and new concepts are being born every day. Elements of spiritual energy and the connection with other realms are inherent in the motion created through hip-hop. Moreover, these stories shared through hip-hop are sensual, a characteristic that appeals to a performance-rooted aesthetic. The telling of these stories are stimulating to the senses and involve the use of body vocabulary as well as other ways of voicing that achieve a connection to community. Toronto-based b-boy QRock shares his experiences,

> I get a really good feeling when I dance. It satisfies the warrior side of my spirit, not just the peace side of my spirit. Really good dancers complement the drum. You

capture the moment, and you do things that you have never done before—appearing as though you have done that all of your life. You did it so well that everyone knew exactly what you meant, your point got made. (QRock personal communication, January 20, 2012)

The metaphor of motion is strong in b-boy and b-girl motivation in the circle. For example, Cree b-boy Mathew CreeAsian described his relationship with one of his movements that resembles a "grass dancer" smudging[11] the atmosphere around him (CreeAsian, M., personal communication, 2007). QRock also describes an "eagle step" and the intent to mimic eagles hovering across stone.

INDIGENOUS MOTION

One of the contributions of hip-hop practitioners to Indigenous contemporary urban thought is the actuation of *Indigenous motion*. As a Cree woman who grew up in urban space, my own experiences with motion compelled me toward hip-hop as a medium to understand contemporary identities and knowledge production. My relationship with Indigenous motion is reflected in how I think about my own history, lineage, and identity. I needed alternative narratives that viewed Indigenous knowledge(s) (IK) rooted within an arts-based/urban dialogue, where IK could become a portal to "other worlds." These other worlds allow the exploration into the depths of my own relationship to creation, mobility, and transformation. In this way I have been guided by my teachers in the world of performance, so that I can begin to find the language to express this motion. My impulse has been to garner an understanding of my own identity as something that is fluid, naturally transforming, multi-layered, and complex. And this reflects my interest in Chippewa scholar Gerald Vizenor's relationship to Native Motion. Perhaps I don't think about Native Motion in the same way that Vizenor does. I see Native motion as a practice of a central nervous system shooting out pulsations to connect Indigenous peoples with and within the cities. I see Native motion mirrored in devices that transmit contemporary expressions of urban thought. These devices, I believe, include the five elements of hip- hop, producing effectual portals or center places of Native motion.

Growing up in urban spaces quite apart from Native communities, I had yearned for narratives that expressed elements of my Indigenous being. I called out for those songs, stories, and feelings that connected me with Indigeneity. Finally, it wasn't until I reached my thirties that I heard the whisperings of this life force emerging from the underground Native hip-hop scene. I immediately found myself connected to a legacy of Indigenous motion. I heard the voices of creation and started tapping into contemporary urban mythologies coming from an underground, underworld space. I began to feel the rhythm and pulsation of this source of intelligence and story that illuminated for me, some of the stories shared by a community of Indigenous knowledge holders in Peterborough, Ontario, and the surrounding area. For instance, on a recent trip to the Petroglyph Provincial Park near Peterborough, Ontario, Anishinaabe Elder Doug Williams, from *Waawshkigaamagki*[12] shared with my theater students his knowledge of petroglyphs. Obvious to all was the quality of time he spends contemplating and reflecting on the images that grace those rocks, impressions marked with ancient stories, etched onto the rocks' porous surfaces. He explained that natural springs flow underneath the rock. Since it was a nighttime visit to the petroglyphs, we all had the opportunity to see the shadows that were cast and to catch a glimpse of what lay beneath the crevice of the rock. Doug described how, through this crevice, we could hear the voices of Nanaboozho. The voices of creation emerge from such special spaces. Creation, according to Doug, does not just take place in the sky world and on the surface of the earth, but rather creation is spherical; it includes those spaces that make up our underworld (Williams, D., personal communication, November, 2011).

In Anishinaabe thought-ways there are beings etched on rock that link human beings to the underworld. Carried in stories, these underwater/underworld beings are present in such places as Bon Echo Park in Ontario. In a similar vein, Rulan Tangen,[13] reflects on the source of creation in her work entitled "human landscapes" (2007). In the following prose, Tangen suggests that we ourselves echo this creation through our bodies. She also speaks of our birth spaces as "deep voids in the earth," expressing origin stories that include our being moulded from mud. These origin stories are also reflected in some of the shape-shifting song lines expressed by contemporary hip-hop artists.

> Arms spiral until palms unfold like golden leaves to behold the dance of body and land. The instant you forget yourself is the moment you become the dance. Whirling, shimmering, in swoops and arcs, you echo the rocks, the arroyos, the deep recesses of wind caves.... The Milky Way was a great female cleft to the Mayans, as slot canyons are to others—the emergence point of humanity and creation. Where does land end and self begin—only you can decide. Creation stories of Indigenous North America speak of us as beings descending from stars, emerging from fog, crawling from deep voids in the earth, floating across waves aloft twiggy nests. As far south as the Mayans, there are stories of humans being formed first of mud, then wood, then golden cornmeal. (Tangen, 2007)

Tangen's vivid imagery and language reveal that, central to our creative being, this mobility stems from creation processes of the underworld. If this were one of the truths of creation, which I undoubtedly believe, contemporary urban myth tellers (such as b-girls and b-boys) contribute to this legacy of movement. This movement takes shape in a collective consciousness that spans generations and reflects an ancient pulsation. Embedded within the voicings of hip-hop artists are those understandings that creation thrives in these "other world spaces," where stars, celestial space, and places underneath us are our connectors to ourselves. Beings that surface from such spaces are messengers.

Urban spaces are the central mainframe of Indigenous motion. Perhaps something that we all share as urban Indians is this sense of being born into motion. It is my understanding that the urban collective carries the potential to be a central mainframe of Indigenous motion. This central space has been accessed by emcees, our underground artists, to inform their storytelling to produce awesome stories of transformation such as Daybi No Doubt's lyrics in "The Quickening" (2009), "we survived, we crow walked and we learned to fly, flutter away to the battle, take it back to what matters in an instant...the gifted shift the axis." This idea of Indigenous motion has a deep relationship to Indigenous forms of dance, where we can adopt Vizenor's term "earth diver" to describe those who bring up the storylines of our ancestors and transpose them onto pavement.

Symbolically, hip-hop artists' positioning in-between the break beats enables them to evade the gaze that marks bodies of "difference" according to overly simplistic categorizations and stereotypes. Through carefully negotiating this terrain and embracing the knowledge and energy of border spaces, contemporary urban artists are beginning to shape and express complex/multi-layered identities. These identities are best articulated by their positioning of self and community through lyricism, movement, and emcee naming practices. According to Vizenor (1981) "the Métis, or mixed blood, dive into unknown urban places now, into the racial darkness in the cities, to create a new consciousness of coexistence" (p. ix). As earth divers, hip-hop artists "*of a Native flavour*"[14] offer a new way of thinking about our contemporary expressions of selves in the city as manifestations of a universe that is in flux and constantly changing. B-boys Sundance and Pow Wow of the Mighty Zulu Kingz crew are expressions of those who dive into these unknown urban places to create a new consciousness.

As earth divers, hip-hop artists bring up the words of our ancestors transposed onto pavement. Describing this subject positioning, Owens (1998) described the "mixblood"/ earth diver as:

> A cultural breaker, break-dancing trickster-fashion through all signs, fracturing the self-reflexive mirror of the dominant center, deconstructing rigid borders, slipping between the seams, embodying contradictions, and contradancing across every boundary. (p. 41)

B-girls and b-boys are natural transgressors of spaces; they work within the break beats in order to reconfigure acceptable Indigenous identities highlighted through the rhythmic elements and accentuated by the break beats. These reconfigurations extend to creating different types of spaces, accommodating the production of different types of social relations. For example, QRock's "eagle step" flows out of an embodied response to an idea that the eagles communicate to us how to relate to each other within our families.

> Watch how the eagles live/
> watch how the eagles live/
> adapt for my people to show the kids the teachings/
> and how to fish your dreams/
> so you don't have to make a wish. (QRock, *Eagle Steps!*, 2011)

QRock's lyrics, layered with his movement, which mimics an eagle once he makes his catch, illustrate a "between space" as a way of teaching these relationships, which are the sources of creativity.

Between spaces describe an important site within the creative processes of hip-hop artists of a Native flavor. This space acts as a creative source linked to the idea of an impulse that is the base of all movement and creation. Hip-hop artists embrace an understanding that the presence of impulse as the spirit or life force lives in between the drum beats. In hip-hop terms, this source dwells in between the break beats. Favel Starr[15] (2005) conveys that Native performance culture concerns itself with the terrain of the impulse and the sources of movement and life. He provides a description of the Cree round dance to identify the basic building blocks of Cree song and dance as starting points for a creative vital action. The round dance was explained to him in the image and action of a duck bobbing in the lake water. This image, Favel Starr understood, provided the basic DNA of the dance step, voice, and drumming.

The spirit of the dance and singing is actually contained in the spaces between the waves of the water and the movement of the duck, between the drum beats and steps and between the dancers. The space between, created through the image of a duck bobbing in the water, allows the dancer to embody the movement and connect with the culturally based impulses of creativity. Native performance culture, according to Favel Starr, involves an investigation of, and a grounding in the Cree and Anishinaabe body. In a similar fashion, emcees interacting with urban environments practice such grounding to create art within the spaces between the drum beats. This space between has also been described within other cultures as a source of creation and spirituality. As described by Favel Starr (2005):

> The Japanese have this word Ma. Ma is the interval, the pause in music and in dance. Butoh artists say that the ancestors and spirits dwell in this interval and pause. It is this we are talking about when we say the dance is in the intervals between the waves, between the movements of the duck from one wave to the next in the drumbeats. (p. 70)

Indigenous poets such as b-girls/b-boys, emcees, dub poets, and spoken word artists are actuating these between spaces that are manifested in a variety of ways. Accessing these spaces, and the life energy and spirituality that they house, can be within the grasp of everyday, urban life. Cree poet Marvin Francis (2002) has employed the term "word drummers" to represent those who embody ancestral processes of retrieving survival strategies and spirituality from unexpected between spaces. In a similar manner, QRock describes the *ethical space*[16] of the circle, "if it was appropriate to offer tobacco, I would. But it's not, the circle doesn't need that. It has different healing elements that are maintained" (QRock, personal communication, January 20, 2012).

Marvin Francis's "word drummers" are those Indigenous poets who carry the words and stories of these between spaces, capturing the resonance of the contemporary landscape to describe modern Indigeneity as an act of survivance. Describing the feeling of this between-space that manifests in the circle, QRock describes, "There is a synergy that is created, especially if there are a lot of people, the energy just gets more intense. Everyone is just building on that same fire that is in the circle. Once someone goes in there and just kills it [sic] (urban slang for 'performing at the highest level'), that's it, the circle is from that point on about fire, it keeps going" (QRock, personal communication, January 20, 2012).

BeatNation: Hip-Hop through Indigenous Culture (2011)[17] is a collective of artists at the forefront of Native hip-hop culture in their use of layering and the creation of between spaces to connect with the pulse of the Native youth movement to actuate change and unity. As a collective, Beat Nation Live introduces a fusion of deejaying, socially conscious lyricism, a digital graffiti wall, film, a digital hand drum, a cello, and spoken word poetry. Beat Nation Live's *Landscapes* contributes to Indigenous performance culture through artfully integrating the practice of layering in order to tell the whole story. In my mind Beat Nation is the embodiment of an entire nation based on fusion through their visual imagery and beats. *Landscapes* addresses the issue of authoritarian control over traditional territory and sacred homelands of the Secwepemc people in British Columbia as the people's central struggle regarding the multi-national corporations' inability to "see" land as a traditional territory with life-sustaining importance. The images introduced through film footage imposed on a scrim in the background illuminate images of the "occupation"[18] by Secwepemc and their supporters, protecting their nation's relationship to their traditional hunting, berry picking, and sacred mountains from a Japanese-owned company, Sun Peaks Resort Company.

Landscapes, recorded and placed on YouTube, was originally performed live in Vancouver in 2011 and begins with all the artists onstage with video footage of "warriors" in the background. Cris Derksen's cello, reminiscent of Northern soundscapes, mimics the natural world and contrasts with images of occupation and camouflaged Native protestors. The layering includes Kinnie Starr's words, echoing, "you think we don't know!"; Archer Pechawis's digital hand drum; and imagery of a camouflaged man sitting behind a female elder (both warriors in my mind). Later in the film/interactive performance, we are faced with the image of a young mother carrying her small child, the eyes of the mother beautiful, brown, and knowing, her hair in small braids around her face sheathed in a camouflage scarf; she carries her son similarly sheathed in a camouflage hat and a scarf covering his mouth.[19] Layered with Starr's words at the end of the piece, "It's the whole story, it's not a part—it's the whole...She knows," we see that word drummers who carry the words and stories of these between spaces use layering to capture the resonance of the contemporary landscape to describe modern Indigeneity as an act of survivance. Hip-hop artists are contemporary manifestations of orality, actualizing metaphor to produce a mirrored reflection of reality and also to express how these observed patterns can be challenged and transformed. While embodying oral tradition, hip-hop voicing is a human response to explain and reflect upon our contemporary place within urban environments.

Embedded within the voicings of hip-hop artists, such as the sweeping movements of b-girls and boys, are those understandings that creation thrives in these "other world spaces," where stars, celestial space, and places underneath us are our connectors to ourselves. It is the artists who can tap into our life force and illustrate these journeys and migrations as tales and stories that are shared to connect us all as an urban community.

Contemporary Urban Indigenous Thought and "The Crew"

Hip-hop crews represent a challenge to the discourse of dominance that asserts that cities are not "Indigenous spaces." The types of activities that take place in crew collectivities also challenge ideas that urban Aboriginal people are cut off culturally from Aboriginal ways of relating within families. For example, hip-hop collectives represent an extended family for emcees. Crews constitute important repositories of transformative energy. As communities held together through a collective activism, these spaces can also create social movements. According to Rose (1994),

> Identity in hip-hop is deeply rooted in the specific, the local experience, and one's attachment to and status in a local group or family. These crews are new kinds of families forged with intercultural bonds that, like the social formation of gangs, provide insulation and support in a complex and unyielding environment that may serve as the basis for new social movements. (p. 34)

Processes that take place within the "crew" as a collective space are incredibly rich and serve as starting points for youth in urban centers. These repositories of youth energy and ways of being in the world inspire visionings of the future that can be useful to carving out spaces for youth in cities. As important elements in youth social movements, crews represent a physical space with kin-based mentalities, oftentimes built on actual familial relationships between cousins, brothers, and sisters[20] (as in hip-hop practiced amongst Native youth). The ability to voice through the family is an element of strength inciting hip-hop's transcendence of struggle.

The crew can be seen as constituting physical and ideological spaces for the transcendence of struggle. Crews represent ideological spaces in the sense that they nurture concepts and meanings that are used in interpreting and expressing new ideas expressed through the storytelling of hip-hop artists. Crew activities such as the creation of dialogue leading to transformation challenge the dominant stereotypes of Aboriginal youth collectives as gangs and Aboriginal youth as gangsters. Effectually the types of practices that take place in these spaces destabilize this stereotype of Aboriginal youth as gangsters. Butler (2004) claims, "representation is an important theme in hip-hop culture. One 'represents' by conducting himself or herself in a way that makes the community proud" (p. 1013). Crews are safe spaces of dialogue for the germination of concepts and ideas that are reinvigorated, in some instances, from oral traditions and which are imbued on city landscapes. In addition, crews are the incubators of intelligence, preserving memory and creating new referents for oralities in the city.

The naming of Native youth within a hip-hop community functions to highlight their creativity as well as mirror the complex fusion of the different elements that embody the whole person. Hip-hop beat maker and b-boy Mathew CreeAsian carries a name that illustrates similar ways of thinking about the creativity embedded in hip-hop's artistic relevance, while formulating new interpretations of Indigeneity. CreeAsian describes his name in the following passage,

> I'm half Native and half Vietnamese. So, my boy was sitting there, and he knew that [I] was half Native and half Asian, he was like "yo, you know what would be a sick name for you? Kree-Azn." You know? Like, a word "creative" like "creation" or two races that click together, you know, like, it does the same with hip-hop, like, there's no certain race you have to be in hip-hop, there's no certain skin colour, it's all about what's inside you, the creativity. (as cited in Lashua, 2006)

Emcee naming practices state one's positioning within the hip-hop community as they approach the circle and enter into storytelling mode. This practice is symbolic in that, for the artist, it also asserts the right for an individual or community to determine the mode of representation to reflect how they want to be seen. Through naming, hip-hop artists shape the context within which their messagings will be received. Further, in many instances, hip-hop names have come to reflect the transformational messages that use to inspire change, as in Eekwol, and CreeAsian.

Embodiment: The Colonial Weight Is Heavy[21]

> You know they really did a number on our minds because our minds are what confuses and makes us do these bad things, wicked things. Our minds are the things that make us pass down these generational curses you know that were never our curses to begin with—but those bad spirits that latched themselves onto us.
>
> Quese IMC, personal communication, August 4, 2007

The intentions of this section are to share with you my understanding of the roles of resistance, struggle, and the dismantling of colonialism within the collective voices of Native hip-hop artists, as they convey, for example, an understanding of colonialism as a time when "those bad spirits...latched onto us." This concept was first introduced to me through Seminole/Pawnee emcee Quese IMC and marks a critical moment for me in recognizing the embodiment of colonialism. Colonialism is the antithesis of the freedom of movement, which I believe is an element of hip-hop that inspires Native youth to participate in the culture/art form. Colonialism is an attempt to thwart our Indigenous motion in many ways. It is my understanding that this freedom of motion has been challenged through colonialism's attempt to contain and control Indigenous motion. Therefore, I look at colonialism's practices as representative of "the struggle" toward which contemporary Native urban hip-hop formulates a response such as those expressed through Battiest's *The Storm*. The ideas understood and shared within the hip-hop community help to shape the way that we think about the past as it influences the future, and it also provides a way of speaking about the contemporary effects of colonialism. The unique approach of hip-hop's embrace of "the struggle" represents a complex way of looking at the effects of colonialism. The creation of hip-hop storylines expressed through b-girling and b-boying, graffiti writing, djing, and emceeing is a multi-voiced response to struggle. Collectively these creators present a "new activism" as these artists bear witness to injustice and use hip-hop as a strategy of resistance. In many cases these artists express a way of thinking about our contemporary world that echoes voices from the past.

Conveying the inspiration behind the movement, Quese IMC relays an important insight in stating that colonialism is a physical manifestation that acts as weight within the body. The idea of colonialism as a physical manifestation was introduced within postcolonial literature by Martinique-born psychiatrist, philosopher, and revolutionary Franz Fanon (2008) in his seminal work *Black Skin, White Masks*. Fanon (2008) described the internalization or "epidermalization" of inferiority (p. xv), thus embracing a similar understanding of embodiment. Visualized as "bad spirits" latching onto Native people, colonialism assumes a new face, the scrutiny of which can assist in understanding the true nature of Native struggle within Canada. Through considering Quese's perspective, we can see how newly emerging concepts and ideas manifest in "movements" with transformative potential. Such understandings contained in the phrase "a time when bad spirits latched themselves onto us" can assist in creating "ethical space" (Ermine, 2005) through our ability to "see" the embodiment of colonialism. Quese's insight—that music contains spirit and impulse to carry us forward— transcends struggle through counteracting the impacts of colonization. According to this lyricist, hip-hop as movement music heals that space within us that embodies that historical past and begins a process of transcendence. This transcendence is the effect of new forms of expression carried forth by those participating in the movement that blends various styles to create a unique visual and aural culture that is hip-hop *"of a Native flavour."*

The contemporary presence of A Tribe Called Red (ATCR)[22] is an example of the creation of a new art form defining contemporary urban Indigeneity through the harnessing of digital sampling, film, and dub step. Similar to the work of Native b-girls/b-boys, ATCR redefines urban Native identity through fusing traditional pow wow with contemporary beats. These artists also critique stereotypical representations of Indigenous culture on the popular screen through infusing these images into the music and performance of the Electric pow wow. ATCR's pivotal contribution within the movement creates a new art form re-envisioning a different kind of relationship between contemporary Native peoples and the popular screen. Reminiscent of QRock's experiences of the circle, there is a momentum within the movement, where the energy of the collective takes over and individual voice becomes part of something greater. As articulated by DJ Bear Witness, a member of ATCR, "we're a unity, always cutting on top of each other, sampling on top of each other and mixing back and forth." He says "when things are going it's hard to even know who is even playing" (as cited in Kinos-Goodin, 2011). In the video *NDNs from All Directions*, Bear Witness contributes to urban thought through illustrating how Indigenous visual culture contours urban cultural landscapes. Cultural landscape is perceived as a mash-up of visual and aural challenges to stereotypical representations of "the Indian" and "the other" as projected on the popular screen.

Through ATCR's work, urban identity is expressed as an "electric pow wow" weaving in and out of these representations through layers of samples and re-mixes of invented Indians. They are using these images as the dominant-cultural raw materials to create alternative identities though mash-ups and the critical use of color, form, and subject matter in film. *NDNs from All Directions* provides snapshots of believable Native American dancers dancing in a circular fashion to pow wow music. These images are juxtaposed with clips of hyper-sexualized British dancers posing as dancing "Indians" and a gun-wielding cowboy. This mash-up creates a visual collage of stereotypical "Indian" dancing: stomping, limbs in angular shapes, unison formations, and the looking-into-the-distance gesture as represented by the flat hand resting above the eyes. Together these images illustrate how repetition, sampling, and layering of storylines have become the toolkit for contemporary youth navigating the complex "ruins" of Indian representations. ATCR's *NDNs from All Directions* actualizes what Rose (1994) describes as a hip-hop principle for social resistance.

One can argue that they (hip hop principles) create and sustain rhythmic motion, continuity, and circularity via flow, accumulate, reinforce and embellish this continuity through layering; and manage threats to these narratives by building in ruptures that highlight the continuity as it momentarily challenges it. (p. 39)

ATCR builds in circularity via flow and incorporates the ruptures in the inclusion of glimpses of gun-wielding cowboy superimposed on the pow wow scene, and with the inclusion of the dancing group of women dressed as "Indian." ATCR has tapped into this energy and used these build-ups as ways to draw attention to stereotypical images, but also to insert breaks in the narrative within which is the space for change and transformation. These ruptures are also implicit in the "freeze," as the moment where you transform the movement. You build up the tempo, the flow, and then you create change.

NDNs from All Directions includes riffs from Super Cat's "Scalp Dem" from their 1994 album *The Good, the Bad, the Ugly, and the Crazy*, and incorporates a segment of the 1970s show "It's Cliff Richards." The segment called "I'm an Indian Too" highlighted Cliff with white women dancers posing as Indian princesses and wearing "native"-style bikinis. Such staged Indian role-playing represents an erasure of Native American people and a stifling of Indigenous movement socially, politically, and physically. This representation of plastic Indians contrasts with another image utilized by ATCR in its video *Red Skin Girl*, where the girl of the title appears as if she is part of the circle. Her dancing image represents an unbounded movement coming out of a space of struggle and a need for movement. Her image seems appropriate, as through my reading, it represents transformation and change amidst the ruins of Indigenous representation. ATCR uses the form of the aural-visual collage as a form of re-appropriation. In doing so, they are nurturing a between space. The "electric pow wow" has become a central hub of Indigenous motion, where nothing is static and identities are continually in flux. Thus, Indegeneity asserts its mobility with YouTube functioning as a catalyst for such multiplicities of motion and identity.

The blending of traditional soundscapes through any of the art forms associated with hip-hop culture creates a portal to strengthen our "urban tribal" connection with ourselves and the city contours we inhabit. I look forward to the next generation of "earth divers" as they continue to tap into a deeper consciousness of contemporary Indigenous thought and "shapeshift" a different world for themselves and those of us who have the privilege to bear witness.

NOTES

1. For an in-depth analysis of the representational use of "the Indian" on the popular screen see *Reel Injuns* (2009).
2. See www.redwiremag.com.
3. KAYA's song weaver's studio program is a free youth recording studio with the goal to empower the voice of Aboriginal youth.
4. See www.rpm.fm. Content manager Ostwelve (Coast Salish-Sto:lo) is a multi-media artist, hip-hop producer, emcee, actor, and writer. He has traveled the world—from the Nokia Jam in Johannesburg to the North American Indigenous Games in Duncan, BC—delegating and performing.
5. Think NDN is created, produced, and hosted by Suzette Amaya (Kwakwak wakw, Cree, Nisga, and Coast Salish.)
6. *Blueprint for Life* is an organization that practices "social work through hip-hop" and offers programming throughout Canada's northern regions and inner cities. B-boy Mathew CreeAsian (Vietnamese/Cree) is a member of *Blueprint for Life*.
7. The content in this section also appears in Recollet (2010).
8. Cree hip-hop photographer, author, and activist.
9. The Mighty Zulu Kingz are an all-star hip-hop crew from across the world chosen to represent the "Zulu Nation," which was founded by the grandfather of hip-hop culture, Afrika Bambaataa.
10. Fancy dancing originated as "Fancy War Dance" by the Hethwska Society in Oklahoma. It was invented by Augustus Hurley, aka "Gus" McDonald (1898–1974) of the Ponca Tribe.
11. A cleansing practice through the use of sage, sweetgrass, or other medicine belonging within the context of an Indigenous nation's knowledge system.
12. Elder Williams is from the First Nation community Waawshkigaamagki which is the Anishinaabemowin (Ojibway) name for Curve Lake. This appears in Simpson (2011, p. 99).
13. Artistic Director and founder of Dancing Earth–Indigenous dance creations
14. This term was introduced to me by emcee Eekwol (aka Lindsay Knight) of Muskoday First Nation in Saskatchewan, Canada. It is useful in challenging the categorization "Native" hip-hop, which can be perceived as restrictive.
15. Cree playwright and actor.
16. This term's context is borrowed from my uncle—Cree scholar Willie Ermine.
17. This project emerged from grunt gallery and debuted live in Vancouver and Paris in June 2011. Performers include Kinnie Starr, Ostwelve (emcee and media artist), electronic cellist

Cris Derksen, video artist Jackson 2Bears, performance artist, singer and co-creator Skeena Reece, Haida Artist Cory Bulpitt, and Larrisa Healy aka Gurl23 with Tangible Interaction Digital Graffiti Wall, creator of digitally triggered video drum Archer Pechawis, special guests Christie Lee Charles, and J.B. the First Lady.

18. I use this term with caution due to the understanding that the nation's historical and contemporary relationship to this place for generations involves extensive occupation and use previous to this struggle.

19. Secwepemc activists have been said to wear camouflage masks "to symbolize the colors of Mother Earth that we show our alliance with. We are speaking for those who cannot be heard, the trees, animals, sky, water, and all life on the land which also depend on our Sacred Mountains.... Our faces will be covered because even when we do speak you do not listen, from the first contact until now, we remain invisible. Why: Sun Peaks Resort Corporation and owner Nippon Cable (a partner of Blackcomb whistler Resort), continue to expand onto our traditional Secwepemc Lands without consent of the Indigenous people" (First Nations land rights and environmentalism in British Columbia).

20. Sibling duos include Cree emcee Eekwol and brother beat maker Mils; and the Seminole Battiest brothers Zack and Spencer, *The Storm*.

21. Some of these ideas appeared in my Ph.D. dissertation *Aural Traditions: Indigenous Youth and the Hip-Hop Movement in Canada*.

22. Ottawa, Ontario–based audio/visual collective consisting of DJ Shub, Deejay NDN, and Bear Witness.

REFERENCES

Alridge, D.P. (2005). From Civil Rights to Hip Hop: Toward a Nexus of Ideas. *The Journal of African American History*, 90 (3), 226–252.

Banes, S. (2004). "Breaking." In *That's the Joint, the Hip-Hop Studies Reader*, edited by M. Forman and M. Neal, 13–20. New York, London: Routledge.

Battiest,Z.,andBattiest,S.(2011).TheStorm.[video]Judd,S.P.(Director).Hollywood:Unconquered Media. Video retrieved from www.youtube.com/watch?v=QawQyLTH7NO.

Bear Witness (2011). *NDNs from All Directions*. Retrieved from http://vimeo.com/27888900.

Beat Nation: Hip Hop through Indigenous Culture. *Beat Nation Live "Landscapes"* (2011). http://www.youtube.com/watch?v=5vDbbjmQhb4

Bennett, A. (1999). "Hip Hop Am Main: The Localization of Rap Music and Hip Hop Culture." *Media, Culture & Society* 21, 77–91.

Boyd, T. (2003). *The New H.N.I.C: the Death of Civil Rights and the Reign of Hip Hop*. New York and London: New York University.

Butler, P. (2004). "Much Respect: Toward a Hip-Hop Theory of Punishment." *Stanford Law Review*, 56 (5), 983–1016.

Peters, E.J. (2004) *Three Myths About Aboriginals in Cities*. Ottawa, Ont.: Canadian Federation for the Humanities and Social Sciences.

Collins, P.H., (2006). *From Black power to Hip Hop: Racism, Nationalism, and Feminism*. Philadelphia: Temple University Press.

Dyson, M. E. (2004). "The Culture of Hip-Hop. In *That's the Joint, the Hip-Hop Studies Reader*, edited by M. Forman and M. Neal, 61–68. New York, London: Routledge.

Ermine, W. (2005). Ethical Space: Transforming Relations. Paper presented for the *National Gatherings on Indigenous Knowledge*, Rankin Inlet, NU. Retrieved from www.traditions. gc.ca/docs/docs_disc_ermine_e.cfm.

Fanon, F. (2008). *Black Skin White Masks*. New Edition. Translated by R. Philcoxx. New York: Grove Press.

Favel Starr, F. (2005). "The Artificial Tree: Native Performance Culture Research, 1991–1996." In *Aboriginal drama and theatre: Critical perspectives on Canadian theatre in English*, vol. 1, edited by R. Appleford. Toronto: Playwrights Canada Press.

Fon, C., Bainbridge, C., and Ludwick, L. (Producers), and Diamond, N. (Director). (2009). *Reel Injun* [Feature Documentary]. Canada: Rezolution Pictures Inc. in cooperation with The National Film Board of Canada.

Francis, M. (2002). *City Treaty: A Long Poem*. Winnipeg, MB: Turnstone Press.

Kinos-Goodin, J. (2011, August 23). "A Tribe Called Red's urban pow wow." *The National Post*. Retrieved from http://arts.nationalpost.com/2011/08/23/a-tribe-called-r eds-urban-powwow/.

Lashua, B. (2006). "The Arts of the Remix: Ethnography and Rap." *Anthropology Matters Journal*, 8 (2). Retrieved from http://www.anthropologymatters.com/index.

No Doubt, D. (2009). The Quickening. On *First contact* [CD]. Montreal, QC: Bombay Records.

Owens, L. (1998). *Mixedblood Messages: Literature, Film, Family, Place*. Norman, OK: University of Oklahoma Press.

Paniccioli, E. (Sept. 2010). *Hip Hop Has Always Been with Us*. So Much to Say MANIFESTO Speaker Series presented in association with Ryerson Student's Union, Ryerson University, Toronto, ON. Retrieved from http://vimeo.com/16037416.

QRock (2011). *1Q Rock- Eagle Steps! (Final HD 1)*. Mp4 Retrieved from www.youtube.ca/ watch?v=x8AohkJc10.

Recollet, K. (2010). *Aural traditions: Indigenous Youth and the Hip-Hop Movement in Canada*. (Unpublished doctoral dissertation). Trent University, Peterborough, Ontario.

Rose, T. (1994). *Black noise: Rap Music and Black Culture in Contemporary America*. Hanover, NH: Wesleyan University Press.

Simpson, L. (2011). *Dancing on Our Turtle's Back: Stories of Nishnaabeg Re-creation, Resurgence and a New Emergence*. Winnipeg, MB: Arbeiter Ring Publishing.

Tangen, R. (2007). Introduction. In Miller, P., and Crane, P., *Human Landscapes: Interpreting the Human Form*. Albuquerque, NM: Fresco Fine Art Publications LLC.

Vizenor, G. (1981). *Earth Divers: Tribal Narratives on Mixed Descent*. Minneapolis, MN: University of Minnesota Press.

Williard, T. (2009). "Medicine Beats and Ancestral Rhymes." *Beat Nation—Hip-Hop as Indigenous Culture*. Retrieved from www.beatnation.org.

CHAPTER 26

DANCING WITH MYSELF: *DANCE CENTRAL*, CHOREOGRAPHY, AND EMBODIMENT

MELISSA BLANCO BORELLI AND DEREK A. BURRILL

PRESS START . . . WARM UP . . .

NOT everyone likes to play video games. Some do not have the patience to stare at a screen and develop good hand-eye coordination, and others lack interest in games that feature guns, in fighting ridiculously animated monsters, or even in becoming a high scorer. However, things changed for this co-author upon attending Dance Technology and the Circulation of the Social v2.0 at Massachusetts Institute of Technology in 2011. Here was a conference dedicated to the intersections among dance, the virtual, the corporeal, and the digital. One of the conference organizers had fortuitously left *Dance Central* for us to play. Dance what? My first instinct was to dismiss it as another passive eye-wasting activity, but when I heard the echoes of well-known pop songs and recognized some choreography from either those songs' music videos or social dance, I drew closer. I watched as several people danced along to the avatar that executed the moves I recognized. Eventually, I found myself playing the game for about an hour, choosing song after song, following routine after routine. Not only was it addicting, but it also prompted some inquiry into the circulation and consumption of dance as a commodity. Here was a game that was trademarking specific choreographies, associating them with songs and avatars and then selling it to the consumer as a way to not only play, but to get fit and to join in a collective consciousness of choreography.

This co-authored chapter has been set up as a dialogue to think about and through the different epistemologies that gaming and dance games in particular set up. We decided to co-author it because this structure mirrors the relationship between the player's body and the player's brain, both working together during the game, yet often in conflict when in comes to that difficult (or simple) move. Our individual research interests—popular dance on screens, primarily music video choreography,[1] and gaming, virtual spaces, and embodiment[2]—enable a fruitful conversation between our disciplinary frames of dance, technology, mediated representations of bodies, and the politics of consumption.

At root, we want to demonstrate how technologies like *Dance Central* (as well as other games played with the body, on the Wii or the Xbox Kinect system, for example) enable new ways of learning and embodiment through social choreographies, while at the same time de- and re-materializing the demonstrative visceral body of the choreographer. In a sense, *Dance Central* and similar games are reconceptualizing both the role of the choreographer and choreography itself. The game sets up a type of consumer choreography that everyone can access and learn, practice and perfect. We find this to be at the core of the power of popular dance and its transmission through screens, networks, and bodies. Thus, this chapter does not purport to completely analyze all of *Dance Central* and its extensive set of choreographies. What it attempts to do is to begin a conversation as well as theorizations about what it means for popular dance to literally dance alongside and through the digital.

GAME ON!

Dance Central is a game developed by Harmonix Music Systems for Microsoft Studios. It was released in November 2010, with *Dance Central 2* appearing almost a year later in October 2011. To play it you must have an Xbox 360 with a Kinect sensor. Kinect, developed by Microsoft as well, is a user interface system that enables advanced human tracking, gesture recognition, and voice control.[3] The player's body controls the avatar on the screen and the motion capture technology senses how one's body is or is not facilitating the action or activity on the screen. Kinect has sold over 18 million units in the past year (2011), garnering a Guinness Book of World Records award for fastest selling consumer electronics device.[4] Recently, Microsoft announced that Kinect would be available in Windows-based PCs, so that voice recognition and movement tracking could be available without an Xbox.[5] Somewhat more cost-prohibitive, Kinect is literally moving quickly into new territories outside of gaming attesting to the speed of technological developments volleying between novelty and obsolescence.[6]

Kinect's indispensible help facilitates the objective of *Dance Central*'s game: to follow a piece of choreography as closely and correctly as possible. The Kinect sensor records the dancer/player's movement execution, thereby determining his or her ability to replicate the choreography. Points are tabulated based on the player's accuracy. A *Dance Central* player chooses his/her avatar from a variety of characters, although each song comes with its pre-assigned avatar and background. The player as the controller can change these at will. The first game has eight avatars: Angel, Miss Aubrey, Dare, Amelia, McCoy, Mo, Oblio, and Taye. A secret avatar exists in the form of the robot Eliot who only appears after one has scored the maximum or has earned four stars. The "human" avatars range in racial appearance and clothing style so that a player has the possibility to choose one with which they can corporeally relate.

With the advent of motion capture technology and its use in making video games, avatars seem more corpo-real—they seem to have gained a new level of "realness." That is, the quality of their movement evokes some qualities that make dancing a material, embodied experience. *Dance Central's* avatars demonstrate various interpretations of space (direct/indirect), weight (strong/light), flow (bound/free), and time (sudden/sustained).[7] Surely the avatar cannot replace a real body showing you how to do the movements in a dance class. There, you get a three-dimensional perspective (often aided by mirrors and other surrounding bodies) that *Dance Central* tries to evoke with the use of the two backup dancing avatars and the bystanders in the background. Furthermore, the ways in which different bodies shift through weight and flow with(in) (a) movement(s) becomes markedly visible in three dimensions. The flat screen with the seemingly "weightless" avatar renders these corporeal manifestations of dance invisible. Whether or not this is successfully executed bears little relevance for the objective—to learn the moves as accurately as possible—since this can be accomplished through the demonstrative body of the avatar, the instructions on the right, and through repetition of the choreography.

Professional choreographers wear the motion-capture technology and create choreographies that are not only easy to "capture," but also work with the music. It is important to note that motion capture is yet another exciting but problematic innovation in a long line of representative technologies, technologies like film, television, virtual reality, and videogames. These technologies all have several things in common. First, they are technologies of representation, not duplication. What is projected on the screen or in the space of the game is a version of some original or referent work, idea, or image. Second, these technologies are about the complicating of space and dimension. The world of the *Lord of the Rings* trilogy, for example, is a mix of real actors filmed in real landscapes as well as meticulously constructed sets with characters constructed through motion capture and CGI. And you'll notice that dance has always been an important part of these technologies' evolution and exegesis, both as something that represents and as something that is represented. This is largely because dance and choreography is itself a technological system of representation (i.e., through particular techniques, with the dancer as a kind of tool and as a discursive technical system) and occurs in space as it simultaneously *invents* that space. So, it should come as no surprise that a game like *Dance Central* operates as a dance theory machine, too.

Dance Central also allows for the player/dancer to have her own improvisational moment during the segment called Freestyle. Here, the avatar disappears from the screen and a heat-sensor outline of the player/dancer's body appears. In this section, the player/dancer moves independently to her own choreographically improvised score and then a moment of this section gets replayed back to the dancer/player in quick edited fast-time for either humorous or technologically whizzy affect. The quality of the improvised section depends on the dancer and YouTube is full of a variety of improvisations ranging from players that seem either lazy or uncomfortable with the concept of improvisation (as evidenced by a dancer/player standing still during this segment) to quite well-choreographed or executed improvisation. In these instances, the dancer/player has taken some of the moves learned and ordered them in his/her own way, adding personal flair. The level of difficulty for the choreography ranges from easy to hard. How is this level of skill determined? And, if a player masters the hard choreography what can s/he do to remain challenged or even interested in the game? Do mastery and (gasp!) virtuosity, in *Dance Central* provide their own reward? Harmonix offers bonus choreographies and avatars that one can purchase with Microsoft Points (which are equal to about $3–6) to access the new material. By the plethora of online communities for its fans, *Dance Central* has made a point to support and indulge the dance competition fantasies of its players. Players can log onto their website and set up points, compare notes, and post videos.

Like massive multiplayer online games (e.g., *Everquest, World of Warcraft*), a great deal of the serious fun of *Dance Central* is the shared, common language and literacies that online social groups and subcultures create, maintain, and propagate. As in all social media (Facebook, MySpace, Match.com, tumblr, Pinterest, Google+, foursquare, et al.), the drive to connect is similar to the drive in real, face-to-face interactions, with an important difference. Online social media allows the user to *customize* and *enhance* their profile and through this optimization, customize and enhance their (online) self. Online, the profile serves as an ever-present chance to alter and perfect what the social circle will see. In a sense, the real body becomes a kind of avatar of the profile. What sets games like *Dance Central* apart (largely *because* of their online social features), is that a moving body, a choreographed self, always leave a trace. But, whereas this trace on Facebook might be a photo, a favorite song, or a funny clip, the individual and particular pieces of people's lives present in *Dance Central* digital communities are truly *shared*—all of the bodies have performed the same moves, the same steps, the same popular dance manifold. Why is this significant? It shows that these new technologies/games/communities let people experience dance at a micro and macro scale simultaneously, while the sharing and dissemination of this form are themselves part of the choreography. So, where (the heck) is the choreographer in all this? Does popular digital dance need them at all? Does the referent body matter, that primary dancer that was motion-captured function as a kind of über-choreographer? Before we consider the role of the choreographer, the crucial component of the music in *Dance Central* bears mentioning. It is the music that determines how the *Dance Central* choreographers create their respective choreographies.

The songs used in both *Dance Central* and *Dance Central 2* mostly come from the US Billboard pop charts. More than likely, a dancer/player is familiar with some, if not all, of them. They follow the formulaic pop song structure of several verses interspersed with a catchy chorus and a bridge. Thus, the song's structure informs its accompanying choreography with certain movement phrases that return during the chorus. This handy, repetitive tactic enables the player/dancer to repeat those phrases several times within the span of the song, thereby enabling an embodied understanding of the phrase after just one game. Clearly not all bodies embody, understand, and learn movement in the same way, yet the repetitive nature of the choreography facilitates some quick muscle memory tactics. For example, in the choreography to Cascada's *Evacuate the Dance Floor* (used in the advertisements for *Dance Central 1*), the movement phrase—hips wider than shoulder width apart, arms bent at the elbow, a little lower than the shoulders with the forearms facing forward, alternate weight shifts (engaged by the quadriceps as the legs should be slightly bent) with the non-weighted foot twisting inward as the arms in ninety-degree angles rotate and alternate from up to down, elbows maintain their lifted position with the head moving to each side that has a lifted arm—pairs consistently chorus, "oh, oh-oh, evacuate the dance floor." The song lasts about two minutes and twenty seconds, and the chorus repeats four times. Feasibly, after four tries a player/dancer can increase her comfort in executing the movement. For those that need more practice and repetition, the game provides a mode called "Break It Down," where the dancer/player can practice the choreography before she decides to go to the "Perform" mode where she will be scored. *Dance Central 2*'s "Break it Down Mode" is now customizable in that the player/dancer can focus on particular moves or movement phrases that produce a challenge rather than the entire choreography.

In "Evacuate the Dance Floor," the screen features a central avatar, Emilia, in her basketball jersey and shorts and accompanied by her two backup dancers. In the background a party scene ensues. The location can be a club, a bridge, a pier, a roof, any place where impromptu social dance activity can start if someone smart enough brings a sound system. The site of the choreography and the background dancers can vary. Sometimes, the clothes the avatar wears can vary as well. The routine varies in its difficulty level— from easy to medium to hard. *Dance Central 2* provides new features that include voice control; the opportunity for two players/dancers to be on the screen at the same time for fun or for competition; drop in/out feature; customizable "Break it Down" mode; new avatars songs; dance crews; and the capability to record and export your performance to social media like Twitter, Facebook, or YouTube and receive comments/feedback from other dancers/players.[8] Who needs a dance class with other live bodies around and specific detailed instructions on how to improve when you can create a virtual community with the mere predilection for one track, one piece of choreography, or one game?

To the right of the screen, boxes appear with a drawing of the choreographic move, and the main part of the body that will be used is highlighted, with the corresponding title of the move above. A small arrow drawn inside the box provides directional instructions (e.g., up, down, circular, reverse). Sometimes, the name of the move is based on the descriptive quality of the movement and it is a mere adjective, for example, "smooth." In another instance, the name stems from a black social dance from the 1980s, the Roger Rabbit. And sometimes the name evokes an image the dancer, avatar, or spectator of the move should conjure up in her mind as she does the movement, such as "phoenix." The main *Dance Central* (2) choreographers, Marcos Aguirre and Frenchy Hernandez, have a significant influence in the naming of the moves. Is this a form of trademarking choreography or is it just following the historical trajectory of (black) popular dance, where moves are executed, circulated, and performed with names that relate to style, song lyric, name of dancer, body part, or popular culture character?[9]

The game plays into a somatic approach to learning, mimicking and ultimately embodying movement, but how many players would consider this? In other words, if the instructions are to do a dance movement called smooth in a *smooth* way (not that it specifically requires this, but one can speculate that the title will have an affect on the understanding of the quality of the movement), what type of effort should the learning body call forth when she is playing/learning/copying? Should she maintain a free, relaxed shoulder as she lifts her arm and flexes it at the elbow joint? Or, if she just follows the instructions, will Kinect just read only her movement, not her effort? If this sensing device becomes the arbiter for flow and effort in a piece of choreography, how might *Dance Central* be shifting the ways in which we consider performance, mastery, or embodiment? How good does one have to be to become a high scorer? Whereas Western theater dance establishes a dance piece's value on factors such as frequency of performance on prestigious stages, level of technical virtuosity, a particular choreographer's legacy, cost of tickets (this involves its historical significance as part of a stage art dance canon), popular dance's value resides in other factors. Dodds addresses this distinct valuation system and argues that value in popular dance must step away from the absolutist and relativist positions of constructing value. She develops the term "embodied value" which is "the multiple enunciations of significance, judgment and worth that are expressed through the movement practices of different communities engaged in popular dance forms.[10] Dodds's analysis enables discussions such as these about social dance via a technology in the privacy of one's home to formulate understandings about the value of popular dance in today's world of consumer capitalism.

This next section provides a quick movement and phenomenological analysis of what it is like to play *Dance Central*. By phenomenological, we mean an analysis based on the experience of dancing through the perception of how one's body is moving and engaging with movement.[11] Every body will have a different set of experiences, given its ability to embody dance technique or style. Thus, popular dance studies provides an analytical frame through which to engage in the variety of analysis and critiques that can come from these other sets of experiences.

> Don't Cha—Pussycat Dolls featuring Busta Rhymes (*Dance Central*, downloadable content)
> Avatar: Miss Aubrey
> Choreographer: Frenchy Hernandez
> Level: Hard
> **Loading**...
> "Say what you will about me, but you know I'm good. Please form an orderly line to wait for my autograph."—Miss Aubrey

Miss Aubrey is the sassy redhead. In one version of the choreography, she wears a gold dress cinched at the waist with a belt, black headband and black shoes that look like a cross between ballet flats and ancient Greek sandals. They call this her Princess look. In another version, she wears her traditional outfit: shorts, red suspenders, knee high argyle socks and a blue button-up short-sleeve shirt. Miss Aubrey gets ready by rolling her shoulders back, or shaking certain parts of the body. She performs a suave confidence, asserting that she *is* the demonstrative body. The beat of the song begins and so does her swagger. She shifts weight and bounces from side to side. On the side, the boxes that signal the choreographic moves are still, waiting for the lyrics to begin. Once they do, these boxes progress as the movement changes.

The choreographic moves for this song include: "smooth," "sassy bounce," "lasso down," "burlesque," "pop it down," "slow hit," "gankitty," "eyepatch," "neck crack," "open hip wind," "shimmy," "djinn," "lava," "phoenix," "the hellion," "slow snatch," "snatch both," "mini wind," "get it," "round hit snap," "round hit sass." Several of them get repeated, depending on their relationship to the music. For example, the chorus of the song features these four: djinn, the hellion, lava, and phoenix. Without the visual stimuli, some of these choreographic moves do not immediately evoke a physical response. The active verbs such as snatch, pop, lasso, snap, or get, offer a direction (lasso *down*) or a qualifier (*slow* snatch) to establish a more nuanced interpretation or embodiment of the move, while other names evoke Orientalist imaginaries (e.g., djinn); names such as hellion and phoenix call to mind monsters/animals and their physical embodiment through a gesture of resemblance.

Like the earlier example of "Evacuate the Dance Floor," "Don't Cha" features specific moves that go along with a song lyric. Frenchy Hernandez, one of the Harmonix's resident choreographers, describes her process to *Wired Magazine*: "Like I sit at my desk and I'm listening to it and just moving around in my chair listening to it," she explained. "And from there I kind of get up and move to a mirror and just freestyle dance."[12] From there, she comes up with movement phrases and routines that "come in at just the right beat or lyric."[13] Interestingly, Hernandez is later filmed performing the choreography. Together with the producer of *Dance Central*, Hernandez determines what movement sequence or specific movements belong in each level: easy, medium, or hard. They also name the moves. Hernandez's role as both cultural insider and dancer/choreographer sets her up to become a brand manager, branding dance for further circulation and consumption. The limits of current motion-capture technology prevent certain moves from appearing in the choreographies (hand movements in front of the torso, for example), so *Dance Central* choreographers have to negotiate and make choices as to what movements and articulated body parts will best be represented and recorded by motion capture and then learned and embodied by the dancer/player (customer).

PERFORM IT!

(This analysis is based on the chorus.)

Lyric	Movement Name	Movement Description
Don't cha wish your girlfriend	Djinn	(Don't cha wish) Legs out, wider than shoulder-width apart. Arms at 90 degrees, elbows at shoulder height, and head bobs downward to punctuate the beat—(your girlfriend). With the elbows staying at shoulder height, the arms come in toward the torso, forearms facing down. Again, head bobs down to punctuate the beat.
Was hot like me?	Lava	Arms lifted straight upward in unison, they trace a circular path, with the torso and hips rotating gently in the same direction.
Don't cha wish your girlfriend	Phoenix	Right foot steps diagonally back, weight is centered while arms swing laterally along the side of the body, sweeping downward to follow the movement of the foot; then arms circle back toward the front.
Was a freak like me?	Hellion	Legs remain in the same position as phoenix while arms open out wide at shoulder height and then shoot upward, elbows straight.
Don't cha? Don't cha?	Slow snatch R, Slow snatch L, Slow snatch both.	The right leg glides in toward the body to join left standing-leg while the right arm circles inward with a grabbing gesture of the hand. This move is repeated on left side, then right leg glides and both arms make smooth snatching gesture inward.
(No lyrics)	Mini wind	Hips/pelvis rotation with arms held loosely in front of torso and flexed at elbow, hands in relaxed fists.
Don't cha wish your girlfriend	Djinn	(Don't cha wish) Legs out, wider than shoulder-width apart. Arms at 90 degrees, elbows at shoulder height, and head bobs downward to punctuate the beat—(your girlfriend). With the elbows staying at shoulder height, the arms come in toward the torso, forearms facing down. Again, head bobs down to punctuate the beat.
Was wrong like me?	Lava	Arms lifted straight upward in unison, they trace a circular path, with the torso and hips rotating gently in the same direction.
Don't cha wish your girlfriend	Phoenix	Right foot steps diagonally back, weight is centered while arms swing laterally along the side of the body, sweeping downward to follow the movement of the foot; then arms circle back toward the front.
Was fun like me?	Get it	Arms in same position as lava, but instead of rotating they pulse to the left 4 times to the beat.
Don't cha? Don't cha?	Slow snatch right, Slow snatch left, Slow snatch both.	The right leg glides in toward the body to join left standing-leg while the right arm circle inward with a grabbing gesture of the hand. This move is repeated on left side, then right leg glides and both arms make smooth snatching gesture inward.

In this particular choreography, we suggest that the verb "to wish" evokes the idea of a genie, a signifier of desire fulfillment. Thus, the djinn movement can be said to operate within the mode of dance representation called *resemblance*. Dance scholar Susan Leigh Foster developed four modes of representation—resemblance, imitation, replication and reflection—in order to facilitate how a particular dance makes meaning in the world.[14] The "djinn" movement, with its head bob and folded arms, resembles the gestures associated with this imaginary figure (particularly in visual culture). "Lava," on the other hand, could be an *imitation*, as the bodily rotations evoke the circle of lava as it bubbles and bursts inside of a volcano. "Hellion," most likely associated with the word "freak" in the lyrics, resembles this monster through the quality of the movement, that is its jerky, sudden shift from "phoenix" beforehand, which was a slower and sustained upward movement used to resemble the beautiful and elegant fairy tale–bird that rises from its ashes. As stated earlier, the limitations of the motion-capture technology prevent certain movements from appearing in the choreography. Despite such parameters, the variety of choreographic gestures and moves that are set is astounding. Additionally, the relationship between words and their corporeal interpretation makes *Dance Central* a potentially rich site for studying how popular dance choreographers envision and create movements, and how their execution and circulation among practitioners/gamers establishes specific types of values to the dance and the game itself.

On YouTube there are fan videos for both versions of the game. Most of them are split screen, with the visceral body on one side and the virtual one on the other. This duet of the visceral and virtual makes for many hours of viewing pleasure. Which body performs better? If the visceral one is replicating a translation of another real body's choreography, what role does the avatar have in the transmission? *Dance Central* functions as the site where choreography gets mediated through the avatar onto the corporeal body playing the game/dancing along. What does the avatar's "presenceness" have to say about embodiment and its relationship to commodity consumer culture? Thirty years into the evolution of dance in music videos, popular dance choreographies no longer need a visible visceral body to labor and transmit the dance.[15] Motion-capture technology has facilitated the translation from body to body through the avatar as an intermediary. However, might this be just a new way to reconceptualize the exchange of dance between bodies? In other words, dance has always been a translation of corporeal technique and vocabulary from one body to the next by watching, trying, mimicking, practicing, and redoing. How then might *Dance Central* complicate notions of the debate between visceral and virtual bodies and the ontological status of bodies and their functionality in dance?

If ontology is the branch of metaphysics that deals with the nature of being, then we have a significant quandary here. Generally speaking, humans like to separate everything in nature into two categories: subject and object. Subjects are "us" humans. Everything else is an object. The problem is, this artificial demarcation functions, at a very basic level, as a means of objectifying whatever is outside the "self." The most familiar and tragic result of this system is that women are notated as objects, particularly in the hyper-dynamics of visual culture. Another familiar problem is that instead of seeing a tree, we see lumber—for a matchstick, a house, or an arc—which has lead us into our current environmental catastrophe. This lies at the heart of the magnificent work of Michel Foucault—how power flows and accumulates during the transactions between objects and subjects. What, then, does this mean for dance and for *Dance Central* in particular? Dance, as a practice, is often about disrupting the simplistic demarcation of subject/object, so that multiple objects and subjects can speak *through* the subject-body, blurring the lines so that power is shared, conjoined, and problematized. In the case of *Dance Central*, we are literally seeing both the body as object (the avatar) and the body as subject (the recorded body), while real bodies watch in real space-time, having provided the "source material" for the entire scenario. Is this a case, then, of dematerialization resulting in a greater fracturing of the subject? If so, is this a bad thing? Or, does this process of ontological slippage allow both subjects and objects to speak in new ways, therefore further sublimating power and power flow into multiple states and sites?

FIVE STARS, 428,011 POINTS, MOVES PASSED 100 PERCENT

Reset/Reload

The two main choreographers used for *Dance Central* are of color: Marcos Aguirre and Frenchy Hernandez. They both hail from Boston, Massachusetts, and have had prolific careers dancing in music videos and touring with well-known pop music acts, such as Rihanna, Ashanti, and Snoop Dogg. How do their training and cultural background impact the kind of dancing corporealities that *Dance Central* is trademarking and mass producing? How do these corporealities circulate globally? A Marxist analysis might suggest these bodies operate as alienated labor, displaying their choreographic skills (and getting paid for it), which then gets circulated and embodied. Can embodiment be branded? Dance scholars have made a case for the branding of embodiment through, for example, a theory of hip(g)nosis which suggests how mulatta women learn, embody, and replicate gendered and racialized choreographies that become branded as mulatta-ness.[16] This hip(g)nosis can then circulate from body to body, outside of racialized notions of essentialized ways of moving/being. This is how both Shakira and Beyoncé, for example, can be proponents of hip(g)nosis even though their cultural and racialized contexts are different and despite their participation in commodity culture's pop celebrity mode of production. So, *Dance Central* operates in a similar register in that it uses the bodies and respective choreographic scores of Aguirre and Hernandez, captures them through motion sensors and technology, animates them through the nine avatars, and then brands the choreography as *Dance Central* so that other bodies can practice, learn, and perhaps even perfect or improve upon the execution; a technological ruse at the expense of choreographic labor and historically or culturally learned corporeality. In other words, their bodies disappear and all that remains is a trace through the avatar, similar to the trails of light that emerge from the avatar's limbs as s/he moves. Undoubtedly, Aguirre and Hernandez receive adequate compensation for their work. Furthermore, the ability to create choreography that will be mass-produced, reproduced, and embodied contributes to the circulation of dance as a social, physical, and cultural experience that cannot be belittled or overlooked.

What does it mean when the labor of a proper flesh-encased choreographer of color is morphed into and onto a white avatar? Is this a version of cyber-racial-appropriation, and if so, what does it say about consumer culture and technology's anthropophagous machinations? Does the avatar function as a palliative against essentialist beliefs that still cloud dance practices, and what type of bodies can or cannot perform certain movements or dance genres? Dance scholar Jane Desmond states that "in cases where a cultural form migrates from a subordinate to a dominant group, the meanings attached to that adoption (and remodeling) are generated within the parameters of the current and historical relations between the two groups, and their constitution of each as "other" and as different in particular ways."[17] In *Dance Central*, this migration involves but is not exclusively based on African American social dance practice and the unique movement vocabularies associated with it; dance moves that developed in a family's living room, among a group of physically nimble teens hanging on the street, or, as in Frenchy Hernandez's case, a Latina choreographer's rented studio space. What kind of historical erasures of the importance and significance of social dance in specific communities is happening through the virtual world of a kinetic utopia that *Dance Central* celebrates? A type of American brand of dance emerges from *Dance Central*, a brand that is a kinesthetic melting pot showcased through mediated dance forms such as music video choreography, television dance competition shows, and films about dance (such as the ones discussed in this anthology), where any body (anybody), if they have the skill and determination, can indeed learn to dance by following mediated bodies, either virtual or visceral.

Many of the issues facing digital culture are enunciating themselves here. What is the nature of work? How do bodies labor and how are they remunerated? Who owns what and what qualifies as intellectual property? Do we have a duty to share and disseminate digital information and art in spite of the copyright, distribution, and fair use laws of capitalism? What is an original? A copy? A shared work of art? Dance is uniquely suited to tackle these questions because it is, at root, about bodies *as* bodies, a uniquely tangible yet malleable mode of production. So, dance studies can take the lead here, by carefully inspecting the body as a laboring instrument, a force of production that is actively being displaced, recreated, and reimagined by digital technologies. There is real power here, for dancing bodies are infamously difficult to tie down as signifying agents, often resisting what digital code does to so much of human production—the reduction of material objects and subjects to a codified system for copy, simulation, and control. Dance's slippery nature is a benefit and a (pleasant) curse, for it forces us to look at the system from a unique vantage point while contemplating and acting upon the new forms of movement manifested by new technologies and the new bodies they produce.

Italo Calvino's *Invisible Cities* suddenly comes to mind. In this story, Marco Polo tells Genghis Khan a tale of a city where Polo encounters uncanny sites, people, and stories. Each city has the name of a woman, and as one reads the book it begins to surface that Polo shrewdly describes only one city, but in a myriad of ways. As an experiment, what would it mean to imagine each setting in *Dance Central* as a different "city" populated with denizens who long for the Greek muse of dance Terpsichore's touch and talent? These "cities" are invisible because they do not exist in the "real," yet they are continually made real each time a player/dancer, like Polo, brings them into being; Polo through rhetoric, the player/dancer through embodiment. These invisible cities of *Dance Central* posit a conflict-free space where the act of learning and embodying a set choreography creates a space of collectivity and healthy competition. As Tracey Rosenthal-Newsom, Harmonix's VP of Production states, "dancing is about creating experiences together, in the real world whether it's in your home or whether it's at a club..." It seems fitting to add the qualifier of social to describe the dancing to which she refers.

Although this essay has not fully delved into the politics of representation—particularly gender or race—occurring in *Dance Central/Dance Central 2*, we welcome further analysis on this rich site of inquiry within the field of dance studies. In a historical moment when the insidious machinations of global consumer capitalism continue to alienate, disembody, and exploit some of us more than others, *Dance Central* offers a moment of respite, where one can "just dance" (like the Lady Gaga song featured in *Dance Central*) and re-"kinect" with other bodies no matter what their age or skill set.[18] As a comment on the Dance Central tumblr attests:

> "Grandmas. Grandpas. 40 year olds. 8 year olds. @Dance_Central turned my living room into a Christmas dance floor. Thanks HMX!"
>
> —@darthhaider5150dancecentral.tmblr.com

NOTES

1. See Blanco Borelli, Melissa, "Dance in Music Video, or How I Learned to Dance Like Janet... Miss Jackson," *International Journal of Screendance* 2, No. 1 (Winter 2012): 52–55.

2. Derek A. Burrill, *Die Tryin': Videogames, Masculinity, and Culture*. New York: Peter Lang, 2008.

3. "Kinect for Windows Commercial Program Announced," http://blogs.msdn.com/b/kinect-forwindows/archive/2012/01/09/kinect-for-windows-commercial-program-announced.aspx (accessed February 27, 2012).

4. Ibid.

5. "Kinect for Windows gesture sensor launched by Microsoft," http://www.bbc.co.uk/news/technology-16836031 (accessed February 27, 2012).

6. For an insightful analysis of how mobile technology and the hyperkinetic developments of such technology affect our daily lives, refer to Jason Farman's *Mobile Interface Theory: Embodied Space and Locative Media*. New York: Routledge, 2011.

7. We use Laban Movement Analysis not to privilege it as a universal method in analyzing movement and/or dancing bodies, but because these efforts or dynamics when applied

to a "real" dancer versus a virtual one create interesting observations that deserve further analytical development by dance/movement scholars.

8. *Dance Central* websites: http://www.dancecentral.com/forums/showthread.php?t=1927 and http://www.dancecentral.com/game (accessed on February 27, 2012).

9. For an overview of the history of black social dance forms, consult Lynn Fauley Emery's *Black Dance from 1619 to Today* (Princeton: Princeton Book Company, 1989). Nadine George-Graves's chapter "Just Like Being at the Zoo: Primitivity and Ragtime Dance" in *Ballroom, Boogie, Shimmy Sham, Shake: A Social Dance Reader*, ed. Julie Malnig (Urbana Champaign: University of Illinois Press) provides background on how black social dances garnered some of their names; Katrina Hazzar-Gordon's *Jookin': The Rise of Social Dance Formations in African-American Culture* (Philadelphia: Temple University Press, 1990) provides another historical examination of black social dance; and lastly, Halifu Osumare's *The African Aesthetic in Global Hip Hop: Power Moves* (New York and London: Palgrave MacMillan, 2008) demonstrates how hip-hop circulates globally, as do the black social dance moves in Dance Central, as well.

10. *Dancing on the Canon* (Basingstoke: Palgrave MacMillan, 2011), 99.

11. Merleau Ponty's theory of phenomenology has informed writers and scholars of dance, as it posits that we perceive the world through our bodies. For Merleau Ponty, the body is both subject and object, a radical proposition for Western philosophical thought, as body has been theorized as pure extension (Descartes) and object. Merleau-Ponty, Maurice. Trans: Colin Smith. *Phenomenology of Perception* (London: Routledge, 2005).

12. Andrew Webster, "Star Choreographer Lends her Moves to Dance Central 2," *Wired Magazine*, October 2011, http://www.wired.com/gamelife/2011/10/dance-central-2-choreography/ (accessed January 30, 2012).

13. Ibid.

14. See Susan Leigh Foster's *Reading Dancing: Bodies and Subjects in Contemporary American Dance* (Berkeley: University of California Press, 1986), particularly chapter 2.

15. The thirty years are tabulated from the beginning of MTV in 1982.

16. See Blanco Borelli in this volume and also Blanco Borelli, "¿Y Ahora qué Vas a Hacer, Mulata? Hip Choreographies in the Mexican Cabaretera Film *Mulata* (1954)." *Women and Performance: A Journal of Feminist Theory.* 2008.

17. Jane Desmond, ed. *Meaning In Motion: New Cultural Studies in Dance* (Durham: Duke University Press), 37.

18. In October 2012, Harmonix issued *Dance Central 3.* New features include crew throwdown (teams of up to four members can dance battle), mini-choreography mode to make up new moves, beginner mode for bodies unfamiliar with dance video games, and party mode, which shuffles songs and difficulty depending on the players' performance scores.

BIBLIOGRAPHY

Baudrillard, Jean. *Simulations*. Semiotext(e): London, 1983.

Burrill, Derek. "Check Out My Moves." *Social Semiotics* 16, No. 1 (April 2006): 17–38.

Burrill, Derek. "Out of the Box: Performance, Drama and Interactive Software." *Modern Drama* 48, No. 3 (Fall 2005): 493–513.

"E3: Microsoft shows off gesture control technology for Xbox 360" Los Angeles Times Technology. http://latimesblogs.latimes.com/technology/2009/06/microsofte3.html

Foucault, Michel. *Discipline and Punish*. 2nd ed. Vintage: London, 1995.

"Starting February 1, 2012: Use the Power of Kinect for Windows to Change the World" *Kinect for Windows Blog*. http://blogs.msdn.com/b/kinectforwindows/archive/2012/01/09/kinect-for-windows-commercial-program-announced.aspx

PART VI

CONCLUSION

CHAPTER 27

....

VALUES IN MOTION:
REFLECTIONS ON
POPULAR SCREEN DANCE

....

SHERRIL DODDS

You want fame? Well fame costs and right here is where you start paying, in sweat!

As popular dance film enthusiasts will know, these words were immortalized in the motion picture *Fame* (1980) by the dance teacher "Lydia" at the fictionalized New York City High School for the Performing Arts. The idea that the popular-screen dance body operates through a framework of value and exchange forms the starting point of this chapter, as I suggest that corporeal values are mobilized in a variety of ways. The styles of dance featured in popular film and television produce measures of cultural capital so that some forms carry greater currency than others. For instance, in *StreetDance 3D* (2010), the cool hip-hop crew introduce the uptight ballet students to a funkier style of movement expression, and in *Strictly Ballroom* (1992), the vernacular *paso doble* signifies considerably more innovation and edge than its restrained and stuffy ballroom version. The popular-screen dance body also constitutes a site through which social values are played out. For example, film scholar Richard Dyer (1993) observes how the couple dances of the Hollywood musical allow heteronormative gender roles to be challenged and maintained, and several authors in this volume reveal how differences of race, class, and gender are articulated, negotiated, and resolved within popular dance film. Furthermore, the screen media act as a vehicle of economic worth, as popular dance film can produce high levels of capital exchange. Whether this is income reaped through box office returns or through its capacity to sell other commodities, such as CDs, DVDs, or advertising space, the mass dissemination of popular-screen dance potentially reaches a wealth of global consumers.

In addition to cultural capital, social value, and economic exchange, the popular-screen dance body occupies a shifting terrain of intellectual worth. Given that I am contributing, along with many others, to a book on popular dance film signals an important reconsideration of academic values within dance scholarship. Several scholars have documented how dance research traditionally focused on theater dance practice and it is only in the last decade or so that popular forms of dance have begun to occupy academic inquiry and the university curriculum (Buckland, 1999; Desmond, 2000; Dodds, 2011). Indeed, my own intellectual history traces this shift, as my doctoral research centered on "screendance"; that is "art dance" for camera, which is primarily screened at specialist film festivals or niche television slots and is created by choreographers and filmmakers whose interests and practices are generally located in theater dance traditions.[1] Yet while this body of work was typically produced and consumed within an art dance paradigm, I also recognized that it frequently shared a similar aesthetic to the dancing bodies that occupied music video, screen advertising, and other forms of popular film and television. At that time, my own values came into play as I concluded that the latter significantly departed from "screendance," as it behaved as a mainstream commercial enterprise that employed dance stereotypes to access broad consumer audiences.

While I see now how this sets up a simplistic binary between art and popular forms of dance, it nevertheless struck me how aesthetically innovative some of these popular forms were and how they offered me huge amounts of viewing pleasure, an issue rarely addressed in relation to art dance practice. Fifteen years on from completing my PhD, and as a scholar now totally immersed in the study of popular dance practice, my aim with this chapter is to revisit what might be central to the way in which we study popular-screen dance, what ought we to value, and what still requires some investment in our intellectual efforts. To do so, I call upon a range of screen dance examples created by television production companies, major Hollywood studios, and independent filmmakers. Through an examination of the issues and trends that shape screen choreography, a discussion of critical reading strategies, and consideration of the economics of popular-screen dance, I hope to offer potential methodological lenses for this diverse field of study.

POPULAR-SCREEN CHOREOGRAPHY

For any dance studies project, we are trained to attend to the body in motion, and this applies equally to the consideration of popular-screen dance. Within this particular context, however, the filmic medium not only demands that we consider the dance styles that are called upon, but also the way in which they are constructed through camerawork, editing, and other special effects. In continuing to explore questions of value, I first examine the genres and styles of dance that have come to typify popular dance film and the aesthetic values invested in them, and secondly focus on how the filmic apparatus participates in the construction of bodies in motion and how those aesthetic decisions create ways of seeing dance that signal measures of worth.

It is hardly surprising that a significant proportion of the dance featured in popular-screen dance is rooted in social and vernacular forms. Ballroom, tap, street dance, and club styles frequently form part of our everyday visual landscape and are perhaps more meaningful to cinema and television audiences unfamiliar with dance on the concert stage. Yet this is not to suggest that art dance forms do not appear within the context of popular film. For instance, ballet often presents a visual trope for "difference" and can be employed to enunciate varied attitudes to the popular: in *Flashdance* (1983) ballet forms a site of aspiration, in *Saturday Night Fever* (1977) it becomes a point of departure, and in *Save the Last Dance* (2001) it offers an opportunity for creative (and racial) fusion. This play between art and popular dance practice not only serves to reinforce the high/low binary that has traditionally divided cultural production but also shows its precarious framework when the popular becomes privileged or when high and low art forms engage in a creative reciprocity.

That said, popular dance film primarily calls upon popular dance practice as its choreographic matter. Yet, while popular dance in its live vernacular context tends to take place in everyday social settings, such as clubs and dancehalls, and is participatory and improvised in nature, in its mediated form, it is clearly "re-choreographed" for the camera. At times, the screen translation seeks to reproduce the social dynamic of a live vernacular setting through scenes of dancing in specific leisure settings or other public spaces where dance might be plausibly located. In spite of this illusion of authenticity, however, the dancing will always remain "presentational," as it is composed specifically for the cinematic gaze. In other instances, however, the social dance origins are simply a starting point for a highly theatricalized staging that bears little relation to its vernacular form. For example, I recall the extended "dance off" sequence that takes place between Moose and Kid Darkness in *Step Up 3D* (2010), which showcases an elaborate and virtuosic hip-hop choreography within the bustling environment of New York City's Central Park, or the sleek swing dance number that features in a Gap clothing advertisement (1998), in which beautiful dancing couples perform direct to the camera from the perspective of stage front.

This re-envisioning of dance is achieved not only through the way that the movement itself is choreographed and performed by "dancer-actors," but also through the filmic apparatus that rechoreographs these bodies through a reworking of time, space, and energy. Some commentators have criticized approaches to filming dance for the way in which the camera work and editing manipulate or distort the movement material. Yet I wonder how fruitful it is to attempt to conceive "a dance" that preexists the film. In many instances, choreography for film is created as a series of short sequences that are designed with specific shots in mind and, even if an entire choreography preceded the film, the screen version inevitably shapes how we see, know, and experience the dance. For instance, the close-up shot can create an intimate relationship between the spectator and dancer or direct us to levels of detail that we would not otherwise see; a rapid edit can produce an illusion of speed so that bodies move in space or traverse environments at an impossibly fast rate; and the motion of the camera can add a layer of mobility that allows spectators to feel that they are also participating in a kinaesthetic experience. These directorial choices, which are formed through aesthetic values, choreographic strategies, and the codes and conventions of filmmaking are central to the construction of the popular-screen dance body. Therefore, what kinds of trends have come into play?

With the combined visuality of the film medium and its capacity to manipulate movement through its technical apparatus, one observable trend is the desire to present dance as spectacular. Whether this is through producing images that are visually breathtaking or through creating superbodies that exceed the physical capacities of the live human body, popular-screen dance demonstrates a preoccupation with spectacle. For example, within the classic era of the Hollywood musical, the film choreographies of Busby Berkeley feature choruses of beautiful young women who are lined up in rows or positioned lying on the ground and, as the camera moves past them or captures them from directly above, their sheer mass produces visually arresting mobile patterns. More recently, popular dance film has employed digital technologies to choreograph bodies that extend beyond perceived limitations of time and space. Although not a dance film as such, *The Matrix* (1999) presents extended movement sequences in which the cybernetic bodies possess superhuman qualities as they run up walls, become suspended mid-motion, and leap way beyond human capacity. Similarly, the rise of 3-D filmmaking disrupts our spatial expectations as bodies are literally extended beyond the 2-D perception that has traditionally characterized film spectatorship. During several of the hip-hop routines in *Step Up 3* we see limbs fly toward us in a manner that feels quite uncanny.

The other tendency that has come to typify popular dance film is the creation of idealized bodies. In the context of live vernacular dance, its bodies are sweaty, disordered, and imperfect. On film, dancers can rest between takes, hair and makeup can be touched up, and mistakes can usually be edited out. The result is a flawless dancing body. Unless a director strategically decides to show a "learning" or "rehearsing" body, the labor of dance is frequently erased. Hence the popular-screen dance body is clean, dry, technically competent, and cosmetically enhanced to appear perfect. This construction of the "rehearsing" versus the "idealized" body forms a common theme across a range of genres and is particularly prevalent within the context of reality television dance shows, such as *Strictly Come Dancing, So You Think You Can Dance?,* and *Got to Dance*. While during the rehearsal period we see dancers in sweaty practice clothes who frequently fail to master the movement, are locked in a frustrating battle of repetition, and express disappointment at their efforts, in the moment of performance and judgment, they are glamorously presented in dazzling costumes and makeup, almost always succeed to execute a technically competent routine, and display immense pride in their achievements. Thus, whereas in the vernacular setting the participatory and experiential is stressed, on film the visual idealization of the body becomes the key point of attraction.

READING POPULAR-SCREEN DANCE

While it is important to consider what genres are featured in popular dance film and how this movement is rechoreographed for the screen, we also need to examine the ways in which the popular-screen dance body participates in the construction of meaning. As always, how the body is choreographed invites us to read it in particular ways and this collection alone clearly signals the complex array of meanings invested in popular-screen dance. Notably, within the context of popular dance film, the choreography rarely operates within the structures of a formalist aesthetic. Instead, it serves to convey ideas and values about the dancing bodies in motion. This then raises the question of how we might find meaning in popular-screen dance.

I would argue that different screen genres prompt the spectator to construct meaning in particular ways. For instance, in television advertising, the style of dance carries a set of meanings that are then routed back to the promotional messages of the product; in reality television shows, discourses of effort, achievement, competition, and evaluation are imbued in the dancing body; and in popular narrative dance films, the dancing body offers important information about the characters, their values and aspirations. Indeed, in a special issue of *Conversations across the Field of Dance Studies* on "Dancing the Popular," screendance artist Marisa C. Hayes (2010) describes how popular dance within the context of mainstream narrative films can be used to express emotions or ideas that cannot easily be reduced to language. While the visual images of film are replete with cultural meaning, as a dance scholar I would urge viewers to reflect on how the dance itself offers an entry to meaning-making.

As a very brief example, I want to examine how a short sequence in *Dirty Dancing* (1987) operates as a metaphor for sexual maturation. This occurs when "Baby," the teenage female protagonist, has offered to stand in for one of the professional dancers at the holiday camp where she is staying, and must learn a mambo duet with the romantic lead protagonist, Johnny. Initially, we see a montage of clips that show Johnny's frustrated attempts to rehearse and discipline Baby's "immature dancing body" and scenes of her practicing around the camp setting in a crude attempt to mimic this sophisticated dance style. The mood changes, however, as the film cuts to a practice session in which Johnny asks Baby to feel the "heartbeat" of the music through touching his chest, and the gentle strains of the rock ballad *Hungry Eyes* strike up.

To begin with, the shots depict Johnny correcting Baby as her dancing body fails to maintain correct posture, close-ups of her feet spinning out of control, or a comical moment in which she accidentally butts him on the head. As the shots progress, however, we see Baby's dress change from cute pink twinsets and sneakers to silver heels and black tights, and her dancing ability moves from clumsy and childlike to articulate and sexual. Throughout this, the verbal interaction disappears and their eyes become increasingly locked in a seductive mutual gaze to the romantic mood of the soundtrack. In the final few shots, we observe the increasing sexual awareness of Baby as Johnny traces his fingers down Baby's raised arm as far as her naked midriff. At first, she giggles each time he reaches her armpit, but then finally relishes in this sexualized physical encounter with her eyes closed and head inclined toward his lips. In this short sequence, the screen choreography allows the spectator to see Baby's sexual transformation from child to woman.

Another approach to reading popular dance film is through the temporal organization of shots, which relates to the preoccupation in film studies with theories of narrative structure (Monaco, 1981; Stam et al., 1992). The classic realist narrative dominates mainstream Hollywood in which an equilibrium is broken and, through a series of cause and effect action, a new equilibrium is brought into balance, which forms the resolution of the plot (Stam et al., 1992). This structuralist paradigm also shapes popular dance film, in which a binary model of narrative conflict is constructed through two opposing sets of dance styles or values. For instance, in *Dirty Dancing*, these oppositions are played out through the middle-class ballroom dance and the working-class Latin American styles; in *Flashdance*, the seedy world of erotic dance is set against the hallowed ground of classical ballet; and in *Step Up 3D*, the wealthy "House of Samurai" crew are pitted against the underdog "House of Pirates" who live together as a "family" on the verge of financial collapse. These tensions then offer opportunities for closure and transformation through which difference can be negotiated and the moral conquest of "good" over "bad" can be resolved. Yet it is important to recognize that not all popular-screen dance follows this same narrative organization. Film scholar Carol Vernallis (2004) has argued that music video employs a structural logic that is far closer to the ordering conventions of popular music than narrative film, and both Bollywood film and the classic Hollywood musical frequently suspend the realist narrative in order to stage elaborate song and dance routines.

A further strategy for reading popular dance film is through understanding the way that it quotes and references other screen examples. This "intertextual strategy" of acknowledging and borrowing visual signifiers from other genres both reflects the playful way in which filmmakers explicitly share a rich vocabulary of images and offers the reader a tool for analyzing dance film.[2] For instance, we draw upon our knowledge of the Hollywood musical and the B-movie horror genre to make sense of the Michael Jackson video *Thriller* (1983), and our visual memory of Jerome Robbins's choreography from *West Side Story* (1961) informs our reading of the Gap "West Side Story" (2000) clothing advertisement, which draws on a strikingly similar movement idiom to promote its sixties-inspired capri pants.

Yet while popular dance film clearly speaks to a media-literate audience able to recognize its visual reference points, it can also "mis-quote" its dance sources. For instance, even though the film is clearly a "horror fantasy," the crude representation of the manipulative and misogynistic ballet director in *The Black Swan* (2010) has exercised ballet audiences. Similarly, the male "body double" hip-hop dancer who stands in for actress Jennifer Beals during the audition scene in *Flashdance* or the character of "ballet dancer" Stephanie in *Saturday Night Fever* who practices her barre work in silver high heels have been a source of much amusement. This failure to offer plausible images of dance raises complex issues of authenticity and illusion.

Given that film and television continue to work primarily within the codes and conventions of a realist tradition, perceived misrepresentations of dance can be a point of frustration for spectators knowledgeable about dance. Indeed, this lack of attention to whether dance is presented with integrity on screen could be read as a devaluation of the discipline. Yet, as dance audiences, we must also recognize that this appropriation and mediation of a concert or vernacular form will inevitably be modified as it is re-presented through a screen medium. These political and ethical questions of authenticity and representation are important to dance in all of its contexts of production and reception and, for me, they signal important issues regarding the role of the spectator-participant. After all, the viewer makes assessments of the veracity of images and the extent to which they reflect or contradict her experiences of dance. The final section of this chapter, therefore, moves to examine audience values and their relationship to capital exchange.

Selling Popular Dance Film

Across the disciplines of film, television, media, and cultural studies, a significant volume of research exists that explores "who" constitutes audiences and "how" spectators read and engage with screen texts (Allen, 1997; Mayne, 1993; Morley, 1992; Stokes and Maltby, 2008). Within the field of dance studies, however, comparatively little work exists that examines dance audiences either in relation to the concert stage or in the reception of screen dance forms. Furthermore, the social values that have underpinned the low cultural worth of popular dance practice have problematically shaped the way in which audiences and participants have been historically conceived. In a study of the diachronic construction of "popular culture," cultural theorist John Storey (2003) describes how the mass production techniques of the late nineteenth and early twentieth centuries brought about social anxieties regarding the new "mass media" of radio, cinema, and television, which were considered homogenous and formulaic in their output. This conception of popular culture positioned its audiences as an indiscriminate mass passively shaped by the culture that was imposed upon them with no ability to actively negotiate its ideological meanings (Storey, 2003). The legacy of popular culture as manipulative, facile, and lacking in cultural worth has clearly influenced its late entry into the arena of serious dance research (Dodds, 2011).

A significant intervention into the role of the audience emerged through the work of feminist film scholar Laura Mulvey (1989), whose critique of gendered modes of "looking" and representation brought about a proliferation of research into film spectatorship. Notably, Mulvey's influence also worked its way into dance studies as scholars began to explore representations of gender within the stage dance arena (Adair, 1994; Burt, 1995). Although her conception of the "male gaze" exposed the problematic nature of the female image as a site of erotic spectacle, her failure to consider the precise constituency of cinema audiences prevented a serious examination of how spectators read images through a multiplicity of subject-positions.

While the development of audience reception studies has since provided far more nuanced understandings of engagement and spectatorship across other disciplines (Nightingale and Ross, 2003; Staiger, 2005), studies of audiences have been slow to emerge within dance studies. A notable exception is the *Watching Dance: Kinesthetic Empathy* project that employs qualitative research methods and neuroscience to examine how audiences perceive dance.[3] In one of the outcomes of this project, dance scholar Dee Reynolds (2010) considers how audiences watch popular dance shows through the concept of the "inner dancer." Yet this attention to matters of spectatorship is a rarity in popular-screen dance scholarship, and I would argue that the field would benefit from further qualitative research into how audiences read and understand popular dance film. The other dimension of audience reception, which has often been overlooked but would enhance understandings of popular-screen dance further, is the political economy of filmmaking and how this impacts both the visual content and matters of spectatorship.

As "mass" media, I suggest that film and television serve as important conduits for enabling dance to be "popular" through their capacity to reach far greater audience numbers than theater dance or presentational vernacular dance could ever hope to achieve. This raises the question of how the relationship between dance and economics affects the dance form and audience reception. In a study of the dance film *Mad Hot Ballroom* (2005), I argue that in spite of its characterization as a realist documentary created by an independent writer and director, it employs the structuring devices of Hollywood fiction to produce a popular narrative fantasy of transformation and escape (Dodds, 2008). This strategy of modeling the documentary on popular dance imagery therefore makes it potentially accessible to the widest possible audience, which in turn ensures high box office sales. Consequently, the use of "popular dance representations" on film and television produces a relatively simple equation in that the more accessible the imagery, the more viewers will "buy" into these visual commodities.

Thus one dimension of a film's "popularity" is certainly measured through box office returns. Although *Mad Hot Ballroom* was reputedly created with an extremely low budget, its distribution rights were bought by Paramount Studios and Nickelodeon Classics (James, 2005) and, following its release, it was positioned as the seventh-highest grossing documentary on record (Cadwalladr, 2005). It therefore comes as no surprise that production studios are quick to capitalize on a successful formula to reap further economic return. The recent run of reality television dance shows and feature films that revolve around street dance crews demonstrates how the screen media are motivated to reproduce lucrative commercial models. For instance, the first *Step Up* (2006) film was produced at an estimated $12,000,000; its worldwide sales have grossed at $114,194,847; and it was swiftly followed by *Step Up 2: The Streets* (2008), *Step Up 3D* (2010), and *Step Up: Revolution* (2012) (imdb.com, accessed August 23, 2012).[4] Due to such high financial reward, the popular-screen dance body serves as a potentially valuable commodity. While the earning capacity of dancers invested in live performance continues to be comparatively low, those who gain employment in film and television benefit from the explicit commercialization of the dancing body. Within some fields of dance practice, however, this can be construed as a form of "selling out." In the area of hip-hop, for example, those dancers immersed in its vernacular form are often critical of its mediated representations, which Banes (1994, p. 139) describes as "theatricalized and sanitized."

Although popular dance film behaves as a commercial enterprise that inevitably commodifies the dancing body and positions the spectator within a consumerist relationship for potential capital exchange, it also offers a significant amount of viewing pleasure that should not be underestimated. As I explain earlier, because of their proclivity toward mass engagement, popular forms have traditionally been derided and dismissed. Yet they also offer opportunities for pleasure that are rarely addressed. As scholars and students of dance, while we have the theoretical apparatus to critique the populist or normative discourses imbued in these images, popular-screen dance also presents enticing moments of virtuosity, transformation, humor, fantasy, and desire, concepts that should not be readily devalued. While our position towards popular dance film might often be one of ambivalence, I urge us to explore all of these complex and contradictory values in motion.

NOTES

1. My doctoral thesis is titled "Video Dance: Hybrid Sites and Fluid Bodies" (1997, University of Surrey) and was developed into a monograph (Dodds, 2001). While this area of dance film practice is currently known as "screendance," at the time of writing my thesis, it was typically referred to as "video dance."
2. For further discussion on intertextuality and dance see Adshead-Lansdale (1999).
3. This was a three-year project across four institutions: University Glasgow, Imperial College London, University of Manchester, and York St John University, funded through the Arts and Humanities Research Council. For further information see: http://www.watchingdance.org/.
4. A breakdown of worldwide sales of *Step Up* is recorded on the International Movie Database http://www.imdb.com/title/tt0462590/business, accessed August 23, 2012). For its United Kingdom release, *Step Up: Revolution* was titled *Step Up 4: Miami Heat* (2012), http://www.imdb.com/find?q=step+up&s=all, accessed August 23, 2012).

BIBLIOGRAPHY

Adair, C. (1994) *Women and Dance: Sylphs and Sirens*. New York: New York University Press.

Adshead-Lansdale, J., ed. (1999). *Dancing Texts*. London: Dance Books.

Allen, R. (1997). *Projecting Illusion: Film Spectatorship and the Impression of Reality* Cambridge: Cambridge University Press.

Buckland, T. (1999). "All Dances are Ethnic, But Some Are More Ethnic Than Others: Some Observations on Dance Studies and Anthropology." *Dance Research* XVII: 1, 3–21.

Burt, R. (1995). *The Male Dancer: Bodies, Spectacle, Sexualities*. London and New York: Routledge.

Cadwalladr, C. (2005). "Dance: How to Foxtrot." *The Observer*, November 20, p. 5.

Desmond, J. (2000). "Terra Incognita: Mapping New Territory in Dance and Cultural Studies." *Dance Research Journal* 32: 1, 43–53.

Dodds, S. (2001). *Dance on Screen: Genres and Media from Hollywood to Experimental Art*. Basingstoke: Palgrave.

——.(2008) "*Mad Hot Ballroom* and the Politics of transformation in *Decentring Texts*, edited by J. Lansdale. Basingstoke: Palgrave.

—— (2011). *Dancing on the Canon: Embodiments of Value in Popular Dance.* Basingstoke: Palgrave.

Dyer, R. (1993). "I Seem to Find the Happiness I Seek": Heterosexuality and Dance in the Musical in *Dance, Gender and Culture*, edited by H. Thomas. Basingstoke: Macmillan.

James, C. (2005). "Nonfiction is Flavor of Moment for Films." *The New York Times*, May 25, E1.

Mayne, J. (1993). *Cinema and Spectatorship*. London and New York: Routledge.

Monaco, J. (1981). *How to Read a Film*. Oxford: Oxford University Press.

Morley, D. (1992). *Television Audiences and Cultural Studies*. London: Routledge.

Mulvey, L. (1989). *Visual and Other Pleasures*. Basingstoke: Macmillan.

Nightingale, V., and Ross, K., eds. (2003). *Critical Readings: Media and Audiences*. Berkshire: Open University Press.

Reynolds, D. (2010). "'Glitz and Glamour' or Atomic Rearrangement: What Do Dance Audiences Want?" *Dance Research* 2010, 28:1, 19–35.

Staiger, J. (2005). *Media Reception Studies*. New York: New York University Press.

Stam, R., Burgoyne, R., and Flitterman-Lewis, S. (1992). *New Vocabularies in Film Semiotics*. London: Routledge.

Stokes, M., and Maltby, R., eds. (2008). *Hollywood Spectatorship: Changing Perceptions of Cinema Audiences*. London: British Film Institute.

Storey, J. (2003). *Inventing Popular Culture*. Oxford: Blackwell.

Vernallis, C. (2004). *Experiencing Music Video: Aesthetics and Cultural Context*. New York: Columbia University Press.

Index

Page numbers followed by *f* indicate figures. Numbers followed by n indicate notes.

Made in the USA
Las Vegas, NV
12 January 2023

65434202R00289